Houghton
Mifflin
Harcourt

OHIO SCIENCE FUSION

fusion [FYOO • zhuhn] a combination of two
or more things that releases energy

This **Write-In Student Edition** belongs to

_____

Teacher/Room

_____

Consulting Authors

Michael A. DiSpezio

Global Educator
North Falmouth, Massachusetts

Michael DiSpezio is a renaissance educator who segued from the research laboratory of a Nobel Prize winner to the K–12 science classroom. He has authored or coauthored numerous textbooks and trade books. For nearly a decade he worked with the JASON Project, under the auspices of the National Geographic Society, where he designed curriculum, wrote lessons, and hosted dozens of studio and location broadcasts. Over the past two decades, DiSpezio has developed supplementary material for organizations and programs that include PBS *Scientific American Frontiers*, *Discover* magazine, and the Discovery Channel. To all his projects, he brings his extensive background in science and his expertise in classroom teaching at the elementary, middle, and high school levels.

Marjorie Frank

Science Writer and Content-Area Reading Specialist
Brooklyn, New York

An educator and linguist by training, a writer and poet by nature, Marjorie Frank has authored and designed a generation of instructional materials in all subject areas, including past HMH Science programs. Her other credits include authoring science issues of an award-winning children's magazine, writing game-based digital assessments, developing blended learning materials for young children, and serving as instructional designer and coauthor of pioneering school-to-work software for a nonprofit organization dedicated to improving reading and math skills for middle and high school learners. In addition, she has served on the adjunct faculty of Hunter, Manhattan, and Brooklyn Colleges, teaching courses in science methods, literacy, and writing.

Acknowledgments for Covers

Front cover: *polar bear* ©Mark Rodger-Snelson/Alamy; *hand x-ray* ©Lester Lefkowitz/Getty Images; *tarsier* ©Bruno Morandi/ The Image Bank/Getty Images; *cells* ©Todd Davidson/Getty Images; *fossils* ©YOSHIHI TANAKA/amana images/Getty Images.

Back cover: *Aurora borealis* ©Wayne R. Bilenduke/Photographer's Choice/Getty Images; *laser lab* ©U. Bellhsuser/ScienceFoto/ Getty Images; *Mars Rover* ©Mark Garlick/Photo Researchers, Inc.; *bee* ©Nathan Griffith/Corbis.

Michael R. Heithaus

Executive Director, School of Environment, Arts, and Society Associate Professor, Department of Biological Sciences
Florida International University
North Miami, Florida

Mike Heithaus joined the Florida International University Biology Department in 2003. He has served as Director of the Marine Sciences Program and is now the Executive Director of the School of Environment, Arts, and Society, which brings together the natural and social sciences and humanities to develop solutions to today's environmental challenges. His research focuses on predator-prey interactions and the ecological roles of large marine species including sharks, sea turtles, and marine mammals. His long-term studies include the Shark Bay Ecosystem Project in Western Australia. He also served as a Research Fellow with National Geographic, using remote imaging in his research and hosting a *Crittercam* television series on the National Geographic Channel.

Donna M. Ogle

Professor of Reading and Language
National-Louis University
Chicago, Illinois

Creator of the well-known KWL strategy, Donna Ogle has directed many staff development projects translating theory and research into school practice in schools throughout the United States. She is a past president of the International Reading Association and has served as a consultant on literacy projects worldwide. Her extensive international experience includes coordinating the Reading and Writing for Critical Thinking Project in Eastern Europe and speaking and consulting on projects in several Latin American countries and in Asia. Her books include *Reading Comprehension: Strategies for Independent Learners*; *All Children Read*; and *Literacy for a Democratic Society*.

Ohio Reviewers

Shila Garg
William F. Harn Professor of Physics
Senior Director of India Initiatives
The College of Wooster
Wooster, OH

Brian Geniusz, M.Ed.
Science Curriculum Leader
Worthington Schools
Worthington, OH

Richard J. Johnson Jr., M.Ed.
Science Department Chair
Eastlake Middle School
Eastlake, OH

Robert Mendenhall
Curriculum Director
Toledo Public Schools
Toledo, OH

Donald J. Stierman, Ph.D.
Associate Professor
Department of Environmental Sciences
The University of Toledo
Toledo, OH

Jessica N. Stried
Science Department Chair
Hyatts Middle School
Powell, OH

Jaimie Thomas, M.Ed.
Olentangy Shanahan Middle School
Lewis Center, OH

Content Reviewers

Arkhat Abzhanov, Ph.D.
Associate Professor
Department of Organismic and Evolutionary Biology
Harvard University
Cambridge, MA

Paul D. Asimow, Ph.D.
Professor of Geology and Geochemistry
Division of Geological and Planetary Sciences
California Institute of Technology
Pasadena, CA

Laura K. Baumgartner, Ph.D.
Biology Instructor
Science Department
Front Range Community College
Longmont, CO

Eileen M. Cashman, Ph.D.
Professor and Department Chair, Environmental Resources Engineering
Research Associate, Schatz Energy Research Center
Humboldt State University
Arcata, CA

Wesley N. Colley, Ph.D.
Senior Research Analyst
Center for Modeling, Simulation, and Analysis
The University of Alabama in Huntsville
Huntsville, AL

Joe W. Crim, Ph.D.
Professor Emeritus
Department of Cellular Biology
The University of Georgia
Athens, GA

Elizabeth A. De Stasio, Ph.D.
Raymond H. Herzog Professor of Science
Professor of Biology
Department of Biology
Lawrence University
Appleton, WI

Julia R. Greer, Ph.D.
Professor of Materials Science and Mechanics
Division of Engineering and Applied Sciences
California Institute of Technology
Pasadena, CA

John E. Hoover, Ph.D.
Professor, Department Chair
Department of Biology
Millersville University
Millersville, PA

William H. Ingham, Ph.D.
Professor Emeritus
Department of Physics and Astronomy
James Madison University
Harrisonburg, VA

Charles W. Johnson, Ph.D.
Associate Professor of Physics, Division Chair
Division of Natural Sciences, Mathematics, and Physical Education
South Georgia State College
Douglas, GA

Tatiana A. Krivosheev, Ph.D.
Professor of Physics
Department of Natural Sciences
Clayton State University
Morrow, GA

Joel Leventhal, Ph.D.
Emeritus Scientist
(formerly *Research Geochemist*)
U.S. Geological Survey
Denver, CO

Joseph A. McClure, Ph.D.
Associate Professor Emeritus
Department of Physics
Georgetown University
Washington, DC

Mark B. Moldwin, Ph.D.
Professor of Space Sciences
Department of Atmospheric, Oceanic and Space Sciences
University of Michigan
Ann Arbor, MI

Sten Odenwald, Ph.D.
Astrophysicist
Director of SpaceMath@NASA
National Institute of Aerospace
Hampton, VA

Patricia M. Pauley, Ph.D.
Meteorologist, Data Assimilation Group
Naval Research Laboratory
Monterey, CA

Stephen F. Pavkovic, Ph.D.
Professor Emeritus
Department of Chemistry
Loyola University of Chicago
Chicago, IL

James L. Pazun, Ph.D.
Professor and Chair
Chemistry and Physics
Pfeiffer University
Misenheimer, NC

L. Jeanne Perry, Ph.D.
Director (Retired)
Protein Expression Technology Center
Institute for Genomics and Proteomics
University of California, Los Angeles
Los Angeles, CA

Kenneth H. Rubin, Ph.D.
Professor
Department of Geology and Geophysics
University of Hawaii
Honolulu, HI

Brandon E. Schwab, Ph.D.
Professor and Chair
Department of Geology
Humboldt State University
Arcata, CA

Adam D. Woods, Ph.D.
Associate Professor
Department of Geological Sciences
California State University, Fullerton
Fullerton, CA

Natalie Zayas, M.S., Ed.D.
Lecturer
Division of Science and Environmental Policy
California State University, Monterey Bay
Seaside, CA

Teacher Reviewers

Karen Cavalluzzi, M.Ed., NBCT
Sunny Vale Middle School
Blue Springs, MO

Katie Demorest, M.A. Ed. Tech.
Marshall Middle School
Marshall, MI

Dave Grabski, M.S. Ed.
P. J. Jacobs Junior High School
Stevens Point, WI

Ben Hondorp
Creekside Middle School
Zeeland, MI

Mary Larsen
Science Instructional Coach
Helena Public Schools
Helena, MT

Angie Larson
Bernard Campbell Middle School
Lee's Summit, MO

Christy Leier
Horizon Middle School
Moorhead, MN

Michele K. Lombard, Ed.D.
Swanson Middle School
Arlington, VA

Helen Mihm, NBCT
Crofton Middle School
Crofton, MD

Jeff Moravec, Sr., M.S. Ed.
Teaching Specialist
Milwaukee Public Schools
Milwaukee, WI

Nancy Kawecki Nega, M.S.T., NBCT, PAESMT
Churchville Middle School
Elmhurst, IL

Mark E. Poggensee, M.S. Ed.
Elkhorn Middle School
Elkhorn, WI

Sherry Rich
Bernard Campbell Middle School
Lee's Summit, MO

Heather Wares, M.Ed.
Traverse City West Middle School
Traverse City, MI

Alexandra Workman, M.Ed., NBCT
Thomas Jefferson Middle School
Arlington, VA

Contents
in Brief

Power Up with Ohio Science Fusion!

Your program fuses...

e-Learning and Virtual Labs

Labs and Activities

Write-In Student Edition

... to generate energy for today's science learner — *you*.

S.T.E.M. Engineering & Technology

...neering Design Process

Objectives
- Explain how a need for clean energy has driven a technological solution.
- Describe two examples of wind-powered generators.
- Design a technological solution to a problem.
- Test and modify a prototype to achieve the desired result.

...lls
- Iden...
- Condu...
- Brainstor... ...ons
- Select a sol...
- ...esign a proto...
- ...ild a prototype...
- ...nd evaluate
- ...to improve
- ...te results

Bui...

During th... human an... manufactu... easier. How... coal, oil, an... Revolution a... ...ut burning ...aste produc... ...ironment. ... will even... a... ...lt, we nee... ...u... ...tand alternative, renewable sou... of energy.

...instor... ...r Solution...
...are many s... ...energy besides fos... One of the m... ...dant renewable ...s is wind. A w... ...ine is a device that ...ergy from the... ...turn an axle. The ...e axle can be att... ...o other equipment ...obs such as pum... ...er, cutting ...or generating e... To generate ...ty, the axle spir... s around a coiled ...is causes electro... w in the wire. ...electrons produ... ...tric current. ...rrent is used to... ...es and ...or electrical ene... ...ored in

...3 Earth's Atmosphere

1 Brainstorm. What are other possible sources of renewable energy that could be used to power a generator?

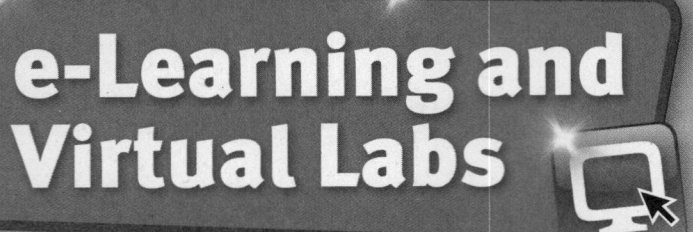

e-Learning and Virtual Labs

Digital lessons and virtual labs provide e-learning options for every lesson of ScienceFusion.

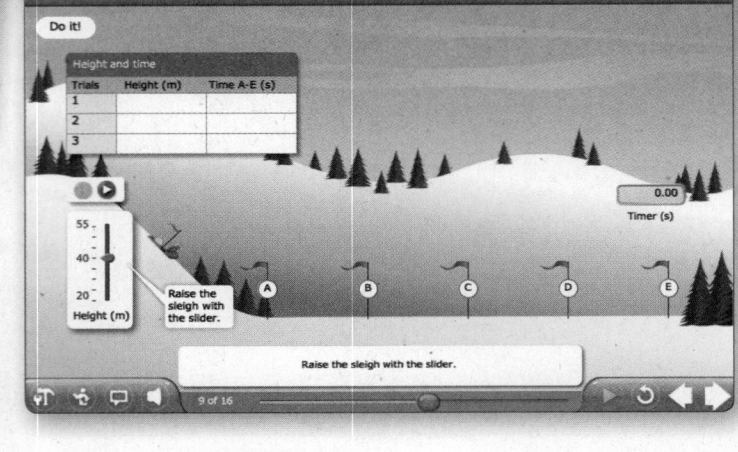

Investigate key science concepts with multiple virtual labs in each unit.

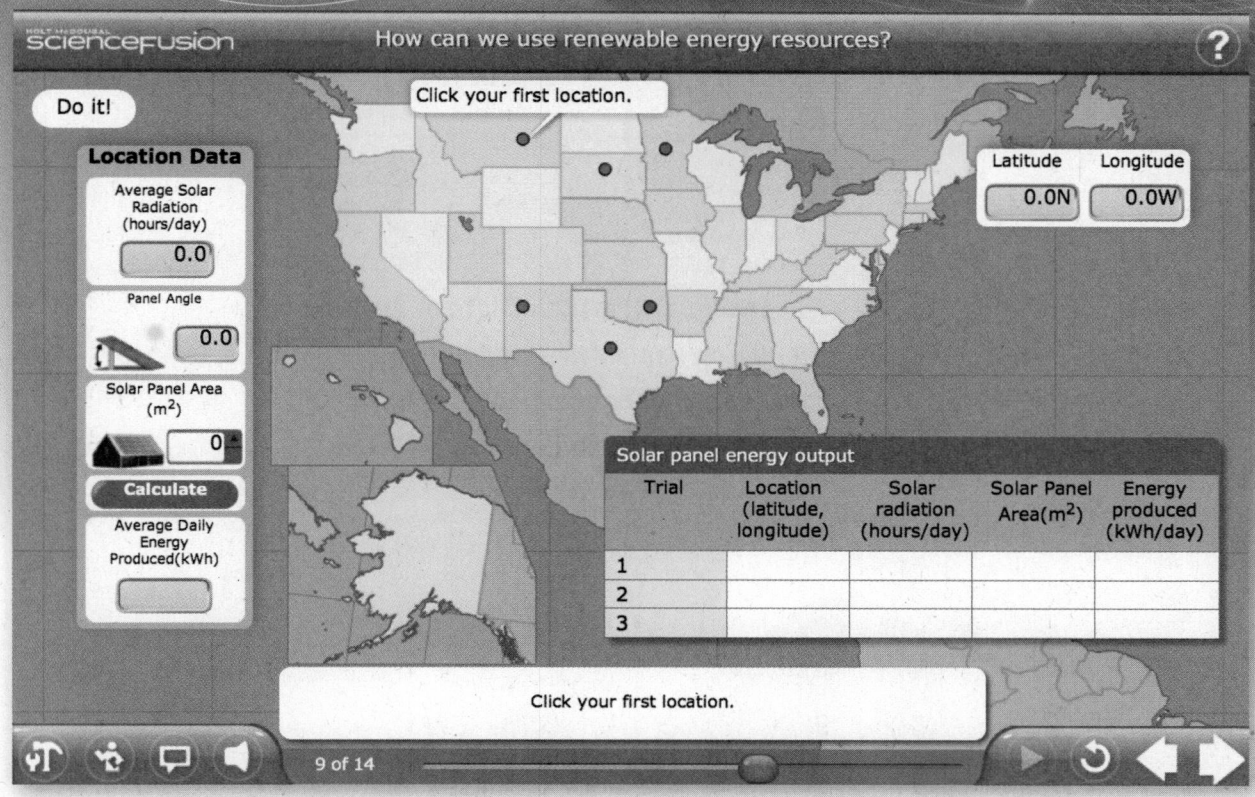

On your own or with a group, explore science concepts in a digital world.

Continue your science explorations with these online tools:

→ **ScienceSaurus**

→ **NSTA SciLinks**

→ **Video-Based Projects**

→ **People in Science**

→ **Media Gallery**

→ **Digital Glossary**

Labs and Activities

ScienceFusion includes lots of exciting hands-on inquiry labs and activities, each one designed to bring science skills and concepts to life and get you involved.

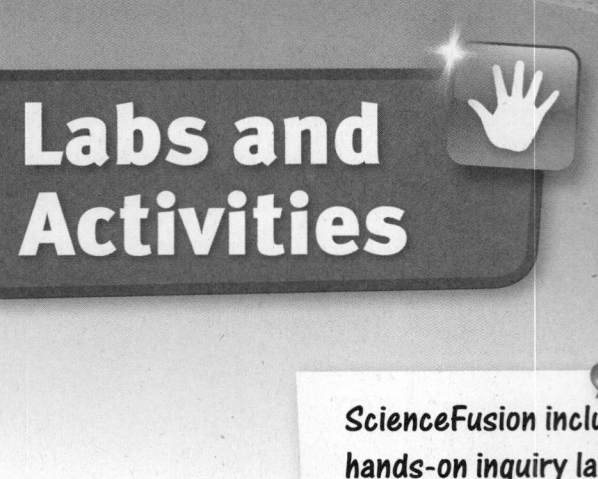

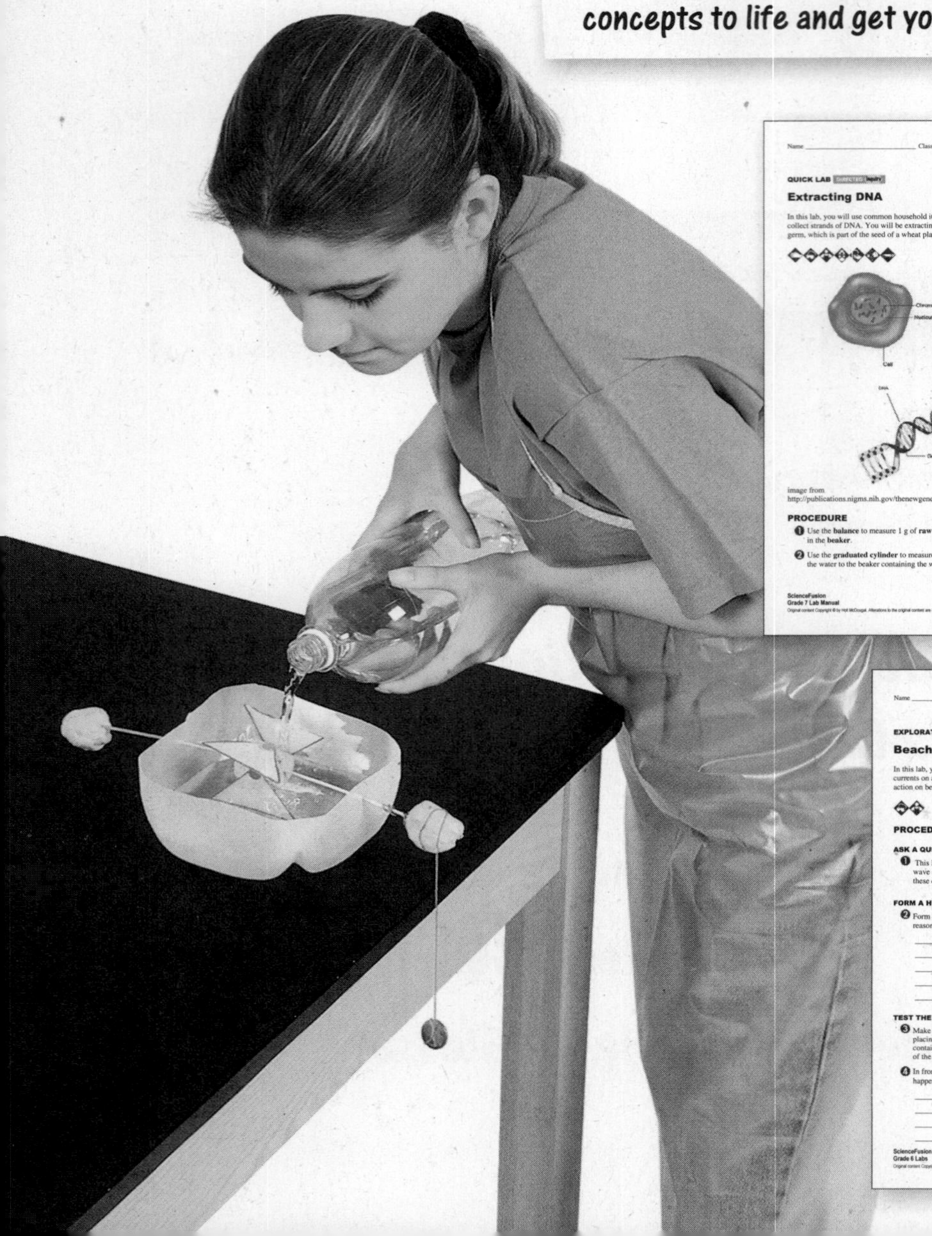

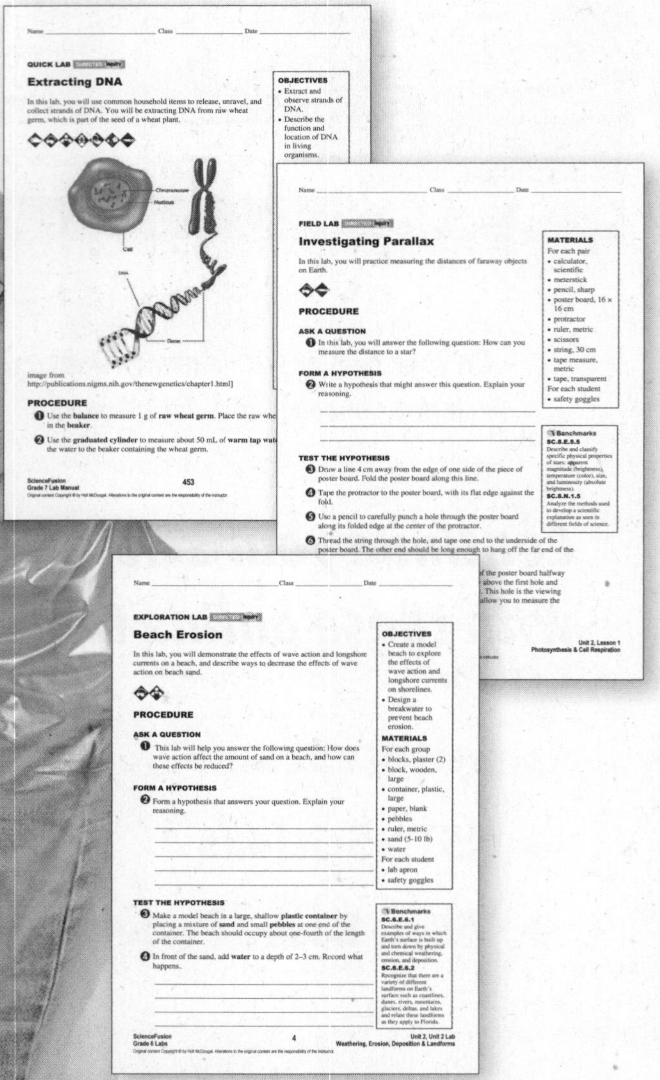

QUICK LAB DIRECTED Inquiry

Extracting DNA

In this lab, you will use common household items to release, unravel, and collect strands of DNA. You will be extracting DNA from raw wheat germ, which is part of the seed of a wheat plant.

OBJECTIVES
- Extract and observe strands of DNA.
- Describe the function and location of DNA in living organisms.

image from http://publications.nigms.nih.gov/thenewgenetics/chapter1.html]

PROCEDURE

1. Use the **balance** to measure 1 g of **raw wheat germ**. Place the raw wheat germ in the **beaker**.

2. Use the **graduated cylinder** to measure about 50 mL of **warm tap water**. Add the water to the beaker containing the wheat germ.

ScienceFusion
Grade 7 Lab Manual   453
Original content Copyright © by Holt McDougal. Alterations to the original content are the responsibility of the instructor.

FIELD LAB DIRECTED Inquiry

Investigating Parallax

In this lab, you will practice measuring the distances of faraway objects on Earth.

PROCEDURE

ASK A QUESTION

1. In this lab, you will answer the following question: How can you measure the distance to a star?

FORM A HYPOTHESIS

2. Write a hypothesis that might answer this question. Explain your reasoning.

TEST THE HYPOTHESIS

3. Draw a line 4 cm away from the edge of one side of the piece of poster board. Fold the poster board along this line.

4. Tape the protractor to the poster board, with its flat edge against the fold.

5. Use a pencil to carefully punch a hole through the poster board along its folded edge at the center of the protractor.

6. Thread the string through the hole, and tape one end to the underside of the poster board. The other end should be long enough to hang off the far end of the

MATERIALS

For each pair
- calculator, scientific
- meterstick
- pencil, sharp
- poster board, 16 × 16 cm
- protractor
- ruler, metric
- scissors
- string, 30 cm
- tape measure, metric
- tape, transparent
For each student
- safety goggles

Benchmarks
SC-8.E.5.5
Describe and classify specific physical properties of stars: apparent magnitude (brightness), temperature (color), size, and luminosity (absolute brightness).
SC-8.N.1.5
Analyze the methods used to develop a scientific explanation as seen in different fields of science.

...of the poster board halfway ...above the first hole and ... This hole is the viewing ...allow you to measure the

Unit 2, Lesson 1
Photosynthesis & Cell Respiration

EXPLORATION LAB DIRECTED Inquiry

Beach Erosion

In this lab, you will demonstrate the effects of wave action and longshore currents on a beach, and describe ways to decrease the effects of wave action on beach sand.

PROCEDURE

ASK A QUESTION

1. This lab will help you answer the following question: How does wave action affect the amount of sand on a beach, and how can these effects be reduced?

FORM A HYPOTHESIS

2. Form a hypothesis that answers your question. Explain your reasoning.

TEST THE HYPOTHESIS

3. Make a model beach in a large, shallow **plastic container** by placing a mixture of **sand** and small **pebbles** at one end of the container. The beach should occupy about one-fourth of the length of the container.

4. In front of the sand, add **water** to a depth of 2–3 cm. Record what happens.

OBJECTIVES
- Create a model beach to explore the effects of wave action and longshore currents on shorelines.
- Design a breakwater to prevent beach erosion.

MATERIALS

For each group
- blocks, plaster (2)
- block, wooden, large
- container, plastic, large
- paper, blank
- pebbles
- ruler, metric
- sand (5–10 lb)
- water
For each student
- lab apron
- safety goggles

Benchmarks
SC-6.E.6.1
Describe and give examples of ways in which Earth's surface is built up and torn down by physical and chemical weathering, erosion, and deposition.
SC-6.E.6.2
Recognize that there are a variety of different landforms on Earth's surface such as coastlines, dunes, rivers, mountains, glaciers, deltas, and lakes and relate these landforms as they apply to Florida.

ScienceFusion
Grade 6 Labs   4
Original content Copyright © by Holt McDougal. Alterations to the original content are the responsibility of the instructor.

Unit 2, Unit 2 Lab
Weathering, Erosion, Deposition & Landforms

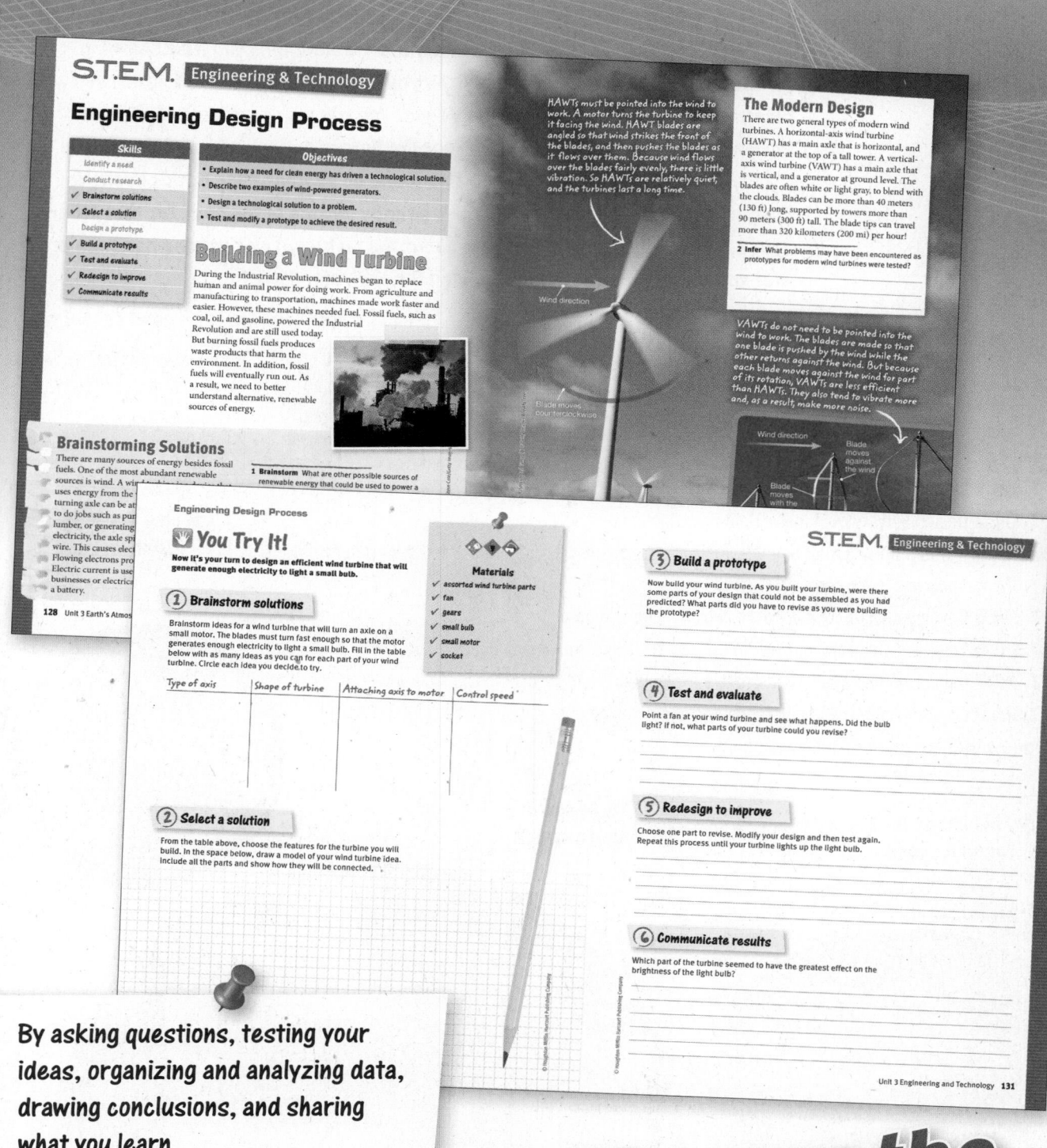

S.T.E.M. Engineering & Technology

Engineering Design Process

Skills
Identify a need
Conduct research
✓ Brainstorm solutions
✓ Select a solution
Design a prototype
✓ Build a prototype
✓ Test and evaluate
✓ Redesign to improve
✓ Communicate results

Objectives
- Explain how a need for clean energy has driven a technological solution.
- Describe two examples of wind-powered generators.
- Design a technological solution to a problem.
- Test and modify a prototype to achieve the desired result.

Building a Wind Turbine

During the Industrial Revolution, machines began to replace human and animal power for doing work. From agriculture and manufacturing to transportation, machines made work faster and easier. However, these machines needed fuel. Fossil fuels, such as coal, oil, and gasoline, powered the Industrial Revolution and are still used today. But burning fossil fuels produces waste products that harm the environment. In addition, fossil fuels will eventually run out. As a result, we need to better understand alternative, renewable sources of energy.

Brainstorming Solutions

There are many sources of energy besides fossil fuels. One of the most abundant renewable sources is wind. A wind turbine is a device that uses energy from the wind to turn an axle. The turning axle can be attached to other machines to do jobs such as pumping water, cutting lumber, or generating electricity. To generate electricity, the axle spins a coil of copper wire. This causes electrons to flow in the wire. Flowing electrons produce an electric current. Electric current is used to power homes, businesses or electrical devices, or is stored in a battery.

1 **Brainstorm** What are other possible sources of renewable energy that could be used to power a

HAWTs must be pointed into the wind to work. A motor turns the turbine to keep it facing the wind. HAWT blades are angled so that wind strikes the front of the blades, and then pushes the blades as it flows over them. Because wind flows over the blades fairly evenly, there is little vibration. So HAWTs are relatively quiet, and the turbines last a long time.

Wind direction

Blade moves counterclockwise

The Modern Design

There are two general types of modern wind turbines. A horizontal-axis wind turbine (HAWT) has a main axle that is horizontal, and a generator at the top of a tall tower. A vertical-axis wind turbine (VAWT) has a main axle that is vertical, and a generator at ground level. The blades are often white or light gray, to blend with the clouds. Blades can be more than 40 meters (130 ft) long, supported by towers more than 90 meters (300 ft) tall. The blade tips can travel more than 320 kilometers (200 mi) per hour!

2 **Infer** What problems may have been encountered as prototypes for modern wind turbines were tested?

VAWTs do not need to be pointed into the wind to work. The blades are made so that one blade is pushed by the wind while the other returns against the wind. But because each blade moves against the wind for part of its rotation, VAWTs are less efficient than HAWTs. They also tend to vibrate more and, as a result, make more noise.

Wind direction

Blade moves against the wind

Blade moves with the

Engineering Design Process

You Try It!

Now it's your turn to design an efficient wind turbine that will generate enough electricity to light a small bulb.

1 Brainstorm solutions

Brainstorm ideas for a wind turbine that will turn an axle on a small motor. The blades must turn fast enough so that the motor generates enough electricity to light a small bulb. Fill in the table below with as many ideas as you can for each part of your wind turbine. Circle each idea you decide to try.

Type of axis	Shape of turbine	Attaching axis to motor	Control speed

2 Select a solution

From the table above, choose the features for the turbine you will build. In the space below, draw a model of your wind turbine idea. Include all the parts and show how they will be connected.

Materials
✓ assorted wind turbine parts
✓ fan
✓ gears
✓ small bulb
✓ small motor
✓ socket

S.T.E.M. Engineering & Technology

3 Build a prototype

Now build your wind turbine. As you built your turbine, were there some parts of your design that could not be assembled as you had predicted? What parts did you have to revise as you were building the prototype?

4 Test and evaluate

Point a fan at your wind turbine and see what happens. Did the bulb light? If not, what parts of your turbine could you revise?

5 Redesign to improve

Choose one part to revise. Modify your design and then test again. Repeat this process until your turbine lights up the light bulb.

6 Communicate results

Which part of the turbine seemed to have the greatest effect on the brightness of the light bulb?

By asking questions, testing your ideas, organizing and analyzing data, drawing conclusions, and sharing what you learn . . .

You are the scientist!

Ohio New Learning Standards for Science

Dear Students and Families,

This book and this class are structured around the Ohio New Learning Standards for Science for Grade 7. As you read, experiment, and study, you will learn the concepts listed on these pages. You will also continue to build your science literacy, which will enrich your life both in and out of school.

Each picture shown below is also found on another page of this book. You can begin your exploration of science this year by looking in the book for that other page, where you can find out more about the picture. The first one has been done for you. (Hint: Look in the units listed for each standard.)

Best wishes for a good school year,

The ScienceFusion Team

OHIO

Science Inquiry and Application

During the years of grades 5–8, all students must use the following scientific processes, with appropriate laboratory safety techniques, to construct their knowledge and understanding in all science content areas:

7.SIA.1 Identify questions that can be answered through scientific investigations.

7.SIA.2 Design and conduct a scientific investigation.

7.SIA.3 Use appropriate mathematics, tools and techniques to gather data and information.

7.SIA.4 Analyze and interpret data.

7.SIA.5 Develop descriptions, models, explanations and predictions.

7.SIA.6 Think critically and logically to connect evidence and explanations.

7.SIA.7 Recognize and analyze alternative explanations and predictions.

7.SIA.8 Communicate scientific procedures and explanations.

Check it out: Unit 1 and pages R28–R53

C This image is found on page

_____

A This image is found on page

21

B This image is found on page

_____

Answers: A. 21; B. 24; C. 40

_____

OHIO

Earth and Space Science

7.ESS.1 The hydrologic cycle illustrates the changing states of water as it moves through the lithosphere, biosphere, hydrosphere and atmosphere.

7.ESS.2 Thermal-energy transfers in the ocean and the atmosphere contribute to the formation of currents, which influence global climate patterns.

7.ESS.3 The atmosphere has different properties at different elevations and contains a mixture of gases that cycle through the lithosphere, biosphere, hydrosphere and atmosphere.

7.ESS.4 The relative patterns of motion and positions of the Earth, moon and sun cause solar and lunar eclipses, tides and phases of the moon.

Check it out: Units 2–5

D This image is found on page

_____

E This image is found on page

_____

F This image is found on page

_____

Answers: D. 104, E. 124, F. 229, G. 321

H This image is found on page

_____

Life Science

7.LS.1 Matter is transferred continuously between one organism to another and between organisms and their physical environments.

7.LS.2 In any particular biome, the number, growth and survival of organisms and populations depend on biotic and abiotic factors.

Check it out: Unit 6

I This image is found on page

_____

Answers: H, 354; I, 413

OHIO

Physical Science

7.PS.1 The properties of matter are determined by the arrangement of atoms.

7.PS.2 Energy can be transformed or transferred but is never lost.

7.PS.3 Energy can be transferred through a variety of ways.

Check it out: Units 7–8

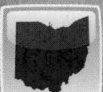

L This image is found on page ______

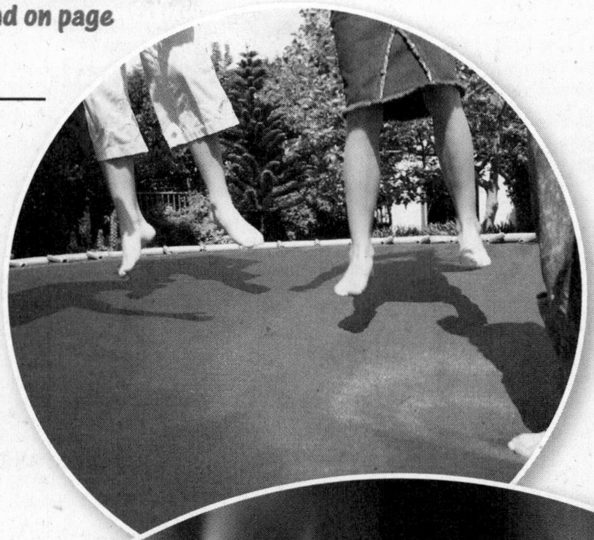

K This image is found on page ______

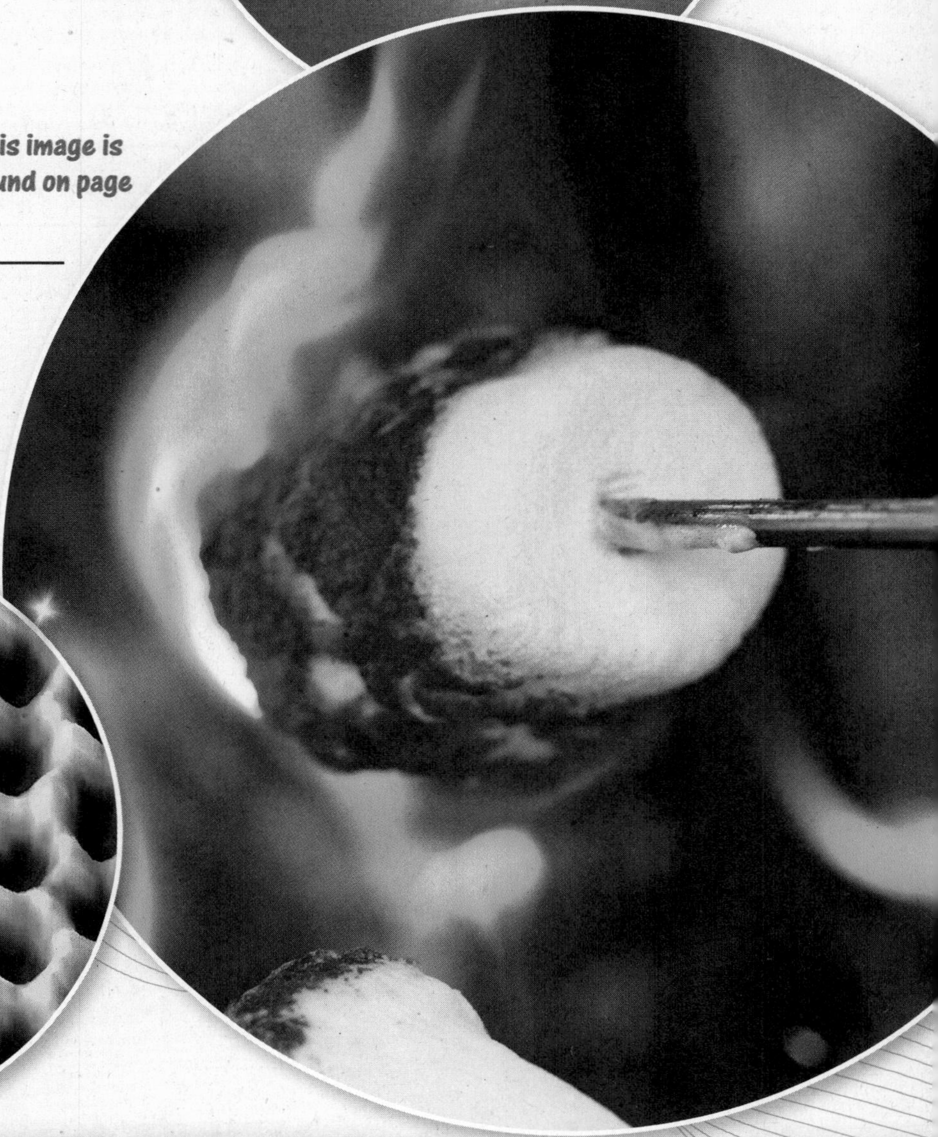

J This image is found on page ______

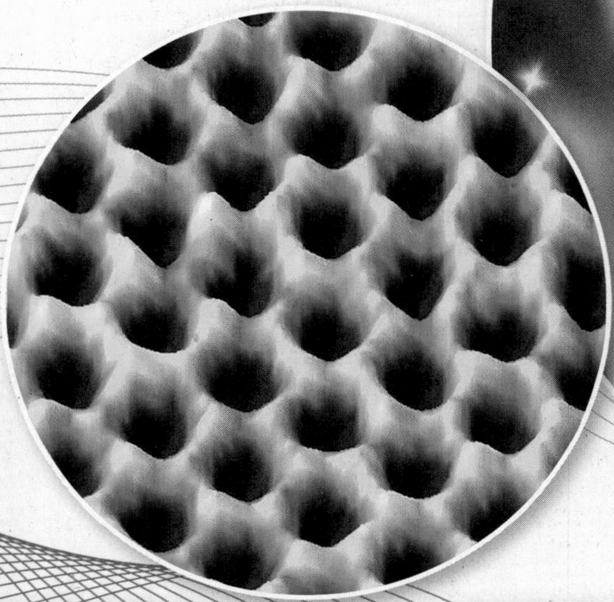

Answers: J. 453; K. 561; L. 583

Contents

What is the scientific explanation for what makes popcorn pop?

These rafters are on a wild ride downriver! They are using the river currents that form as water flows from higher elevations to lower elevations.

Some green sea turtles migrate over 2,000 km on ocean currents in the Atlantic Ocean.

Contents (continued)

What happens when solar wind particles reach the upper atmosphere over the Arctic? The aurora borealis!

© Houghton Mifflin Harcourt Publishing Company • Image Credits: ©John Warden/Stone/Getty Images

Although humans don't have thick fur or the ability to survive without drinking water for months, we have found other ways to live in extreme environments.

Contents (continued)

Imagine living where the sun never sets! That's what summer is like north of the Arctic Circle.

Hawks eat a variety of smaller animals such as lizards, fish, mice, and squirrels. Hawks are usually at the top of the food web, which means they are rarely eaten by other animals.

© Houghton Mifflin Harcourt Publishing Company • Image Credits: ©James McLaughlin/Alamy

Contents (continued)

You cannot see atoms with the naked eye. However, atoms make up everything you see, including each grain of sand in this sand castle.

During a lightning strike, electrical energy can be transferred from a cloud to the ground—or to a lightning rod.

Assignments:

_____

_____

_____

_____

_____

_____

_____

_____

_____

_____

_____

_____

_____

_____

_____

_____

_____

_____

_____

_____

_____

_____

_____

_____

_____

_____

_____

_____

_____

_____

_____

Science, Technology, and Engineering

Big Idea

Scientists and engineers use careful observations and clear reasoning to understand the world around us and to design technology to meet a variety of needs.

This skier is testing aerodynamic properties in a wind tunnel.

What do you think?

Scientists perform tests and experiments to answer questions, increase our knowledge, and improve the products we use. How can you apply scientific thought in your everyday activities?

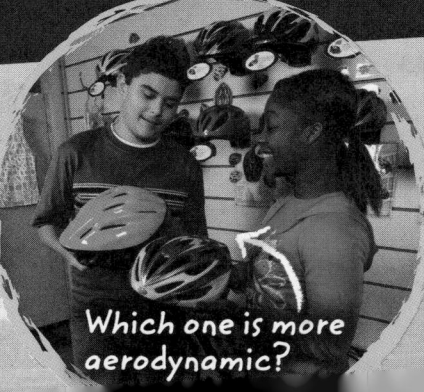

Which one is more aerodynamic?

Unit 1
Science, Technology, and Engineering

CITIZEN SCIENCE
Weather Myths

People have passed down many stories about predicting weather. Groundhog Day is a holiday based on a myth about predicting the end of winter. The story says that if a groundhog leaves its hole and does not see its shadow, winter will end in six weeks. This traditional method for predicting weather has no basis in science. Are any weather myths supported by science?

① Think About It

Many people believe that the number of times a cricket chirps in a given time period is a way to determine the temperature. Why is it possible that this myth could be scientifically supported?

_____
_____
_____

✔ Count the number of chirps in 14 seconds, then add 40 to get the temperature in degrees Fahrenheit.

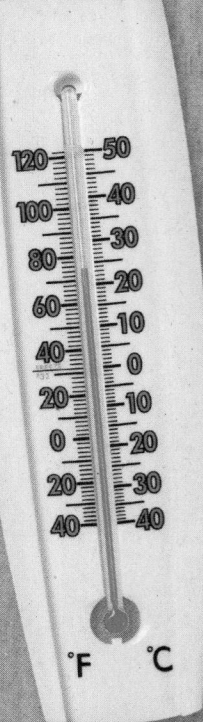

② Ask A Question

How can people test whether or not this is accurate?

As a class, design a plan for testing whether or not cricket chirps can accurately determine the temperature. Remember that crickets do not chirp all day long.

Things to Consider

☐ Is the temperature the same where your thermometer and cricket are located?

☐ Have you collected enough data and performed enough trials?

③ Apply Your Knowledge

A Determine what materials you will need to carry out your class plan.

_____
_____
_____

B Describe the procedure you will use to run your experiment. What will you specifically do to ensure your data lead to reliable results?

_____
_____
_____
_____
_____
_____
_____
_____

C Carry out your plan to test the cricket chirp theory. Record your data and results in a notebook. Analyze your results and write your conclusion below.

_____
_____
_____
_____
_____
_____
_____

Take It Home

Research other weather myths, especially any that are unique to your area. Do they have any basis in science? Share your findings with your class.

What Is Science?

ESSENTIAL QUESTION

How is science different from other fields of study?

By the end of this lesson, you should be able to identify what distinguishes science and scientific explanations from other forms of knowledge and to recognize creativity in science.

A scientist studies the genetic code. To most people, this looks impossible to understand. To her eyes, it's a wealth of information.

OHIO 7.SIA.1 Identify questions that can be answered through scientific investigations.

OHIO 7.SIA.6 Think critically and logically to connect evidence and explanations.

OHIO 7.SIA.7 Recognize and analyze alternative explanations and predictions.

Engage Your Brain

1 Predict Check T or F to show which statement is true or false.

T   F

☐   ☐   Science can determine what book you will enjoy.

☐   ☐   Scientists can often be creative when designing experiments.

☐   ☐   Because they are well educated, scientists do not need to make many observations before coming to a conclusion.

☐   ☐   Scientific results can be proven incorrect.

2 Contrast The pottery in the photo is known for its unique appearance. This is partly because of the glaze used on it. What is one question a scientist might ask about this pottery and one question a nonscientist might ask?

_____

_____

_____

_____

_____

_____

Active Reading

3 Apply Use context clues to write your own definition for the underlined word.

Example sentence
Having watched frogs in ponds her whole childhood, Reilley had a lot of <u>empirical</u> evidence about how they behaved.

empirical:

_____

_____

_____

Vocabulary Terms

• science
• empirical evidence

4 Identify As you read, place a question mark next to any words that you don't understand. When you finish reading the lesson, go back and review the text that you marked. If the information is still confusing, consult a classmate or teacher.

Science Is Everywhere

What does science study?

One way to define **science** is as the systematic study of natural events and conditions. It is a logical, structured way of thinking about the world. Scientists ask questions about nature. They try to give explanations to describe what they observe. Any explanation a scientist gives must rely on information available to everyone. It must be an explanation others can test.

You probably have done science yourself without knowing it. If you have looked around you and tried to explain what you saw in a way that could be tested, you have done science.

Active Reading

5 Apply As you read, underline examples of subjects that can be studied by science.

The Natural World

Science is subdivided into different branches. Each branch considers a different part of the world. Each branch, however, studies the world in the same logical and structured way.

Biology, or life science, is the study of all living things, from the smallest, one-celled organisms to mammals. Geology, or earth science, studies Earth, from the materials that make it up to the processes that shape it. Astronomy, the study of objects in outer space, often is included under Earth science. Physical science is the study of energy and all nonliving matter. Physical science includes both physics and chemistry.

These branches of science can and often do overlap. You might hear a scientist called a *biochemist* or *geophysicist*. Such terms refer to those whose work falls a little in each branch.

Think Outside the Book Inquiry

6 Infer List three questions you would like to have answered. Categorize them as scientific or nonscientific. For the nonscientific questions, can you rephrase them in a scientific way? Do you think you can answer every question scientifically?

Testable Ideas

What are types of questions scientists ask? Scientists ask questions that can be tested. They ask questions that have answers they can measure in some way. An explanation in science is usually agreed upon by many people and not just someone's opinion.

One way to understand how scientific thinking differs from other activities is to think of a sculptor making a piece of art. For example, consider the ice sculptor on the next page. Different people can have different ideas of the value of the art. Some may think it is beautiful. Others may find it ugly. Still another may think it's beautiful one day and ugly the next. These are all opinions. No one's opinion is more correct than another's. The types of books you like, the clothes you like to wear, or the foods you like to eat are not questions science normally addresses.

However, now think of other things the sculptor or onlooker might wonder about the piece. How long will an ice sculpture like this last before it melts? Might the sculpture stay frozen longer if something is used to treat the ice? Would using warmer tools make sculpting ice easier? Questions like these have testable answers. The results can be measured and compared. More important, they can be proved false. This is what distinguishes scientific questions from other kinds.

Visualize It!

7 Apply This sculptor wonders whether the piece may start to melt before it's finished. Is this a question he can investigate scientifically? Explain.

_____

_____

_____

_____

_____

Tools like this thermometer help scientists make measurements.

8 Explain This sculptor wonders if making the wings thinner would make the sculpture look more graceful. Is this a question that could be tested by science? Explain.

_____

_____

_____

_____

_____

9 Discriminate What other testable questions might one ask about the statue?

_____

_____

"Give me an explanation ..."

EVIDENCE

What is a scientific explanation?

A scientific explanation describes a natural process. It relies heavily on evidence gained from direct observation and testing. It is an explanation that others can test and refute.

Evidence gained from observation is empirical evidence. **Empirical evidence** includes observations, measurements, and other types of data scientists gather. Scientists use these data to support scientific explanations. Personal feelings and opinions are not empirical evidence.

A scientist never should hide any evidence he or she claims supports a scientific explanation. Whatever that evidence might be, the scientist must disclose all of it, if he or she wants to be taken seriously. If one scientist does an experiment, other scientists must be able to do the same experiment and get the same results. This openness is what makes scientific explanations strong.

LOGIC

Scientific explanation can be complex and, perhaps, even unintelligible to nonscientists. This should not discourage you from at least trying to evaluate explanations you hear like a scientist would.

For example, what makes popcorn pop? You most likely have seen it pop. You probably even have some idea as to how it happens. Here is a scientific explanation for it you can evaluate.

The corn pops because of a change in temperature. All plants contain water. Maybe the rise in temperature causes that water in the shell to boil. When the water turns into a gas, it pushes the kernel apart. The popcorn "pops" when the hard outer shell explodes. This is an explanation you can evaluate.

Active Reading **10 List** Give two examples of things that are not empirical evidence.

_____

_____

TESTS

How is a scientific explanation evaluated?

Now that you have an explanation for what makes popcorn pop, you can try to evaluate it as a scientist might. Here is how you might proceed. For each step, some sample responses are provided. Try to think of others.

First, look at any empirical evidence. Think of all the evidence that might support the explanation. Think of the times you've seen popcorn pop. What have you noticed?

Second, consider if the explanation is logical. Does it contradict anything else you know? What about it don't you understand? What else might you also wish to know?

Third, think of other tests you could do to support your ideas. Could you think of a test that might contradict the explanation?

Last, evaluate the explanation. Do you think it has stood up to logic and testing? What about it might be improved?

> **The Scientific Explanation:**
> Popcorn pops because the rise in temperature causes the water in it to expand and "pop" the kernel outward.

The Evidence

For the first step, identify all the evidence you can think of for what causes popcorn to pop.

11 Identify What have you observed about how and when popcorn pops?

- Pops when placed in a microwave
- Pops on a stove top

The Logic

Second, consider if the explanation is consistent with other evidence you have seen.

12 Infer Describe how well your explanation agrees with all of the evidence you have and with all that you know.

- See that water does turn to a gas when heated
- Other things expand when heated

The Tests

Think of other tests you could do that would support the explanation.

13 Predict What other ways might you pop popcorn if this explanation is correct?

- Could pop it in a solar cooker
- Could pop it using hot air

The Conclusion

Last, evaluate the explanation. Describe its strong points. Describe how it might be improved.

14 Evaluate How strong do you think the explanation is? How might it be improved?

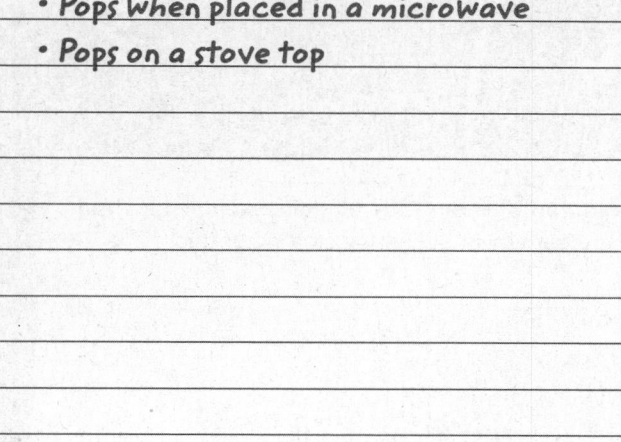

Creative Expression

How do scientists show creativity?

Scientists must rely only on what they can observe. They must always try to think logically. Indeed, this might seem dull. However, the best scientists are very creative. They can be creative both in the experiments they design and in the explanations they draw from them.

15 Apply Underline examples of creative solutions used by scientists to solve problems.

In Designing Experiments

How might creativity help in designing experiments? In one case, environmental scientists in the Washington, DC, area were looking for a method to detect harmful substances in drinking water. It would be too dangerous to have people drink the water directly, so they had to be creative.

Scientists knew bluegills are very sensitive to some contaminants. The fish "cough" to expel dirty water from their gills. Some scientists thought to use the fish coughing to identify contaminated water. They set bluegills in tanks in different locations. Sensors hooked up to the tanks detected the fishes' coughing and alerted monitors to potential harm. To ensure each fish's safety, a fish stayed in the tank only a short time.

The bluegill's "coughing" expels contaminants from its gills.

16 Infer How does the bluegill example illustrate creativity in designing experiments?

_____

_____

_____

_____

_____

Newton claimed he got the idea for gravity when he saw an apple fall from a tree.

In Explaining Observations

Sometimes, a creative mind can put old evidence together in a new way. New explanations can often be as important as new observations.

Isaac Newton claimed the law of gravity came to him when he saw an apple fall. He reasoned that some force, gravity, pulled the apple to the ground. The question was why didn't gravity pull the moon to the ground as well?

Newton claimed it did. He explained the moon just didn't reach the Earth because it was moving too fast. To understand the idea, think of what would happen if you threw an apple as hard as you could. The harder you throw it, the farther it goes before gravity pulls it to the ground. What if you threw it so hard that it would travel once around the Earth before it reached the ground? This is what is happening to the moon. As it moves, Earth's gravity attracts it. It just moves too fast to fall to the ground.

Newton's explanation changed the understanding of motion forever. He had taken something many had seen, the fall of an apple, and explained it in a new way.

17 Devise Write a caption for this figure explaining how Newton related the moon to an apple falling to the ground.

_____

_____

_____

_____

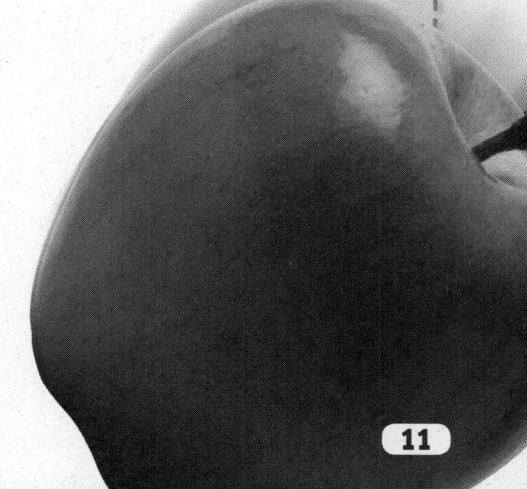

Visual Summary

To complete this summary, circle the correct word or phrase. Then use the key below to check your answers. You can use this page to review the main concepts of the lesson.

What Is Science?

Science is the systematic study of the natural world.

18 The natural sciences are normally divided into the life, earth, and physical / behavioral branches.

19 Science can / can't explain why you think a particular sculpture looks good.

Scientific explanations are supported by empirical evidence.

20 Empirical evidence includes observations / personal beliefs.

21 Scientific explanations are / are not able to be proved false.

Science can seem to be very dull work, but scientists are often very creative people.

22 Scientists are often creative in designing / comparing experiments.

23 Creative explanations must / need not rely on new observations.

Answers: 18 physical; 19 can't; 20 observations; 21 are; 22 designing; 23 need not

24 **Hypothesize** Why is it important that a scientist be both very logical and very creative?

Lesson Review

Vocabulary

Fill in the blanks with the term that best completes the following sentences.

1 The study of _____ involves the study of the natural world.

2 Science uses _____ to support its explanations.

Key Concepts

3 Distinguish You just bought a book titled *The Most Beautiful Artworks of the Century*. Is this likely to be a science book? Explain.

_____

_____

_____

_____

4 Determine A manufacturer claims its cleanser works twice as fast as any other. Could tests be performed to support the claim? Explain.

_____

_____

_____

_____

5 Contrast What is empirical evidence and what is it not?

_____

_____

_____

_____

_____

6 Identify What are two ways in which scientists can show creativity?

_____

_____

_____

_____

_____

Critical Thinking

Use this table to answer the following questions.

Color of flower	Number of butterfly visits	Number of moth visits
Red	11	0
Yellow	13	1
White	0	24

7 Distinguish For a science fair project, Ina wanted to investigate if flower color influenced the attraction of butterflies and moths. She made the table after observing the visits of butterflies and moths over a one-day period. Did she collect empirical evidence? Explain.

_____

_____

_____

_____

_____

8 Infer Ina concludes that color does influence the attraction of butterflies and moths. Do you think this was a logical conclusion? Explain.

_____

_____

_____

_____

_____

_____

9 Judge Does being creative in doing science mean that a scientist should make things up? Why?

_____

_____

_____

_____

_____

My Notes

S.T.E.M.

Analyzing Technology

Skills
✔ Identify benefits and risks
✔ Evaluate cost of technology
✔ Evaluate environmental impact
Propose improvements
Propose risk reduction
Compare technology
✔ Communicate results

Objectives
• Identify the benefits of a specific technology.
• Identify the risks of a specific technology.
• Conduct a risk-benefit analysis of a specific technology.

Risks and Benefits of Electric Transportation

The growing population in many areas has led to significant transportation problems. People need to move around to get to work, school, or shopping areas. However, without other options, they often end up driving around in cars all by themselves. This contributes to traffic problems, wear and tear on the roads, pollution, and wasted fuel.

Many traffic problems are caused by too many cars on the roads.

1 Observe From a safe place, observe the number of cars driving by your school or driving on a main street in your neighborhood. Record how many cars drive by in a certain amount of time and also how many of those cars contain only the driver.

Cars	Only driver

2 Infer What are some of the benefits of people driving around in cars, even though they may often be by themselves?

_____

_____

_____

_____

Electric Scooters

Electric scooters are small, open vehicles that use a battery-operated electric motor to propel the rider. Some people say electric scooters are the solution to modern transportation problems. A benefit is something that provides an advantage. Some benefits are that electric scooters take up less space on the road and in parking lots. Electric scooters also do not emit exhaust and can be cheaper to own and operate than cars. A risk is the chance of a dangerous or undesirable outcome.

3 Infer What are some of the problems or risks that could result from the widespread use of electric scooters?

_____

_____

_____

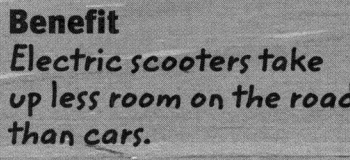

Risk
Even though electric vehicles don't emit exhaust, the power plants that deliver their electricity do have negative environmental effects.

Benefit
Electric scooters take up less room on the road than cars.

 **You Try It!** →

Now it's your turn to evaluate the risks and benefits of students using electric scooters to travel to and from your school.

 # You Try It!

Now it's your turn to evaluate the risks and benefits of students using electric scooters to travel to and from your school.

1 Identify Risks and Benefits

Suppose all of the students at your school used electric scooters to ride from home to school and back. Think of all the positive and negative aspects of all students riding electric scooters. In the table below, list all of these risks and benefits. List any negative aspects under the "Risks" heading and list any positive aspects under the "Benefits" heading. You may need to add to the table as you complete the rest of this activity.

Risks	Benefits

2 Evaluate Cost of Technology

A Imagine that every student in your school rides the school bus. Research the cost per student per year of your school's bus system. To do this, estimate how many miles the students have to ride to and from school and how much gas is needed to travel that distance.

_____

_____

_____

B Research the cost of electric scooters that students might be able to use to get to and from your school. How much would it cost each student to buy a scooter? What other costs do you need to consider?

_____

_____

③ Evaluate Environmental Impact

In what specific ways would the environment be affected by all students riding electric scooters to and from your school? Be sure to think about both positive and negative effects on the environment.

_____

_____

_____

_____

_____

_____

④ Communicate Results

A Based on all the risks and benefits you listed, what conclusion would you make about whether all students should drive electric scooters to and from your school? Explain your answer.

_____

_____

_____

_____

_____

_____

_____

B Write a persuasive letter to your local school board attempting to convince members to adopt your conclusion about the use of electric scooters at your school. Be sure to support your argument with facts from your risk-benefit analysis.

_____

_____

_____

_____

_____

_____

_____

_____

Scientific Investigations

ESSENTIAL QUESTION

How do scientists discover things?

By the end of this lesson, you should be able to summarize the processes and characteristics of different kinds of scientific investigations.

DNA placed in a special gel is separated into smaller pieces during gel electrophoresis.

OHIO 7.SIA.1 Identify questions that can be answered through scientific investigations.

OHIO 7.SIA.2 Design and conduct a scientific investigation.

OHIO 7.SIA.3 Use appropriate mathematics, tools and techniques to gather data and information.

OHIO 7.SIA.8 Communicate scientific procedures and explanations.

🖐 Lesson Labs

Quick Labs
- Design Procedures
- Revising Your Hypothesis

Field Lab
- Investigating Soil Microorganisms

 Engage Your Brain

1 Discriminate Circle the word or phrase that best completes the following sentences.

A *hypothesis / dependent variable* is a possible explanation of a scientific problem.

Scientists carry out controlled experiments because this method allows them to test the effects of a single *variable / theory*.

Graphing of results is most often done as part of *writing hypotheses / analyzing data*.

Making observations *in the field / in laboratories* allows a scientist to collect data about wildlife in their natural environments.

2 Explain Draw a picture of what you think a scientific investigation might look like. Write a caption to go with your picture.

🖊 Active Reading

3 Synthesize Many English words have their roots in other languages. Use the Latin words below to make an educated guess about the meaning of the words *experiment* and *observation*.

Latin word	Meaning
experiri	to try
observare	to watch

Example sentence
Shaun's favorite <u>experiment</u> involved pouring vinegar onto baking soda.

Experiment:

_____

_____

Example sentence
Microscopes are used to make <u>observations</u>.

Observation:

_____

_____

Vocabulary Terms

- experiment
- observation
- hypothesis
- independent variable
- dependent variable
- constant
- data

4 Apply As you learn the definition of each vocabulary term in this lesson, write a sentence that includes the term to help you remember it.

Scientists at Work!

What are some types of scientific investigations?

Scientists carry out investigations to learn about the natural world—everything from the smallest particles to the largest structures in the universe. The two main types of scientific investigations are *experiments* and field *observations*.

Scientific Investigations

Experiments

An **experiment** is an organized procedure to study something under controlled conditions. Experiments are often done in a laboratory. This makes it easier to control factors that can affect a result. For example, a scientist notices that a particular kind of fish is becoming less common in a lake near his home. He knows that some fish need more oxygen than others. To find out if this local fish species is being harmed by decreased oxygen levels, he might do the following experiment. First, he measures oxygen levels in the lake. Then, he sets up three tanks of water in a laboratory. The water in each tank has a different level of oxygen. Other factors that might affect fish, such as temperature, are the same in all three tanks. The scientist places the same number of fish in each tank. Then he collects information on the health of the fish.

---

5 Infer Why would the scientist in the example want the temperature to be the same in all three tanks?

_____

_____

_____

_____

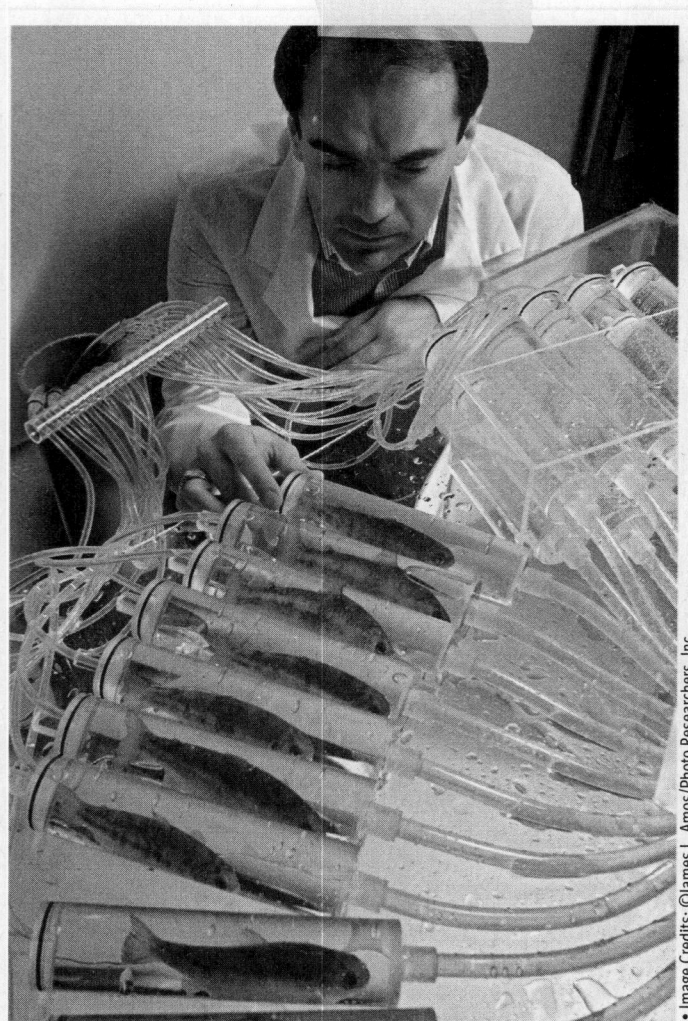

This scientist is studying salmon in a controlled laboratory experiment.

© Houghton Mifflin Harcourt Publishing Company • Image Credits: ©James L. Amos/Photo Researchers, Inc.

Visualize It!

6 Analyze List the factors that the scientists cannot control in the field investigation shown in this picture.

_____

_____

_____

_____

This scientist is observing salmon in their natural environment in Mongolia.

7 Identify As you read, underline reasons why a scientist might choose to do observations that do not involve experiments.

Observations and Models

Observation is the process of obtaining information by using the senses. Observation is also the term for the information gathered by using the senses or tools. Scientists routinely make observations during experiments. However, many things in the natural world cannot be studied under controlled conditions. For example, it is impossible to create or manipulate a star. But astronomers can observe stars using telescopes, cameras, and other equipment.

Observations of the natural world differ from observations made in experiments because of the many factors that scientists cannot control. However, such observations may give a better description of what actually happens in nature.

The scientist who experiments with fish and oxygen levels in the example you read on the opposite page might observe a lake to find out which fish and plants live in it. The scientist's observations of the fishes' natural habitat may or may not support the findings of the laboratory experiment.

Another type of investigation is the creation of models. Models are representations of an object or system. Models are useful for studying things that are too small, large, or complex to observe directly. For example, computer models of Earth's atmosphere can help scientists forecast the weather.

© Houghton Mifflin Harcourt Publishing Company • Image Credits: ©Matthieu Paley/Corbis

Why Ask Why?

What are some parts that make up scientific investigations?

The work that scientists do can vary greatly. Some scientists spend much of their time outdoors. Others mostly work in laboratories. Yet all scientific investigations have some basic things in common.

Hypothesis

A **hypothesis** (hy•PAHTH•ih•sis) is a testable idea or explanation that leads to scientific investigation. A scientist may develop a hypothesis after making observations of his or her own, or after reading findings from other scientists' investigations. The hypothesis can be tested by experiment or observation.

For example, imagine that after a snowstorm, you notice that the leaves of the outdoor plants seem to be alive. You wonder how the leaves stayed alive while the temperature was below freezing during the storm. You know that heat does not pass as easily through snow as it does through air. With this information, you could make the following hypothesis: "The leaves on the plants stayed alive because the snow cover slowed their loss of heat." This is a hypothesis that could be tested by an experiment.

Prediction

A prediction is similar to a hypothesis because it also makes a statement about what will happen under certain conditions. However, a prediction does not include any explanation of relationships among factors. For example, a prediction about the leaves could be as follows: "The leaves on a plant will stay alive if they are covered by snow."

These scientists are removing a mummy discovered in Peru. Because Peru's climate is so dry, some DNA is preserved.

Mummies such as this one have been preserved by the cold, dry climate of the Andes Mountains in Peru.

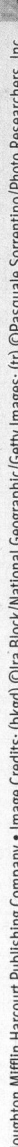

This scientist is analyzing DNA found in a mummy from Peru.

Variables

Active Reading **8 Identify** As you read, underline the three types of variables in an investigation.

A variable is any factor that can change in an experiment, observation, or model. The **independent variable** is the factor that is deliberately changed in order to test the effect of the change on another variable. This other variable, the **dependent variable**, is the factor that is measured to gather results. A **constant** is a variable that is not allowed to change in the investigation.

In an experiment, there is only one independent variable. Everything else is kept the same. This allows scientists to conclude that changes to the dependent variable were caused by the change in the independent variable. For example, imagine an experiment testing how temperature affects plant growth. In the experiment, several plants are grown at different temperatures, and plant height is measured. In this case, temperature is the independent variable that is deliberately changed. Plant height is the dependent variable that is measured to determine the influence of temperature on plant growth. All the other factors that could affect plant growth are kept the same for all plants. They are the constants in the experiment.

Observations and Data

Data are measurements and information gathered during an investigation that can be used in calculating or reasoning. Everything a scientist observes in an investigation must be recorded. The setup and procedure of an experiment also need to be recorded. By carefully recording this information, scientists make sure that they will not forget important details.

The biologist shown in the photo above would record the results of her analysis of mummy DNA. In addition, she would identify the type of tissue that was examined—whether it came from a tooth or bone, for example. She would also record the type of instrument used to examine the tissue and the procedures that she followed. All of these details may be important when she reports her findings. The information will also help other scientists evaluate her work.

9 Compare What is the difference between a constant and a dependent variable?

_____

_____

_____

_____

_____

Many Methods

What are some scientific methods?

Scientific methods are the ways in which scientists answer questions and solve problems. There is no single formula for an investigation. Scientists do not all use the same steps in every investigation or use steps in the same order. They may even repeat some of the steps. The following graphic shows one path a scientist might follow when conducting an experiment.

 **Visualize It!**

10 Diagram Using a different color, draw arrows showing another path a scientist might follow if he or she were observing animals in the wild.

Defining a Problem

After making observations or reading scientific reports, a scientist might be curious about some unexplained aspect of a topic. A scientific problem is a specific question that a scientist wants to answer. The problem must be well-defined, or precisely stated, so that it can be investigated.

Planning an Investigation

A scientific investigation must be carefully planned so that it tests a hypothesis in a meaningful way. Scientists need to decide whether an investigation should be done in the field or in a laboratory. They must also determine what equipment and technology are required and how materials for the investigation will be obtained.

Forming a Hypothesis and Making Predictions

When scientists form a hypothesis, they are offering a potential explanation for a problem. A hypothesis must be tested to see if it is supported or not. Before testing a hypothesis, scientists often make predictions about what will happen in an investigation. A prediction is a statement that shows a cause-and-effect relationship.

Identifying Variables

Before conducting a controlled experiment, scientists identify all the variables that can affect the results. Then they decide which variable should change and which ones should stay constant. Some variables may be impossible to control. Researchers may have more control over variables in the laboratory than in the field.

Collecting and Organizing Data

The data collected in an investigation must be recorded and properly organized so that they can be analyzed. Data such as measurements and numbers are often organized into tables, spreadsheets, or graphs. Data from multiple trials are often compared using tables.

Interpreting Data and Analyzing Information

After they finish collecting data, scientists must analyze this information. Their analysis will help them draw conclusions about the results. Scientists may have different interpretations of the same data because they analyze them using different methods.

Defending Conclusions

Scientists conclude whether the results of their investigation support the hypothesis. If the hypothesis is not supported, scientists may think about the problem some more and try to come up with a new hypothesis to test. When they publish the results of their investigation, scientists must be prepared to defend their conclusions if they are challenged by other scientists.

Life Lessons

Do these birds learn their songs from older birds? Or are their songs inherited?

How are scientific methods used?

Scientific methods are used in physical, life, and earth sciences. The methods that are used depend on the type of investigation that is to be conducted.

Different Situations Require Different Methods

Scientists choose the setting for an investigation very carefully. Some problems are well suited for field investigations. For example, many life scientists work in the field in order to study living things in their natural habitat. Many geologists begin in the field, collecting rocks and samples. But those same geologists might then study their samples in a laboratory, where certain conditions can be controlled.

Sometimes scientists study things that are very large, very small, or that occur over a very long period of time. In these cases, scientists can investigate the phenomenon by studying models. A scientific model is a representation of an object or a process that allows scientists to study something in detail. Scientists can conduct detailed research using models.

Think Outside the Book (Inquiry)

11 **Describe** Do research to learn about a new hypothesis that has replaced an older explanation of something in the natural world. Describe the process that led to this change in thinking.

When finches were first isolated, they didn't sing like wild finches. But later generations of isolated finches sang just like wild birds.

Scientific Methods Are Used in Life Science

Active Reading 12 **Identify** As you read, underline the scientific methods used in the study.

Life scientists use scientific methods to study how traits are passed from parents to offspring.

One team of scientists recently studied birds called zebra finches. Zebra finches learn songs by imitating the songs of older relatives. But the scientists thought that genes might play a role in how the birds learn their songs.

To test this hypothesis, they isolated a group of young zebra finches from older finches. When these young birds grew up, they sang different songs than wild finches did. Then the scientists placed another group of young male finches in with the isolated finches. The younger finches imitated the songs of the older ones, but the younger finches' songs were slightly different. As the scientists continued to add new groups of young finches in with the isolated ones, the song of each new generation was more like that of wild finches. The scientists concluded that genes influence the way zebra finches learn their songs.

To make this conclusion, scientists had to control other variables that could affect how the finches sang. Factors such as the environment the finches lived in, how often they came in contact with people, and diet would all have to remain constant. Otherwise, the song the finches sang could be caused by differences in these factors.

13 **Identify** Fill in the blanks to identify the variables and constants in the experiment with the zebra finches.

Dependent variable	Independent variable	Constants

Your Ducks in a Row

What makes a good scientific investigation?

The standards for scientific investigations are demanding. Potential sources of error in the design of an experiment should be identified and actions taken to avoid these errors. The investigation should be recorded clearly. Carrying out repeated trials, or repetition, ensures results are more reliable. Together, these checks help ensure that scientific practices are followed.

Using a Control

It is important to know that the results of a scientific experiment are due to changes in the independent variable. One way to confirm this is by using a control. A control is a part of an experiment for which the independent variable is not changed. Scientists use controls as a way to determine the reliability of experimental results. If the control remains unchanged, observed changes are due to the independent variable.

Repetition and Replication

There are two ways that scientific investigations can be retested. First, the scientist who conducted the original investigation can repeat the study. Multiple repetitions of an investigation with similar results provide support for the original findings. Second, other scientists can replicate the investigation. Replication of the findings by different scientists in different locations also provides support for the experimental results.

Repetition occurs when an activity is repeated by the same person. When a person bakes a cake several times using the same recipe, the cake should be the same each time. When a scientist repeats her experiment, she should achieve similar results each time.

14 Apply Explain how you could replicate the baking of a cake.

_____

_____

_____

What are experimental errors?

15 Identify As you read, underline the differences between experimental error and design error.

An experimental error is not the same as a error in the design of an experiment. Experimental errors are caused by the process of taking measurements. They can be caused by the small imprecisions that occur in the tools making the measurements, or by rounding measurements up or down during calculations. Errors in the design of experiments are caused by such things as not having a control and not having a large enough sample size.

Errors of Measurement

Measuring tools need to work reliably to obtain accurate measurements. Scientists also need to read the tools correctly. Tools can be calibrated, or adjusted to make sure they measure accurately. For example, a balance must first be tared, or set to zero, to obtain accurate measurements of mass. Also, the volume of a liquid should be read at eye level for a correct measurement. The precision of measurements can also be affected by estimating a quantity smaller than the scale on the measuring tool. For example, estimating length to a fraction of a centimeter by using a ruler that does not have millimeter graduations will cause inconsistent results. Taking several measurements can help reduce such errors.

Actually taking a measurement can also influence the outcome. For example, placing a thermometer into warm liquid to take its temperature may change the temperature of the liquid.

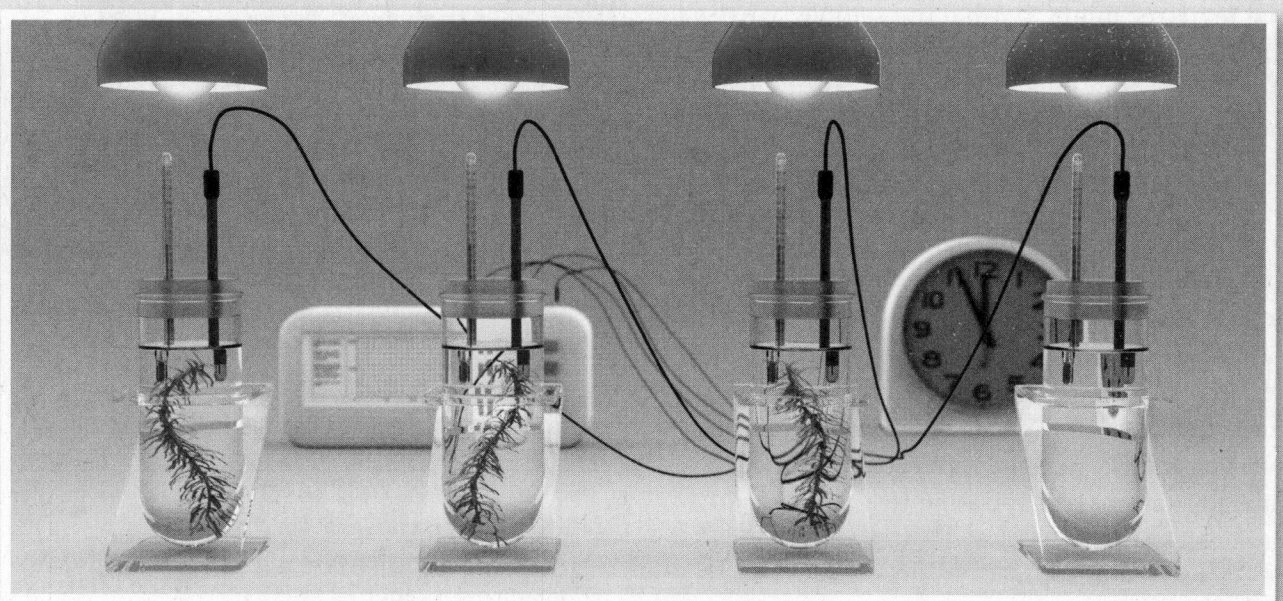

16 Analyze This picture shows the setup for an experiment to test the rate of photosynthesis under certain conditions. Which parts of the design help minimize errors in this experiment?

_____

_____

_____

Getting It Right

What are some ways to confirm that an investigation is valid?

Scientific investigations should be carried out with great care. But scientists are only human. Sometimes they fail to plan properly. They may make mistakes in collecting or analyzing data. Fortunately, there are procedures that help expose flawed investigations. On rare occasions, irresponsible scientists produce false results on purpose. This usually ends a scientist's career.

Evaluating Investigations

Peer Review

Before a study is published, it is reviewed by scientists who were not involved in the study. These peer reviewers evaluate the methods used in a study and the conclusions reached by its authors. For example, a reviewer could decide that an experiment was not properly controlled. Or a reviewer might say that the sample size used in a study was too small to be meaningful. Even after a study is published, scientists must answer questions raised by other scientists.

Replication

An important way to confirm an investigation is for other scientists to replicate it, or to do the investigation and get the same findings. To make this possible, scientists must explain the methods and materials used in the original study when they publish their findings. Not every investigation needs to be replicated exactly. But if a study cannot be supported by the results of similar investigations, it will not be accepted by the scientific community.

WEEKLY

NEWS
Special Edition

FUSION OR FICTION?

Was this experiment flawed?

WHY CAN'T RESULTS BE REPLICATED?

In 1989 a pair of scientists reported that they had accomplished cold nuclear fusion. The possibility of a cheap source of energy excited the public. However, other scientists doubted the claim. Attempts to replicate the findings failed.

Think Outside the Book

17 Evaluate Research the cold fusion news reported in 1989. Write a few paragraphs about the study. Did the study exhibit the characteristics of a good scientific investigation? Explain.

© Houghton Mifflin Harcourt Publishing Company • Image Credits: © Yves Forestier/Sygma/Corbis

How can you evaluate the quality of scientific information?

Scientific information can be found on the Internet, in magazines, and in newspapers. It can be difficult to decide which information should be trusted. The most reliable scientific information is published in scientific journals.

The most reliable information on the Internet is on government or academic webpages. Other sites should be studied closely for errors or bias, especially if they are selling things.

Although the lab reports that you prepare for school might not be published, you should try to meet the same standards of published studies. For example, you should provide enough information so that other students can replicate your results.

Visualize It!

18 Apply List two examples of poor scientific methodology found in this student's lab report.

_____

_____

_____

_____

Problem: How does the amount of sunlight affect the growth of plants?

Hypothesis: Plants that spend more time in the sunlight will grow taller because plants grow taller in warm conditions.

Changed variables: amount of time in the sunlight and type of plant

Constant variables: amount of water

Materials: plants, water, sunlamp, ruler

Procedure: Take the plants and put them under the sunlamp. Leave some of them under the lamp for longer amounts of time than others.

Data Table:

Plant number	Length of time in sunlight per day	Height after 2 weeks
1	5 hours	8 inches
2	8 hours	12 inches

19 Assess Would you believe this result, or would you be skeptical of it? Explain your answer.

_____

_____

_____

_____

_____

© Houghton Mifflin Harcourt Publishing Company

Visual Summary

To complete this summary, circle the correct word from each set of words. Then use the key below to check your answers. You can use this page to review the main concepts of the lesson.

Scientists carry out investigations through experiments and observation.

20 Scientific investigations that involve testing a single variable are called models / experiments / theories.

21 Hypotheses / Controls / Observations are often made before other types of investigations are done.

Scientists use scientific methods to answer questions and solve problems.

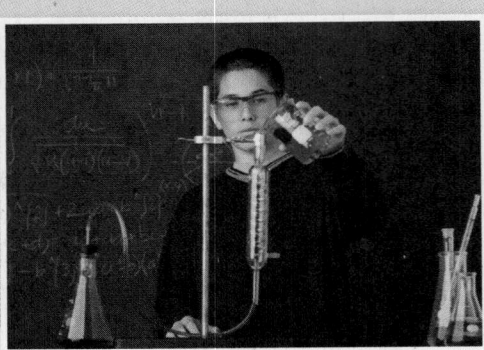

22 A problem / hypothesis / variable must be tested to see if it is supported.

23 Scientists must decide which data / hypotheses / variables will stay constant in an experiment.

Scientific Investigations

There are procedures and high standards that separate good scientific investigations from flawed ones.

24 The findings of experiments are generally not accepted until they are modeled / proven / replicated.

25 The most reliable scientific information comes from reporters / scientists / companies working in a particular field.

Answers: 20 experiments; 21 observations; 22 hypothesis; 23 variables; 24 replicated; 25 scientists

26 Relate What is the relationship between a scientific problem and a hypothesis?

Lesson Review

Vocabulary

Fill in the blank with the term that best completes the following sentences.

1 A(n) _____ determines what will be tested in a scientific experiment.

2 All of the _____ gathered in an investigation must be recorded.

3 A good scientific _____ can be repeated by someone else, and the same results will be found.

Key Concepts

Example	Scientific Method
4 Identify Scientists use instruments to record the strength of earthquakes in an area.	
5 Identify Scientists decide that in an experiment on fish, all the fish will be fed the same amount of food.	

6 Identify What are two key characteristics of a good scientific investigation?

_____

_____

_____

_____

7 Explain Describe at least two ways that a researcher can minimize experimental errors in an investigation.

_____

_____

_____

Critical Thinking

Use this drawing to answer the following questions.

8 Analyze Which variable changes in the investigation depicted in the drawing?

_____

_____

9 Conclude Identify one variable that is kept constant for both groups in this experiment.

_____

_____

10 Infer What kind of data might be collected for this experiment?

_____

_____

_____

11 Evaluate Which is less likely to be a reliable source of information, the webpage of a university or the webpage of a scientist who is trying to sell a new invention? Explain.

_____

_____

_____

_____

_____

_____

My Notes

Scientific Tools & Measurement

ESSENTIAL QUESTION

What are the tools and units used in science?

By the end of this lesson, you should be able to describe the different tools and units of measurement used in scientific investigations.

OHIO **7.SIA.3** Use appropriate mathematics, tools and techniques to gather data and information.

An important part of a scientist's job is picking the right tool for a measurement. For this measurement, calipers are more accurate than a metric ruler.

🤚 Lesson Labs

Quick Labs
- Investigate Making Measurements
- Investigating Density

Field Lab
- Use a Sextant to Make a Map

🧠 Engage Your Brain

1 Predict Check T or F to show whether you think each statement is true or false.

T	F	
☐	☐	A lab journal or notebook is considered a scientific tool.
☐	☐	Scientists worldwide use the same units of measurement.
☐	☐	It is sometimes appropriate for scientists to estimate measurements.
☐	☐	Precision describes how close a measured value comes to the true value of the measurement.

2 Infer Describe how the scientist might use this electron microscope for a scientific investigation.

_____

_____

_____

✏️ Active Reading

3 Apply Use context clues to write your own definition for the term *standard*.

Example sentence
A scientist uses a <u>standard</u> unit of measurement to compare the lengths of different bacteria.

standard:

_____

_____

Vocabulary Terms
- measurement
- scientific notation
- accuracy
- precision

4 Apply As you learn the definition of each vocabulary term in this lesson, create your own definition or sketch to help you remember the meaning of the term.

For Good Measure

What is measurement?

In science, the ability to describe an observation is an important skill. A description is a statement that reports what has been observed. Often, a scientist uses a measurement to describe an observation. A **measurement** is a description that includes a number and a unit.

Why do we use standard units of measurement?

Measurements were once based on parts of the body, such as arms or feet, but this method caused problems with accuracy. Body parts vary in size from one person to another, which made it difficult for two people to get the same measurement for an object.

Over time, societies realized that they needed to make units of measurement standard. Using standard units makes it possible for a person in one place to work with the same quantity as someone many kilometers away. Standard units also allow scientists to repeat one another's experiments. Experiments must be repeatable to determine if the results are valid.

Whether you are in the kitchen or the laboratory, it is difficult to work with nonstandard units of measurement.

ggs
dash of vanilla
pinch of salt
3 cups all-purpo
1 teaspoon bak

Visualize It!

6 List Which units of measurement in this recipe are not standard?

_____
_____
_____

Active Reading

5 Compare What is the difference between a description and a measurement?

_____
_____
_____
_____

1 tsp.

1 tsp.

What is the International System of Units?

In the late 1700s, the French government requested that the French Academy of Sciences improve their own existing official measurement system. The academy responded by creating the original metric system. The system has undergone several changes over the years. The modern metric system is now called the International System of Units (SI). The SI units are the language for all scientific measurement. There are seven base SI units. They are used to express the following quantities: length, mass, time, temperature, amount of substance, electric current, and light intensity. Each SI unit is represented by a symbol. Each quantity can also be measured with a specific tool or set of tools.

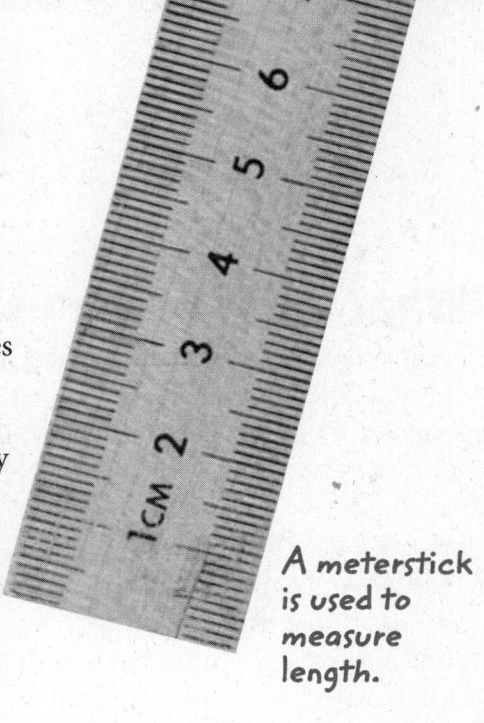

A meterstick is used to measure length.

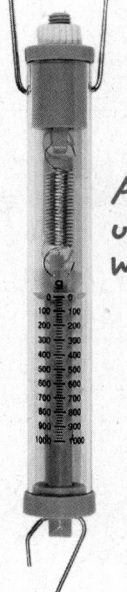

A spring scale is used to measure weight.

A brass weight may be used when measuring the mass of an object.

A volumetric flask can be used to measure liquid volume.

What are the advantages of using the SI?

There are many advantages of using the SI rather than other systems of measurement. One advantage is that SI measurements provide a common international language for scientists. Scientists worldwide can share and compare their observations and results. A second advantage is that changing from one unit to another is easier in SI than in other systems. Almost all SI units are based on the number 10. You can convert from one unit to another by multiplying or dividing by a multiple of 10. Conversions in non-SI systems are more complicated, as when converting between inches, feet, and yards.

Think Outside the Book

7. Apply Do ONE of the following: Write a blog entry from the viewpoint of a member of the 1790 French National Assembly on the need for a standard measurement system. OR Research the history of a common measurement, such as the yard, and write a report explaining how it came into use.

Made to Measure

What are the SI units?

Earlier we mentioned that there are seven base SI units. There are also units that are derived, or formed from, these base units. Let's take a look at the units you will use in the lab.

SI Base Units

Most often, you will use the base units for these four quantities in the lab: *length*, *mass*, *time*, and *temperature*. The unit of length is the *meter* (m). Length can be measured using a meterstick, ruler, or measuring tape. The *kilogram* (kg) is the SI unit for mass. Mass is measured using a balance. The SI unit for time is the *second* (s). Time can be measured using a stopwatch. The *kelvin* (K) is the SI unit used for temperature. Temperature is measured using a thermometer.

Derived Units

The unit for volume is an example of a derived unit because it is calculated from a base unit, length. Volume is the amount of space that something occupies. The SI unit for volume is the cubic meter (m^3), but liquid volume is often expressed in *liters* (L), which is not an SI unit. One liter is equal to one cubic decimeter. One *milliliter* (mL) is equal to one cubic centimeter (cm^3). Liquid volume can be measured using graduated cylinders and beakers.

The SI unit for weight is the *newton* (N). Weight is a measurement of the gravitational force on an object. It depends on the object's mass. Weight is measured using a spring scale. Measurements such as density must be calculated. Density is the amount of matter in a given volume. Density is calculated by dividing an object's mass by its volume.

Visualize It!

8 Label Using the table, identify the measurement associated with each tool in the image below.

Measurement	Base unit	Symbol
length	meter	m
mass	kilogram	kg
time	second	s
temperature	kelvin	K

Measurement	Derived unit	Symbol
volume	cubic decimeter (liter)	dm^3 or L
weight	newton	N
density	grams per cubic centimeter (milliliter)	g/cm^3 or g/mL

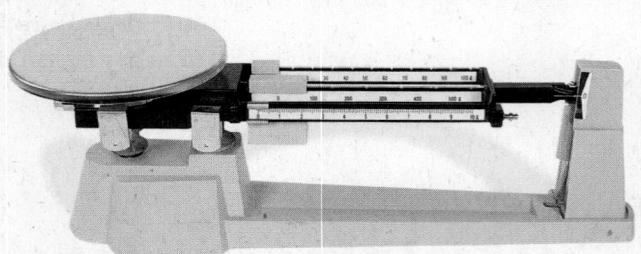

triple beam balance

A _____

stopwatch

B _____

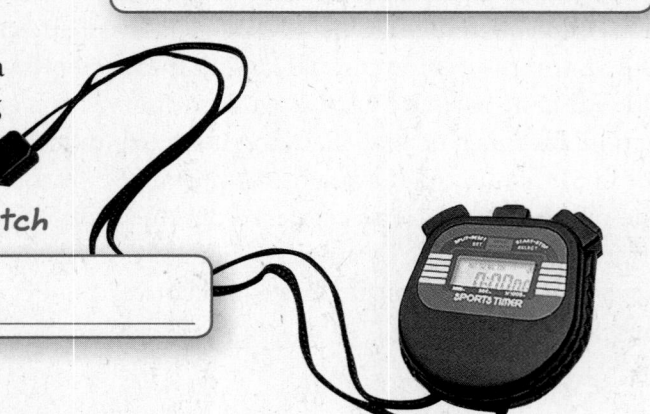

How can we make very large or small measurements easy to work with?

Some scientific numbers are much smaller or much larger than those we use in everyday life. Measurements that are very big or very small can be confusing to work with. There are two ways that scientists can make working with very large or very small numbers easier: using prefixes and scientific notation.

We Can Use Prefixes

A prefix is one or more letters or syllables added to the beginning of a word to change its meaning. In the SI, a prefix is used to express an SI unit that is larger or smaller than a base unit. For example, *kilo-* means 1,000 times, so a kilometer is 1,000 meters. The prefix *milli-* indicates 1/1,000 times, so a millimeter is 1/1,000 of a meter. The prefix used depends on the size of the object being measured. The table below shows common SI prefixes.

9 Identify As you read, underline the prefix that means "1/1,000."

SI Prefixes		
Prefix	**Symbol**	**Factor**
kilo–	k	1,000
hecto–	h	100
deca–	da	10
		1
deci–	d	0.1
centi–	c	0.01
milli–	m	0.001
micro–	µ	0.000001

10 Apply The table below shows how prefixes can be used with the unit for length. Complete the table by filling in the blanks.

Prefix with the base unit meter	Symbol	Number of meters
kilometer	km	
	hm	100
decameter	dam	
millimeter		0.001

We Can Use Scientific Notation

Scientific notation is a short way of representing very large numbers or very small numbers. Numbers in scientific notation are written in the form $a \times 10^b$. For example, the speed of light in standard notation is 300,000,000 m/s. It is 3×10^8 m/s in scientific notation.

The value for a is usually a number between 1 and 10. To find a, first locate the decimal point. For 300,000,000 m/s, the decimal point is at the right of the last 0. Then move the decimal point to the left until it is to the right of the number 3. The exponent b tells how many places the decimal is moved. When the decimal moves to the left, b is a positive number. For numbers less than 0, the decimal moves to the right, so b is a negative number.

To convert from scientific notation to standard notation, look at the exponent. If the exponent is positive, move the decimal point b places to the right. If the exponent is negative, move the decimal point b places to the left. For the speed of light, 3×10^8 m/s, the exponent is 8, and is positive, so move the decimal eight places to the right to write it as 300,000,000 m/s again.

Do the Math

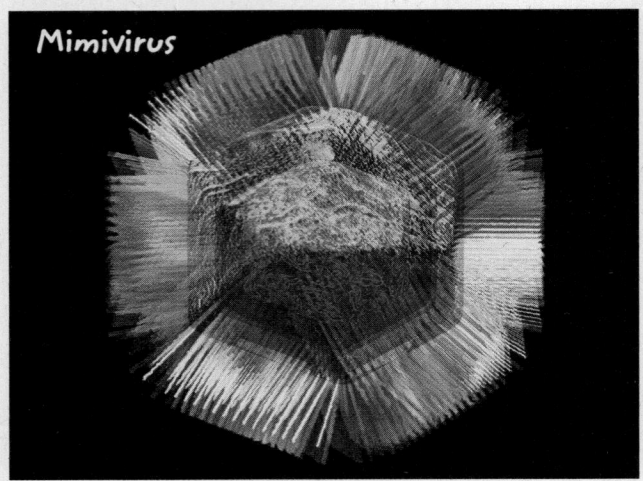
Mimivirus

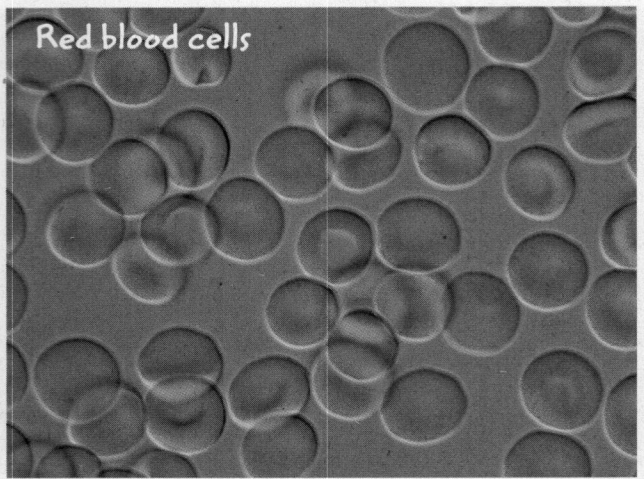
Red blood cells

Sample Problem

The diameter of this mimivirus is 0.000000750 m. Write this number in scientific notation.

Use the form $a \times 10^b$. The first nonzero number(s) given $= a$. The number of decimal places to move $= b$.

To get a, move the decimal 7 places to the right.

$$a = 7.5, b = -7$$

$$0.000000750\ m = 7.5 \times 10^{-7}\ m$$

You Try It

11 Calculate The diameter of a human red blood cell is 0.000006 m. Write the diameter in scientific notation.

Why are accuracy and precision important?

A scientist wants to use tools that can provide a measurement very close to the actual value. **Accuracy** is a description of how close a measurement is to the true value of the quantity measured. The smaller the difference between the measurement and the true value, the more accurate the measurement is.

 Precision is the exactness of a measurement. A precise measurement is repeatable and reliable. If a high-precision measurement is repeated, the number obtained will be the same or very nearly the same.

In a game of horseshoes, the most accurate and precise player wins. Accurate throws are close to the stake. Precise throws are close together.

Visualize It!

12 Illustrate Draw a fourth set of horseshoes that represents low accuracy and low precision.

Low accuracy, high precision

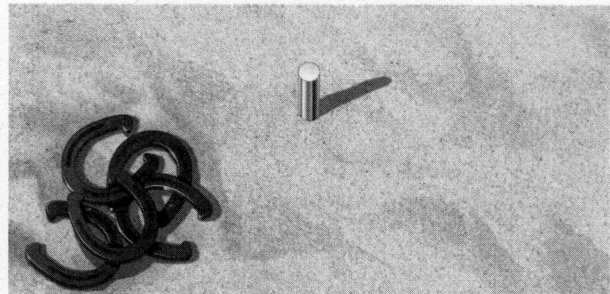

High accuracy, low precision

High accuracy, high precision

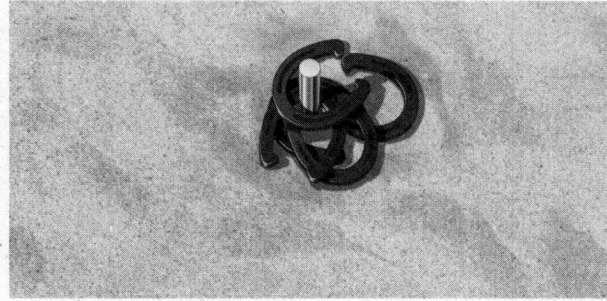

Low accuracy, low precision

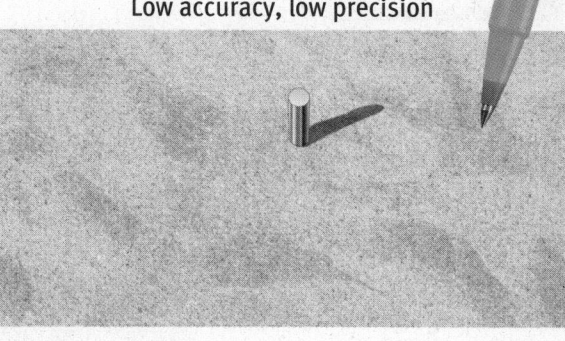

Why do scientists sometimes estimate measurements?

People estimate measurements doing everyday tasks such as making salsa or rearranging furniture. Scientists also make estimates of measurements. Scientists may use estimates to see if the data they collected are reasonable. Scientists may also use estimates to determine which tool is best suited for making the measurements they need.

Think Outside the Book Inquiry

13 Apply Choose an everyday object, and design a method to measure that object that is both accurate and precise. What tool or tools would you use? Explain your answer.

Tools of the Trade

How are tools used in science?

A scientist needs tools to perform experiments. Hot plates can be used to increase the temperature of a substance. Test tubes are common containers for holding samples of materials. Test-tube racks hold test tubes upright. Pipettes can be used to transfer liquids. Lab journals or lab notebooks and pencils are tools that scientists use to record data and observations.

Scientists also need tools to make observations or measurements that cannot be detected by senses alone. A hand lens can be used to magnify small objects. For very small objects, compound light microscopes or electron microscopes can be used. Light microscopes use a series of lenses to magnify objects. Electron microscopes use tiny particles called electrons to produce clearer and more detailed images than light microscopes. Two types of electron microscopes are scanning electron microscopes and transmission electron microscopes.

Scientists also use digital cameras to record images of objects or environments. These images can be used later to discover details that they did not notice or remember.

Active Reading

14 **Distinguish** What is the difference between a compound light microscope and an electron microscope?

_____

_____

_____

_____

Visualize It!

15 **Identify** List the tools in this image that are necessary for performing an experiment.

_____

_____

_____

_____

_____

Tools are used to perform experiments and make observations.

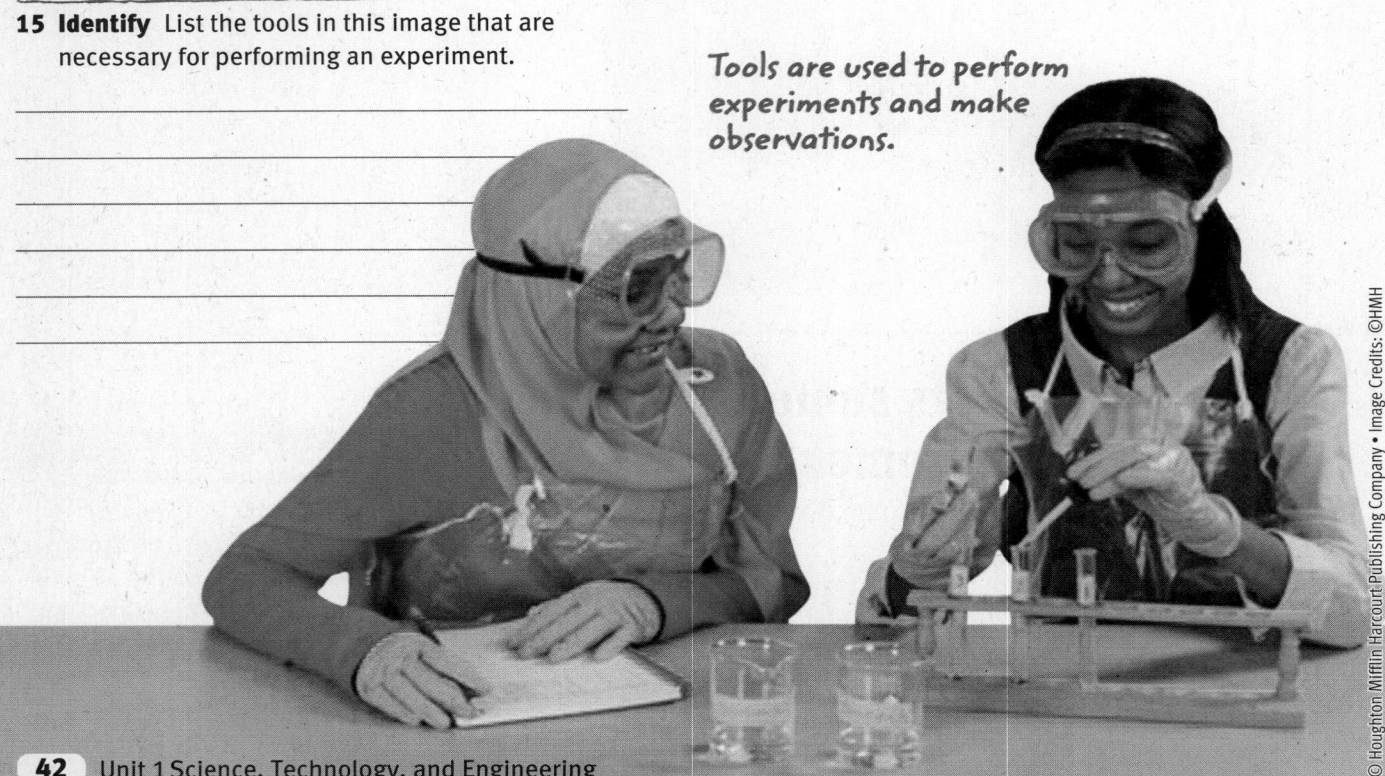

How are computers and technology used by scientists?

The use of science for practical purposes is called technology. Scientists use technology to find information and solve problems. Technology also contributes to the progress of science. Calculators and computers are two types of technological devices. They allow scientists to make quick and accurate calculations. They can also analyze data by creating graphs and solving complex equations. Scientists use computers to make spreadsheets, create models, or run simulations. Computers also help scientists share data and ideas with one another and publish reports about their research.

Scientists may also use probeware, which is a measuring tool linked to a computer. Probeware can be used to obtain and display the values of a quantity such as temperature, oxygen concentration, or pH. Probeware also allows scientists to interpret and analyze data. It is often used in long-term projects such as environmental quality monitoring.

When new technology is developed, scientists often learn new information. For example, cells were not discovered until the light microscope was developed. Now electron microscopes can make images of individual atoms. Just as technology leads to new scientific discoveries, new scientific discoveries lead to the development of new technologies. Thanks to the discovery of semiconductors, you can put an entire computer in your lap. The first computers filled up large rooms!

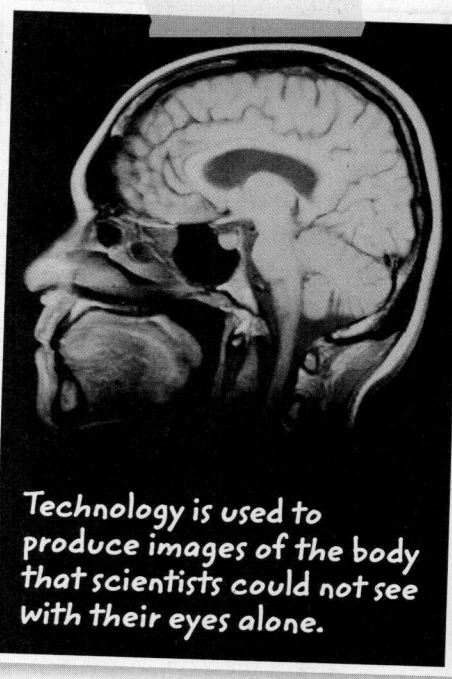

Technology is used to produce images of the body that scientists could not see with their eyes alone.

Magnetic resonance imaging

16 Hypothesize Magnetic resonance imaging (MRI) scanners use electromagnetic waves to generate images of the inside of a person's body. How might MRI technology be used to investigate how the brain works?

_____

_____

_____

_____

_____

_____

_____

_____

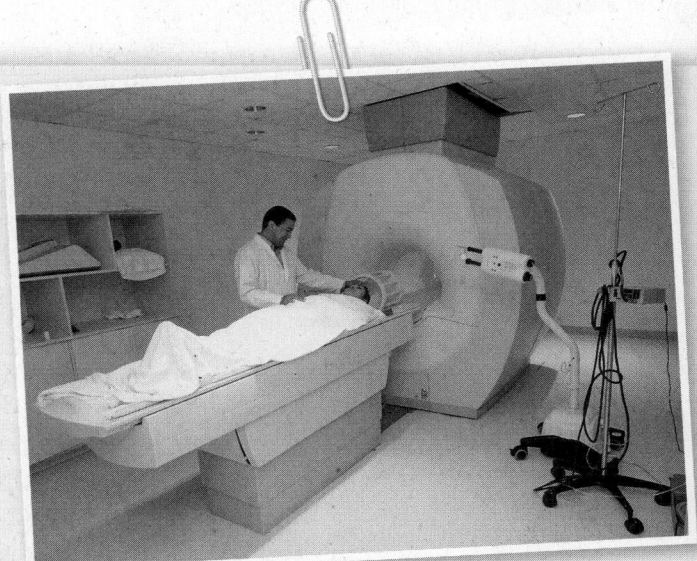

MRI scans allow the inside of a body to be seen in great detail.

Visual Summary

To complete this summary, circle the correct word or phrase. Then, use the key below to check your answers. You can use this page to review the main concepts of the lesson.

Scientific Tools & Measurement

The International System of Units (SI) is the standard system of measurement used in science.

17 The SI unit for mass is the kilogram / newton.

18 The SI unit for time is the hour / second.

Scientific tools are used to make observations, collect and analyze data, and share results.

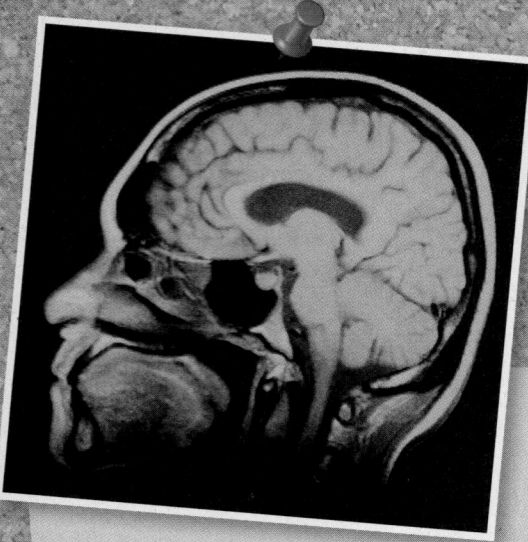

19 A series of lenses is used to magnify small objects in a compound light microscope / scanning electron microscope.

20 A common container in the laboratory used for holding small samples of liquid is a hot plate / test tube.

21 Computers may be used at every stage / only to calculate results of a scientific investigation.

22 A sensor that connects directly to a computer to collect data is called a calculator / probeware.

Technology is used to conduct research and to share ideas and results.

Answers: 17 kilogram; 18 second; 19 compound light microscope; 20 test tube; 21 at every stage; 22 probeware

23 **Summarize** Why are tools and technology important for scientific investigations?

Lesson Review

Vocabulary

Draw a line to connect the following terms to their definitions.

1 precision   **A** closeness to the true value

2 accuracy   **B** description with a unit

3 measurement   **C** way to write very large or small numbers

4 scientific notation **D** the repeatability of a measurement

Key Concepts

5 Summarize Which of the following is not an advantage of using SI units?

A allows scientists to compare observations and results

B can compare measurements made years apart

C based on the number 5, which is easy to use in calculations

D uses prefixes to express measurements that are small or large

6 Calculate What is 0.003 in scientific notation?

A 10×10^3

B 3×10^{-3}

C 3×10^3

D 10×3^{-10}

7 Identify What is the SI unit for temperature?

A the kelvin

B degrees Celsius

C degrees Fahrenheit

D the newton

Critical Thinking

Use this photo to answer the following questions.

8 Conclude Name the type of measurement the student in the photo is making.

_____

9 Apply The prefix for the measurement the student is making is *milli–*. What does *milli–* mean?

_____

10 Evaluate The student measured the volume of water as 80.0 mL. She discovered that the actual volume was 80.1 mL. Is her measurement accurate? Explain.

_____
_____
_____
_____

11 Compare How might the student's recorded data differ if she were simply describing the liquid instead of measuring it?

_____
_____
_____
_____

My Notes

Representing Data

ESSENTIAL QUESTION

How do scientists make sense of data?

By the end of this lesson, you should be able to use tables, graphs, models, and simulations to represent data, phenomena, and systems.

The letters here represent just a tiny portion of the human genome. The letters correspond to the bases that make up DNA, the carrier of genetic information. These letters are part of a genetics exhibition panel located in the French museum City of Science and Industry.

OHIO **7.SIA.4** Analyze and interpret data.
OHIO **7.SIA.5** Develop descriptions, models, explanations and predictions.

© Houghton Mifflin Harcourt Publishing Company • Image Credits: ©Mauro Fermariello/Photo Researchers, Inc.

Lesson Labs

Quick Labs
- Interpreting Models
- Simulating Competition in the Food Web

Exploration Lab
- Plant Pollinators

Engage Your Brain

1 Describe Fill in the blank with the word or phrase that you think correctly completes the following sentences.

Graphs are visual representations of

_____.

A map of the United States is an example of a(n)

_____.

_____ help show patterns, or trends, in data.

2 Evaluate Identify two things you can understand by looking at this model that would be difficult to see without it.

_____
_____
_____
_____
_____
_____
_____
_____
_____

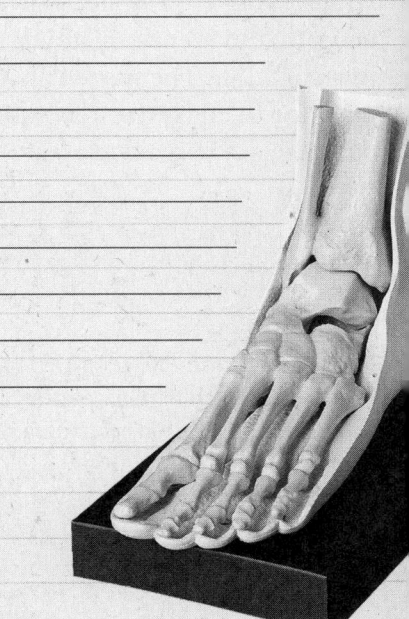

Active Reading

3 Apply Many words, such as *model,* have multiple meanings. Use context clues to write your own definition for each meaning of the word *model.*

Example sentence
Sports stars are role <u>models</u> for thousands of young people.

model:

_____
_____

Example sentence
They used a computer to <u>model</u> the possible effects of global warming.

model:

_____
_____

Vocabulary Terms

- mean
- model
- simulation

4 Apply As you learn the definition of the vocabulary term in this lesson, create your own definition or sketch to help you remember the meaning of the term.

Get Organized!

How do scientists make sense of data?

There are many different kinds of scientific investigations, all of which involve the collection of data. *Data* are the facts, figures, and other evidence scientists gather when they conduct an investigation. The more data a scientist collects, the greater is the need for the data to be organized in some way. Data tables are one useful way to organize a lot of data.

5 Identify Underline the title of the table below. This table has three columns, each with a heading on top. The headings tell what data are in the column. This table also has four rows. Write the headings of the rows below.

_____

_____

_____

2010 Summer Tomato Yield

Month	Plant without Fertilizer	Plant with Fertilizer (1 tsp mixed into soil)
June	1	1
July	10	9
August	11	13

A data table has a title, columns, and rows.

The data table above shows the number of tomatoes produced each month from an unfertilized and a fertilized tomato plant.

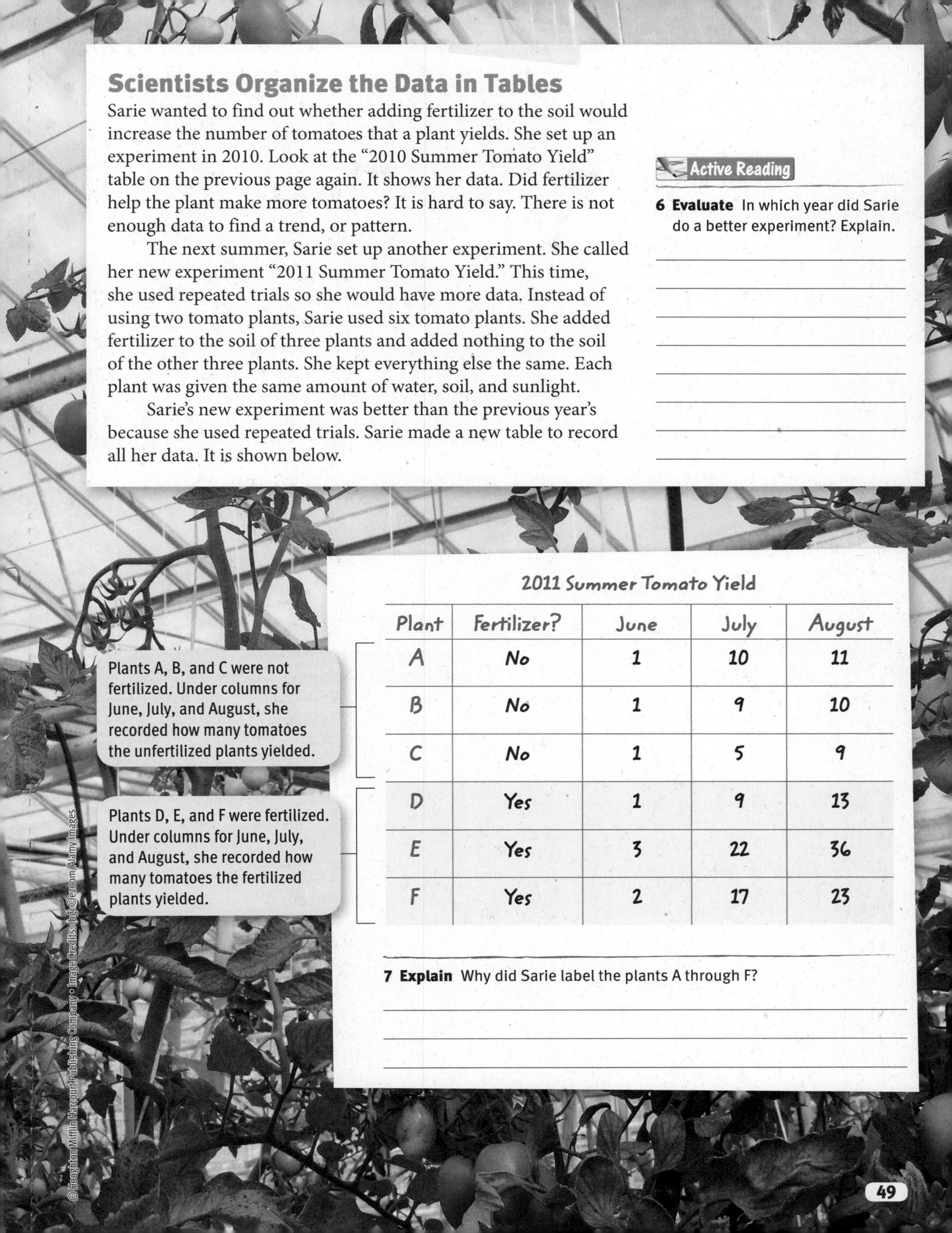

Scientists Organize the Data in Tables

Sarie wanted to find out whether adding fertilizer to the soil would increase the number of tomatoes that a plant yields. She set up an experiment in 2010. Look at the "2010 Summer Tomato Yield" table on the previous page again. It shows her data. Did fertilizer help the plant make more tomatoes? It is hard to say. There is not enough data to find a trend, or pattern.

The next summer, Sarie set up another experiment. She called her new experiment "2011 Summer Tomato Yield." This time, she used repeated trials so she would have more data. Instead of using two tomato plants, Sarie used six tomato plants. She added fertilizer to the soil of three plants and added nothing to the soil of the other three plants. She kept everything else the same. Each plant was given the same amount of water, soil, and sunlight.

Sarie's new experiment was better than the previous year's because she used repeated trials. Sarie made a new table to record all her data. It is shown below.

🖊 **Active Reading**

6 Evaluate In which year did Sarie do a better experiment? Explain.

_____

_____

_____

_____

_____

_____

_____

Plants A, B, and C were not fertilized. Under columns for June, July, and August, she recorded how many tomatoes the unfertilized plants yielded.

Plants D, E, and F were fertilized. Under columns for June, July, and August, she recorded how many tomatoes the fertilized plants yielded.

2011 Summer Tomato Yield

Plant	Fertilizer?	June	July	August
A	No	1	10	11
B	No	1	9	10
C	No	1	5	9
D	Yes	1	9	13
E	Yes	3	22	36
F	Yes	2	17	23

7 Explain Why did Sarie label the plants A through F?

_____

_____

Scientists Graph and Analyze the Data

To analyze data for trends, scientists construct graphs. The type of graph depends upon the type of data collected and the trends they want to show. All graphs need a title to explain what the graph shows.

One type of graph is a line graph. A line graph shows changes over time. Line graphs are useful for showing changes over time. A line graph has an *x*-axis and a *y*-axis. The *x*-axis goes across the bottom of the graph. The *x*-axis usually represents time. The *y*-axis goes up and down the side of a graph. The *y*-axis usually represents units being measured. For example, the numbers on the *y*-axis of a line graph could represent tomato yields. The *x*-axis could represent growing-season months.

Data are represented with dots or other marks called data points. Lines connecting these points show changes over time. A line of a different color or style represents each category. A key shows what the color or style means.

How To Calculate the Mean

The **mean**, also called the average, is the sum of the data values divided by the number of data values. Comparing means is a good way to compare data sets. The mean number of tomatoes on fertilized plants in August is:

$$\underset{\text{Plant D}}{13} + \underset{\text{Plant E}}{36} + \underset{\text{Plant F}}{23} = \underset{\text{Sum}}{72}$$

$$\underset{\text{Sum}}{72} \div \underset{\text{Number of data values}}{3} = \underset{\text{Mean}}{24}$$

Visualize It!

8 Interpret Data recorded in a table can be used to create a line graph. What do the numbers on the *y*-axis of this graph stand for?

_____

_____

2010 Summer Tomato Yield		
Month	**Plant without Fertilizer**	**Plant with Fertilizer**
June	1	1
July	10	9
August	11	13

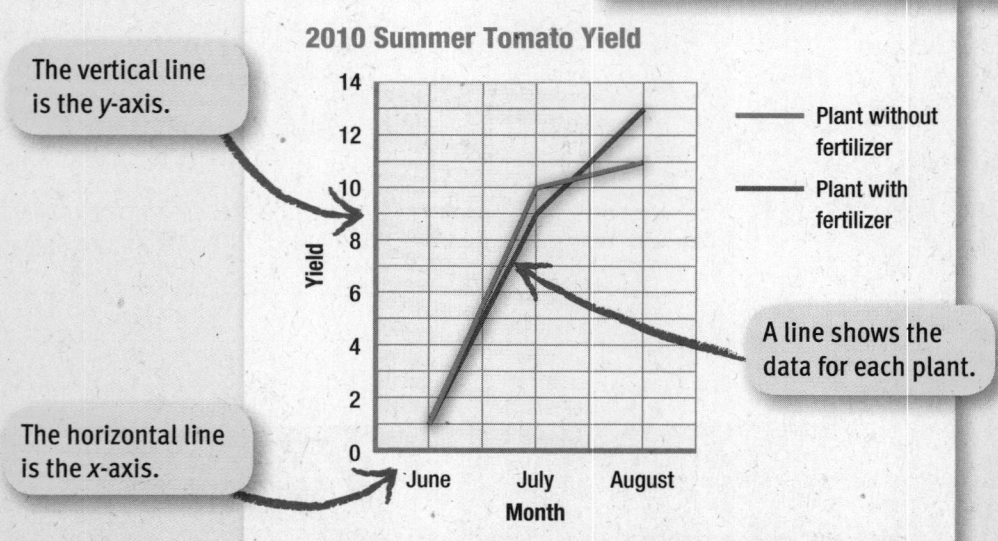

2010 Summer Tomato Yield

The vertical line is the *y*-axis.

The horizontal line is the *x*-axis.

A line shows the data for each plant.

Plant without fertilizer

Plant with fertilizer

Do the Math You Try It

9 Analyze Help Sarie organize and graph her 2011 data.

Calculate the Mean

Calculate Using data in the data table, find the mean for all unfertilized and fertilized tomato plants for each summer month.

Use this formula for unfertilized plants for each month:

$$\underline{} + \underline{} + \underline{} = \underline{}$$

Plant A   Plant B   Plant C   Sum

$$\underline{} \div \underline{} = \underline{}$$

Sum   Number of months   Mean

Now use the same formula for the fertilized plants.

2011 Summer Tomato Yield				
Plant	Fertilizer?	June	July	August
A	No	1	10	11
B	No	1	9	10
C	No	1	5	9
D	Yes	1	9	13
E	Yes	3	22	36
F	Yes	2	17	23

Graph the Data

Step 1:
Write the means in the data table under the correct columns and in the correct rows.

Step 2:
Label the axes. Mark the months on the *x*-axis and numbers of tomatoes on the *y*-axis. Make sure your numbers go high enough. If needed, write every other number only (2, 4, 6, etc.).

Step 3:
Plot the data points on the graph. Connect the data points using one color to show fertilized plants and another color to show unfertilized plants. Make a key to show what the colors stand for.

Step 4:
Write a title that describes what the graph shows.

2011 Mean Summer Tomato Yield

Month	Plants without Fertilizer	Plants with Fertilizer
June		
July		
August		24

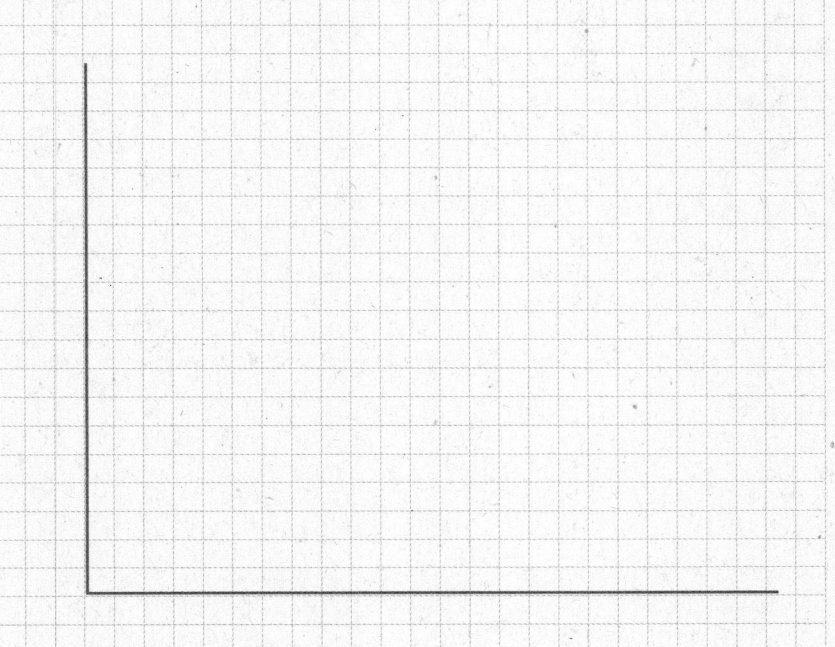

Circle Up!

What do graphs show?

Graphs show data in a visual way. Data shown in a graph are often easier to understand than data shown in a table. There are many kinds of graphs.

A *circle graph,* or pie chart, is used when showing how each group of data relates to all of the data. A *bar graph* is used to display and compare data in a number of categories. A *line graph* is most often used to show continuous change. Line graphs are useful for showing changes in variables over time.

Do the Math | You Try It

Jon observes the bird feeder in his yard for 3 hours at the same time each day for 3 days. He writes down the types and numbers of birds that visit the feeder. In total, he sees 60 birds. His data are shown at the right.

Cardinal	JHT JHT JHT
Finch	JHT IIII
Mockingbird	JHT JHT JHT JHT IIII
Wren	JHT JHT II

10 Calculate Use the table below to organize the data that Jon collected. In the last column, find the percentage of each bird that Jon saw by dividing the number of each type of bird by the total number of birds and multiplying by 100%.

Type of bird	Number of birds	Percentage of birds

Visualize It!

The circle graph below is divided into equal sections that are 5% of the total circle. Remember that a complete circle is 100%.

11 Graph Make a circle graph using the percentages you calculated for the bird study. Make appropriately sized pie-shaped slices of the graph for each type of bird. Label each section of the graph with the name of the bird type and the total number of birds of that type counted. Then add an appropriate title.

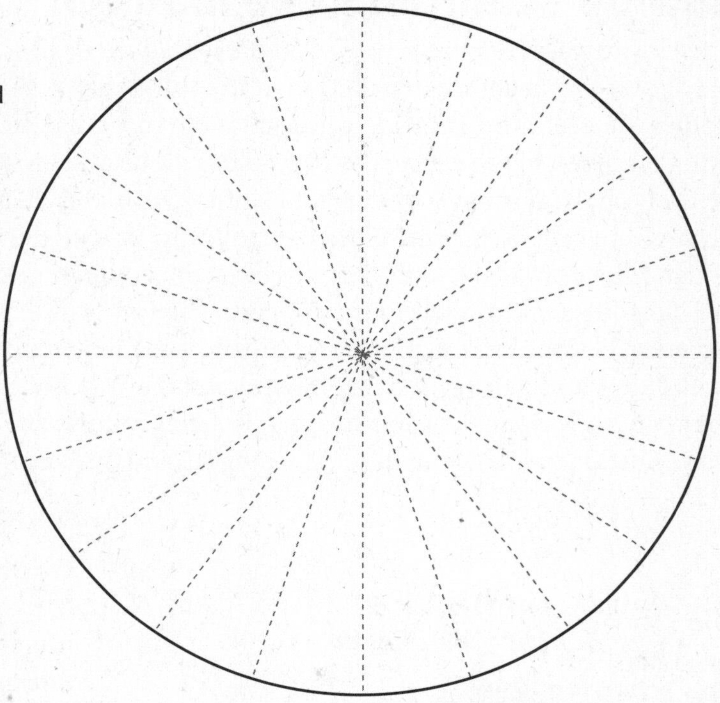

12 Identify Describe something that is easier to see in the circle graph than it is to see in the table.

_____

_____

_____

13 Interpret How does the size of each section of your circle graph relate to the percentage that it represents?

_____

_____

_____

Think Outside the Book Inquiry

14 Graph Plot the results of the bird study in a bar graph. Which variable will be shown on the horizontal axis, and which will be shown on the vertical axis?

Test Drive the New Model

How do scientists use models?

A scientific **model** is a pattern, plan, representation, or description that shows the structure or function of the thing that is studied. Models are useful for showing things that are too small, too large, or too complex to see easily. For example, a globe and an atlas are both physical models of Earth. Scientists who study Earth's atmosphere use mathematical models to try to imitate Earth's climate. Other models, like diagrams, are conceptual models.

Scientists use models in many ways. They use models to make predictions before an investigation as well as to represent the results after an investigation. Scientists must use models wisely. They must always make sure the models are as accurate as possible. They must be aware of the model's strengths and limitations.

Active Reading

15 Apply As you read, underline examples of scientific models.

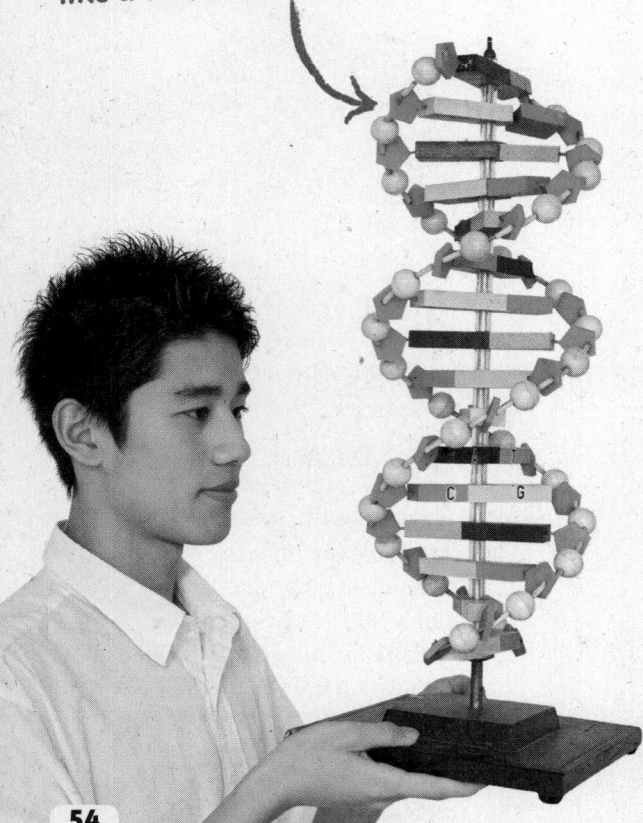

The structure of DNA is a double helix, which is shaped like a twisted ladder.

To Explain and Represent Data

One famous scientific model is that of the DNA (deoxyribonucleic acid) double helix. DNA is the molecule that passes genetic information from one generation to the next. Data from biology, chemistry, and physics went into developing the DNA model. The model, in a way, is a representation of that data and evidence.

Models can be created out of a variety of materials. They can be simple or complex. For example, a DNA double helix model can be brightly colored and three-dimensional, similar to the one at the left, or it can be lines on a piece of paper. The important thing is for the model to show what it must in order to be a useful representation.

16 Infer Why is it valuable for some objects to be shown by more than one kind of model?

_____
_____
_____
_____

Visualize It!

17 Compare Both the photo and model below show a plant cell. Identify an advantage and a disadvantage for using the model instead of the photo to study cells.

_____

_____

_____

_____

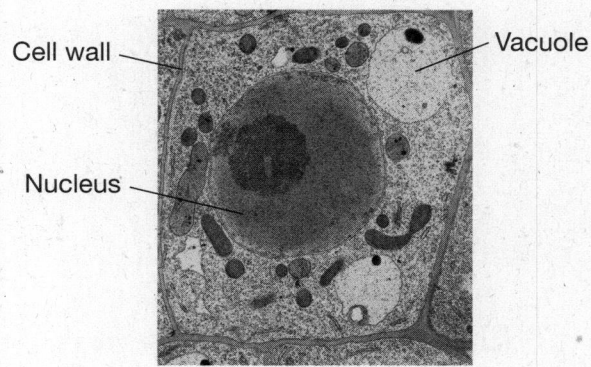

Cell wall

Vacuole

Nucleus

The details of the actual plant cell in this photograph can be fuzzy.

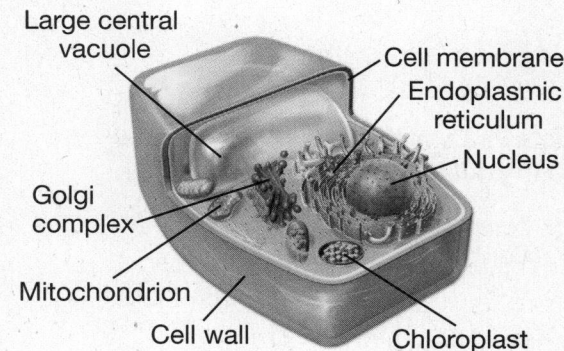

Large central vacuole

Cell membrane

Endoplasmic reticulum

Nucleus

Golgi complex

Mitochondrion

Cell wall

Chloroplast

The model of the plant cell shows distinct parts.

How can simulations explain scientific phenomena?

A **simulation** uses a model to show how an object or system behaves or functions. Simulations can be simple animations, such as one showing how a lever works. Many simulations that scientists use are complex computer simulations based on mathematical models. These simulations show how something very small or very complex could behave or function. Scientists can test a hypothesis about a function with a simulation.

Scientists use computer simulations to explain why DNA looks like a twisted ladder. These simulations show the "rungs" of the "ladder" coming apart in the middle. The DNA ladder splits into two half-ladders. Pieces of DNA with matching rungs can attach, forming a new DNA ladder. Scientists use this simulation to explain how genetic information is passed from parents to offspring.

Simulations May Predict Future Events

Scientists also use simulations to predict how objects or systems could change. For example, they could make a change in a simulation of DNA as it splits. They could predict how this change might affect offspring. Designers of aircraft and automobiles use simulations to study how air flows around a vehicle. A design change could cause more or less drag, or friction, on the vehicle body caused by air. The simulations help designers predict how a change in the body of a vehicle could affect how much fuel it uses.

A major use of simulations involves predicting the weather. Meteorologists create mathematical models of weather systems. They use the models to simulate how a change in wind or air temperature might cause a weather system to behave differently. You can see these models and simulations on television news programs every day.

Visual Summary

To complete this summary, check the box that indicates true or false. Then use the key below to check your answers. You can use this page to review the main concepts of the lesson.

Representing Data

Scientists organize and analyze data using calculations, tables, and graphs.

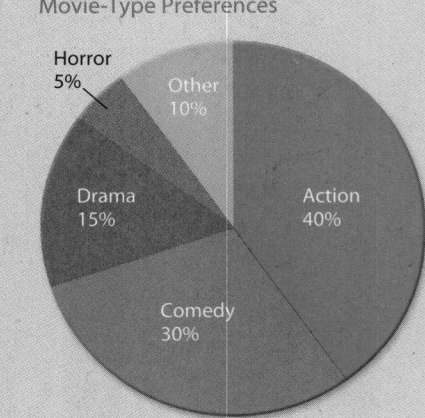

Movie-Type Preferences

- Horror 5%
- Other 10%
- Action 40%
- Drama 15%
- Comedy 30%

T F

19. ☐ ☐ According to this circle graph, more students preferred horror movies than comedies.

Models and simulations represent and explain phenomena and systems.

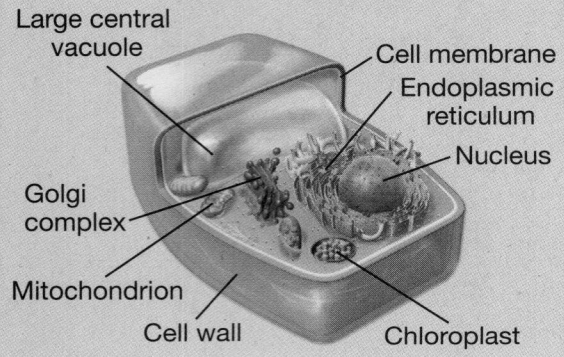

- Large central vacuole
- Cell membrane
- Endoplasmic reticulum
- Nucleus
- Golgi complex
- Mitochondrion
- Cell wall
- Chloroplast

T F

18. ☐ ☐ Because models are simplified versions of real objects, they often have limitations.

Answers: 18 True; 19 False; 20 True

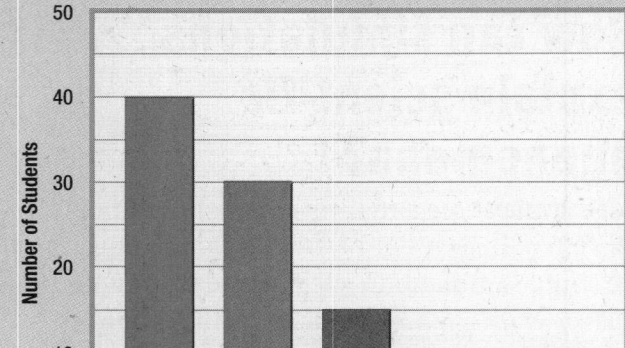

Movie-Type Preferences

Number of Students (y-axis: 0, 10, 20, 30, 40, 50)

Type of Movie: Action, Comedy, Drama, Horror, Other

T F

20. ☐ ☐ A bar graph is used to compare data in categories.

21 **Model** Sketch a simple model of your yard or a neighborhood park. Include some animals, some plants, and some environmental factors.

Lesson Review

Vocabulary

Circle the term that best completes each of the following sentences.

1 A(n) *hypothesis/simulation* can be used to imitate how a system functions.

2 A *model/law* uses familiar things to describe unfamiliar things.

3 The *mean/graph* is an average of the data.

Key Concepts

4 Define What is a model?

_____

_____

_____

_____

5 Describe Give an example in which a scientist might calculate the mean of a data set.

_____

_____

_____

_____

6 Explain Why do scientists use data tables?

_____

_____

_____

_____

7 Define What is a simulation?

_____

_____

_____

8 Explain Could you use a circle graph to show data about how body mass changes with height? Explain your answer.

_____

_____

_____

Critical Thinking

Use this photo to answer the following questions.

9 Compare How similar is this physical model to a real object?

_____

_____

_____

10 Apply How might this model be useful?

_____

_____

_____

_____

11 Hypothesize Identify a possible limitation of a model, and describe why it might make a model less useful than it could be.

_____

_____

_____

My Notes

OHIO 7.SIA.4 Analyze and interpret data.
OHIO 7.SIA.5 Develop descriptions, models, explanations and predictions.

Making Conclusions from Evidence

In scientific investigations, you will be asked to collect data and summarize your findings. Sometimes, a set of data can be interpreted in more than one way and lead to more than one conclusion. A reliable investigation will allow you to make conclusions that are supported by the data you have collected, and that reflect the findings of other scientists.

Tutorial

Take these steps as you analyze findings and evaluate a conclusion made from the findings.

Flu Prevention Breakthrough

A medical study has shown that a new drug, Compound Z, protected children from the flu. The results of the study that was conducted last year showed that only 5% of students who were taking Compound Z were affected by the flu. During the same period of time, 20% of the general population was affected by the flu.

Researchers do not know exactly how Compound Z protects children from the flu.

1 What conclusion is made by the study? Identify the conclusion or interpretation of the data that is being made in the study.

2 What evidence or data is given and does the data support the conclusion? Identify all the observations and findings that are presented to support the conclusion. Decide whether the findings support the conclusion. Look for information and data in other studies that replicate the experiments and verify the conclusion.

3 Should other data be considered before accepting the conclusion as true? There may be more than one way to interpret findings of scientific work, and important questions left unanswered. When this happens, plan to make observations, look for more information, or do further experiments that could eliminate one explanation as a possibility.

Other data should be considered before the conclusion above can be supported. For example, data should be gathered to determine the percentage of children who were not taking Compound Z and got the flu. And, within the 20% of the general population who got the flu, what percentage were children?

You Try It!

Climate change is one of the most debated issues in modern science.

In the past 100 years, Earth's average global temperature has risen more than 0.74 °C. In 2008, the cold La Niña current in the Pacific caused the average global temperature to drop, but the global average was still warmer than any year from 1880 to 1996. The concentration of the greenhouse gas carbon dioxide (CO_2), rose from by about 76 parts per million from 1958 to 2008. Many people interpret this to mean that human activity is causing global climate change. However, evidence from the geologic record shows that Earth's climate has experienced even larger climate changes in the past.

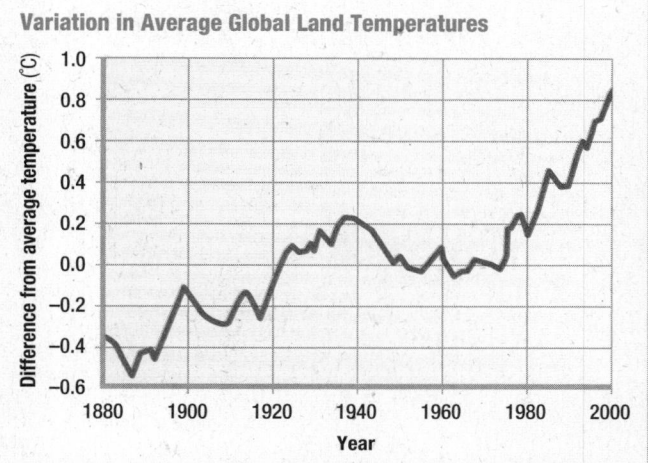

Variation in Average Global Land Temperatures

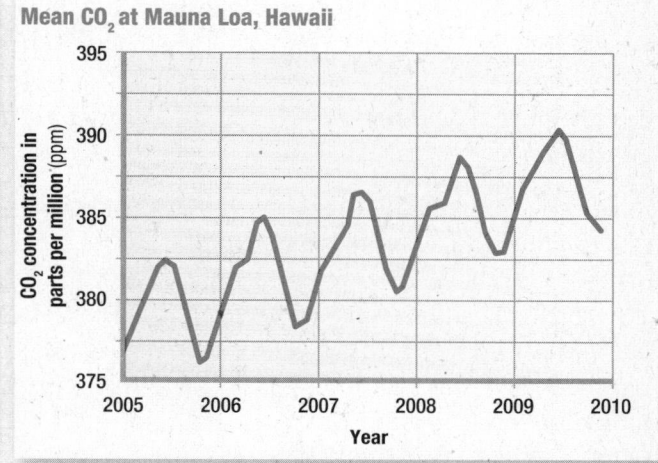

Mean CO_2 at Mauna Loa, Hawaii

1 Gathering Data The graphs shown above are taken from a study on climate change. Identify trends or patterns that you observe in the graphs.

_____

_____

_____

_____

2 Making a Conclusion Draw a conclusion that is supported by the data you describe. Summarize your conclusion in a single paragraph.

_____

_____

_____

_____

_____

3 Analyzing Data Which conclusions are supported by the data in the graphs? Which conclusions are not supported by the data?

_____

_____

_____

_____

4 Making Predictions What other data do you need to further support your conclusion?

_____

_____

_____

Take It Home

Find an article that makes a conclusion based on a scientific study. Evaluate the conclusion and determine whether the evidence given supports the conclusion. Bring the article to class and be prepared to discuss.

Lesson 5

The Engineering Design Process

ESSENTIAL QUESTION

What is the engineering design process?

By the end of this lesson, you should be able to explain how the engineering design process is used to develop solutions to meet people's needs.

In 2008, Olympic swimmers competed in a large pool inside the Beijing National Aquatics Center, also known as the Beijing Water Cube. It now houses water rides, a wave pool, and a spa.

OHIO 7.SIA.3 Use appropriate mathematics, tools and techniques to gather data and information.

OHIO 7.SIA.5 Develop descriptions, models, explanations and predictions.

OHIO 7.SIA.8 Communicate scientific procedures and explanations.

🖐 Lesson Labs

Quick Labs
- Technology in Science
- Evaluate a Prototype

S.T.E.M. Lab
- Using Engineering to Solve a Problem

🌎 Engage Your Brain

1 Predict Check T or F to show whether you think each statement is true or false.

T	F	
☐	☐	The Beijing Water Cube is an example of technology.
☐	☐	Creativity is not part of the engineering design process.
☐	☐	Nature can inspire new designs.

2 Observe Both the shape of a structure and the shapes of its individual parts affect the overall strength of a structure. Identify the repeating shapes in each image. List at least two differences between the walls of the Water Cube and the milk bubbles.

_____

_____

_____

_____

📖 Active Reading

3 Synthesize You can often define an unknown word if you know the meanings of its word parts. Use the word parts and sentence below to make an educated guess about the meaning of the word *technology*.

Word part	Meaning
techno	skill
logy	study of

Example sentence:
The development of smartphones is viewed as an important advance in computer technology.

technology:

_____

_____

Vocabulary Terms
- engineering
- technology
- prototype

4 Identify This list contains the vocabulary terms you'll learn in this lesson. As you read, underline the vocabulary words whenever they appear in the text.

It's All Relative

How does the goal of science compare to the goal of engineering?

Scientists observe, collect data, and form hypotheses. **Engineering** is the use of scientific and mathematical knowledge to solve practical problems. The goal of engineering is to meet the needs of society while the goal of science is to understand the natural world. Scientists study how the parts of nature work alone and together. Engineers develop ways of improving the quality of life for human beings.

Science Strives to Explain the Natural World

Scientists work in an orderly, logical way. They ask questions about the natural world and gather experimental evidence to address those questions. In order to form a scientific explanation, scientists observe, measure, test, and record data. Scientific research is careful, but it can also be creative. Creativity is expressed in the design of experiments and in the scientific explanations of observations.

Engineering Strives to Meet the Needs of Society

Humans have always needed tools, such as knives and fire, to help them survive. Beginning in the 1700s, people have increasingly used industrial processes. There is a growing need for energy to operate machines and services to support urban populations. Engineers apply scientific discoveries to develop technologies such as electrical power, sanitation systems, and new ways of communicating.

Active Reading **5 Explain** How do engineers contribute to the area where you live?

_____

_____

Visualize It!

6 Compare In what ways is the modern lamp a better design than the antique lamp? Explain.

_____

_____

_____

A wick carries oil into the globe of this lamp where it burns to produce light.

This light-emitting diode (LED) boat light stays cool. Almost 100% of its energy production is light.

© Houghton Mifflin Harcourt Publishing Company • Image Credits: (bl) ©Juha Eronen/Alamy; (br) ©Chris Hondros/Getty Images News/Getty Images

What is the relationship between technology, engineering, math, and science?

Science is the study of the natural world. Engineering applies knowledge to develop technology to solve real-life problems. **Technology** includes the use of tools, materials, or processes to meet human needs. Scientists depend on technology such as digital cameras and instruments to observe and measure when they collect data. With computers, they analyze data to support scientific explanations. Engineers build advances in science into new instruments and processes. Science and engineering support one another to advance our knowledge of the natural world and create technologies to manipulate it. Engineers use science and math to develop new technologies. Scientists use technology in research, and engineers use research results to develop technology.

Visualize It!

7 Apply Insert the terms *science, technology, engineering,* and *math* into the graphic organizer to see how they are all related.

Inquiry

8 Infer How could a biologist studying bird migration use global positioning satellite (GPS) technology?

9 Explain Why does the graphic show arrows between technology and both science and engineering?

The Right Tool For the Job

How is technology used in scientific investigations?

Scientists investigate the natural world by making observations and doing experiments. They use tools to measure, collect, and analyze data. Many investigations focus on things that are very big or very small, or located in places that are dangerous or hard to reach. Scientists and engineers design specialized technologies for these investigations. For example, biologists observe bacteria through microscopes. Huge accelerators produce high energy collisions between atoms and other particles. Astronomers probe deep into space using digital cameras with telescopes. Robots transmit data from distant planets and ocean depths. The purpose of all of these tools is to collect samples, take pictures, and acquire data.

Think Outside the Book

11 **Apply** Imagine a place or situation that would be interesting to explore but is inaccessible to humans. Design, sketch, and label your own explorer. Think about the tasks that the explorer will need to do and the environment in which it will be working.

Visualize It!

10 **Identify** Label each part with one of the following tasks: generating energy, measuring properties, recording information, communicating data.

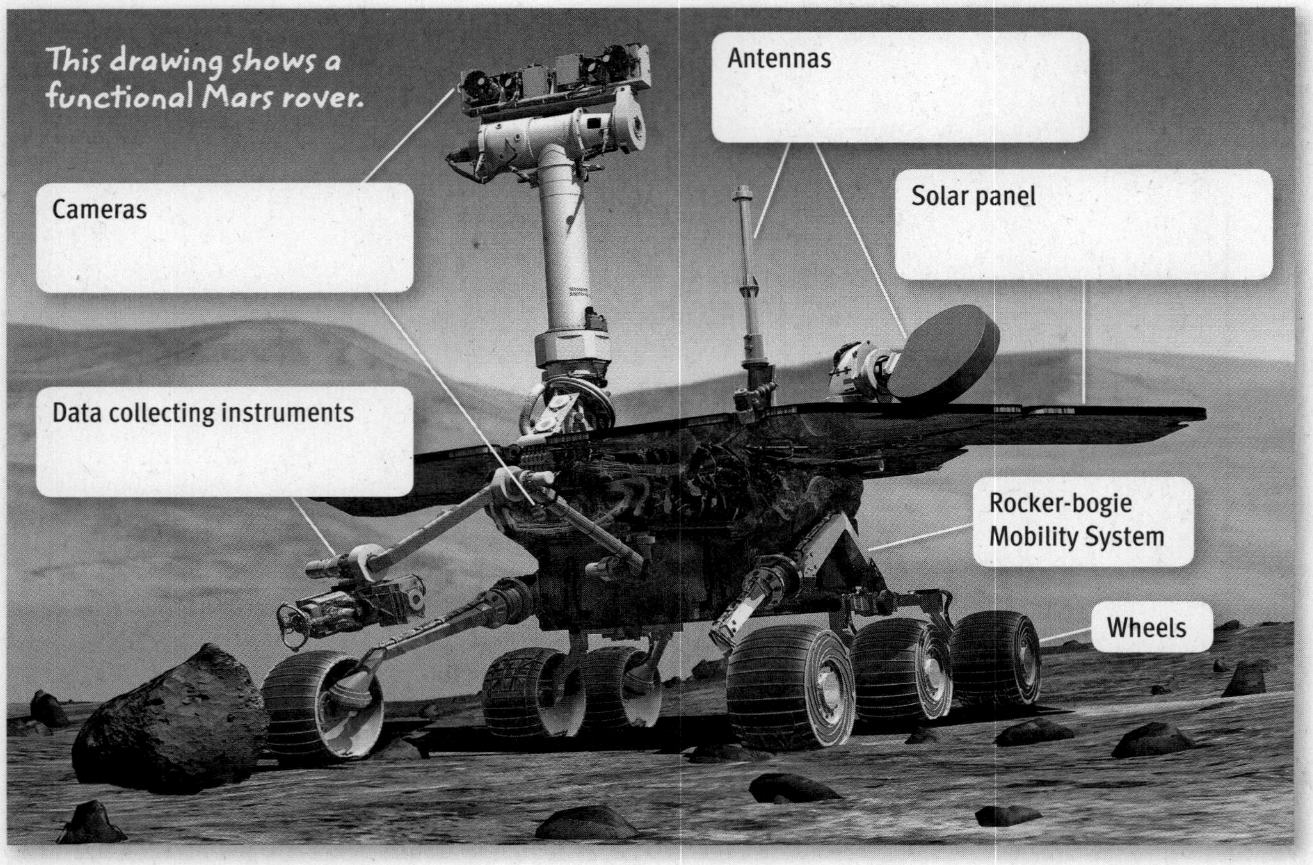

This drawing shows a functional Mars rover.

Antennas

Cameras

Solar panel

Data collecting instruments

Rocker-bogie Mobility System

Wheels

Students learning about engineering design develop such technical skills as learning to build and test a prototype.

What skills are needed for engineering design?

Look at the world around you. You see computers, cell phones, microwave ovens, and machines for washing dishes and clothes. You see motor vehicles on roads and bridges. You see a world that was designed by engineers.

The goal of engineering design is to meet people's needs. When engineers design solutions to problems, they employ a set of skills that work together.

Active Reading

12 Apply Which type of skills below do you use most often? Give an example.

_____

_____

_____

Research Skills

Engineering design starts with good research skills. Engineers learn all they can about the problem they want to solve, including how similar problems were tackled in the past. Then they must determine whether previous solution attempts were successful and how to adapt them to the current problem. To build on existing approaches, engineers examine new scientific research and apply the results to their design. These adaptations often improve on or replace the previous solutions.

Technical Skills

In solving practical problems, engineers must apply their technical skills in math and science. For example, determining how much weight a bridge can bear requires knowledge of materials and structure and the ability to perform complex calculations. Modern engineering design depends on computer skills in using specialized software for computer-aided design and analysis. Engineering design also requires skill in building **prototypes**, special models built to test a product.

Thinking Skills

Methodical, orderly thinking skills are essential for engineers who must carefully go through every step in the design process. While engineers must pay close attention to every detail in building and testing a prototype, the engineering design process also calls for creativity. Engineers form teams to brainstorm ways of thinking about a problem and proposing solutions. Sometimes they turn a disadvantage into an advantage by finding creative ways to use existing knowledge to solve problems.

Step Right Up

What are the steps of the engineering design process?

When you need to solve a problem, an organized approach leads to the best solution. The steps in the engineering design process provide a logical way of developing a new product or system to solve a real-world problem. People using the process often work in teams. As you will see on the next page, once the need has been identified, the steps of the process often become a cycle.

Active Reading **13 Identify** What is the purpose of breaking the engineering design process into specific steps?

_____

_____

1. Identifying a Need

What is the problem? Who has the problem? Why must it be solved? These are the types of questions that identify a problem that needs a technical solution.

2. Conducting Research

By doing research, the design team learns as much as possible about the need that must be met or the problem that must be solved. The research frequently turns up similar problems and the different solutions that have been tried. The design team works more efficiently by learning from the past efforts of others and by identifying new resources and possibilities.

3. Brainstorming and Selecting Solutions

Team members think of possible solution ideas during a brainstorming session. The goal of brainstorming is to come up with as many engineering design solutions as possible. Any idea, even if it does not seem promising, is open for discussion. Then each idea is evaluated: Is the device or product safe? Does it address the problem? What would it cost? Would it be easy to make? The team selects the best solution based on how well it meets the requirements of the need or problem.

4. Building a Prototype

The design team builds a prototype of the device or product they selected as the best technical solution to the need or problem. The team uses the prototype as a working model to test and evaluate how well the product works under real-life conditions. A prototype usually does not work perfectly right away. The team uses the prototype to find out how the solution can be improved and for troubleshooting—finding out why parts of the product or device do not work as expected.

 **Visualize It!**

14 Design In the space provided, sketch a prototype device for rescuing the trapped cat.

5. Testing, Evaluating, and Redesigning a Prototype

The engineering design process calls for testing and changing the prototype until a solution is reached. The team tests the prototype and records the results. After discussing the results, changes are made to improve the prototype design. Testing and redesigning the prototype continues until the prototype addresses the need.

6. Communicating Results

The final step in the engineering design process is communicating the results. It is very important to take good notes and communicate all details about the product or solution. Such details enable others to duplicate the results. Student teams can communicate the results to others in a final report or by posting their results on a display board. Professional engineers often communicate their results through reports in engineering journals.

15 List You want to tell others how you rescued the cat. How will you communicate the results? List two possible ways below.

_____

_____

How does the engineering design process work?

The steps of the engineering design process call for engineers to use both technical skills and creativity. From identifying a need to finding a good solution, engineers are always asking questions. Instead of simply moving from one step to the next, the process goes back and forth between the steps. In the chart below, the rectangles contain steps, and the diamonds contain questions or decision points. Try answering the questions in different ways and see how the path that you follow through the design process depends on the answers to the questions. Keep in mind that the goal is to design a solution to a problem, whether it is rescuing a cat or focusing a beam of charged particles on a tiny target.

Active Reading

16 **Infer** How does asking questions help the engineering design process?

_____

_____

_____

_____

_____

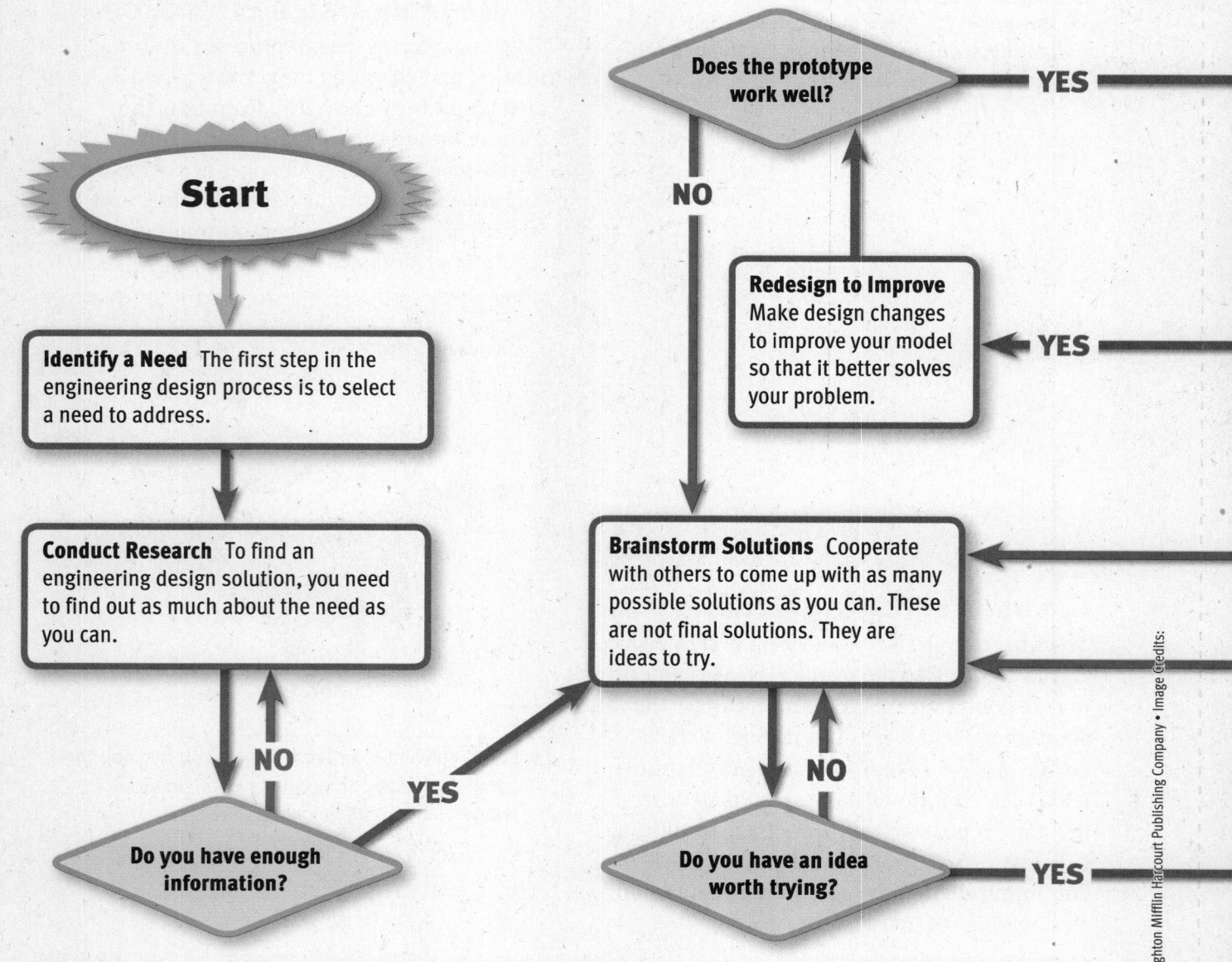

Start

Identify a Need The first step in the engineering design process is to select a need to address.

Conduct Research To find an engineering design solution, you need to find out as much about the need as you can.

Do you have enough information?

NO

YES

Brainstorm Solutions Cooperate with others to come up with as many possible solutions as you can. These are not final solutions. They are ideas to try.

Do you have an idea worth trying?

NO

YES

Does the prototype work well?

YES

NO

Redesign to Improve Make design changes to improve your model so that it better solves your problem.

YES

© Houghton Mifflin Harcourt Publishing Company • Image Credits:

This superconducting magnet assembly is one of many magnets designed to focus a beam of charged particles on a target the size of an atom in the Large Hadron Collider. Engineers followed the engineering design process to develop every component of the magnet.

Communicate Your Results When your prototype is finished, you have designed a solution to your problem. Tell others how you did it!

End!

Test and Evaluate Your prototype probably won't be perfect the first time you try it, but it should be on the right track.

Does the prototype show promise?

NO

Build a Prototype Your prototype should be a working model of your solution to the problem.

YES

NO **Can you make a prototype?**

Select a Solution Which of your ideas do you want to try? Pick one, and plan how you want to try it.

Visualize It!

17 Apply Oh, no! The test results of your most recent prototype indicate that it doesn't meet the need it was designed for. List the next four steps that your design might go through.

_____

_____

_____

_____

Visual Summary

To complete this summary, fill in each blank with the correct word or phrase. Then use the key below to check your answers. You can use this page to review the main concepts of this lesson.

> The goal of science is to understand the natural world. The goal of engineering is to meet the needs of society.

18 Engineering applies _____ and math to develop technology.

The Engineering Design Process

> The first steps in the process are identifying and doing research about a need.
> The next steps involve brainstorming and selecting a solution.

20 Before selecting the final design, engineers built and tested a _____

> Engineering design starts with good research skills. Engineering design requires a variety of technical skills.

19 Engineering design calls for both logical and creative _____ skills.

Answers: 18. science; 19. thinking; 20. prototype

21 **Design** As part of an engineering team, you are designing a tool for tracking packages being shipped. Make some suggestions to be discussed as part of the brainstorming process.

Lesson Review

Vocabulary

Fill in the blank with the term that best completes the following sentences.

1 Engineers solve real-life problems by developing new _____.

2 Developing new products and systems that meet human needs is the goal of _____.

3 A working model that engineers use to test a design is called a _____.

Key Concepts

4 Relate How are scientific discoveries used in engineering design?

_____

_____

_____

5 Summarize List the basic steps in the engineering design process.

_____

_____

_____

_____

6 Describe Explain why engineering design calls for good research skills.

_____

_____

_____

7 Conclude Explain why the engineering design process does not move smoothly from step to step but instead goes back and forth between the steps.

_____

_____

_____

Critical Thinking

8 Infer After an engineering design team communicates its results, how could those results be used?

_____

_____

_____

Use this diagram to answer the following questions.

9 Predict What qualities could engineers use the prototype of this bicycle to test?

_____

_____

_____

10 Design Suggest one or more changes that could be made to this prototype to reduce wind resistance and increase speed.

_____

_____

_____

_____

_____

_____

_____

My Notes

Unit 1

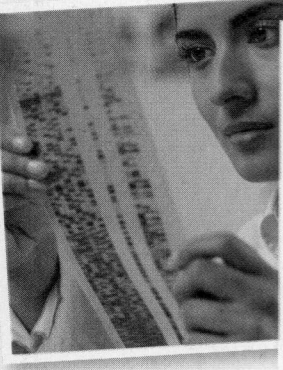

Lesson 1
ESSENTIAL QUESTION
How is science different from other fields of study?

Distinguish science and scientific explanations from other forms of knowledge, and recognize creativity in science.

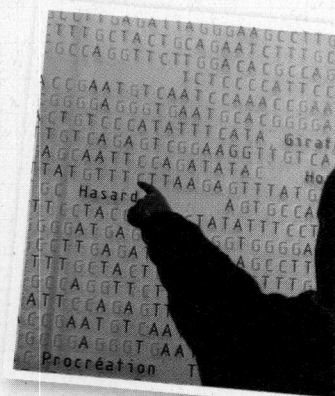

Lesson 4
ESSENTIAL QUESTION
How do scientists make sense of data?

Use tables, graphs, models, and simulations to represent data, phenomena, and systems.

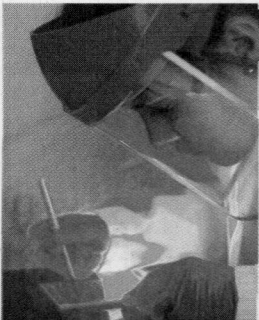

Lesson 2
ESSENTIAL QUESTION
How do scientists discover things?

Summarize the processes and characteristics of different kinds of scientific investigations.

Lesson 5
ESSENTIAL QUESTION
What is the engineering design process?

Explain how the engineering design process is used to develop solutions to meet people's needs.

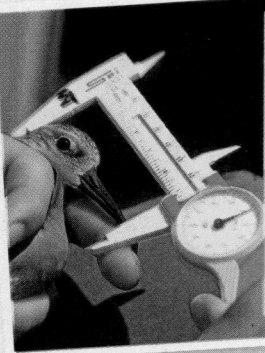

Lesson 3
ESSENTIAL QUESTION
What are the tools and units used in science?

Describe the different tools and units of measurement used in scientific investigations.

Think Outside the Book

2 Synthesize Choose one of these activities to help synthesize what you have learned in this unit.

☐ Using what you learned in Lessons 2 and 4, demonstrate the importance of repeated trials by conducting a coin-toss experiment. Record the number of trials it takes to reach 50% heads and 50% tails, which is the probability for each outcome.

☐ Using what you learned in Lessons 1 and 5, create a timeline of scientific discovery to illustrate ways that science has affected engineering throughout history. Choose a field of engineering that interests you, and research scientific discoveries in your chosen field. Illustrate your timeline.

Connect ESSENTIAL QUESTIONS
Lessons 1 and 2

1 Evaluate In what ways might the type of investigations conducted by physicists and chemists differ from the type of investigations conducted by biologists and geologists?

_____

_____

_____

_____

© Houghton Mifflin Harcourt Publishing Company • Image Credits: (tl) © Andrew Brookes/Corbis; (tr) © Mauro Fermariello/Photo Researchers, Inc.; (cl) © Richard T. Nowitz/Photo Researchers, Inc.; (bl) © fStop/Alamy; (br) © Milk Photographie/Corbis

Unit 1 Review

Name _____

Vocabulary

Fill in each blank with the term that best completes the following sentences.

1 A(n) _____ is a factor that is not allowed to change.

2 A _____ is a description of something that includes a number and a unit.

3 The sum of all values in a data set divided by the total number of values in the set is the _____ .

4 A scientific _____ is a well-supported and widely accepted explanation of nature.

5 _____ is the application of science and math to solve real-life problems.

Key Concepts

Read each question below, and circle the best answer.

6 Which of the following is a scientific question?

A Which plant is my favorite?

B Why do plants grow taller in sunlight?

C Which plant looks best in this room?

D Which plant will sell well in the store?

7 Scientists use which one of the following units to measure mass?

A pounds

B meters

C kilograms

D ounces

8 All of the following products are the result of using the engineering design process. Which product was engineered to address the needs of a person who has lost a body part such as an arm or a leg?

A lasers

B prosthetics

C steam engine

D voice-recording devices

9 The table shows events that led to the current theory that the sun is the center of the solar system.

	Event
1	Scientists observe planetary motion that cannot be explained if Earth is the center of the universe.
2	Scientists accept the theory that the planets and sun travel around Earth.
3	Scientists develop the theory that the planets travel around the sun.

Which sequence of events is correct?

A 1, 2, 3

B 1, 3, 2

C 2, 1, 3

D 3, 1, 2

10 Good experiments follow organized procedures. Which of these phrases describes another characteristic of a good scientific experiment?

A repeated trials

B uncontrolled surroundings

C small sample size for collecting data

D variable procedures for obtaining data

11 Controlled experiments include variables. Which statement describes the difference between an independent variable and a dependent variable?

A The dependent variable does not change, and the independent variable does change.

B The independent variable does not change, and the dependent variable does not change.

C The dependent variable is the control, and the independent variable is the result.

D The dependent variable changes based on the independent variable.

12 Which is a tool that scientists would least likely use in a lab?

A test tube

C electron microscope

B hot plate

D yardstick

13 Neil drops a ball from four different heights. The table shows how long it took the ball to reach the ground each time.

Time to Drop from Various Heights

Trial	?	Time (s)
A	5	1
B	20	2
C	40	3
D	80	4

Which of the following is the best label for the second column?

A Speed

C Height (m)

B Mass of the ball

D Length of drop

Critical Thinking

Answer the following questions in the spaces provided.

14 Explain how a scatter plot can be used to show precision in data measurements.

_____

_____

_____

_____

15 A biologist used the terrarium below to model the interactions of plants and animals in a forest ecosystem.

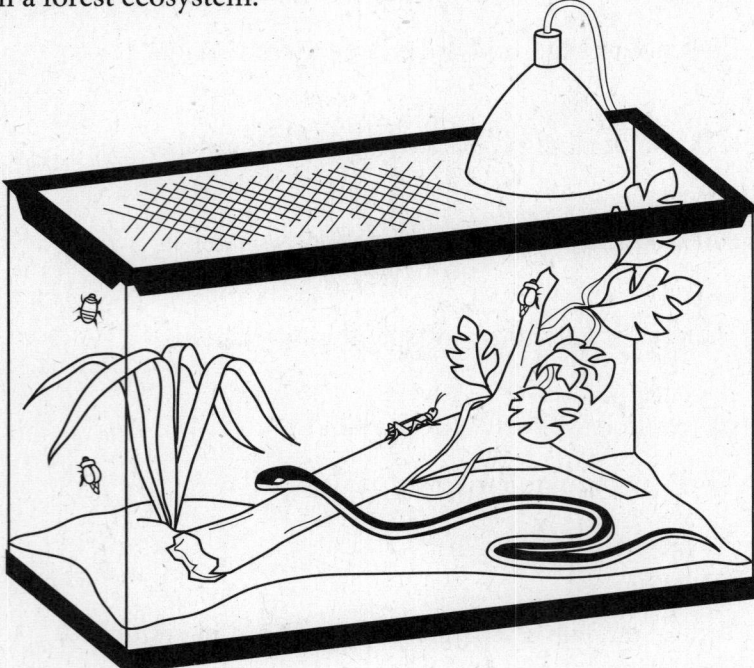

A Identify one benefit of using this model to study organism interactions.

_____

_____

B Identify one limitation of using this model to study organism interactions.

_____

_____

Connect **ESSENTIAL QUESTIONS**
Lessons 2 and 3

Answer the following question in the space provided.

16 One student thinks that marigold plants grow better when they receive 10 h of light each day. Another student thinks they grow better with only 8 h per day. Design an experiment that could test this idea. Identify the independent variable and the dependent variable, and describe how the data will be collected, describe how it will be controlled, and show how the data should be recorded.

_____

_____

_____

_____

_____

Earth's Water

Big Idea

Water moves through Earth's atmosphere, oceans, land, and living things in a cycle.

Waterfalls show the important role gravity plays in moving Earth's water.

What do you think?

Fresh water is found in ponds, lakes, streams, rivers, and underground in aquifers. Where does the water in your school come from?

Humans rely on water to stay healthy.

CITIZEN SCIENCE

Conserving Water

Fresh water evaporates into the air and then condenses to form clouds. It falls from the sky as precipitation and then flows over Earth's surface in streams and rivers. It seeps underground through soil and rocks. Fresh water makes up only a small fraction of Earth's water and is not evenly distributed.

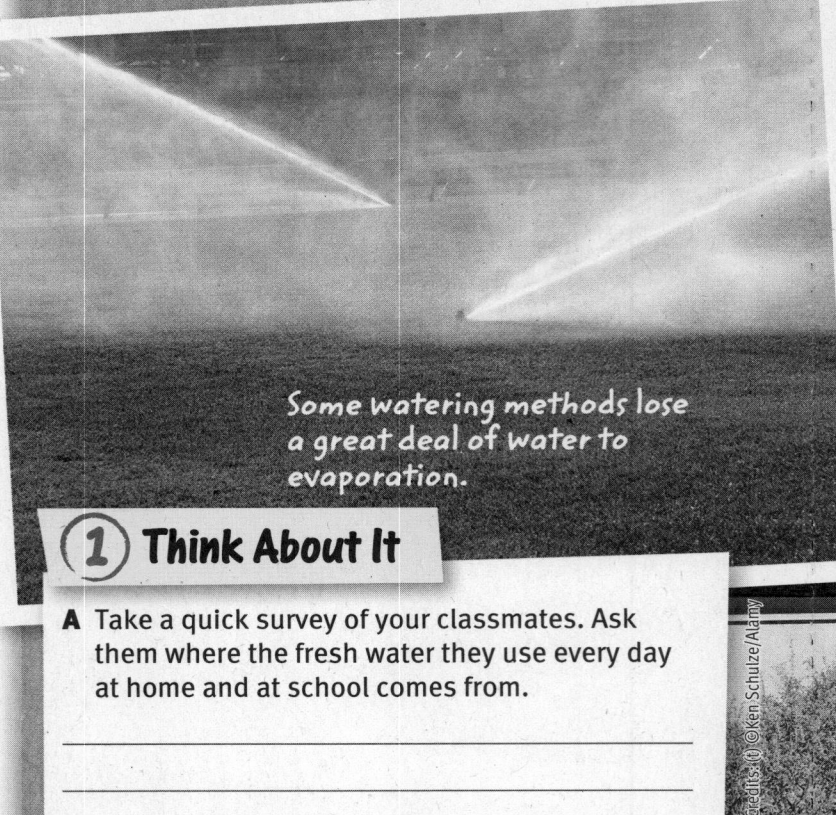

Some watering methods lose a great deal of water to evaporation.

1 Think About It

A Take a quick survey of your classmates. Ask them where the fresh water they use every day at home and at school comes from.

_____

_____

_____

B Ask your classmates to identify different uses of water at your school.

_____

_____

_____

② Ask a Question

How do you conserve water?

Water is an essential resource for everyone, but it is a limited resource. What are some ways that your school may be wasting water?

_____

_____

_____

_____

_____

_____

_____

_____

Xeriscaping is a method of landscaping by using plants that require less water.

③ Make a Plan

A Make a list of five ways in which the school can conserve water.

_____

_____

_____

_____

_____

B In the space below, sketch out a design for a pamphlet or a poster that you can place in the hallways to promote water conservation at your school.

Take It Home

Take a pamphlet or a poster home. With an adult, talk about ways in which water can be conserved in and around your home.

Water and Its Properties

ESSENTIAL QUESTION

What makes water so important?

By the end of this lesson, you should be able to describe water's structure, its properties, and its importance to Earth's systems.

Not all liquids form round droplets, but water does. Water's unique properties have to do with the way water molecules interact.

OHIO **7.ESS.1** The hydrologic cycle illustrates the changing states of water as it moves through the lithosphere, biosphere, hydrosphere and atmosphere.

Engage Your Brain

1 Predict Check T or F to show whether you think each statement is true or false.

T   F

☐ ☐ Most of the water on Earth is fresh water.

☐ ☐ Water exists in three different states on Earth.

☐ ☐ Water can dissolve many different substances, such as salt.

☐ ☐ Flowing water can be used to generate electricity.

2 Identify The drawing below shows a water molecule. What do each of the three parts represent?

_____

_____

_____

 Active Reading

3 Synthesize You can often define an unknown word if you know the meaning of its word parts. Use the word parts and sentence below to make an educated guess about the meaning of the word *cohesion*.

Word part	Meaning
co-	with, together
-hesion	sticking, joined

Example sentence
When water forms droplets, it is displaying the property of <u>cohesion</u>.

Cohesion:

_____

_____

_____

Vocabulary Terms
• polarity   • specific heat
• cohesion   • solvent
• adhesion

4 Apply As you learn the definition of each vocabulary term in this lesson, create your own definition or sketch to help you remember the meaning of the term.

Watered Down

What are some of water's roles on Earth?

Water shapes Earth's surface and influences Earth's weather. Water is also vital for life. In fact, you are over 70% water. You depend on clean, fresh drinking water to maintain that 70% of you. But a limited amount of fresh water is available on Earth. Only 3% of Earth's water is drinkable. Of this 3% of water that is drinkable, over 75% is frozen in the polar icecaps and is not readily available for our use. Therefore, it is important that we protect our water resources.

Influencing Weather

 **Active Reading** **6 Identify** As you read, underline four different forms of water that fall on Earth's surface.

All weather is related to water. Water constantly moves from Earth's surface to the atmosphere, where it may form clouds. Water falls back to Earth's surface again as rain, snow, hail, or sleet. Weather also depends on the amount of moisture in the air.

Shaping Earth's Surface

Over time, water can completely reshape a landscape. Water slowly wears away rock and carries away sediment and soil. Flowing rivers and pounding ocean waves are also examples of water shaping Earth's surface. Frozen water shapes Earth's surface, too. Glaciers, for example, scrape away rock and soil, depositing the sediment elsewhere when the glacier melts.

Do the Math

You Try It

5 Graph About 3% of water on Earth is fresh water. The rest is salt water. Fill out the percentage grid to show the percentage of fresh water on Earth.

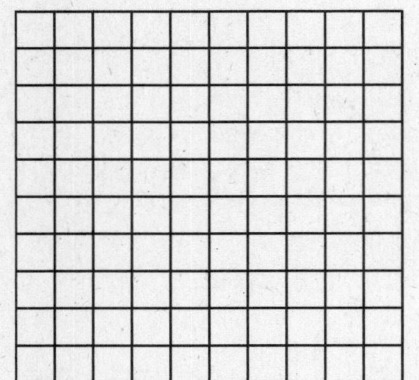

Supporting Life

Every living thing is largely made up of water, and nearly all biological processes use water. All of an organism's cellular chemistry depends on water. Water regulates temperature and helps transport substances. Without water, animals and plants would dry up and die.

For humans, clean water is vital for good health. People must have clean water to drink in order to survive. Contaminated water sources are a major public health problem in many countries. Contaminated water is also harmful to plants, animals, and can affect crops that provide food for humans.

Supporting Human Activities

Clean drinking water is necessary for all humans. Many humans use water at home for bathing, cleaning, and watering lawns and gardens.

More fresh water is used in industry than is used in homes. Over 20% of the fresh water used by humans is used for industrial purposes—to manufacture goods, cool power stations, clean industrial products, extract minerals, and generate energy by using hydroelectric dams.

More water is used for agriculture than industry. Most water used for agriculture is used to irrigate crops. It is also used to care for farm animals.

Visualize It!

7 List List at least four roles of water in this scene.

_____

_____

_____

_____

Molecular Attraction

What is the structure of a water molecule?

Matter is made up of tiny particles called *atoms*. Atoms can join with other atoms to make molecules. A water molecule is made up of two hydrogen atoms and one oxygen atom—in other words, H_2O. Each hydrogen atom is linked to the oxygen atom, forming a shape like a cartoon mouse's ears sticking out from its head.

What makes water a polar molecule?

In a water molecule, the hydrogen atoms have a small positive charge. The oxygen atom has a small negative charge. So the water molecule has a partial positive charge at one end (mouse ears) and a partial negative charge at the other (mouse chin). Anything that has a positive charge at one end and negative charge at the other end is said to have **polarity**. A water molecule is therefore a polar molecule. In liquid water, the negative end of one water molecule is attracted to the positive end of another water molecule. Each water molecule interacts with the surrounding water molecules.

👁 Visualize It!

8 Label Indicate the polarity of water by writing a + or − next to each atom that makes up the water molecule.

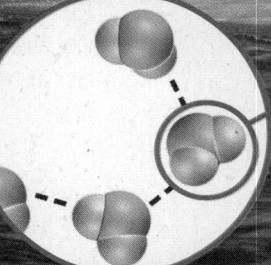

Because of polarity, the positive end of one water molecule interacts with the negative end of another molecule.

Water molecules have a positive end and a negative end.

What states of water occur on Earth?

Active Reading **9 Identify** As you read, underline the three states of water that occur on Earth.

Most of Earth's water is in liquid form. Earth is the only planet in our solar system with abundant liquid water. Gravity causes liquid water to flow downhill and to rest in low-lying areas. As a result, Earth has rivers, lakes, and oceans. Like other liquids, liquid water takes the shape of whatever contains it.

Liquid water can change into an invisible gas called water vapor, or it can freeze into solid ice or snow. Like liquid water, water vapor and ice also have the chemical formula H_2O. So liquid water, water vapor, and ice are simply varieties, or states, of water. Conditions on Earth allow water to exist in these three different states. The three states of water can change into one another. When water changes state, it either takes up or releases energy.

Water vapor is a gas, so most water vapor is found in Earth's atmosphere. Water vapor cannot be seen. Clouds form when water vapor in the atmosphere condenses into liquid water droplets. Like all gases, water vapor expands or contracts to fill available space.

Unlike other liquids, water expands when it freezes. Molecules in liquid water, therefore, are closer together than are the molecules of solid water. In other words, there is more open space between the water molecules in ice. Due to this fact, solid water, or ice, is less dense than liquid water. So ice floats on liquid water.

Visualize It!

10 Describe Using your own words in the spaces provided, identify the state of water, and describe the properties of each state of water.

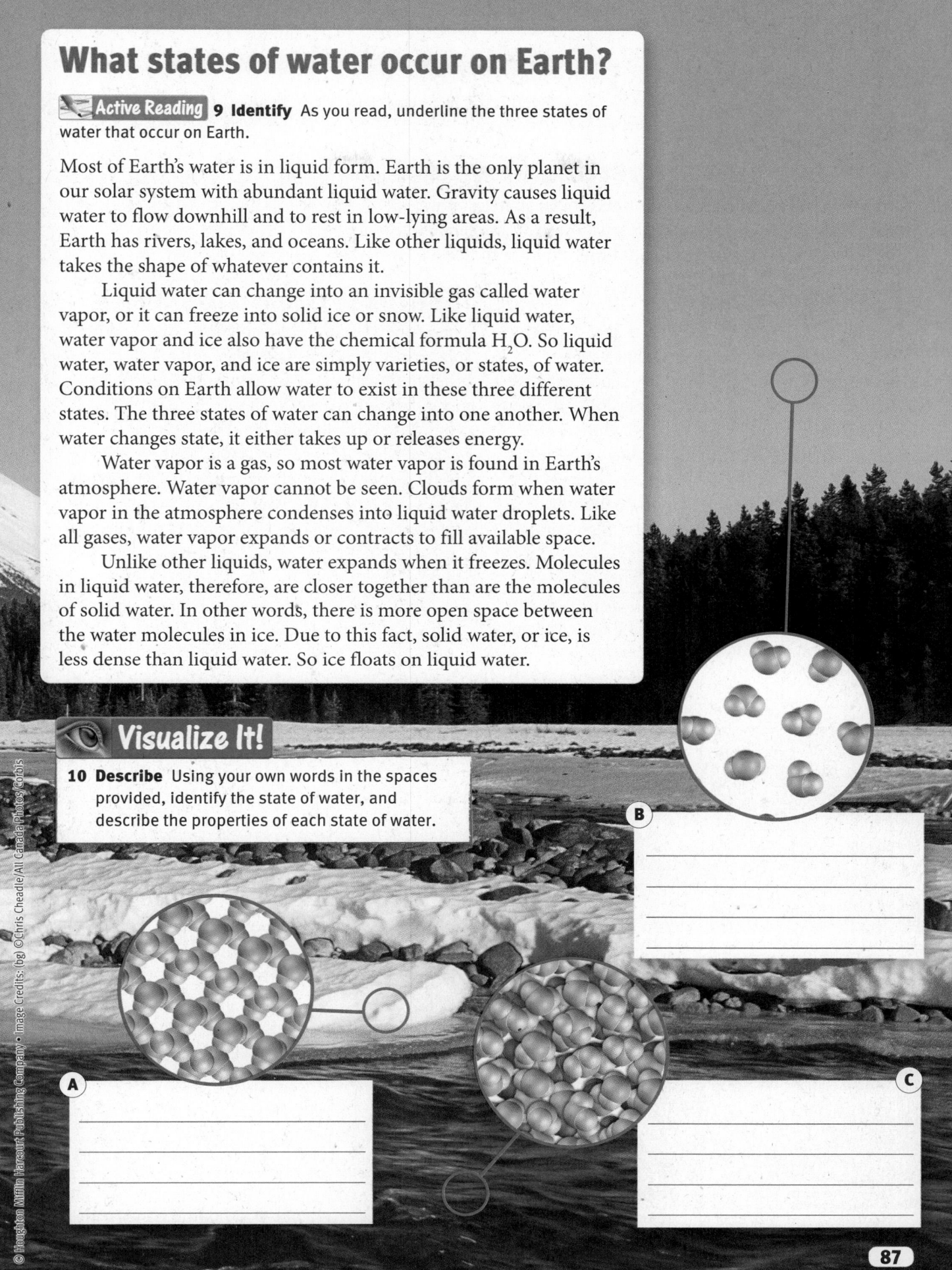

B

_____
_____
_____
_____

A

_____
_____
_____
_____

C

_____
_____
_____
_____

The Universal Solvent

What are four properties of water?

The polarity of water molecules affects the properties of water. This is because water's polarity affects how water molecules interact with one another and with other types of molecules.

It Sticks to Itself

The property that holds molecules of a substance together is **cohesion**. Water molecules stick together tightly because of their polarity, so water has high cohesion. Because of cohesion, water forms droplets. And water poured gently into a glass can fill it above the rim because cohesion holds the water molecules together. Some insects can walk on still water because their weight does not break the cohesion of the water molecules.

It Sticks to Other Substances

The property that holds molecules of different substances together is **adhesion**. Polar substances other than water can attract water molecules more strongly than water molecules attract each other. These substances are called "wettable" because water adheres, or sticks, to them so tightly. Paper towels, for example, are wettable. Water drops roll off unwettable, or "waterproof," surfaces, which are made of non-polar molecules.

Visualize It!

11 Label Identify each photo as representing either adhesion or cohesion. Then write captions explaining the properties of water shown by each photo.

A

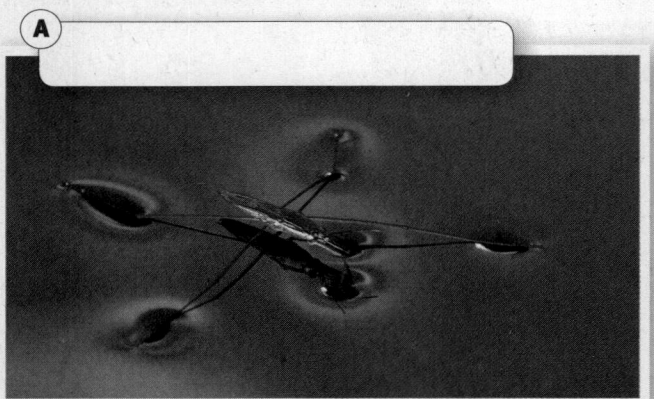

B

© Houghton Mifflin Harcourt Publishing Company • Image Credits: (t) ©blickwinkel/Alamy; (b) ©Ocean/Corbis

These stalactites formed as water dripped down and left dissolved minerals behind.

It Can Absorb Large Amounts of Energy

The energy needed to heat a substance by a particular amount is called its **specific heat**. As water is warmed, its molecules are separated a little as the water expands. The attraction between polar water molecules means that separating them takes a great deal of energy, so the specific heat of water is very high. Because of its high specific heat, water can absorb more energy than many other substances can.

Warm water stores more energy than cold water does. And water vapor stores much more energy than liquid water does. The stored energy is released when warm water cools and when water vapor cools to form liquid. This ability of water to store and release heat is very important in weather and climate.

It Dissolves Many Things

A liquid that dissolves substances is called a **solvent**. Because of its polarity, water dissolves many substances. Therefore, water is often called the universal solvent. Salt, or NaCl, is a familiar substance that water dissolves.

Water as a solvent is very important to living things. Water transports vital dissolved substances through organisms. And most of the chemical reactions that take place inside organisms involve substances dissolved in water.

Only this one doesn't dissolve quickly in water.

12 **Summarize** What characteristic of water accounts for its properties of adhesion, cohesion, high specific heat, and nature as a solvent?

_____

Think Outside the Book Inquiry

13 **Apply** Water dissolves a substance until the water becomes saturated and can dissolve no more of the substance. Starting with 100 ml water, determine how much salt or sugar can be dissolved before the solution is saturated.

Visual Summary

To complete this summary, fill in the blanks. Then use the key below to check your answers. You can use this page to review the main concepts of the lesson.

Water and Its Properties

Water plays many roles in Earth's systems.

14 Water has the following four major roles on Earth:

_____

_____

_____

Water has high cohesion, high adhesion to polar substances, high specific heat, and is a good solvent.

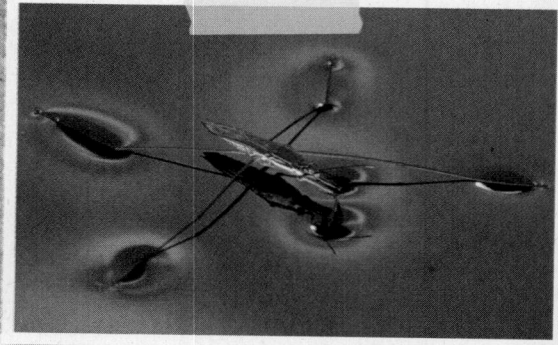

Water is a polar molecule. On Earth, water may be found as a liquid, a solid, and a gas.

15 Water is made up of two _____ atoms and one _____ atom.

16 Because water molecules have a negative end and a positive end, they have _____

17 Water gets soaked up by a paper towel because of the property of _____

18 Water is a commonly used _____ because it dissolves most substances.

Answers: 14 influencing weather, shaping Earth's surface, supporting life, use in human activities; 15 hydrogen, oxygen; 16 polarity; 17 adhesion; 18 solvent

19 **Synthesize** Which properties of water make it useful for washing and cleaning? Explain your answer.

_____

Lesson Review

Vocabulary

Fill in the blanks with the terms that best complete the following sentences.

1 Because a water molecule has a negative end and a positive end, it displays _____

2 Water's high _____ means that a large amount of energy is required to change the water's temperature.

3 When water molecules stick to the molecules of other substances, the molecules are displaying _____

Key Concepts

4 Summarize Why is water important to living things?

_____
_____
_____
_____

5 Describe Draw a water molecule in the space below. Label the atoms that make up the molecule, as well as their partial charges.

_____

6 Explain Why does water have high cohesion?

_____
_____
_____
_____

Critical Thinking

Use the graph to answer the following questions.

Household Water Use in the United States

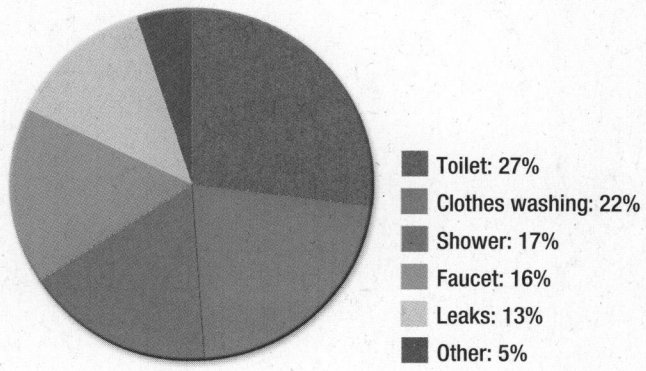

- ■ Toilet: 27%
- ■ Clothes washing: 22%
- ■ Shower: 17%
- ■ Faucet: 16%
- ■ Leaks: 13%
- ■ Other: 5%

Source: American Water Works Association Research Foundation, 1999

7 Identify In an average household, what is most water used for?

_____

8 Infer What do you think are the three biggest changes a household could make to reduce its use of water?

_____
_____
_____
_____

9 Explain Why do you think conserving fresh water might be important?

_____
_____
_____

10 Evaluate Which states of water can you find in your home? Explain.

_____
_____
_____
_____
_____

My Notes

The Water Cycle

ESSENTIAL QUESTION

How does water change state and move around on Earth?

By the end of this lesson, you should be able to describe the water cycle and the different processes that are part of the water cycle on Earth.

Water from the ocean evaporates, forms clouds, then falls back into the ocean when it rains. Can you think of other ways water travels between Earth and Earth's atmosphere?

OHIO **7.ESS.1** The hydrologic cycle illustrates the changing states of water as it moves through the lithosphere, biosphere, hydrosphere and atmosphere.

OHIO **7.SIA.5** Develop descriptions, models, explanations and predictions.

✋ **Lesson Labs**

Quick Labs
• Modeling the Water Cycle
• Can You Make It Rain in a Jar?

Exploration Lab
• Changes in Water

Engage Your Brain

1 Predict Circle the word or phrase that best completes the following sentences.

The air inside a glass of ice would feel *warm/cold/room temperature*.

Ice would *melt/evaporate/remain frozen* if it were left outside on a hot day.

Water vapor will *condense on/evaporate from/ melt into* the glass of ice from the air.

The ice *absorbs energy from/maintains its energy/releases energy into* the surroundings when it melts.

2 Analyze Using the photo above, solve the word scramble to answer the question: What happens to ice as it warms up?

TI GACNSEH EASTT

_____

Active Reading

3 Synthesize You can often define an unknown word if you know the meaning of the word's origin. Use the meaning of the words' origins and the sentence below to make an educated guess about the meaning of *precipitation* and *evaporation*.

Latin word	Meaning
praecipitare	fall
evaporare	spread out in vapor or steam

Vocabulary Terms

• water cycle   • sublimation
• evaporation   • condensation
• transpiration   • precipitation

4 Apply As you learn the definition of each vocabulary term in this lesson, write out a sentence using that term to help you remember the meaning of the term.

Example sentence
<u>Precipitation</u>, in the form of rain, helps replace the water lost by <u>evaporation</u> from the lake.

precipitation:

_____

evaporation:

_____

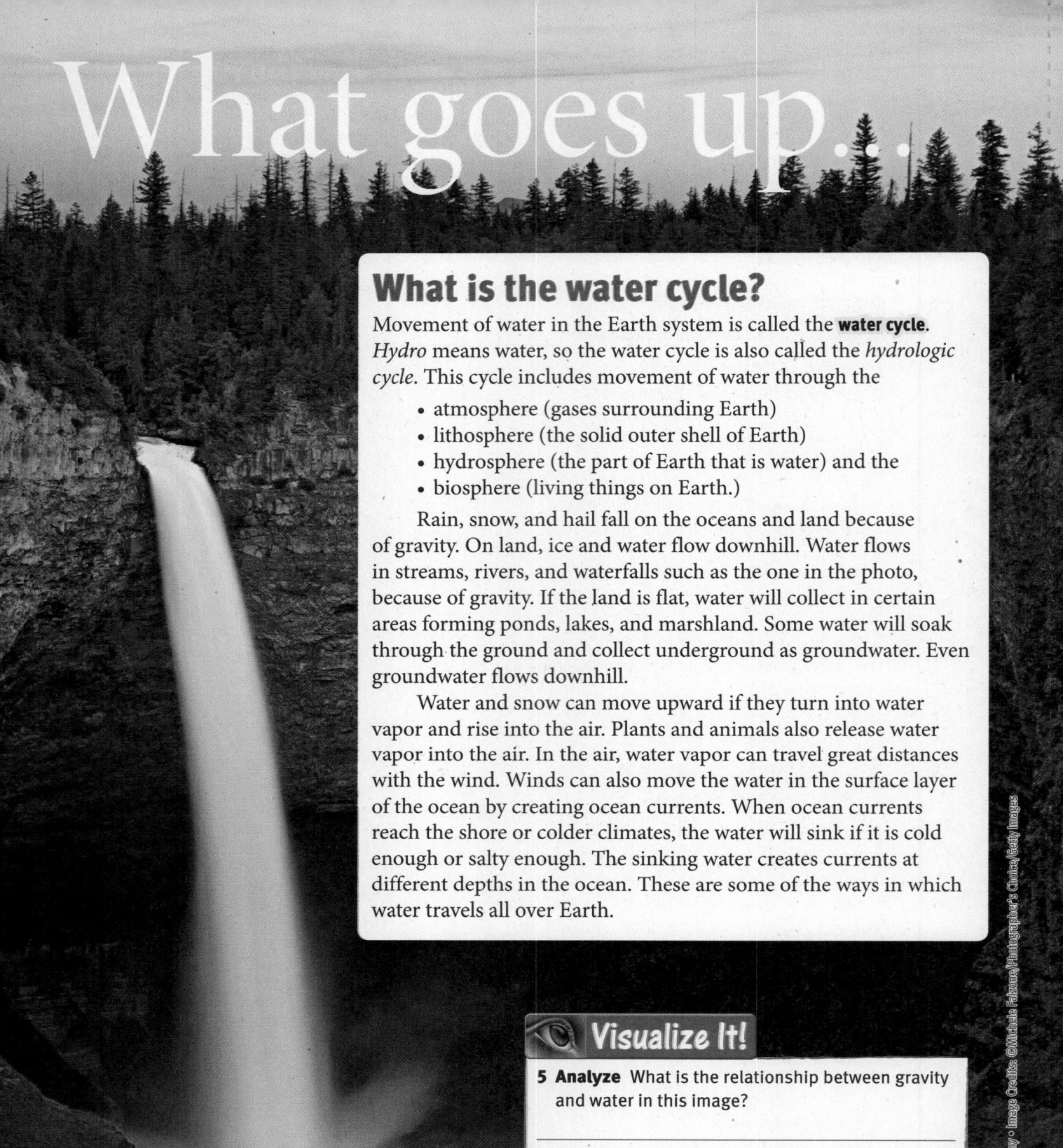

What goes up...

What is the water cycle?

Movement of water in the Earth system is called the **water cycle**. *Hydro* means water, so the water cycle is also called the *hydrologic cycle*. This cycle includes movement of water through the

- atmosphere (gases surrounding Earth)
- lithosphere (the solid outer shell of Earth)
- hydrosphere (the part of Earth that is water) and the
- biosphere (living things on Earth.)

Rain, snow, and hail fall on the oceans and land because of gravity. On land, ice and water flow downhill. Water flows in streams, rivers, and waterfalls such as the one in the photo, because of gravity. If the land is flat, water will collect in certain areas forming ponds, lakes, and marshland. Some water will soak through the ground and collect underground as groundwater. Even groundwater flows downhill.

Water and snow can move upward if they turn into water vapor and rise into the air. Plants and animals also release water vapor into the air. In the air, water vapor can travel great distances with the wind. Winds can also move the water in the surface layer of the ocean by creating ocean currents. When ocean currents reach the shore or colder climates, the water will sink if it is cold enough or salty enough. The sinking water creates currents at different depths in the ocean. These are some of the ways in which water travels all over Earth.

Visualize It!

5 Analyze What is the relationship between gravity and water in this image?

_____

_____

_____

How does water change state?

Water is found in three states on Earth: as liquid water, as solid water ice, and as gaseous water vapor. Water is visible as a liquid or a solid, but it is invisible as a gas in the air. Water can change from one state to another as energy is transferred to or from the water.

Energy is transferred to water from its surroundings as water *melts* from solid to liquid. Water also absorbs energy when it *evaporates* from liquid to gas, or when it *sublimates* from solid to gas. Energy is transferred from water into its surroundings when water *condenses* from gas to liquid. Water also releases energy when it *freezes* from liquid to solid, or *deposits* from gas to solid. No water is lost during any of these changes.

Active Reading

6 Identify As you read, underline each process in which energy is transferred to or from water.

Visualize It!

7 Analyze Under each photo, write an example of where you might find water in that state of matter.

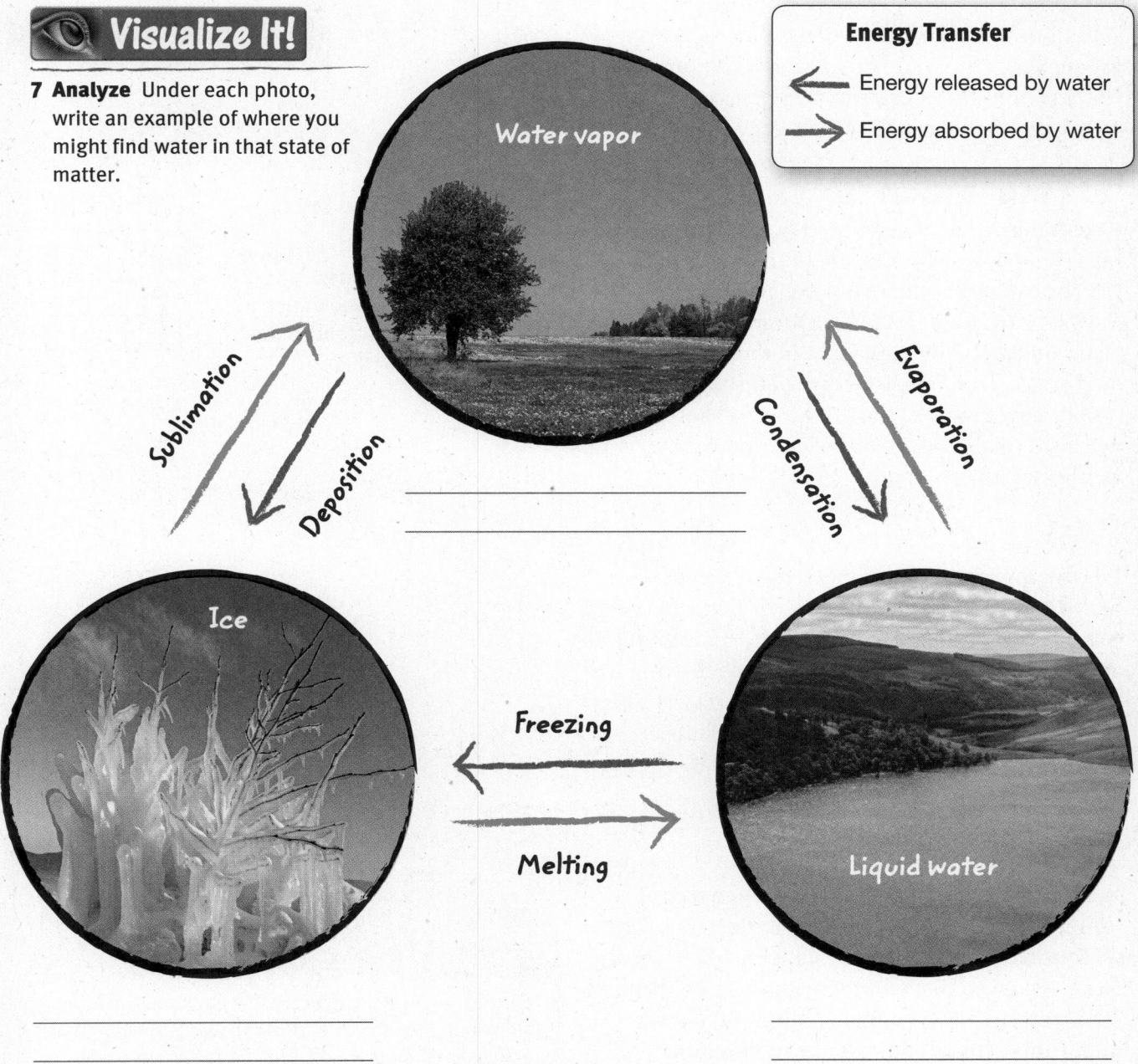

Energy Transfer

← Energy released by water

→ Energy absorbed by water

Water vapor

Sublimation

Deposition

Condensation

Evaporation

Ice

Freezing

Melting

Liquid water

_____

_____

_____

© Houghton Mifflin Harcourt Publishing Company • Image Credits: (t) ©Andrzej Tokarski/Alamy; (bl) ©Peter Lilja/The Image Bank/Getty Images; (br) ©Vincent MacNamara/Alamy

The evaporating water leaves behind a dry, cracked lake bed.

How does water reach the atmosphere?

Water reaches the atmosphere as water vapor in three ways: evaporation (i•VAP•uh•ray•shuhn), transpiration (tran•spuh•RAY•shuhn), and sublimation (suhb•luh•MAY•shuhn). It takes a lot of energy for liquid or solid water to turn into water vapor. The energy for these changes comes mostly from the sun, as solar energy.

◯ Evaporation

Evaporation occurs when liquid water changes into water vapor. About 90% of the water in the atmosphere comes from the evaporation of Earth's water. Some water evaporates from the water on land. However, most of the water vapor evaporates from Earth's oceans. This is because oceans cover most of Earth's surface. Therefore, oceans receive most of the solar energy that reaches Earth.

◯ Transpiration

Like many organisms, plants release water into the environment. Liquid water turns into water vapor inside the plant and moves into the atmosphere through stomata. Stomata are tiny holes that are found on some plant surfaces. This release of water vapor into the air by plants is called **transpiration**. About 10% of the water in the atmosphere comes from transpiration.

◯ Sublimation

When solid water changes directly to water vapor without first becoming a liquid, it is called **sublimation**. Sublimation can happen when dry air blows over ice or snow, where it is very cold and the pressure is low. A small amount of the water in the atmosphere comes from sublimation.

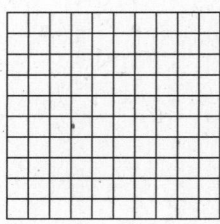

Do the Math **You Try It**

8 Graph Show the percentage of water vapor in the atmosphere that comes from evaporation by coloring the equivalent number of squares in the grid.

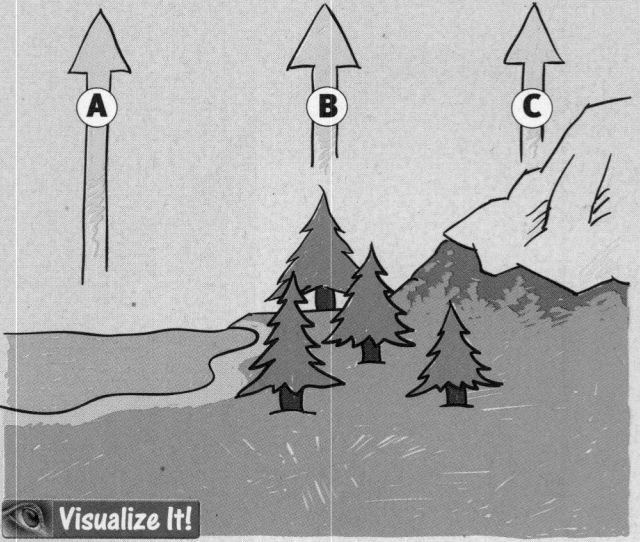

Water moves into the air.

A B C

Visualize It!

9 Identify Fill in the circles beside each red heading at left with the label of the arrow showing the matching process in this diagram.

What happens to water in the atmosphere?

Water reaches the atmosphere as water vapor. In the atmosphere, water vapor mixes with other gases. To leave the atmosphere, water vapor must change into liquid or solid water. Then the liquid or solid water can fall to Earth's surface.

◯ Condensation

Remember, **condensation** (kahn•den•SAY•shuhn) is the change of state from a gas to a liquid. If air that contains water vapor is cooled enough, condensation occurs. Some of the water vapor condenses on small particles, such as dust, forming little balls or tiny droplets of water. These water droplets float in the air as clouds, fog, or mist. At the ground level, water vapor may condense on cool surfaces as dew.

◯ Precipitation

In clouds, water droplets may collide and "stick" together to become larger. If a droplet becomes large enough, it falls to Earth's surface as precipitation (pri•sip•i•TAY•shuhn). **Precipitation** is any form of water that falls to Earth from clouds. Three common kinds of precipitation shown in the photos are rain, snow, and hail. Snow and hail form if the water droplets freeze. Most rain falls into the oceans because most water evaporates from ocean surfaces and oceans cover most of Earth's surface. But winds carry clouds from the ocean over land, increasing the amount of precipitation that falls on land.

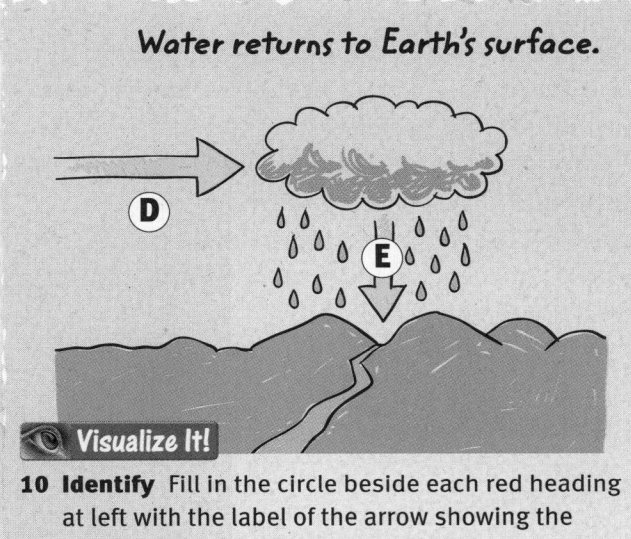

Water returns to Earth's surface.

Visualize It!

10 Identify Fill in the circle beside each red heading at left with the label of the arrow showing the matching process in this diagram.

11 Summarize Fill in the boxes to describe how precipitation forms.

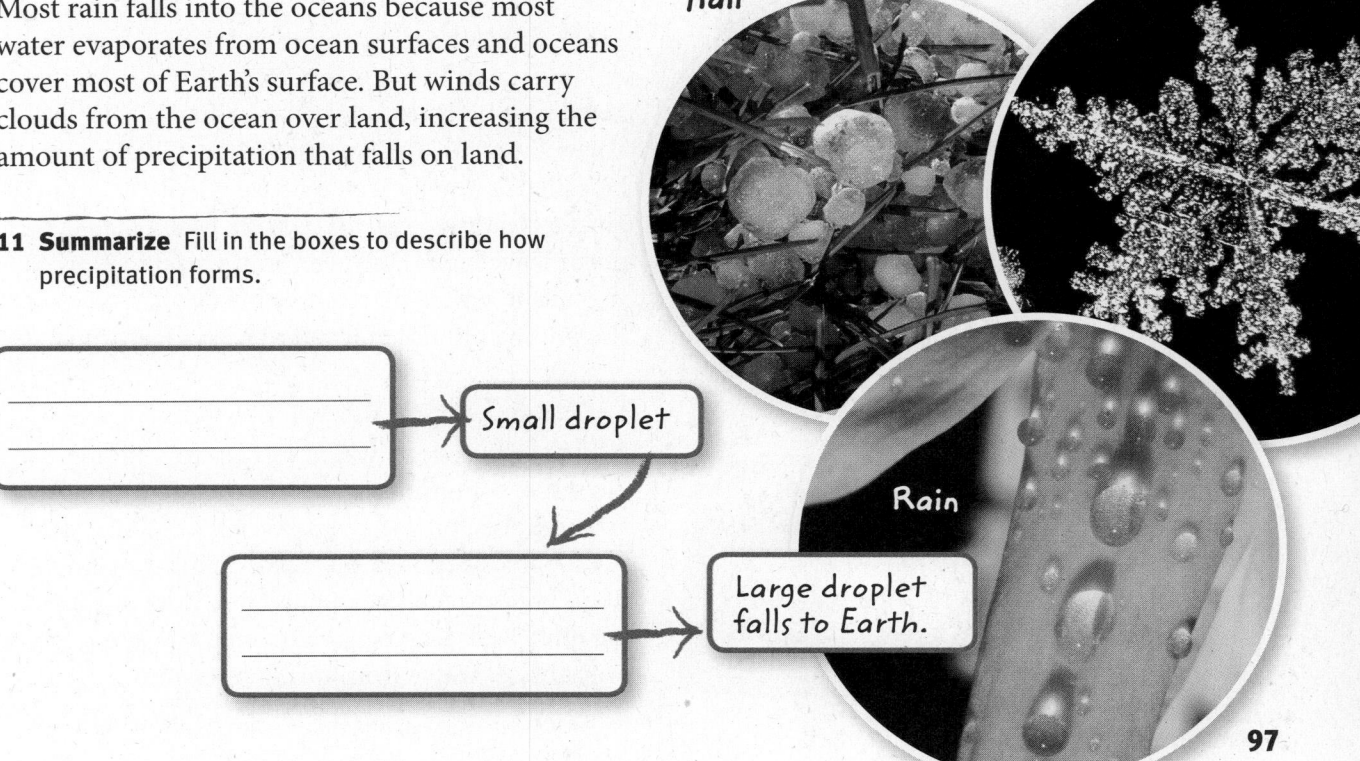

Hail

Snow

Rain

Small droplet

Large droplet falls to Earth.

How does water move on land and in the oceans?

After water falls to Earth, it flows and circulates all over Earth. On land, water flows downhill, both on the surface and underground. However, most of Earth's precipitation falls into the oceans. Ocean currents move water around the oceans.

Runoff and Infiltration

All of the water on land flows downhill because of gravity. Streams, rivers, and the water that flows over land are types of *runoff*. Runoff flows downhill toward oceans, lakes, and marshlands.

Some of the water on land seeps into the ground. This process is called *infiltration* (in•fil•TRAY•shuhn). Once undergound, the water is called *groundwater*. Groundwater also flows downhill through soil and rock.

 **Active Reading**

12 Compare How do runoff and groundwater differ?

_____

_____

_____

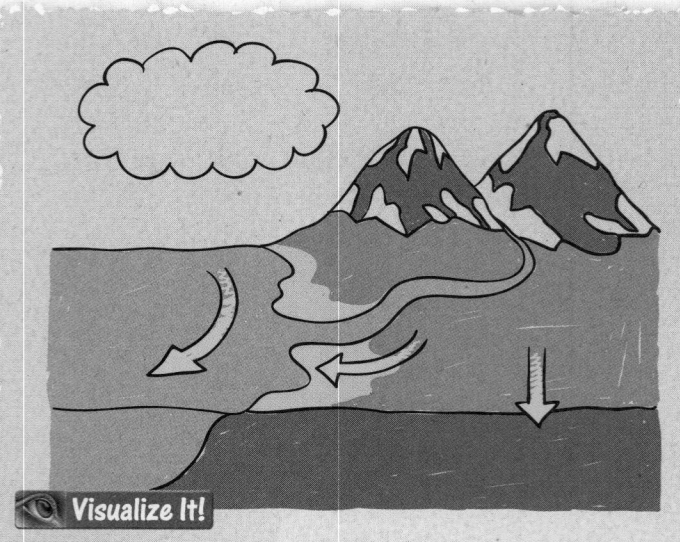

Visualize It!

13 Summarize Write a caption describing how water is moving in the diagram above.

_____

_____

Icebergs can be carried over long distances by ocean currents.

Ice Flow

Much of Earth's ice is stored in large ice caps in Antarctica and Greenland. Some ice is stored in glaciers at high altitudes all over Earth. Glaciers cover about 10% of Earth's surface. Glaciers can be called "rivers of ice" because gravity also causes glaciers to flow slowly downhill. Many glaciers never leave land. However, some glaciers flow to the ocean, where pieces may break off, as seen in the photo, and float far out to sea as icebergs.

Ocean Circulation

Winds move ocean water on the surface in great currents, sometimes for thousands of miles. At some shores, or if the water is very cold or salty, it will sink deep into the ocean. This movement helps create deep ocean currents. Both surface currents and deep ocean currents transport large amounts of water from ocean to ocean.

© Houghton Mifflin Harcourt Publishing Company • Image Credits: (bl) ©Marco Simoni/Robert Harding World Imagery/Getty Images

Water Works

What does the water cycle transport?

In the water cycle, each state of water has some energy in it. This energy is released into or absorbed from its surroundings as water changes state. The energy in each state of water is then transported as the water moves from place to place. Matter is also transported as water and the materials in the water move all over Earth. So, the water cycle moves energy and matter through Earth's atmosphere, lithosphere, hydrosphere, and biosphere.

Energy

Energy is transported in the water cycle through changes of state and by the movement of water from place to place. For example, water that evaporates from the ocean carries energy into the atmosphere. This movement of energy can generate hurricanes. Also, cold ocean currents can cool the air along a coastline by absorbing the energy from the air and leaving the air cooler. This energy is carried away quickly as the current continues on its path. Such processes affect the weather and climate of an area.

Matter

Earth's ocean currents move vast amounts of water all over the world. These currents also transport the solids in the water and the dissolved salts and gases. Rivers transfer water from land into the ocean. Rivers also carry large amounts of sand, mud, and gravel as shown below. Rivers form deltas and floodplains, where some of the materials from upstream collect in areas downstream. Rivers also carve valleys and canyons, and carry the excess materials downstream. Glaciers also grind away rock and carry the ground rock with them as they flow.

Visualize It!

15 **Identify** What do rivers, such as the ones in the photo, transport?

_____

_____

Visualize It! **The Water Cycle**

Water is continuously changing state and moving from place to place in the water cycle. This diagram shows these processes and movements.

16 Identify Label each arrow to show which process the arrow represents.

17 Identify Shade in the arrows that indicate where water is changing state.

Condensation

Evaporation

_____

_____

_____

_____

_____

_____

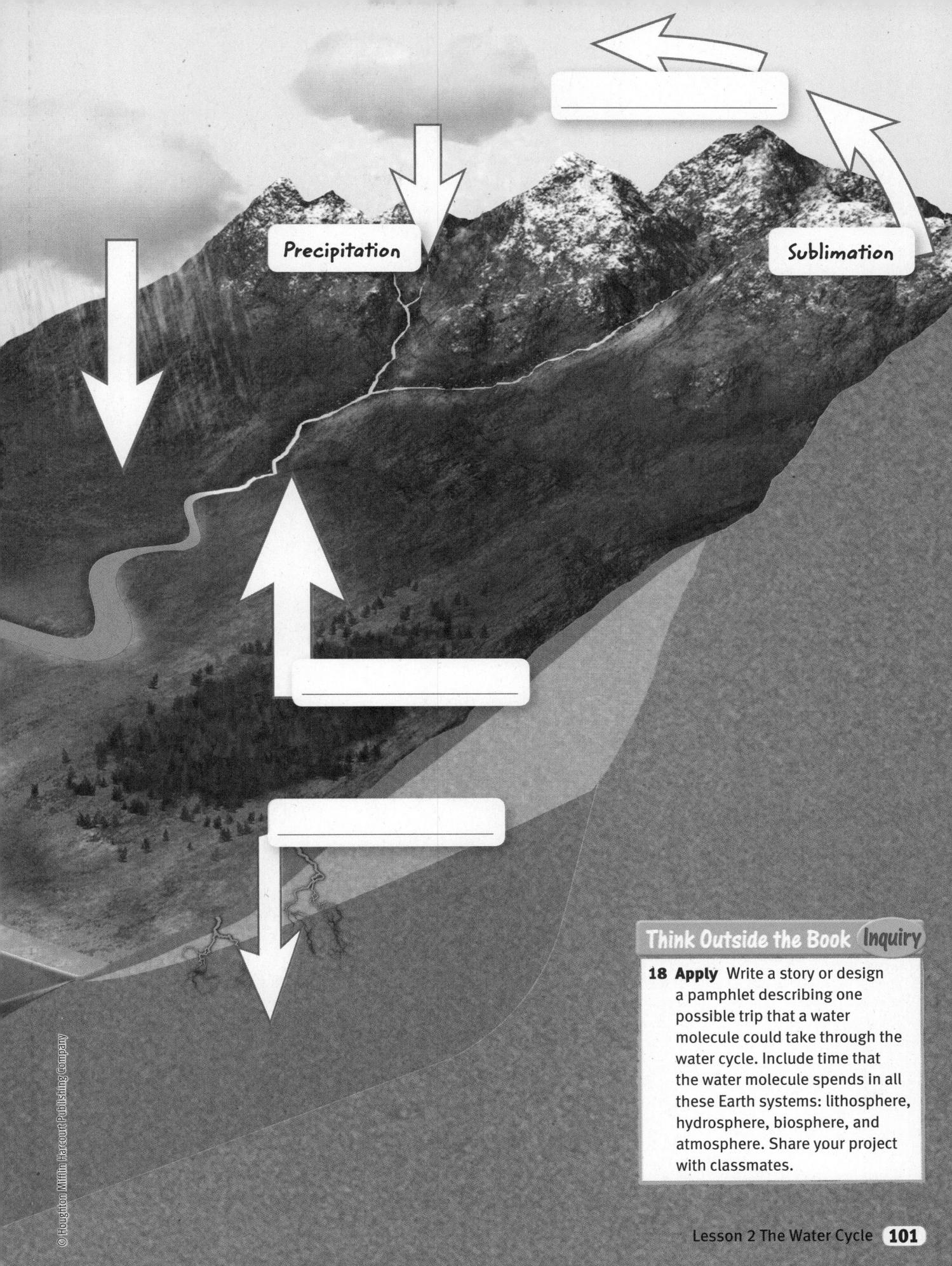

Precipitation

Sublimation

Think Outside the Book Inquiry

18 Apply Write a story or design
a pamphlet describing one
possible trip that a water
molecule could take through the
water cycle. Include time that
the water molecule spends in all
these Earth systems: lithosphere,
hydrosphere, biosphere, and
atmosphere. Share your project
with classmates.

Visual Summary

To complete this summary, write one or more terms that describe the process or processes happening in each of the images. Then use the key below to check your answers. You can use this page to review the main concepts of the lesson.

Water moves in the atmosphere.

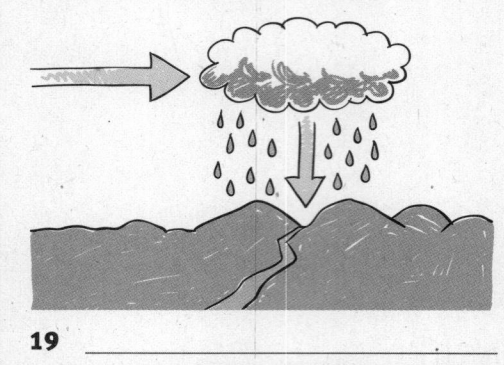

19 _____

The Water Cycle

Water moves into the atmosphere.

21 _____

Water moves on land and in oceans.

20 _____

Answers: 19 condensation or precipitation; 20 iceflow, runoff, infiltration, or ocean current; 21 evaporation, transpiration, or sublimation

22 Predict Describe what might happen to the water cycle if less solar energy reached Earth and how Earth's climate would be affected.

Lesson Review

Vocabulary

Write the correct label A, B, C, or D under each term to indicate the definition of that term.

1 water cycle
_____

2 evaporation
_____

3 precipitation
_____

4 condensation
_____

A The change of state from a liquid to a gas

B The change of state from a gas to a liquid

C The movement of water between the atmosphere, land, oceans, and living things

D Any form of water that falls to Earth's surface from the clouds

Key Concepts

5 Identify List the three ways in which water reaches the atmosphere and tell which way accounts for most of the water in the atmosphere.

_____

_____

_____

6 Classify Which of the processes of the water cycle occur by releasing energy?

_____

_____

7 Identify What happens to water once it reaches Earth's surface?

_____

_____

_____

8 Summarize Describe how three common types of precipitation form.

_____

_____

_____

_____

_____

_____

Critical Thinking

Use the image below to answer the following question.

9 Apply Describe the energy changes occurring in the process shown above.

_____

_____

10 Infer Why does the amount of water that flows in a river change during the year?

_____

_____

11 Predict During a storm, a tree fell over into a river. What might happen to this tree?

_____

_____

_____

12 Evaluate Warm ocean currents cool as they flow along a coastline, away from the equator. Explain what is transported and how.

_____

_____

_____

_____

_____

My Notes

Surface Water and Groundwater

ESSENTIAL QUESTION

How does fresh water flow on Earth?

By the end of this lesson, you should be able to explain the processes involved in the flow of water, both above and below the ground.

Fresh water flows on Earth's surface, sometimes tumbling over waterfalls like these.

OHIO **7.ESS.1** The hydrologic cycle illustrates the changing states of water as it moves through the lithosphere, biosphere, hydrosphere and atmosphere.

Lesson Labs

Quick Labs
• Modeling Groundwater
• Model a Stream

Exploration Lab
• Aquifers and Development

Engage Your Brain

1 Identify Read over the following vocabulary terms. In the spaces provided, place a + if you know the term well, a ~ if you have heard of the term but are not sure what it means, and a ? if you are unfamiliar with the term. Then write a sentence that includes one of the words you are most familiar with.

_____ tributary
_____ surface water
_____ aquifer

Sentence using known word:

_____

_____

_____

_____

2 Describe Write your own caption for this photo.

_____

_____

_____

_____

_____

Active Reading

3 Apply Many scientific words, such as *channel*, also have everyday meanings. Use context clues to write your own definition for each meaning of the word *channel*.

Example sentence:
She didn't like the TV show, so she changed the <u>channel</u>.

channel:

_____

_____

Example sentence:
The <u>channel</u> of the river was broad and deep.

channel:

_____

_____

Vocabulary Terms
• surface water   • tributary
• groundwater   • watershed
• water table   • divide
• channel   • aquifer

4 Identify As you read, create a reference card for each vocabulary term. On one side of the card, write the term and its meaning. On the other side, draw an image that illustrates or makes a connection to the term. These cards can be used as bookmarks in the text so that you can refer to them while studying.

Getting Your Feet Wet

Where on Earth is fresh water found?

About 97% of Earth's water is salty, which leaves only 3% as fresh water. Most of that small amount of fresh water is frozen as ice and snow, so only about 1% of Earth's water is fresh liquid water. This fresh liquid water is found both on and below Earth's surface.

This tiny percentage of Earth's water must meet the large demand that all living things have for fresh, clean water. In addition to providing drinking water, fresh water is used for agriculture, industry, transportation, and recreation. It also provides a place to live for many plants and animals.

On Earth's Surface

Active Reading 5 **Identify** As you read, underline three examples of surface water.

Water above Earth's surface is called **surface water**. Surface water is found in streams, rivers, and lakes. It either comes from precipitation, such as rain, or from water that comes up from the ground to Earth's surface. Springs are an example of underground water coming up to the surface. Surface water flows from higher ground to lower ground. Water that flows across Earth's surface is called *runoff*. Eventually, runoff can enter bodies of water.

Beneath Earth's Surface

Active Reading 6 **Identify** As you read, underline how surface water becomes groundwater.

Not all runoff becomes surface water. Some runoff and surface water seep down into the ground. Water drains through the soil and filters down into underground rock, collecting in spaces between rock particles. The water found in the spaces between rock particles below Earth's surface is called **groundwater**.

Most drinking water in the United States comes from groundwater supplies. To use these supplies, people drill down to the water table to reach reservoirs of groundwater. The **water table** is the upper boundary, or surface, of groundwater.

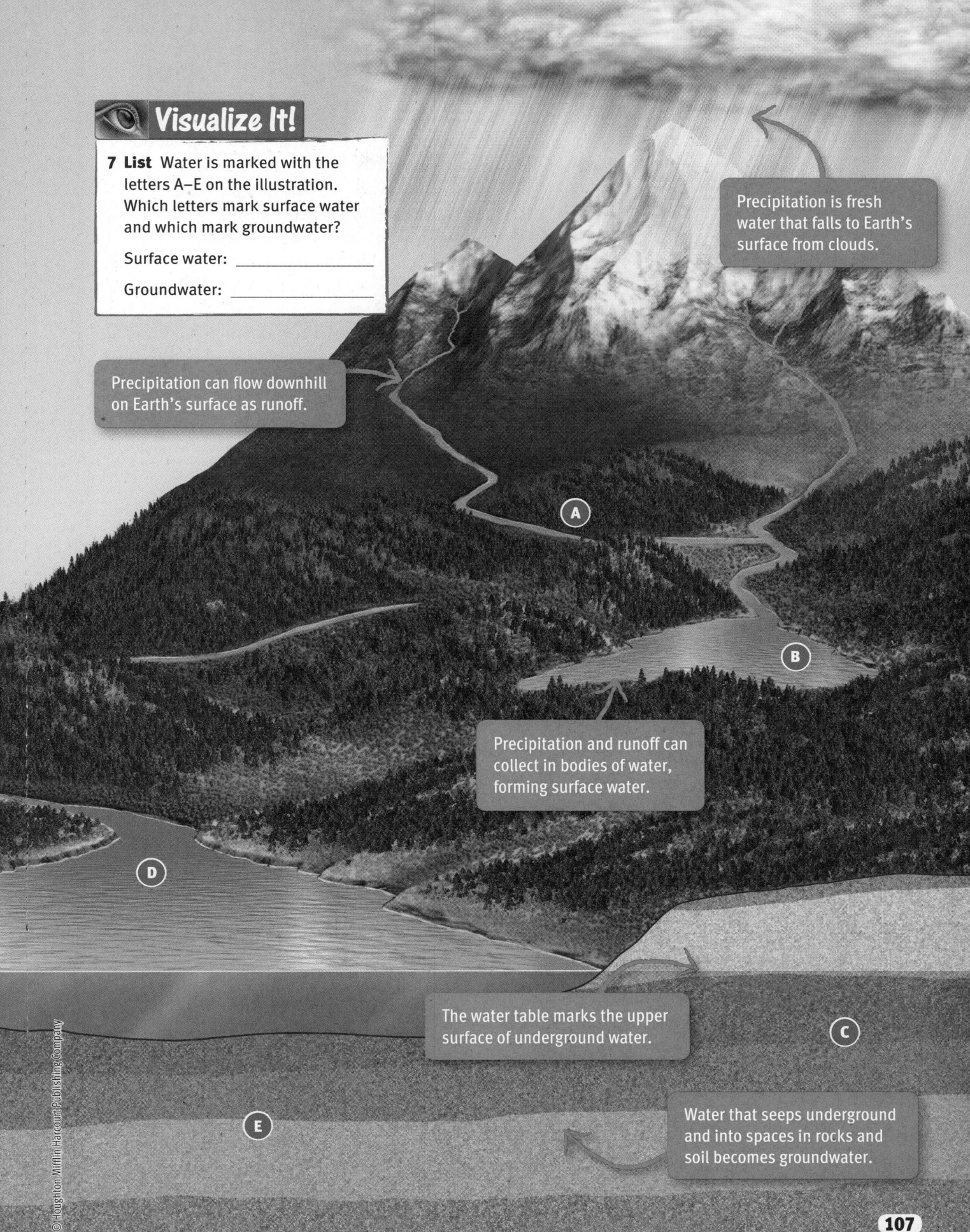

Visualize It!

7 List Water is marked with the letters A–E on the illustration. Which letters mark surface water and which mark groundwater?

Surface water: _____

Groundwater: _____

Precipitation is fresh water that falls to Earth's surface from clouds.

Precipitation can flow downhill on Earth's surface as runoff.

Precipitation and runoff can collect in bodies of water, forming surface water.

The water table marks the upper surface of underground water.

Water that seeps underground and into spaces in rocks and soil becomes groundwater.

Cry Me a River

How does water move on Earth's surface?

As precipitation falls on Earth's surface, it flows from higher to lower areas. The water that does not seep below the surface flows together and forms streams. The water erodes rocks and soil, eventually forming channels. A **channel** is the path that a stream follows. Over time, a channel gets wider and deeper, as the stream continues to erode rock and soil.

A **tributary** is a smaller stream that feeds into a river and eventually into a river system. A river system is a network of streams and rivers that drains an area of its runoff.

B

A

8 Identify Label *tributary*, *river*, *divide*, and *stream load* in the spaces provided on the illustration.

C

Within Watersheds

A **watershed** is the area of land that is drained by a river system. Streams, rivers, flood plains, lakes, ponds, wetlands, and groundwater all contribute water to a watershed. Watersheds are separated from one other by a ridge or an area of higher ground called a **divide**. Precipitation that falls on one side of a divide enters one watershed while the precipitation that falls on the other side of a divide enters another watershed.

The largest watershed in the United States is the Mississippi River watershed. It has hundreds of tributaries. It extends from the Rocky Mountains, in the west, to the Appalachian Mountains, in the east, and down the length of the United States, from north to south.

Many factors affect the flow of water in a watershed. For example, plants slow runoff and reduce erosion. The porosity and permeability of rocks and sediment determine how much water can seep down into the ground. The steepness of land affects how fast water flows over a watershed.

Active Reading **9 State** Which land feature separates watersheds?

_____

_____

In Rivers and Streams

Gradient is a measure of the change in elevation over a certain distance. In other words, gradient describes the steepness, or slope, of the land. The higher the gradient of a river or stream, the faster the water moves. The faster the water moves, the more energy it has to erode rock and soil.

A river's *flow* is the amount of water that moves through the river channel in a given amount of time. Flow increases during a major storm or when warm weather rapidly melts snow. An increase in flow causes an increase in a river's speed.

Materials carried by a stream are called *stream load*. Streams with a high flow carry a larger stream load. The size of the particles depends on water speed. Faster streams can carry larger particles. Streams eventually deposit their stream loads where the speed of the water decreases. This commonly happens as streams enter lakes and oceans.

Active Reading **10 Summarize** How would an increase in gradient affect the speed of water?

_____

_____

How does groundwater flow?

Although you can see some of Earth's fresh water in streams and lakes, you cannot see the large amount of water that flows underground as groundwater. Earth has much more fresh groundwater than fresh surface water.

It Trickles Down from Earth's Surface

Water from precipitation or streams may seep below the surface and become groundwater. Groundwater is either stored or it flows underground. It can enter back into streams and lakes, becoming surface water again. An **aquifer** is a body of rock or sediment that stores groundwater and allows it to flow.

Recall that the water table is the upper surface of underground water. The water table can rise or fall depending on the amount of water in the aquifer. In wet regions, the water table can be at or just beneath the soil's surface. In wetland areas, the water table is above the soil's surface.

It Fills Tiny Spaces Underground

An aquifer stores water in open spaces, or *pores,* between particles of rock or sediment. The storage space in an aquifer is measured by *porosity,* the percentage of the rock that is composed of pore space. The greater the pore space is, the higher the porosity is. A cup of gravel, for example, has higher porosity than a cup of sand does.

Permeability is a measure of how easily water can flow through an aquifer. High permeability means that many pores in the aquifer are connected, so water can flow easily. Aquifers with both high porosity and high permeability are useful as a water resource.

Visualize It!

11 Label Draw an arrow, ↑ (high) or ↓ (low), to indicate the porosity and permeability of each rock sample. One is already completed as an example.

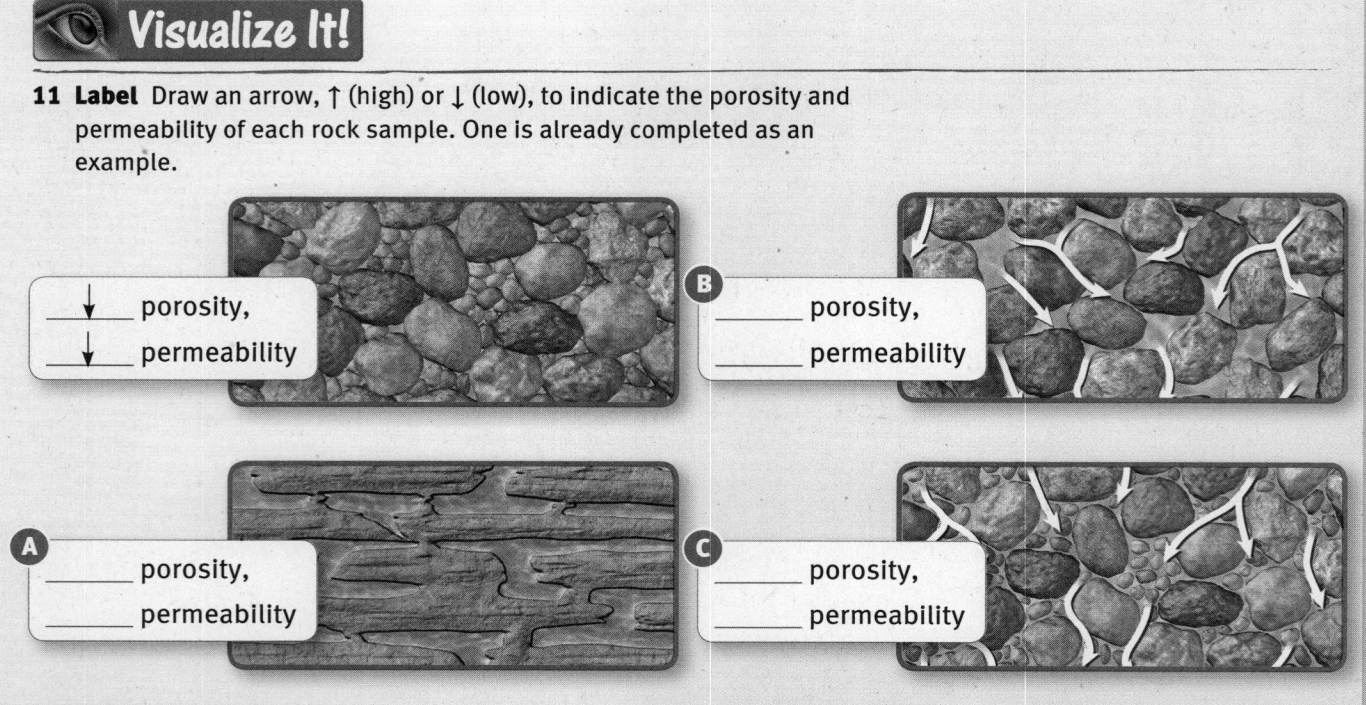

_____ ↓ porosity, _____ ↓ permeability

B _____ porosity, _____ permeability

A _____ porosity, _____ permeability

C _____ porosity, _____ permeability

It Is Recharged and Discharged

Surface water that trickles down into the ground can reach the water table and enter an aquifer. This process is called *recharge*, and occurs in an area called the *recharge zone*.

Where the water table meets the surface, water may pool to form a wetland or may flow out as a spring. The process by which groundwater becomes surface water is called *discharge* and happens in *discharge zones*. Discharge can feed rivers, streams, and lakes. Groundwater is also discharged where water is extracted from wells that are drilled down into the water table. Through discharge and recharge, the same water circulates between surface water and groundwater.

Visualize It!

12 **Label** On the illustration below, write a caption for *discharge zone* and for *aquifer*.

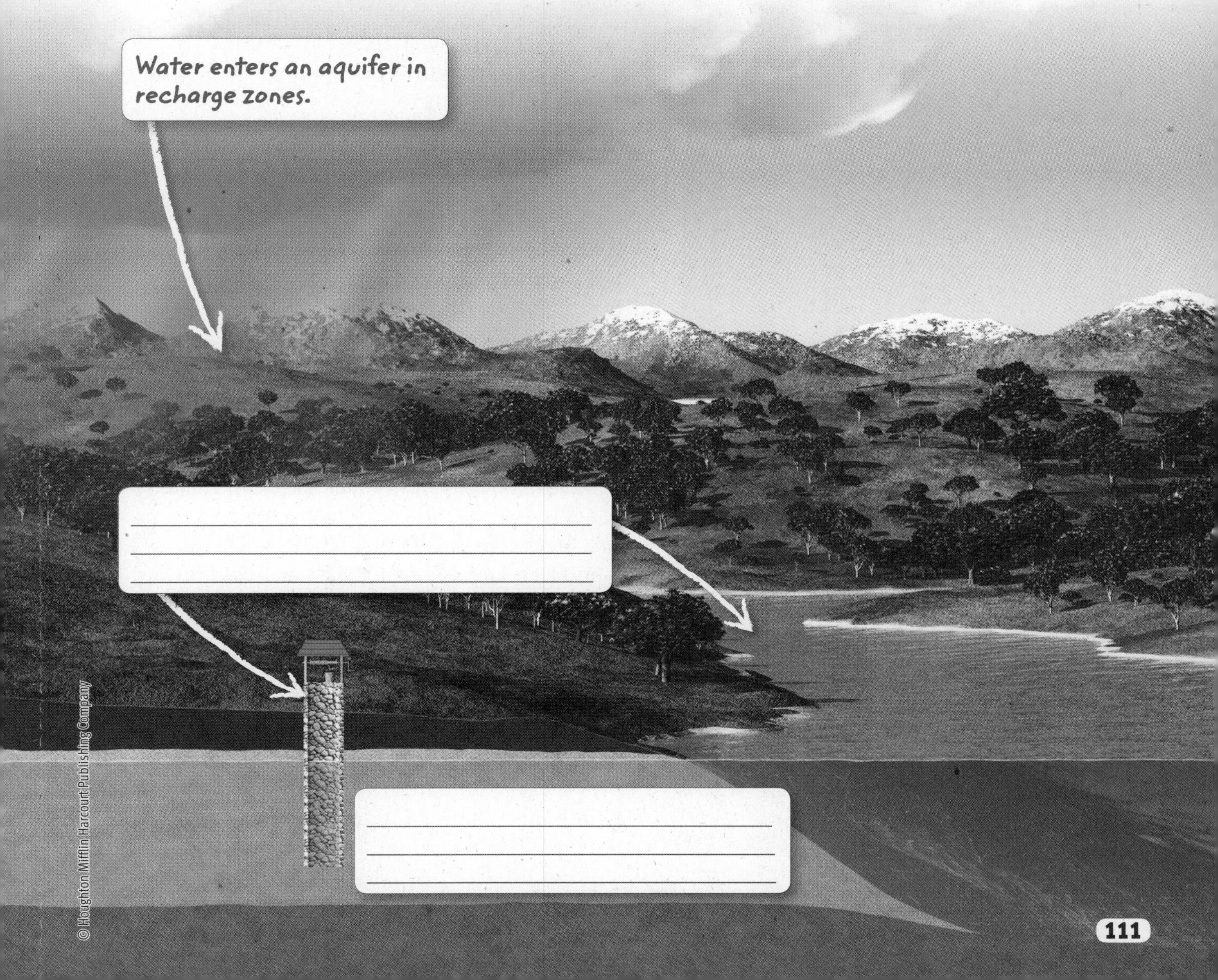

Water enters an aquifer in recharge zones.

Making a Splash

How do people use surface water and groundwater?

Active Reading

14 Identify As you read this page, underline how water is used in a typical home.

About 75% of all the fresh water used in the United States comes from surface water. The other 25% comes from groundwater. But surface water and groundwater are connected. In human terms, they are one resource. People use this freshwater resource in many different ways.

For Drinking and Use at Home

Groundwater is an important source of drinking water. Surface water is used for drinking, too. Fresh water is also used in many other ways in homes. In a typical home, about 50% of all water used is for washing clothes, bathing, washing dishes, and flushing toilets. About 33% is used to water lawns and gardens. The rest is used for drinking, cooking, and washing hands.

For Agriculture

Activities like growing crops and raising livestock use about 40% of fresh water used in the United States. These activities account for about 70% of all groundwater use. A little over half the water used in agriculture comes from surface water. A little less than half comes from groundwater.

For Industry

Almost half of the fresh water used in the United States is used for industry. Only about 20% of this water comes from groundwater. The rest is surface water. About 40% of water used in industry helps cool elements in power plants.

For Transportation and Recreation

Surface water is also used to transport products and people from place to place. In addition, people use rivers, streams, and lakes for swimming, sailing, kayaking, water skiing, and other types of recreation.

These rafters enjoy the exhilaration of river rapids.

Troubled Waters

Each hour, about 15,114 babies are born around the world. The human population has skyrocketed over the last few hundred years. But the amount of fresh water on Earth has remained roughly the same. The limited supply of fresh water is an important resource that must be managed so that it can meet the demands of a growing population.

Scientists are developing technologies for obtaining clean, fresh water to meet global needs. Here, a boy uses a water purifier straw that filters disease-causing microbes and certain other contaminants from surface water. The straw is inexpensive and can filter 700 L of water before it needs to be replaced—that's about how much water the average person drinks in one year.

Like many places on Earth, Zimbabwe is experiencing severe water shortages. The country has been plagued by droughts since the 1980s. Scientists estimate that about 1 billion people around the world do not have an adequate supply of clean, fresh water.

Extend

Inquiry

15 Infer Most of Earth is covered by water. How can we be experiencing shortages of drinking water?

16 Research Find out which diseases are caused by microbes found in untreated surface water. How might the water purifier straw reduce the number of people getting these diseases?

17 Recommend Conserving water is one way to ensure adequate supplies of drinking water. Work with a group to develop a plan to reduce water use at school. Present your plan to the class. As a class, select the best aspects of each group's plan. Combine the best suggestions into a document to present to the school administration.

Visual Summary

To complete this summary, fill in the blank with the correct word or phrase. Then, use the key below to check your answers. You can use this page to review the main concepts of the lesson.

Surface Water and Groundwater

Fresh surface water is found in streams, rivers, and lakes.

18 Smaller streams, or _____, flow into the main river channel.

Groundwater is found in pore spaces in rocks and sediment below Earth's surface.

19 The surface area where water enters an aquifer is called the _____ zone.

People use fresh water in homes, agriculture, and industry, for transportation, and for recreation.

20 Most industrial fresh water comes from rivers and other sources of _____

21 **Relate** Describe how a raindrop could become surface water, then groundwater, and then end up back on Earth's surface again.

Lesson Review

Vocabulary

In your own words, define the following terms.

1 surface water

_____

_____

2 watershed

_____

_____

3 groundwater

_____

_____

4 water table

_____

_____

5 aquifer

_____

_____

Key Concepts

6 Identify What three factors describe the movement of surface water in streams and rivers?

_____

_____

_____

7 Explain How does the gradient of a river affect its flow?

_____

_____

_____

8 Describe How quickly would groundwater flow through rock with high porosity and high permeability? Explain your answer.

_____

_____

_____

Critical Thinking

9 Conclude An area's rate of groundwater recharge exceeds its rate of groundwater discharge. What can you conclude about the area's groundwater supply?

_____

_____

_____

_____

Use this graph to answer the following questions.

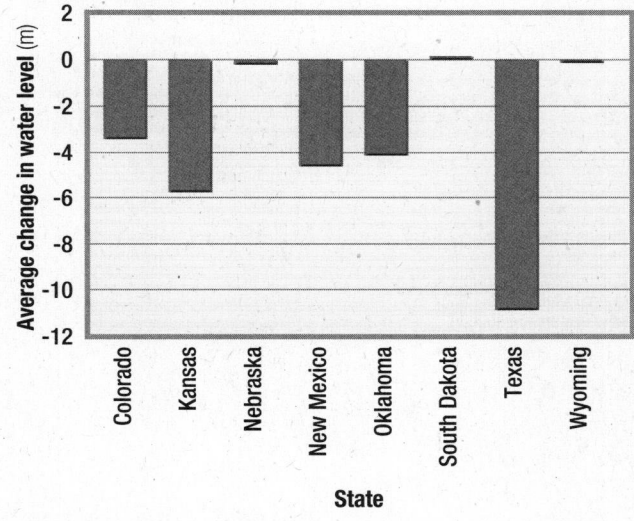

Average Water-Level Changes in the High Plains Aquifer by State (1950-2005)

10 Analyze What has happened to the amount of water in the High Plains Aquifer over time?

_____

_____

11 Infer What might account for the changes described in question 10?

_____

_____

_____

_____

_____

_____

_____

My Notes

Ocean Currents

ESSENTIAL QUESTION

How does water move in the ocean?

By the end of this lesson, you should be able to describe the movement of ocean water, explain what factors influence this movement, and explain why ocean circulation is important in the Earth system.

This iceberg off the coast of Newfoundland broke off an Arctic ice sheet and drifted south on ocean surface currents.

OHIO 7.ESS.2 Thermal-energy transfers in the ocean and the atmosphere contribute to the formation of currents, which influence global climate patterns.

 **Lesson Labs**

Quick Labs
- Modeling the Coriolis Effect
- The Formation of Deep Currents
- Can Messages Travel on Ocean Water?

Engage Your Brain

1 Predict Check T or F to show whether you think each statement is true or false.

T	F	
☐	☐	Ocean currents are always cold.
☐	☐	Continents affect the directions of currents.
☐	☐	Currents only flow near the surface of the ocean.
☐	☐	Wind affects currents.
☐	☐	The sun affects currents near the surface of the ocean.

2 Analyze What can you learn about ocean currents from this image?

_____

_____

_____

_____

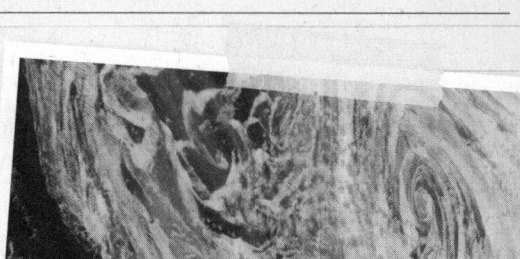

This image shows sea ice caught in ocean currents.

Active Reading

3 Synthesize You can often define an unknown word if you know the meaning of its word parts. Use the word parts and sentence below to make an educated guess about the meaning of the word *upwelling*.

Word part	Meaning
up-	from beneath the ground or water
well	to rise

Example Sentence
In areas where <u>upwelling</u> occurs, plankton feed on nutrients from deep in the ocean.

upwelling:

_____

_____

Vocabulary Terms

- ocean current
- surface current
- Coriolis effect
- deep current
- convection current
- upwelling

4 Apply As you learn the definition of each vocabulary term in this lesson, create your own definition or sketch to help you remember the meaning of the term.

Going with the Flow

What are ocean currents?

The oceans contain streamlike movements of water called **ocean currents**. Ocean currents that occur at or near the surface of the ocean, caused by wind, are called **surface currents**. Most surface currents reach depths of about 100 m, but some go deeper. Surface currents also reach lengths of several thousand kilometers and can stretch across oceans. An example of a surface current is the Gulf Stream. The Gulf Stream is one of the strongest surface currents on Earth. The Gulf Stream transports, or moves, more water each year than is transported by all the rivers in the world combined.

Infrared cameras on satellites provide images that show differences in temperature. Scientists add color to the images afterward to highlight the different temperatures, as shown below.

What affects surface currents?

Surface currents are affected by three factors: continental deflections, the Coriolis effect, and global winds. These factors keep surface currents flowing in distinct patterns around Earth.

Active Reading

5 Identify As you read, underline three factors that affect surface currents.

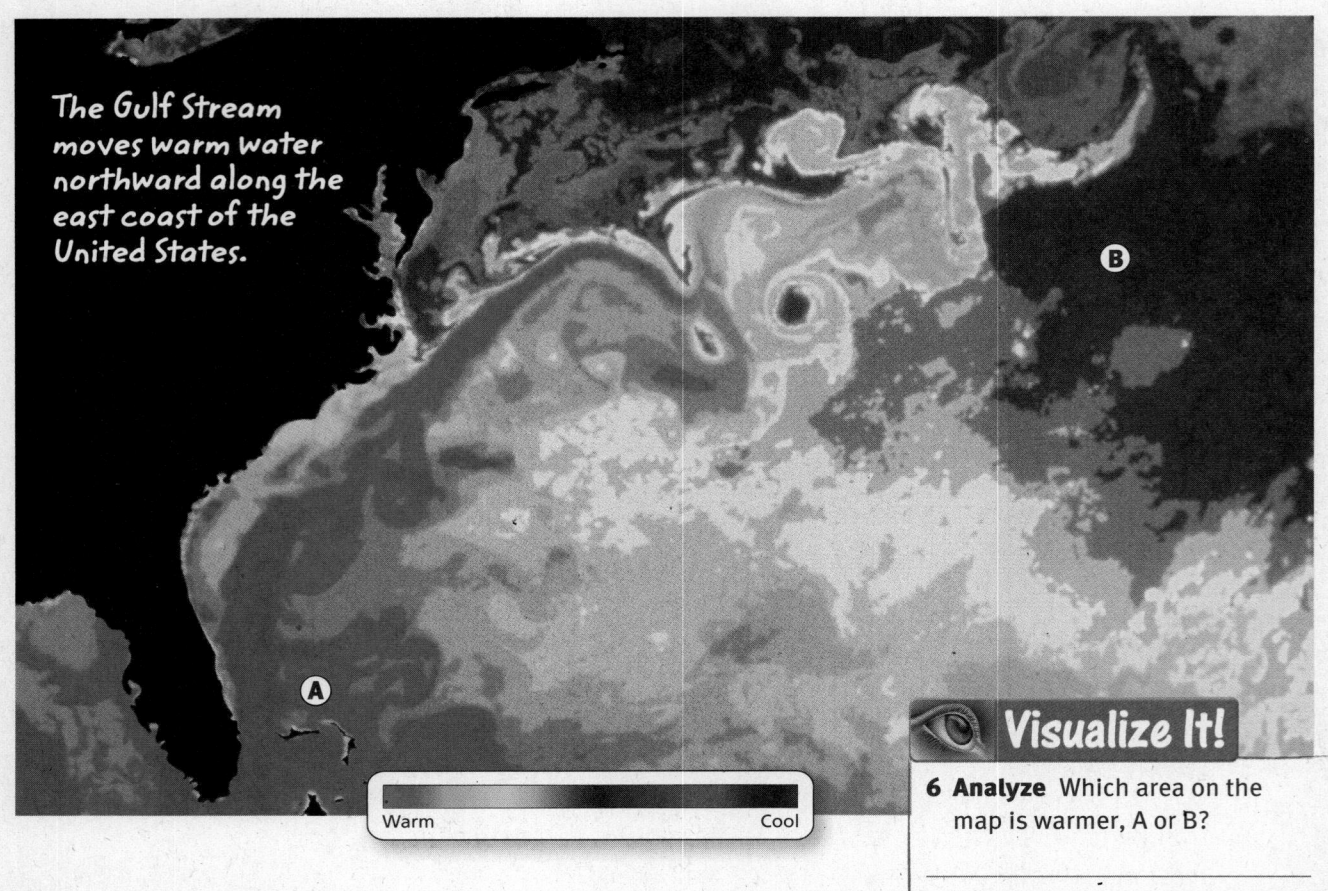

The Gulf Stream moves warm water northward along the east coast of the United States.

Warm — Cool

Visualize It!

6 Analyze Which area on the map is warmer, A or B?

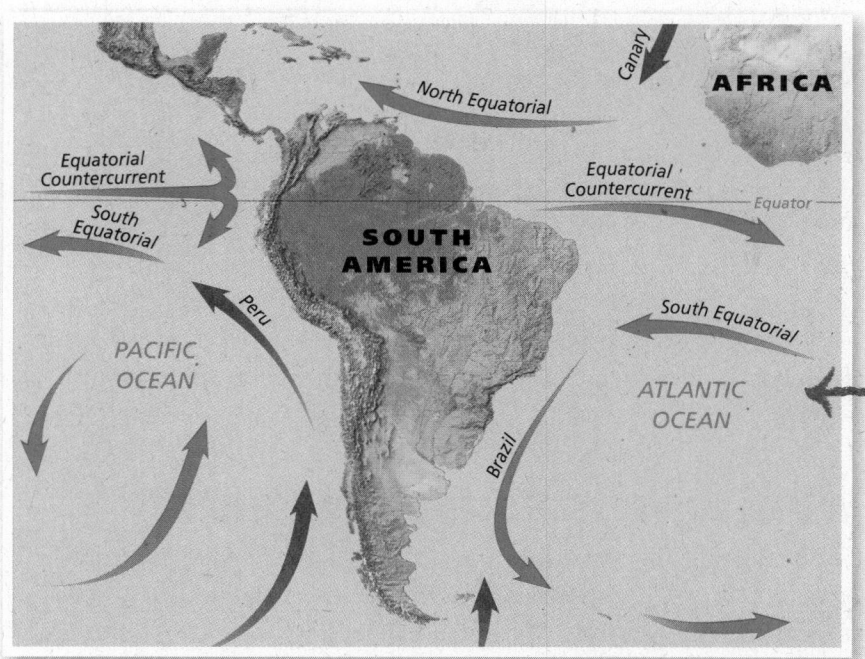

7 Identify Circle areas on the map where ocean currents have been deflected by a land mass.

Currents change direction when they meet continents.

Continental Deflections

If Earth's surface were covered only with water, surface currents would simply travel continually in one direction. However, water does not cover the entire surface of Earth. Continents rise above sea level over about one-third of Earth's surface. When surface currents meet continents, the currents are deflected and change direction. For example, the South Equatorial Current turns southward as it meets the coast of South America.

The Coriolis Effect

Earth's rotation causes all wind and ocean currents, except on the equator, to be deflected from the paths they would take if Earth did not rotate. The deflection of moving objects from a straight path due to Earth's rotation is called the **Coriolis effect** (kawr•ee•OH•lis ih•FEKT). Earth is spherical, so Earth's circumference at latitudes above and below the equator is shorter than the circumference at the equator. But the period of rotation is always 24 hours. Therefore, points on Earth near the equator travel faster than points closer to the poles.

The difference in speed of rotation causes the Coriolis effect. For example, wind and water traveling south from the North Pole actually go toward the southwest instead of straight south. Wind and water deflect to the right because the wind and water move east more slowly than Earth rotates beneath them. In the Northern Hemisphere, currents are deflected to the right. In the Southern Hemisphere, currents are deflected to the left.

The Coriolis effect is most noticeable for objects that travel over long distances, without any interruptions. Over short distances, the difference in Earth's rotational speed from one point to another point is not great enough to cause noticeable deflection.

In the Northern Hemisphere, currents are deflected to the right.

Direction of Earth's rotation

→ Path of wind without Coriolis effect
→ Approximate path of wind with Coriolis effect

Global Winds

Have you ever blown gently on a cup of hot chocolate? You may have noticed that your breath makes ripples that push the hot chocolate across the surface of the liquid. Similarly, winds that blow across the surface of Earth's oceans push water across Earth's surface. This process causes surface currents in the ocean.

Different winds cause currents to flow in different directions. For example, near the equator, the winds blow east to west for the most part. Most surface currents in the same area follow a similar pattern.

What powers surface currents?

The sun heats air near the equator more than it heats air at other latitudes. Pressure differences form because of these differences in heating. For example, the air that is heated near the equator is warmer and less dense than air at other latitudes. The rising of warm air creates an area of low pressure near the equator. Pressure differences in the atmosphere cause the wind to form. So, the sun causes winds to form, and winds cause surface currents to form. Therefore, the major source of the energy that powers surface currents is the sun.

8 Analyze Fill in the cause-and-effect chart to show how the sun's energy powers surface ocean currents.

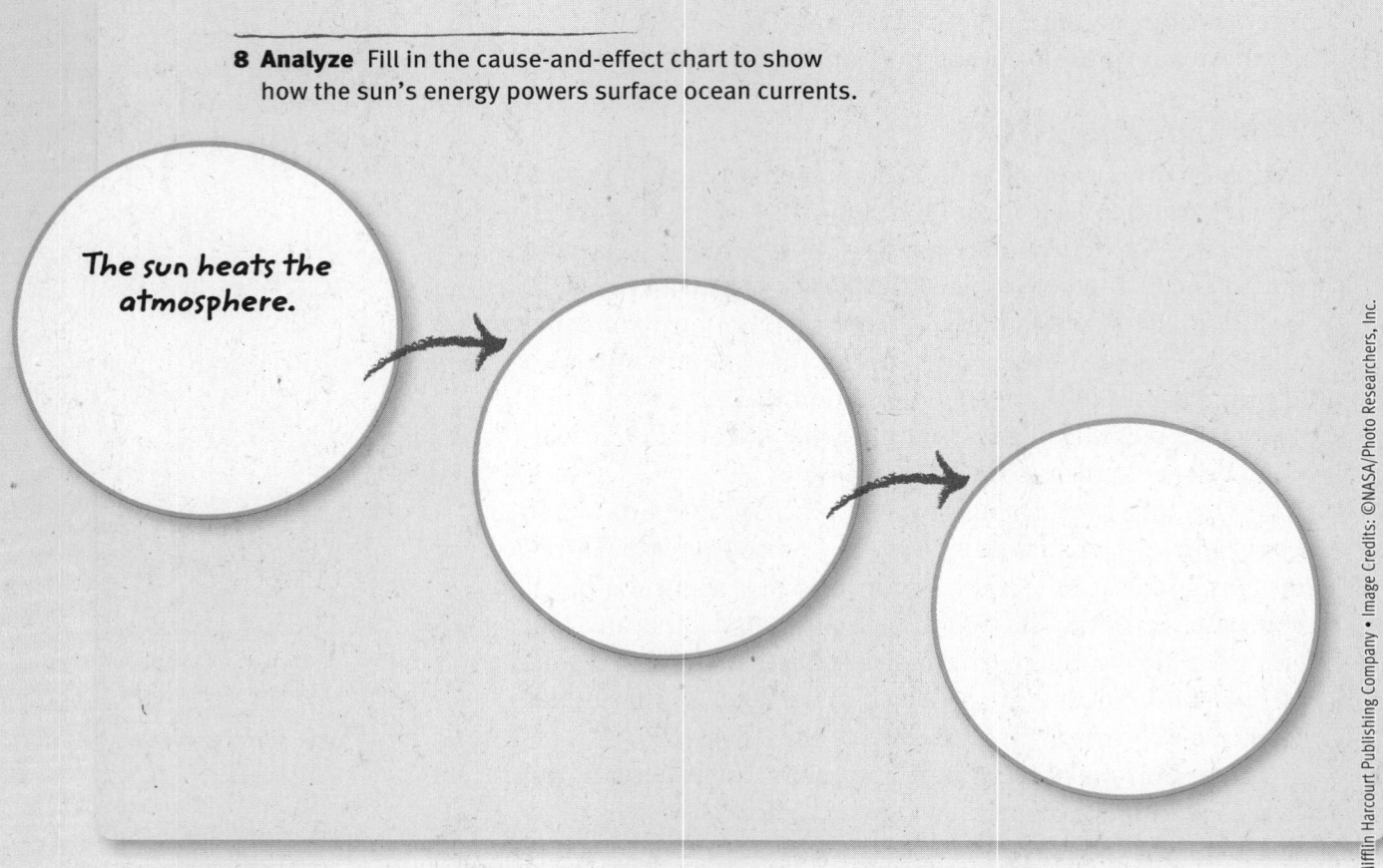

The sun heats the atmosphere.

Global Surface Winds

NORTH AMERICA

EUROPE

ASIA

PACIFIC OCEAN

PACIFIC OCEAN

AFRICA

Equator

SOUTH AMERICA

INDIAN OCEAN

AUSTRALIA

ATLANTIC OCEAN

SOUTHERN OCEAN

ANTARCTICA

→ Ocean surface wind

Global Surface Currents

ARCTIC OCEAN

Oyashio

Alaska

Labrador

Norwegian

North Pacific

NORTH AMERICA

North Atlantic Drift

EUROPE

ASIA

Oyashio

PACIFIC OCEAN

California

Gulf Stream

Canary

Kuroshio

North Pacific

PACIFIC OCEAN

North Equatorial

North Equatorial

Equatorial Countercurrent

Equatorial Countercurrent

AFRICA

Equator

INDIAN OCEAN

South Equatorial

SOUTH AMERICA

South Equatorial

Peru

ATLANTIC OCEAN

Brazil

Benguela

Agulhas

AUSTRALIA

West Australian

East Australian

Antarctic Circumpolar

SOUTHERN OCEAN

Antarctic Circumpolar

ANTARCTICA

→ Warm current
→ Cold current

9 Analyze Circle the same area on each map. Describe what you observe about these two areas.

_____

_____

_____

Current Events

How do deep currents form?

Active Reading

10 Identify As you read, underline the cause of deep currents.

Movements of ocean water far below the surface are called **deep currents**. Deep currents are caused by differences in water density. *Density* is the amount of matter in a given space or volume. The density of ocean water is affected by salinity (suh•LIN•ih•tee) and temperature. *Salinity* is a measure of the amount of dissolved salts or solids in a liquid. Water with high salinity is denser than water with low salinity. And cold water is denser than warm water. When water cools, it contracts and the water molecules move closer together. This contraction makes the water denser. When water warms, it expands and the water molecules move farther apart. The warm water is less dense, so it rises above the cold water.

When ocean water at the surface becomes denser than water below it, the denser water sinks. The water moves from the surface to the deep ocean, forming deep currents. Deep currents flow along the ocean floor or along the top of another layer of denser water. Because the ocean is so deep, there are several layers of water at any location in the ocean. The deepest and densest water in the ocean is Antarctic Bottom Water, near Antarctica.

Polar region

Convection current

B Warm water from surface currents cools in polar regions, becomes denser, and sinks toward the ocean floor.

C Deep currents carry colder, denser water in the deep ocean from polar regions to other parts of Earth.

Visualize It!

11 Illustrate Complete the drawing at part B on the diagram.

What are convection currents?

As you read about convection currents, refer to the illustration below. Surface currents and deep currents are linked in the ocean. Together they form convection currents. In the ocean, a **convection current** is a movement of water that results from density differences. Convection currents can be vertical, circular, or cyclical. Think of convection currents in the ocean as a conveyor belt. Surface currents make up the top part of the belt. Deep currents make up the bottom part of the belt. Water from a surface current may become a deep current in areas where water density increases. Deep current water then rises up to the surface in areas where the surface current is carrying low-density water away.

How do convection currents transfer energy?

Convection currents transfer energy. Water at the ocean's surface absorbs energy from the sun. Surface currents carry this energy to colder regions. The warm water loses energy to its surroundings and cools. As the water cools, it becomes denser and it sinks. The cold water travels along the ocean bottom. Then, the cold water rises to the surface as warm surface water moves away. The cold water absorbs energy from the sun, and the cycle continues.

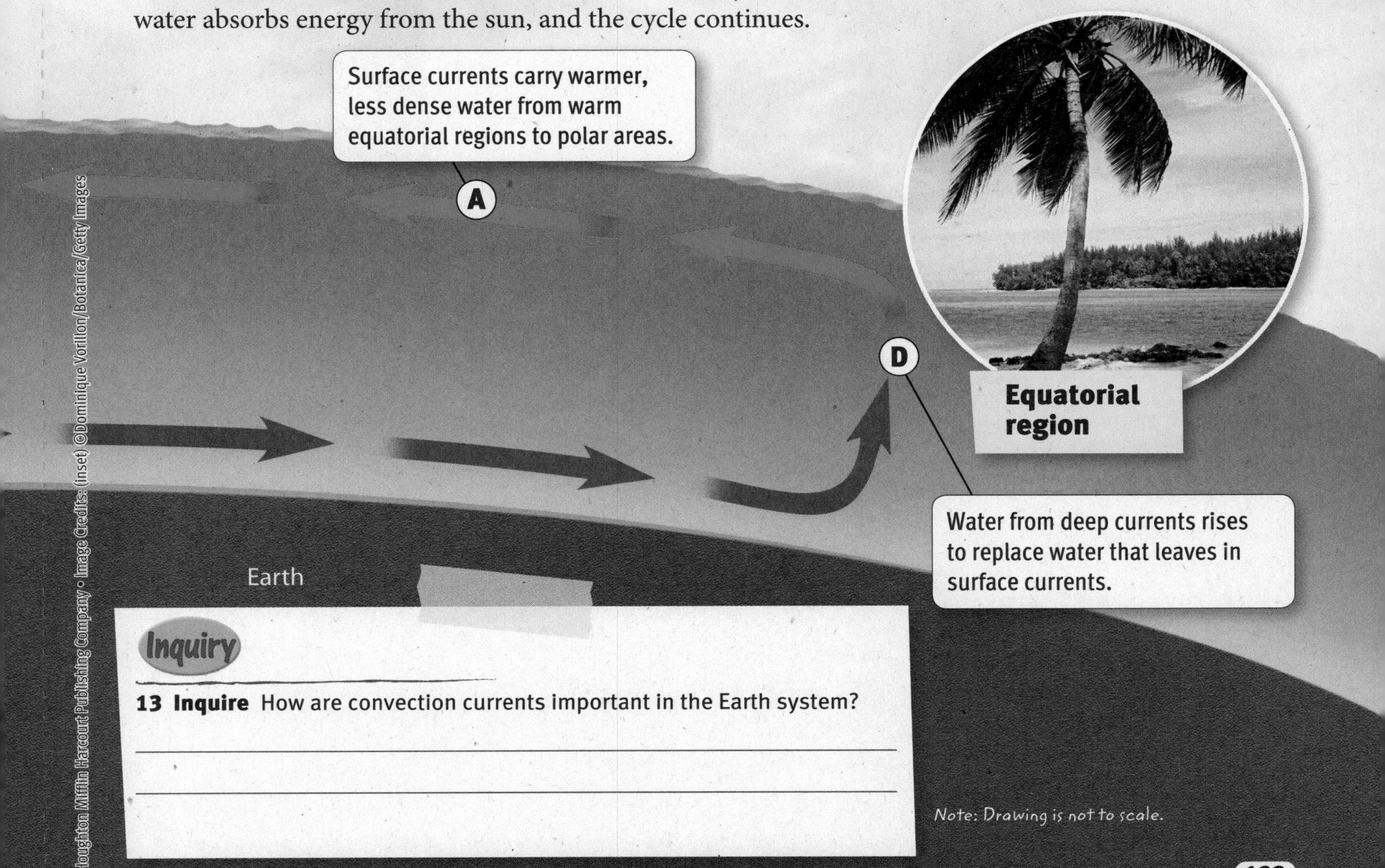

Surface currents carry warmer, less dense water from warm equatorial regions to polar areas.

A

D

Equatorial region

Water from deep currents rises to replace water that leaves in surface currents.

Earth

Note: Drawing is not to scale.

> ## Think Outside the Book (Inquiry)
>
> **12 Apply** Write an interview with a water molecule following a convection current. Be sure to include questions and answers. Can you imagine the temperature changes the molecule would experience?

Inquiry

13 Inquire How are convection currents important in the Earth system?

_____

_____

That's Swell!

![Active Reading]

14 Identify As you read, underline the steps that occur in upwelling.

What is upwelling?

At times, winds blow toward the equator along the northwest coast of South America and the west coast of North America. These winds cause surface currents to move away from the shore. The warm surface water is then replaced by cold, nutrient-rich water from the deep ocean in a process called **upwelling**. The deep water contains nutrients, such as iron and nitrate.

Upwelling is extremely important to ocean life. The nutrients that are brought to the surface of the ocean support the growth of phytoplankton (fy•toh•PLANGK•tuhn) and zooplankton. These tiny plants and animals are food for other organisms, such as fish and seabirds. Many fisheries are located in areas of upwelling because ocean animals thrive there. Some weather conditions can interrupt the process of upwelling. When upwelling is reduced, the richness of the ocean life at the surface is also reduced.

15 Predict What might happen to the fisheries if upwelling stopped?

_____

_____

_____

_____

_____

_____

The livelihood of these Peruvian fishermen depends on upwelling.

On the coast of California, upwelling sustains large kelp forests.

During upwelling, cold, nutrient-rich water from the deep ocean rises to the surface.

Wind

Warm surface water

Why It Matters

Hitching a Ride!

What do coconuts, plankton, and sea turtles have in common? They get free rides on ocean currents.

Sprouting Coconuts!
This sprouting coconut may be transported by ocean currents to a beach. This transport explains why coconut trees can grow in several areas.

World Travel
When baby sea turtles are hatched on a beach, they head for the ocean. They can then pick up ocean currents to travel. Some travel from Australia to South America on currents.

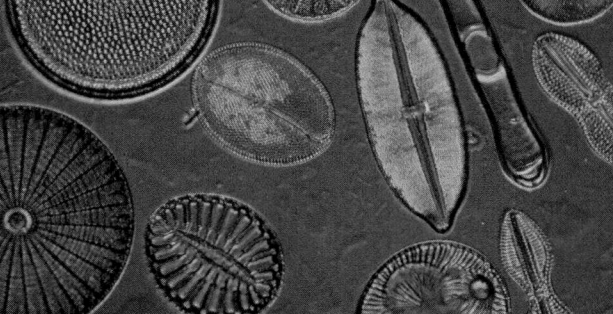

Fast Food
Diatoms are a kind of phytoplankton. They are tiny, one-celled plants that form the basis of the food chain. Diatoms ride surface currents throughout the world.

Extend

Inquiry

16 Identify List three organisms transported by ocean currents.

17 Research Investigate the Sargasso Sea. State why a lot of plastic collects in this sea. Find out whether any plastic collects on the shoreline nearest you.

18 Explain Describe how plastic and other debris can collect in the ocean by doing one of the following:
- make a poster
- write a song
- write a poem
- write a short story

Traveling the World

What do ocean currents transport?

Ocean water circulates through all of Earth's ocean basins. The paths are like the main highway on which ocean water flows. If you could follow a water molecule on this path, you would find that the molecule takes more than 1,000 years to return to its starting point! Along with water, ocean currents also transport dissolved solids, dissolved gases, and energy around Earth.

Active Reading

19 Identify As you read, underline the description of how energy reaches the poles.

20 Describe Choose a location on the map. Using your finger, follow the route you would take if you could ride a current. Describe your route. Include the direction you go and the landmasses you pass.

_____

_____

_____

_____

_____

Antarctica is not shown on this map, but the currents at the bottom of the map circulate around Antarctica.

Ocean Currents Transport Energy

Global ocean circulation is very important in the transport of energy in the form of heat. Remember that ocean currents flow in huge convection currents that can be thousands of kilometers long. These convection currents carry about 40% of the energy that is transported around Earth's surface.

Near the equator, the ocean absorbs a large amount of solar energy. The ocean also absorbs energy from the atmosphere. Ocean currents carry this energy from the equator toward the poles. When the warm water travels to cooler areas, the energy is released back into the atmosphere. Therefore, ocean circulation has an important influence on Earth's climate.

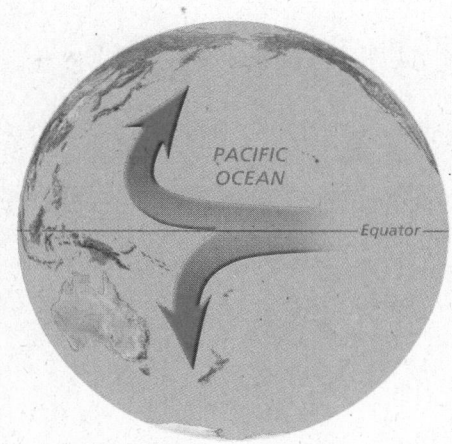

In the Pacific Ocean, surface currents transport energy from the tropics to latitudes above and below the equator.

Ocean Currents Transport Matter

Besides water, ocean currents transport whatever is in the water. The most familiar dissolved solid in ocean water is sodium chloride, or table salt. Other dissolved solids are important to marine life. Ocean water contains many nutrients—such as nitrogen and phosphorus—that are important for plant and animal growth.

Ocean water also transports gases. Gases in the atmosphere are absorbed by ocean water at the ocean surface. As a result, the most abundant gases in the atmosphere—nitrogen, oxygen, argon, and carbon dioxide—are also abundant in the ocean. Dissolved oxygen and carbon dioxide are necessary for the survival of many marine organisms.

21 List Write three examples of matter besides water that are transported by ocean currents.

_____

_____

_____

_____

_____

Visual Summary

To complete this summary, draw an arrow to show each type of ocean current. Fill in the blanks with the correct word. Then use the key below to check your answers. You can use this page to review the main concepts of the lesson.

Surface currents are streamlike movements of water at or near the surface of the ocean.

22 The direction of a surface current is affected by

_____,

_____,

and _____

Deep currents are streamlike movements of ocean water located far below the surface.

23 Deep currents form where the

_____

of ocean water increases.

Ocean Currents

A convection current in the ocean is any movement of matter that results from differences in density.

24 A convection current in the ocean transports matter and

_____

Upwelling is the process in which warm surface water is replaced by cold water from the deep ocean.

25 The cold water from deep in the ocean contains

_____

Answers: 22 continental deflections, the Coriolis effect, global winds; 23 density; 24 energy; 25 nutrients

26 **Describe** State the two general patterns of global ocean circulation.

Lesson Review

Vocabulary

Fill in the blanks with the terms that best complete the following sentences.

1 _____ are streamlike movements of water in the ocean.

2 The _____ causes currents in open water to move in a curved path rather than a straight path.

3 _____ causes cold, nutrient-rich waters to move up to the ocean's surface.

Key Concepts

4 Explain List the steps that show how the sun provides the energy for surface ocean currents.

_____

_____

_____

_____

_____

5 Explain State how a deep current forms.

_____

_____

_____

_____

_____

6 Describe Explain how a convection current transports energy around the globe.

_____

_____

_____

_____

7 List Write the three factors that affect surface ocean currents.

_____

_____

_____

Critical Thinking

Use this diagram to answer the following questions.

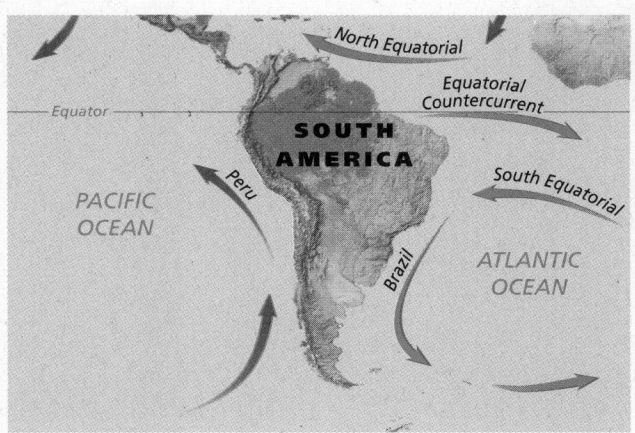

8 Apply Explain why the direction of the South Equatorial current changes.

_____

_____

_____

_____

9 Apply If South America were not there, explain how the direction of the South Equatorial current would be different.

_____

_____

_____

_____

10 Apply Describe how surface currents would be affected if Earth did not rotate.

_____

_____

_____

_____

_____

_____

My Notes

Evaluating Technological Systems

Analyzing Water Power

A system is a group of interacting parts that work together to do a job. Technological systems process inputs and generate outputs. An input is any matter, energy, or information that goes into a system. Outputs are matter, energy, or information that come out of the system. Most systems also generate some waste as an output.

Inputs and Outputs

Most renewable energy produced in the United States is generated using the energy of moving water. A hydroelectric dam is a system that changes the mechanical energy in moving water into electrical energy. Water is the input to a hydroelectric dam. Huge tunnels, called *penstocks,* carry water into the dam to fan-like turbines. Water flowing past the blades of the turbines causes the turbines to spin. This causes wire coils in the generator to spin. Spinning coiled wire in a magnetic field produces an electric current. Electric current is one output of the hydroelectric dam system. Water flowing out of the dam is another output. In a hydroelectric dam, some of the energy from the flowing water is wasted in the form of heat from the friction of the spinning turbines and coils.

1 Identify What are the inputs and outputs of a hydroelectric dam?

_____

_____

"Workers use bicycles or tricycles to travel from one turbine to the next over the length of the dam because the turbines are so large."

Feedback and Control

Feedback is information from one step in a process that affects a previous step in the process. Feedback can be used to regulate a system by applying controls. In a hydroelectric dam system, information about how much electricity is produced is sent back into the system. This information is used to regulate the amount of electricity that is produced. When more electricity is needed, giant gates, called *sluice gates,* are opened to allow water to flow. When less electricity is required, some gates are closed. The sluice gates act as the control in this system.

2 Analyze In the image below, place the terms *input, output,* and *control* in the boxes that correspond to the correct part of the hydroelectric dam system.

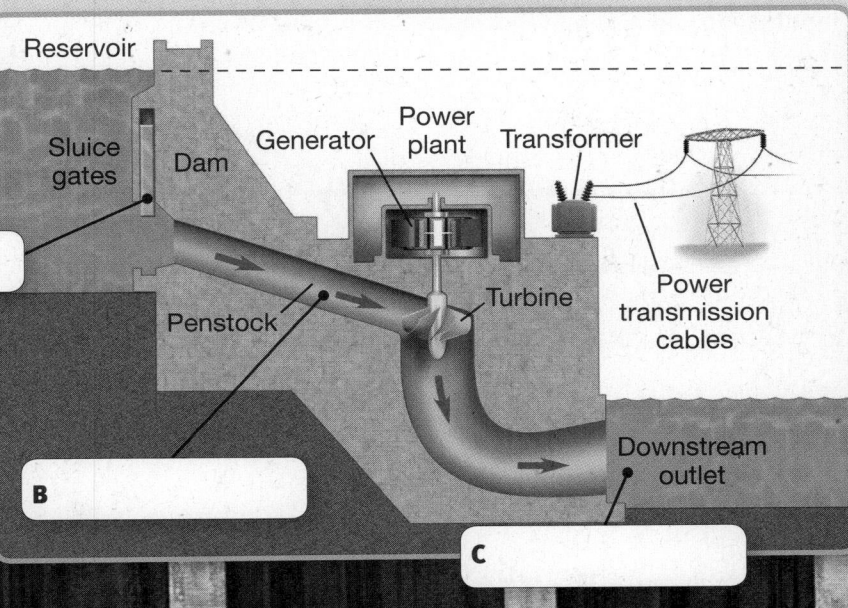

Water flowing through a dam spins a turbine. This spins a generator, which produces electric current. Transformers convert the current so that it can be used in homes, businesses, and factories.

✋ You Try It! ⟶

Now it's your turn to identify inputs, outputs, feedback, and controls.

👋 You Try It!

Now it's your turn to identify inputs, outputs, feedback and controls in a system that uses water power. Working with a partner, think of another way that you could use moving water to do a job. For example, flowing water in water mills has been used to spin large cutting blades in saw mills or to grind grain in flour mills. You can use one of these systems or use your imagination to create your own system that uses moving water to do a job.

① Identify Inputs

In the oval below, enter a name for your system. Recall that inputs can be matter, energy, or information. List the inputs into your system on the lines above the arrows. If there are more than three inputs, you can add more arrows.

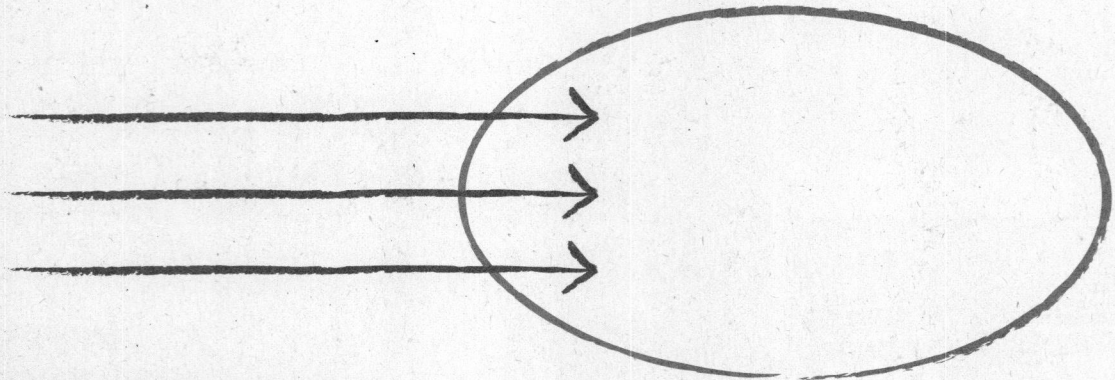

② Identify Outputs

As with the inputs, the outputs of a system can be matter, energy, or information. Keep in mind that most systems also generate some waste as an output. In the oval, write the name of your system. Use the arrows below to list the outputs of your system. If there are more than three outputs, you can add more arrows.

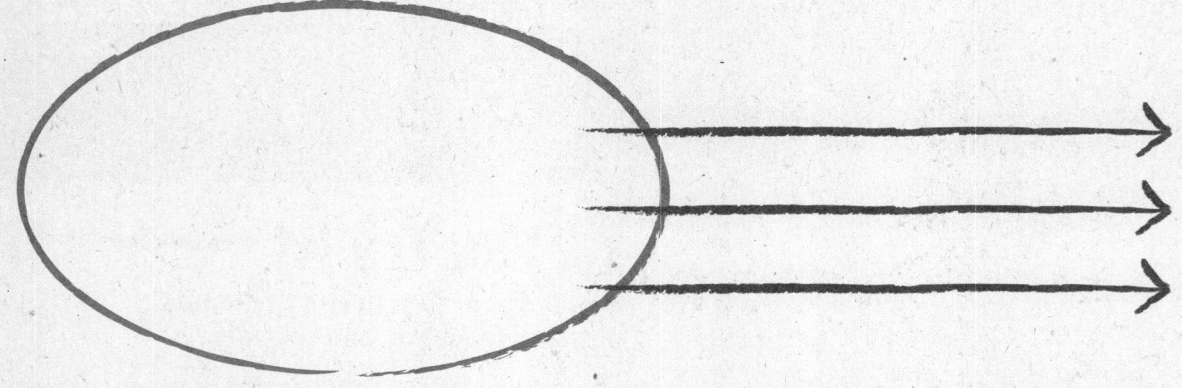

③ Evaluate System Feedback

Now, consider which steps in your system could be used as feedback to regulate the system. Which outputs need to be monitored and why?

_____

_____

_____

_____

④ Apply System Controls

Using the feedback you identified in the last step, propose one or more controls for your system that will keep the system working properly.

_____

_____

_____

_____

⑤ Communicate Results

In the space below, draw a sketch of the system you developed. Label the inputs, outputs, feedback and controls.

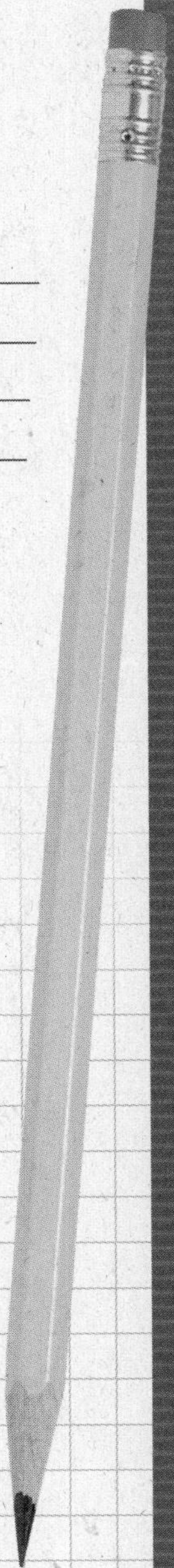

Human Impact on Water

ESSENTIAL QUESTION

What impact can human activities have on water resources?

By the end of this lesson, you should be able to explain the impacts that humans can have on the quality and supply of fresh water.

Humans and other organisms depend on clean water to survive. More than half of the material inside humans is water.

OHIO **7.ESS.1** The hydrologic cycle illustrates the changing states of water as it moves through the lithosphere, biosphere, hydrosphere and atmosphere.

OHIO **7.SIA.6** Think critically and logically to connect evidence and explanations.

OHIO **7.SIA.7** Recognize and analyze alternative explanations and predictions.

Lesson Labs

Quick Labs
• Ocean Pollution From Land
• Turbidity and Water Temperature

Field Lab
• Investigating Water Quality

 **Engage Your Brain**

1 Analyze Write a list of the reasons humans need water. Next to this list, write a list of reasons fish need water. Are there similarities between your two lists?

2 Identify Circle the word that correctly completes the following sentences.
The man in this photo is testing *water/air* quality.
The flowing body of water next to the man is a *river/lake*.

 **Active Reading**

3 Synthesize You can often define an unknown word if you know the meaning of its word parts. Use the word parts and the sentence below to make an educated guess about the meaning of the word *nonrenewable*.

Word part	Meaning
renew	restore, make like new
-able	able to be
non-	not

Example sentence
Some of Earth's <u>nonrenewable</u> resources include coal and oil.

nonrenewable:

_____

_____

_____

_____

Vocabulary Terms

• water pollution
• point-source pollution
• nonpoint-source pollution
• thermal pollution
• eutrophication
• potable
• reservoir

4 Identify This list contains the key terms you'll learn in this lesson. As you read, circle the definition of each term.

Close up of a mayfly larva

Water, Water

Organisms need clean water for life and good health. For example, young mayflies live in water, humans drink water, and brown pelicans eat fish they catch in water.

Why is water important?

Earth is the only planet with large amounts of water. Water shapes Earth's surface and affects Earth's weather and climates. Most importantly, water is vital for life. Every living thing is made mostly of water. Most life processes use water. Water is an important natural resource. For humans and other organisms, access to clean water is important for good health.

There is lots of water, so what's the problem?

About 97% of Earth's water is salty, which leaves only 3% as fresh water. However, as you can see from the graph, over two-thirds of Earth's fresh water is frozen as ice and snow. But a lot of the liquid water seeps into the ground as groundwater. That leaves much less than 1% of Earth's fresh liquid water on the surface. Water is vital for people, so this small volume of fresh surface and groundwater is a limited resource.

Areas with high densities of people, such as cities, need lots of fresh water. Cities are getting bigger, and so the need for fresh water is increasing. *Urbanization* (ER•buh•ny•zhay•shuhn) is the growth of towns and cities that results from the movement of people from rural areas into the urban areas. The greater demand for fresh water in cities is threatening the availability of water for many people. Fresh water is becoming a natural resource that cannot be replaced at the same rate at which it is used.

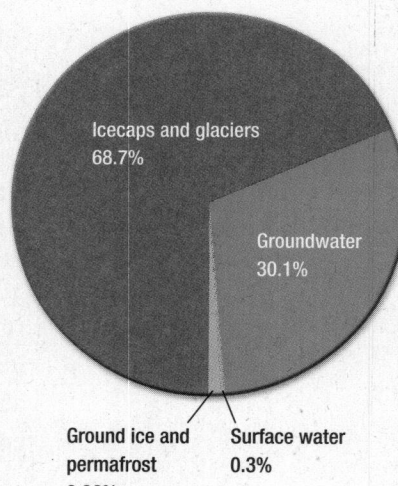

Distribution of Earth's Fresh Water

- Icecaps and glaciers 68.7%
- Groundwater 30.1%
- Ground ice and permafrost 0.86%
- Surface water 0.3%

Visualize It!

5 Interpret What percentage of fresh water on Earth is frozen? What percentage of fresh water is liquid?

_____

_____

Everywhere...

Where do we get fresh water?

Fresh water may fall directly as precipitation, or may melt from ice and snow. Earth's fresh liquid water is found as surface water and groundwater. *Surface water* is any body of water above the ground. It includes liquid salt or fresh water, or solid water, like snow and ice. Water may seep below the surface to become *groundwater*. Groundwater is found under Earth's surface, in spaces in rocks or in soil, where it can be liquid or frozen.

Active Reading

6 List What are the different sources of fresh water?

Aquifers and Groundwater

Aquifers and ground ice are forms of groundwater. An *aquifer* is a body of rock or sediment that can store a lot of water, and that allows water to flow easily through it. Aquifers store water in spaces, called *pores,* between particles of rock or sediment. Wells are dug into aquifers to reach the water. In polar regions, water is often frozen in a layer of soil called *permafrost.*

Think Outside the Book **Inquiry**

7 Observe Keep a water diary for a day. Record every time you use water at school, at home, or elsewhere. At the end of the day, review your records. How could you reduce your water usage?

Rivers, Streams, and Lakes

Rivers, streams, and most lakes are fresh surface waters. A stream or river may flow into a bowl-shaped area, which may fill up to form a lake. Many millions of people around the world depend on fresh water that is taken from rivers and fresh water lakes.

What are water quality and supply?

Water quality is a measure of how clean or polluted water is. Water quality is important because humans and other organisms depend on clean water to survive. It is vital for living things to not only have water, but also to have clean water. Dirty, contaminated water can make us sick or even kill us.

Water supply is the availability of water. Water supply influences where and when farmers grow crops, and where people can build cities. *Water supply systems* carry water from groundwater or surface waters so people can use the water. The systems can be a network of underground pipes, or a bucket for scooping water from a well. A shortage of clean, fresh water reduces quality of life for people. Many people in developing countries do not have access to clean, fresh water.

Many people do not have a water supply to their homes. Instead, they have to go to a local stream, well, or pump to gather water for cooking, cleaning, and drinking.

Under Threat

What threatens fresh water quality?

When waste or other material is added to water so that it is harmful to organisms that use it or live in it, **water pollution** (WAW•ter puh•LOO•shuhn) occurs. It is useful to divide pollution sources into two types. **Point-source pollution** comes from one specific site. For example, a major chemical spill is point-source pollution. Usually this type of pollution can be controlled once its source is found. **Nonpoint-source pollution** comes from many small sources and is more difficult to control. Most nonpoint-source pollution reaches water supplies by runoff or by seeping into groundwater. The main sources of nonpoint-source pollution are city streets, roads and drains, farms, and mines.

 **Active Reading**

8 Identify As you read, underline the sources of water pollution.

Thermal Pollution

Any heating of natural water that results from human activity is called **thermal pollution**. For example, water that is used for cooling some power plants gets warmed up. When that water is returned to the river or lake it is at a higher temperature than the lake or river water. The warm water has less oxygen available for organisms that live in the water.

Chemical Pollution

Chemical pollution occurs when harmful chemicals are added to water supplies. Two major sources of chemical pollution are industry and agriculture. For example, refineries that process oil or metals and factories that make metal or plastic products or electronic items all produce toxic chemical waste. Chemicals used in agriculture include pesticides, herbicides, and fertilizers. These pollutants can reach water supplies by seeping into groundwater. Once in groundwater, the pollution can enter the water cycle and can be carried far from the pollution source. *Acid rain* is another form of chemical pollution. It forms when gases formed by burning fossil fuels mix with water in the air. Acid rain can harm both plants and animals. It can lower the pH of soil and water, and make them too acidic for life.

Biological Pollution

Many organisms naturally live in and around water, but they are not normally polluters. *Biological pollution* occurs when live or dead organisms are added to water supplies. Wastewater may contain disease-causing microbes from human or animal wastes. *Wastewater* is any water that has been used by people for such things as flushing toilets, showering, or washing dishes. Wastewater from feed lots and farms may also contain harmful microbes. These microbes can cause diseases such as dysentery, typhoid, or cholera.

Eutrophication

Fresh water often contains nutrients from decomposing organisms. An increase in the amount of nutrients in water is called **eutrophication** (yoo•TRAWF•ih•kay•shuhn). Eutrophication occurs naturally in water. However, *artificial eutrophication* occurs when human activity increases nutrient levels in water. Wastewater and fertilizer runoff that gets into waterways can add extra nutrients which upset the natural biology of the water. These extra nutrients cause the fast growth of algae over the water surface. An overgrowth of algae and aquatic plants can reduce oxygen levels and kill fish and other organisms in the water.

Visualize It!

Water can become polluted by human activities in many different ways.

Chemical Pollution
Sulfur in smoke and vehicle exhausts contributes to the acidification of rain, leading to acid rain. Acid rain can affect areas far from the point of pollution.

Biological pollution

Biological Pollution
Animal and human wastes can get washed into a water supply in runoff, or through leaking pipes.

Thermal pollution

Eutrophication

Chemical pollution

9 Describe How is human activity impacting water quality in this image?

_____

_____

_____

_____

10 Apply Identify one point-source and one nonpoint-source of pollution in this image.

_____

_____

_____

_____

How is water quality measured?

Before there were scientific methods of testing water, people could only look at water, taste it, and smell it to check its quality. Scientists can now test water with modern equipment, so the results are more reliable. Modern ways of testing water are especially important for finding small quantities of toxic chemicals or harmful organisms in water.

Water is a good solvent. So, water in nature usually contains dissolved solids, such as salt and other substances. Because most dissolved solids cannot be seen, it is important to measure them. Measurements of water quality include testing the levels of dissolved oxygen, pH, temperature, dissolved solids, and the number and types of microbes in the water. Quality standards depend on the intended use for the water. For example, drinking water needs to meet much stricter quality standards than environmental waters such as river or lake waters do.

Water Quality Measurement

Quality measurement	What is it?	How it relates to water quality
Dissolved solids	a measure of the amount of ions or microscopic suspended solids in water	Some dissolved solids could be harmful chemicals. Others such as calcium could cause scaling or build-up in water pipes.
pH	a measure of how acidic or alkaline water is	Aquatic organisms need a near neutral pH (approx. pH 7). Acid rain can drop the pH too low (acidic) for aquatic life to live.
Dissolved oxygen (DO)	the amount of oxygen gas that is dissolved in water	Aquatic organisms need oxygen. Animal waste and thermal pollution can decrease the amount of oxygen dissolved in water.
Turbidity	a measure of the cloudiness of water that is caused by suspended solids	High turbidity increases the chance that harmful microbes or chemicals are in the water.
Microbial load	the identification of harmful bacteria, viruses or protists in water	Microbes such as bacteria, viruses, and protists from human and animal wastes can cause diseases.

11 Predict Why might increased turbidity increase the chance of something harmful being in the water? _____

_____

How is water treated for human use?

Active Reading 12 Identify As you read, number the basic steps in the water treatment process.

Natural water may be unsafe for humans to drink. So, water that is to be used as drinking water is treated to remove harmful chemicals and organisms. Screens take out large debris. Then chemicals are added that make suspended particles stick together. These particles drop out of the water in a process called *flocculation*. Flocculation also removes harmful bacteria and other microbes. Chlorine is often added to kill microbes left in the water. In some cities, fluoride is added to water supplies to help prevent tooth decay. Finally, air is bubbled through the water. Water that is suitable to drink is called **potable** water. Once water is used, it becomes wastewater. It enters the sewage system where pipes carry it to a wastewater treatment plant. There the wastewater is cleaned and filtered before being released back into the environment.

Drinking water is often mixed in large basins to help remove chemicals and harmful organisms. Paddles stir the water in the basins.

Who monitors and protects our water quality?

Active Reading 13 Identify As you read, underline the government agency that is responsible for enforcing water quality rules.

If a public water supply became contaminated, many people could get very sick. As a result, public water supplies are closely monitored so that any problems can be fixed quickly. The Safe Drinking Water Act is the main federal law that ensures safe drinking water for people in the United States. The act sets strict limits on the amount of heavy metals or certain types of bacteria that can be in drinking water, among other things. The Environmental Protection Agency (EPA) has the job of enforcing this law. It is responsible for setting the standards drinking water must meet before the water can be pumped into public water systems. Water quality tests can be done by trained workers or trained volunteers.

Samples of water are routinely taken to make sure the water quality meets the standards required by law.

© Houghton Mifflin Harcourt Publishing Company • Image Credits: (t) ©Lawrence Migdale/Photo Researchers, Inc.; (b) ©Will & Deni McIntyre/Photo Researchers, Inc.

Supply and Demand

How does water get to the faucet?

In earlier times, humans had to live near natural sources of fresh water. Over time, engineers developed ways to transport and store large amounts of water. So, humans can now live in places where fresh water is supplied by water pipes and other infrastructure. The ability to bring fresh water safely from its source to a large population has led to the urbanization of cities.

Creating Water Supply Systems

Freshwater supply is often limited, so we have found ways to store and transport water far from its source to where it is used. Surface water is collected and pumped to places where people need it. Groundwater can be found by digging wells into aquifers. Water can be lifted from a well by hand in buckets. It can be pumped into pipes that supply homes, farms, factories and cities. Piped water supply systems can deliver water over great distances to where humans need it. Water supply and storage systems are expensive to build and maintain.

Visualize It!

A public water supply includes the water source, the treatment facilities, and the pipes and pumps that send it to homes, industries, businesses, and public facilities.

Water treatment and distribution

A Water can be moved far away from its source by pumping it through pipes to large urban areas.

Intake

Chemicals added

Lake

Mixing basins

Settling basins

Tunnels

Water treatment plant

B Water is treated to make it potable.

© Houghton Mifflin Harcourt Publishing Company • Image Credits: ©NASA image by Marit Jentoft-Nilsen, based on data from NOAA GOES. Blue Marble Imagery by NASA's Earth Observatory Team, ©artpartner-images/Photographer's Choice/Getty Images.

Changing the Flow of Water

Pumping and collecting groundwater and surface waters changes how water flows in natural systems. For example, a **reservoir** (REZ•uhr•vwohr) is a body of water that usually forms behind a dam. Dams stop river waters from flowing along their natural course. The water in a reservoir would naturally have flowed to the sea. Instead, the water can be diverted into a pipeline or into artificial channels called *canals* or *aqueducts*.

What threatens our water supply?

Active Reading **14 Identify** As you read, underline the things that are a threat to water supply.

As the human use of water has increased, the demand for fresh water has also increased. Demand is greater than supply in many areas of the world, including parts of the United States. The larger a population or a city gets, the greater the demand for fresh water. Increased demand for and use of water can cause water shortages. Droughts or leaking water pipes can also cause water shortages. Water is used to keep our bodies clean and healthy. It is also used to grow crops for food. Water shortages threaten these benefits.

15 Infer Why would a larger city have a larger demand for water?

_____

_____

_____

_____

_____

C The infastructure shown here is used to supply clean water. Once water is used, it becomes wastewater. A different system, called a sewage system, carries wastewater away from urban areas to wastewater treatment plants.

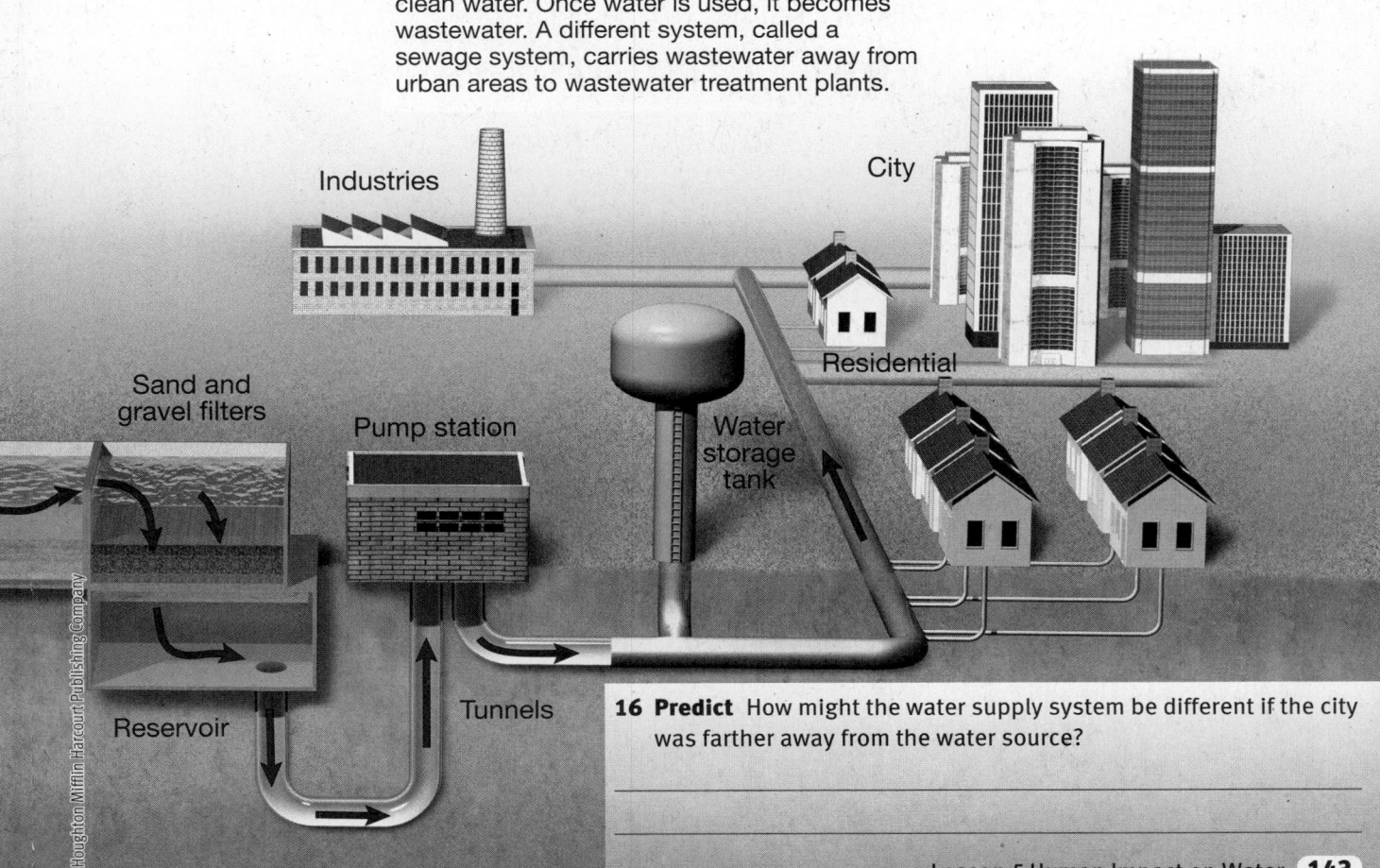

Industries

City

Residential

Sand and gravel filters

Pump station

Water storage tank

Reservoir

Tunnels

16 Predict How might the water supply system be different if the city was farther away from the water source?

_____

_____

How do efforts to supply water to humans affect the environment?

Growing urban populations place a greater demand on water supplies. Efforts to increase water supply can affect the environment. For example, building dams and irrigation canals changes the natural flow of water. The environment is physically changed by construction work. The local ecology changes too. Organisms that live in or depend on the water may lose their habitat and move away.

Aquifers are often used as freshwater sources for urban areas. When more water is taken from an aquifer than can be replaced by rain or snow, the water table can drop below the reach of existing wells. Rivers and streams may dry up and the soil that once held aquifer waters may collapse, or *subside*. In coastal areas, the overuse of groundwater can cause seawater to seep into the aquifer in a process called *saltwater intrusion*. In this way, water supplies can become contaminated with salt water.

Increasing population in an area can also affect water quality. The more people that use a water supply in one area, the greater the volume of wastewater that is produced in that area. Pollutants such as oil, pesticides, fertilizers, and heavy metals from city runoff, from industry, and from agriculture may seep into surface waters and groundwater. In this way, pollution could enter the water supply. This pollution could also enter the water cycle and be carried far from the initial source of the pollution.

Active Reading

17 Relate How can the increased demand on water affect water quality?

_____

_____

_____

_____

_____

_____

Digging irrigation canals changes the flow of rivers.

Building dams disrupts water flow and affects the ecology of the land and water.

Irrigating arid areas changes the ecology of those areas.

© Houghton Mifflin Harcourt Publishing Company • Image Credits: (l) ©Travel Ink/Gallo Images/Getty Images; (r) ©Derrick Francis Furlong/Alamy; (bc) ©Tony Roberts/Corbis

Why It Matters

Death of a Sea

The Aral Sea in Central Asia was once the world's fourth-largest inland salty lake. But it has been shrinking since the 1960s. In the 1940s, the courses of the rivers that fed the lake were changed to irrigate the desert, so that crops such as cotton and rice could be grown. By 2004, the lake had shrunk to 25% of its original size. The freshwater flow into the lake was reduced and evaporation caused the lake to become so salty that most of the plants and animals in it died or left the lake.

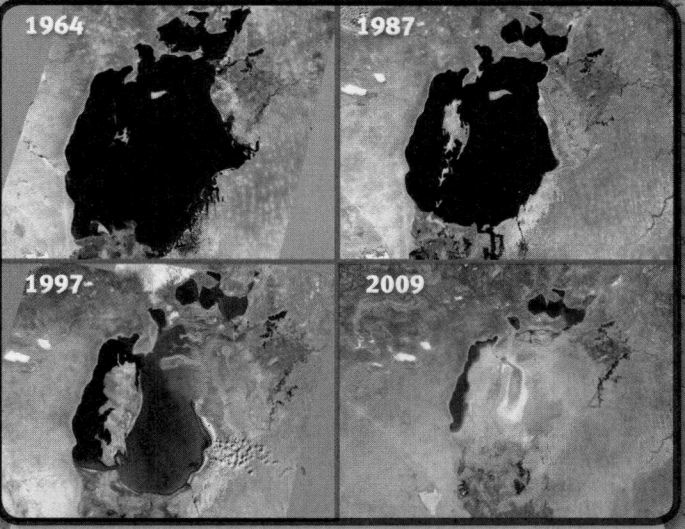

1964
1987
1997
2009

By 2007, the lake had shrunk to 10% of its original size and had split into three separate, smaller lakes.

Polluted Land

The Aral Sea is also heavily polluted by industrial wastes, pesticides, and fertilizer runoff. Salty dust that is blown from the dried seabed damages crops and pollutes drinking water. The salt- and dust-laden air cause serious public health problems in the Aral Sea region. One of the more bizarre reminders of how large the lake once was are the boats that lie abandoned on the exposed sea floor.

Extend

Inquiry

18 Identify What human activity has created the situation in the Aral Sea?

19 Apply Research the impact that of one of these two large water projects has had on people and on the environment: The Three Gorges Dam or the Columbia Basin Project.

20 Relate Research a current or past water project in the area where you live. What benefits will these projects have for people in the area? What risks might there be to the environment?

EYE ON THE ENVIRONMENT

© Houghton Mifflin Harcourt Publishing Company • Image Credits: (bkgd) ©Gerd Ludwig/Corbis; (inset) ©NASA/Photo Researchers, Inc.

145

Visual Summary

To complete this summary, fill in the blanks with the correct word or phrase. Then use the key below to check your answers. You can use this page to review the main concepts of the lesson.

Human Impact on Water

Organisms need clean water for life and good health.

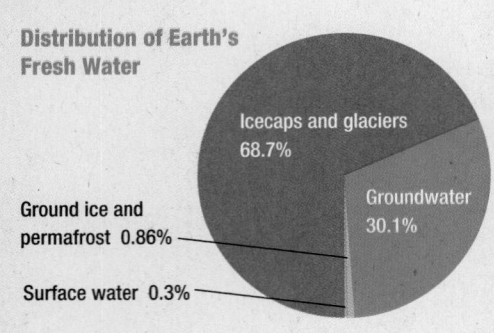

Distribution of Earth's Fresh Water

- Icecaps and glaciers 68.7%
- Groundwater 30.1%
- Ground ice and permafrost 0.86%
- Surface water 0.3%

21 Earth's fresh liquid water is found as surface water and _____

Water pollution can come from many different sources.

22 Runoff from farmland into a river is an example of _____ source pollution.

Federal laws set the standards for potable water quality. Water quality is constantly monitored.

23 Dissolved solids, pH, temperature, and dissolved oxygen are measures of _____.

Ensuring a constant supply of water for people can change the environment.

24 A _____ is a body of water that forms when a dam blocks a river.

Answers: 21 groundwater; 22 nonpoint; 23 water quality; 24 reservoir

25 Compare What is the difference between water quality and water supply?

Lesson Review

Vocabulary

Fill in the blank with the term that best completes the following sentences.

1 _Potable_ water is a term used to describe water that is safe to drink.

2 The addition of nutrients to water by human activity is called artificial _Eutrophication_.

3 _Non-point source_ pollution comes from many small sources.

Key Concepts

Complete the table below with the type of pollution described in each example.

Example	Type of pollution (chemical, thermal, or biological)
4 **Identify** A person empties an oil can into a storm drain.	chemical
5 **Identify** A factory releases warm water into a local river.	Thermal
6 **Identify** Untreated sewage is washed into a lake during a rain storm.	biological

7 **Describe** Name two ways in which humans can affect the flow of fresh water.
By puting baterica in it they might not know and polluing it.

8 **Explain** Why does water quality need to be monitored?
So if any goes wrong even the tiniest thing it can harm you so it need to be monitered

Critical Thinking

Use this graph to answer the following questions.

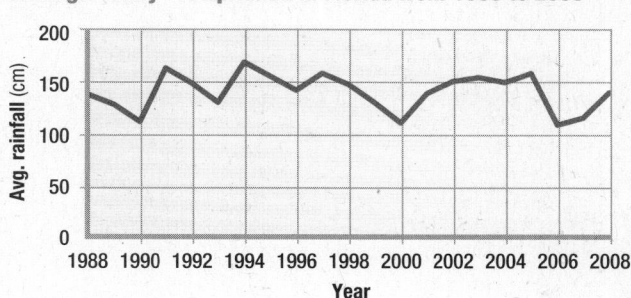

Average Yearly Precipitation in Florida from 1988 to 2008

Source: Florida State University Climate Center

9 **Analyze** Which year had the least precipitation?
_2006_

10 **Infer** What effect might many years of low precipitation have on water supply?
It might make us have not enough water

11 **Explain** Could a single person or animal be a cause of point-source pollution? Explain.
Yes, because they can do something to it and might not know

12 **Apply** In times of hot, dry, weather, some cities ban the use of garden sprinklers. Why do you think there is such a rule?
It might change something that is why

My Notes

Unit 2 [Big Idea] Water moves through Earth's atmosphere, oceans, land, and living things in a cycle.

Lesson 1
ESSENTIAL QUESTION
What makes water so important?

Describe water's structure, its properties, and its importance to Earth's systems.

Lesson 4
ESSENTIAL QUESTION
How does water move in the ocean?

Explain what factors influence this movement, and explain why ocean circulation is important in the Earth system.

Lesson 2
ESSENTIAL QUESTION
How does water change state and move around on Earth?

Describe the water cycle and the different processes that are part of the water cycle on Earth.

Lesson 5
ESSENTIAL QUESTION
What impact can human activities have on water resources?

Explain the impacts that humans can have on the quality and supply of fresh water.

Lesson 3
ESSENTIAL QUESTION
How does fresh water flow on Earth?

Explain the processes involved in the flow of water, both above and below the ground.

[Connect] ESSENTIAL QUESTIONS
Lessons 2 and 3

1 Synthesize Explain why precipitation on Earth's surface is less common over land than it is over the oceans. Base your answer on the water cycle.

_____

_____

_____

Think Outside the Book

2 Synthesize Choose one of these activities to help synthesize what you have learned in this unit.

☐ Using what you learned in lessons 1, 2, and 4, make a poster to show how the stored energy in water is released to the environment during certain changes in state.

☐ Using what you learned in lessons 1, 2, 3, and 4, make a flipbook to show how gravity affects the movement and flow of water.

Unit 2 Review

Name _____

Vocabulary

Fill in each blank with the term that best completes the following sentences.

1 Water is a _____ molecule because its hydrogen atoms have a small positive charge and its oxygen atom has a small negative charge.

2 Water is called the universal _____ because it dissolves a large number of substances.

3 The continuous movement of water between the atmosphere, the land, the oceans, and living things is called the _____.

4 Any form of water that falls to Earth's surface from the clouds is called _____.

5 A _____ is the area of land that is drained by a river system.

Key Concepts

Choose the letter of the best answer.

6 A glass of ice water is shown below before and after it reaches room temperature.

Which of the following correctly explains something that occurred in the time between these two images?

A The ice cubes expanded in volume as they melted into liquid water.

B As water vapor condensed on the glass, it absorbed energy.

C The water droplets outside the glass absorbed energy as they evaporated.

D Some liquid water inside the glass sublimated into water vapor in the air.

7 Which of these circle graphs most correctly shows the approximate proportions of fresh water and salt water on the surface of Earth?

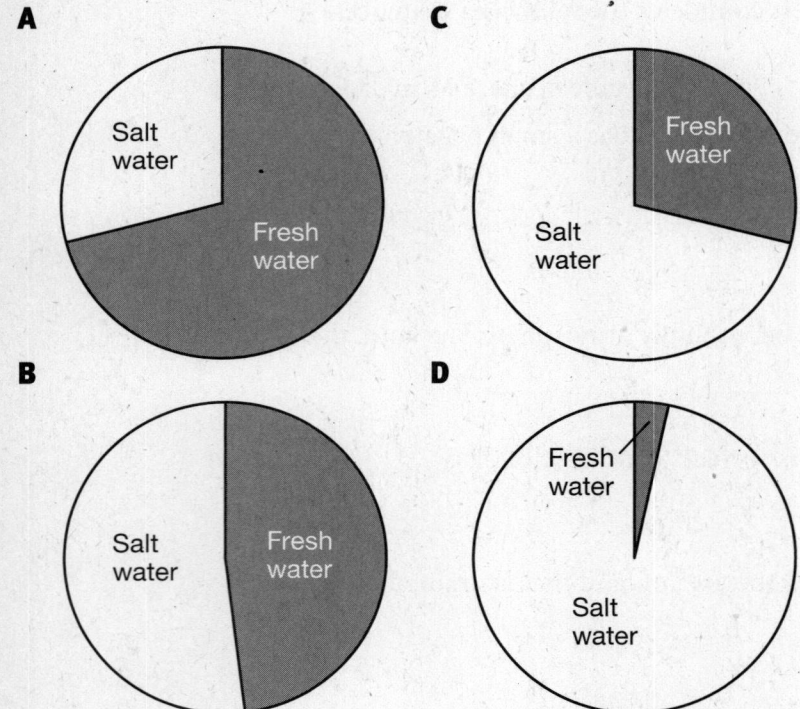

A

Salt water

Fresh water

C

Fresh water

Salt water

B

Salt water

Fresh water

D

Fresh water

Salt water

8 Which of the following correctly shows the chain of energy transfers that creates surface currents on the ocean?

A solar energy —> wind energy —> surface currents.

B wind energy —> solar energy —> surface currents.

C tidal energy —> wind energy —> surface currents.

D geothermal energy —> wind energy —> surface currents.

9 Which of the following correctly explains why icebergs float in the ocean?

A Ice is less dense than liquid water because water contracts when it freezes, filling in open space between molecules.

B Ice is less dense than liquid water because there is more open space between molecules in ice than in liquid water.

C Ice is more dense than liquid water because there is less open space between molecules in ice than in water.

D Water is a polar molecule, so the net positive electrical charges in the water repel the net positive electrical charges inside the iceberg.

10 A certain percentage of water that falls to Earth's surface as precipitation does not become surface water or groundwater and does not evaporate back into the atmosphere. Which of the following most likely explains what happens to this water?

A The water falls into the ocean, where it evaporates back into the atmosphere.

B The water is stored as snow and ice on Earth's surface.

C The water molecules are broken down into hydrogen and oxygen atoms.

D The water is absorbed and used by plants.

11 A manufacturing plant is built on the bank of the Mississippi River. Water is diverted into the plant to use in the making of a product and is then piped back into the river. If the water that is released back into the river is contaminated, what is this form of pollution called?

A thermal pollution

B biological pollution

C point-source pollution

D nonpoint-source pollution

12 Which of the following is the name for all the materials carried by a stream other than the water itself?

A discharge   **C** gradient

B flow   **D** stream load

Critical Thinking

Answer the following questions in the spaces provided.

13 Most of the energy that powers ocean waves and ocean currents ultimately comes from the sun. Describe how ocean waves and ocean currents transfer solar energy around the globe.

_____
_____
_____
_____
_____

14 The diagram below shows the changes among the three states of water.

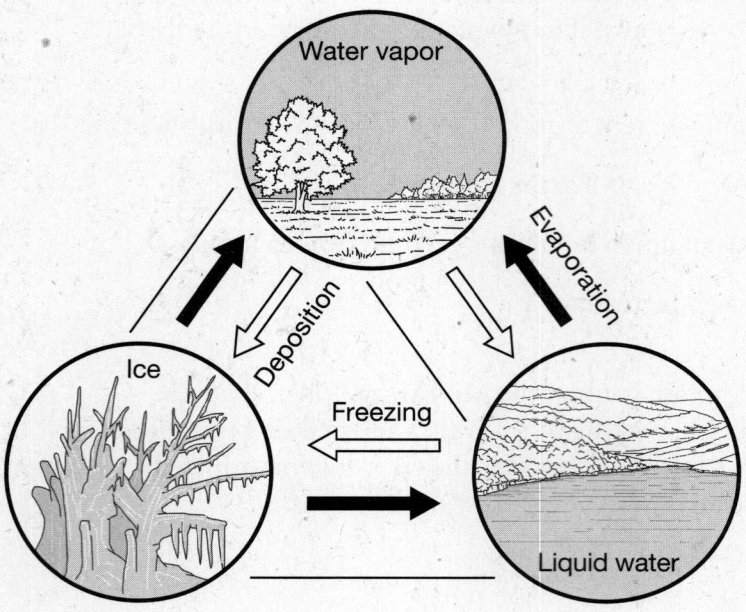

⇦ Energy absorbed / released by water

➡ Energy absorbed / released by water

Fill in each of the three blank lines with the correct term for the change of state shown by the arrows. In the key, circle the correct word to show whether water absorbs or releases energy in the changes of state shown by that type of arrow.

Connect ESSENTIAL QUESTIONS
Lessons 3 and 5

Answer the following question in the space provided.

15 Urbanization has major effects on Earth's land and water. Natural vegetation is removed in order to make room for buildings, roads, and parking lots. How does paving parking lots and roads with concrete or asphalt affect surface water and groundwater?

_____

_____

_____

_____

_____

_____

_____

UNIT 3

Earth's Atmosphere

Earth's atmosphere is divided into different layers. These clouds have formed in the troposphere, the lowest layer of the atmosphere where most weather occurs.

Big Idea

Earth's atmosphere is a mixture of gases that interacts with solar energy.

Wind is the movement of air caused by differences in air pressure.

What do you think?

Like other parts of the Earth system, energy is transferred through Earth's atmosphere. What are the three processes by which energy is transferred through the atmosphere?

Unit 3
Earth's Atmosphere

CITIZEN SCIENCE

Clearing the Air

In some areas, there are many vehicles on the roads every day. Some of the gases from vehicle exhausts react with sunlight to form ozone. There are days when the concentration of ozone is so high that it becomes a health hazard. Those days are especially difficult for people who have problems breathing. What can you do to reduce gas emissions?

① Think About It

A How do you get to school every day?

_____

_____

_____

B How many of the students in your class come to school by car?

_____

_____

Gas emissions are high during rush-hour traffic.

② Ask A Question

How can you reduce the number of vehicles students use to get to school one day each month?

With your teacher and classmates, brainstorm different ways in which you can reduce the number of vehicles students use to get to school.

Ride a bicycle to school.

Check off the points below as you use them to design your plan.

☐ how far a student lives from school

☐ the kinds of transportation students may have available to them

③ Make A Plan

A Write down different ways that you can reduce the number of vehicles that bring students to school.

_____

_____

_____

_____

_____

_____

B Create a short presentation for your principal that outlines how the whole school could become involved in your vehicle-reduction plan. Write down the points of your presentation in the space below.

_____

_____

_____

_____

_____

_____

_____

_____

C In the space below, design a sign-up sheet that your classmates will use to choose how they will come to school on the designated day.

Take It Home

Give your presentation to an adult. Then, have the adult brainstorm ways to reduce their daily gas emissions.

The Atmosphere

ESSENTIAL QUESTION

What is the atmosphere?

By the end of this lesson, you should be able to explain how the layers of the atmosphere are defined by differences in composition and physical properties.

The atmosphere is a very thin layer of gases that surrounds Earth. It keeps Earth warm, provides organisms with air to breathe, and protects organisms from the harmful effects of the sun.

OHIO 7.ESS.3 The atmosphere has different properties at different elevations and contains a mixture of gases that cycle through the lithosphere, biosphere, hydrosphere and atmosphere.

Lesson Labs

Quick Labs
- Modeling Air Pressure
- Modeling Air Pressure Changes with Altitude

Field Lab
- Measuring Oxygen in the Air

Engage Your Brain

1 Predict Check T or F to show whether you think each statement is true or false.

T F

☐ ☐ Oxygen is in the air we breathe.

☐ ☐ Pressure is not a property of air.

☐ ☐ The air around you is part of the atmosphere.

☐ ☐ As you climb up a mountain, the air temperature usually gets warmer.

2 Explain Does the air in this balloon have mass? Why or why not?

_____
_____
_____
_____

Active Reading

3 Synthesize Many English words have their roots in other languages. Use the ancient Greek words below to make an educated guess about the meanings of the words *atmosphere* and *mesosphere*.

Greek word	Meaning
atmos	vapor
mesos	middle
sphaira	ball

Vocabulary Terms

- atmosphere
- air pressure
- troposphere
- stratosphere
- ozone layer
- mesosphere
- thermosphere
- greenhouse effect

4 Apply As you learn the definition of each vocabulary term in this lesson, create your own definition or sketch to help you remember the meaning of the term.

atmosphere:

_____
_____

mesosphere:

_____
_____

Up and Away!

What is Earth's atmosphere?

The mixture of gases that surrounds Earth is the **atmosphere**. This mixture is most often referred to as air. The atmosphere has many important functions. It protects living things from the sun's harmful rays. It also keeps Earth warm enough for life to exist. The fact that there is so much liquid water on the planet is due to the temperature range that the atmosphere makes possible. Many of the components of the atmosphere are necessary for life, such as oxygen, which nearly all living things need to live.

A Mixture of Gases and Small Particles

As shown below, the atmosphere is made mostly of nitrogen gas (78%), oxygen gas (21%), and a very small amount (1%) of other gases. The atmosphere also contains small particles that include dust, volcanic ash, sea salt, and smoke. There are even small pieces of skin, bacteria, and pollen found in the atmosphere!

Water is also found in the atmosphere. This includes liquid water, such as the water droplets that form clouds, and solid water, such as snow and ice crystals. However, most water in the atmosphere exists as an invisible gas called *water vapor*. Under certain conditions, water vapor can change into solid or liquid water. Then, snow or rain might fall from the sky.

Visualize It!

5 Identify Fill in the missing percentage for oxygen.

Nitrogen is the most abundant gas in the atmosphere.

Oxygen is the second most abundant gas in the atmosphere.

The remaining 1% of the atmosphere is made up of argon, carbon dioxide, water vapor, and other gases.

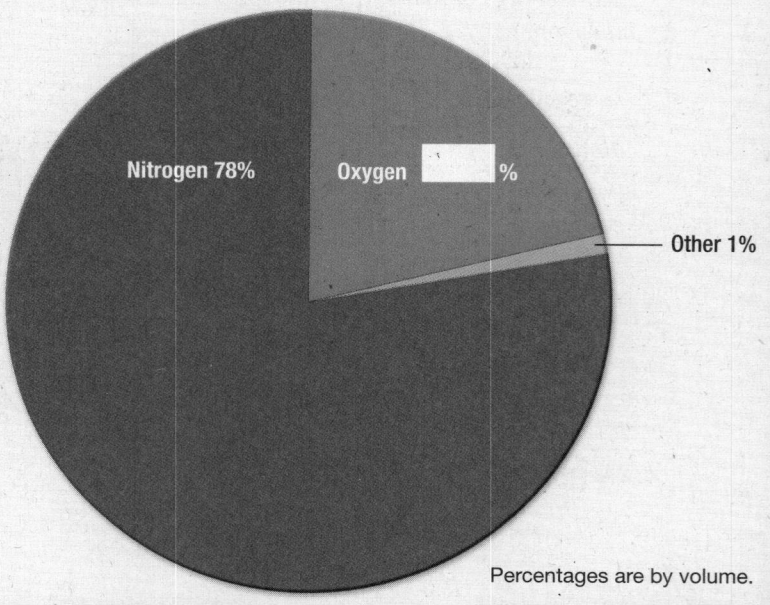

Composition of the Atmosphere

Nitrogen 78%

Oxygen ___ %

Other 1%

Percentages are by volume.

How do pressure and temperature change in the atmosphere?

Active Reading

6 Identify As you read, underline what happens to temperature and to pressure as altitude increases.

The atmosphere is held around Earth by gravity. Gravity pulls gas molecules in the atmosphere toward Earth's surface, causing air pressure. **Air pressure** is the measure of the force with which particles in the air push on an area of a surface. At sea level, air pressure is over 2 lbs. for every square centimeter of your body. That is like balancing a 2 lb. weight on the tip of your finger!

Air pressure, however, is not the same throughout the atmosphere. Although there are many gases that surround you on Earth, gas molecules become increasingly farther apart as you move away from Earth's surface. So, as altitude increases, air pressure decreases. As air pressure decreases, it becomes harder and harder, and, eventually, impossible for organisms to breathe.

As altitude increases, air temperature changes. These changes are due to the way solar energy is absorbed in the atmosphere. Some parts of the atmosphere are warmer because they contain a high percentage of gases that absorb solar energy. Other parts of the atmosphere contain less of these gases and are cooler.

Inquiry

7 Explain Why does a mountain climber need an oxygen supply at very high altitudes, even though the air still contains 21% oxygen?

_____

_____

_____

At high altitudes, such as the top of Mount Everest, air pressure and temperature are lower than they are at sea level.

Layer upon Layer

What are the layers of the atmosphere?

Gas molecules become increasingly farther apart as the distance from Earth's surface increases. Eventually, the molecules become so far apart that the atmosphere ends.

The atmosphere changes between Earth's surface and space. Air pressure decreases as the distance from Earth's surface increases. Temperature and the chemical composition also change. At certain altitudes, the temperature in the atmosphere changes dramatically. Scientists use these temperature differences to divide the atmosphere into four layers. These layers are the troposphere, stratosphere, mesosphere, and thermosphere.

Think Outside the Book

8 Relate Research the *ionosphere*. Describe the aurora borealis, and explain how it relates to the ionosphere.

The aurora borealis occurs in the thermosphere.

The Troposphere

You live in the troposphere. The **troposphere** (TROH poh SFIR) is the lowest layer of the atmosphere and has an average thickness of 10 to 12 km. It is the layer that provides the oxygen that most organisms need and is where most weather takes place.

The troposphere contains almost 90% of the total mass of the atmosphere. The air is denser than it is in the other layers of the atmosphere. Gas molecules in the troposphere are closer together because Earth's gravity is greatest near Earth's surface.

The temperature of the troposphere is also greatest near Earth's surface. Solar radiation warms land and water, which then warm the air above. The warm air expands and rises. It is cooled as it transfers heat to cooler, denser air at higher altitudes. Air continues to rise up to about 12 km above the surface. Here, temperature stops decreasing and cool air sinks back toward the surface. This defines the upper boundary of the troposphere. Once the air sinks back to the surface, it is rewarmed and rises again.

The rising and sinking of gas particles mixes the gases in the troposphere. As a result, the chemical composition of the troposphere is fairly uniform. However, the amounts of natural and human pollutants and water vapor do vary.

Active Reading

9 Summarize Describe how the temperature and chemical composition of the troposphere vary.

_____
_____
_____
_____
_____
_____

The Stratosphere

The layer of atmosphere above the troposphere is the **stratosphere** (STRAT uh SFIR). The top of the stratosphere is an average of 50 km above the surface of Earth. There are few clouds in the stratosphere, because this layer contains little water vapor.

In the stratosphere, temperature increases with altitude. Warmer air is located above cooler air. As a result, air in the stratosphere does not mix like it does in the troposphere.

The chemical composition of this layer depends on altitude. The area of the stratosphere that is located between 15 km and 40 km above Earth's surface contains a relatively large amount of ozone. It is called the **ozone layer**. The ozone layer protects Earth by absorbing large amounts of harmful ultraviolet radiation from the sun. The air in the stratosphere is warmed by the absorbed radiation. So, temperature in this layer increases as altitude increases.

 **Visualize It!**

10 Describe What is the altitude of the ozone layer and in which layer of the atmosphere is it located?

_____

_____

_____

_____

The ozone layer has a large amount of ozone as well as other gases found in air.

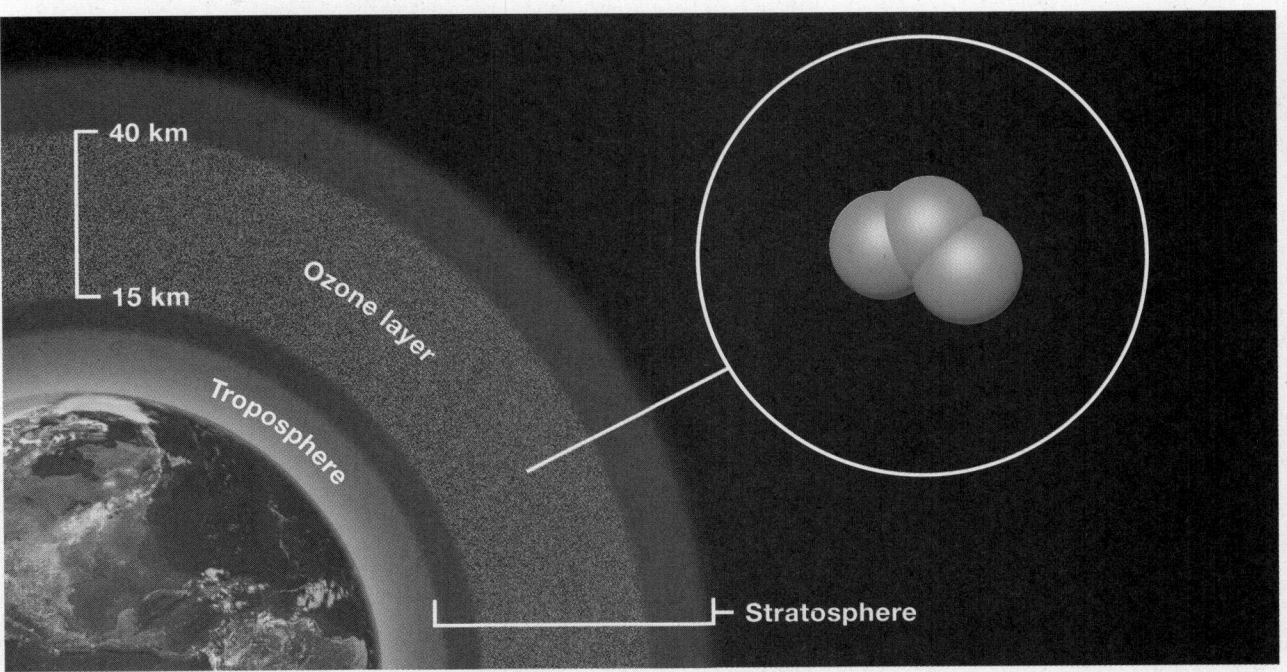

(Graphic is not to scale.)

The Mesosphere

The atmospheric layer above the stratosphere is called the **mesosphere** (MES oh SFIR). The mesosphere does not have an ozone layer to absorb ultraviolet radiation and warm the air. So, temperatures in the mesosphere decrease as altitude increases. The lower mesosphere is warmed by the stratosphere. The top of the mesosphere is the coldest part of the atmosphere.

The mesosphere is a very difficult layer of the atmosphere to study. This is due to the fact that it is located higher than aircraft can fly and lower than satellites can orbit.

Active Reading **11 Explain** Why do temperatures in the mesosphere decrease as altitude increases?

_____

_____

_____

The Thermosphere

The uppermost layer of the atmosphere is the **thermosphere** (THUHR moh SFIR). Around 80 km above the surface, between the mesosphere and thermosphere, air temperature stops decreasing and begins increasing. The top of the thermosphere is 500 to 1,000 km above Earth.

To transfer thermal energy, particles at different temperatures must touch. However, in the thermosphere, particles are spread very far apart. This means that particles rarely collide, so there is very little transfer of thermal energy.

Solar radiation breaks apart molecules of nitrogen (N_2) and oxygen (O_2). As a result, atomic nitrogen (N) and atomic oxygen (O) are common in the thermosphere. Atomic oxygen in the thermosphere absorbs solar radiation. So, the temperature of the thermosphere increases with altitude. The temperatures at the top of the thermosphere are very high. However, the air would not feel hot because there are so few particles to collide and transfer thermal energy.

Visualize It!

12 Analyze Using the image below, explain the relationship between air pressure, altitude, and the transfer of thermal energy.

_____

_____

_____

The thermosphere is less dense than the troposphere. So, although particles are moving very fast, they do not transfer much thermal energy.

The troposphere is denser than the thermosphere. So, although particles in the troposphere are moving much slower than particles in the thermosphere, they can transfer much more thermal energy.

Temperature in the Troposphere and Thermosphere

 **Visualize It!**

In the graph, the green line shows pressure change with altitude.
The red line shows temperature change with altitude.

Lower   Pressure   Higher

Altitude (km) (not to scale)

500

100

90

Thermosphere

80

70

Mesosphere

60

50

40

Temperature

Stratosphere

30

Ozone layer

20

Pressure

10

Troposphere

0

Lower   Temperature   Higher

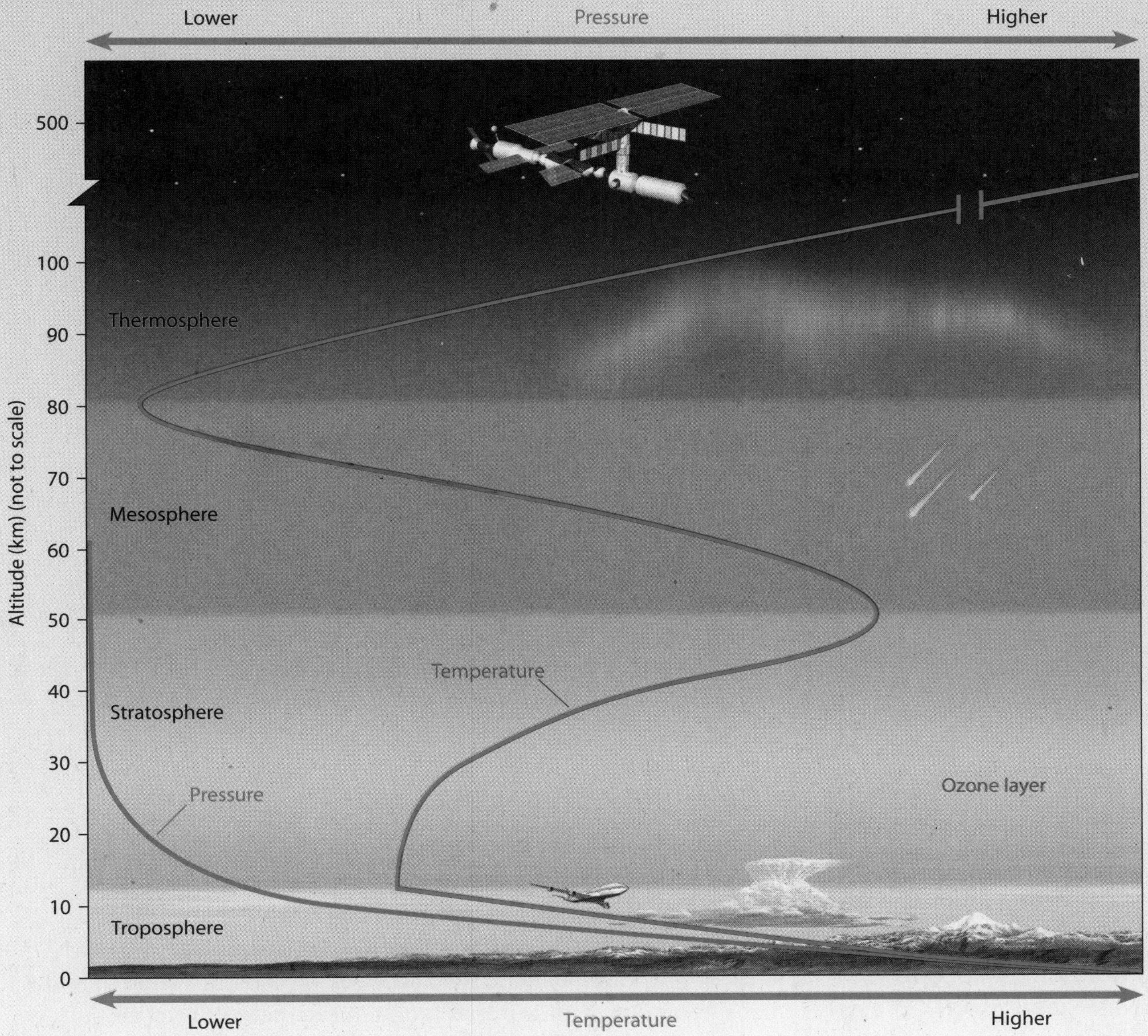

The layers of the atmosphere are defined by changes in temperature.

13 Analyze Using the graph and descriptions provided, indicate if air pressure and temperature increase or decrease with increased altitude in each layer of the atmosphere. One answer has been provided for you.

Layer	Air pressure	Temperature
Thermosphere	decreases	
Mesosphere		
Stratosphere		
Troposphere		

How does the atmosphere protect life on Earth?

The atmosphere surrounds and protects Earth. The atmosphere provides the air we breathe. It also protects Earth from harmful solar radiation and from meteorites that enter the Earth system. In addition, the atmosphere controls the temperature on Earth.

By Absorbing or Reflecting Harmful Radiation

Earth's atmosphere reflects or absorbs most incoming solar radiation. The ozone layer absorbs most of the radiation from the sun. Although its thickness varies with season and location, the volume of ozone in the ozone layer has been steadily decreasing. This is shown in the illustrations at the left. Scientists think that this decrease is due to the use of certain chemicals by people. These chemicals enter the stratosphere. There, they react with ozone and convert it to other compounds. Ozone levels are particularly low over the South Pole during some times of the year. The area where the ozone layer is very thin is referred to as the "ozone hole."

By Maintaining the Right Temperature Range

Without the atmosphere, Earth's average temperature would be very low. How does Earth remain warm? The answer is the greenhouse effect. The **greenhouse effect** is the process by which gases in the atmosphere, such as water vapor and carbon dioxide, absorb and give off infrared radiation. Radiation from the sun warms Earth's surface, and Earth's surface gives off infrared radiation. Greenhouse gases in the atmosphere absorb some of this infrared radiation and then reradiate it. Some of this energy is absorbed again by Earth's surface, while some energy goes out into space. Because greenhouse gases keep energy in the Earth system longer, Earth's average surface temperature is kept at around 15°C (59°F). In time, all the energy ends up back in space.

Active Reading 15 **List** Name two examples of greenhouse gases.

_____

_____

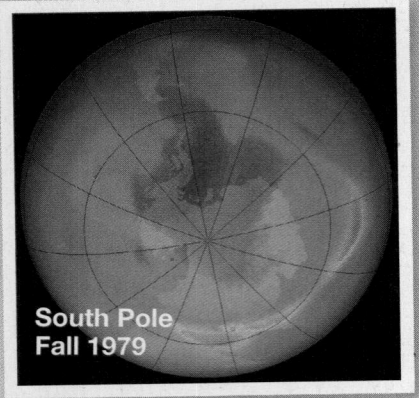

South Pole
Fall 1979

Less ozone   More ozone

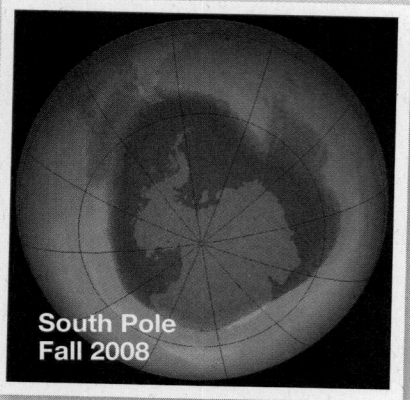

South Pole
Fall 2008

14 Compare How did the ozone layer over the South Pole change between 1979 and 2008?

_____

_____

_____

the Sun ...

The Greenhouse Effect

Greenhouse gas molecules absorb and emit infrared radiation.

Atmosphere without Greenhouse Gases

Without greenhouse gases in Earth's atmosphere, radiation from Earth's surface is lost directly to space.

Average Temperature: -18°C

Atmosphere with Greenhouse Gases

With greenhouse gases in Earth's atmosphere, radiation from Earth's surface is lost to space more slowly, which makes Earth's surface warmer.

Average Temperature: 15°C

sunlight   infrared radiation

The atmosphere is much thinner than shown here.

Visualize It!

16 Illustrate Draw your own version of how greenhouse gases keep Earth warm.

Visual Summary

To complete this summary, fill in each blank with the correct word or phrase. Then, use the key below to check your answers. You can use this page to review the main concepts of the lesson.

Both air pressure and temperature change within the atmosphere.

The atmosphere protects Earth from harmful radiation and helps to maintain a temperature range that supports life.

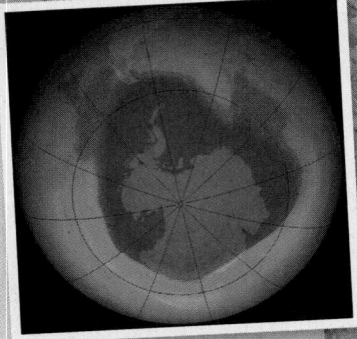

17 As altitude increases, air pressure _____ .
_____

18 Earth is protected from harmful solar radiation by the
_____

The Atmosphere

The atmosphere is divided into four layers according to temperature and other properties.

19 The four layers of the atmosphere are the
_____
_____
_____
_____

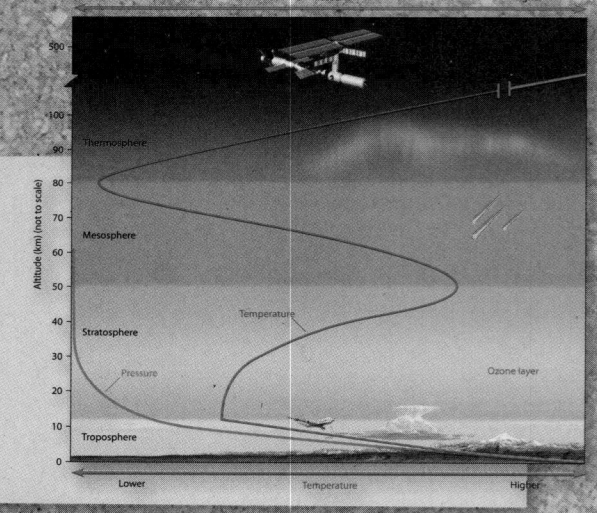

20 Predict What do you think Earth's surface would be like if Earth did not have an atmosphere?
_____

Lesson Review

Vocabulary

Fill in the blanks with the terms that best complete the following sentences.

1 The _____ is a mixture of gases that surrounds Earth.

2 The measure of the force with which air molecules push on a surface is called _____ .

3 The _____ is the process by which gases in the atmosphere absorb and reradiate heat.

Key Concepts

4 List Name three gases in the atmosphere.

_____

_____

5 Compare How does temperature change in the troposphere differ from the stratosphere?

_____

_____

_____

_____

6 Identify Which layer contains almost 90% of the atmosphere's total mass?

_____

7 Describe How and why does temperature change with altitude in the mesosphere?

_____

_____

_____

_____

_____

8 Explain Why would it feel cold in the upper thermosphere, where the temperature is high?

_____

_____

_____

Critical Thinking

9 Predict What would happen to life on Earth if the ozone layer were not present?

_____

_____

_____

10 Criticize A friend says that temperature increases as altitude increases because you're moving closer to the sun. Is this true? Explain.

_____

_____

_____

11 Predict Why would increased levels of greenhouse gases contribute to higher temperatures on Earth?

_____

_____

_____

Use this graph to answer the following questions.

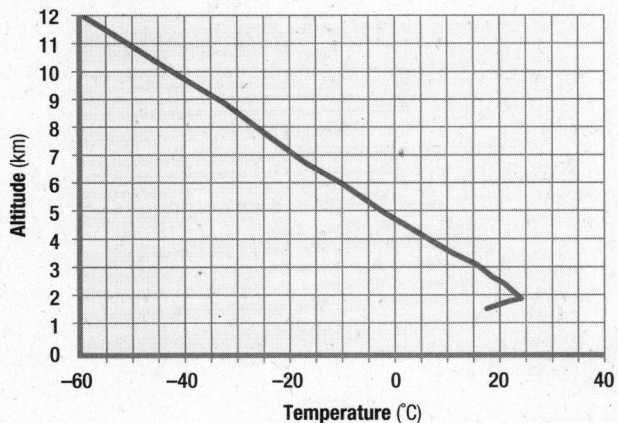

Changes in Temperature with Altitude

Source: National Weather Service. Data taken at Riverton, Wyoming, 2001

12 Analyze The top of Mount Everest is at about 8,850 m. What would the approximate air temperature be at that altitude? _____

13 Analyze What is the total temperature change between 3 km and 7 km above Earth's surface? _____

My Notes

Energy Transfer

ESSENTIAL QUESTION

How does energy move through Earth's system?

By the end of this lesson, you should be able to summarize the three mechanisms by which energy is transferred through Earth's system.

Ice absorbs energy from the sun. This can cause ice to melt—even these icicles in Antarctica.

OHIO **7.ESS.2** Thermal-energy transfers in the ocean and the atmosphere contribute to the formation of currents, which influence global climate patterns.

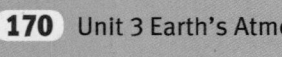
© Houghton Mifflin Harcourt Publishing Company • Image Credits: ©Frans Lanting/Corbis

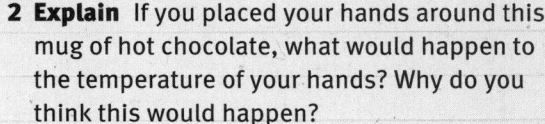

Lesson Labs

Quick Labs
- The Sun's Angle and Temperature
- How Does Color Affect Temperature?
- Modeling Convection

S.T.E.M. Lab
- Heat from the Sun

Engage Your Brain

1 Describe Fill in the blank with the word or phrase that you think correctly completes the following sentences.

An example of something hot is

_____

An example of something cold is

_____

The sun provides us with

_____

A thermometer is used to measure

_____

2 Explain If you placed your hands around this mug of hot chocolate, what would happen to the temperature of your hands? Why do you think this would happen?

_____

_____

_____

_____

_____

_____

Active Reading

3 Apply Many scientific words, such as *heat*, are used to convey different meanings. Use context clues to write your own definition for each meaning of the word *heat*.

The student won the first <u>heat</u> of the race.

heat:

_____

_____

The man wondered if his rent included <u>heat</u>.

heat:

_____

_____

Energy in the form of <u>heat</u> was transferred from the hot pan to the cold counter.

heat:

_____

_____

Vocabulary Terms

- temperature
- thermal energy
- thermal expansion
- heat
- radiation
- convection
- conduction

4 Identify This list contains the vocabulary terms you'll learn in this lesson. As you read, circle the definition of each term.

Hot and Cold

How are energy and temperature related?

All matter is made up of moving particles, such as atoms or molecules. When particles are in motion, they have kinetic energy. Because particles move at different speeds, each has a different amount of kinetic energy.

Temperature (TEMM•per•uh•choor) is a measure of the average kinetic energy of particles. The faster a particle moves, the more kinetic energy it has. As shown below, the more kinetic energy the particles of an object have, the higher the temperature of the object. Temperature does not depend on the number of particles. A teapot holds more tea than a cup. If the particles of tea in both containers have the same average kinetic energy, the tea in both containers is at the same temperature.

Thermal energy is the total kinetic energy of particles. A teapot full of tea at a high temperature has more thermal energy than a teapot full of tea at a lower temperature. Thermal energy also depends on the number of particles. The more particles there are in an object, the greater the object's thermal energy. The tea in a teapot and a cup may be at the same temperature, but the tea in the pot has more thermal energy because there is more of it.

Visualize It!

5 Analyze Which container holds particles with the higher average kinetic energy?

_____

_____

particle motion

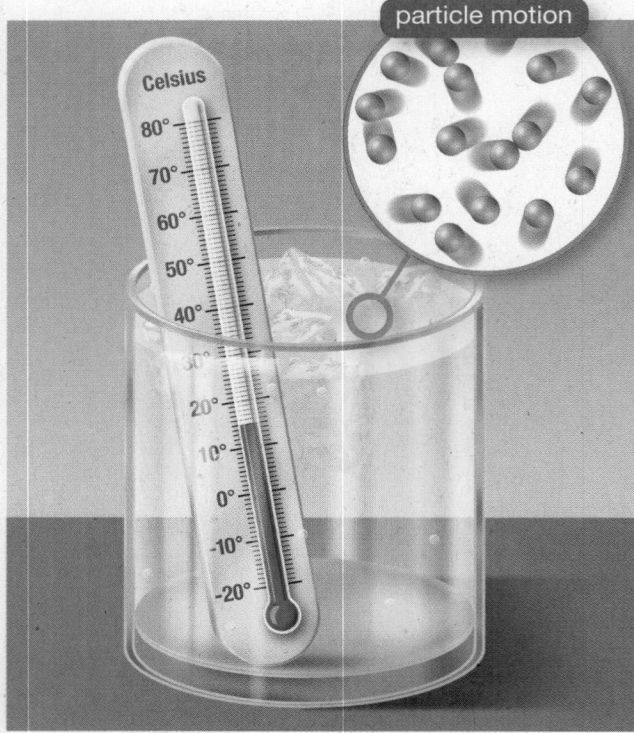

particle motion

What is thermal expansion?

When the temperature of a substance increases, the substance's particles have more kinetic energy. Therefore, the particles move faster and move apart. As the space between the particles increases, the substance expands. The increase in volume that results from an increase in temperature is called **thermal expansion**. Most substances on Earth expand when they become warmer and contract when they become cooler. Water is an exception. Cold water expands as it gets colder and then freezes to form ice.

Thermal expansion causes a change in the density of a substance. *Density* is the mass per unit volume of a substance. When a substance expands, its mass stays the same but its volume increases. As a result, density decreases. Differences in density that are caused by thermal expansion can cause movement of matter. For example, air inside a hot-air balloon is warmed, as shown below. The air expands as its particles move faster and farther apart. As the air expands, it becomes less dense than the air outside the balloon. The less-dense air inside the balloon is forced upward by the colder, denser air outside the balloon. This same principle affects air movement in the atmosphere, water movement in the oceans, and rock movement in the geosphere.

7 Apply Why would an increase in the temperature of the oceans contribute to a rise in sea level?

_____

_____

_____

_____

6 Predict What might happen to the hot-air balloon if the air inside it cooled down?

_____

_____

When the air in this balloon becomes hotter, it becomes less dense than the surrounding air. So, the balloon goes up, up, and away!

Getting Warm

What is heat?

Active Reading

8 Identify As you read, underline the direction of energy transfer between objects that are at different temperatures.

You might think of the word *heat* when you imagine something that feels hot. But heat also has to do with things that feel cold. In fact, heat is what causes objects to feel hot or cold. You may often use the word *heat* to mean different things. However, in this lesson, the word *heat* has only one meaning. **Heat** is the energy that is transferred between objects that are at different temperatures.

Energy Transferred Between Objects

When objects that have different temperatures come into contact, energy will be transferred between them until both objects reach the same temperature. The direction of this energy transfer is always from the object with the higher temperature to the object with the lower temperature. When you touch something cold, energy is transferred from your body to that object. When you touch something hot, like the pan shown below, energy is transferred from that object to your body.

Visualize It!

9 Predict Draw an arrow to show the direction in which energy is transferred between the pan and the oven mitts.

This pan is being removed from the oven and is very hot.

Why can the temperatures of land, air, and water differ?

When the same amount of energy is being transferred, some materials will get warmer or cooler at a faster rate than other materials. Suppose you are walking along a beach on a sunny day. You may notice that the land feels warmer than the air and the water, even though they are all exposed to the same amount of energy from the sun. This is because the land warms up at a faster rate than the water and air do.

Specific Heat

The different rates at which materials become warmer or cooler are due to a property called *specific heat*. A substance that has a high specific heat requires a lot of energy to show an increase in temperature. A substance with a lower specific heat requires less energy to show the same increase in temperature. Water has a higher specific heat than land. So, water warms up more slowly than land does. Water also cools down more slowly than land does.

10 Predict Air has a lower specific heat than water. Once the sun goes down, will the air or the water cool off faster? Why?

_____

_____

_____

The temperatures of land, water, and air may differ— even when they are exposed to the same amount of energy from the sun.

Heat

How is energy transferred by radiation?

On a summer day, you can feel warmth from the sun on your skin. But how did that energy reach you from the sun? The sun transfers energy to Earth by radiation. **Radiation** is the transfer of energy as electromagnetic (ee•LEK•troh•mag•NEH•tik) waves. Radiation can transfer energy between objects that are not in direct contact with each other. Many objects other than the sun also radiate energy as light and heat. These include a hot burner on a stove and a campfire, shown below.

Electromagnetic Waves

Energy from the sun is called *electromagnetic radiation*. This energy travels in waves. You are probably familiar with one form of radiation called *visible light*. You can see the visible light that comes from the sun. Electromagnetic radiation includes other forms of energy, which you cannot see. Most of the warmth that you feel from the sun is infrared radiation. This energy has a longer wavelength and lower energy than visible light. Higher-energy radiation includes x-rays and ultraviolet light.

Visualize It!

11 Analyze Write a caption for the campfire photo on the right. Make sure the caption relates the image to radiation.

_____

_____

_____

Energy from this hot burner is being transferred by radiation.

Energy from the sun is transferred through space.

Where does radiation occur on Earth?

We live almost 150 million km from the sun. Yet almost all of the energy on Earth is transmitted from the sun by radiation. The sun is the major source of energy for processes at Earth's surface. Receiving that energy is absolutely vital for life on Earth. The electromagnetic waves from the sun also provide energy that drives the water cycle.

When solar radiation reaches Earth, some of the energy is reflected and scattered by Earth's atmosphere. But much of the energy passes through Earth's atmosphere and reaches Earth's surface. Some of the energy that Earth receives from the sun is absorbed by the atmosphere, geosphere, and hydrosphere. Then, the energy is changed into thermal energy. This thermal energy may be reradiated into the Earth system or into space. Much of the energy is transferred through Earth's systems by the two other ways—convection and conduction.

Think Outside the Book

13 Apply Research ultraviolet radiation from the sun and its role in causing sunburns.

12 Summarize Give two examples of what happens when energy from the sun reaches Earth.

_____

_____

_____

_____

Heating Up

How is energy transferred by convection?

Have you ever watched a pot of boiling water, such as the one below? If so, you have seen convection. **Convection** (kun•VECK•shuhn) is the transfer of energy due to the movement of matter. As water warms up at the bottom of the pot, some of the hot water rises. At the same time, cooler water from other parts of the pot sink and replace the rising water. This water is then warmed and the cycle continues.

Convection Currents

Convection involves the movement of matter due to differences in density. Convection occurs because most matter becomes less dense when it gets warmer. When most matter becomes warmer, it undergoes thermal expansion and a decrease in density. This less-dense matter is forced upward by the surrounding colder, denser matter that is sinking. As the hot matter rises, it cools and becomes more dense. This causes it to sink back down. This cycling of matter is called a *convection current*. Convection most often occurs in fluids, such as water and air. But convection can also happen in solids.

wax

© Houghton Mifflin Harcourt Publishing Company

energy sources

convection current

Visualize It! Inquiry

14 Apply How is convection related to the rise and fall of wax in lava lamps?

_____

_____

_____

_____

Where does convection occur on Earth?

If Earth's surface is warmer than the air, energy will be transferred from the ground to the air. As the air becomes warmer, it becomes less dense. This air is pushed upward and out of the way by cooler, denser air that is sinking. As the warm air rises, it cools and becomes denser and begins to sink back toward Earth's surface. This cycle moves energy through the atmosphere.

Convection currents also occur in the ocean because of differences in the density of ocean water. More dense water sinks to the ocean floor, and less dense water moves toward the surface. The density of ocean water is influenced by temperature and the amount of salt in the water. Cold water is denser than warmer water. Water that contains a lot of salt is more dense than less-salty water.

Energy produced deep inside Earth heats rock in the mantle. The heated rock becomes less dense and is pushed up toward Earth's surface by the cooler, denser surrounding rock. Once cooled near the surface, the rock sinks. These convection currents transfer energy from Earth's core toward Earth's surface. These currents also cause the movement of tectonic plates.

Active Reading **15 Name** What are three of Earth's spheres in which energy is transferred by convection?

_____

_____

Visualize It!

16 Apply Draw the convection current that could occur in the body of water in this image.

Convection currents occur throughout the Earth system.

Ouch!

These desert sands would feel hot because of conduction.

How is energy transferred by conduction?

Have you ever touched an ice cube and wondered why it feels cold? An ice cube has only a small amount of energy, compared to your hand. Energy is transferred to the ice cube from your hand through the process of conduction. **Conduction** (kun•DUHK•shuhn) is the transfer of energy from one object to another object through direct contact.

Direct Contact

Remember that the atoms or molecules in a substance are constantly moving. Even a solid block of ice has particles in constant motion. When objects at different temperatures touch, their particles interact. Conduction involves the faster-moving particles of the warmer object transferring energy to the slower-moving particles in the cooler object. The greater the difference in energy of the particles, the faster the transfer of energy by conduction occurs.

Active Reading **17 Apply** Name two examples of conduction that you experience every day.

_____

_____

_____

_____

Where does conduction occur on Earth?

Energy can be transferred between the geosphere and the atmosphere by conduction. When cooler air molecules come into direct contact with the warm ground, energy is passed to the air by conduction. Conduction between the ground and the air happens only within a few centimeters of Earth's surface.

Conduction also happens between particles of air and particles of water. For example, if air transfers enough energy to liquid water, the water may evaporate. If water vapor transfers energy to the air, the kinetic energy of the water decreases. As a result, the water vapor may condense to form liquid water droplets.

Inside Earth, energy transfers between rock particles by conduction. However, rock is a poor conductor of heat, so this process happens very slowly.

Visualize It!

18 Compare Does conduction also occur in a city like the one shown below? Explain.

_____
_____
_____
_____
_____

19 Summarize Complete the following spider map by describing the three types of energy transfer. One answer has been started for you.

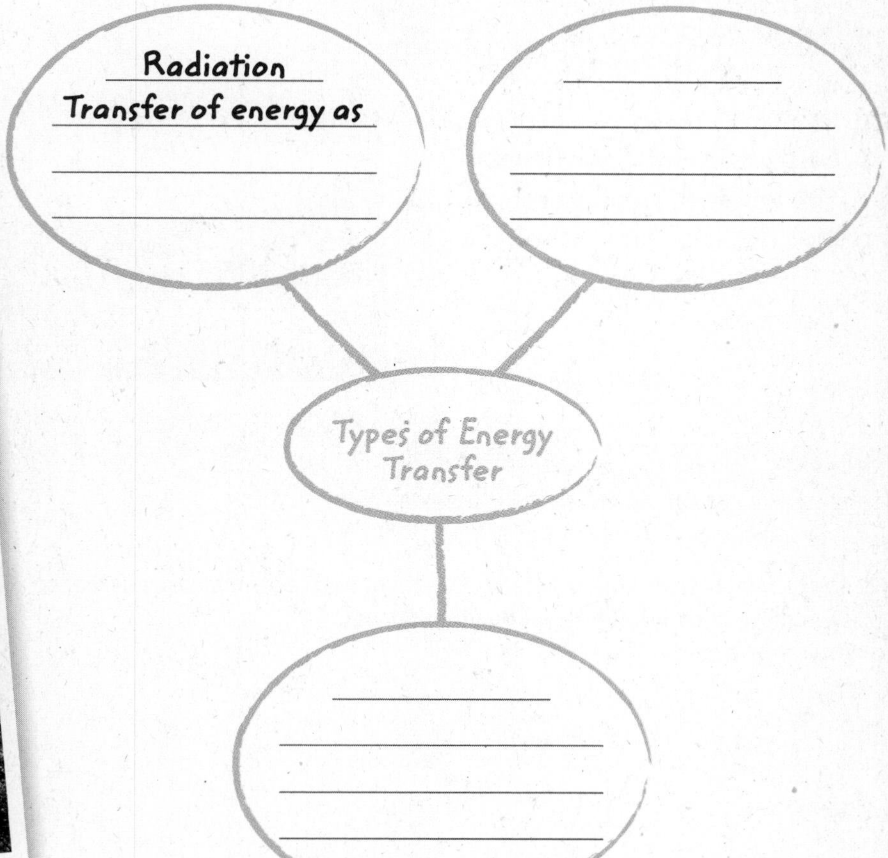

Radiation
Transfer of energy as
_____
_____

_____
_____
_____

Types of Energy Transfer

_____
_____
_____

Visual Summary

To complete this summary, fill in the blanks with the correct word or phrase. Then, use the key below to check your answers. You can use this page to review the main concepts of the lesson.

Energy Transfer

Heat is the energy that is transferred between objects that are at different temperatures.

20 The particles in a hot pan have _____ kinetic energy than the particles in a cool oven mitt.

Energy can be transferred in different ways.

21 The three ways that energy can be transferred are labeled in the image as

A: _____

B: _____

C: _____

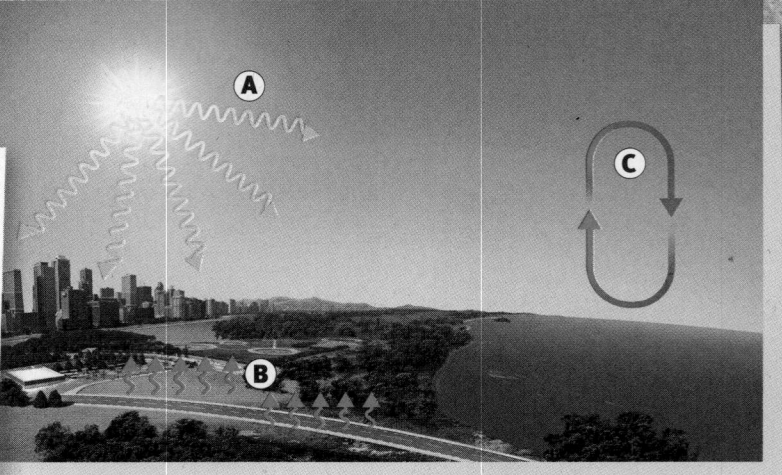

Answers: 20 more; 21 A: radiation, B: conduction, C: convection

22 **Apply** What type of energy transfer is responsible for making you feel cold when you are swimming in cool water? Explain your answer.

Lesson Review

Vocabulary

In your own words, define the following terms.

1 radiation

_____

_____

2 convection

_____

_____

3 conduction

_____

_____

Key Concepts

4 Compare What is the difference between temperature, thermal energy, and heat?

_____

_____

_____

_____

5 Describe What is happening to a substance undergoing thermal expansion?

_____

_____

_____

6 Explain What is the main source of energy for most processes at Earth's surface?

_____

7 Summarize What happens when two objects at different temperatures touch? Name one place where it occurs in Earth's system.

_____

_____

_____

8 Identify What is an example of convection in Earth's system?

_____

Critical Thinking

9 Apply Why can metal utensils get too hot to touch when you are cooking with them?

_____

_____

_____

10 Predict You are doing an experiment outside on a sunny day. You find the temperature of some sand is 28°C. You also find the temperature of some water is 25°C. Explain the difference in temperatures.

_____

_____

_____

_____

Use this image to answer the following questions.

11 Analyze Name one example of where energy transfer by radiation is occurring.

_____

12 Analyze Name one example of where energy transfer by conduction is occurring.

_____

13 Analyze Name one example of where energy transfer by convection is occurring.

_____

My Notes

Wind in the Atmosphere

ESSENTIAL QUESTION

What is wind?

By the end of this lesson, you should be able to explain how energy provided by the sun causes atmospheric movement, called wind.

Although you cannot see wind, you can see how it affects things like these kites.

OHIO **7.ESS.2** Thermal-energy transfers in the ocean and the atmosphere contribute to the formation of currents, which influence global climate patterns

OHIO **7.SIA.4** Analyze and interpret data.

© Houghton Mifflin Harcourt Publishing Company • Image Credits: ©Martin Bennett/Alamy

Engage Your Brain

1 Predict Check T or F to show whether you think each statement is true or false.

T   F

☐   ☐   The atmosphere is often referred to as air.

☐   ☐   Wind does not have direction.

☐   ☐   During the day, there is often a wind blowing toward shore from the ocean or a large lake.

☐   ☐   Cold air rises and warm air sinks.

2 Explain if you opened the valve on this bicycle tire, what would happen to the air inside of the tire? Why do you think that would happen?

_____

_____

_____

Active Reading

3 Synthesize You can often define an unknown phrase if you know the meaning of its word parts. Use the word parts below to make an educated guess about the meanings of the phrases *local wind* and *global wind*.

Word part	Meaning
wind	movement of air due to differences in air pressure
local	involving a particular area
global	involving the entire Earth

Vocabulary Terms

- wind
- Coriolis effect
- global wind
- jet stream
- local wind

4 Identify This list contains the vocabulary terms you'll learn in this lesson. As you read, circle the definition of each term.

local wind:

_____

_____

global wind:

_____

_____

Blow It Out!

What causes wind?

The next time you feel the wind blowing, you can thank the sun! The sun does not warm the whole surface of the Earth in a uniform manner. This uneven heating causes the air above Earth's surface to be at different temperatures. Cold air is more dense than warmer air is. Colder, denser air sinks. When denser air sinks, it places greater pressure on the surface of Earth than warmer, less-dense air does. This results in areas of higher air pressure. Air moves from areas of higher pressure toward areas of lower pressure. The movement of air caused by differences in air pressure is called **wind**. The greater the differences in air pressure, the faster the air moves.

Areas of High and Low Pressure

Cold, dense air at the poles creates areas of high pressure at the poles. Warm, less-dense air at the equator forms an area of lower pressure. This pressure gradient results in global movement of air. However, instead of moving in one circle between the equator and the poles, air moves in smaller circular patterns called *convection cells,* shown below. As air moves from the equator, it cools and becomes more dense. At about 30°N and 30°S latitudes, a high-pressure belt results from the sinking of air. Near the poles, cold air warms as it moves away from the poles. At around 60°N and 60°S latitudes, a low-pressure belt forms as the warmed air is pushed upward.

Visualize It!

5 Identify In the white oval area on the map, draw the convection cell that was left out. Use a pencil to indicate warm air and a pen to indicate cool air.

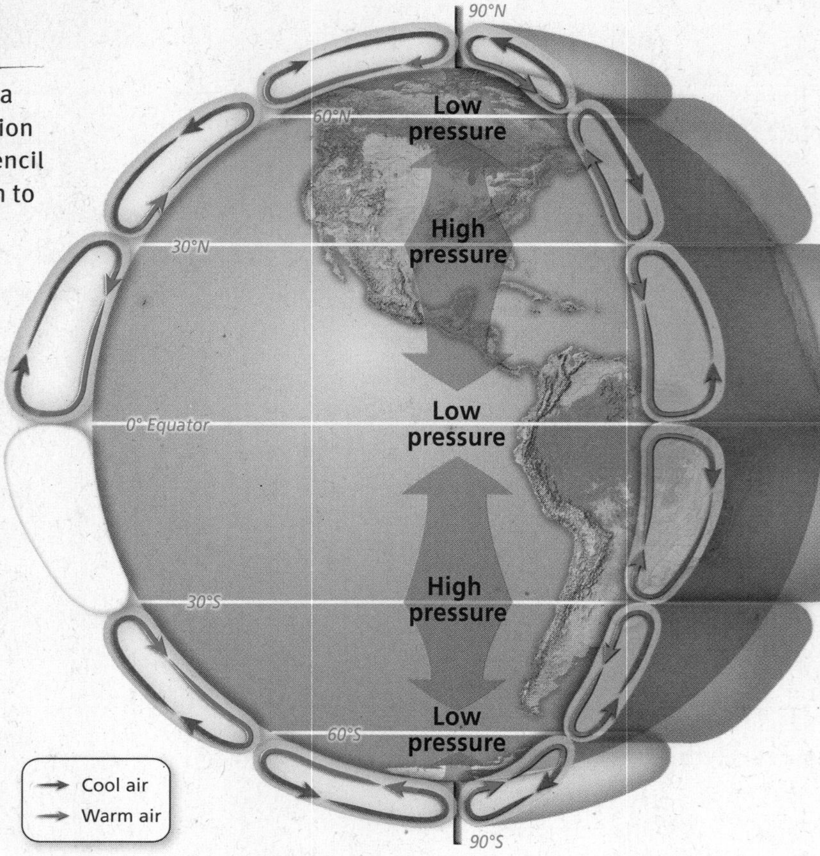

The warming and cooling of air produces pressure belts every 30° of latitude.

90°N

60°N — Low pressure

High pressure

30°N

0° Equator — Low pressure

High pressure

30°S

60°S — Low pressure

90°S

→ Cool air
→ Warm air

© Houghton Mifflin Harcourt Publishing Company • Image Credits: (t) ©Alejandro Ernesto/epa/Corbis

How does Earth's rotation affect wind?

![Active Reading]

6 Identify As you read, underline how air movement in the Northern Hemisphere is influenced by the Coriolis effect.

Pressure differences cause air to move between the equator and the poles. If Earth was not rotating, winds would blow in a straight line. However, winds are deflected, or curved, due to Earth's rotation, as shown below. The apparent curving of the path of a moving object from an otherwise straight path due to Earth's rotation is called the **Coriolis effect** (kawr•ee•OH•lis ih•FEKT). This effect is most noticeable over long distances.

Because each point on Earth makes one complete rotation every day, points closer to the equator must travel farther and, therefore, faster than points closer to the poles do. When air moves from the equator toward the North Pole, it maintains its initial speed and direction. If the air travels far enough north, it will have traveled farther east than a point on the ground beneath it. As a result, the air appears to follow a curved path toward the east. Air moving from the North Pole to the equator appears to curve to the west because the air moves east more slowly than a point on the ground beneath it does. Therefore, in the Northern Hemisphere, air moving to the north curves to the east and air moving to the south curves to the west.

![Visualize It!]

7 Label In the white ovals on the map, draw the direction and path of the winds that would occur at those locations on Earth.

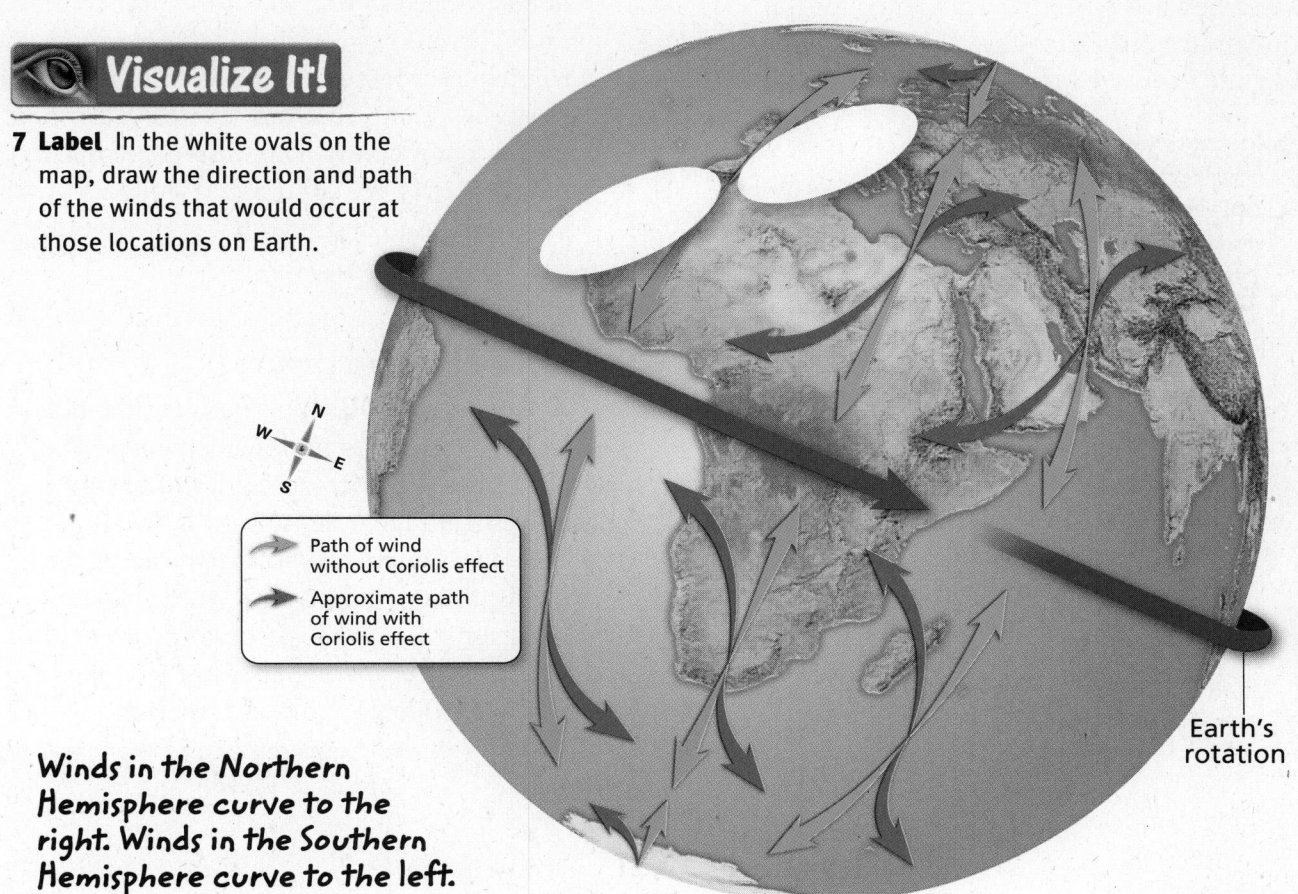

Path of wind without Coriolis effect

Approximate path of wind with Coriolis effect

Earth's rotation

Winds in the Northern Hemisphere curve to the right. Winds in the Southern Hemisphere curve to the left.

Blowin' Around

What are examples of global winds?

Recall that air travels in circular patterns called convection cells that cover approximately 30° of latitude. Pressure belts at every 30° of latitude and the Coriolis effect produce patterns of calm areas and wind systems. These wind systems occur at or near Earth's surface and are called **global winds**. As shown at the right, the major global wind systems are the *polar easterlies* (EE•ster•leez), the *westerlies* (WES•ter•leez), and the *trade winds*. Winds such as polar easterlies and westerlies are named for the direction from which they blow. Calm areas include the doldrums and the horse latitudes.

Active Reading

8 Explain If something is being carried by westerlies, what direction is it moving toward?

_____

_____

Think Outside the Book Inquiry

9 Model Winds are described according to their direction and speed. Research wind vanes and what they are used for. Design and build your own wind vane.

Trade Winds

The trade winds blow between 30° latitude and the equator in both hemispheres. The rotation of Earth causes the trade winds to curve to the west. Therefore, trade winds in the Northern Hemisphere come from the northeast, and trade winds in the Southern Hemisphere come from the southeast. These winds became known as the trade winds because sailors relied on them to sail from Europe to the Americas.

Westerlies

The westerlies blow between 30° and 60° latitudes in both hemispheres. The rotation of Earth causes these winds to curve to the east. Therefore, westerlies in the Northern Hemisphere come from the southwest, and westerlies in the Southern Hemisphere come from the northwest. The westerlies can carry moist air over the continental United States, producing rain and snow.

Polar Easterlies

The polar easterlies blow between the poles and 60° latitude in both hemispheres. The polar easterlies form as cold, sinking air moves from the poles toward 60°N and 60°S latitudes. The rotation of Earth causes these winds to curve to the west. In the Northern Hemisphere, polar easterlies can carry cold Arctic air over the majority of the United States, producing snow and freezing weather.

Visualize It!

10 Identify Label the polar easterlies, the westerlies, and the trade winds in the white boxes on the map.

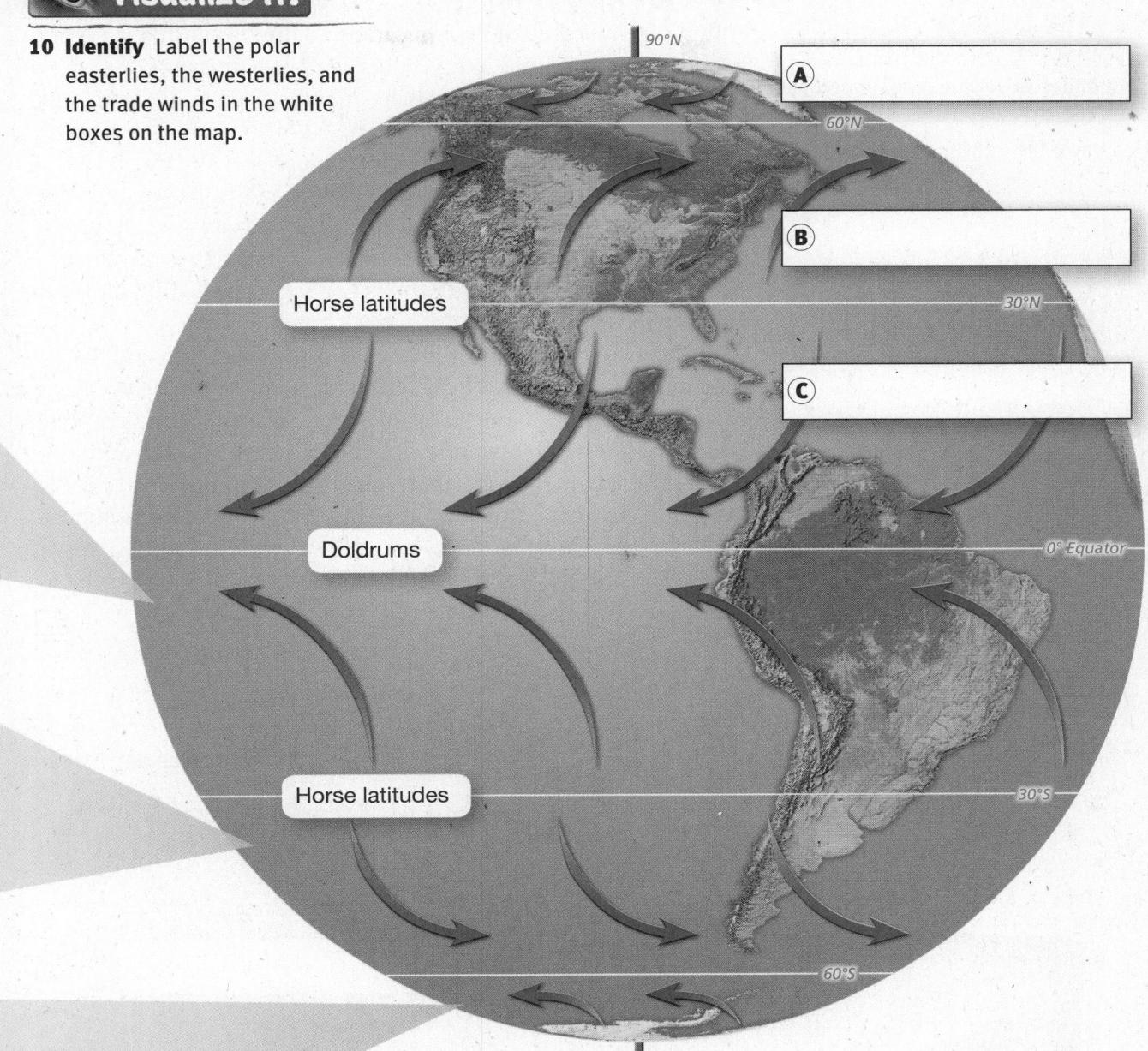

A

B

Horse latitudes

C

Doldrums

Horse latitudes

90°N
60°N
30°N
0° Equator
30°S
60°S
90°S

The Doldrums and Horse Latitudes

The trade winds of both hemispheres meet in a calm area around the equator called the *doldrums* (DOHL•druhmz). Very little wind blows in the doldrums because the warm, less-dense air results in an area of low pressure. The name doldrums means "dull" or "sluggish." At about 30° latitude in both hemispheres, air stops moving and sinks. This forms calm areas called the *horse latitudes*. This name was given to these areas when sailing ships carried horses from Europe to the Americas. When ships were stalled in these areas, horses were sometimes thrown overboard to save water.

The Jet Streams

A flight from Seattle to Boston can be 30 min faster than a flight from Boston to Seattle. Why? Pilots can take advantage of a jet stream. **Jet streams** are narrow belts of high-speed winds that blow from west to east, between 7 km and 16 km above Earth's surface. Airplanes traveling in the same direction as a jet stream go faster than those traveling in the opposite direction of a jet stream. When an airplane is traveling "with" a jet stream, the wind is helping the airplane move forward. However, when an airplane is traveling "against" the jet stream, the wind is making it more difficult for the plane to move forward.

The two main jet streams are the polar jet stream and the subtropical (suhb•TRAHP•i•kuhl) jet stream, shown below. Each of the hemispheres experiences these jet streams. Jet streams follow boundaries between hot and cold air and can shift north and south. In the winter, as Northern Hemisphere temperatures cool, the polar jet stream moves south. This shift brings cold Arctic air to the United States. When temperatures rise in the spring, this jet stream shifts to the north.

Active Reading

11 Identify As you read, underline the direction that the jet streams travel.

Visualize It!

12 Identify Label the polar jet stream and the subtropical jet stream in the Northern Hemisphere.

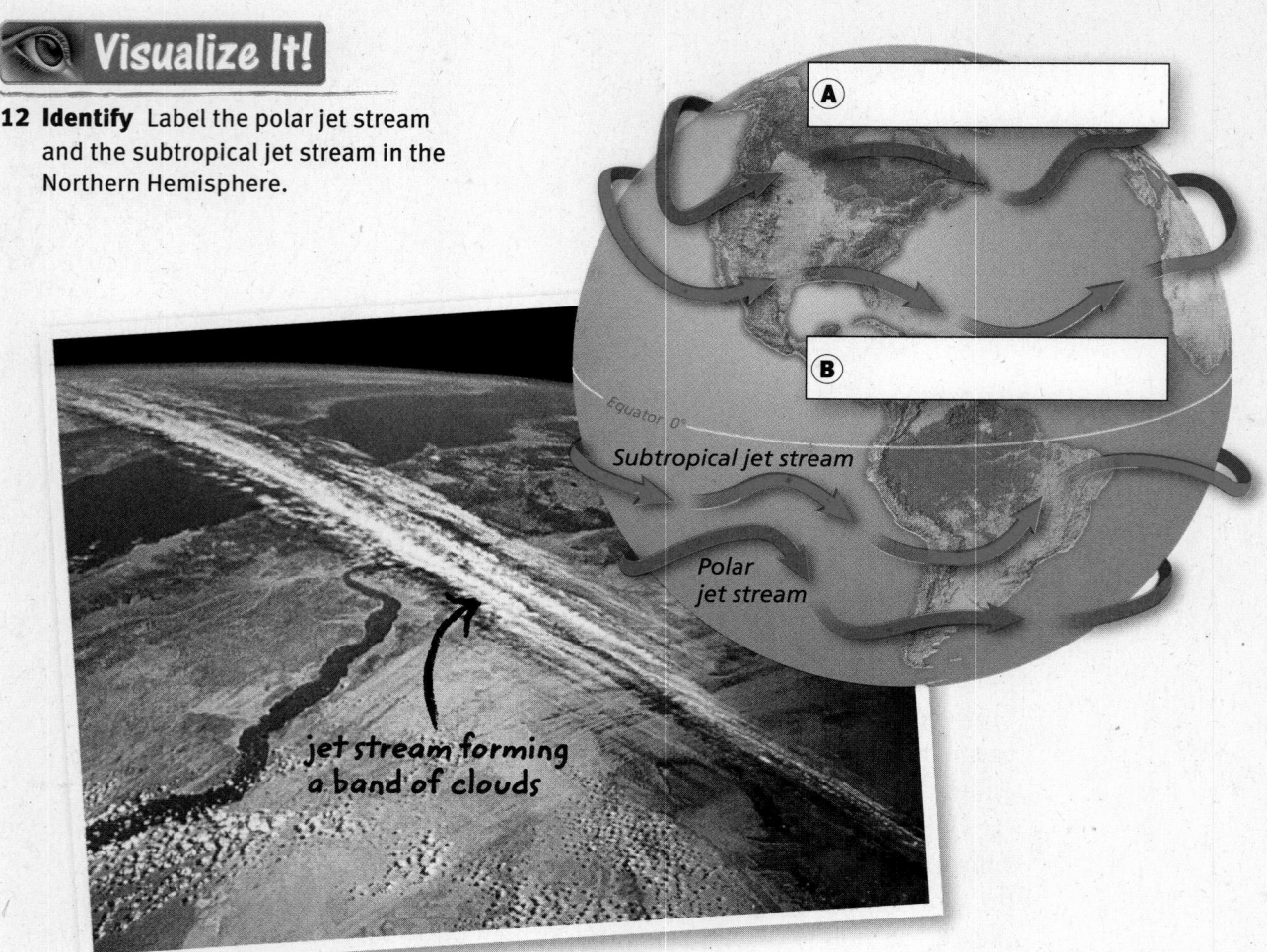

A

B

Equator 0°

Subtropical jet stream

Polar jet stream

jet stream forming a band of clouds

Desert Trades

How does some of the Sahara end up in the Americas? Global winds carry it.

Trade Wind Carriers
Trade winds can carry Saharan dust across the Atlantic Ocean to Florida and the Caribbean.

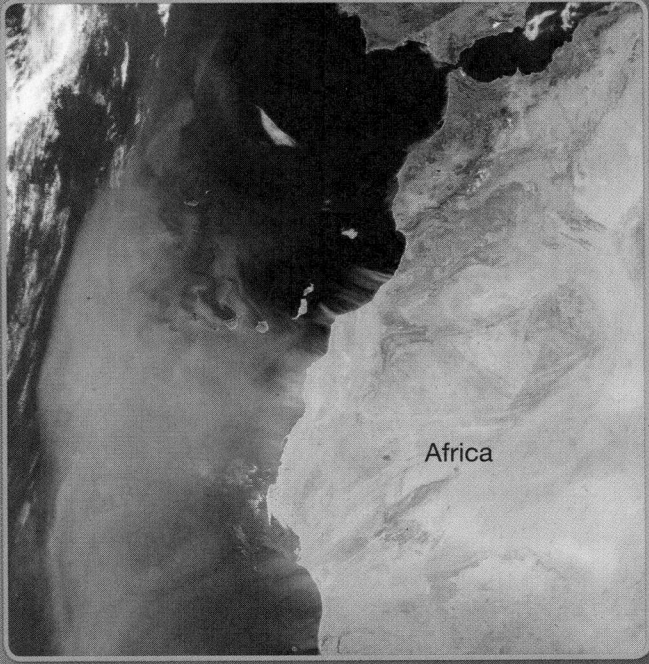

Africa

Florida Meets the Sahara
This hazy skyline in Miami is the result of a dust storm. Where did the dust come from? It all started in the Sahara.

The Sahara
The Sahara is the world's largest hot desert. Sand and dust storms that produce skies like this are very common in this desert.

Extend

Inquiry

13 Explain Look at a map and explain how trade winds carry dust from the Sahara to the Caribbean.

14 Relate Investigate the winds that blow in your community. Where do they usually come from? Identify the wind system that could be involved.

15 Apply Investigate how winds played a role in distributing radioactive waste that was released after an explosion at the Chernobyl Nuclear Power Plant in Ukraine. Present your findings as a map illustration or in a poster.

Feelin' Breezy

What are examples of local winds?

Local geographic features, such as a body of water or a mountain, can produce temperature and pressure differences that cause local winds. Unlike global winds, **local winds** are the movement of air over short distances. They can blow from any direction, depending on the features of the area.

Sea and Land Breezes

Have you ever felt a cool breeze coming off the ocean or a lake? If so, you were experiencing a sea breeze. Large bodies of water take longer to warm up than land does. During the day, air above land becomes warmer than air above water. The colder, denser air over water flows toward the land and pushes the warm air on the land upward. While water takes longer to warm than land does, land cools faster than water does. At night, cooler air on land causes a higher-pressure zone over the land. So, a wind blows from the land toward the water. This type of local wind is called a land breeze.

Active Reading

16 Identify As you read, underline two examples of geographic features that contribute to the formation of local winds.

Visualize It!

17 Analyze Label the areas of high pressure and low pressure.

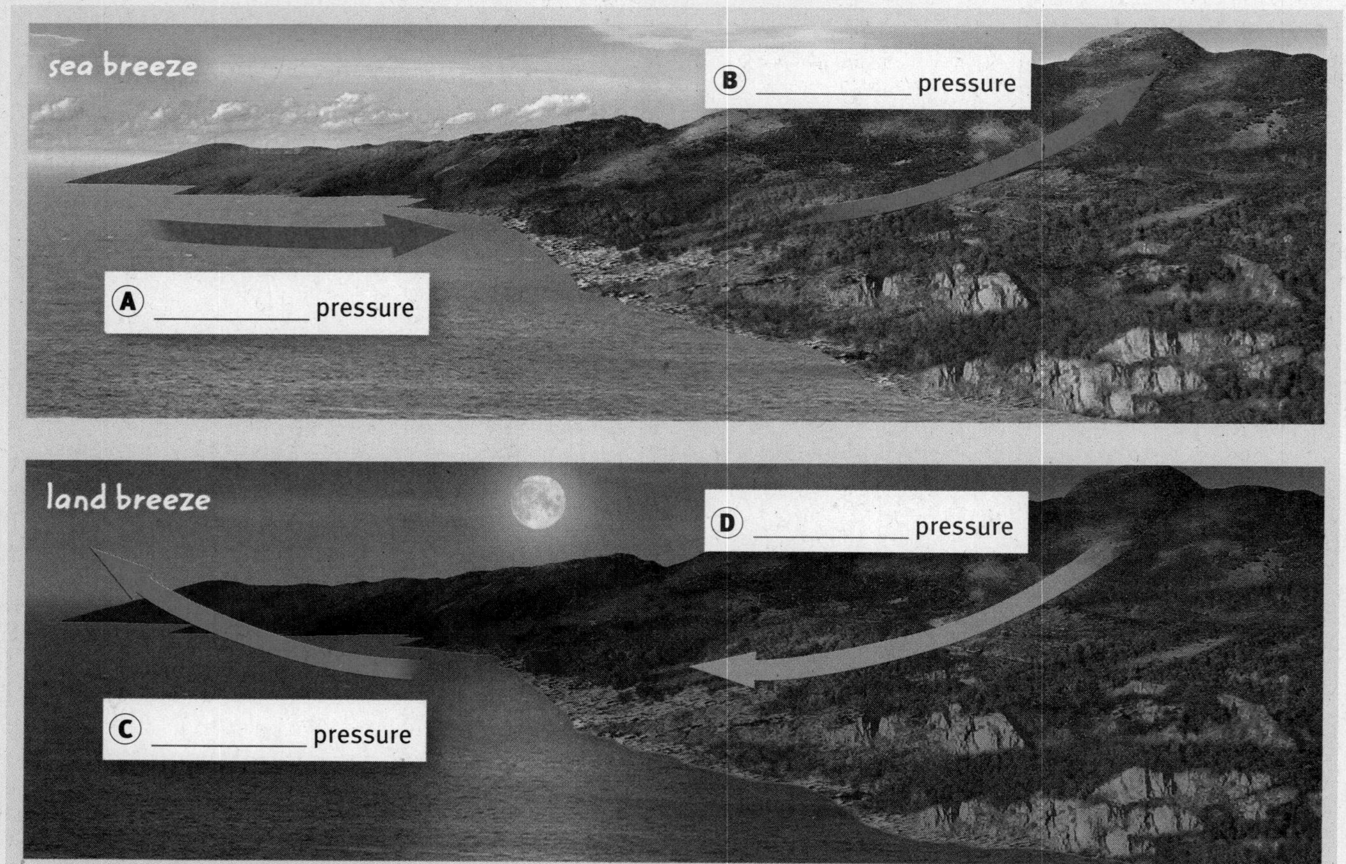

sea breeze

B _____ pressure

A _____ pressure

land breeze

D _____ pressure

C _____ pressure

Valley and Mountain Breezes

Areas that have mountains and valleys experience local winds called mountain and valley breezes. During the day, the sun warms the air along the mountain slopes faster than the air in the valleys. This uneven heating results in areas of lower pressure near the mountain tops. This pressure difference causes a valley breeze, which flows from the valley up the slopes of the mountains. Many birds float on valley breezes to conserve energy. At nightfall, the air along the mountain slopes cools and moves down into the valley. This local wind is called a mountain breeze.

Visualize It!

18 Analyze Label the areas of high pressure and low pressure.

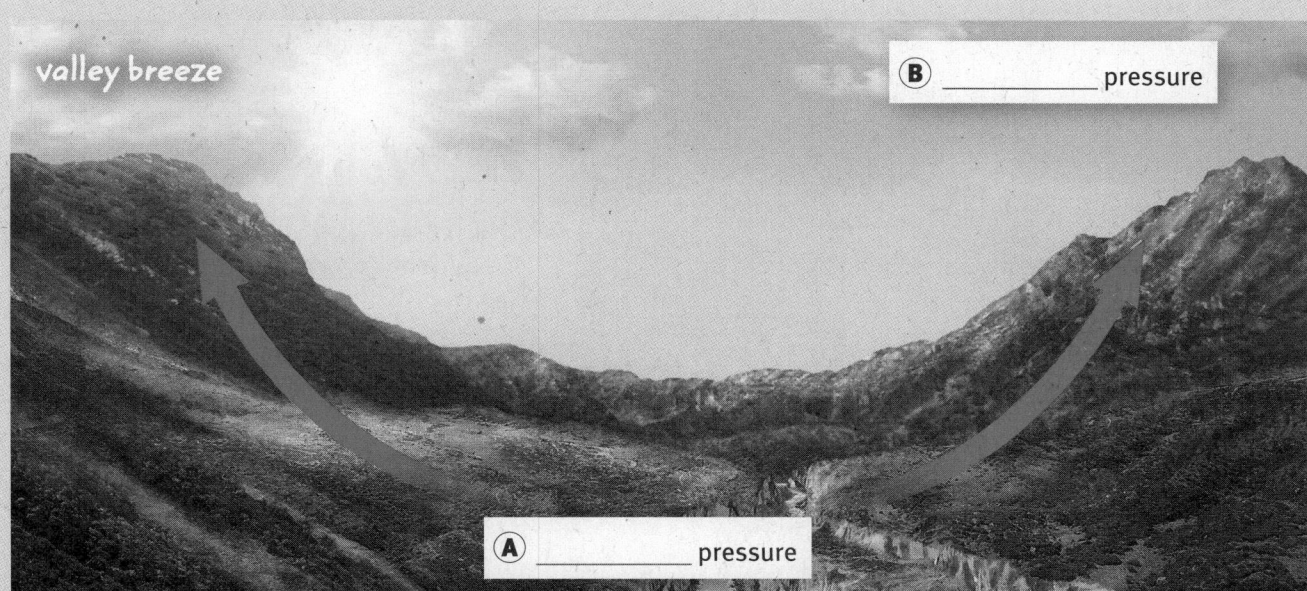

valley breeze

(B) _____ pressure

(A) _____ pressure

mountain breeze

(D) _____ pressure

(C) _____ pressure

Visual Summary

To complete this summary, circle the correct word or phrases. Then use the key below to check your answers. You can use this page to review the main concepts of the lesson.

Wind is the movement of air from areas of higher pressure to areas of lower pressure.

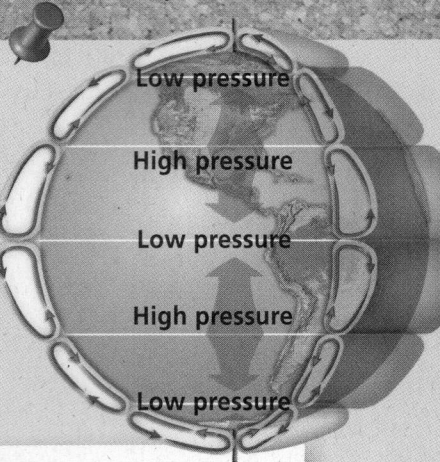

Low pressure

High pressure

Low pressure

High pressure

Low pressure

19 Cool air sinks, causing an area of high / low air pressure.

Global wind systems occur on Earth.

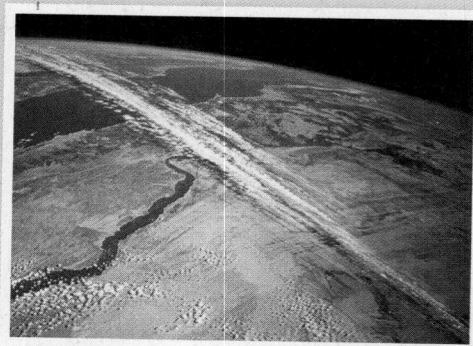

20 High-speed wind between 7 km and 16 km above Earth's surface is a jet stream / mountain breeze.

Wind in the Atmosphere

Geographic features can produce local winds.

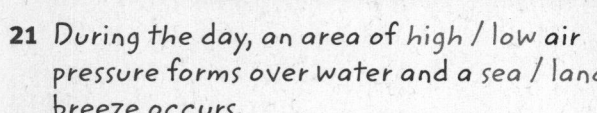

21 During the day, an area of high / low air pressure forms over water and a sea / land breeze occurs.

Answers: 19 high; 20 jet stream; 21 high, sea

22 Explain Would there be winds if the air above Earth's surface was the same temperature everywhere? Explain your answer.

Lesson Review

Vocabulary

Fill in the blanks with the term that best completes the following sentences.

1 Another term for air movement caused by differences in air pressure is

_____

2 Pilots often take advantage of the _____ , which are high-speed winds between 7 km and 16 km above Earth's surface.

3 The apparent curving of winds due to Earth's rotation is the _____

Key Concepts

4 Explain How does the sun cause wind?

_____
_____
_____

5 Predict If Earth did not rotate, what would happen to the global winds? Why?

_____
_____
_____

6 Explain How do convection cells in Earth's atmosphere cause high- and low-pressure belts?

_____
_____
_____
_____

7 Describe What factors contribute to global winds? Identify areas where winds are weak.

_____
_____
_____
_____

8 Identify Name a latitude where each of the following occurs: polar easterlies, westerlies, and trade winds.

_____
_____

Critical Thinking

9 Predict How would local winds be affected if water and land absorbed and released heat at the same rate? Explain your answer.

_____
_____
_____

10 Compare How is a land breeze similar to a sea breeze? How do they differ?

_____
_____
_____
_____

Use this image to answer the following questions.

11 Analyze What type of local wind would you experience if you were standing in the valley? Explain your answer.

_____
_____
_____

12 Infer Would the local wind change if it was nighttime? Explain.

_____
_____
_____

My Notes

Engineering Design Process

Skills
Identify a need
Conduct research
✓ Brainstorm solutions
✓ Select a solution
Design a prototype
✓ Build a prototype
✓ Test and evaluate
✓ Redesign to improve
✓ Communicate results

Objectives
• Explain how a need for clean energy has driven a technological solution.
• Describe two examples of wind-powered generators.
• Design a technological solution to a problem.
• Test and modify a prototype to achieve the desired result.

Building a Wind Turbine

During the Industrial Revolution, machines began to replace human and animal power for doing work. From agriculture and manufacturing to transportation, machines made work faster and easier. However, these machines needed fuel. Fossil fuels, such as coal, oil, and gasoline, powered the Industrial Revolution and are still used today. But burning fossil fuels produces waste products that harm the environment. In addition, fossil fuels will eventually run out. As a result, we need to better understand alternative, renewable sources of energy.

Brainstorming Solutions

There are many sources of energy besides fossil fuels. One of the most abundant renewable sources is wind. A wind turbine is a device that uses energy from the wind to turn an axle. The turning axle can be attached to other equipment to do jobs such as pumping water, cutting lumber, or generating electricity. To generate electricity, the axle spins magnets around a coiled wire. This causes electrons to flow in the wire. Flowing electrons produce an electric current. Electric current is used to power homes and businesses or electrical energy can be stored in a battery.

1 Brainstorm What are other possible sources of renewable energy that could be used to power a generator?

_____

_____

_____

_____

_____

_____

HAWTs must be pointed into the wind to work. A motor turns the turbine to keep it facing the wind. HAWT blades are angled so that wind strikes the front of the blades, and then pushes the blades as it flows over them. Because wind flows over the blades fairly evenly, there is little vibration. So HAWTs are relatively quiet, and the turbines last a long time.

Wind direction

Blade moves counterclockwise

The Modern Design

There are two general types of modern wind turbines. A horizontal-axis wind turbine (HAWT) has a main axle that is horizontal, and a generator at the top of a tall tower. A vertical-axis wind turbine (VAWT) has a main axle that is vertical, and a generator at ground level. The blades are often white or light gray, to blend with the clouds. Blades can be more than 40 meters (130 ft) long, supported by towers more than 90 meters (300 ft) tall. The blade tips can travel more than 320 kilometers (200 mi) per hour!

2 Infer What problems may have been encountered as prototypes for modern wind turbines were tested?

_____

_____

_____

VAWTs do not need to be pointed into the wind to work. The blades are made so that one blade is pushed by the wind while the other returns against the wind. But because each blade moves against the wind for part of its rotation, VAWTs are less efficient than HAWTs. They also tend to vibrate more and, as a result, make more noise.

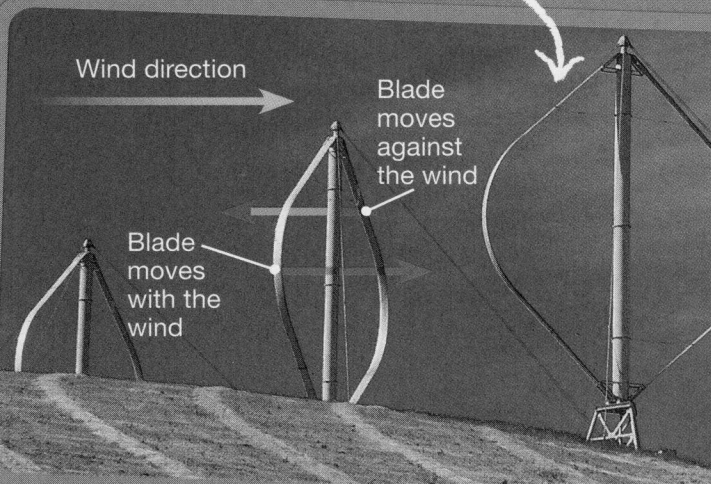

Wind direction

Blade moves against the wind

Blade moves with the wind

✋ You Try It! ⟶

Now it's your turn to design a wind turbine that will generate electricity and light a small bulb.

 # You Try It!

Now it's your turn to design an efficient wind turbine that will generate enough electricity to light a small bulb.

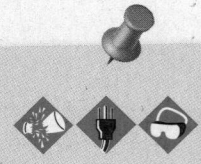

Materials

- ✓ assorted wind turbine parts
- ✓ fan
- ✓ gears
- ✓ small bulb
- ✓ small motor
- ✓ socket

① Brainstorm solutions

Brainstorm ideas for a wind turbine that will turn an axle on a small motor. The blades must turn fast enough so that the motor generates enough electricity to light a small bulb. Fill in the table below with as many ideas as you can for each part of your wind turbine. Circle each idea you decide to try.

Type of axis	Shape of turbine	Attaching axis to motor	Control speed

② Select a solution

From the table above, choose the features for the turbine you will build. In the space below, draw a model of your wind turbine idea. Include all the parts and show how they will be connected.

③ Build a prototype

Now build your wind turbine. As you built your turbine, were there some parts of your design that could not be assembled as you had predicted? What parts did you have to revise as you were building the prototype?

_____
_____
_____
_____

④ Test and evaluate

Point a fan at your wind turbine and see what happens. Did the bulb light? If not, what parts of your turbine could you revise?

_____
_____
_____
_____

⑤ Redesign to improve

Choose one part to revise. Modify your design and then test again. Repeat this process until your turbine lights up the light bulb.

_____
_____
_____
_____

⑥ Communicate results

Which part of the turbine seemed to have the greatest effect on the brightness of the light bulb?

_____
_____
_____
_____
_____
_____

Human Impact on the Atmosphere

ESSENTIAL QUESTION

How do humans impact Earth's atmosphere?

By the end of this lesson, you should be able to identify the impact that humans have had on Earth's atmosphere.

OHIO 7.ESS.3 The atmosphere has different properties at different elevations and contains a mixture of gases that cycle through the lithosphere, biosphere, hydrosphere and atmosphere.

OHIO 7.SIA.4 Analyze and interpret data.

OHIO 7.SIA.6 Think critically and logically to connect evidence and explanations.

Human activities that involve burning fuels, such as driving vehicles and keeping buildings cool, can cause air pollution.

🧠 Engage Your Brain

1 Identify Check T or F to show whether you think each statement is true or false.

T F

☐ ☐ Human activities can cause air pollution.

☐ ☐ Air pollution cannot affect you if you stay indoors.

☐ ☐ Air pollution does not affect places outside of cities.

☐ ☐ Air pollution can cause lung diseases.

2 Analyze The photo above shows the same city as the photo on the left, but on a different day. How are these photos different?

_____

_____

_____

_____

✏️ Active Reading

3 Apply Use context clues to write your own definitions for the words *contamination* and *quality*.

Example sentence
You can help prevent food <u>contamination</u> by washing your hands after touching raw meat.

contamination:

_____

_____

Example sentence
The good sound <u>quality</u> coming from the stereo speakers indicated they were expensive.

quality:

_____

_____

Vocabulary Terms

• **greenhouse effect**   • **acid precipitation**
• **air pollution**   • **air quality**
• **particulate**
• **smog**

4 Apply As you learn the definition of each vocabulary term in this lesson, create your own definition or sketch to help you remember the meaning of the term.

AIR
What Is It Good For?

Why is the atmosphere important?

If you were lost in a desert, you could survive a few days without food and water. But you wouldn't last more than a few minutes without air. Air is an important natural resource. The air you breathe forms part of Earth's atmosphere. The *atmosphere* (AT•muh•sfeer) is a mixture of gases that surrounds Earth. Most organisms on Earth have adapted to the natural balance of gases found in the atmosphere.

It Provides Gases That Organisms Need to Survive

Oxygen is one of the gases that make up Earth's atmosphere. It is used by most living cells to get energy from food. Every breath you take brings oxygen into your body. The atmosphere also contains carbon dioxide. Plants need carbon dioxide to make their own food through photosynthesis (foh•toh•SYN•thuh•sys).

It Absorbs Harmful Radiation

High-energy radiation from space would harm life on Earth if it were not blocked by the atmosphere. Fast-moving particles, called *cosmic rays,* enter the atmosphere every second. These particles collide with oxygen, nitrogen, and other gas molecules and are slowed down. A part of the atmosphere called the *stratosphere* contains ozone gas. The ozone layer absorbs most of the high-energy radiation from the sun, called *ultraviolet radiation* (UV), that reaches Earth.

It Keeps Earth Warm

Without the atmosphere, temperatures on Earth would not be stable. It would be too cold for life to exist. The **greenhouse effect** is the way by which certain gases in the atmosphere, such as water vapor and carbon dioxide, absorb and reradiate thermal energy. This slows the loss of energy from Earth into space. The atmosphere acts like a warm blanket that insulates the surface of Earth, preventing the sun's energy from being lost. For this reason, carbon dioxide and water vapor are called *greenhouse gases.*

Active Reading **5 Explain** How is Earth's atmosphere similar to a warm blanket?

_____

_____

© Houghton Mifflin Harcourt Publishing Company • Image Credits: ©NASA

What is air pollution?

The contamination of the atmosphere by pollutants from human and natural sources is called **air pollution**. Natural sources of air pollution include volcanic eruptions, wildfires, and dust storms. In cities and suburbs, most air pollution comes from the burning of fossil fuels such as oil, gasoline, and coal. Oil refineries, chemical manufacturing plants, dry-cleaning businesses, and auto repair shops are just some potential sources of air pollution. Scientists classify air pollutants as either gases or particulates.

Visualize It!

7 Analyze Which one of these images could be both a natural or a human source of air pollution? Give reasons for your answer.

_____

_____

_____

_____

_____

Factory emissions

Vehicle exhaust

Forest fires and wildfires

Gases

Gas pollutants include carbon monoxide, sulfur dioxide, nitrogen oxide, and ground-level ozone. Some of these gases occur naturally in the atmosphere. These gases are considered pollutants only when they are likely to cause harm. For example, ozone is important in the stratosphere, but at ground level it is harmful to breathe. Carbon monoxide, sulfur dioxide, and nitrogen dioxide are released from burning fossil fuels in vehicles, factories, and homes. They are a major source of air pollution.

Particulates

Particle pollutants can be easier to see than gas pollutants. A **particulate** (per•TIK•yuh•lit) is a tiny particle of solid that is suspended in air or water. Smoke contains ash, which is a particulate. The wind can pick up particulates such as dust, ash, pollen, and tiny bits of salt from the ocean and blow them far from their source. Ash, dust, and pollen are common forms of air pollution. Vehicle exhaust also contains particulates. The particulates in vehicle exhaust are a major cause of air pollution in cities.

It Stinks!

What pollutants can form from vehicle exhaust?

In urban areas, vehicle exhaust is a common source of air pollution. Gases such as carbon monoxide and particulates such as soot and ash are in exhaust fumes. Vehicle exhaust may also react with other substances in the air. When this happens, new pollutants can form. Ground-level ozone and smog are two types of pollutants that form from vehicle exhaust.

Active Reading

8 Identify As you read, underline how ground-level ozone and smog can form.

Ground-Level Ozone

Ozone in the ozone layer is necessary for life, but ground-level ozone is harmful. It is produced when sunlight reacts with vehicle exhaust and oxygen in the air. You may have heard of "Ozone Action Days" in your community. When such a warning is given, people should limit outdoor activities because ozone can damage their lungs.

Smog

Smog is another type of pollutant formed from vehicle exhaust. **Smog** forms when ground-level ozone and vehicle exhaust react in the presence of sunlight. Smog is a problem in large cities because there are more vehicles on the roads. It can cause lung damage and irritate the eyes and nose. In some cities, there can be enough smog to make a brownish haze over the city.

Visualize It!

Some compounds in smoke and exhaust are harmful by themselves. And some compounds in smoke and exhaust can react in the atmosphere to form other pollutants such as smog and acid precipitation.

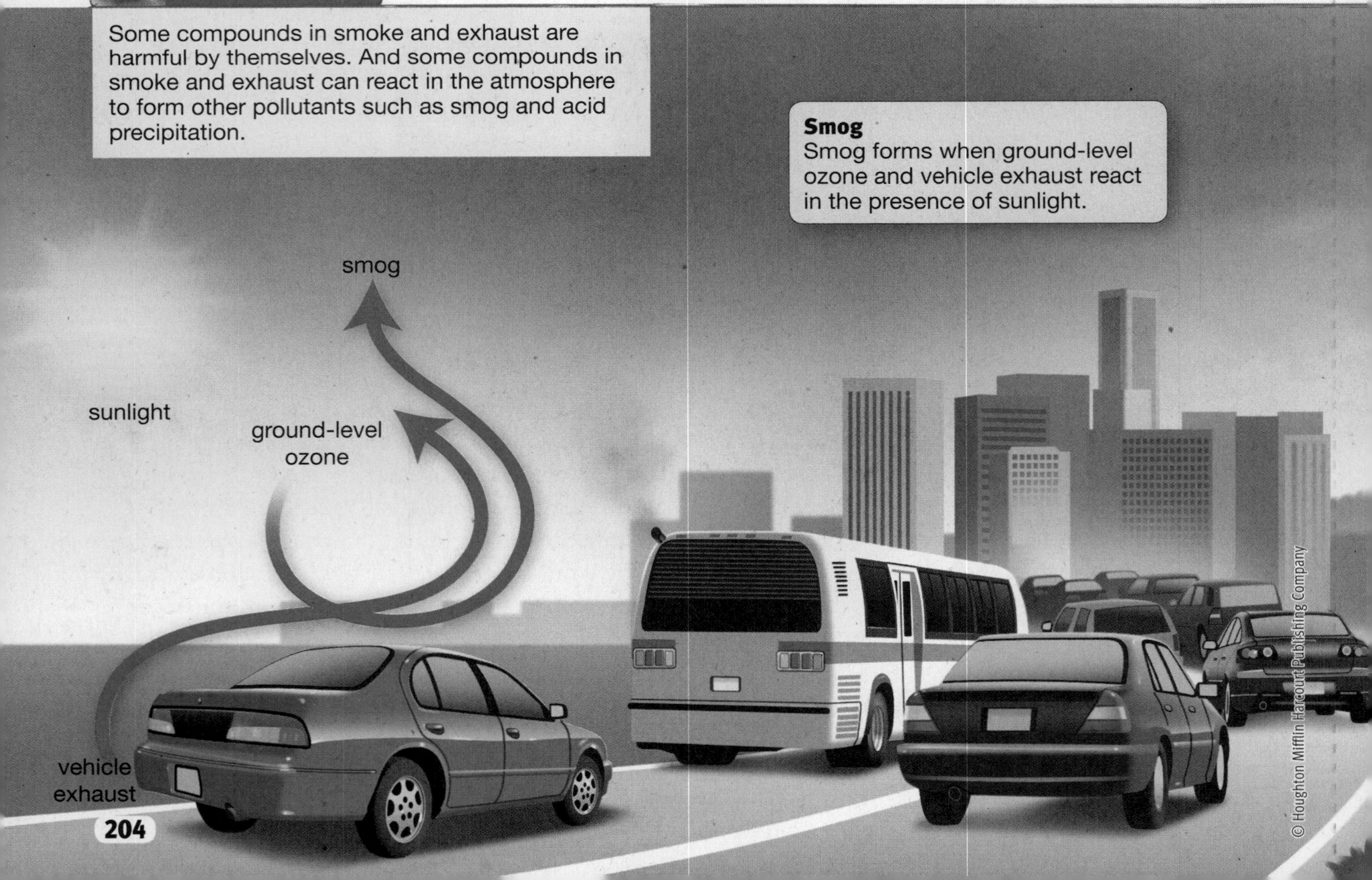

Smog
Smog forms when ground-level ozone and vehicle exhaust react in the presence of sunlight.

smog

sunlight

ground-level ozone

vehicle exhaust

How does pollution from human activities produce acid precipitation?

Active Reading **9 Identify** As you read, underline how acid precipitation forms.

Precipitation (prih•sip•ih•TAY•shuhn) such as rain, sleet, or snow that contains acids from air pollution is called **acid precipitation**. Burning fossil fuels releases sulfur dioxide and nitrogen oxides into the air. When these gases mix with water in the atmosphere, they form sulfuric acid and nitric acid. Precipitation is naturally slightly acidic. When carbon dioxide in the air and water mix, they form carbonic acid. Carbonic acid is a weak acid. Sulfuric acid and nitric acid are strong acids. They can make precipitation so acidic that it is harmful to the environment.

What are some effects of acid precipitation?

Acid precipitation can cause soil and water to become more acidic than normal. Plants have adapted over long periods of time to the natural acidity of the soils in which they live. When soil acidity rises, some nutrients that plants need are dissolved. These nutrients get washed away by rainwater. Bacteria and fungi that live in the soil are also harmed by acidic conditions.

Acid precipitation may increase the acidity of lakes or streams. It also releases toxic metals from soils. The increased acidity and high levels of metals in water can sicken or kill aquatic organisms. This can disrupt habitats and result in decreased biodiversity in an ecosystem. Acid precipitation can also erode the stonework on buildings and statues.

blowing winds

Smoke and fumes from factories and vehicles contain sulfur dioxide and nitrogen oxide gases, which can be blown long distances by winds.

10 Analyze Explain how pollution from one location can affect the environment far away from the source of the pollution.

_____

_____

_____

_____

Acid Precipitation
These gases dissolve in water vapor, and form sulfuric acids and nitric acids, which fall to Earth as acid precipitation.

How's the AIR?

What are measures of air quality?

Measuring how clean or polluted the air is tells us about **air quality**. Pollutants reduce air quality. Two major threats to air quality are vehicle exhausts and industrial pollutants. The air quality in cities can be poor. As more people move into cities, the cities get bigger. This leads to increased amounts of human-made pollution. Poor air circulation, such as a lack of wind, allows air pollution to stay in one area where it can build up. As pollution increases, air quality decreases.

Air Quality Index

The Air Quality Index (AQI) is a number used to describe the air quality of a location such as a city. The higher the AQI number, the more people are likely to have health problems that are linked to air pollution. Air quality is measured and given a value based on the level of pollution detected. The AQI values are divided into ranges. Each range is given a color code and a description. The Environmental Protection Agency (EPA) has AQIs for the pollutants that pose the greatest risk to public health, including ozone and particulates. The EPA can then issue advisories to avoid exposure to pollution that may harm health.

Indoor Air Pollution

The air inside a building can become more polluted than the air outside. This is because buildings are insulated to prevent outside air from entering the building. Some sources of indoor air pollution include chlorine and ammonia from household cleaners and formaldehyde from furniture. Harmful chemicals can be released from some paints and glues. Radon is a radioactive gas released when uranium decays. Radon can seep into buildings through gaps in their foundations. It can build up inside well-insulated buildings. *Ventilation,* or the mixing of indoor and outside air, can reduce indoor air pollution. Another way to reduce indoor air pollution is to limit the use of items that create the pollution.

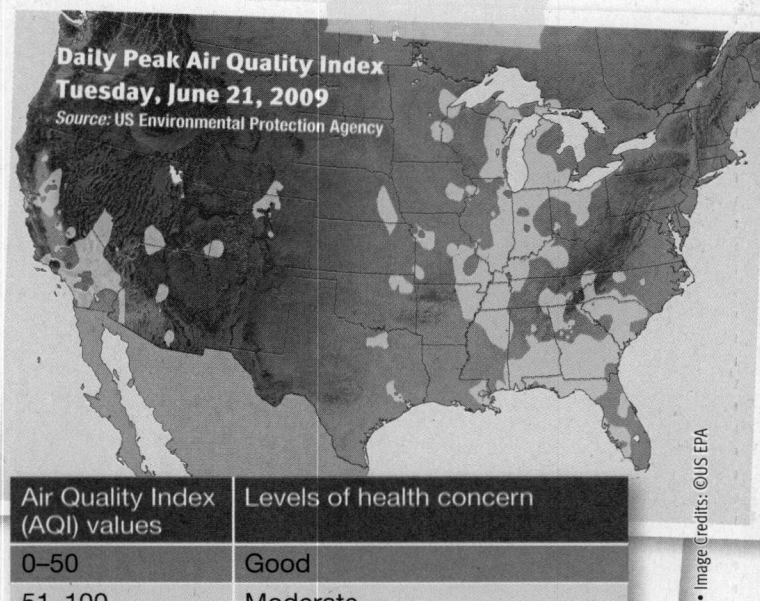

Daily Peak Air Quality Index
Tuesday, June 21, 2009
Source: US Environmental Protection Agency

Air Quality Index (AQI) values	Levels of health concern
0–50	Good
51–100	Moderate
101–150	Unhealthy for sensitive groups
151–200	Unhealthy
201–300	Very unhealthy

Source: **US Environmental Protection Agency**

Color codes based on the Air Quality Index show the air quality in different areas.

Visualize It!

11 Recommend If you were a weather reporter using this map, what would you recommend for people living in areas that are colored orange?

_____

_____

_____

_____

_____

12 Apply If this was your house, how might you decrease the sources of indoor air pollution?

_____
_____
_____
_____

Nitrogen oxides from unvented gas stove, wood stove, or kerosene heater

Fungi and bacteria from dirty heating and air conditioning ducts

Chlorine and ammonia from household cleaners

Chemicals from paint strippers and thinners

Chemicals from dry cleaning

Gasoline from car and lawn mower

Formaldehyde from furniture, carpeting, particleboard, and foam insulation

Carbon monoxide from car left running

How can air quality affect health?

Daily exposure to small amounts of air pollution can cause serious health problems. Children, elderly people, and people with asthma, allergies, lung problems, and heart problems are especially vulnerable to the effects of air pollution. The short-term effects of air pollution include coughing, headaches, and wheezing. Long-term effects, such as lung cancer and emphysema, are dangerous because they can cause death.

Think Outside the Book Inquiry

13 Evaluate Think about the community in which you live. What different things in your community and the surrounding areas might affect the air quality where you live?

Air Pollution and Your Health

Short-term effects	Long-term effects
coughing	asthma
headaches	emphysema
difficulty breathing	allergies
burning/itchy eyes	lung cancer
	chronic bronchitis

14 Identify Imagine you are walking next to a busy road where there are a lot of exhaust fumes. Circle the effects listed in the table that you are most likely to have while walking.

Things Are CHANGING

How might humans be changing Earth's climates?

The burning of fossil fuels releases greenhouse gases, such as carbon dioxide, into the atmosphere. The atmosphere today contains about 37% more carbon dioxide than it did in the mid-1700s, and that level continues to increase. Average global temperatures have also risen in recent decades.

Many people are concerned about how the greenhouse gases from human activities add to the observed trend of increasing global temperatures. Earth's atmosphere and other systems work together in complex ways, so it is hard to know exactly how much the extra greenhouse gases change the temperature. Climate scientists make computer models to understand the effects of climate change. Models predict that average global temperatures are likely to rise another 1.1 to 6.4 °C (2 to 11.5 °F) by the year 2100.

A Sunlight (radiant energy) passes through the windows of the car.

B Energy as heat is trapped inside by the windows.

C The temperature inside the car increases.

Visualize It!

15 Synthesize How is a car with closed windows a good analogy of the atmosphere's greenhouse effect?

_____

_____

_____

_____

What are some predicted effects of climate change?

Active Reading **16 Identify** As you read, underline some effects of an increasing average global temperature.

Scientists have already noticed many changes linked to warmer temperatures. For example, some glaciers and the Arctic sea ice are melting at the fastest rates ever recorded. A warmer Earth may lead to changes in rainfall patterns, rising sea levels, and more severe storms. These changes will have many negative impacts for life on Earth. Other predicted effects include drought in some regions and increased precipitation in others. Farming practices and the availability of food is also expected to be impacted by increased global temperatures. Such changes will likely have political and economic effects on the world, especially in developing countries.

Melt water pours from an iceberg that broke away from the Jakobshavn Glacier in West Greenland.

How is the ozone layer affected by air pollution?

In the 1980s, scientists reported an alarming discovery about Earth's protective ozone layer. Over the polar regions, the ozone layer was thinning. Chemicals called *chlorofluorocarbons* (klor•oh•flur•oh•kar•buhns) (CFCs) were causing ozone to break down into oxygen, which does not block harmful ultraviolet (UV) rays. The thinning of the ozone layer allows more UV radiation to reach Earth's surface. UV radiation is dangerous to organisms, including humans, as it causes sunburn, damages DNA (which can lead to cancer), and causes eye damage.

CFCs once had many industrial uses, such as coolants in refrigerators and air-conditioning units. CFC use has now been banned, but CFC molecules can stay in the atmosphere for about 100 years. So, CFCs released from a spray can 30 years ago are still harming the ozone layer today. However, recent studies show that breakdown of the ozone layer has slowed.

The dark blue area on this map shows the size of the ozone hole over the South Pole.

17 Infer How might these penguins near the South Pole be affected by the ozone hole?

_____

_____

_____

Source: NASA

Satellite image of Arctic summer sea ice in September 1979.

Source: NASA

Satellite image of Arctic summer sea ice in September 2007.

Inquiry

18 Relate What effect might melting sea ice have for people who live in coastal areas?

_____

_____

_____

© Houghton Mifflin Harcourt Publishing Company • Image Credits: (bkgd) ©Paul Souders/Corbis; (tl) ©NASA Images courtesy Goddard Space Flight Center Ozone Processing Team; (tr) Kyodo via AP Images; (bl) ©NASA/Goddard Space Flight Center Scientific Visualization Studio. Thanks to Rob Gerston (GSFC) for providing the data.; (br) ©NASA/Goddard Space Flight Center Scientific Visualization Studio. Thanks to Rob Gerston (GSFC) for providing the data.

Visual Summary

To complete this summary, fill in the blanks with the correct word or phrase. Then use the key below to check your answers. You can use this page to review the main concepts of the lesson.

Human activities are a major cause of air pollution.

19 Two types of air pollutants are gases and _____.

smog

Car exhaust is a major source of air pollution in cities.

20 _____ is formed when exhausts and ozone react in the presence of sunlight.

Human Impact on the Atmosphere

Air quality and levels of pollution can be measured.

Air Quality Index (AQI) values	Levels of health concern
0–50	Good
51–100	Moderate
101–150	Unhealthy for sensitive groups
151–200	Unhealthy
201–300	Very unhealthy

21 As pollution increases, _____ decreases.

Climate change may lead to dramatic changes in global weather patterns.

22 The melting of polar ice is one effect of _____ .

23 Apply Explain in your own words what the following statement means: Each of your breaths, every tree that is planted, and every vehicle on the road affects the composition of the atmosphere.

© Houghton Mifflin Harcourt Publishing Company • Image Credits: (t) ©Steve Cole/PhotoDisc/Getty Images; (b) ©NASA/Goddard Space Flight Center Scientific Visualization Studio. Thanks to Rob Gerston (GSFC) for providing the data.

Lesson Review

Lesson **4**

Vocabulary

Draw a line to connect the following terms to their definitions.

1 Air pollution

2 Greenhouse effect

3 Air quality

4 Particulate

5 Smog

A tiny particle of solid that is suspended in air or water

B the contamination of the atmosphere by the introduction of pollutants from human and natural sources

C pollutant that forms when ozone and vehicle exhaust react with sunlight

D a measure of how clean or polluted the air is

E the process by which gases in the atmosphere, such as water vapor and carbon dioxide, absorb and release energy as heat

Key Concepts

6 Identify List three effects that an increase in urbanization can have on air quality.

_____

_____

7 Relate How are ground-level ozone and smog related?

_____

_____

8 Explain How can human health be affected by changes in air quality?

_____

_____

_____

Critical Thinking

Use this graph to answer the following questions.

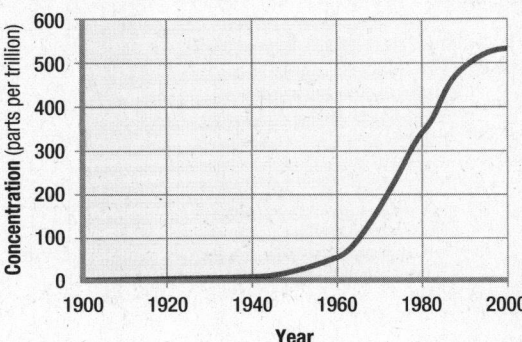

Concentration of a CFC in the Atmosphere Over Time

9 Analyze At what time in the graph did CFCs begin building up in the atmosphere?

_____

_____

10 Synthesize Since the late 1970s, the use of CFCs has been reduced, with a total ban in 2010. But CFCs can stay in the atmosphere for up to 100 years. In the space below, draw a graph showing the concentration of CFCs in the atmosphere over the next 100 years.

11 Apply Do you think it is important that humans control the amount of human-made pollution? Explain your reasoning.

_____

_____

_____

_____

My Notes

Unit 3 [Big Idea] Earth's atmosphere is a mixture of gases that interacts with solar energy.

Lesson 1
ESSENTIAL QUESTION
What is the atmosphere?

Describe the composition and structure of the atmosphere, and explain how the atmosphere protects life and insulates Earth.

Lesson 2
ESSENTIAL QUESTION
How does energy move through Earth's system?

Summarize the three mechanisms by which energy is transferred through Earth's system.

Lesson 3
ESSENTIAL QUESTION
What is wind?

Explain how energy provided by the sun causes atmospheric movement, called wind.

Lesson 4
ESSENTIAL QUESTION
How do humans impact Earth's atmosphere?

Identify the impact that humans have had on Earth's atmosphere.

Connect ESSENTIAL QUESTIONS
Lessons 2 and 3

1 Synthesize Explain how the uneven warming of Earth causes air to move.

_____

_____

_____

_____

Think Outside the Book

2 Synthesize Choose one of these activities to help synthesize what you have learned in this unit.

☐ Using what you learned in lessons 2 and 3, make a poster presentation explaining the role that radiation, conduction, and convection play in the transfer of energy in Earth's atmosphere.

☐ Using what you learned in lessons 1, 2, and 4, explain how solar radiation contributes to the greenhouse effect. Include the terms *radiation* and *reradiation* in your explanation.

Unit 3 Review

Name _____

Vocabulary

Check the box to show whether each statement is true or false.

T	F	
☐	☐	**1** <u>Radiation</u> is a measure of the average kinetic energy of the particles in an object.
☐	☐	**2** <u>Thermal expansion</u> is the increase in volume that results from an increase in temperature.
☐	☐	**3** <u>Air quality</u> is a measure of how clean or polluted the air is.
☐	☐	**4** A <u>jet stream</u> is a wide band of low-speed winds that flow in the middle atmosphere.
☐	☐	**5** The curving of the path of a moving object as a result of Earth's rotation is called the <u>Coriolis effect</u>.

Key Concepts

Choose the letter of the best answer.

6 The picture below shows all three methods of energy transfer.

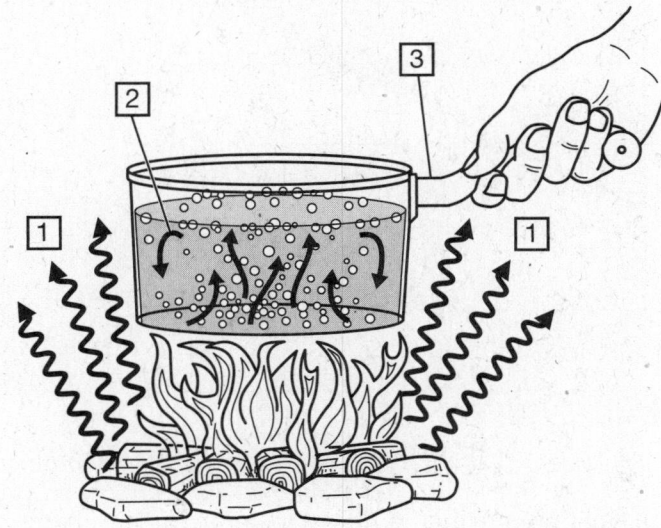

Which of these correctly identifies the three methods of energy transfer?

A 1: convection   2: radiation   3: conduction

B 1: radiation   2: conduction   3: convection

C 1: conduction   2: convection   3: radiation

D 1: radiation   2: convection   3: conduction

7 Which of the following is a source of indoor air pollution?

A greenhouse gases

B steam from a hot shower

C chemicals from certain cleaning products

D radiation from sunlight entering windows

8 A plastic spoon that has a temperature of 78 °F is placed into a bowl of soup that has a temperature of 84 °F. Which of these correctly describes what will happen?

A Energy as heat moves from the spoon to the soup.

B Energy as heat does not move, because the spoon is plastic.

C Energy as heat moves from the soup to the spoon.

D Energy as heat does not move, because the temperature difference is too small.

9 The graph below shows how the amount of carbon dioxide (CO_2) in our atmosphere has changed since 1960.

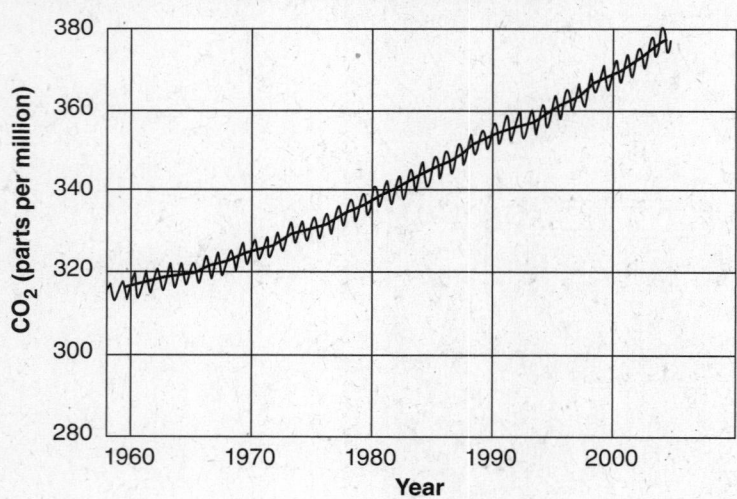

Amount of Atmospheric Carbon Dioxide per Year

Based on the information given in the graph, which of these phenomena has likely increased since 1960?

A land erosion

B coastal erosion

C ozone depletion

D greenhouse effect

10 An astronomer studying planets outside our solar system has analyzed the atmospheres of four planets. Which of these planets' atmospheres would be most able to support a colony of humans?

A Planet A: 76% nitrogen, 23% oxygen, 1% other

B Planet B: 82% nitrogen, 11% oxygen, 7% other

C Planet C: 78% nitrogen, 1% oxygen, 21% other

D Planet D: 27% nitrogen, 3% oxygen, 70% other

11 Refer to the picture below to answer the question.

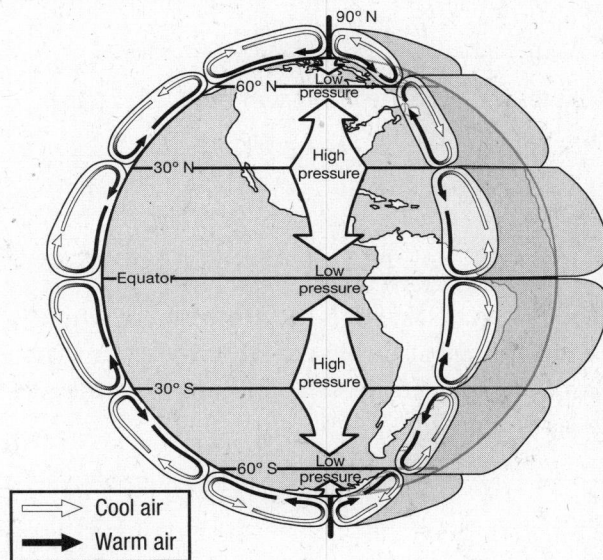

Which of the following is most responsible for the moving bands of air around Earth that are shown in the picture above?

A conduction   **C** Coriolis effect

B convection   **D** greenhouse effect

12 Which of the following describes the general pattern of winds near the equator?

A Winds are generally weak because the equator is a region where low and high air pressure atmospheric bands come together.

B Winds are generally strong because the equator is a region where low and high air pressure atmospheric bands come together.

C Winds are generally strong because the equator is a region of mostly high air pressure.

D Winds are generally weak because the equator is a region of mostly low air pressure.

Critical Thinking

Answer the following questions in the spaces provided.

13 The picture below shows a situation that causes local winds.

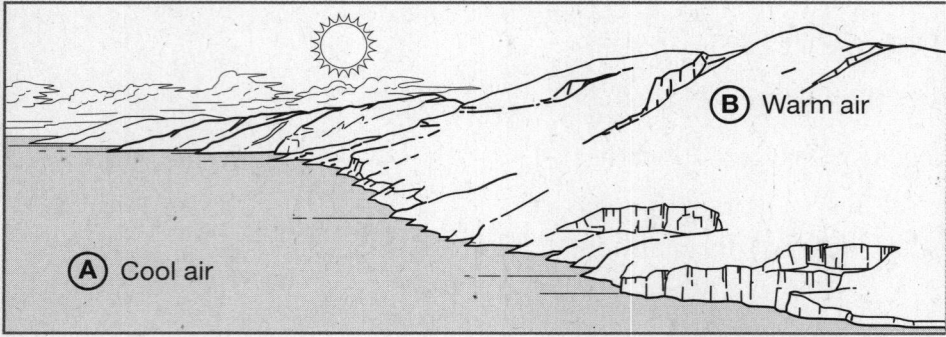

Draw an arrow on the picture to show which way the wind will blow. Describe why the wind blows in that direction, and name this type of local wind.

_____

_____

14 Suppose you were a superhero who could fly up through the atmosphere while feeling the temperature and air pressure change around you. Describe your trip in a paragraph, naming the four main atmospheric layers and telling how the temperature and air pressure change as you pass through each.

_____

_____

_____

_____

_____

Connect ESSENTIAL QUESTIONS
Lessons 1, 2, and 3

Answer the following question in the space provided.

15 Explain how Earth gets energy from the sun and what the atmosphere does with that energy to help life survive on Earth.

_____

_____

_____

_____

Weather and Climate

Strong winds create huge waves that crash on shore.

Big Idea

Air pressure, temperature, air movement, and humidity in the atmosphere affect both weather and climate.

What do you think?

The weather can change very quickly. In severe weather, people and pets can get hurt, and property can be damaged. Can you think of ways to keep people, pets, and property safe?

Warning flags are used to show how safe this beach is.

Unit 4
Weather and Climate

CITIZEN SCIENCE
Exit Strategy

When there is an emergency, knowing what to do helps keep people as safe as possible. So what's the plan?

1 Think About It

A Do you know what to do if there were a weather emergency while you were in school?

_____

_____

B What kinds of information might you need to stay safe? List them below.

_____

_____

_____

_____

_____

Floods can happen very quickly during a bad storm.

② Ask A Question

How well do you know your school's emergency evacuation plan? Obtain a copy of the school's emergency evacuation plan. Read through the plan and answer the following questions as a class.

A Is the emergency evacuation plan/map easy for students to understand?

_____

B How would you know which way to go?

_____

_____

C How often do you have practice drills?

_____

③ Propose and Apply Improvements

A Using what you have learned about your school's emergency evacuation plan, list your ideas for improvements below.

_____

_____

_____

_____

_____

B Develop and give a short oral presentation to your principal about your proposal on ways to improve the school's emergency evacuation plan. Write the main points of your presentation below.

_____

_____

_____

_____

C As a class, practice the newly improved emergency evacuation plan. Describe how well the improved emergency evacuation plan worked.

_____

_____

_____

_____

_____

_____

_____

Take It Home

With an adult, create an emergency evacuation plan for your family or evaluate your family's emergency evacuation plan and propose improvements.

Lesson 1

Elements of Weather

ESSENTIAL QUESTION

What is weather and how can we describe different types of weather conditions?

By the end of this lesson, you should be able to describe elements of weather and explain how they are measured.

Weather stations placed all around the world allow scientists to measure the elements, or separate parts, of weather.

A researcher checks an automatic weather station on Alexander Island, Antarctica.

OHIO 7.ESS.2 Thermal-energy transfers in the ocean and the atmosphere contribute to the formation of currents, which influence global climate patterns.

OHIO 7.SIA.5 Develop descriptions, models, explanations and predictions.

Quick Labs
- Investigate the Measurement of Rainfall
- Classifying Features of Different Types of Clouds

Field Lab
- Comparing Different Ways to Estimate Wind Speed

Engage Your Brain

1 Predict Check T or F to show whether you think each statement is true or false.

T F

☐ ☐ Weather can change every day.

☐ ☐ Temperature is measured by using a barometer.

☐ ☐ Air pressure increases as you move higher in the atmosphere.

☐ ☐ Visibility is a measurement of how far we can see.

2 Describe Use at least three words that might describe the weather on a day when the sky looks like the picture above.

_____

_____

_____

_____

Active Reading

3 Distinguish The words *weather, whether,* and *wether* all sound alike but are spelled differently and mean entirely different things. You may have never heard of a wether—it is a neutered male sheep or ram.

Circle the correct use of the three words in the sentence below.

The farmer wondered *weather / whether / wether* the cold *weather / whether / wether* had affected his *weather / whether / wether*.

Vocabulary Terms

- weather
- humidity
- relative humidity
- dew point
- precipitation
- air pressure
- wind
- visibility

4 Apply As you learn the definition of each vocabulary term in this lesson, create your own definition or sketch to help you remember the meaning of the term.

Wonder about Weather?

What is weather?

Weather is the condition of Earth's atmosphere at a certain time and place. Different observations give you clues to the weather. If you see plants moving from side to side, you might infer that it is windy. If you see a gray sky and wet, shiny streets, you might decide to wear a raincoat. People talk about weather by describing factors such as temperature, humidity, precipitation, air pressure, wind, and *visibility* (viz•uh•BIL•i•tee).

What is temperature and how is it measured?

Temperature is a measure of how hot or cold something is. An instrument that measures and displays temperature is called a *thermometer*. A common type of thermometer uses a liquid such as alcohol or mercury to display the temperature. The liquid is sealed in a glass tube. When the air gets warmer, the liquid expands and rises in the tube. Cooler air causes the liquid to contract and fill less of the tube. A scale, often in Celsius (°C) or Fahrenheit (°F), is marked on the glass tube.

Another type of thermometer is an electrical thermometer. As the temperature becomes higher, electric current flow increases through the thermometer. The strength of the current is then translated into temperature readings.

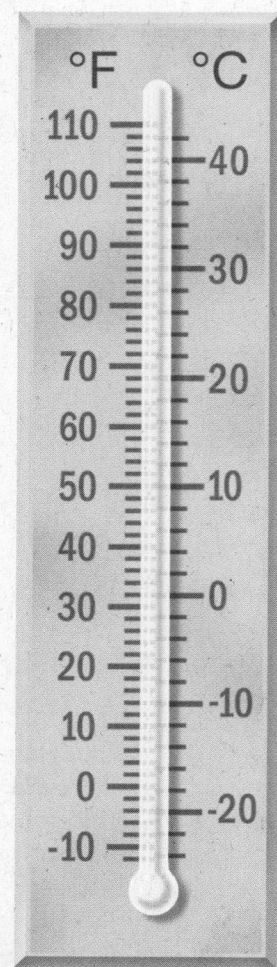

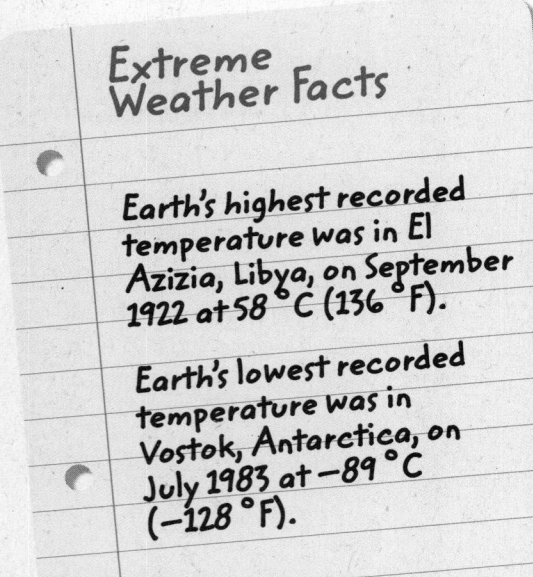

Extreme Weather Facts

Earth's highest recorded temperature was in El Azizia, Libya, on September 1922 at 58°C (136°F).

Earth's lowest recorded temperature was in Vostok, Antarctica, on July 1983 at −89°C (−128°F).

Visualize It!

5 Identify Color in the liquid in the thermometer above to show Earth's average temperature in 2009 (58 °F). Write the Celsius temperature that equals 58 °F on the line below.

_____

What is humidity and how is it measured?

As water evaporates from oceans, lakes, and ponds, it becomes water vapor, or a gas that is in the air. The amount of water vapor in the air is called **humidity**. As more water evaporates and becomes water vapor, the humidity of the air increases.

Humidity is often described through relative humidity. **Relative humidity** is the amount of water vapor in the air compared to the amount of water vapor needed to reach saturation. As shown below, when air is saturated, the rates of evaporation and condensation are equal. Saturated air has a relative humidity of 100%. A psychrometer (sy•KRAHM•i•ter) is an instrument that is used to measure relative humidity.

Air can become saturated when evaporation adds water vapor to the air. Air can also become saturated when it cools to its dew point. The **dew point** is the temperature at which more condensation than evaporation occurs. When air temperature drops below the dew point, condensation forms. This can cause dew on surfaces cooler than the dew point. It also can form fog and clouds.

Active Reading

6 Identify Underline the name of the instrument used to measure relative humidity.

Visualize It!

7 Sketch In the space provided, draw what happens in air that is below the dew point.

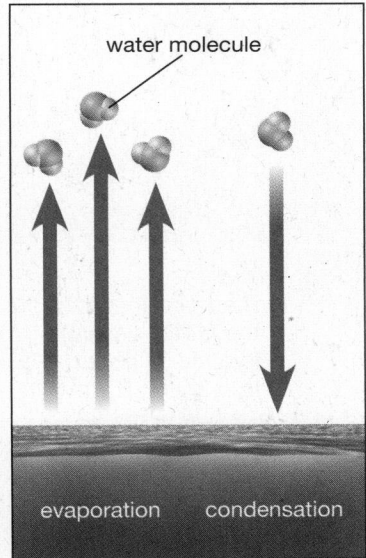

In unsaturated air, more water evaporates into the air than condenses back into the water.

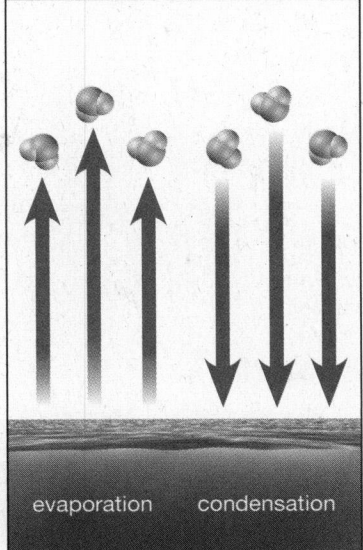

In saturated air, the amount of water that evaporates equals the amount that condenses.

When air cools below its dew point, more water vapor condenses into water than evaporates.

8 Explain Why does dew form on grass overnight?

_____

_____

What is precipitation and how is it measured?

Water vapor in the air condenses not only on Earth's surfaces, but also on tiny particles in the air to form clouds. When this water from the air returns to Earth's surface, it falls as precipitation. **Precipitation** is any form of water that falls to Earth's surface from the clouds. The four main forms of precipitation are rain, snow, hail, and sleet.

Rain is the most common form of precipitation. Inside a cloud, the droplets formed by condensation collide and form larger droplets. They finally become heavy enough to fall as raindrops. Rain is measured with a rain gauge, as shown in the picture below. A funnel or wide opening at the top of the gauge allows rain to flow into a cylinder that is marked in centimeters.

Snow forms when air temperatures are so low that water vapor turns into a solid. When a lot of snow has fallen, it is measured with a ruler or meterstick. When balls or lumps of ice fall from clouds during thunderstorms it is called *hail*. Sleet forms when rain falls through a layer of freezing air, producing falling ice.

Visualize It! Inquiry

9 Synthesize What are two ways in which all types of precipitation are alike?

_____

_____

_____

Snow
Snow can fall as single ice crystals or ice crystals can join to form snowflakes.

Rain
Rain occurs when the water droplets in a cloud get so big they fall to Earth.

Sleet
Small ice pellets fall as sleet when rain falls through cold air.

Hail
Hailstones are layered lumps of ice that fall from clouds.

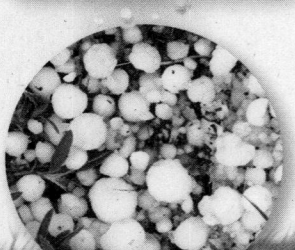

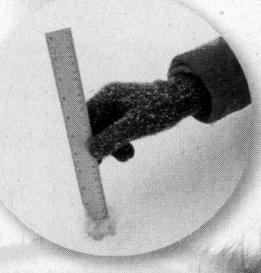

10 Measure How much rain has this rain gauge collected?

_____

Why It Matters

Watching Clouds

Cirrus Clouds

Cumulus Clouds

Stratus Clouds

As you can see above, cirrus (SIR•uhs) clouds appear feathery or wispy. Their name means "curl of hair." They are made of ice crystals. They form when the wind is strong.

Cumulus (KYOOM•yuh•luhs) means "heap" or "pile." Usually these clouds form in fair weather but if they keep growing taller, they can produce thunderstorms.

Stratus (STRAY•tuhs) means "spread out." Stratus clouds form in flat layers. Low, dark stratus clouds can block out the sun and produce steady drizzle or rain.

If you watch the sky over a period of time, you will probably observe different kinds of clouds. Clouds have different characteristics because they form under different conditions. The shapes and sizes of clouds are mainly determined by air movement. For example, puffy clouds form in air that rises sharply or moves straight up and down. Flat, smooth clouds covering large areas form in air that rises gradually.

Extend

Inquiry

11 Reflect Think about the last time you noticed the clouds. When are you most likely to notice what type of cloud is in the sky?

12 Research Word parts are used to tell more about clouds. Look up the word parts -*nimbus* and *alto*-. What are cumulonimbus and altostratus clouds?

The Air Out There

What is air pressure and how is it measured?

Scientists use an instrument called a *barometer* (buh•RAHM•i•ter) to measure air pressure. **Air pressure** is the force of air molecules pushing on an area. The air pressure at any area on Earth depends on the weight of the air above that area. Although air is pressing down on us, we don't feel the weight because air pushes in all directions. So, the pressure of air pushing down is balanced by the pressure of air pushing up.

Air pressure and density are related; they both decrease with altitude. Notice in the picture that the molecules at sea level are closer together than the molecules at the mountain peak. Because the molecules are closer together, the pressure is greater. The air at sea level is denser than air at high altitude.

Air pressure and density are lower at a high altitude.

Air pressure and density are higher at sea level.

Visualize It!

13 Identify Look at the photos below and write whether wind direction or wind speed is being measured.

Anemometer

An anemometer measures:

_____

Wind vane

A wind vane measures:

_____

What is wind and how is it measured?

Wind is air that moves horizontally, or parallel to the ground. Uneven heating of Earth's surface causes pressure differences from place to place. These pressure differences set air in motion. Over a short distance, wind moves directly from higher pressure toward lower pressure.

An anemometer (an•uh•MAHM•i•ter) is used to measure wind speed. It has three or four cups attached to a pole. The wind causes the cups to rotate, sending an electric current to a meter that displays the wind speed.

Wind direction is measured by using a wind vane or a windsock. A wind vane has an arrow with a large tail that is attached to a pole. The wind pushes harder on the arrow tail due to its larger surface area. This causes the wind vane to spin so that the arrow points into the wind. A windsock is a cone-shaped cloth bag open at both ends. The wind enters the wide end and the narrow end points in the opposite direction, showing the direction the wind is blowing.

What is visibility and how is it measured?

Visibility is a measure of the transparency of the atmosphere. Visibility is the way we describe how far we can see, and it is measured by using three or four known landmarks at different distances. Sometimes not all of the landmarks will be visible. Poor visibility can be the result of air pollution or fog.

Poor visibility can be dangerous for all types of travel, whether by air, water, or land. When visibility is very low, roads may be closed to traffic. In areas where low visibility is common, signs are often posted to warn travelers.

 **Active Reading**

14 Explain What are two factors that can affect visibility?

_____

_____

Fog forms as land cools overnight, causing water vapor in the air above the land to condense.

What are some ways to collect weather data?

Many forms of technology are used to gather weather data. The illustration below shows some ways weather information can be collected. Instruments within the atmosphere can make measurements of local weather conditions. Satellites can collect data from above the atmosphere.

 **Visualize It!** Inquiry

15 Infer What are the benefits of stationary weather collection? Moving weather collection?

_____

_____

_____

_____

Satellite

Airplane

Ground station

Stationary
Some forms of technology provide measurements from set locations.

Moving
Some forms of technology report changing measurements along their paths.

Weather buoy

Ship

Visual Summary

To complete this summary, fill in the blanks with the correct word or phrase. Then use the key below to check your answers. You can use this page to review the main concepts of the lesson.

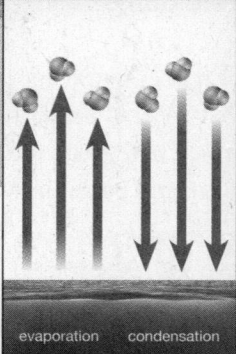

Elements of Weather

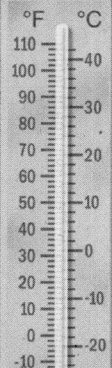

Weather is a condition of the atmosphere at a certain time and place.

16 Weather is often expressed by describing _____, humidity, precipitation, air pressure, wind, and visibility.

Humidity describes the amount of water vapor in the air.

17 The amount of moisture in the air is commonly expressed as _____ humidity.

evaporation   condensation

Uneven heating of Earth's surface causes air pressure differences and wind.

18 Wind moves from areas of _____ pressure to areas of _____ pressure.

Visibility describes how far into the distance objects can be seen.

19 Visibility can be affected by air pollution and _____.

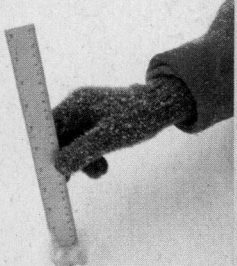

Precipitation occurs when the water that condenses as clouds falls back to Earth in solid or liquid form.

20 The main types of precipitation are hail, snow, _____, and rain.

21 **Synthesize** What instruments would you take along if you were going on a 3-month field study to measure how the weather on a mountaintop changes over the course of a season?

Lesson Review

Vocabulary

In your own words, define the following terms.

1 weather _____

_____

_____

2 humidity _____

_____

_____

3 air pressure _____

_____

_____

4 visibility _____

_____

_____

Key Concepts

Weather element	Instrument
5 Identify Measures temperature	
	6 Identify Is measured by using a barometer
7 Identify Measures relative humidity	
	8 Identify Is measured by using a rain gauge or meterstick
9 Identify Measures wind speed	

10 List What are four types of precipitation?

_____

_____

Critical Thinking

11 Apply Explain how wind is related to the uneven heating of Earth's surfaces by the sun.

_____

_____

_____

_____

12 Explain Why does air pressure decrease as altitude increases?

_____

_____

_____

13 Synthesize What is the relative humidity when the air temperature is at its dew point?

_____

_____

The weather data below was recorded from 1989–2009 by an Antarctic weather station similar to the station in the photo at the beginning of this lesson. Use these data to answer the questions that follow.

	Jan.	Apr.	July	Oct.
Mean max. temp. (°C)	2.1	−7.4	−9.9	−8.1
Mean min. temp. (°C)	−2.6	−14.6	−18.1	−15.1
Mean precip. (mm)	9.0	18.04	28.5	16.5

14 Identify Which month had the lowest mean minimum and maximum temperatures?

_____

15 Infer The precipitation that fell at this location was most likely in what form?

_____

My Notes

Lesson 2

What Influences Weather?

ESSENTIAL QUESTION

How do the water cycle and other global patterns affect local weather?

By the end of this lesson, you should be able to explain how global patterns in Earth's system influence weather.

The weather doesn't always turn out the way you want. But learning about the factors that affect weather can help you plan your next outing.

OHIO **7.ESS.2** Thermal-energy transfers in the ocean and the atmosphere contribute to the formation of currents, which influence global climate patterns.

OHIO **7.SIA.4** Analyze and interpret data.

Lesson Labs

Quick Labs
• Analyze Weather Patterns
• Coastal Climate Model

Exploration Lab
• Modeling El Niño

Engage Your Brain

1 Predict Check T or F to show whether you think each statement is true or false.

T	F	
☐	☐	The water cycle affects weather.
☐	☐	Air can be warmed or cooled by the surface below it.
☐	☐	Warm air sinks, cool air rises.
☐	☐	Winds can bring different weather to a region.

2 Explain How can air temperatures along this coastline be affected by the large body of water that is nearby?

_____

_____

_____

Active Reading

3 Infer A military front is a contested armed frontier between opposing forces. A *weather front* occurs between two air masses, or bodies of air. What kind of weather do you think usually happens at a weather front?

_____

_____

_____

_____

_____

_____

_____

Vocabulary Terms

• air mass
• front
• jet stream

4 Apply As you learn the definition of each vocabulary term in this lesson, create your own definition or sketch to help you remember the meaning of the term.

Water, Water

How does the water cycle affect weather?

Weather is the short-term state of the atmosphere, including temperature, humidity, precipitation, air pressure, wind, and visibility. These elements are affected by the energy received from the sun and the amount of water in the air. To understand what influences weather, then, you need to understand the water cycle.

The *water cycle* is the continuous movement of water between the atmosphere, the land, the oceans, and living things. In the water cycle, shown to the right, water is constantly being recycled between liquid, solid, and gaseous states. The water cycle involves the processes of evaporation, condensation, and precipitation.

Evaporation occurs when liquid water changes into water vapor, which is a gas. Condensation occurs when water vapor cools and changes from a gas to a liquid. A change in the amount of water vapor in the air affects humidity. Clouds and fog form through condensation of water vapor, so condensation also affects visibility. Precipitation occurs when rain, snow, sleet, or hail falls from the clouds onto Earth's surface.

Active Reading

5 List Name at least 5 elements of weather.

_____

_____

_____

Visualize It!

6 Summarize Describe how the water cycle influences weather by completing the sentences on the picture.

Ⓐ Evaporation affects weather by _____

_____

_____

Everywhere . . .

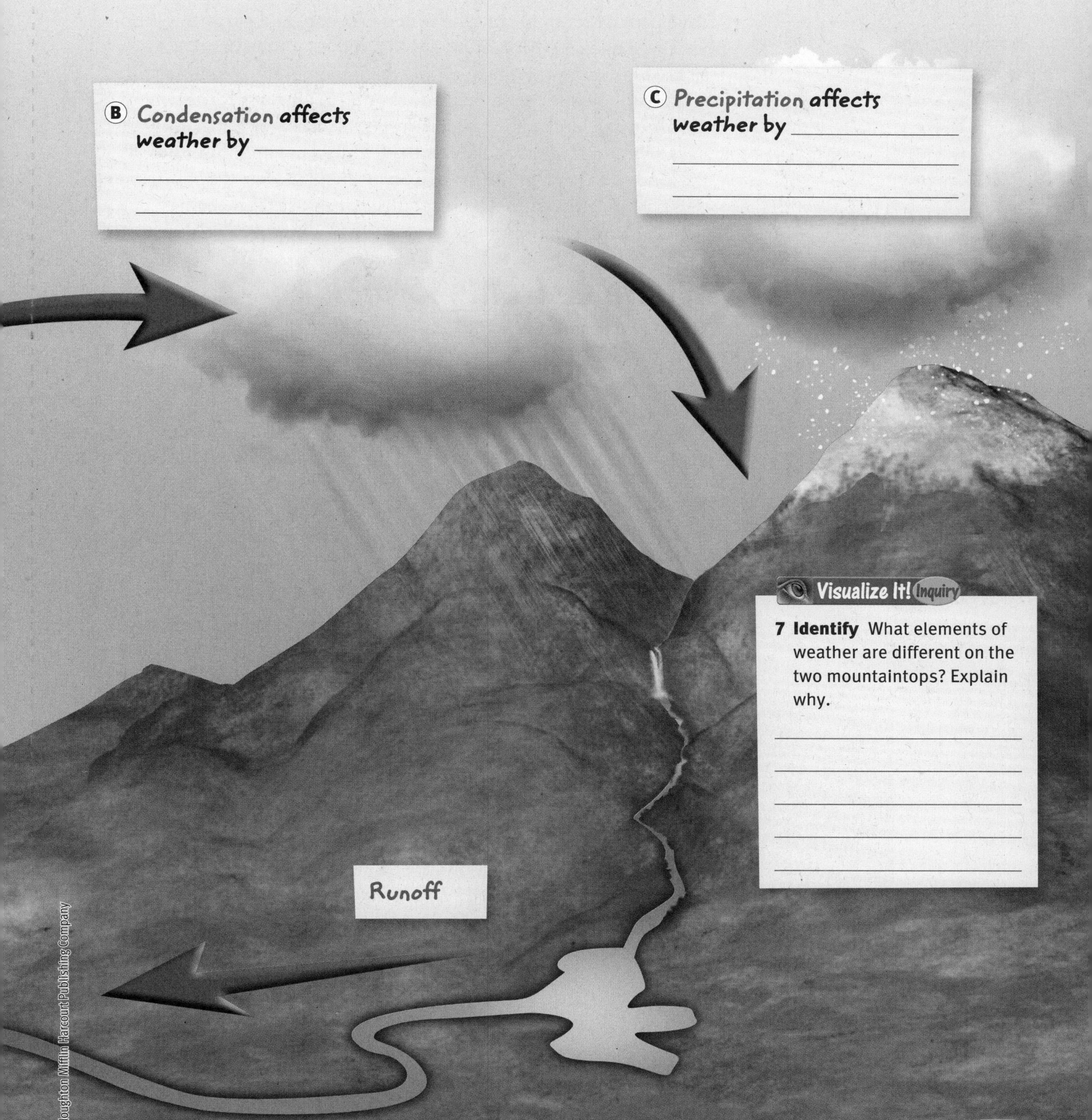

B Condensation affects
weather by _____
_____
_____

C Precipitation affects
weather by _____
_____
_____

Runoff

Visualize It! Inquiry

7 Identify What elements of
weather are different on the
two mountaintops? Explain
why.

_____
_____
_____
_____
_____

Putting Up a Front

How do air masses affect weather?

Active Reading

8 Identify As you read, underline how air masses form.

You have probably experienced the effects of air masses—one day is hot and humid, and the next day is cool and pleasant. The weather changes when a new air mass moves into your area. An **air mass** is a large volume of air in which temperature and moisture content are nearly the same throughout. An air mass forms when the air over a large region of Earth stays in one area for many days. The air gradually takes on the temperature and humidity of the land or water below it. When an air mass moves, it can bring these characteristics to new locations. Air masses can change temperature and humidity as they move to a new area.

Where do fronts form?

When two air masses meet, density differences usually keep them from mixing. A cool air mass is more dense than a warm air mass. A boundary, called a **front**, forms between the air masses. For a front to form, one air mass must run into another air mass. The kind of front that forms depends on how these air masses move relative to each other, and on their relative temperature and moisture content. Fronts result in a change in weather as they pass. They usually affect weather in the middle latitudes of Earth. Fronts do not often occur near the equator because air masses there do not have big temperature differences.

The boundary between air masses, or front, cannot be seen, but is shown here to illustrate how air masses can take on the characteristics of the surface below them.

Air masses that form above water are moist.

Air masses that form above land are dry.

Cold Fronts Form Where Cold Air Moves under Warm Air

Warm air is less dense than cold air is. So, a cold air mass that is moving can quickly push up a warm air mass. If the warm air is moist, clouds will form. Storms that form along a cold front are usually short-lived but can move quickly and bring heavy rain or snow. Cooler weather follows a cold front.

9 Apply If you hear that a cold front is headed for your area, what type of weather might you expect?

_____

_____

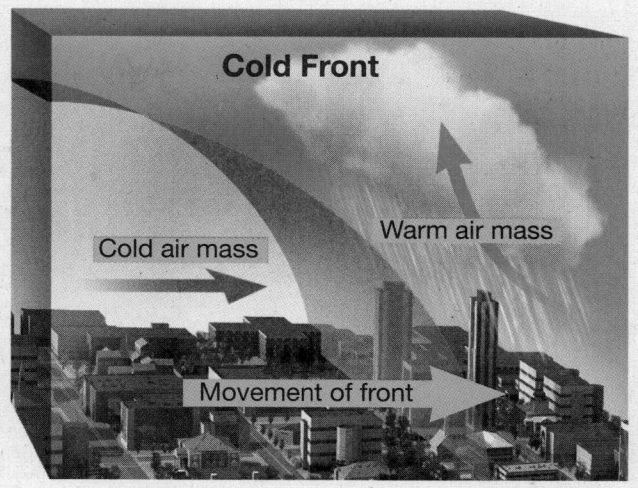

Cold Front

Cold air mass

Warm air mass

Movement of front

Warm Fronts Form Where Warm Air Moves over Cold Air

A warm front forms when a warm air mass follows a retreating cold air mass. The warm air rises over the cold air, and its moisture condenses into clouds. Warm fronts often bring drizzly rain and are followed by warm, clear weather.

10 Identify The rainy weather at the edge of a warm front is a result of

☐ the cold air mass that is leaving.

☐ the warm air rising over the cold air.

☐ the warm air mass following the front.

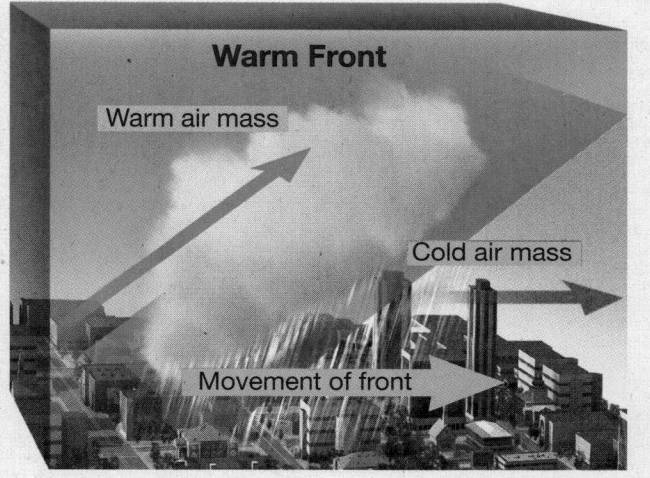

Warm Front

Warm air mass

Cold air mass

Movement of front

Stationary Fronts Form Where Cold and Warm Air Stop Moving

In a stationary front, there is not enough wind for either the cold air mass or the warm air mass to keep moving. So, the two air masses remain in one place. A stationary front can cause many days of unchanging weather.

11 Infer When could a stationary front become a warm or cold front?

_____

_____

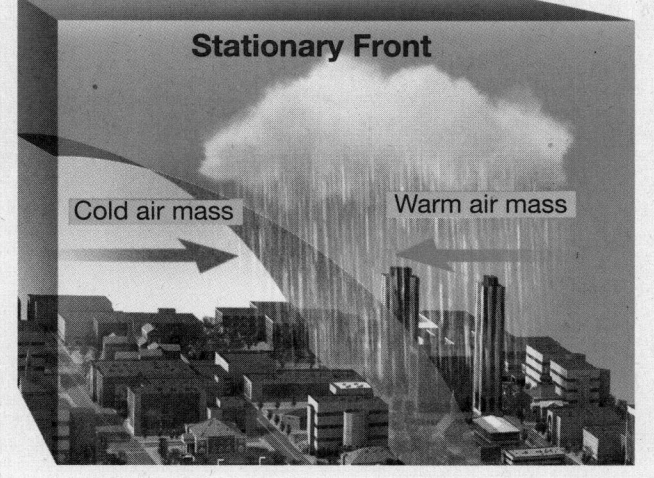

Stationary Front

Cold air mass

Warm air mass

© Houghton Mifflin Harcourt Publishing Company

Feeling the Pressure!

What are pressure systems, and how do they interact?

Areas of different air pressure cause changes in the weather. In a *high-pressure system*, air sinks slowly down. As the air nears the ground, it spreads out toward areas of lower pressure. Most high-pressure systems are large and change slowly. When a high-pressure system stays in one location for a long time, an air mass may form. The air mass can be warm or cold, humid or dry.

In a *low-pressure system*, air rises and so has a lower air pressure than the areas around it. As the air in the center of a low-pressure system rises, the air cools.

The diagram below shows how a high-pressure system can form a low-pressure system. Surface air, shown by the black arrows, moves out and away from high-pressure centers. Air above the surface sinks and warms. The green arrows show how air swirls from a high-pressure system into a low-pressure system. In a low-pressure system, the air rises and cools.

Visualize It!

12 Identify Choose the correct answer for each of the pressure systems shown below.

A high-pressure system can spiral into a low-pressure system, as illustrated by the green arrows below. In the Northern Hemisphere, air circles in the directions shown.

(A) In a high-pressure system, air

☐ rises and cools.

☐ sinks and warms.

(B) in a low-pressure system, air

☐ rises and cools.

☐ sinks and warms.

How do different pressure systems affect us?

When air pressure differences are small, air doesn't move very much. If the air remains in one place or moves slowly, the air takes on the temperature and humidity of the land or water beneath it. Each type of pressure system has it own unique weather pattern. By keeping track of high- and low-pressure systems, scientists can predict the weather.

High-Pressure Systems Produce Clear Weather

High-pressure systems are areas where air sinks and moves outward. The sinking air is denser than the surrounding air, and the pressure is higher. Cooler, denser air moves out of the center of these high-pressure areas toward areas of lower pressure. As the air sinks, it gets warmer and absorbs moisture. Water droplets evaporate, relative humidity decreases, and clouds often disappear. A high-pressure system generally brings clear skies and calm air or gentle breezes.

Low-Pressure Systems Produce Rainy Weather

Low-pressure systems have lower pressure than the surrounding areas. Air in a low-pressure system comes together, or converges, and rises. As the air in the center of a low-pressure system rises, it cools and forms clouds and rain. The rising air in a low-pressure system causes stormy weather.

A low-pressure system can develop wherever there is a center of low pressure. One place this often happens is along a boundary between a warm air mass and a cold air mass. Rain often occurs at these boundaries, or fronts.

Visualize It!

13 Match Label each picture as a result of a high- or low-pressure system. Then, draw a line from each photo to its matching air-pressure diagram.

(A)

(B)

Warm air rises

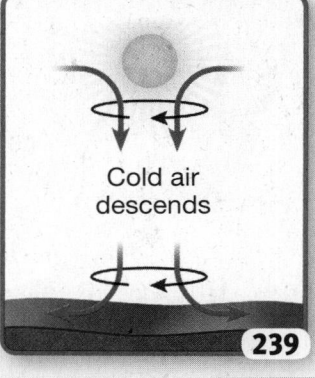
Cold air descends

Windy Weather

How do global wind patterns affect local weather?

Winds are caused by unequal heating of Earth's surface—which causes air pressure differences—and can occur on a global or on a local scale. On a local scale, air-pressure differences affect both wind speed and wind direction at a location. On a global level, there is an overall movement of surface air from the poles toward the equator. The heated air at the equator rises and forms a low-pressure belt. Cold air near the poles sinks and creates high-pressure centers. Because air moves from areas of high pressure to areas of low pressure, it moves from the poles to the equator. At high altitudes, the warmed air circles back toward the poles.

Temperature and pressure differences on Earth's surface also create regional wind belts. Winds in these belts curve to the east or the west as they blow, due to Earth's rotation. This curving of winds is called the *Coriolis effect* (kawr•ee•OH•lis eff•EKT). Winds would flow in straight lines if Earth did not rotate. Winds bring air masses of different temperatures and moisture content to a region.

Belts of global winds circle Earth. The winds in these belts curve to the east or west. Between the global wind belts are calm areas.

Visualize It!

14 Apply Trade winds bring

☐ cool air to the warmer equatorial regions.

☐ warm air to the cooler, higher latitudes.

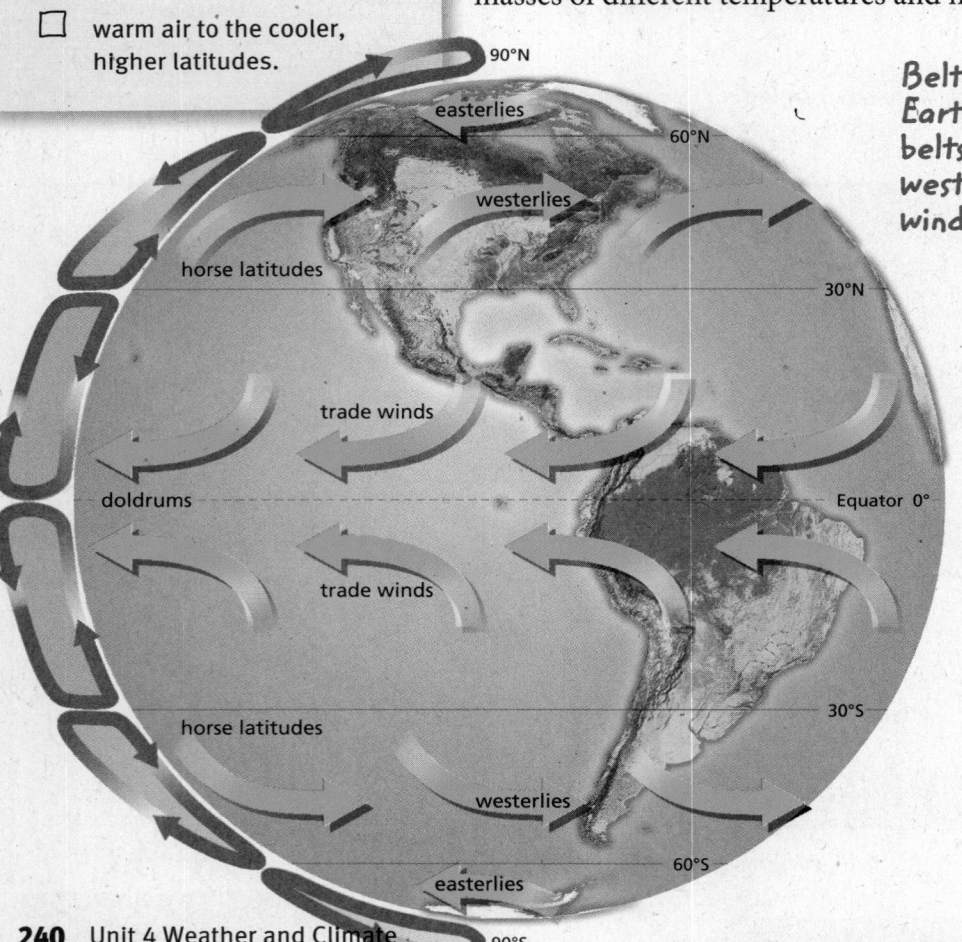

- easterlies — 90°N, 60°N
- westerlies — 60°N
- horse latitudes — 30°N
- trade winds
- doldrums — Equator 0°
- trade winds
- horse latitudes — 30°S
- westerlies — 60°S
- easterlies — 90°S

How do jet streams affect weather?

Long-distance winds that travel above global winds for thousands of kilometers are called **jet streams**. Air moves in jet streams with speeds that are at least 92 kilometers per hour and are often greater than 180 kilometers per hour. Like global and local winds, jet streams form because Earth's surface is heated unevenly. They flow in a wavy pattern from west to east.

Each hemisphere usually has two main jet streams, a polar jet stream and a subtropical jet stream. The polar jet streams flow closer to the poles in summer than in winter. Jet streams can affect temperatures. For example, a polar jet stream can pull cold air down from Canada into the United States and pull warm air up toward Canada. Jet streams also affect precipitation patterns. Strong storms tend to form along jet streams. Scientists must know where a jet stream is flowing to make accurate weather predictions.

Active Reading **15 Identify** What are two ways jet streams affect weather?

_____

_____

_____

_____

In winter months, the polar jet stream flows across much of the United States.

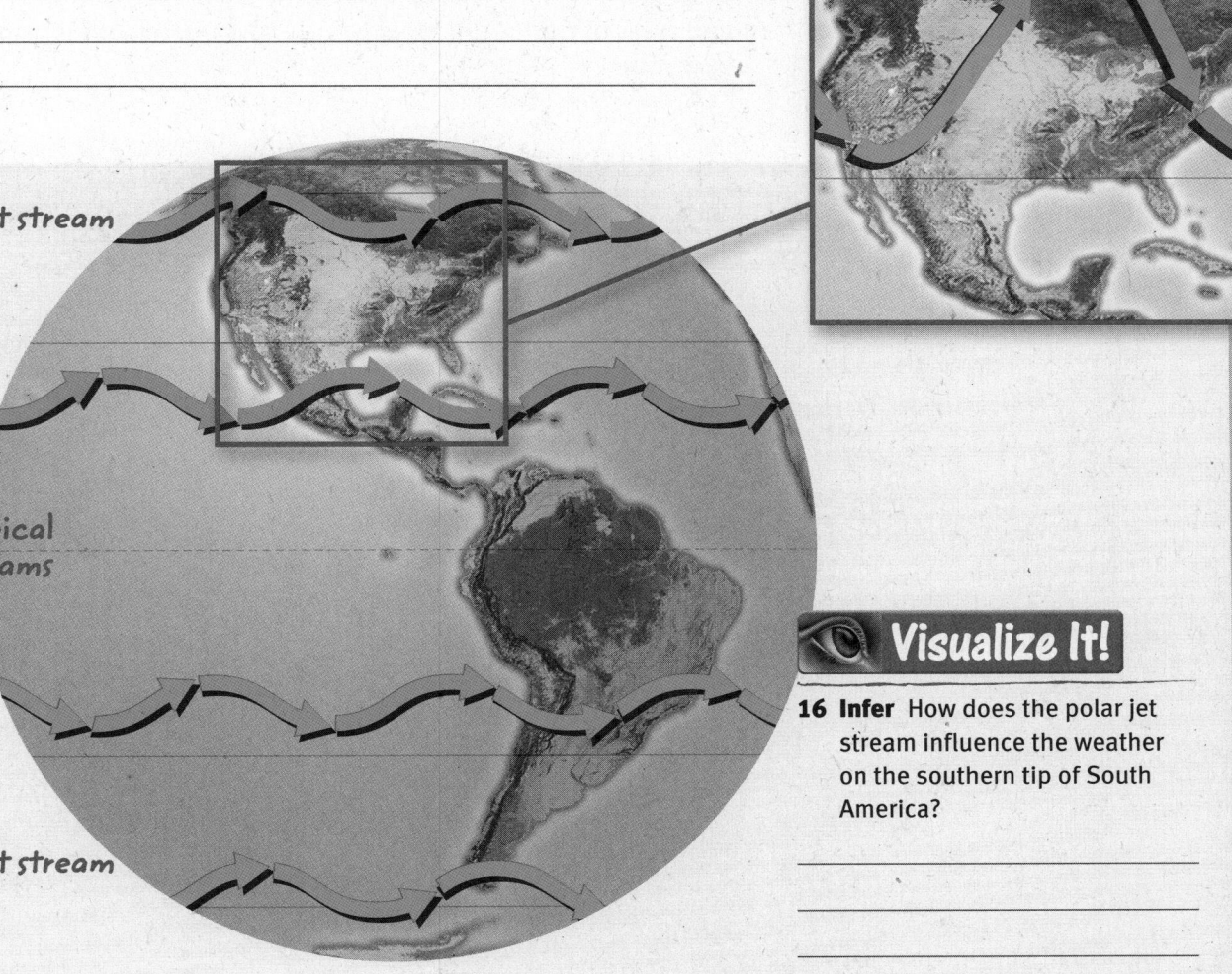

Polar jet stream

Subtropical jet streams

Polar jet stream

Visualize It!

16 Infer How does the polar jet stream influence the weather on the southern tip of South America?

_____

_____

_____

_____

Ocean Effects

How do ocean currents influence weather?

The same global winds that blow across the surface of Earth also push water across Earth's oceans, causing surface currents. Different winds cause currents to flow in different directions. The flow of surface currents moves energy as heat from one part of Earth to another. As the map below shows, both warm-water and cold-water currents flow from one ocean to another. Water near the equator carries energy from the sun to other parts of the ocean. The energy from the warm currents is transferred to colder water or to the atmosphere, changing local temperatures and humidity.

Oceans also have an effect on weather in the form of hurricanes and monsoons. Warm ocean water fuels hurricanes. Monsoons are winds that change direction with the seasons. During summer, the land becomes much warmer than the sea in some areas of the world. Moist wind flows inland, often bringing heavy rains.

Warm current
Cold current

Surface currents are caused by winds. They distribute energy across Earth's surface, changing local temperature and humidity.

Cool Ocean Currents Lower Coastal Air Temperatures

As currents flow, they warm or cool the atmosphere above, affecting local temperatures. The California current is a cold-water current that keeps the average summer high temperatures of coastal cities such as San Diego around 26 °C (78 °F). Cities that lie inland at the same latitude have warmer averages. The graph below shows average monthly temperatures for San Diego and El Centro, California.

👁 Visualize It!

18 Explain Why are temperatures in San Diego, California, usually cooler than they are in El Centro, California?

_____

_____

_____

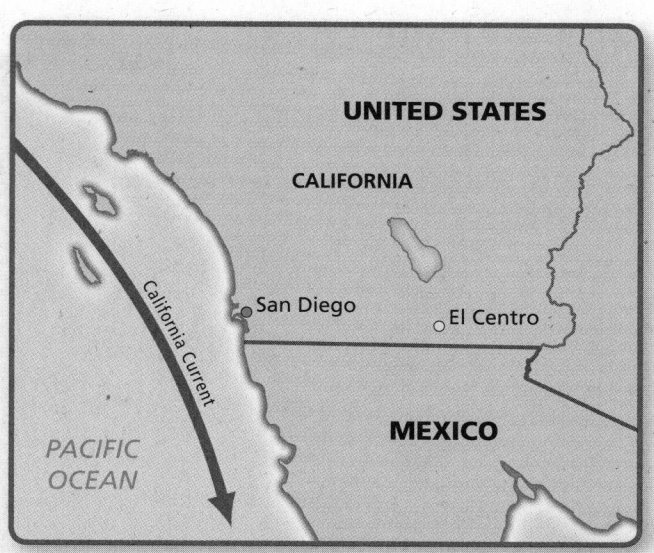

Average Monthly Temperatures

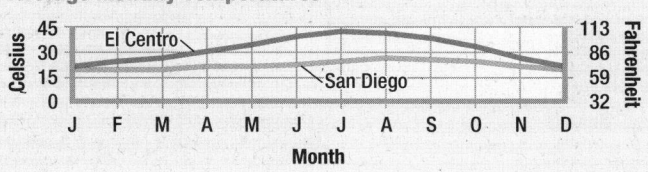

Source: weather.com

Warm Ocean Currents Raise Coastal Air Temperatures

In areas where warm ocean currents flow, coastal cities have warmer winter temperatures than inland cities at similar latitudes. For example, temperatures vary considerably from the coastal regions to the inland areas of Norway due to the warmth of the North Atlantic Current. Coastal cities such as Bergen have relatively mild winters. Inland cities such as Lillehammer have colder winters but temperatures similar to the coastal cities in summer.

👁 Visualize It!

19 Identify Circle the city that is represented by each color in the graph.

■ Lillehammer/Bergen

■ Lillehammer/Bergen

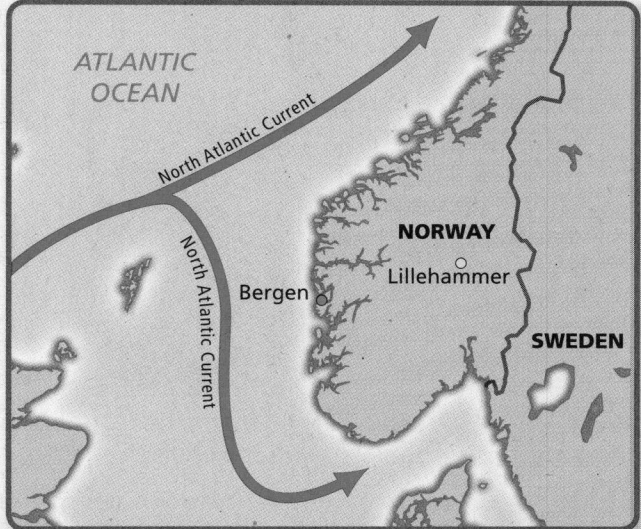

Average Monthly High Temperatures

Source: worldweather.org

Visual Summary

To complete this summary, circle the correct word. Then, use the key below to check your answers. You can use this page to review the main concepts of the lesson.

Influences of Weather

A front forms where two air masses meet.

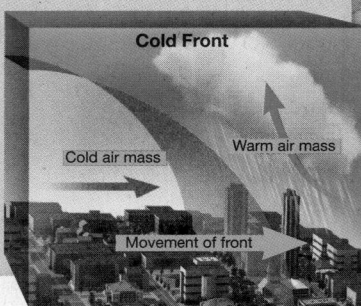

Cold Front

Cold air mass

Warm air mass

Movement of front

21 When a warm air mass and a cool air mass meet, the warm / cool air mass usually moves upward.

Pressure differences from the uneven heating of Earth's surface cause predictable patterns of wind.

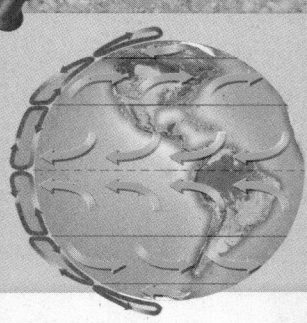

23 Global wind patterns occur as, due to temperature differences, air rises / sinks at the poles and rises / sinks at the equator.

Understanding the water cycle is key to understanding weather.

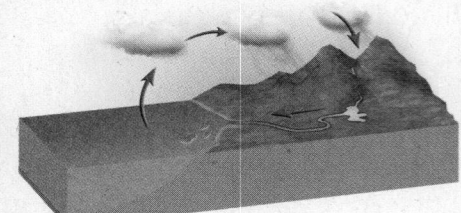

20 Weather is affected by the amount of oxygen / water in the air.

Low-pressure systems bring stormy weather, and high-pressure systems bring dry, clear weather.

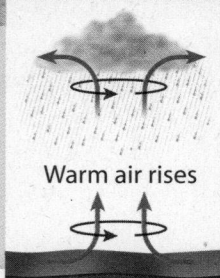

Warm air rises

22 In a low-pressure system, air moves upward / downward.

Global ocean surface currents can have warming or cooling effects on the air masses above them.

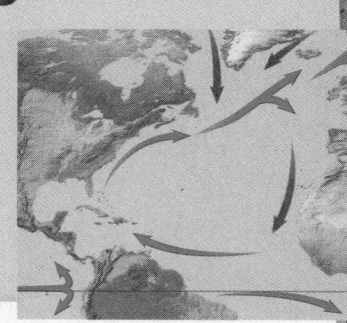

24 Warm currents have a warming / cooling effect on the air masses above them.

Answers: 20 water; 21 warm; 22 upward; 23 sinks, rises; 24 warming

25 Synthesize How do air masses cause weather changes?

Lesson Review

Vocabulary

For each pair of terms, explain how the meanings of the terms differ.

1 *front* and *air mass*

_____

_____

_____

2 *high-pressure system* and *low-pressure system*

_____

_____

_____

3 *jet streams* and *global wind belts*

_____

_____

_____

Key Concepts

4 Apply If the weather becomes stormy for a short time and then becomes colder, which type of front has most likely passed?

_____

5 Describe Explain how an ocean current can affect the temperature and the amount of moisture of the air mass above the current and above nearby coastlines.

_____

_____

_____

_____

6 Synthesize How does the water cycle affect weather?

_____

_____

_____

_____

_____

Critical Thinking

Use the diagram below to answer the following question.

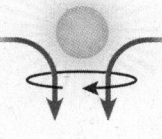 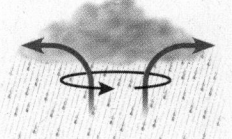

Cool air descends   Warm air rises

 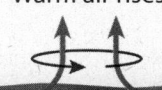

7 Interpret How does the movement of air affect the type of weather that forms from high-pressure and low-pressure systems?

_____

_____

_____

_____

_____

8 Explain How does the polar jet stream affect temperature and precipitation in North America?

_____

_____

_____

_____

_____

9 Describe Explain how changes in weather are caused by the interaction of air masses.

_____

_____

_____

_____

_____

_____

My Notes

J. Marshall Shepherd

METEOROLOGIST AND CLIMATOLOGIST

Dr. Marshall Shepherd, who works at the University of Georgia, has been interested in weather since he made his own weather-collecting instruments for a school science project. Although the instruments he uses today, like computers and satellites, are much larger and much more powerful than the ones he made in school, they give him some of the same information.

In his work, Dr. Shepherd tries to understand weather events, such as hurricanes and thunderstorms, and relate them to current weather and climate change. He once led a team that used space-based radar to measure rainfall over urban areas. The measurements confirmed that the areas downwind of major cities experience more rainfall in summer than other areas in the same region. He explained that the excess heat retained by buildings and roads changes the way the air circulates, and this causes rain clouds to form.

While the most familiar field of meteorology is weather forecasting, research meteorology is also used in air pollution control, weather control, agricultural planning, climate change studies, and even criminal and civil investigations.

J. Marshall Shepherd

Social Studies Connection

An almanac is a type of calendar that contains various types of information, including weather forecasts and astronomical data, for every day of the year. Many people used almanacs before meteorologists started to forecast the weather. Use an almanac from the library or the Internet to find out what the weather was on the day that you were born.

JOB BOARD

Atmospheric Scientist

What You'll Do: Collect and analyze data on Earth's air pressure, humidity, and winds to make short-range and long-range weather forecasts. Work around the clock during weather emergencies like hurricanes and tornadoes.

Where You Might Work: Weather data collecting stations, radio and television stations, or private consulting firms.

Education: A bachelor's degree in meteorology, or in a closely related field with courses in meteorology, is required. A master's degree is necessary for some jobs.

Airplane Pilot

What You'll Do: Fly airplanes containing passengers or cargo, or for crop dusting, search and rescue, or fire-fighting. Before flights, check the plane's control equipment and weather conditions. Plan a safe route. Pilots communicate with air traffic control during flight to ensure a safe flight and fill out paperwork after the flight.

Where You Might Work: Flying planes for airlines, the military, radio and tv stations, freight companies, flight schools, farms, national parks, or other businesses that use airplanes.

Education: Most pilots will complete a four-year college degree before entering a pilot program. Before pilots become certified and take to the skies, they need a pilot license and many hours of flight time and training.

Snow Plow Operator

What You'll Do: In areas that receive snowfall, prepare the roads by spreading a mixture of sand and salt on the roads when snow is forecast. After a snowfall, drive snow plows to clear snow from roads and walkways.

Where You Might Work: For public organizations or private companies in cities and towns that receive snowfall.

Education: In most states, there is no special license needed, other than a driver's license.

Climate

ESSENTIAL QUESTION

How is climate affected by energy from the sun and variations on Earth's surface?

By the end of this lesson, you should be able to describe the main factors that affect climate and explain how scientists classify climates.

Earth has a wide variety of climates, including polar climates like the one shown here. What kind of climate do you live in?

OHIO **7.ESS.2** Thermal-energy transfers in the ocean and the atmosphere contribute to the formation of currents, which influence global climate patterns.

OHIO **7.SIA.4** Analyze and interpret data.

✋ **Lesson Labs**

Quick Labs
• Determining Climate
• Factors That Affect Climate
• The Angles of the Sun's Rays

Field Lab
• How Land Features Affect Climate

Engage Your Brain

1 Predict Check T or F to show whether you think each statement is true or false.

T	F	
☐	☐	Locations in Florida and Oregon receive the same amount of sunlight on any given day.
☐	☐	Temperature is an important part of determining the climate of an area.
☐	☐	The climate on even the tallest mountains near the equator is too warm for glaciers to form.
☐	☐	Winds can move rain clouds from one location to another.

2 Infer Volcanic eruptions can send huge clouds of gas and dust into the air. These dust particles can block sunlight. How might the eruption of a large volcano affect weather for years to come?

_____

_____

_____

_____

_____

Active Reading

3 Synthesize You can often define an unknown word if you know the meaning of its word parts. Use the word parts and sentence below to make an educated guess about the meaning of the word *topography*.

Word part	Meaning
topos-	place
-graphy	writing

Example sentence
The <u>topography</u> of the area is varied, because there are hills, valleys, and flat plains all within a few square miles.

topography:

_____

_____

Vocabulary Terms

• weather	• topography
• climate	• elevation
• latitude	• surface currents

4 Apply As you learn the definition of each vocabulary term in this lesson, create your own definition or sketch to help you remember the meaning of the term.

How's the **Climate?**

What determines climate?

Weather conditions change from day to day. **Weather** is the condition of Earth's atmosphere at a particular time and place. **Climate**, on the other hand, describes the weather conditions in an area over a long period of time. For the most part, climate is determined by temperature and precipitation (pree•SIP•uh•tay•shuhn). But what factors affect the temperature and precipitation rates of an area? Those factors include latitude, wind patterns, elevation, locations of mountains and large bodies of water, and nearness to ocean currents.

Temperature

Temperature patterns are an important feature of climate. Although the average temperature of an area over a period of time is useful information, using only average temperatures to describe climate can be misleading. Areas that have similar average temperatures may have very different temperature ranges.

A temperature range includes all of the temperatures in an area, from the coldest temperature extreme to the warmest temperature extreme. Organisms that thrive in a region are those that can survive the temperature extremes in that region. Temperature ranges provide more information about an area and are unique to the area. Therefore, temperature ranges are a better indicator of climate than are temperature averages.

_____

_____

_____

_____

Desert region

Polar region

Precipitation

Precipitation, such as rain, snow, or hail, is also an important part of climate. As with temperature, the average yearly precipitation alone is not the best way to describe a climate. Two places that have the same average yearly precipitation may receive that precipitation in different patterns during the year. For example, one location may receive small amounts of precipitation throughout the year. This pattern would support plant life all year long. Another location may receive all of its precipitation in a few months of the year. These months may be the only time in which plants can grow. So, the pattern of precipitation in a region can determine the types of plants that grow there and the length of the growing season. Therefore, the pattern of precipitation is a better indicator of the local climate than the average precipitation alone.

Think Outside the Book Inquiry

8 Apply With a classmate, discuss what condition, other than precipitation, is likely related to better plant growth in the temperate area shown directly below than in the desert on the bottom right.

Visualize It!

7 Interpret Match the climates represented in the bar graph below to the photos by writing *A*, *B*, or *C* in the blank circles.

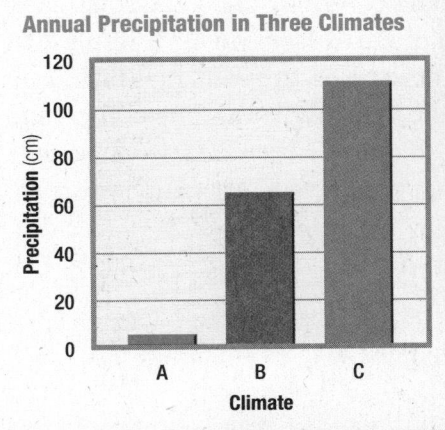

Annual Precipitation in Three Climates

There are enough resources in the area for plants to thickly cover the ground.

Some plants that grow in deserts have long roots to reach the water deep underground.

Conditions in a tropical forest allow lots of plants to grow quickly and closely together.

Here Comes the Sun!

How is the sun's energy related to Earth's climate?

Active Reading

9 Identify As you read, underline how solar energy affects the climate of an area.

The climate of an area is directly related to the amount of energy from the sun, or *solar energy*, that the area receives. This amount depends on the latitude (LAHT•ih•tood) of the area. **Latitude** is the angular distance in degrees north and south from the equator. Different latitudes receive different amounts of solar energy. The available solar energy powers the water cycle and winds, which affect the temperature, precipitation, and other factors that determine the local climate.

Latitude Affects the Amount of Solar Energy an Area Receives and that Area's Climate

Latitude helps determine the temperature of an area, because latitude affects the amount of solar energy an area receives. The figure below shows how the amount of solar energy reaching Earth's surface varies with latitude. Notice that the sun's rays travel in lines parallel to one another. Near the equator, the sun's rays hit Earth directly, at almost a 90° angle. At this angle, the solar energy is concentrated in a small area of Earth's surface. As a result, that area has high temperatures. At the poles, the sun's rays hit Earth at a lesser angle than they do at the equator. At this angle, the same amount of solar energy is spread over a larger area. Because the energy is less concentrated, the poles have lower temperatures than areas near the equator do.

Visualize It!

10 Analyze What is the difference between the sun's rays that strike at the equator and the sun's rays that strike at the poles?

_____

_____

_____

_____

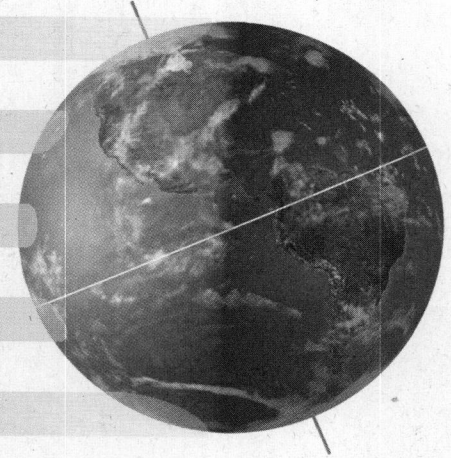

The amount of solar energy an area receives depends on latitude.

Drawing is not to scale.

The Sun Powers the Water Cycle

It is easy to see how the water cycle affects weather and climate. For example, when it rains or snows, you see precipitation. In the water cycle, energy from the sun warms the surface of the ocean or other body of water. Some of the liquid water evaporates, becoming invisible water vapor, a gas. When cooled, some of the vapor condenses, turning into droplets of liquid water and forming clouds. Some water droplets collide, becoming larger. Once large enough, they fall to Earth's surface as precipitation.

11 Apply Using the figure below, explain how the water cycle affects the climate of an area.

_____

_____

_____

_____

_____

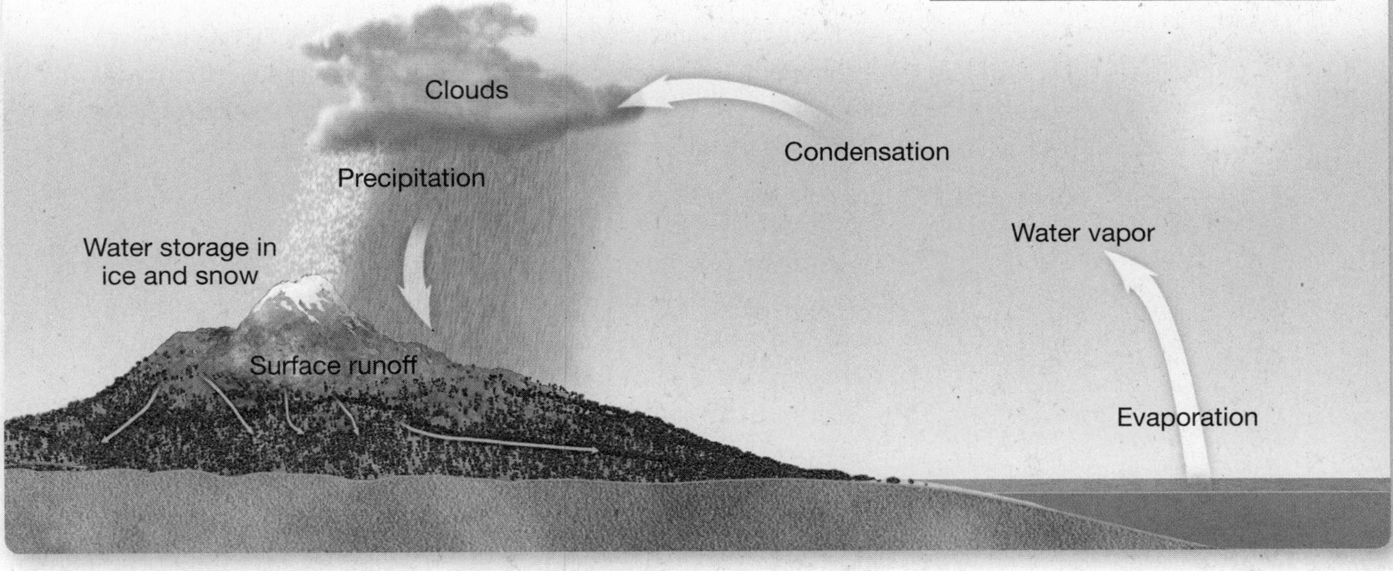

Clouds

Condensation

Precipitation

Water vapor

Water storage in ice and snow

Surface runoff

Evaporation

The Sun Powers Wind

The sun warms Earth's surface unevenly, creating areas of different air pressure. As air moves from areas of higher pressure to areas of lower pressure, it is felt as wind, as shown below. Global and local wind patterns transfer energy around Earth's surface, affecting global and local temperatures. Winds also carry water vapor from place to place. If the air cools enough, the water vapor will condense and fall as precipitation. The speed, direction, temperature, and moisture content of winds affect the climate and weather of the areas they move through.

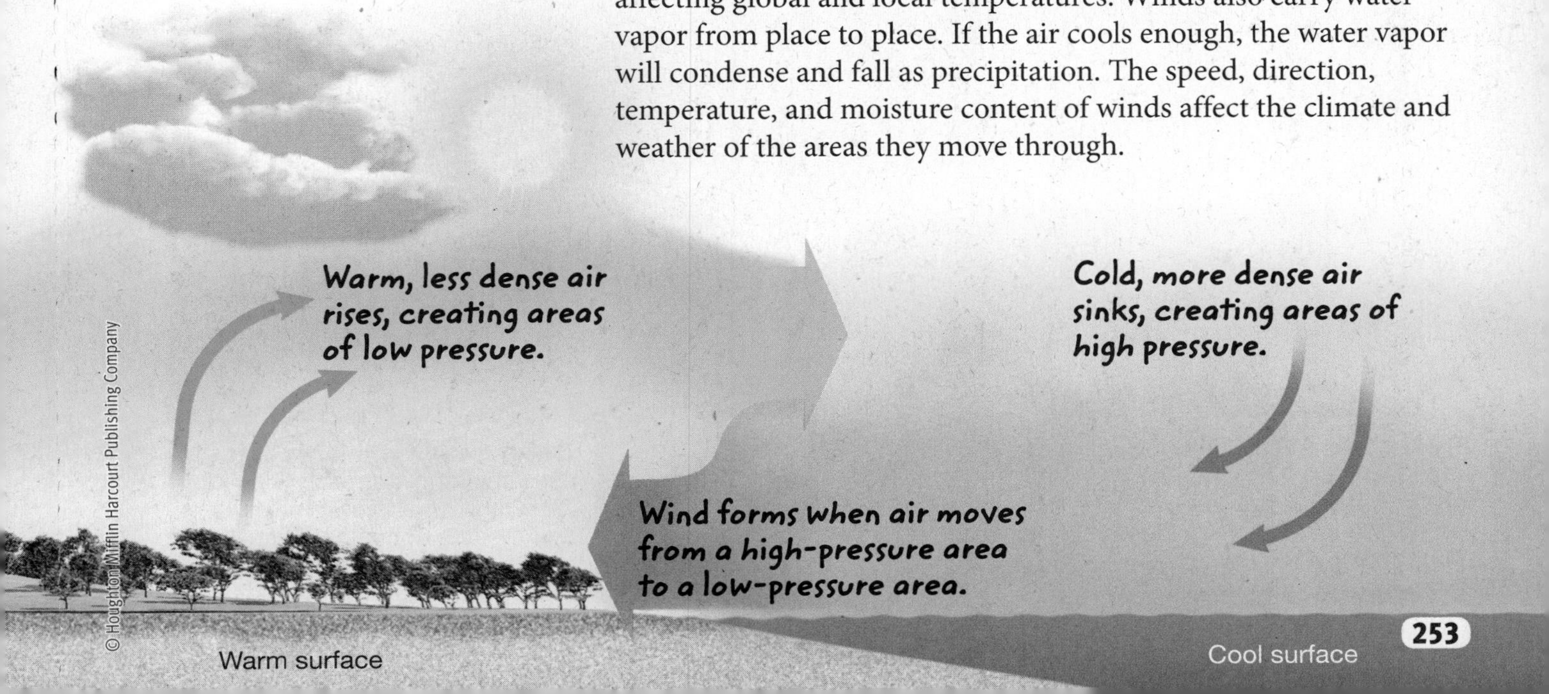

Warm, less dense air rises, creating areas of low pressure.

Cold, more dense air sinks, creating areas of high pressure.

Wind forms when air moves from a high-pressure area to a low-pressure area.

Warm surface

Cool surface

Latitude Isn't Everything

How do Earth's features affect climate?

On land, winds have to flow around or over features on Earth's surface, such as mountains. The surface features of an area combine to form its **topography** (tuh•POG•ruh•fee). Topography influences the wind patterns and the transfer of energy in an area. An important aspect of topography is elevation. **Elevation** refers to the height of an area above sea level. Temperature changes as elevation changes. Thus, topography and elevation affect the climate of a region.

Topography Can Affect Winds

Even the broad, generally flat topography of the Great Plains gives rise to unique weather patterns. On the plains, winds can flow steadily over large distances before they merge. This mixing of winds produces thunderstorms and even tornadoes.

Mountains can also affect the climate of an area, as shown below. When moist air hits a mountain, it is forced to rise up the side of the mountain. The rising air cools and often releases rain, which supports plants on the mountainside. The air that moves over the top of the mountain is dry. The air warms as it descends, creating a dry climate, which supports desert formation. Such areas are said to be in a *rain shadow*, because the air has already released all of its water by the time that it reaches this side of the mountain.

Active Reading

12 Identify As you read, underline how topography affects the climate of a region.

Visualize It!

13 Apply Circle the rain gauge in each set that corresponds to how much rain each side of the mountain is likely to receive.

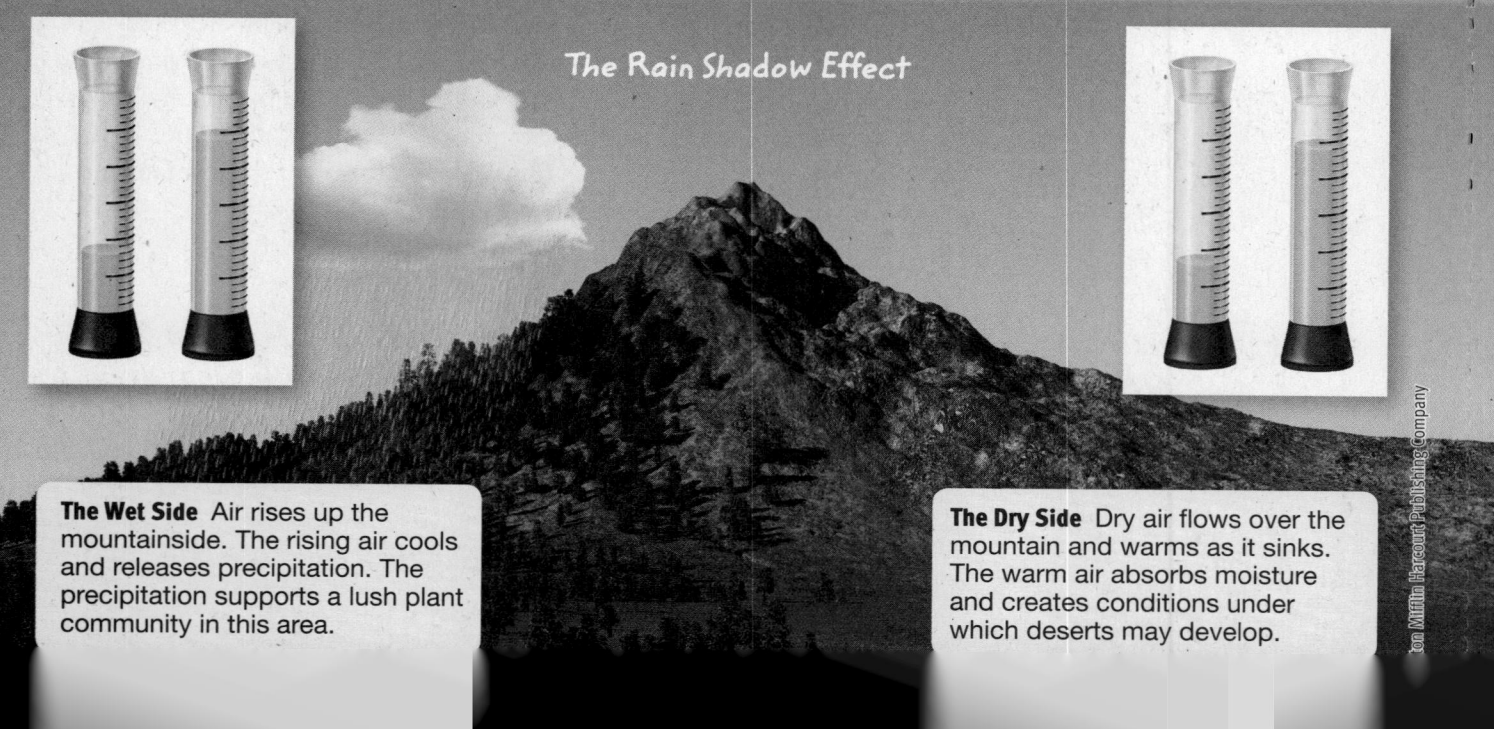

The Rain Shadow Effect

The Wet Side Air rises up the mountainside. The rising air cools and releases precipitation. The precipitation supports a lush plant community in this area.

The Dry Side Dry air flows over the mountain and warms as it sinks. The warm air absorbs moisture and creates conditions under which deserts may develop.

Elevation Influences Temperature

Elevation has a very strong effect on the temperature of an area. If you rode a cable car up a mountain, the temperature would decrease by about 6.5 °C (11.7 °F) for every kilometer you rose in elevation. Why does it get colder as you move higher up? Because the lower atmosphere is mainly warmed by Earth's surface that is directly below it. The warmed air lifts to higher elevations, where it expands and cools. Even close to the equator, temperatures at high elevations can be very cold. For example, Mount Kilimanjaro in Tanzania is close to the equator, but it is still cold enough at the peak to support a permanent glacier. The example below shows how one mountain can have several types of climates.

Visualize It!

14 Apply Circle the thermometer that shows the most likely temperature for each photo at different elevations.

Effects of Elevation

Haleakala, Maui

Elevation: 3,048 m (10,000 ft)

Elevation: 0 m (sea level)

15 Infer Generally, why are there no trees above a certain elevation on very tall mountains?

_____

_____

© Houghton Mifflin Harcourt Publishing Company • Image Credits: (t) ©Douglas Peebles Photography/Alamy; (bl) ©Randy Barnes/Aurora/Getty Images; (br) ©Tina Poole/Alamy

Waterfront Property

How do large bodies of water affect climate?

Large bodies of water, such as the ocean, can influence an area's climate. Water absorbs and releases energy as heat more slowly than land does. So, water helps moderate the temperature of nearby land. Sudden or extreme temperature changes rarely take place on land near large bodies of water. The state of Michigan, which is nearly surrounded by the Great Lakes, has more moderate temperatures than places far from large bodies of water at the same latitude. California's coastal climate is also influenced by a large body of water—the ocean. Places that are inland, but that are at the same latitude as a given place on California's coast, experience wider ranges of temperature.

Crescent City, California
Temperature Range:
4 °C to 19 °C
Latitude 41.8°N

Council Bluffs, Iowa
Temperature Range:
-11 °C to 30.5 °C
Latitude 41.3°N

Cleveland, Ohio
Temperature Range:
-4 °C to 28 °C
Latitude 41.4°N

GULF STREAM

ANTILLES CURRENT

CARIBBEAN CURRENT

Visualize It!

16 Apply Explain the difference in temperature ranges between Crescent City, Council Bluffs, and Cleveland.

_____

_____

_____

_____

_____

_____

How do ocean currents affect climate?

An *ocean current* is the movement of water in a certain direction. There are many different currents in the oceans. Ocean currents move water and distribute energy and nutrients around the globe. The currents on the surface of the ocean are called **surface currents.** Surface currents are driven by winds and carry warm water away from the equator and carry cool water away from the poles.

Cold currents cool the air in coastal areas, while warm currents warm the air in coastal areas. Thus, currents moderate global temperatures. For example, the Gulf Stream is a surface current that moves warm water from the Gulf of Mexico northeastward, toward Great Britain and Europe. The British climate is mild because of the warm Gulf Stream waters. Polar bears do not wander the streets of Great Britain, as they might in Natashquan, Canada, which is at a similar latitude.

NORWAY CURRENT

Natashquan, Canada
Temperature Range:
-18 °C to 14 °C
Latitude: 50.2°N

LABRADOR CURRENT

NORTH ATLANTIC CURRENT

London, England
Temperature Range:
2 °C to 22 °C
Latitude 51.5°N

GULF STREAM

ATLANTIC OCEAN

17 Summarize How do currents distribute heat around the globe?

_____

_____

_____

Visualize It!

18 Infer How do you think that the Canary current affects the temperature in the Canary Islands?

_____

_____

_____

CANARY CURRENT

Canary Islands, Spain
Temperature Range:
12 °C to 26 °C
Latitude 28°N

NORTH EQUATORIAL CURRENT

Zoning Out

What are the three major climate zones?

Earth has three major types of climate zones: tropical, temperate, and polar. These zones are shown below. Each zone has a distinct temperature range that relates to its latitude. Each of these zones has several types of climates. These different climates result from differences in topography, winds, ocean currents, and geography.

Temperate

Temperate climates have an average temperature below 18 °C (64 °F) in the coldest month and an average temperature above 10 °C (50 °F) in the warmest month. There are five temperate zone subclimates: marine west coast climates, steppe climates, humid continental climate, humid subtropical climate, and Mediterranean climate. The temperate zone is characterized by lower temperatures than the tropical zone. It is located between the tropical zone and the polar zone.

Visualize It!

20 Label What climate zone is this?

_____

Polar

The polar zone, at latitudes of 66.5° and higher, is the coldest climate zone. Temperatures rarely rise above 10 °C (50 °F) in the warmest month. The climates of the polar regions are referred to as the *polar climates*. There are three types of polar zone subclimates: subarctic climates, tundra climates, and polar ice cap climates.

ARCTIC OCEAN

NORTH AMERICA

ATLANTIC OCEAN

23.5°N

0°–Equator

PACIFIC OCEAN

SOUTH AMERICA

23.5°S

66.5°S

SOUTH

21 Summarize Fill in the table for either the factor that affects climate or the effect on climate the given factor has.

Factor	Effect on climate
Latitude	
	Cooler temperatures as you travel up a tall mountain
Winds	
	Moderates weather so that highs and lows are less extreme
Surface ocean currents	
	Impacts wind patterns and the transfer of energy in an area

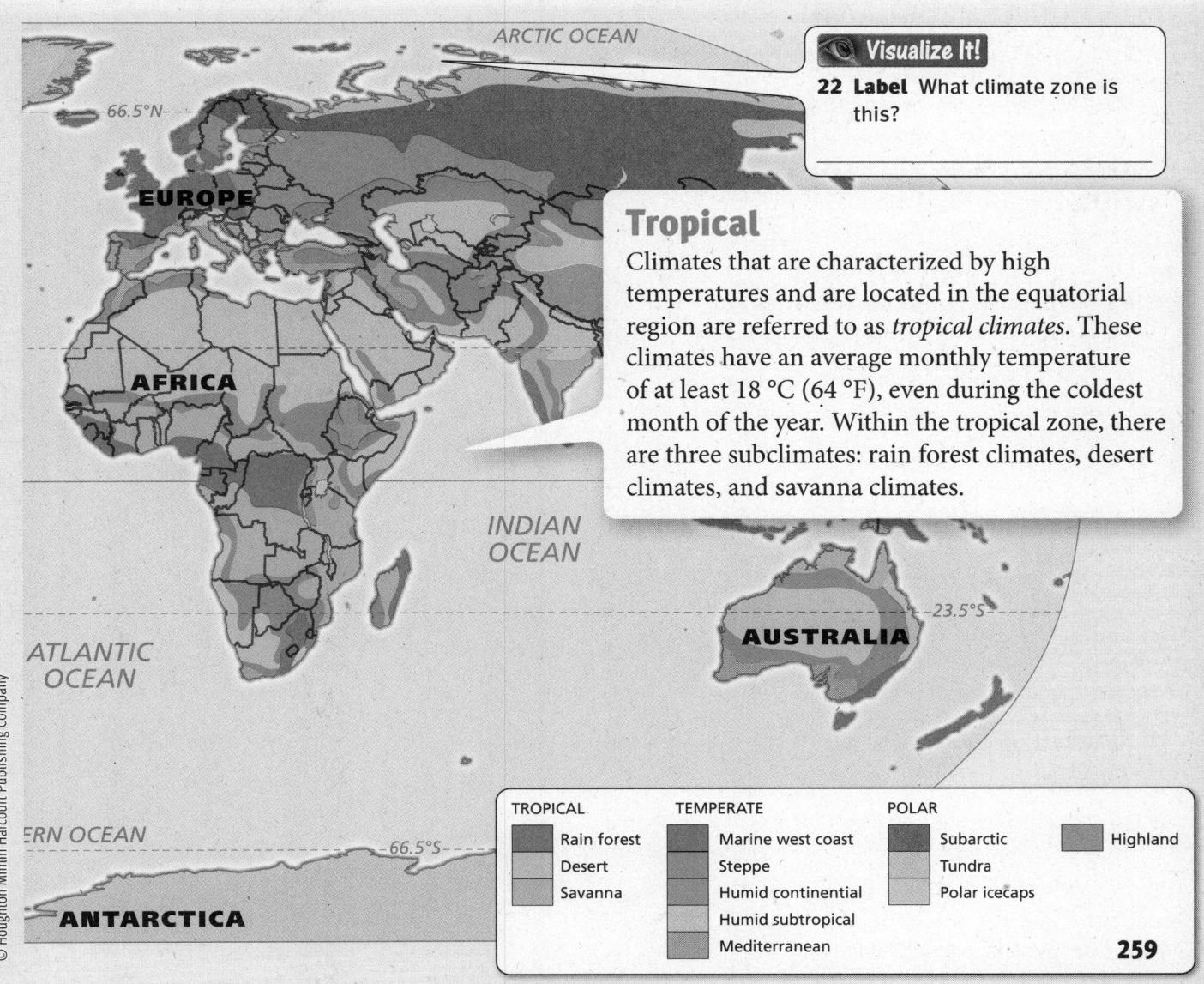

Visualize It!

22 Label What climate zone is this?

Tropical

Climates that are characterized by high temperatures and are located in the equatorial region are referred to as *tropical climates*. These climates have an average monthly temperature of at least 18 °C (64 °F), even during the coldest month of the year. Within the tropical zone, there are three subclimates: rain forest climates, desert climates, and savanna climates.

ARCTIC OCEAN

66.5°N

EUROPE

AFRICA

INDIAN OCEAN

ATLANTIC OCEAN

AUSTRALIA

23.5°S

ERN OCEAN

66.5°S

ANTARCTICA

TROPICAL	TEMPERATE	POLAR	
Rain forest	Marine west coast	Subarctic	Highland
Desert	Steppe	Tundra	
Savanna	Humid continental	Polar icecaps	
	Humid subtropical		
	Mediterranean		

Visual Summary

To complete this summary, circle the correct word or phrase. Then, use the key below to check your answers. You can use this page to review the main concepts of the lesson.

Climate

Temperature and precipitation are used to describe climate.

23 Climate is the characteristic weather conditions in a place over a short/long period.

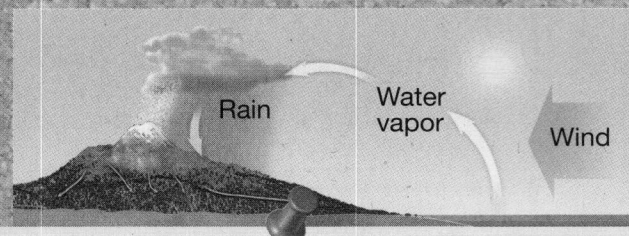

Rain   Water vapor   Wind

Winds transfer energy and moisture to new places.

24 Winds can affect the amount of precipitation in/elevation of an area.

Both topography and elevation affect climate.

25 Temperatures decrease as elevation increases/decreases.

Large bodies of water and ocean currents both affect climate.

26 Large bodies of water affect the climate of nearby land when cool waters absorb energy as heat from the warm air/cold land.

There are three main climate zones and many subclimates within those zones.

27 The three main types of climate zones are polar, temperate, and equatorial/tropical.

28 The three main climate zones are determined by elevation/latitude.

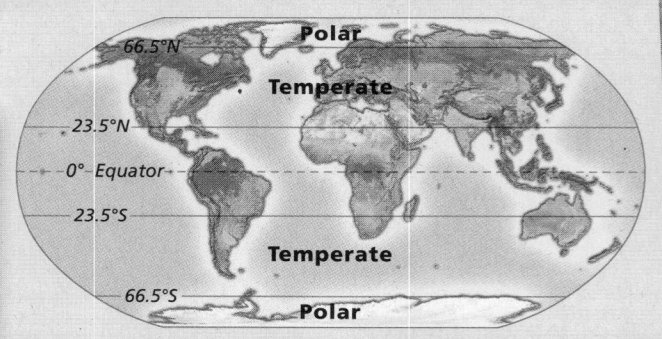

Polar
66.5°N
Temperate
23.5°N
0° Equator
23.5°S
Temperate
66.5°S
Polar

Answers: 23 long; 24 precipitation; 25 increases; 26 warm air; 27 tropical; 28 latitude

29 **Analyze** How does temperature change with elevation and latitude?

Lesson Review

Vocabulary

In your own words, define the following terms.

1 topography

_____

_____

2 climate

_____

_____

Key Concepts

Fill in the table below.

Factor	Effect on Climate
3 Identify Latitude	
4 Identify Elevation	
5 Identify Large bodies of water	
6 Identify Wind	

7 Explain What provides Great Britain with a moderate climate? How?

_____

_____

_____

8 Identify What are two characteristics used to describe the climate of an area?

_____

Critical Thinking

Use the image below to answer the following question.

9 Explain Location A receives nearly 200 cm of rain each year, while Location B receives only 30 cm. Explain why Location A gets so much more rain. Use the words *rain shadow* and *precipitation* in your answer.

_____

_____

_____

_____

_____

_____

10 Analyze What climate zone are you in if the temperatures are always very warm? Where is this zone located on Earth?

_____

11 Analyze How does the sun's energy affect the climate of an area?

_____

_____

_____

_____

_____

My Notes

Lesson 4

Climate Change

ESSENTIAL QUESTION

What are the causes and effects of climate change?

By the end of this lesson, you should be able to describe climate change and the causes and effects of climate change.

Temperatures are rising in the Arctic. Warmer temperatures cause the ice sheets to freeze later and melt sooner. With less time on the ice to hunt for seals, polar bears are struggling to survive.

OHIO **7.ESS.2** Thermal-energy transfers in the ocean and the atmosphere contribute to the formation of currents, which influence global climate patterns.

OHIO **7.SIA.4** Analyze and interpret data.

OHIO **7.SIA.5** Develop descriptions, models, explanations and predictions.

OHIO **7.SIA.6** Think critically and logically to connect evidence and explanations.

🌎 Engage Your Brain

1 Predict Check T or F to show whether you think each statement is true or false.

T   F

☐   ☐ There have been periods on Earth when the climate was colder than the climate is today.

☐   ☐ The ocean does not play a role in climate.

☐   ☐ Earth's climate is currently warming.

☐   ☐ Humans are contributing to changes in climate.

2 Describe Write your own caption relating this photo to climate change.

_____

_____

_____

✏️ Active Reading

3 Apply Many scientific terms, such as *greenhouse effect,* also have everyday meanings. Use context clues to write your own definition for the words *greenhouse* and *effect.*

Example sentence
The <u>greenhouse</u> is filled with tropical plants that are found in Central America.

greenhouse:

_____

_____

_____

Example sentence
What are some of the <u>effects</u> of staying up too late?

effect:

_____

_____

_____

Vocabulary Terms

• ice age
• greenhouse effect
• global warming

4 Identify As you read, create a reference card for each vocabulary term. On one side of the card, write the term and its meaning. On the other side, draw an image that illustrates or makes a connection to the term. These cards can be used as bookmarks in the text so that you can refer to them while studying.

The Temps are a–**Changin'**

What are some natural causes of climate change?

The weather conditions in an area over a long period of time are called *climate*. Natural factors have changed Earth's climate many times during our planet's history. Natural changes in climate can be long-term or short-term.

Movement of Tectonic Plates

Tectonic plate motion has contributed to long-term climate change over billions of years. And Earth's plates are still moving!

The present continents once fit together as a single landmass called *Pangaea* (pan•JEE•uh). Pangaea began to break up about 200 million years ago. By 20 million years ago, the continents had moved close to their current positions. Some continents grew warmer as they moved closer to the equator. Other continents, such as Antarctica, moved to colder, higher latitudes.

The eruption of Mt. Pinatubo sent ash and gases as high as 34 km into the atmosphere.

Visualize It!

5 Infer Today, Antarctica is the coldest desert on Earth. But fossils of trees and dinosaurs have been found on this harsh continent. Explain how life could thrive on ancient Antarctica.

_____

_____

_____

_____

_____

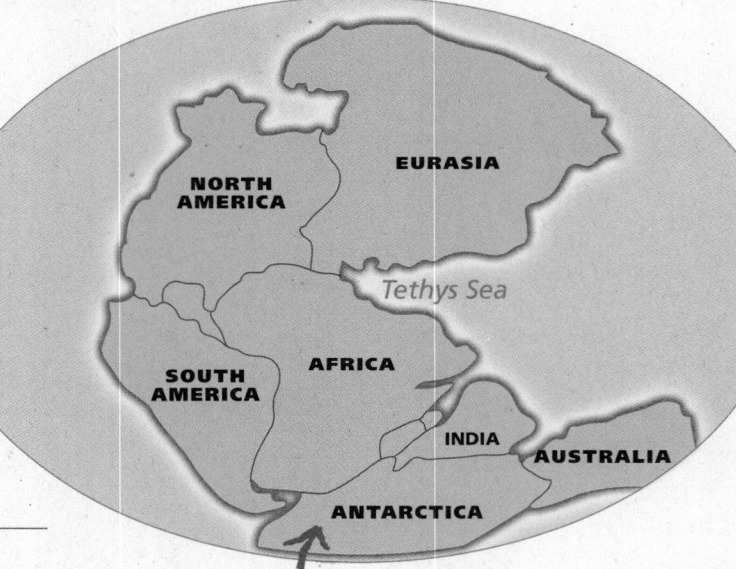

Antarctica was part of the supercontinent Pangaea about 250 million years ago. Antarctica is located at the South Pole today.

If you look closely at the current shapes of the continents, you can see how they once fit together to form Pangaea.

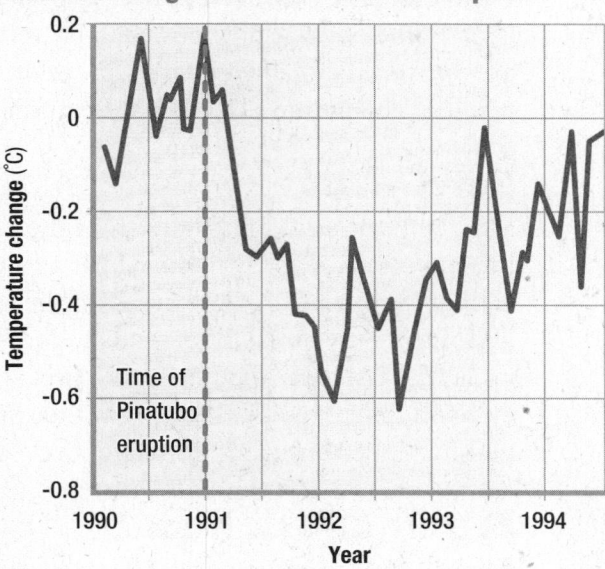

Climate Change After Mt. Pinatubo Eruption

Temperature change (°C) vs. Year (1990–1994)

Time of Pinatubo eruption

Source: Goddard Institute for Space Studies, NASA, 1997

This graph shows the *change* in average global temperature, not the actual temperature.

Particles in the Atmosphere

Short-term changes in climate can be due to natural events that send *particulates* into the atmosphere. Particulates are tiny, solid particles that are suspended in air or water. They absorb some of the sun's energy and reflect some of the sun's energy back into space. This process temporarily lowers temperatures on Earth.

Where do particulates come from? Asteroid impacts throw large amounts of dust into the atmosphere. Dust from the asteroid that struck near Mexico around 65 million years ago would have blocked the sun's rays. This reduction in sunlight may have limited photosynthesis in plants. The loss of plant life may have caused the food chain to collapse and led to dinosaur extinction.

Volcanic eruptions also release enormous clouds of ash and gases into the atmosphere. Particulates from large eruptions can circle Earth. The average global surface temperature fell by about 0.5 °C for several years after the 1991 eruption of Mt. Pinatubo in the Philippines. Twenty million tons of sulfur dioxide and 5 km³ of ash were blasted into the atmosphere. The sulfur-rich gases combined with water to form an Earth-cooling haze.

Active Reading **7 Describe** Give one example of a long-term and one example of a short-term change in climate caused by natural factors.

_____

_____

Visualize It!

6 Analyze What happened to global temperatures after the eruption of Mt. Pinatubo? How long did this effect last?

_____

_____

_____

© Houghton Mifflin Harcourt Publishing Company • Image Credits: (t) ©StockTrek/Photodisc/Getty Images

What are some causes of repeating patterns of climate change?

From day to day, or even year to year, the weather can change quite a lot. Some of these changes are relatively unpredictable, but others are due to predictable patterns or cycles. These patterns are the result of changes in the way energy is distributed around Earth.

Sun Cycles

Most of Earth's energy comes from the sun. And the output from the sun is very slightly higher during times of higher sunspot activity. Sunspots are dark areas on the sun that appear and disappear. Sunspot activity tends to increase and decrease in a cycle that lasts approximately 11 years. The effect of this sunspot cycle on global temperatures is not dramatic. But studies show a possible link between the sunspot cycle and global rain patterns.

El Niño and La Niña

Changes in ocean temperature also affect climate. During El Niño years, ocean temperatures are higher than usual in the tropical Pacific Ocean. The warmer water causes changes in global weather patterns. Some areas are cooler and wetter than normal. Other areas are warmer and dryer than normal.

The opposite effect occurs during La Niña years. Ocean temperatures are cooler than normal in the equatorial eastern Pacific Ocean. El Niño and La Niña conditions usually alternate, and both can lead to conditions such as droughts and flooding.

During El Niño years, heavy rains fall in the usually dry southwestern United States. This rain can cause floods that wash out roads.

 Do the Math

8 Calculate About what percentage of years are El Niño years, with warmer than average ocean temperatures? About what percentage are La Niña years? About what percentage are neither El Niño or La Niña years?

_____

_____

Cycles of El Niño and La Niña

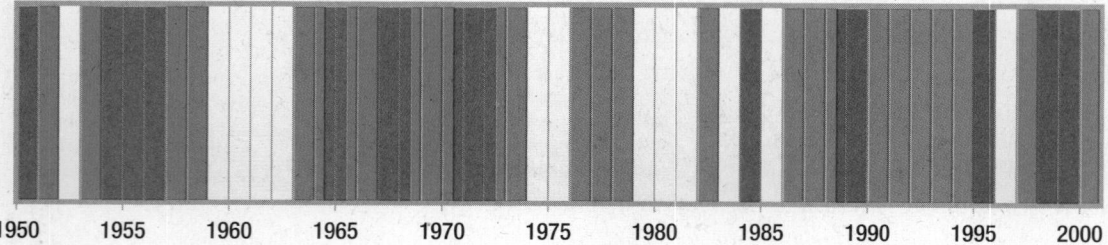

1950   1955   1960   1965   1970   1975   1980   1985   1990   1995   2000

■ La Niña years
■ El Niño years

Source: International Research Institute for Climate and Society, Columbia University, 2007

During the last 2 million years, continental ice sheets have expanded far beyond the polar regions. There have been multiple advances of ice sheets (glacial periods) and retreats of ice sheets (interglacial periods). The timeline shows recent glacial and interglacial periods.

Cycles of the Recent Ice Age

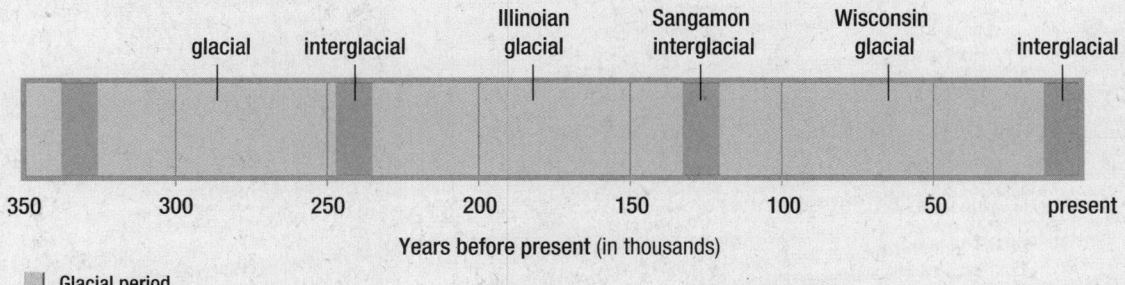

| glacial | interglacial | Illinoian glacial | Sangamon interglacial | Wisconsin glacial | interglacial |

350   300   250   200   150   100   50   present

Years before present (in thousands)

☐ Glacial period
☐ Interglacial period

Source: NOAA Paleoclimatology, 2007

Much of North America was covered with thick ice sheets during the last glacial period. This glacial period ended 10,000 to 14,000 years ago.

PACIFIC OCEAN

NORTH AMERICA

ATLANTIC OCEAN

☐ Land covered by ice
— Ice Age shoreline
— Present-day shoreline
— Present-day border

Ice Ages

The geological record shows that at different times Earth's climate has been both cooler *and* warmer than it is today. Earth's history contains multiple extremely cold periods when thick sheets of ice covered much of the continents. These periods are called *ice ages*. An **ice age** is a long period of cooling during which ice sheets spread beyond the polar regions. The exact cause of ice ages is not fully understood. Some hypotheses propose that ice ages include changes in Earth's orbit, shifts in the balance of incoming and outgoing solar radiation, and changes in heat exchange rates between the equator and the poles.

Geologic evidence indicates that ice ages occur over widely spaced intervals of time—approximately every 200 million years. Each ice age lasts for millions of years. The most recent ice age began about 2 million years ago, with its peak about 20,000 years ago. Large ice sheets still cover Greenland and Antarctica.

Active Reading **10 List** What are some possible causes of ice ages?

_____

9 Infer Locate your home state on the map. Then, describe the climate your state likely experienced during the last glacial period.

_____

_____

_____

Is It Getting HOTTER?

How do humans affect climate change?

Although natural events cause climate change, human activities may also affect Earth's climate. Human activities can cause the planet to warm when greenhouse gases are released into the atmosphere. Certain gases in the atmosphere, known as *greenhouse gases*, warm Earth's surface and the lower atmosphere by a process called the *greenhouse effect*. The **greenhouse effect** is the process by which gases in the atmosphere absorb and radiate energy as heat back to Earth. Greenhouse gases include carbon dioxide (CO_2), water vapor, methane, and nitrous oxide. Without greenhouse gases, energy would escape into space, and Earth would be colder. Two ways that humans release greenhouse gases into the atmosphere are by burning fossil fuels and by deforestation.

Active Reading 11 **List** What are four greenhouse gases?

Smokestacks from a coal-burning power plant release water vapor and carbon dioxide into the atmosphere. Water vapor and carbon dioxide are greenhouse gases.

By Burning Fossil Fuels

There is now evidence to support the idea that humans are causing a rise in global CO_2 levels. Burning fossil fuels, such as gasoline and coal, adds greenhouse gases to the atmosphere. Since the 1950s, scientists have measured increasing levels of CO_2 and other greenhouse gases in the atmosphere. During this same period, the average global surface temperature has also been rising.

Correlation is when two sets of data show patterns that can be related. Both CO_2 level and average global surface temperature have been increasing over the same period of time, as shown by the graphs on the following page. So, there is a correlation between CO_2 levels in Earth's atmosphere and rising temperature. However, even though the two trends can be correlated, this does not show causation, or that one causes the other. In order to show causation, an explanation for how one change causes another has to be accepted. The explanation lies in the greenhouse effect. CO_2 is a greenhouse gas. An increase in greenhouse gases will warm Earth's surface and lower atmosphere. As greenhouse gas levels in the atmosphere have been rising, Earth's surface temperatures have been increasing, and so have temperatures in Earth's lower atmosphere. This shows that it is likely that rising CO_2 levels are causing global warming.

By Deforestation

Some processes, such as burning fossil fuels, add CO_2 and other carbon-based gases to the atmosphere. Processes that emit carbon into the atmosphere are called *carbon sources*. Processes such as the growth of plants and trees remove carbon from the atmosphere. Processes that remove carbon from the atmosphere are called *carbon sinks*. Deforestation is the mass removal of trees for farming, timber, and land development. The loss of trees represents the loss of an important carbon sink. Deforestation often includes the burning of trees, which is another source of carbon dioxide. So deforestation affects the amount of carbon in the atmosphere by converting a carbon sink into a carbon source.

Scientists think that the deforestation of rain forests plays a large role in greenhouse gas emissions. Tropical deforestation is thought to release 1.5 billion tons of carbon each year.

Active Reading **12 Describe** How does deforestation affect the amount of carbon dioxide that is in the atmosphere?

_____

_____

Deforestation is one of the leading sources of greenhouse gases.

Visualize It!

13 Apply Based on the trend shown in the graph, how do you expect CO_2 levels to change over the next 20 years?

_____

_____

14 Explain Describe the changes in average global temperature during the years represented by the CO_2 graph.

_____

_____

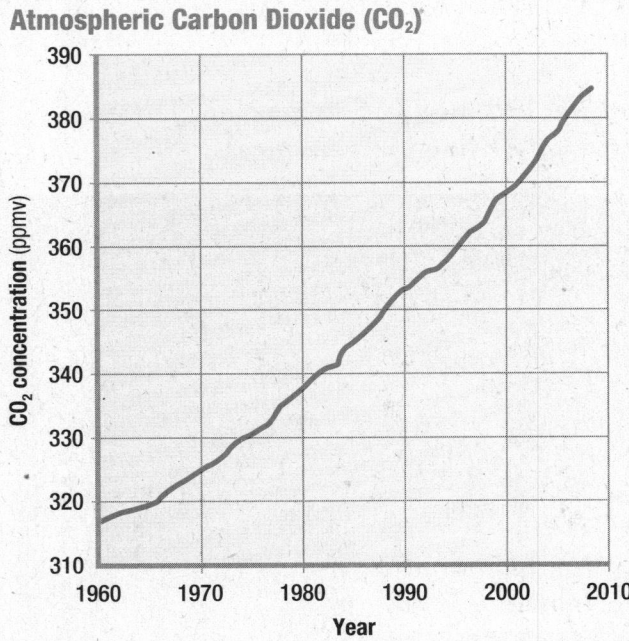

Atmospheric Carbon Dioxide (CO_2)

Source: Scripps Institution of Oceanography, UCSD, 2010

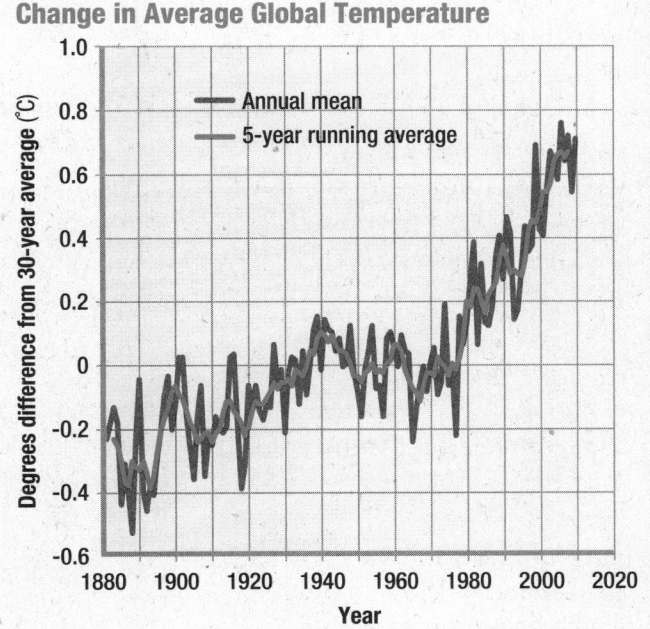

Change in Average Global Temperature

Source: Goddard Institute for Space Studies, NASA, 2010

What are some predicted effects of climate change?

Data show that the world's climate has been warming in recent years. **Global warming** is a gradual increase in average global temperature. Global warming will affect global weather patterns, global sea level, and life on Earth.

Effects on the Atmosphere

Studies show that the average global surface temperature has increased by about 0.3 °C to 0.8 °C over the last 100 years. Even small changes in temperature can greatly affect weather and precipitation. Scientists predict that warming will generate more severe weather. Predictions suggest that storms will be more powerful and occur more frequently. It has also been predicted that as much as half of Earth's surface may be affected by drought.

Effects on the Hydrosphere and Cryosphere

Much of the ice on Earth occurs in glaciers in mountains, arctic sea ice, and ice sheets that cover Greenland and Antarctica. As temperatures increase, some of this ice will melt. A 2010 report observed record-setting hot temperatures, which resulted in record ice melt of the Greenland ice sheet.

When ice on land melts, global sea level rises because water flows into the ocean. Global sea level rose by 10 to 20 cm during the 1900s. Scientists project that sea level may rise 60 cm by 2100. Higher sea level is expected to increase flooding in coastal areas, some of which are highly populated. New York City; Shanghai, China; and Mumbai, India; are some cities that could be affected.

15 Infer How do melting ice caps and glaciers affect sea level?

_____

_____

_____

Mt. Kilimanjaro has lost much of its glacier in recent years due to rising temperatures.

Mt. Kilimanjaro February 1993

Mt. Kilimanjaro February 2000

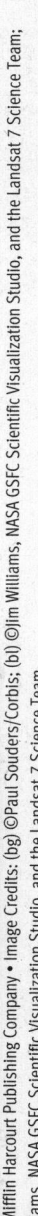© Houghton Mifflin Harcourt Publishing Company • Image Credits: (bg) ©Paul Souders/Corbis; (bl) ©Jim Williams, NASA GSFC Scientific Visualization Studio, and the Landsat 7 Science Team; (br) ©Jim Williams, NASA GSFC Scientific Visualization Studio, and the Landsat 7 Science Team

A warmer climate may force some species northward, including sugar maples.

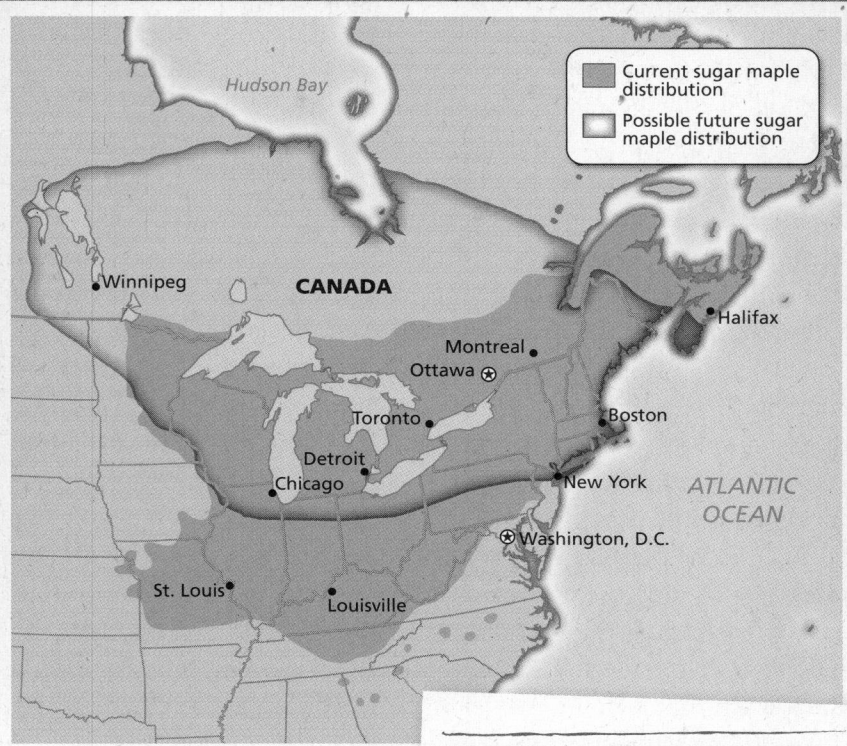

Hudson Bay

Current sugar maple distribution
Possible future sugar maple distribution

Winnipeg

CANADA

Halifax

Montreal
Ottawa ⊛
Toronto
Detroit
Chicago
Boston
New York
Washington, D.C. ⊛

ATLANTIC OCEAN

St. Louis
Louisville

Effects on the Biosphere

Active Reading **17 Summarize** Underline some of the effects of predicted climate change on the biosphere.

Scientists predict that global warming will change ecosystems. These changes may threaten the survival of many plant and animal species. Some species may move to cooler areas or even go extinct. Some butterflies, foxes, and alpine plants have already moved north to cooler climates. In Antarctica, emperor penguin populations could be reduced by as much as 95 percent by the end of this century if sea ice loss continues at its current rate. On the other hand, some species may benefit from expanded habitats in a warmer world.

Changes in temperature and precipitation will affect crops and livestock. If Earth warms more than a few degrees Celsius, many of the world's farms could suffer. Higher temperatures, reduced rainfall, and severe flooding can reduce crop production. Changes in weather will especially affect developing countries with large rural areas, such as countries in South Asia. A less severe warming would actually help agriculture in some regions by lengthening the growing season.

Warmer temperatures could increase the number of heat-related deaths and deaths from certain diseases, such as malaria. However, deaths associated with extreme cold could decrease.

16 Infer Some plant home ranges are shifting northward due to regional warming. What might happen to plant populations that are unable to spread northward?

_____

_____

_____

_____

How are climate predictions made?

Instruments have been placed in the atmosphere, in the oceans, on land, and in space to collect climate data. NASA now has more than a dozen spacecraft in orbit that are providing continuous data on Earth's climate. These data are added to historical climate data that are made available to researchers at centers worldwide. The data are used to create climate models. *Climate models* use mathematical formulas to describe how different variables affect Earth's climate. Today, there are about a dozen climate models that can be used to simulate different parts of the Earth system and the interactions that take place between them.

When designing a model to predict future climate change, scientists first model Earth's current climate system. If the model does a good job describing current conditions, then the variables are changed to reflect future conditions. Scientists usually run the model multiple times using different variables.

Climate models are the means by which scientists predict the effects of an increase in greenhouse gases on future global climate. These models use the best data available about the ways in which Earth's systems interact. No climate model can perfectly reproduce the system that is being modeled. However, as our understanding of Earth's systems improves, models of climate change are becoming more accurate.

Visualize It!

18 Predict As Earth is warming, the oceans are rising. This is due to both melting ice and the expansion of water as it warms. Predict what the change in sea level will be by the year 2020 if the current trend continues. You may draw on the graph to extend the current trend.

_____

_____

Sea level has been rising steadily since the late 1800s. By the year 2000, global average sea level had risen 50 mm above mean sea level, represented by 0 on the graph.

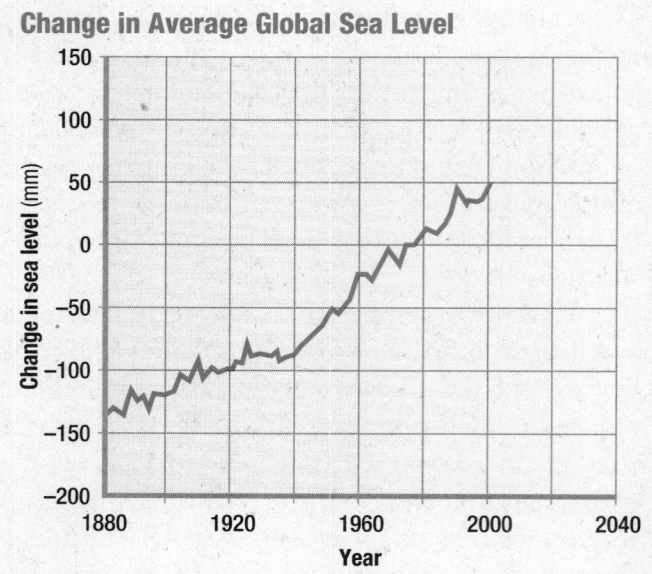

Change in Average Global Sea Level

Source: National Climatic Data Center, NOAA, 2007

Think Clean and Green

How can people reduce their impact on climate change?

People can take action to reduce climate change and its effects. Countries are working together to reduce their impact on Earth's climate. Communities and individuals are also doing their part to reduce greenhouse gas emissions.

Reduce Greenhouse Gas Emissions

The Kyoto Protocol, an international environmental agreement to reduce greenhouse gas emissions, was adopted in 1997. The Kyoto Protocol is the only existing international treaty in which nations have agreed to reduce CO_2 emissions. As of 2010, 191 countries had signed the protocol. At present, the Kyoto Protocol faces many complex challenges. One of the greatest challenges is that developing nations, which will be the largest future sources of CO_2 emissions, did not sign the protocol.

Individuals can reduce their impact on climate by conserving energy, increasing energy efficiency, and reducing the use of fossil fuels. Greenhouse gas emissions can be reduced by driving less and by switching to nonpolluting energy sources. Simple energy conservation solutions include turning off lights and replacing light bulbs. Recycling and reusing products also reduce energy use.

For most materials, recycling uses less energy than making products from scratch. That means less greenhouse gases are emitted.

Do the Math — You Try It

19 Calculate How much energy is saved by using recycled aluminum to make new aluminum cans instead of making aluminum cans from raw materials?

_____

_____

20 Calculate By what percentage does recycling aluminum reduce energy use?

_____

_____

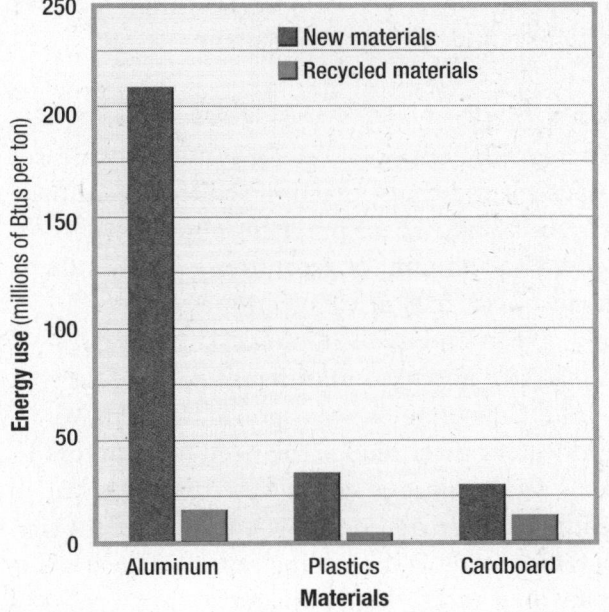

Energy Use for New vs. Recycled Materials

Source: US EPA Solid Waste Management and Greenhouse Gases, 2002

- Reduce use of automobile.
- Use new, cleaner technologies.
- Plant a tree.

Reduce the Rate of Deforestation

Deforestation contributes up to 20 percent of greenhouse gases globally. Planting trees and supporting reforestation programs are ways that carbon sources can be balanced by carbon sinks. Another solution is to educate people about the importance of the carbon that is stored in forests for stabilizing climate. In 2008, the United Nations began a program called REDD, or *Reducing Emissions from Deforestation and Forest Degradation*. REDD offers incentives to developing countries to reduce deforestation. The program also teaches conservation methods, which include forestry management.

Use New Technologies

Energy-efficient practices for homes, businesses, industry, and transportation reduce greenhouse gas emissions. These practices not only reduce the amount of greenhouse gases in the atmosphere, they also save money.

Clean-energy technologies are being researched and used in different parts of the world. New biofuels, solar power, wind power, and water power reduce the need to burn fossil fuels. In the United States, water power is the leading source of renewable energy, and the use of wind power is increasing rapidly. However, many new technologies are currently more expensive than fossil fuels.

21 Summarize Use the table to summarize ways in which sources of greenhouse gases in the atmosphere can be reduced.

Sources of greenhouse gases	Ways to reduce greenhouse gases
cars	Walk or use bikes more often.

What are some economic and political issues related to climate change?

![icon] **Active Reading** **22 Identify** Underline some of the economic and political issues that are related to climate change.

Climate change affects the entire Earth, no matter where greenhouse gases are produced. This makes climate change a global issue. The scientific concerns that climate change poses are not the only issues that have to be taken into account. There are economic and political issues involving climate change that are equally important.

Climate change is an economic issue. The cost of climate change includes the costs of crop failure, storm damage, and human disease. However, developing countries may not be able to afford technologies needed to reduce human impact on climate.

Climate change is also a political issue. Political action can lead to regulations that reduce greenhouse gas emissions. However, these laws may be challenged by groups who disagree with the need for change or disagree about what needs to change. No matter what choices are made to handle the challenges of climate change, it will take groups of people working together to make a difference.

Think Outside the Book **Inquiry**

23 Apply Research a recent extreme weather event from anywhere in the world. How might this event be related to climate change? Present your findings to the class as a news report or poster.

Climate change may make unusual weather the new norm. Rome, Italy, was brought to a standstill by unusually cold and snowy weather in 2010.

In Australia, years of unusually dry and hot weather led to devastating forest fires in 2009. Australia also suffered damaging floods in 2010.

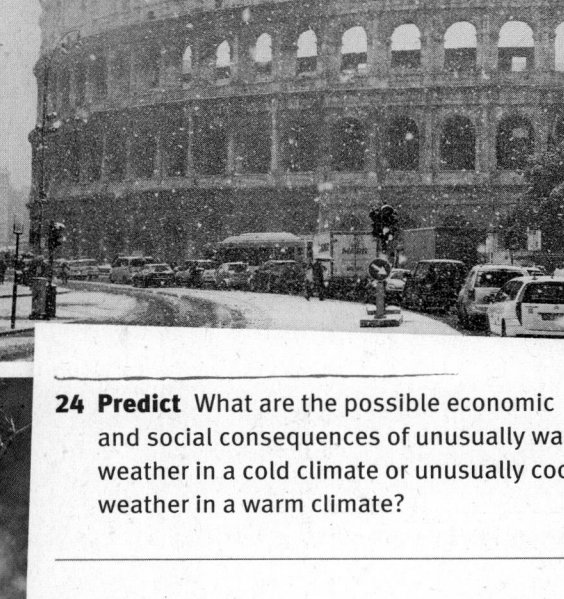

24 Predict What are the possible economic and social consequences of unusually warm weather in a cold climate or unusually cool weather in a warm climate?

_____

_____

_____

Visual Summary

To complete this summary, fill in the blanks with the missing word or phrase. Then, use the key below to check your answers. You can use this page to review the main concepts of the lesson.

Natural factors have changed Earth's climate many times during Earth's history.

25 _____ have moved across Earth's surface over time and once formed a supercontinent called Pangaea.

Global warming affects many of Earth's systems.

27 If average global surface temperature continues to rise, then severe storms may become more _____.

Climate Change

Greenhouse gases have a warming effect on the surface of Earth.

26 Scientists think that there is a connection between rising levels of _____ and rising _____

There are steps that people can take to reduce their impact on climate change.

28 People can reduce their impact on climate change by reducing greenhouse emissions and deforestation, and by _____

29 Synthesize How can burning fossil fuels cause global warming?

Lesson Review

Vocabulary

Fill in the blank with the term that best completes the following sentences.

1 _____ is a gradual increase in average global surface temperature.

2 A long period of climate cooling during which ice sheets spread beyond the polar regions is called a(n) _____

3 The warming of Earth's surface and lower atmosphere that occurs when greenhouse gases absorb and reradiate energy is called the

_____

Key Concepts

4 Identify What are some natural events that have caused changes in Earth's climate?

_____
_____
_____
_____
_____

5 Identify What are some predicted effects of climate change linked to global warming?

_____
_____
_____
_____
_____
_____

6 Summarize List ways in which humans can reduce the rate of climate change.

_____
_____
_____
_____
_____
_____

Critical Thinking

Use the graph to answer the following questions.

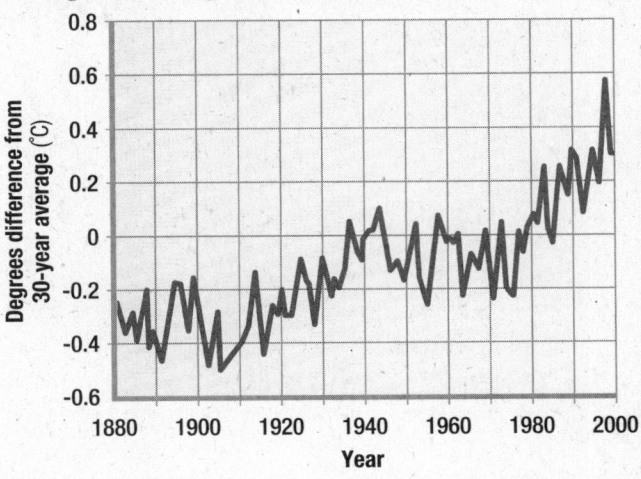

Change in Average Global Temperature

Source: Goddard Institute for Space Studies, NASA, 2010

7 Analyze Describe the trend shown in this graph. Why is it helpful to have many decades of data to make a graph such as this?

_____
_____
_____
_____

8 Infer What might cause average global surface temperature to rise and fall from year to year?

_____
_____
_____
_____
_____

9 Infer Why might some countries be more reluctant than others to take steps to reduce levels of greenhouse gases?

_____
_____
_____
_____
_____
_____

My Notes

Unit 4 [Big Idea]

Air pressure, temperature, air movement, and humidity in the atmosphere affect both weather and climate.

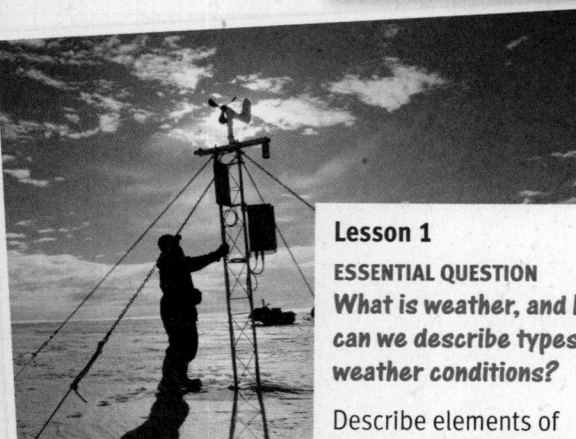

Lesson 1

ESSENTIAL QUESTION
What is weather, and how can we describe types of weather conditions?

Describe elements of weather, and explain how they are measured.

Lesson 2

ESSENTIAL QUESTION
How do the water cycle and other global patterns affect local weather?

Explain how global patterns in Earth's system influence weather.

Lesson 3

ESSENTIAL QUESTION
How is climate affected by energy from the sun and variations on Earth's surface?

Describe the main factors that affect climate, and explain how scientists classify climates.

Lesson 4

ESSENTIAL QUESTION
What are the causes and effects of climate change?

Describe climate change and the causes and effects of climate change.

Connect ESSENTIAL QUESTIONS
Lessons 1 and 2

1 Synthesize Explain how a change in air pressure can signal a change in weather.

_____
_____
_____
_____
_____
_____
_____

Think Outside the Book

2 Synthesize Choose one of these activities to help synthesize what you have learned in this unit.

☐ Using what you learned in lessons 1 and 2, present a poster to explain how latitude affects global weather patterns.

☐ Using what you learned in lessons 2, 3, and 4, explain in a short essay how weather predictions might change if additional greenhouse gases in Earth's atmosphere caused Earth to warm by several degrees C.

Unit 4 Review

Name _____

Vocabulary

Fill in each blank with the term that best completes the following sentences.

1 _____ is the ratio of the amount of water vapor in the air to the amount of water vapor needed to reach saturation at a given temperature.

2 The temperature at which more condensation than evaporation occurs is called the _____ .

3 _____ is any form of water that falls to Earth's surface from the clouds.

4 _____ is the characteristic weather conditions in an area over a long period of time.

5 A long period of climate cooling during which ice sheets spread beyond the polar regions is called a(n) _____.

Key Concepts

Choose the letter of the best answer.

6 The graph shows the temperatures recorded at school one day.

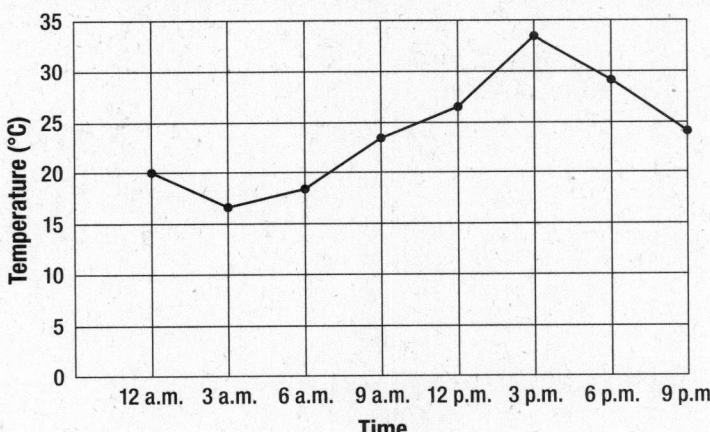

What can these temperature data tell us?

A The highest temperature of the day occurred at 6 p.m.

B The amount of water vapor in the air changed that day.

C The amount of energy as heat in the air changed during that day.

D The climate changed between 3 a.m. and 3 p.m.

7 Which of these types of weather data is measured using a barometer?

A air pressure   **C** relative humidity

B precipitation   **D** wind speed

8 Refer to the regions A, B, C, and D shown on the U.S. map below.

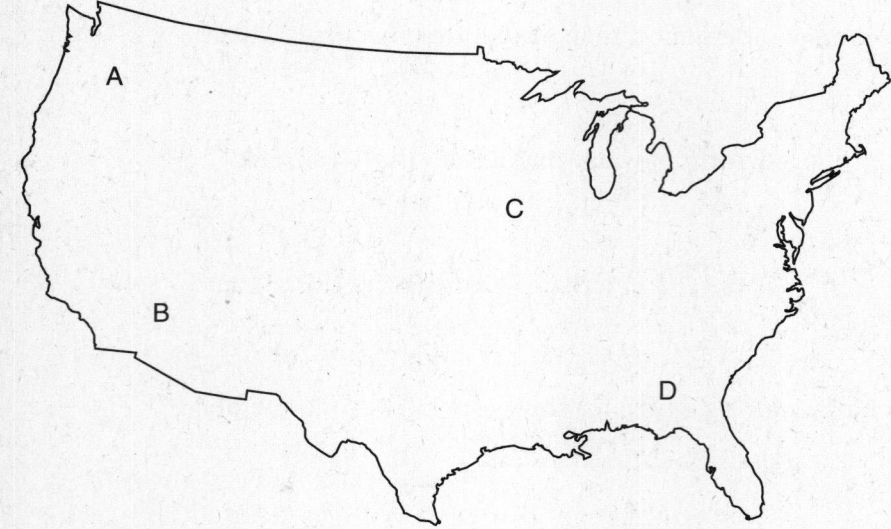

In which of these directions is the jet stream most likely to flow?

A from D to C   **C** from C to A

B from A to C   **D** from C to B

9 What are the two main factors that determine climate?

A temperature and wind

B temperature and precipitation

C air pressure and humidity

D wind and precipitation

10 The picture below shows an exaggerated side view of an ocean on the left and a mountain range on the right. The arrows indicate the movement of air and moisture from the ocean.

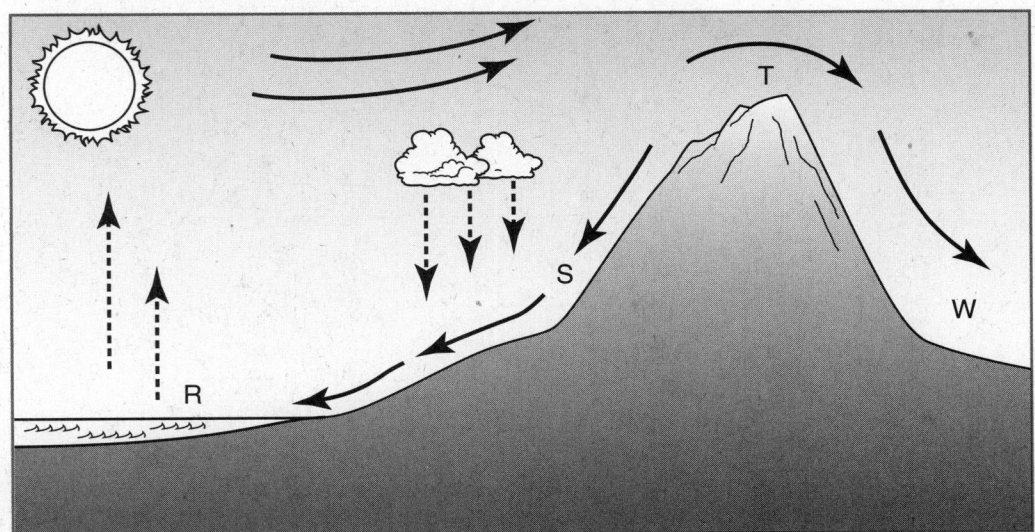

Which region is most likely to have a dry, desert-like climate?

A region R

B region S

C region T

D region W

11 Which of these is not a currently predicted effect of global climate change?

A rising sea levels

B increased precipitation everywhere on the globe

C reduction in Arctic sea ice

D more severe storms

Critical Thinking

Answer the following questions in the spaces provided.

12 How can humans be considered a negative factor in the issue of climate change and global warming? How can humans be considered a positive factor in the issue of climate change and global warming?

_____

_____

_____

_____

13 The map below shows the three different climate zones on Earth.

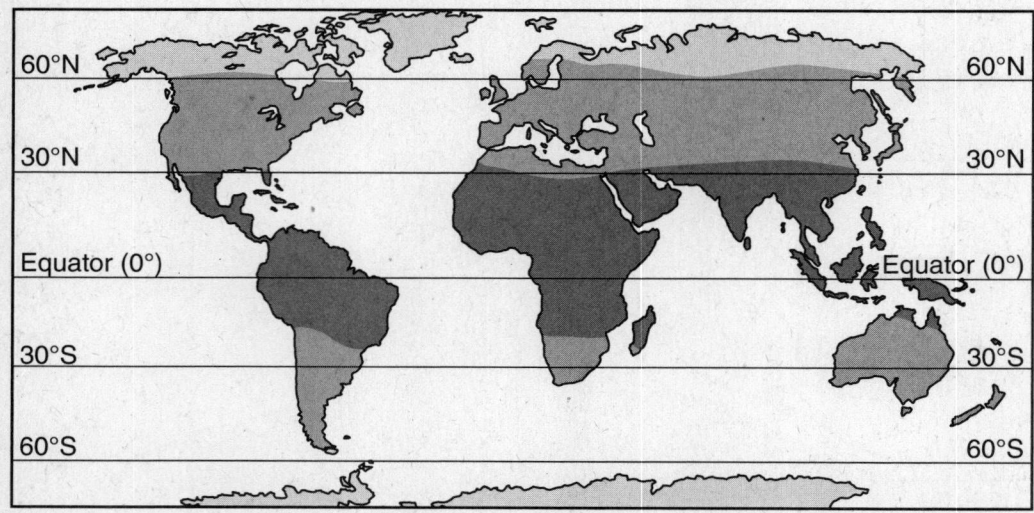

Label each climate zone on the map. Then describe the temperature and precipitation typical of each zone.

_____

_____

_____

Explain how latitude affects the climate of each zone.

_____

_____

_____

Connect **ESSENTIAL QUESTIONS**
Lessons 1, 2, and 3

Answer the following question in the space provided.

14 Even if you do not live on a coast, the movement of water in the oceans and water vapor in the atmosphere over the oceans does affect your weather. Describe how the global movement of water through ocean currents and winds affect the climate of your local region.

_____

_____

_____

_____

_____

_____

The Earth-Moon-Sun System

Big Idea

Earth and the moon move in predictable ways and have predictable effects on each other as they orbit the sun.

What do you think?

Earth is affected by its sun and moon. The sun provides light and energy. The sun and moon regulate Earth's tides. How do tides affect life on Earth?

Tidal pool exposed by low tide

Measuring Shadows

One way to learn more about Earth's rotation and orbit is to study the shadows created by the sun throughout the year. Help students with an ongoing research project, called the Sun Shadows Project. The results are presented at the American Geophysical Union's Annual Conference every year.

① Think About It

Students at James Monroe Middle School in Albuquerque, New Mexico, asked the following questions: The seasons change, but do the length of shadows? How could this be measured? What do you think?

_____

_____

_____

Scientists in Antarctica measure shadows.

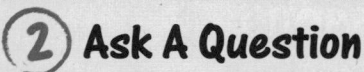

② Ask A Question

What effects do seasons have on the lengths of shadows in your area?

As a class, come up with a prediction. Then, research what students at James Monroe Middle School are doing to gather information.

Things to Consider

Some parts of the world participate in Daylight Savings Time. People move their clocks forward by an hour in the spring and back by an hour in the fall. Daylight Savings Time may affect the way that you will need to collect data in comparison to students at James Monroe Middle School. Make sure to take your measurements when shadows are shortest.

③ Apply Your Knowledge

A List the materials your class will need in order to make and record the measurements to gather the information needed by the students at James Monroe Middle School.

_____

_____

_____

_____

B Decide on a time frame for your class project. Will you participate for an entire season? What factors influence your decision?

_____

_____

_____

_____

_____

C Track the information gathered by your class and draw your own preliminary conclusions.

_____

_____

_____

_____

Take It Home

Who else is participating in the Sun Shadows Project? Research the various national and international groups taking part, such as the U.S. Antarctic Program.

Earth's Days, Years, and Seasons

ESSENTIAL QUESTION

How are Earth's days, years, and seasons related to the way Earth moves in space?

By the end of this lesson, you should be able to relate Earth's days, years, and seasons to Earth's movement in space.

In many parts of the world, blooming flowers are one of the first signs that spring has arrived. Spring flowers start blooming with the warmer temperatures of spring, even if there is still snow on the ground.

OHIO **7.ESS.4** The relative patterns of motion and positions of the Earth, moon and sun cause solar and lunar eclipses, tides and phases of the moon.

✋ **Lesson Labs**

Quick Labs
• Earth's Rotation and Revolution
• Seasons Model

Field Lab
• Sunlight and Temperature

 Engage Your Brain

1 Predict Check T or F to show whether you think each statement is true or false.

T	F	
☐	☐	A day is about 12 hours long.
☐	☐	A year is about 365 days long.
☐	☐	When it is summer in the Northern Hemisphere, it is summer all around the world.

2 Apply Write your own caption for this photo of leaves in the space below.

_____

_____

_____

_____

_____

 Active Reading

3 Synthesize The term *rotation* can be tricky to remember because it is used somewhat differently in science than it is in everyday life. In baseball, a pitching *rotation* lists the order of a team's starting pitchers. The order starts over after the last pitcher on the list has played. On the lines below, write down any other examples you can think of that use the term *rotation*.

rotation:

_____

_____

_____

Vocabulary Terms

• rotation	• season
• day	• equinox
• revolution	• solstice
• year	

4 Apply As you learn the definition of each vocabulary term in this lesson, create your own definition or sketch to help you remember the meaning of the term.

Spinning In

What determines the length of a day?

Each planet spins on its axis. Earth's axis (ACK•sis) is an imaginary straight line that runs from the North Pole to the South Pole. The spinning of a body, such as a planet, on its axis is called **rotation**. The time it takes a planet to complete one full rotation on its axis is called a **day**.

![Active Reading]

5 Identify As you read, underline the places on Earth's surface at which the ends of Earth's axis would be.

The Time It Takes for Earth to Rotate Once

Earth rotates in a counterclockwise motion around its axis when viewed from above the North Pole. This means that as a location on Earth's equator rotates from west to east, the sun appears to rise in the east. The sun then appears to cross the sky and set in the west.

As Earth rotates, only one-half of Earth faces the sun at any given time. People on the half of Earth facing the sun experience daylight. This period of time in daylight is called *daytime*. People on the half of Earth that faces away from the sun experience darkness. This period of time in darkness is called *nighttime*.

Earth's rotation is used to measure time. Earth completes one rotation on its axis in 24 hours, or in one day. Most locations on Earth's surface move through daylight and darkness in that time.

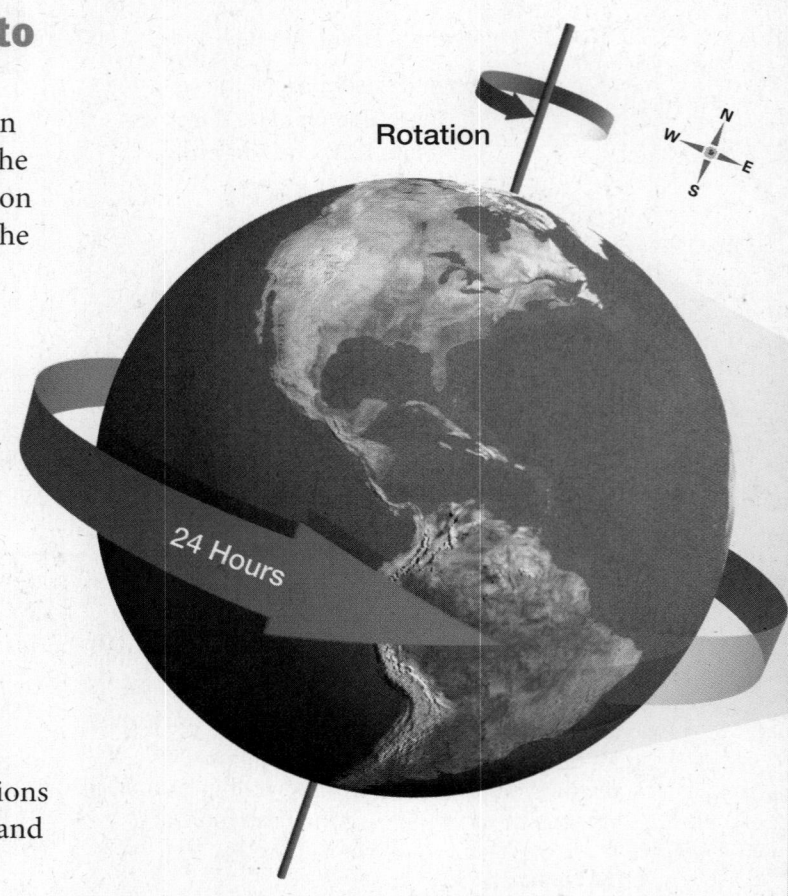

Rotation

24 Hours

Earth's motion is used to measure the length of an Earth day.

Circles

What determines the length of a year?

As Earth rotates on its axis, Earth also revolves around the sun. Although you cannot feel Earth moving, it is traveling around the sun at an average speed of nearly 30 km/s. The motion of a body that travels around another body in space is called **revolution** (reh•vuh•LOO•shun). Earth completes a full revolution around the sun in 365 ¼ days, or about one **year**. We have divided the year into 12 months, each month lasting from 28 to 31 days.

   Earth's orbit is not quite a perfect circle. In January, Earth is about 2.5 million kilometers closer to the sun than it is in July. You may be surprised that this distance makes only a tiny difference in temperatures on Earth.

Visualize It!

7 Apply Imagine that Earth's current position is at point A below. Write the label B to show Earth's position 6 months from now in the same diagram.

This drawing is not to scale.

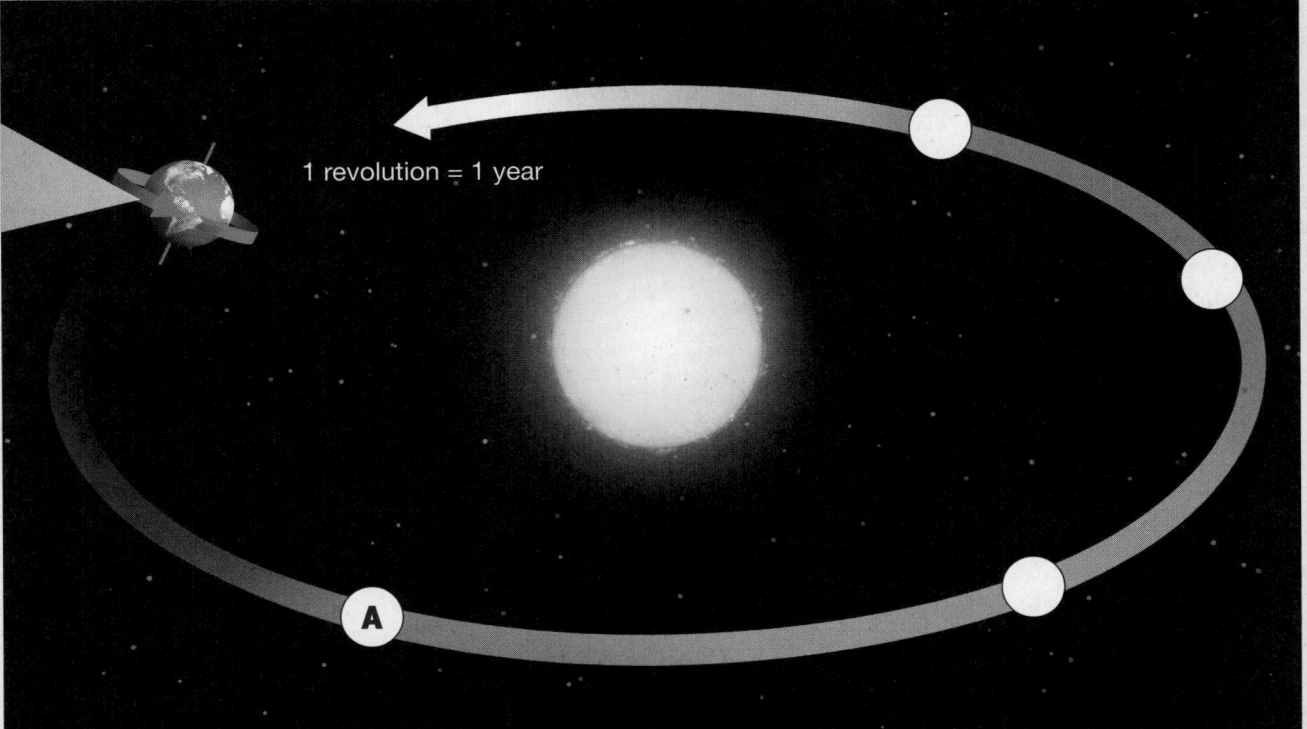

1 revolution = 1 year

A

© Houghton Mifflin Harcourt Publishing Company

Tilt-a-Whirl

What conditions are affected by the tilt of Earth's axis?

Earth's axis is tilted at 23.5°. Earth's axis always points toward the North Star as Earth revolves around the sun. Thus, during each revolution, the North Pole may be tilted toward the sun or away from the sun, as seen below. When the North Pole is tilted toward the sun, the Northern Hemisphere (HEHM•ih•sfeer) has longer periods of daylight than does the Southern Hemisphere. When the North Pole is tilted away from the sun, the opposite is true.

The direction of tilt of Earth's axis remains the same throughout Earth's orbit around the sun.

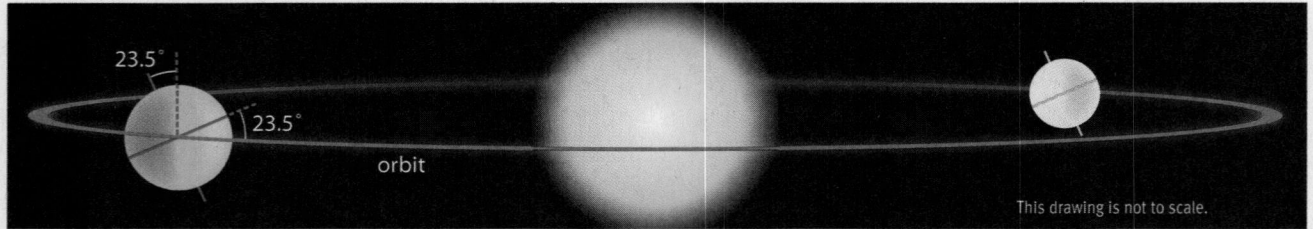

23.5°
23.5°
orbit
This drawing is not to scale.

Temperature

The angle at which the sun's rays strike each part of Earth's surface changes as Earth moves in its orbit. When the North Pole is tilted toward the sun, the sun's rays strike the Northern Hemisphere more directly. Thus, the region receives a higher concentration of solar energy and is warmer. When the North Pole is tilted away from the sun, the sun's rays strike the Northern Hemisphere less directly. When the sunlight is less direct, the solar energy is less concentrated and the region is cooler.

The spherical shape of Earth also affects how the sun warms up an area. Temperatures are high at point A in the diagram. This is because the sun's rays hit Earth's surface at a right angle and are focused in a small area. Toward the poles, the sun's rays hit Earth's surface at a lesser angle. Therefore, the rays are spread out over a larger area and the temperatures are cooler.

Visualize It!

8 Apply Which location on the illustration of Earth below receives more direct rays from the sun?
- [ ] A
- [ ] B
- [ ] They receive equal amounts.

9 Identify Which location is cooler? _____

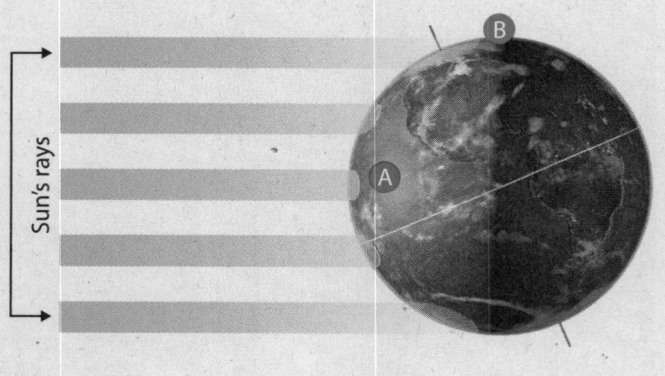

Sun's rays

B

A

Daylight Hours

All locations on Earth experience an *average* of 12 hours of light a day. However, the *actual* number of daylight hours on any given day of the year varies with location. Areas around Earth's equator receive about 12 hours of light a day. Areas on Earth's surface that are tilted toward the sun have more hours of daylight. These areas travel a longer path through the lit part of Earth than areas at the equator. Areas on Earth's surface that are tilted away from the sun have less than 12 hours of light a day. These areas travel a shorter path through the lit part of Earth, as shown below.

This drawing is not to scale.

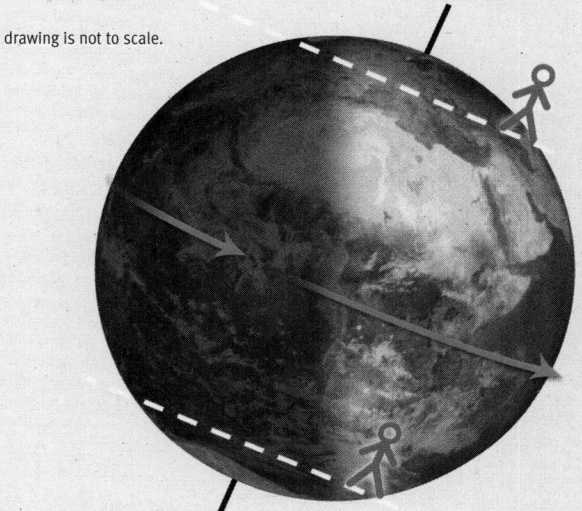

Sun's Rays

During summer in the Northern Hemisphere, a person has already had many daylight hours by the time a person in the Southern Hemisphere reaches daylight.

About twelve hours later, the person in the Northern Hemisphere is close to daylight again, while the person in the Southern Hemisphere still has many hours of darkness left.

Midnight Sun

When it is summer in the Northern Hemisphere, the time in each day that it is light increases as you move north of the equator. Areas north of the Arctic Circle have 24 hours of daylight, called the "midnight sun," as seen in the photo. At the same time, areas south of the Antarctic Circle receive 24 hours of darkness, or "polar night." When it is winter in the Northern Hemisphere, conditions in the polar areas are reversed.

Visualize It! (Inquiry)

10 Synthesize Why isn't the area in the photo very warm even though the sun is up all night long?

_____

_____

_____

This composite image shows that the sun never set on this Arctic summer day.

Seasons change...

What causes seasons?

Most locations on Earth experience seasons. Each **season** is characterized by a pattern of temperature and other weather trends. Near the equator, the temperatures are almost the same year-round. Near the poles, there are very large changes in temperatures from winter to summer. We experience seasons due to the changes in the intensity of sunlight and the number of daylight hours as Earth revolves around the sun. So, both the tilt of Earth's axis and Earth's spherical shape play a role in Earth's changing seasons.

As Earth travels around the sun, the area of sunlight in each hemisphere changes. At an **equinox** (EE•kwuh•nahks), sunlight shines equally on the Northern and Southern Hemispheres. Half of each hemisphere is lit, and half is in darkness. As Earth moves along its orbit, the sunlight reaches more of one hemisphere than the other. At a **solstice** (SAHL•stis), the area of sunlight is at a maximum in one hemisphere and at a minimum in the other hemisphere.

- **September Equinox** When Earth is in this position, sunlight shines equally on both poles.
- **December Solstice** About three months later, Earth has traveled a quarter of the way around the sun, but its axis still points in the same direction into space. The North Pole leans away from the sun and is in complete darkness. The South Pole is in complete sunlight.
- **March Equinox** After another quarter of its orbit, Earth reaches another equinox. Half of each hemisphere is lit, and the sunlight is centered on the equator.
- **June Solstice** This position is opposite to the December solstice. Now the North Pole leans toward the sun and is in complete sunlight, and the south pole is in complete darkness.

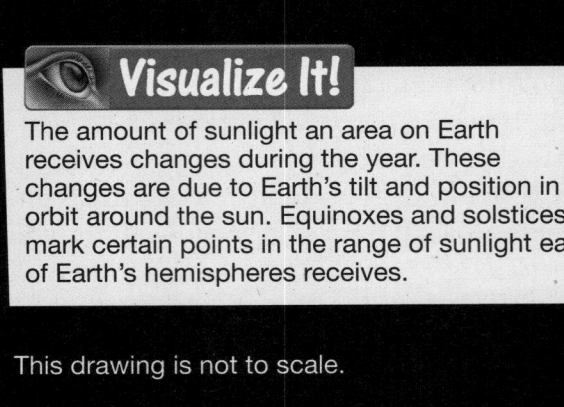

Visualize It!

The amount of sunlight an area on Earth receives changes during the year. These changes are due to Earth's tilt and position in its orbit around the sun. Equinoxes and solstices mark certain points in the range of sunlight each of Earth's hemispheres receives.

This drawing is not to scale.

March Equinox

April

May

June Solstice

11 Apply In what month does winter begin in the Southern Hemisphere?

_____

12 Infer During which solstice would the sun be at its highest point in the sky in the Northern Hemisphere?

_____

_____

Solstices

The seasons of summer and winter begin on days called *solstices*. Each year on June 21 or 22, the North Pole's tilt toward the sun is greatest. This day is called the *June solstice*. This solstice marks the beginning of summer in the Northern Hemisphere. By December 21 or 22, the North Pole is tilted to the farthest point away from the sun. This day is the December solstice.

February

January

December
Solstice

November

October

July

August

September
Equinox

Equinoxes

The seasons fall and spring begin on days called *equinoxes*. The hours of daylight and darkness are approximately equal everywhere on Earth on these days. The *September equinox* occurs on September 22 or 23 of each year. This equinox marks the beginning of fall in the Northern Hemisphere. The March equinox on March 20 or 21 of each year marks the beginning of spring.

13 Infer In which parts of the world is an equinox most different from other days of the year?

_____

_____

Visual Summary

To complete this summary, circle the correct word. Then use the key below to check your answers. You can use this page to review the main concepts of the lesson.

The length of a day is determined by Earth's rotation.

14 It takes Earth 24 seconds/hours to make one rotation on its axis.

The length of a year is determined by Earth's revolution around the sun.

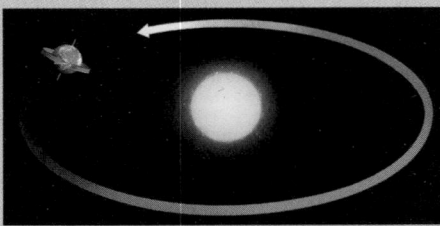

15 It takes Earth about 365 hours/days to revolve around the sun.

Earth's
Days, Years, and Seasons

Earth's tilt affects temperatures and daylight hours at different locations on Earth.

16 Earth's temperatures and hours of daylight stay the most constant at the equator/poles.

This diagram shows how seasons change in the Northern Hemisphere as Earth orbits the sun.

Spring

Summer

Winter

Fall

17 When it is summer in the Northern Hemisphere, it is summer/winter in the Southern Hemisphere.

Answers: 14 hours; 15 days; 16 equator; 17 winter

18 **Predict** How would conditions on Earth change if Earth stopped rotating on its axis?

Lesson Review

Vocabulary

In the space provided below, describe how each set of words are related.

1 revolution, year

_____

_____

2 rotation, day

_____

_____

3 season, equinox, solstice

_____

_____

_____

_____

Key Concepts

4 Identify About how many days are in an Earth year? And how many hours in an Earth day?

_____

5 Describe How does the tilt of Earth's axis affect how the sun's rays strike Earth?

_____

_____

_____

_____

6 Synthesize How does the tilt of Earth's axis affect the number of daylight hours and the temperature of a location on Earth?

_____

_____

_____

_____

_____

Critical Thinking

Use this image to answer the questions below.

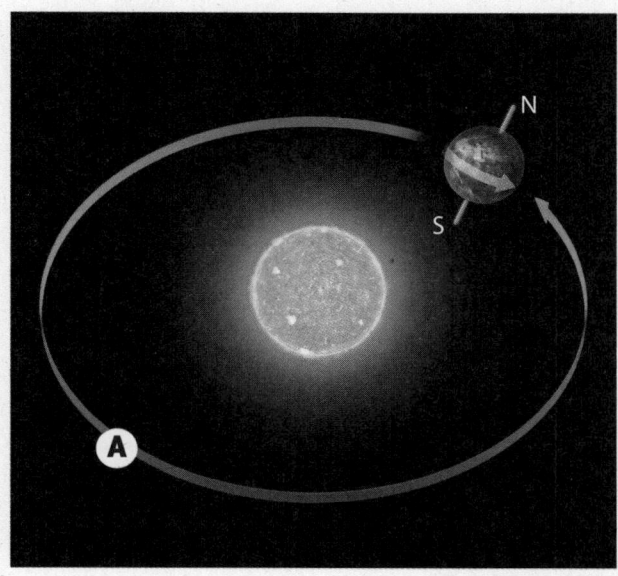

This drawing is not to scale.

7 Identify What season is the Northern Hemisphere experiencing in the image above?

_____

8 Explain How do the tilt of Earth's axis and Earth's movements around the sun cause seasons?

_____

_____

_____

_____

_____

_____

_____

_____

9 Describe If the Earth moves to point A in the image above, what season will the Northern Hemisphere experience?

_____

_____

My Notes

Analyzing Scientific Explanations

OHIO **7.SIA.6** Think critically and logically to connect evidence and explanations.
OHIO **7.SIA.7** Recognize and analyze alternative explanations and predictions.
OHIO **7.SIA.8** Communicate scientific procedures and explanations.

Scientists use different methods to develop scientific explanations in different fields of study. Scientists base their explanations on data collected through observation and measurement. After scientists make observations and collect data, they analyze current explanations for what they observed. If a new observation doesn't fit an existing explanation, scientists might work to revise the explanation or to offer a new one.

Tutorial

The text below describes how Ptolemy, a Greek astronomer in the second century C.E., described the universe. Consider the following steps as you analyze scientific explanations.

As Aristotle put forth, Earth is at the center of the universe. All other planets and the Sun revolve around Earth, each on its own sphere. The spheres follow this order outward from Earth: Mercury, Venus, the Moon, the Sun, Mars, Jupiter, Saturn, and the Fixed Stars. Each sphere turns at its own steady pace. Bodies do appear to move backward during their wanderings, but that does not mean the spheres do not keep a steady pace. This is explained by the movement of the bodies along smaller spheres that turn along the edge of the larger spheres. My calculations and models agree with and predict the motions of the spheres. The constant turning of the spheres also moves the bodies closer to Earth and farther from Earth, which explains why the bodies appear brighter or darker at different times. Thus, the heavens remain perfect. This perfection leads to music in the heavens, created by the spheres.

Identify the evidence that supports the explanation. At least two different lines of evidence are needed to be considered valid.

Identify any evidence that does not support the explanation. A single line of evidence can disprove an explanation. Often, new evidence makes scientists reevaluate an explanation. By the 1500s, Ptolemy's model was not making accurate predictions. In 1543, Copernicus, a Polish astronomer, proposed a new explanation of how planets move.

Identify any additional lines of evidence that should be considered. They might point to additional investigations to further examine the explanation. The gravitational force between objects was not known in Ptolemy's time. However, it should be considered when explaining the motion of planets.

Decide whether the original explanation is supported by enough evidence. An alternative explanation might better explain the evidence or might explain a wider range of observations.

If possible, propose an alternative explanation that could fit the evidence. Often, a simpler explanation is better if it fits the evidence. Copernicus explained the apparent backward movement and changing brightness of planets by placing the sun at the center of the solar system with the planets revolving around it.

You Try It!

In 2006, an official definition of a planet was determined. Read and analyze the information below concerning the classification of the largest Main Belt asteroid, Ceres.

The members of the International Astronomical Union (IAU) voted for the official definition of a planet to be a celestial body that

1. orbits the sun,
2. has enough mass so that its gravity helps it to maintain a nearly round shape,
3. has cleared the neighborhood around its orbit.

A group suggests that Ceres be considered a planet under the new definition. As the largest Main Belt asteroid, Ceres orbits the sun along with thousands of smaller asteroids. Images of Ceres clearly show its nearly round shape. These points, says the group's leader, should qualify Ceres as a planet.

1 Making Observations Underline lines of evidence that support the explanation.

2 Evaluating Data Circle any lines of evidence that do not support the proposed explanation. Explain why this evidence does not support the classification.

_____

_____

_____

_____

3 Applying Concepts Identify any additional evidence that should be considered when evaluating the explanation.

_____

_____

_____

4 Communicating Ideas If possible, propose an alternative explanation that could fit the evidence.

_____

_____

_____

_____

_____

_____

_____

Take It Home

Pluto was recently reclassified. What was it changed to and why? Identify the evidence that supported the decision. How does this compare to the proposed reclassification of Ceres? List similarities of the two explanations in a chart.

Moon Phases and Eclipses

ESSENTIAL QUESTION

How do Earth, the moon, and the sun affect each other?

By the end of this lesson, you should be able to describe the effects the sun and the moon have on Earth, including gravitational attraction, moon phases, and eclipses.

Why is part of the moon orange? Because Earth is moving between the moon and the sun, casting a shadow on the moon.

OHIO 7.ESS.4 The relative patterns of motion and positions of the Earth, moon and sun cause solar and lunar eclipses, tides and phases of the moon.

Lesson Labs

Quick Labs
- Moon Phases
- Lunar Eclipse

S.T.E.M. Lab
- What the Moon Orbits

Engage Your Brain

1 Identify Fill in the blanks with the word or phrase you think correctly completes the following sentences.

We can see the moon because it _____ the light from the sun.

The moon's _____ affects the oceans' tides on Earth.

The impact craters on the moon were created by collisions with _____, meteorites, and asteroids.

2 Describe Write your own caption for this photo in the space below.

_____

_____

_____

_____

_____

Active Reading

3 Synthesize You can often define an unknown word if you know the meaning of its word parts. Use the word parts and sentence below to make an educated guess about the meaning of the word *penumbra*.

Word part	Meaning
umbra	shade or shadow
pen-, from the Latin *paene*	almost

Example sentence
An observer in the <u>penumbra</u> experiences only a partial eclipse.

penumbra:

_____

_____

_____

Vocabulary Terms

- satellite
- gravity
- lunar phases
- eclipse
- umbra
- penumbra

4 Apply As you learn the definition of each vocabulary term in this lesson, create your own definition or sketch to help you remember the meaning of the term.

© Houghton Mifflin Harcourt Publishing Company • Image Credits: (bkgd) ©Detlev Van Ravenswaay/Photo Researchers, Inc.; (tr) ©Larry Landolfi/Photo Researchers, Inc.

'Round and 'Round They Go!

How are Earth, the moon, and the sun related in space?

Earth not only spins on its axis, but like the seven other planets in our solar system, Earth also orbits the sun. A body that orbits a larger body is called a **satellite** (SAT'l•yt). Six of the planets in our solar system have smaller bodies that orbit around each of them. These natural satellites are also called moons. Our moon is Earth's natural satellite.

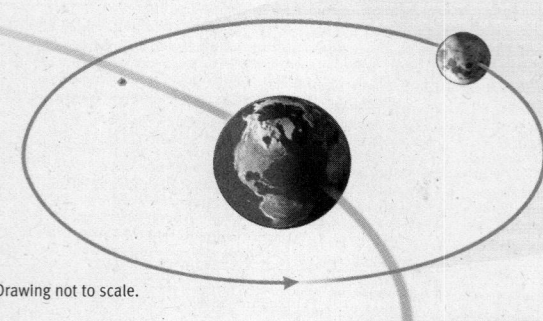

Earth revolves around the sun as the moon revolves around Earth.

Drawing not to scale.

📖 **Active Reading**

5 Identify As you read, underline the reason that the moon stays in orbit around Earth.

Earth and the Moon Orbit the Sun

All bodies that have mass exert a force that pulls other objects with mass toward themselves. This force is called **gravity.** The mass of Earth is much larger than the mass of the moon, and therefore Earth's gravity exerts a stronger pull on the moon than the moon does on Earth. It is Earth's gravitational pull that keeps the moon in orbit around Earth, forming the Earth–moon system.

The Earth–moon system is itself in orbit around the sun. Even though the sun is relatively far away, the mass of the sun exerts a large gravitational pull on the Earth–moon system. This gravitational pull keeps the Earth–moon system in orbit around the sun.

The Moon Orbits Earth

The pull of Earth's gravity keeps the moon, Earth's natural satellite, in orbit around Earth. Even though the moon is Earth's closest neighbor in space, it is far away compared to the sizes of Earth and the moon themselves.

The distance between Earth and the moon is roughly 383,000 km (238,000 mi)—about a hundred times the distance between New York and Los Angeles. If a jet airliner could travel in space, it would take about 20 days to cover a distance that huge. Astronauts, whose spaceships travel much faster than jets, need about 3 days to reach the moon.

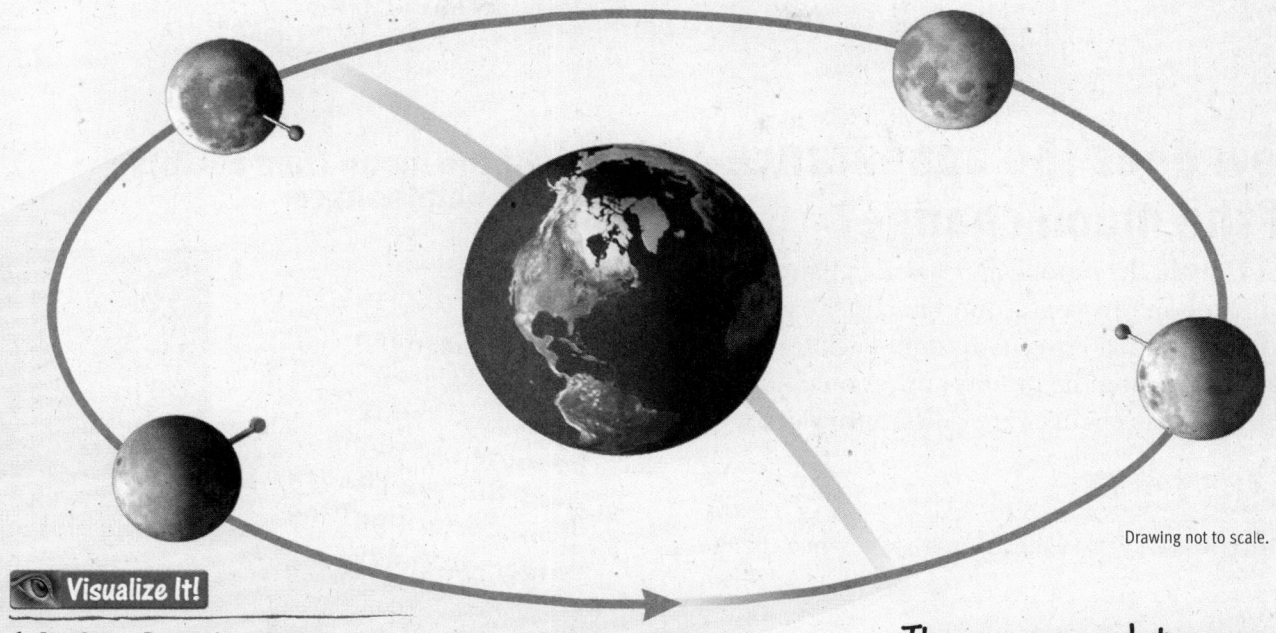

Drawing not to scale.

Visualize It!

6 Analyze Draw the correct position of the pin when the moon is in the position shown in the top right corner of this figure.

The moon completes one rotation for every revolution it makes around Earth.

What does the moon look like from Earth?

The moon is only visible from Earth when it reflects the sunlight that reaches the moon. Although the moon is most easily seen at night, you have probably also seen it during daytime on some days. In the daytime, the moon may only be as bright as a thin cloud and can be easily missed. On some days you can see the moon during both the daytime and at night, whereas on other days, you may not see the moon at all.

When you can look at the moon, you may notice darker and lighter areas. Perhaps you have imagined them as features of a face or some other pattern. People around the world have told stories about the animals, people, and objects they have imagined while looking at the light and dark areas of the moon. The dark and light spots do not change over the course of a month because only one side of the moon faces Earth, often called the near side of the moon. This is because the moon rotates once on its own axis each time it orbits Earth. The moon takes 27.3 days or about a month to orbit Earth once.

Inquiry

7 Analyze How would the moon appear to an observer on Earth if the moon did not rotate?

_____
_____
_____
_____

It's Just a Phase!

How does the appearance of the moon change?

From Earth, the moon's appearance changes. As the moon revolves around Earth, the portion of the moon that reflects sunlight back to Earth changes, causing the moon's appearance to change. These changes are called **lunar phases.**

 Active Reading

8 Describe Why does the moon's appearance change?

_____

_____

Lunar Phases Cycle Monthly

The cycle begins with a new moon. At this time, Earth, the moon, and the sun are lined up, such that the near side of the moon is unlit. And so there appears to be no moon in the sky.

As the moon moves along its orbit, you begin to see the sunlight on the near side as a thin crescent shape. The crescent becomes thicker as the moon waxes, or grows. When half of the near side of the moon is in the sunlight, the moon has completed one-quarter of its cycle. This phase is called the *first quarter.*

More of the moon is visible during the second week, or the *gibbous* (GIB•uhs) *phase.* This is when the near side is more than half lit but not fully lit. When the moon is halfway through its cycle, the whole near side of the moon is in sunlight, and we see a full moon.

During the third week, the amount of the moon's near side in the sunlight decreases and it seems to shrink, or wane. When the near side is again only half in sunlight, the moon is three-quarters of the way through its cycle. The phase is called the *third quarter.*

In the fourth week, the area of the near side of the moon in sunlight continues to shrink. The moon is seen as waning crescent shapes. Finally, the near side of the moon is unlit—*new moon.*

Views of the moon from Earth's northern hemisphere

The waxing moon appears to grow each day. This is because the sunlit area that we can see from Earth is getting larger each day.

Waxing gibbous

Full moon

Waning gibbous

Think Outside the Book

9 Apply Look at the night sky and keep a moon journal for a series of nights. What phase is the moon in now?

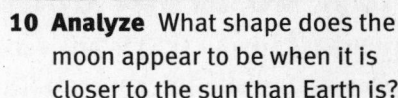
10 Analyze What shape does the moon appear to be when it is closer to the sun than Earth is?

First quarter

Waxing crescent

Drawing not to scale.

New moon

Waning crescent

Third quarter

The waning moon appears to shrink each day. When the moon is waning, the sunlit area is getting smaller. Notice above that even as the phases of the moon change, the total amount of sunlight that the moon gets remains the same. Half the moon is always in sunlight, just as half of Earth is always in sunlight. The moon phases have a period of 29.5 days.

Exploring Eclipses

How do lunar eclipses occur?

An **eclipse** (ih•KLIPS) is an event during which one object in space casts a shadow onto another. On Earth, a lunar eclipse occurs when the moon moves through Earth's shadow. There are two parts of Earth's shadow, as you can see in the diagram below. The **umbra** (UHM•bruh) is the darkest part of a shadow. Around it is a spreading cone of lighter shadow called the **penumbra** (pih•NUHM•bruh). Just before a lunar eclipse, sunlight streaming past Earth produces a full moon. Then the moon moves into Earth's penumbra and becomes slightly less bright. As the moon moves into the umbra, Earth's dark shadow seems to creep across and cover the moon. The entire moon can be in darkness because the moon is small enough to fit entirely within Earth's umbra. After an hour or more, the moon moves slowly back into the sunlight that is streaming past Earth. A total lunar eclipse occurs when the moon passes completely into Earth's umbra. If the moon misses part or all of the umbra, part of the moon stays light and the eclipse is called a partial lunar eclipse.

You may be wondering why you don't see solar and lunar eclipses every month. The reason is that the moon's orbit around Earth is tilted—by about 5°—relative to the orbit of Earth around the sun. This tilt is enough to place the moon out of Earth's shadow for most full moons and Earth out of the moon's shadow for most new moons.

This composite photo shows the partial and total phases of a lunar eclipse over several hours.

Lunar eclipse

👁 Visualize It!

11 Identify Fill in the boxes with the type of eclipse that would occur if the moon were in the areas being pointed to.

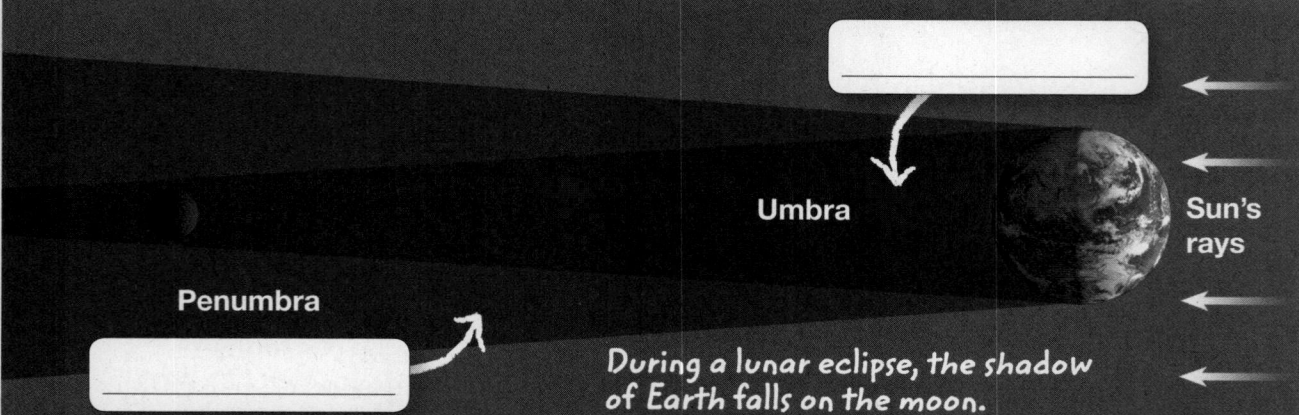

Umbra

Sun's rays

Penumbra

During a lunar eclipse, the shadow of Earth falls on the moon.

Drawing not to scale.

How do solar eclipses occur?

When the moon is directly between the sun and Earth, the shadow of the moon falls on a part of Earth and causes a solar eclipse. During a total solar eclipse, the sun's light is completely blocked by the moon, as seen in this photo. The umbra falls on the area of Earth that lies directly in line with the moon and the sun. Outside the umbra, but within the penumbra, people see a partial solar eclipse. The penumbra falls on the area that immediately surrounds the umbra.

The umbra of the moon is too small to make a large shadow on Earth's surface. The part of the umbra that hits Earth during an eclipse, is never more than a few hundred kilometers across, as shown below. So, a total eclipse of the sun covers only a small part of Earth and is seen only by people in particular parts of Earth along a narrow path. A total solar eclipse usually lasts between one to two minutes at any one location. A total eclipse will not be visible in the United States until 2017, even though there is a total eclipse somewhere on Earth about every one to two years.

Solar eclipse

During a solar eclipse, the moon passes between the sun and Earth so that the sun is partially or totally obscured.

 **Active Reading**

12 Explain Why is it relatively rare to observe a solar eclipse?

_____
_____
_____
_____

Visualize It!

13 Describe Explain what happens during a solar eclipse.

_____
_____
_____

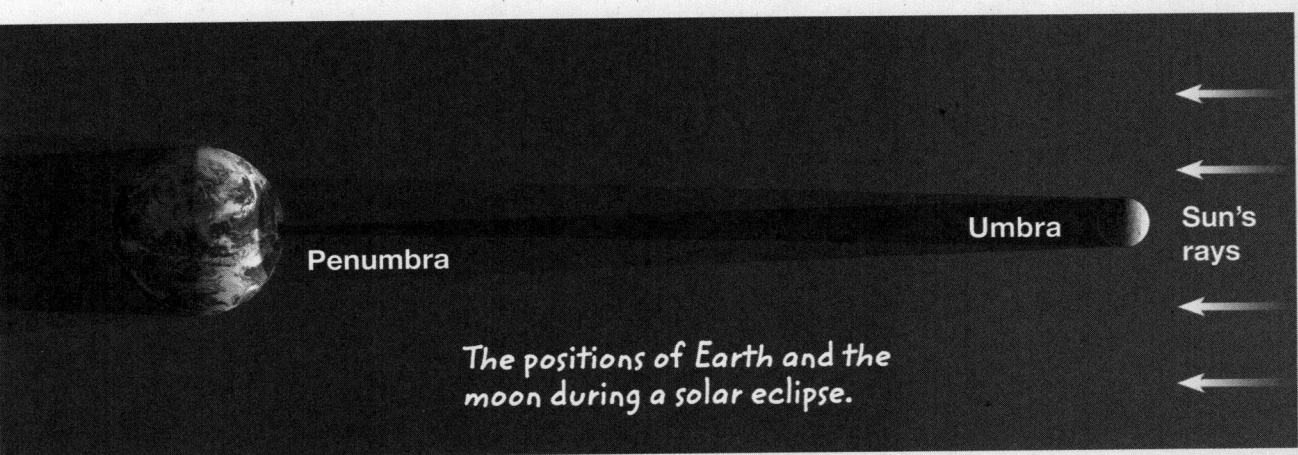

Penumbra

Umbra

Sun's rays

The positions of Earth and the moon during a solar eclipse.

Drawing not to scale.

Visual Summary

To complete this summary, circle the correct word. Then use the key below to check your answers. You can use this page to review the main concepts of the lesson.

Moon Phases and Eclipses

The Earth–moon system orbits the sun.

14 The moon takes about one day/month/year to orbit Earth.

Shadows in space cause eclipses.

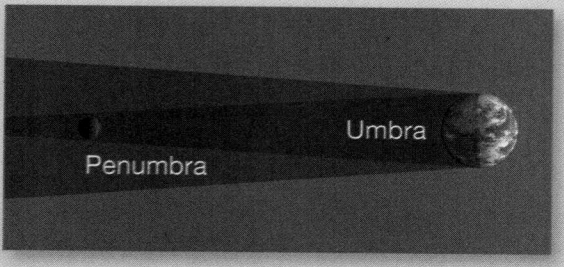

Umbra

Penumbra

15 When the moon is in Earth's umbra, a total solar/lunar eclipse is occurring.

The appearance of the moon depends on the positions of the sun, the moon, and Earth.

16 The fraction of the moon that receives sunlight always/never changes.

Answers:14 month; 15 lunar; 16 never

17 Describe What causes the lunar phases that we see from Earth?

Lesson Review

Vocabulary

In your own words, define the following terms.

1 gravity

_____

_____

_____

2 satellite

_____

_____

_____

3 umbra

_____

_____

Key Concepts

4 Describe What are two phases of a waxing moon, and how do they appear?

_____

_____

_____

_____

_____

_____

5 Identify Explain why the moon can be seen from Earth.

_____

_____

_____

6 Describe What is the relationship between Earth, the sun, and the moon in space?

_____

_____

_____

_____

_____

Critical Thinking

Use the image below to answer the following question.

7 Identify What type of eclipse is shown in the diagram?

_____

8 Describe Where is the moon in its orbit at the time of a solar eclipse?

_____

9 Infer What phase is the moon in when there is a total solar eclipse?

_____

10 Predict Which shape of the moon will you never see during the daytime, after sunrise and before sunset? *Hint:* Consider the directions of the sun and moon from Earth.

_____

11 Synthesize If you were an astronaut in the middle of the near side of the moon during a full moon, how would the ground around you look? How would Earth, high in your sky look? Describe what is in sunlight and what is in darkness.

_____

_____

_____

_____

_____

My Notes

Engineering Design Process

Skills
Identify a need
Conduct research
Brainstorm solutions
✓ Select a solution
✓ Design a prototype
✓ Build a prototype
✓ Test and evaluate
✓ Redesign to improve
✓ Communicate results

Objectives
• Explain several advantages of tidal energy over conventional energy sources.
• Design a technological solution to harnessing changing water levels.
• Test and modify a prototype to raise a mass as water levels change.

Harnessing Tidal Energy

Our society uses a lot of electrical energy. If the energy is generated by nuclear power plants or by burning fossil fuels, the waste products tend to harm the environment. However, in many places, these methods of obtaining energy are still used.

Scientists and engineers have been investigating alternative energy sources, such as solar, wind, and tidal energy. Tidal energy is energy from *tides,* the daily, predictable changes in the level of ocean water. The mechanical energy of the moving water can be transformed to other forms of energy that are useful in human activities. Tidal power facilities have less of an impact on nature and have low operating costs. And unlike fossil fuels or the uranium ore used in nuclear power plants, water is not used up in the generation of tidal energy. Generating electrical energy from tides and other alternative energy sources can be less harmful to the environment, but challenges must still be overcome.

Barrage tidal power facility at La Rance, France

1 Compare What are some advantages of generating electrical energy from tides instead of from fossil fuels?

_____

_____

_____

Types of Tidal Power Generators

There are three main types of tidal energy generators. One type is a system that uses a dam with turbines. The dam is called a *barrage*. The barrage allows water in during high tide and releases water during low tide. Barrage tidal power stations can affect marine life behind the barrage. Also, silt settles behind the barrage and must be dredged up and hauled out to sea. This is an older system of generating electrical energy from tides.

The other two types of tidal power generators are *horizontal-axis turbines* and *vertical-axis turbines*. These systems are like huge underwater fans turned by tidal currents instead of by wind. Because water is denser than air, slow-moving water can still produce a lot of power. These facilities have fewer effects on the environment.

2 Compare What is an advantage of using horizontal-axis turbines and vertical-axis turbines instead of barrage tidal power stations?

_____

_____

_____

_____

Four vertical-axis tidal power turbines are seen here. The blades rotate on an axis perpendicular to the ocean floor.

Two horizontal-axis tidal power turbines are seen here. The blades rotate on an axis parallel to the ocean floor.

✋ You Try It! ⟶

Now it's your turn to design and build a tidal power device.

You Try It!

Now it's your turn to design and build a tidal power device that will lift two masses. You will lift the masses by harnessing energy from the changing water levels in a sink or tub. Adding water to the sink or tub will simulate a rising tide, and removing water will simulate a falling tide. One mass must be raised when the tide rises, and the other mass must be raised when the tide falls. Both masses must be outside the sink or tub.

You Will Need

- ✔ block, wooden or foam
- ✔ bucket
- ✔ dowels, wooden
- ✔ duct tape
- ✔ masses, 50 g or 100 g (2)
- ✔ milk jug, 1 gallon, empty
- ✔ siphon hose
- ✔ string
- ✔ tub, plastic or sink
- ✔ water

① Select a Solution

A How will you use the falling tide to raise a mass?

_____

_____

_____

_____

B How will you use the rising tide to raise a mass?

_____

_____

_____

_____

② Design a Prototype

In the space below, draw and label a prototype of your tidal power device. You may have one idea for harnessing the falling tide and a different idea for harnessing the rising tide.

(3) Build a Prototype

Now build your tidal power device. As you built your device, were there some aspects of your design that could not be assembled as you had predicted? What aspects did you have to revise as you were building the prototype?

_____

_____

_____

_____

(4) Test and Evaluate

Place your device in the tub. Add water to the tub to simulate a rising tide. Then drain water from the tub. Observe the motion of the masses as the tide rises and falls, and record your observations.

_____

_____

_____

_____

(5) Redesign to Improve

Keep making revisions, one at a time, until your tidal power device can lift both masses. Describe the revisions you made.

_____

_____

_____

(6) Communicate Results

Were you able to raise a mass more easily when the simulated tide was rising or falling? Why do you think that was? Record your ideas below. Then, compare your results with those of your classmates.

_____

_____

_____

_____

_____

Lesson 3
Earth's Tides

ESSENTIAL QUESTION

What causes tides?

By the end of this lesson, you should be able to explain what tides are and what causes them in Earth's oceans and to describe variations in the tides.

You may wonder why this boat is sitting in such shallow water. This photo was taken at low tide, when the ocean water is below average sea level.

OHIO **7.ESS.4** The relative patterns of motion and positions of the Earth, moon and sun cause solar and lunar eclipses, tides and phases of the moon.

OHIO **7.SIA.5** Develop descriptions, models, explanations and predictions.

Engage Your Brain

1 Describe Fill in the blank with the word that you think correctly completes the following sentences.

The motion of the _____ around Earth is related to tides.

The daily rotation of _____ is also related to tides.

During a _____ tide, the water level is higher than the average sea level.

During a _____ tide, the water level is lower than the average sea level.

2 Label Draw an arrow to show where you think high tide might be.

Low tide ▶

✎ Active Reading

3 Synthesize The word *spring* has different meanings. Use the meanings of the word *spring* and the sentence below to make an educated guess about the meaning of the term *spring tides*.

Meanings of *spring*
the season between winter and summer
a source of water from the ground
jump, or rise up
a coiled piece of metal

Example Sentence
During <u>spring tides</u>, the sun, the moon, and Earth are in a straight line, resulting in very high tides.

spring tides:

_____

_____

_____

Vocabulary Terms
- tide
- tidal range
- spring tide
- neap tide

4 Apply As you learn the definition of each vocabulary term in this lesson, create your own definition or sketch to help you remember the meaning of the term.

A Rising Tide of Interest

What causes tides?

The photographs below show the ocean at the same location at two different times. **Tides** are daily changes in the level of ocean water. Tides are caused by the difference in the gravitational force of the sun and the moon across Earth. This difference in gravitational force is called the *tidal force*. The tidal force exerted by the moon is stronger than the tidal force exerted by the sun because the moon is much closer to Earth than the sun is. So, the moon is mainly responsible for tides on Earth.

How often tides occur and how tidal levels vary depend on the position of the moon as it revolves around Earth. The gravity of the moon pulls on every particle of Earth. But because liquids move more easily than solids do, the pull on liquids is much more noticeable than the pull on solids is. The moon's gravitational pull on Earth decreases with the moon's distance from Earth. The part of Earth facing the moon is pulled toward the moon with the greatest force. So, water on that side of Earth bulges toward the moon. The solid Earth is pulled more strongly toward the moon than the ocean water on Earth's far side is. So, there is also a bulge of water on the side of Earth farthest from the moon.

At low tide, the water level is low, and the boats are far below the dock.

At high tide, the water level has risen, and the boats are close to the dock.

What are high tides and low tides?

The bulges that form in Earth's oceans are called high tides. *High tide* is a water level that is higher than the average sea level. Low tides form in the areas between the high tides. *Low tide* is a water level that is lower than the average sea level. At low tide, the water levels are lower because the water is in high-tide areas.

As the moon moves around Earth and Earth rotates, the tidal bulges move around Earth. The tidal bulges follow the motion of the moon. As a result, many places on Earth have two high tides and two low tides each day.

This grizzly bear in Alaska is taking advantage of low tide by digging for clams.

Visualize It!

6 Identify Label the areas where high tides form and the area where the other low tide forms.

Note: Drawing is not to scale.

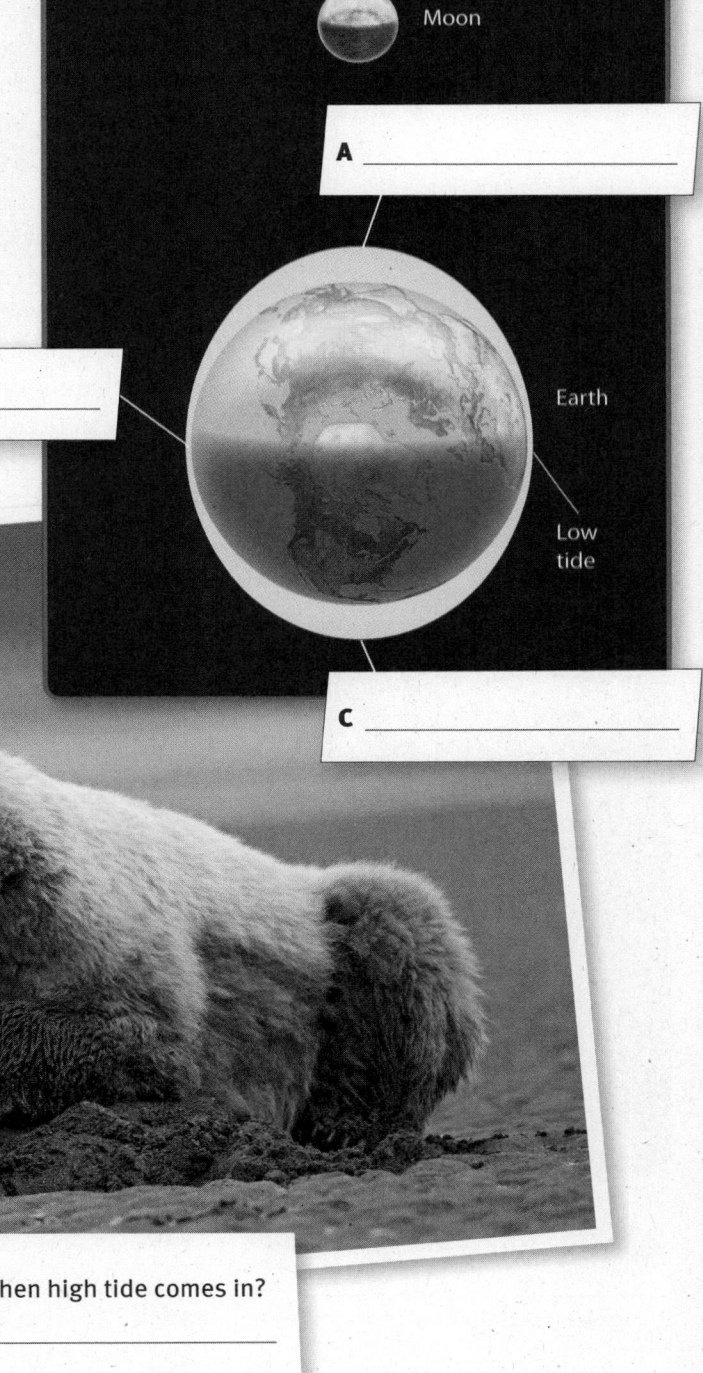

Moon

A _____

B _____

Earth

Low tide

C _____

7 Predict What happens to the bear when high tide comes in?

_____

_____

Tide Me Over

8 Identify As you read, underline the two kinds of tidal range.

What are two kinds of tidal ranges?

Tides are due to the *tidal force*, the difference between the force of gravity on one side of Earth and the other side of Earth. Because the moon is so much closer to Earth than the sun is, the moon's tidal force is greater than the sun's tidal force. The moon's effect on tides is twice as strong as the sun's effect. The combined gravitational effects of the sun and the moon on Earth result in different tidal ranges. A **tidal range** is the difference between the levels of ocean water at high tide and low tide. Tidal range depends on the positions of the sun and the moon relative to Earth.

Spring Tides: The Largest Tidal Range

Tides that have the largest daily tidal range are **spring tides**. Spring tides happen when the sun, the moon, and Earth form a straight line. So, spring tides happen when the moon is between the sun and Earth and when the moon is on the opposite side of Earth, as shown in the illustrations below. In other words, spring tides happen during the new moon and full moon phases, or every 14 days. During these times, the gravitational effects of the sun and moon add together, causing one pair of very large tidal bulges. Spring tides have nothing to do with the season.

Note: Drawings are not to scale.

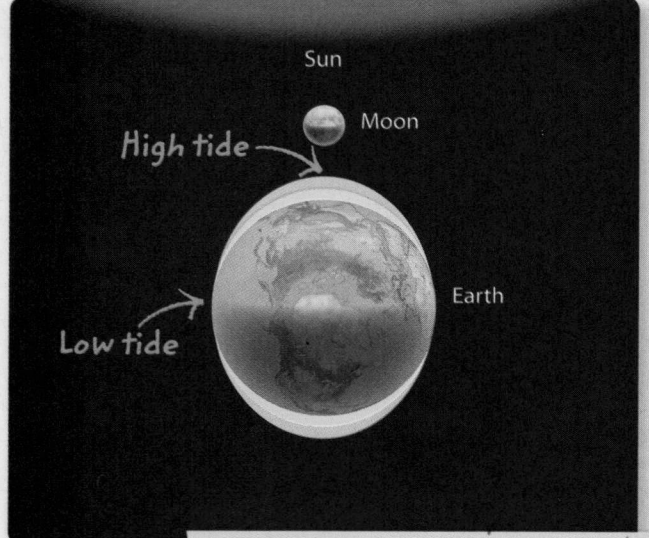
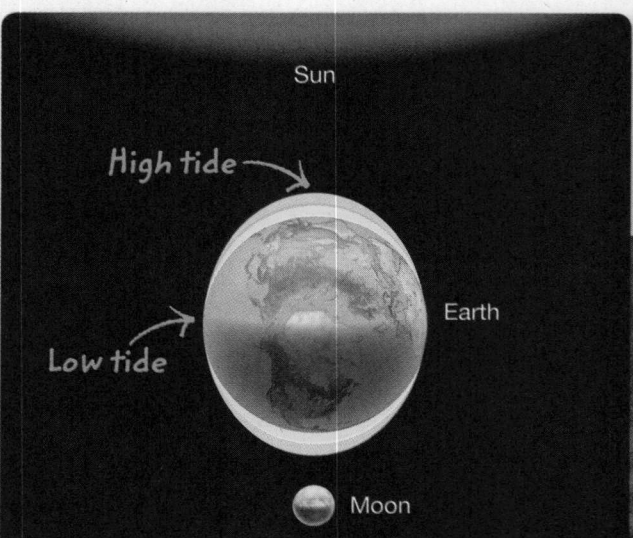

During spring tides, the tidal force of the sun on Earth adds to the tidal force of the moon. The tidal range increases.

Inquiry

9 Inquire Explain why spring tides happen twice a month.

_____

_____

_____

Neap Tides: The Smallest Tidal Range

Tides that have the smallest daily tidal range are **neap tides**. Neap tides happen when the sun, Earth, and the moon form a 90° angle, as shown in the illustrations below. During a neap tide, the gravitational effects of the sun and the moon on Earth do not add together as they do during spring tides. Neap tides occur halfway between spring tides, during the first quarter and third quarter phases of the moon. At these times, the sun and the moon cause two pairs of smaller tidal bulges.

Note: Drawings are not to scale.

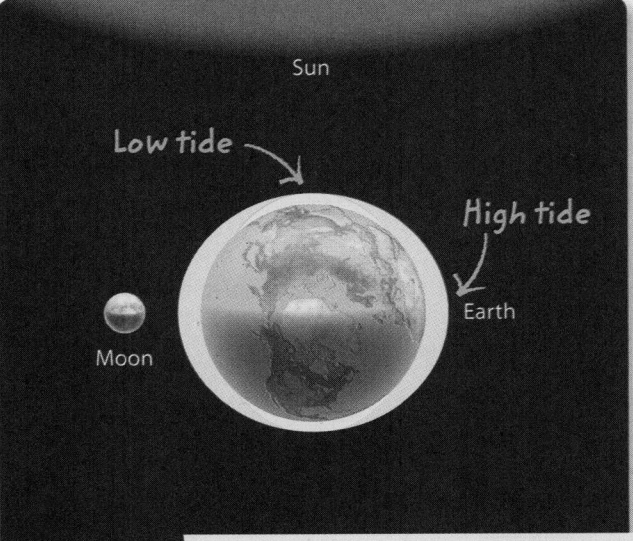

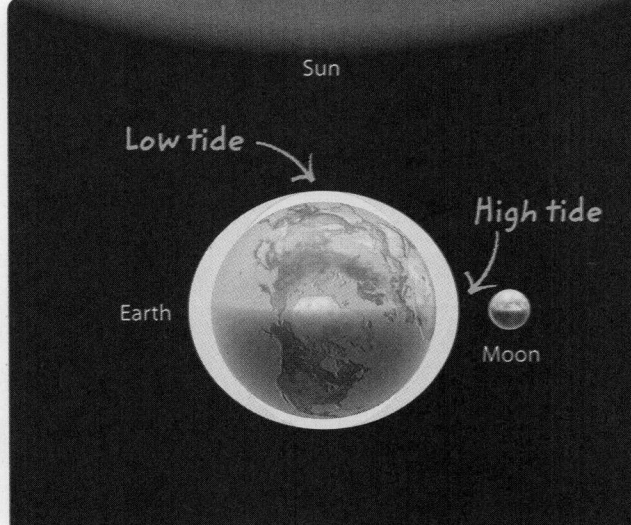

During neap tides, the gravitational effects of the sun and the moon on Earth do not add together. The tidal range decreases.

10 Compare Fill in the Venn diagram to compare and contrast spring tides and neap tides.

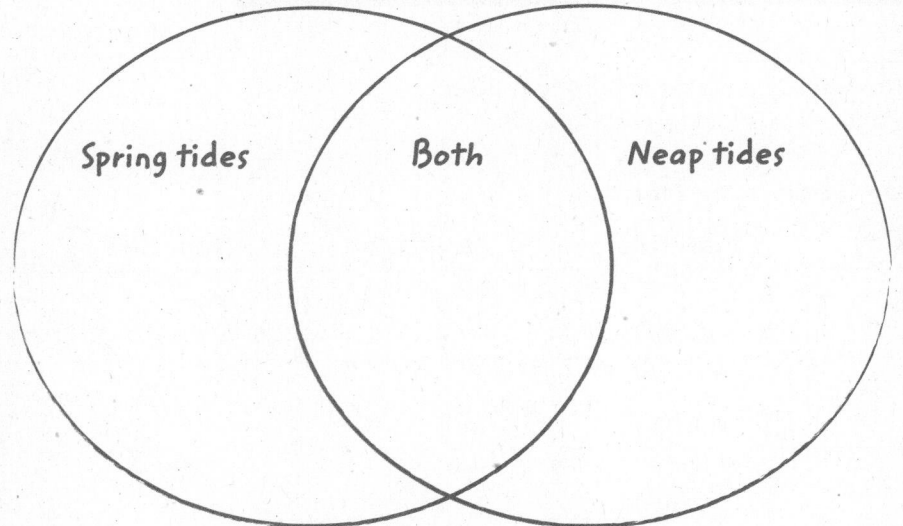

Spring tides   Both   Neap tides

What causes tidal cycles?

The rotation of Earth and the moon's revolution around Earth determine when tides occur. Imagine that Earth rotated at the same speed that the moon revolves around Earth. If this were true, the same side of Earth would always face the moon. And high tide would always be at the same places on Earth. But the moon revolves around Earth much more slowly than Earth rotates. A place on Earth that is facing the moon takes 24 h and 50 min to rotate to face the moon again. So, the cycle of high tides and low tides at that place happens 50 min later each day.

In many places there are two high tides and two low tides each day. Because the tide cycle occurs in 24 h and 50 min intervals, it takes about 6 h and 12.5 min (one-fourth the time of the total cycle) for water in an area to go from high tide to low tide. It takes about 12 h and 25 min (one-half the time of the total cycle) to go from one high tide to the next high tide.

Note: Drawings are not to scale.

Tuesday 11:00 a.m.

Wednesday 11:50 a.m.

The moon moves only a fraction of its orbit in the time that Earth rotates once.

Think Outside the Book (Inquiry)

11 Inquire Draw a diagram of Earth to show what Earth's tides would be like if the moon revolved around Earth at the same speed that Earth rotates.

12 Predict In the table, predict the approximate times of high tide and low tide for Clearwater, Florida.

Tide Data for Clearwater, Florida

Date (2009)	High tide	Low tide	High tide	Low tide
August 19	12:14 a.m.		12:39 p.m.	
August 20	1:04 a.m.	7:17 a.m.		
August 21				

Extreme Living Conditions

Some organisms living along ocean coastlines must be able to tolerate extreme living conditions. At high tide, much of the coast is under water. At low tide, much of the coast is dry. Some organisms must also survive the constant crashing of waves against the shore.

Barnacle Business
Barnacles must be able to live in water as well as out of water. They must also tolerate the air temperature, which may differ from the temperature of the water.

Ghostly Crabs
Ghost crabs live near the high tide line on sandy shores. They scurry along the sand to avoid being underwater when the tide comes in. Ghost crabs can also find cover between rocks.

Stunning Starfish
Starfish live in tidal pools, which are areas along the shore where water remains at low tide. Starfish must be able to survive changes in water temperature and salinity.

Extend

Inquiry

13 Identify Describe how living conditions change for two tidal organisms.

14 Research and Record List the names of two organisms that live in the high tide zone or the low tide zone along a coastline of your choice.

15 Describe Imagine a day in the life of an organism you researched in question 14 by doing one of the following:
- make a poster
- write a play
- record an audio story
- make a cartoon

Visual Summary

To complete this summary, fill in the blanks with the correct word. Then use the key below to check your answers. You can use this page to review the main concepts of the lesson.

In many places, two high tides and two low tides occur every day.

16 The type of tide shown here is

_____

The gravitational effects of the moon and the sun cause tides.

17 Tides on Earth are caused mainly by the

_____

Moon

Earth

Tides on Earth

Note: Drawings are not to scale.

There are two kinds of tidal ranges: spring tides and neap tides.

Sun

Moon

Earth

18 During a spring tide, the sun, moon, and Earth are in a/an

_____

Sun

Moon

Earth

19 During a neap tide, the sun, moon, and Earth form a/an

_____

Answers: 16 low tide; 17 moon; 18 straight line; 19 90° angle

20 **Describe** State how the moon causes tides.

Lesson Review

Vocabulary

Answer the following questions in your own words.

1 Use *tide* and *tidal range* in the same sentence.

_____

_____

_____

2 Write an original definition for *neap tide* and for *spring tide*.

_____

_____

_____

_____

Key Concepts

3 Describe Explain what tides are. Include *high tide* and *low tide* in your answer.

_____

_____

_____

_____

4 Explain State what causes tides on Earth.

_____

_____

_____

5 Identify Write the alignment of the moon, the sun, and Earth that causes a spring tide.

_____

_____

_____

6 Describe Explain why tides happen 50 min later each day.

_____

_____

_____

_____

Critical Thinking

Use this diagram to answer the next question.

Note: Drawing is not to scale.

Last quarter moon

7 Analyze What type of tidal range will Earth have when the moon is in this position?

_____

_____

8 Apply How many days pass between the minimum and the maximum of the tidal range in any given area? Explain your answer.

_____

_____

_____

_____

_____

9 Apply How would the tides on Earth be different if the moon revolved around Earth in 15 days instead of 30 days?

_____

_____

_____

_____

_____

_____

_____

My Notes

Unit 5   Big Idea ◀   Earth and the moon move in predictable ways and have predictable effects on each other as they orbit the sun.

Lesson 1

ESSENTIAL QUESTION
How are Earth's days, years, and seasons related to the way Earth moves in space?

Relate Earth's days, years, and seasons to Earth's movement in space.

Lesson 2

ESSENTIAL QUESTION
How do Earth, the moon, and the sun affect each other?

Describe the effects the sun and the moon have on Earth, including gravitational attraction, moon phases, and eclipses.

Lesson 3

ESSENTIAL QUESTION
What causes tides?

Explain what tides are and what causes them in Earth's oceans, and describe variations in the tides.

Connect   ESSENTIAL QUESTIONS
Lessons 1, 2, and 3

1 Synthesize Name the natural cycles that occur as a result of the Earth-moon-sun system.

_____

_____

_____

_____

Think Outside the Book

2 Synthesize Choose one of these activities to help synthesize what you have learned in this unit.

☐ Using what you learned in lessons 2 and 3, make a flipbook showing the importance of the alignment of Earth, the moon, and the sun in the Earth-moon-sun system.

☐ Using what you learned in lessons 1, 2, and 3, describe the hierarchical relationship of gravitational attraction in the Earth-moon-sun system using a poster presentation.

Name _____

Vocabulary

Fill in each blank with the term that best completes the following sentences.

1 A _____ is the periodic rise and fall of the water level in the oceans and other large bodies of water.

2 A _____ is the motion of a body that travels around another body in space.

3 The force of _____ keeps Earth and other planets of the solar system in orbit around the sun and keeps the moon in orbit around Earth.

4 A natural or artificial body that revolves around a celestial body that is greater in mass is called a _____.

5 _____ is the counterclockwise spin of a planet or moon as seen from above a planet's north pole.

Key Concepts

Read each question below, and circle the best answer.

6 Look at the table of tide information.

Date	High tide time	High tide height (m)	Low tide time	Low tide height (m)
June 3	6:04 a.m.	6.11	12:01 a.m.	1.76
June 4	6:58 a.m.	5.92	12:54 a.m.	1.87
June 5	7:51 a.m.	5.80	1:47 a.m.	1.90
June 6	8:42 a.m.	5.75	2:38 a.m.	1.87
June 7	9:30 a.m.	5.79	3:27 a.m.	1.75
June 8	10:16 a.m.	5.90	4:13 a.m.	1.56
June 9	11:01 a.m.	6.08	4:59 a.m.	1.32
June 10	11:46 a.m.	6.28	5:44 a.m.	1.05
June 11	12:32 p.m.	6.47	6:30 a.m.	0.78

What was the tidal range on June 9?

A 4.76 m

B 7.40 m

C 6.08 m

D 4.76 ft

7 Aside from Earth's tilt, what other factor contributes to Earth's seasons?

   A the time of the day

   B the energy as heat from the moon

   C the angle of the sun's rays and the number of hours of daylight

   D cold or warm air blowing from the oceans

8 Ann is looking at the night sky. There is a first-quarter moon. What does she see?

   A a moon shaped like a crescent

   B a moon shaped like a half circle

   C a moon shaped like a circle, shining brightly

   D no moon in the sky

9 Which is a similarity between a neap tide and a spring tide?

   A Neap tides occur once a year in fall and spring tides once a year in spring.

   B Each occurs twice a year and relates to the phases of the moon.

   C A neap tide occurs at night, and a spring tide occurs during the day.

   D Each tide occurs twice a month, and is determined by the pull of gravity of the moon.

10 The diagram below shows the relative positions of the sun, the moon, and Earth.

   What does the diagram show?

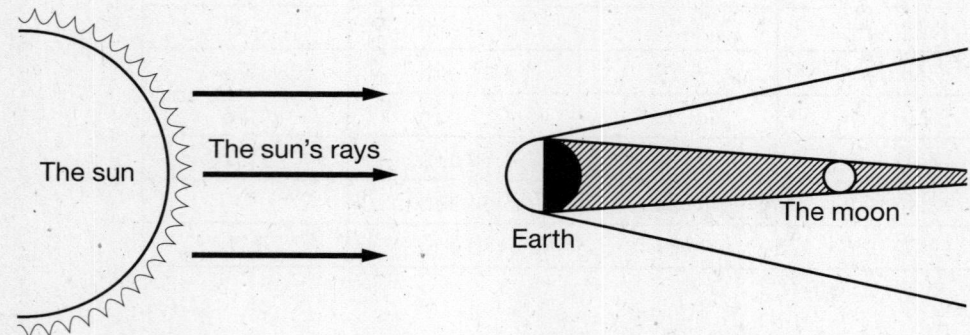

   A a solar eclipse   **C** a first-quarter moon

   B a lunar eclipse   **D** a third-quarter moon

Name _____

11 During equinox, the sun's rays strike Earth at a 90-degree angle along the equator. What is the result of the equinox?

   A the hours of daylight and the hours of darkness are about the same

   B the hours of daylight are longer than the hours of darkness

   C the hours of darkness are longer than the hours of daylight

   D an unseasonably warm day in the midst of winter

12 Examine the diagram below.

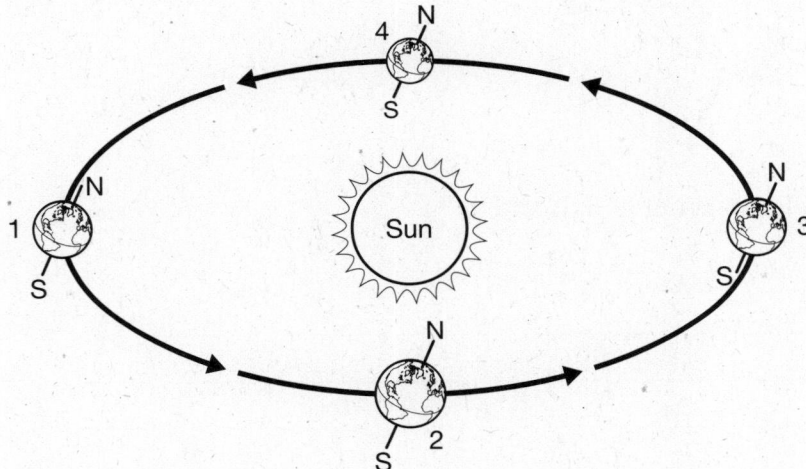

The position labeled "1" represents the season of summer in—

   A the Southern Hemisphere.   **C** the Eastern Hemisphere.

   B Antarctica.   **D** the Northern Hemisphere.

Critical Thinking

Answer the following questions in the space provided.

13 Janais lives near the ocean. How do Earth, the sun, and the moon interact to affect Janais's life?

_____

_____

_____

_____

_____

_____

14 Look at the diagram of Earth.

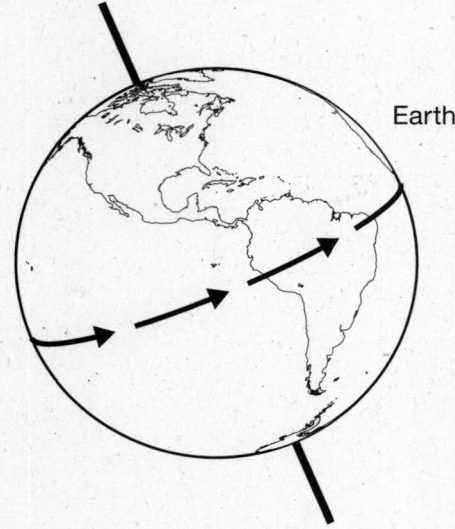

Earth

Describe the rotation of Earth about its axis and why an Earth day is 24 hours long.

_____

_____

_____

_____

_____

_____

_____

Connect ESSENTIAL QUESTIONS
Lessons 2 and 3

Answer the following question in the space provided.

15 Explain what causes tides on Earth and why high and low tides occur.

_____

_____

_____

_____

_____

_____

_____

UNIT 6
Earth's Biomes and Ecosystems

Mangroves

What do you think?

Mangroves and Roseate Spoonbills are both found in Florida. How do organisms like these get and use matter and energy?

Roseate Spoonbill

Unit 6
Earth's Biomes and Ecosystems

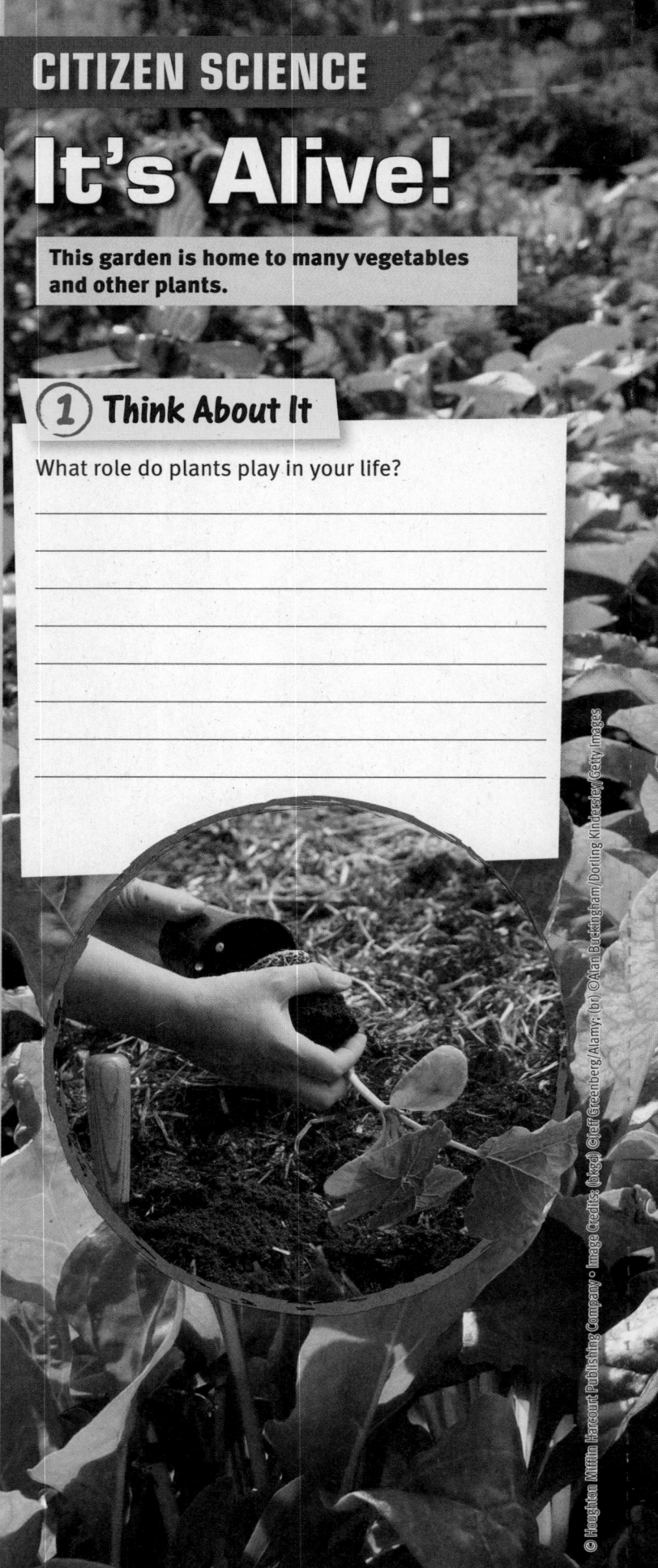

CITIZEN SCIENCE
It's Alive!

This garden is home to many vegetables and other plants.

1 Think About It

What role do plants play in your life?

_____

_____

_____

_____

_____

_____

_____

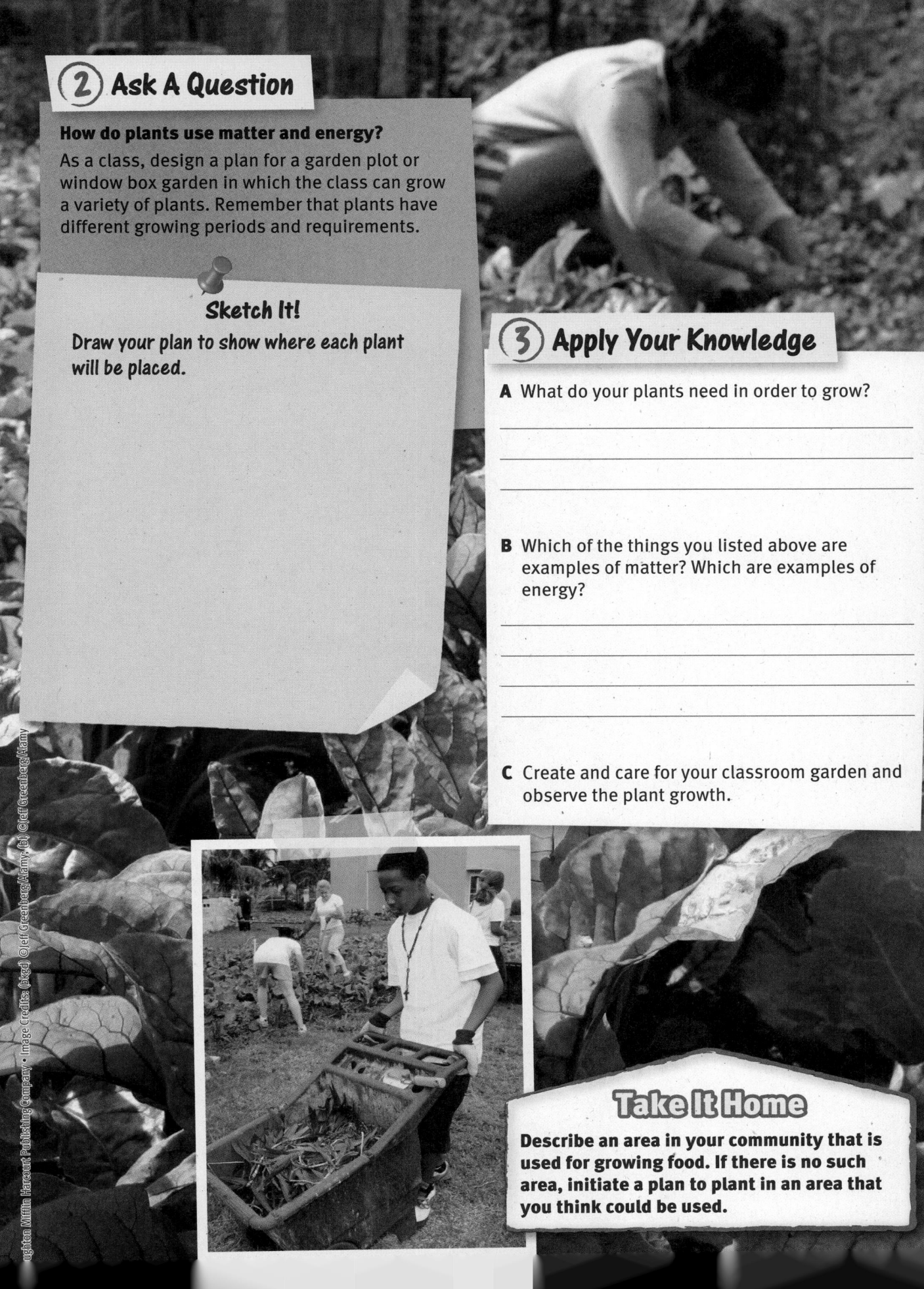

② Ask A Question

How do plants use matter and energy?

As a class, design a plan for a garden plot or window box garden in which the class can grow a variety of plants. Remember that plants have different growing periods and requirements.

Sketch It!

Draw your plan to show where each plant will be placed.

③ Apply Your Knowledge

A What do your plants need in order to grow?

_____

_____

_____

B Which of the things you listed above are examples of matter? Which are examples of energy?

_____

_____

_____

_____

C Create and care for your classroom garden and observe the plant growth.

Take It Home

Describe an area in your community that is used for growing food. If there is no such area, initiate a plan to plant in an area that you think could be used.

Photosynthesis and Cellular Respiration

ESSENTIAL QUESTION

How do cells get and use energy?

By the end of this lesson, you should be able to explain how cells capture and release energy.

Sunflowers capture light energy and change it to chemical energy, but people need to eat to get energy.

OHIO 7.LS.1 Matter is transferred continuously between one organism to another and between organisms and their physical environments.

Lesson Labs

Quick Labs
• Plant Cell Structure
• Investigate Carbon Dioxide

S.T.E.M. Lab
• Investigate Rate of Photosynthesis

Engage Your Brain

1 Predict Check T or F to show whether you think each of the following statements is true or false.

T F

☐ ☐ All living things must eat other living things for food.

☐ ☐ Plants can make their own food.

☐ ☐ Plants don't need oxygen, only carbon dioxide.

☐ ☐ Animals eat plants or other animals that eat plants.

☐ ☐ Many living things need oxygen to release energy from food.

2 Infer Look at the photo. Describe the differences between the plants. What do you think caused these differences?

_____

_____

_____

_____

_____

_____

_____

Active Reading

3 Synthesize You can often define an unknown word if you know the meaning of its word parts. Use the word parts and sentence below to make an educated guess about the meaning of the term *chlorophyll*.

Word part	Meaning
chloro-	green
-phyll	leaf

Example sentence
Chlorophyll is a pigment that captures light energy.

chlorophyll:

_____

_____

Vocabulary Terms

• photosynthesis   • cellular respiration
• chlorophyll

4 Apply As you learn the definition of each vocabulary term in this lesson, write your own definition or make a sketch to help you remember the meaning of the term.

Energize!

How do the cells in an organism function?

Active Reading 5 **Identify** As you read, underline sources of energy for living things.

How do you get the energy to run around and play soccer or basketball? How does a tree get the energy to grow? All living things, from the tiniest single-celled bacterium to the largest tree, need energy. Cells must capture and use energy or they will die. Cells get energy from food. Some living things can make their own food. Many living things get their food by eating other living things.

Your cells use energy all the time, whether you are active or not.

Cells Need Energy

Growing, moving, and other cell functions use energy. Without energy, a living thing cannot replace cells, build body parts, or reproduce. Even when a living thing is not very active, it needs energy. Cells constantly use energy to move materials into and out of the cell. They need energy to make different chemicals. And they need energy to get rid of wastes. A cell could not survive for long if it did not have the energy for all of these functions.

Active Reading 6 **Relate** Why do living things need energy at all times?

_____

_____

Cells Get Energy from Food

The cells of all living things need chemical energy. Food contains chemical energy. Food gives living things the energy and raw materials needed to carry out life processes. When cells break down food, the energy of the chemical bonds in food is released. This energy can be used or stored by the cell. The atoms and molecules in food can be used as building blocks for the cell.

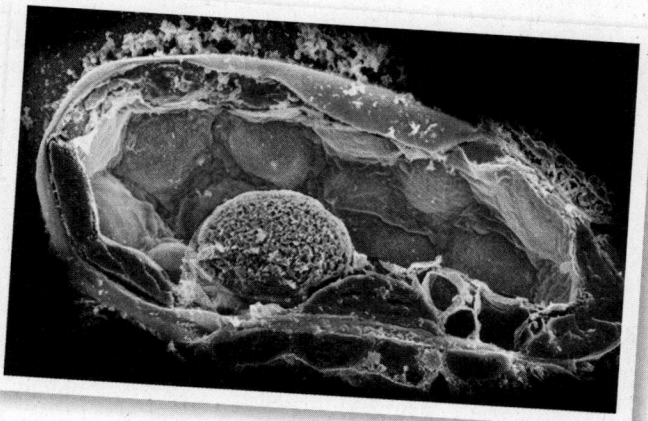

Plant cells make their own food using energy from the sun.

Living things get food in different ways. In fact, they can be grouped based on how they get food. Some living things, such as plants and many single-celled organisms, are called *producers* (proh•DOO•suhrz). Producers can make their own food. Most producers use energy from the sun. They capture and store light energy from the sun as chemical energy in food. A small number of producers, such as those that live in the deepest parts of the ocean, use chemicals to make their own food. Producers use most of the food they produce for energy. The unused food is stored in their bodies.

Many living things, such as people and other animals, are *consumers* (kun•SOO•muhrz). Consumers must eat, or consume, other living things to get food. Consumers may eat producers or other consumers. The cells of consumers break down food to release the energy it contains. A special group of consumers is made up of *decomposers* (dee•cum•POH•zhurhz). Decomposers break down dead organisms or the wastes of other organisms. Fungi and many bacteria are decomposers.

7 Compare Use the Venn diagram below to describe how producers and consumers get energy.

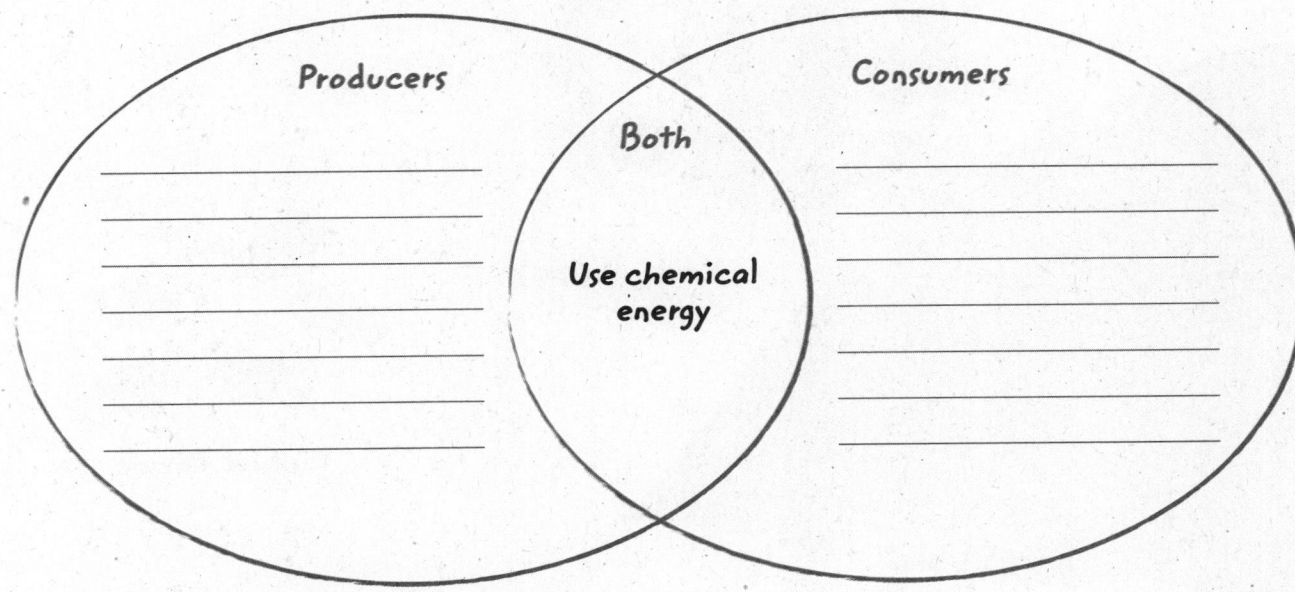

Producers

Both

Consumers

Use chemical energy

Cooking with Chloroplasts

How do plant cells make food?

Nearly all life on Earth gets energy from the sun. Plants make food with the energy from the sun. So, plants use energy from the sun directly. Animals use energy from the sun indirectly when they eat a plant or another animal.

In a process called **photosynthesis** (foh•toh•SYN•thuh•sys), plants use energy from sunlight, carbon dioxide, and water to make sugars. Plants capture light energy from the sun and change it to chemical energy in sugars. These sugars are made from water and carbon dioxide. In addition to sugars, photosynthesis also produces oxygen gas. The oxygen gas is given off into the air.

 **Active Reading**

8 Identify What is the source of energy for nearly all life on Earth?

 **Visualize It!**

Photosynthesis In many plants, photosynthesis takes place in the leaf. Chlorophyll, which is located in chloroplasts, captures light energy from the sun. This light energy is converted to chemical energy in sugars.

Plant cell

Chloroplast

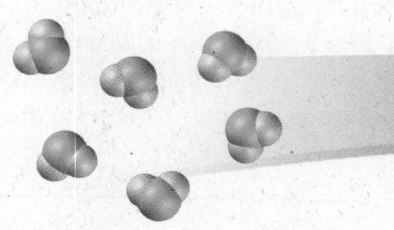

Water

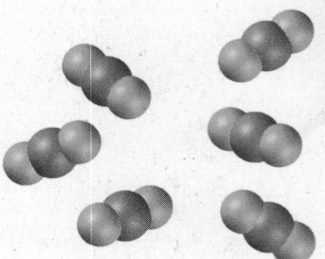

Carbon dioxide

Capturing Light Energy

Energy from sunlight powers the process of photosynthesis. The light energy is converted to chemical energy, which is stored in the bonds of the sugar molecules made during photosynthesis.

Photosynthesis takes place in organelles called *chloroplasts* (KLOHR•oh•plahstz). These organelles are found only in the cells of plants and other organisms that undergo photosynthesis. They are not found in animal or fungal cells. Chloroplasts contain a green pigment called **chlorophyll** (KLOHR•oh•fill). Chlorophyll captures energy from sunlight. This energy is used to combine carbon dioxide (CO_2) and water (H_2O), forming the sugar glucose ($C_6H_{12}O_6$) and oxygen gas (O_2). Photosynthesis is a series of reactions summarized by the following chemical equation:

$$6CO_2 + 6H_2O + \text{light energy} \longrightarrow C_6H_{12}O_6 + 6O_2$$

Chloroplast

Light energy

Oxygen

Sugar

9 Infer How do you think water and carbon dioxide used for photosynthesis get into the plant's leaf?

_____

_____

_____

_____

_____

Storing Chemical Energy

Glucose (GLOO•kohs) is a sugar that stores chemical energy. It is the food that plants make. Plant cells break down glucose for energy. Excess sugars are stored in the body of the plant. They are often stored as starch in the roots and stem of the plant. When another organism eats the plant, the organism can use these stored sugars for energy.

Mighty Mitochondria

How do cells get energy from food?

When sugar is broken down, energy is released. It is stored in a molecule called *adenosine triphosphate* (ATP). ATP powers many of the chemical reactions that enable cells to survive. The process of breaking down food to produce ATP is called **cellular respiration** (SELL•yoo•lahr ress•puh•RAY•shuhn).

Mitochondria are found in both plant cells and animal cells.

Mitochondrion

Cellular Respiration During cellular respiration, cells use oxygen gas to break down sugars and release energy.

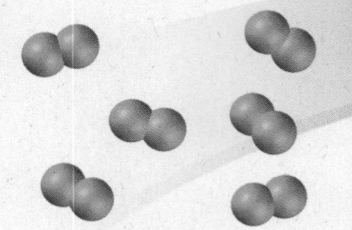

Oxygen

3-carbon molecules

Sugar from photosynthesis

Using Oxygen

Cellular respiration takes place in the cytoplasm and cell membranes of prokaryotic cells. In eukaryotic cells, cellular respiration takes place in organelles called *mitochondria* (singular, *mitochondrion*). Mitochondria are found in both plant and animal cells. The starting materials of cellular respiration are glucose and oxygen.

In eukaryotes, the first stage of cellular respiration takes place in the cytoplasm. Glucose is broken down into two 3-carbon molecules. This releases a small amount of energy. The next stage takes place in the mitochondria. This stage requires oxygen. Oxygen enters the cell and travels into the mitochondria. As the 3-carbon molecules are broken down, energy is captured and stored in ATP.

Releasing Energy

The products of cellular respiration are chemical energy (ATP), carbon dioxide, and water. The carbon dioxide formed during cellular respiration is released by the cell. In many animals, the carbon dioxide is carried to the lungs and exhaled during breathing.

Some of the energy produced during cellular respiration is released as heat. However, much of the energy produced during cellular respiration is transferred to ATP. ATP can be carried throughout the body. When ATP is broken down, the energy released is used for cellular activities. The steps of cellular respiration can be summarized by the following equation:

$$C_6H_{12}O_6 + 6O_2 \rightarrow 6CO_2 + 6H_2O + chemical\ energy\ (ATP)$$

Think Outside the Book Inquiry

11 **Identify** With a partner, write a creative story or play that describes the process of cellular respiration.

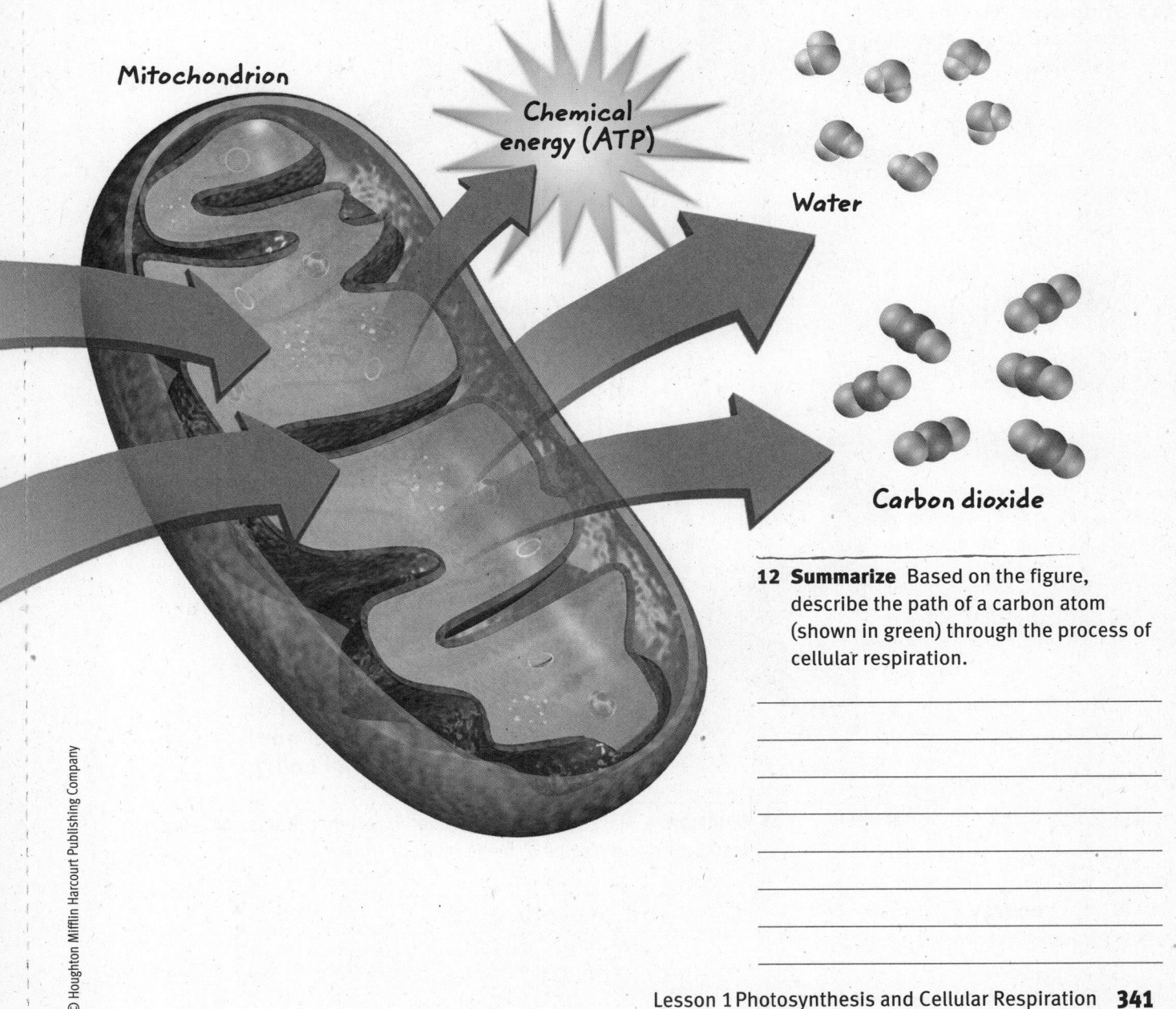

Mitochondrion

Chemical energy (ATP)

Water

Carbon dioxide

12 **Summarize** Based on the figure, describe the path of a carbon atom (shown in green) through the process of cellular respiration.

_____
_____
_____
_____
_____
_____
_____
_____
_____

Merry-Go-Round!

How are photosynthesis and cellular respiration connected?

Most of the oxygen in the atmosphere was made during photosynthesis. Nearly all organisms use this oxygen during cellular respiration. They produce carbon dioxide and release it into the environment. In turn, plants use the carbon dioxide to make sugars. So, photosynthesis and respiration are linked, each depending on the products of the other.

Ⓐ _____
energy

👁 Visualize It!

13 Synthesize Fill in the missing labels, and draw in the missing molecules.

Ⓓ _____

Used in

Produces

Chloroplast
(in plant cells)

Oxygen

Carbon dioxide

Ⓑ _____

Used in

Produces

Mitochondrion
(in plant and animal cells)

Ⓒ _____
energy

14 Summarize How are the starting materials and products of cellular respiration and photosynthesis related?

_____

_____

_____

Why It Matters

Out of Air

When there isn't enough oxygen, living things can get energy by anaerobic respiration (AN•uh•roh•bick ress•puh•RAY•shuhn). *Anaerobic* means "without oxygen." Like cellular respiration, anaerobic respiration produces ATP. However, it does not produce as much ATP as cellular respiration.

Rising to the Top

Fermentation is a type of anaerobic respiration. Many yeasts rely on fermentation for energy. Carbon dioxide is a product of fermentation. Carbon dioxide causes bread to rise, and gives it air pockets.

Feel the Burn!

The body uses anaerobic respiration during hard exercise, such as sprinting. This produces lactic acid, which can cause muscles to ache after exercise.

Extend

Inquiry

15 Compare What products do both cellular and anaerobic respiration have in common?

16 Research Blood delivers oxygen to the body. If this is the case, why does the body rely on anaerobic respiration during hard exercise? Research the reasons why the body switches between cellular and anaerobic respiration.

17 Compare Research and compare cellular respiration and fermentation. How are they similar? How do they differ? Summarize your results by doing one of the following:
- make a poster
- draw a comic strip
- write a brochure
- make a table

Visual Summary

To complete this summary, check the box that indicates true or false. Then, use the key below to check your answers. You can use this page to review the main concepts of the lesson.

Cells get and use energy

Living things need energy to survive.

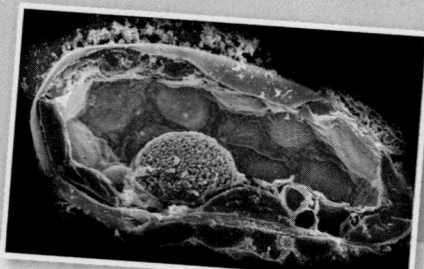

	T	F	
18	☐	☐	Organisms get energy from food.
19	☐	☐	A producer eats other organisms.

Plants make their own food.

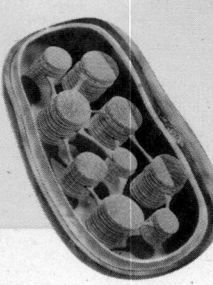

	T	F	
20	☐	☐	Photosynthesis is the process by which plants make their own food.
21	☐	☐	Chlorophyll captures light energy during photosynthesis.

Cells release energy from food during cellular respiration.

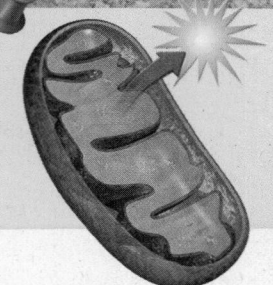

	T	F	
22	☐	☐	Carbon dioxide is required for cellular respiration.
23	☐	☐	Cellular respiration takes place in chloroplasts.

Photosynthesis and cellular respiration are interrelated.

	T	F	
24	☐	☐	The products of photosynthesis are the starting materials of cellular respiration.

Answers: 18 T; 19 F; 20 T; 21 T; 22 F; 23 F; 24 T

25 **Identify** Describe how the cells in your body get energy and then use that energy.

© Houghton Mifflin Harcourt Publishing Company • Image Credits: (tl) ©Dr. David Furness, Keele University/SPL/Photo Researchers, Inc.

Lesson Review

Vocabulary

Fill in the blank with the term that best completes the following sentences.

1 _____ takes place in organelles called *chloroplasts*.

2 Light energy is captured by the green pigment _____

3 Cells use oxygen to release energy during _____

Key Concepts

Use the figure to answer the following questions.

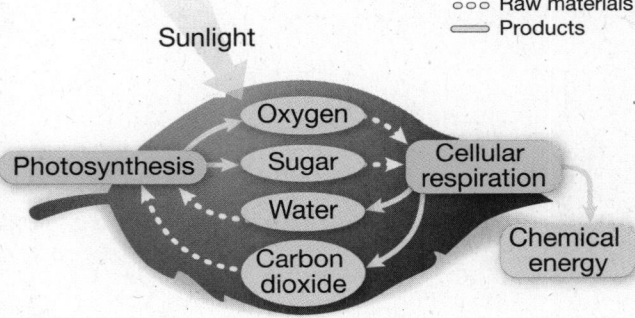

4 Identify What are the starting materials and products of photosynthesis and cellular respiration?

_____

_____

_____

_____

_____

5 Relate What does the diagram above reveal about the connections between photosynthesis and cellular respiration?

_____

_____

_____

_____

6 Contrast How do plants and animals get their energy in different ways?

_____

_____

_____

_____

_____

Critical Thinking

7 Infer Does your body get all its energy from the sun? Explain.

_____

_____

_____

_____

_____

8 Synthesize Could cellular respiration happen without photosynthesis? Explain your reasoning.

_____

_____

_____

_____

_____

9 Apply Plants don't move around, so why do they need energy?

_____

_____

_____

_____

_____

My Notes

Ecology and Energy Transfer

ESSENTIAL QUESTION

How does energy flow through an ecosystem?

By the end of this lesson, you should be able to describe how energy is transferred between organisms in food chains and food webs within an ecosystem.

Energy is transferred from the sun to producers, such as kelp. It flows through the rest of the ecosystem.

This fish also needs energy to live. How do you think it gets this energy?

OHIO **7.LS.1** Matter is transferred continuously between one organism to another and between organisms and their physical environments.
OHIO **7.SIA.5** Develop descriptions, models, explanations and predictions.

© Houghton Mifflin Harcourt Publishing Company • Image Credits: ©Steven Trainoff Ph.D./Flickr/Getty Images

Lesson Labs

Quick Labs
- Making Compost
- Energy Role Game
- Where Does All the Energy Flow?

Field Lab
- Food Webs

Engage Your Brain

1 Describe Most organisms on Earth get energy from the sun. How is energy flowing through the ecosystem pictured on the opposite page?

_____

_____

_____

_____

_____

2 Predict List two of your favorite foods. Then, explain how the sun's energy helped make those foods available to you.

_____

_____

_____

_____

_____

Active Reading

3 Synthesize You can often define an unknown word if you know the meaning of its word parts. Use the word parts and sentences below to make an educated guess about the meaning of the words *herbivore* and *carnivore*.

Word part	Meaning
-vore	to eat
herbi-	plant
carni-	meat

Example sentence
A koala is an <u>herbivore</u> that eats leaves from eucalyptus trees.

herbivore:

_____

_____

_____

Example sentence
A great white shark is a <u>carnivore</u> that eats fish and other marine animals.

carnivore:

_____

_____

_____

Vocabulary Terms

- ecosystem
- habitat
- producer
- decomposer
- consumer
- herbivore
- carnivore
- omnivore
- food chain
- food web

4 Apply As you learn the definition of each vocabulary term in this lesson, create your own definition or sketch to help you remember the meaning of the term.

We're All in This Together

What are the parts of an ecosystem?

A neighborhood park might have trees and a grassy lawn. It might also have animals such as birds and squirrels. A park is an example of an **ecosystem**. An ecosystem is a community of living organisms and their nonliving environment. Living parts of an ecosystem can include fungi, plants, animals, and bacteria. Nonliving parts of an ecosystem can include sunlight, rocks, water, soil, and air.

Ecosystems are found on land and in water. Ecosystems on land include forests, grasslands, and deserts. Aquatic ecosystems include ponds, rivers, lakes, wetlands, and ocean areas. Living and nonliving parts interact with each other in every ecosystem.

Visualize It!

5 Identify Place a check mark next to living and nonliving parts of this ecosystem.

Common loon
- [ ] living
- [ ] nonliving

Water
- [ ] living
- [ ] nonliving

Fern
- [ ] living
- [ ] nonliving

Rock
- [ ] living
- [ ] nonliving

Sunlight
- [ ] living
- [ ] nonliving

Air
- [ ] living
- [ ] nonliving

The living things in this ecosystem depend on each other and their nonliving environment for survival.

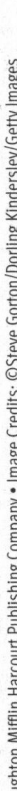

A microhabitat is small, but it still provides certain species with basic needs.

Visualize It!

6 Identify What microhabitats can you identify in this schoolyard?

_____

_____

_____

_____

_____

_____

What determines where a population can live in an ecosystem?

Living things have basic needs. These needs include water, shelter, and food for energy. Each population of organisms has different specific needs. Maple trees need soil nutrients, water, and sunlight to make food and grow. Robins need trees for nesting and insects or berries to eat. Every population has a different place and role within an ecosystem that let its members grow and survive.

Habitat

A **habitat** is the place where an organism lives within an ecosystem. Miles of grassland can be a habitat for a coyote. A pool in a forest stream can be a habitat for a snail. In other words, habitats can be large or small. The smallest habitats are called *microhabitats*. The underside of a rock is a microhabitat that provides shelter for a population of ants. A single leaf is a microhabitat that provides food for leaf miner insects. You can find many microhabitats right outside your school. Patches of grass in an athletic field or bushes growing next to the school can be thriving microhabitats.

Niche

A *niche* (NICH) is the position or role a species has in an ecosystem. A niche includes how an organism gets food and shelter. A niche also includes how an organism interacts with other organisms and the environment. For example, gray squirrels in a maple forest eat seeds from trees. They also build nests made of leaves high in the trees for shelter. Eating seeds and building nests is the squirrels' niche in this forest. In an ecosystem, each species is adapted to its environment and has its own niche.

Active Reading

7 Compare How does a niche differ from a habitat?

_____

_____

_____

© Houghton Mifflin Harcourt Publishing Company • Image Credits: ©Steve Gorton/Dorling Kindersley/Getty Images

Get Energized!

How do organisms get energy?

Energy is all around you. Chemical energy is stored in the bonds that hold molecules together. The energy from food is chemical energy in the bonds of food molecules. All living things need a source of chemical energy to survive.

Active Reading **8 Identify** As you read, underline examples of producers, decomposers, and consumers.

Producers Convert Energy into Food

A **producer**, also called an autotroph, uses energy to make food. Most producers use sunlight to make food in a process called *photosynthesis*. During photosynthesis, producers use light energy to make food from water, carbon dioxide, and nutrients found in water and soil. This food contains chemical energy and can be used immediately or stored for later use. All green plants, such as grasses and trees, are producers. Algae and some bacteria are also producers. The food that these producers make supplies the energy for other living things in an ecosystem.

Decomposers Break Down Matter

An organism that gets energy and nutrients by breaking down the remains of other organisms is a **decomposer**. Fungi, such as the mushrooms on this log, and some bacteria are decomposers. Decomposers are nature's recyclers. By converting dead organisms and animal and plant waste into materials such as water and nutrients, decomposers help move matter through ecosystems. Decomposers make these simple materials available to other organisms.

These mushrooms are decomposers. They break down the remains of plants and animals.

This plant is a producer. Producers make food using light energy from the sun.

Consumers Eat Other Organisms

A **consumer** is an organism that eats other organisms. Consumers use the energy and nutrients stored in other living organisms because they cannot make their own food. A consumer that eats only plants, such as a grasshopper or bison, is called an **herbivore**. A **carnivore**, such as a badger or a wolf, eats other animals. An **omnivore** eats both plants and animals. A *scavenger* is a specialized consumer that feeds on dead organisms. Scavengers, such as turkey vultures, eat dead animals, including leftovers of the meals of other animals.

This wolf is a consumer. It eats other organisms to get energy.

Consumers

Visualize It!

9 Apply Beside each image, place a check mark next to the word that matches the type of consumer the animal is.

Name: Hedgehog
What I eat: leaves, earthworms, insects

What am I?
☐ herbivore
☐ omnivore
☐ carnivore

Name: Moose
What I eat: grasses, fruits

What am I?
☐ herbivore
☐ omnivore
☐ carnivore

Name: Komodo dragon
What I eat: insects, birds, mammals

What am I?
☐ herbivore
☐ omnivore
☐ carnivore

10 Infer Explain how carnivores might be affected if the main plant species in a community were to disappear.

_____

_____

_____

Energy Transfer

How is energy transferred among organisms?

Organisms change energy from the environment or from their food into other types of energy. Some of this energy is used to fuel the organism's activities, such as breathing or moving. Some of the energy is saved within the organism to use later. If an organism is eaten or decomposes, the consumer or decomposer takes in the energy stored in the original organism. Only chemical energy that an organism has stored in its tissues is available to consumers. In this way, energy is transferred from organism to organism.

Active Reading **11 Infer** When a grasshopper eats grass, only some of the energy from the grass is stored in the grasshopper's body. How does the grasshopper use the rest of the energy?

_____

_____

This tree gets its energy from the sun.

12 Identify By what process does this tree get its energy?

_____

_____

This ant eats plants, such as the mesquite tree, and other insects.

13 Apply What type of energy is this ant consuming?

_____

_____

© Houghton Mifflin Harcourt Publishing Company • Image Credits: (bkgd) ©Jamie Pham/Alamy; (l) ©Dave Watts/Alamy; (r) © Peremnot Nuridsany/ Photo Researchers, Inc.

Energy Flows Through a Food Chain

A **food chain** is the path of energy transfer from producers to consumers. Energy moves from one organism to the next in one direction. The arrows in a food chain represent the transfer of energy, as one organism is eaten by another. Arrows represent the flow of energy from the body of the consumed organism to the body of the consumer of that organism.

Producers form the base of food chains. Producers transfer energy to the first, or primary, consumer in a food chain. The secondary consumer in a food chain consumes the primary consumer. A tertiary consumer can eat the secondary consumer. Decomposers in a food chain recycle matter back to the soil.

This hawk eats the lizard. It is at the top of the food chain.

Visualize It!

The photographs below show a typical desert food chain. Answer the following four questions from left to right based on your understanding of how energy flows in a food chain.

15 Predict If no consumers ever eat this hawk, what might eventually happen to the energy that is stored in its body?

_____

_____

This lizard eats mostly insects.

14 Apply What does the arrow between the ant and the lizard represent?

_____

_____

World Wide Webs

How do food webs show the flow of energy through living systems?

Few organisms eat just one kind of food. The energy flow and nutrient connections in living systems are more complicated than a simple food chain can show. A **food web** shows the feeding relationships among many different organisms in an ecosystem. Food webs are made up of many food chains.

The next page shows a coastal food web. Most of the organisms in this food web live in the water. The web also includes some birds that live on land and eat fish. Tiny organisms called phytoplankton form the base of this food web. Like plants on land, phytoplankton are producers. Tiny consumers called zooplankton eat phytoplankton. Larger animals, such as fish and squid, eat zooplankton. At the top of each chain are top predators, animals that eat other animals but are rarely eaten. In this food web, the killer whale is a top predator. Can you identify how many different energy paths lead from phytoplankton to the killer whale?

Think Outside the Book

16 Diagram Draw a food web that is different from the ones in this lesson. Circle one food chain within your food web.

Visualize It!

17 Apply Complete the statements to the right with the correct organism names from the food web.

ENERGY

ENERGY

Energy flows up the food web when

_____ eat puffins.

Puffins are connected to many organisms in the food web.

Puffins get energy by eating

_____,

_____,

and _____.

Food Web

© Houghton Mifflin Harcourt Publishing Company • Image Credits: (tl) ©Stockbyte/Getty Images; (tc) ©ImageState/Alamy; (tr) ©WILDLIFE GmbH/Alamy; (cl) ©Doug Allan/The Image Bank/Getty Images; (cc) ©Jeff Rotman/Photo Researchers, Inc.; (cr) ©blickwinkel/Alamy; (bl) ©blickwinkel/Alamy; (bc) ©CLICK_HERE/Alamy; (br) ©PictureScotland/Alamy; (inset top) ©Natural Visions/Alamy; (inset bottom) ©Science Photo Library/Alamy

The top predator is shown at the top of the food web. What is the top predator in this food web?

Killer whale

Gull

Seal

Cod

Squid

Zooplankton

Phytoplankton

Herring

Puffin

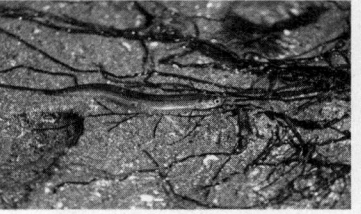

Sand lance

Consumers can eat producers and other consumers.

Producers, such as these phytoplankton, form the base of the food web.

How are organisms connected by food webs?

Living organisms can be connected by many different food webs. Food webs that begin on land or in the water can be connected by many different feeding relationships. For example, zooplankton in a water-based food web might be eaten by a fish. That fish might then be eaten by a bird that also eats insects in a land-based food web. Adult dragonflies that eat insects on land lay their eggs in the water. Some fish eat these eggs and also eat the dragonfly nymphs that hatch from them. Because food webs are interconnected, removing one organism from a food web may affect other organisms in many different ecosystems.

 **Visualize It!**

Imagine how these organisms would be affected if herring disappeared from the food web. Answer the questions starting at the bottom of the page.

■ Puffin

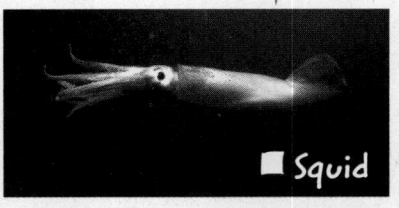
■ Squid

Herring

18 Identify Put a check mark next to the organisms that eat herring.

20 Infer Gulls don't eat herring, but they are still part of the food web below. How might gull populations be affected if herring disappeared?

_____

_____

_____

■ Gull

■ Cod

19 Predict With no herring to eat, how might the eating habits of cod change?

_____

_____

_____

_____

_____

_____

_____

Dangerous Competition

Sometimes species are introduced into a new area. These invasive species can disrupt energy flow in an ecosystem by competing with native species for sunlight or food.

Full Coverage
The kudzu plant was introduced to stop soil erosion. However, it also outgrew many native plants, preventing them from getting sunlight. Sometimes kudzu completely covers houses or cars!

Destructive Zebras
The zebra mussel is one of the most destructive invasive species in the United States. It eats by filtering tiny organisms out of the water, often leaving nothing for native mussel species to eat.

Across the Grass
The walking catfish can move from one pond to another by walking across land! When it enters a new pond, the catfish can compete with native species for food.

Extend

Inquiry

21 Relate Describe how the competition between invasive and native species might affect a food web.

22 Describe Give an example of competition for a food resource that may occur in an ecosystem near you.

23 Illustrate Provide an illustration of your example of competition in a sketch or a short story. Be sure to include the important aspects of food webs that you learned in the lesson.

Visual Summary

To complete this summary, circle the correct word. Then, use the key below to check your answers. You can use this page to review the main concepts of the lesson.

An ecosystem is made up of organisms interacting with their environment.

24 The fungi on a rotting log are an example of living / nonliving things in an ecosystem.

Habitat and niche determine where and how an organism lives in an ecosystem.

25 A tree can be a microhabitat / niche for insects in a schoolyard.

Ecology and Energy Transfer

Organisms can be classified according to how they obtain energy.

26 A producer / decomposer obtains energy through photosynthesis.

Food chains and food webs show how energy is transferred among organisms.

27 A producer / predator can be at the top of a food chain.

Answers: 24 living; 25 microhabitat; 26 producer; 27 predator

28 **Diagram** Construct a food chain for a meadow ecosystem. Sketch and label the organisms in the food chain. Use arrows to show the flow of energy from one organism to another.

Lesson Review

Vocabulary

Fill in the blanks with the term that best completes the following sentences.

1 _____ use energy from their environment to make food.

2 A _____ is the place an organism lives in an ecosystem.

3 A _____ contains many food chains.

4 _____ is the process by which light energy from the sun is converted to food.

Key Concepts

5 Describe What are the roles of producers, consumers, and decomposers in an ecosystem?

_____
_____
_____
_____
_____
_____

6 Compare How is a habitat different from an ecosystem?

_____
_____
_____
_____

7 Explain How could a food web based in water be connected to a food web based on land? Give an example.

_____
_____
_____
_____
_____

Use the figure to answer the following questions.

8 Apply The figure shows an apple tree, a caterpillar, and a cardinal. What feeding role does each organism fill in this food chain (producer, consumer, or decomposer)?

_____
_____
_____
_____
_____
_____

9 Explain What do the arrows represent in the figure above?

_____
_____
_____

Critical Thinking

10 Predict Give an example of a decomposer. Explain what would happen if decomposers were absent from a forest ecosystem.

_____
_____
_____
_____

11 Apply How would a food web be affected if a species disappeared from an ecosystem?

_____
_____
_____
_____
_____

My Notes

Kenneth Krysko

ECOLOGIST

Snakes have fascinated Dr. Kenneth Krysko since he was four years old. Now he is an ecologist specializing in herpetology—the study of snakes. You can often find him in the Florida Everglades looking for Burmese pythons. He tracks these pythons to help limit the effect they have on Florida ecosystems.

Burmese pythons can grow to be 6 meters long. They are native to southeast Asia and were illegally brought to Florida as pets. Many owners released them into the wild when the snakes grew too large. The snakes breed well in Florida's subtropical climate. And they eat just about any animal they can swallow, including many native species. Dr. Krysko tracks down these invasive pythons. Through wildlife management, molecular genetics, and other areas of study, he works with other scientists to search for ways to reduce the python population.

Dr. Krysko studies many other invasive species, that is, nonnative species that can do harm in Florida ecosystems. He shares what he learns, including ways to identify and deal with invasive species with other ecologists. Along with invasion ecology, he has done research in reproduction and conservation biology. Dr. Krysko also works as a collections manager in the herpetology division at the Florida Museum of Natural History.

Dr. Krysko works to get a handle on what to do about the invasive pythons.

JOB BOARD

Park Naturalist

What You'll Do: Teach visitors at state and national parks about the park's ecology, geology, and landscape. Lead field trips, prepare and deliver lectures with slides, and create educational programs for park visitors. You may participate in research projects and track organisms in the park.

Where You Might Work: State and national parks

Education: An advanced degree in science and teacher certification

Other Job Requirements: You need to be good at communicating and teaching. Having photography and writing skills helps you prepare interesting educational materials.

Conservation Warden

What You'll Do: Patrol an area to enforce rules, and work with communities and groups to help educate the public about conservation and ecology.

Where You Might Work: Indoors and outdoors in state and national parks and ecologically sensitive areas

Education: A two-year associate's degree or at least 60 fully accredited college-level credits

Other Job Requirements: To work in the wild, good wilderness skills, map-reading, hiking, and excellent hearing are useful.

PEOPLE IN SCIENCE NEWS

Phil McCRORY

Saved by a Hair!

Phil McCrory, a hairdresser in Huntsville, Alabama, asked a brilliant question when he saw an otter whose fur was drenched with oil from the Exxon Valdez oil spill. If the otter's fur soaked up oil, why wouldn't human hair do the same? McCrory gathered hair from the floor of his salon and performed his own experiments. He stuffed hair into a pair of pantyhose and tied the ankles together. McCrory floated this bundle in his son's wading pool and poured used motor oil into the center of the ring. When he pulled the ring closed, not a drop of oil remained in the water! McCrory's discovery was tested as an alternative method for cleaning up oil spills. Many people donated their hair to be used for cleanup efforts. Although the method worked well, the engineers conducting the research concluded that hair is not as useful as other oil-absorbing materials for cleaning up large-scale spills.

Lesson 3

Energy and Matter in Ecosystems

ESSENTIAL QUESTION

How do energy and matter move through ecosystems?

By the end of this lesson, you should be able to explain the flow of energy and the cycles of matter in ecosystems.

Living things get energy from food. Plants can make their own food, but people have to eat other organisms.

OHIO 7.ESS.3 The atmosphere has different properties at different elevations and contains a mixture of gases that cycle through the lithosphere, biosphere, hydrosphere and atmosphere.

OHIO 7.LS.1 Matter is transferred continuously between one organism to another and between organisms and their physical environments.

OHIO 7.PS.2 Energy can be transformed or transferred but is never lost.

Engage Your Brain

1 Predict Organisms get energy from food. Underline the organisms in the list below that get food by eating other organisms.

Lizard	Butterfly
Pine tree	Cactus
Grass	Mountain lion
Salamander	Bluebird
Turtle	Moss

2 Diagram Choose a nearby ecosystem, and draw a diagram below of the flow of energy from the sun to the organisms in the ecosystem.

Active Reading

3 Apply Many scientific words, such as *energy*, also have everyday meanings. Use context clues to write your own definition for each meaning of the word *energy*.

You could feel the <u>energy</u> in the crowd during the homecoming game.

_____

_____

When she had the flu, Eliza slept all day because she felt completely drained of <u>energy</u>.

_____

_____

The brightly colored painting was full of <u>energy</u>.

_____

_____

Vocabulary Terms

- energy
- matter
- law of conservation of energy
- law of conservation of mass
- energy pyramid
- water cycle
- nitrogen cycle
- carbon cycle

4 Apply As you learn the definition of each vocabulary term in this lesson, create your own definition or sketch to help remember the meaning of the term.

Soak Up the Sun

How do organisms get energy and matter?

To live, grow, and reproduce, all organisms need matter and energy. **Matter** is anything that has mass and takes up space. Organisms use matter in chemical processes, such as digestion and breathing. For these processes to occur, organisms need energy. **Energy** is the ability to do work and enables organisms to use matter in life processes. Organisms have different ways of getting matter and energy from their environment.

From the Sun

Organisms called *producers* use energy from their surroundings to make their own food. In most ecosystems, the sun is the original source of energy. Producers, like most plants and algae, use sunlight to convert water and carbon dioxide into sugars. In a few ecosystems, producers use chemical energy instead of light energy to make food. Producers take in matter, such as carbon dioxide, nitrogen, and water from air and soil.

From Other Organisms

Consumers are organisms that get energy by eating producers or other consumers. They get materials such as carbon, nitrogen, and phosphorus from the organisms they eat. So, consumers take in both energy and matter when they eat other organisms.

Active Reading

5 Identify As you read, underline the characteristics of producers and consumers.

Roots help trees get matter, such as water and nutrients, from the soil.

6 Infer Use this table to identify where producers and consumers get energy and matter.

Type of organism	How it gets energy	How it gets matter
Producer		
Consumer		

What happens to energy and matter in ecosystems?

Energy and matter are constantly moving through ecosystems. Organisms need energy and matter for many functions, such as moving, growing, and reproducing. Some producers use carbon dioxide and water to make sugars, from which they get energy. They also collect materials from their environment for their life processes. Consumers get energy and matter for their life processes by eating other organisms. During every process, some energy is lost as heat. And, matter is returned to the physical environment as wastes or when organisms die.

Energy and Matter Are Conserved

The **law of conservation of energy** states that energy cannot be created or destroyed. Energy changes forms. Some producers change light energy from the sun to chemical energy in sugars. When sugars are used, some energy is given off as heat. Much of the energy in sugars is changed to another form of chemical energy that cells can use for life functions. The **law of conservation of mass** states that mass cannot be created or destroyed. Instead, matter moves through the environment in different forms.

Energy and Matter Leave Ecosystems

Ecosystems do not have clear boundaries, so energy and matter can leave them. Matter and energy can leave an ecosystem when organisms move. For example, some birds feed on fish in the ocean. When birds fly back to land, they take the matter and energy from the fish out of the ocean. Matter and energy can leave ecosystems in moving water and air. Even though the matter and energy enter and leave an ecosystem, they are never destroyed.

Visualize It!

7 Analyze How might energy and matter leave the ecosystem shown in the picture above?

_____

_____

_____

_____

8 Compare Use the Venn diagram below to relate how energy and matter move through ecosystems.

Energy

Matter

Both

Energy and matter are conserved.

Cycle and Flow

How does energy move through an ecosystem?

Energy enters most ecosystems as sunlight, which some producers use to make food. Primary consumers, such as herbivores, get energy by consuming producers. Secondary consumers, such as carnivores, get energy by eating primary consumers, and so on up the food chain. An organism uses most of the energy it takes in for life processes. However, some energy is lost to the environment as heat. A small amount of energy is stored within an organism. Only this stored energy can be used by a consumer that eats the organism.

An **energy pyramid** is a tool that can be used to trace the flow of energy through an ecosystem. The pyramid's shape shows that there is less energy and fewer organisms at each level. At each step in the food chain, energy is lost to the environment. Because less energy is available, fewer organisms can be supported at higher levels. The bottom level—the producers—has the largest population and the most energy. The other levels are consumers. At the highest level, consumers will have the smallest population because of the limited amount of energy available to them.

The amount of energy available and population size decrease as you go up the energy pyramid.

Tertiary consumers

Secondary consumers

Primary consumers

Producers

Visualize It!

9 Analyze Describe how energy flows through each level in this energy pyramid. Is all the matter and energy from one level transferred to the next level?

_____

_____

_____

_____

_____

_____

_____

_____

© Houghton Mifflin Harcourt Publishing Company

How does matter move through an ecosystem?

Matter cycles through an ecosystem. For example, water evaporates from Earth's surface into the atmosphere and condenses to form clouds. After forming clouds, water falls back to Earth's surface, completing a cycle.

Carbon and nitrogen also cycle through an ecosystem. Producers take in compounds made of carbon and nitrogen from the physical environment. They use these compounds for life processes. Primary consumers get matter by consuming producers.

Secondary consumers eat primary consumers. The matter in primary consumers is used in chemical processes by secondary consumers. In this way, carbon and nitrogen flow from producers through all levels of consumers.

Consumers do not use all of the matter that they take in. Some of the matter is turned into waste products. Decomposers, such as bacteria and fungi, break down solid waste products and dead organisms, returning matter to the physical environment. Producers can then reuse this matter for life processes, starting the cycles of matter again.

All of these cycles can take place over large areas. Matter leaves some ecosystems and enters other ecosystems. For example, water that evaporates from a lake in the middle of a continent can later fall into an ocean. Because matter can enter and leave an ecosystem, it is called an *open system*.

Active Reading **10 Identify** What is the role of decomposers in cycling matter?

_____

_____

_____

Visualize It!

11 Analyze Describe how water is moving through the ecosystem on this page.

_____

_____

_____

_____

_____

What is the water cycle?

The movement of water between the oceans, atmosphere, land, and living things is known as the **water cycle**. Three ways water can enter the atmosphere are evaporation, transpiration, and respiration. During *evaporation*, the sun's heat causes water to change from liquid to vapor. Plants release water vapor from their leaves in *transpiration*. Organisms release water as waste during *respiration*.

In *condensation*, the water vapor cools and returns to liquid. The water that falls from the atmosphere to the land and oceans is *precipitation*. Rain, snow, sleet, and hail are forms of precipitation. Most precipitation falls into the ocean. The precipitation that falls on land and flows into streams and rivers is called *runoff*. Some precipitation seeps into the ground and is stored underground in spaces between or within rocks. This water, called *groundwater*, will slowly flow back into the soil, streams, rivers, and oceans.

Active Reading

12 Explain How does water from the atmosphere return to Earth's surface?

_____

_____

_____

_____

_____

_____

Visualize It!

13 Label Use the terms *evaporation*, *transpiration*, and *respiration* to correctly complete the diagram. Be sure the arrow for each term leads from the proper source.

Condensation

Precipitation

Water vapor in air

Runoff

Groundwater

A

B

C

The water cycle describes how water travels from Earth's surface to the atmosphere and back.

What is the nitrogen cycle?

Organisms need nitrogen to build proteins and DNA for new cells. The movement of nitrogen between the environment and living things is called the **nitrogen cycle**. Most of Earth's atmosphere is nitrogen gas. But most organisms cannot use nitrogen gas directly. However, bacteria in the soil are able to change nitrogen gas into forms that plants can use. This process is called *nitrogen fixation*. Lightning can also fix nitrogen into usable compounds. Plants take in and use fixed nitrogen. Consumers can then get the nitrogen they need by eating plants or other organisms.

When organisms die, decomposers break down their remains. Decomposition releases a form of nitrogen into the soil that plants can use. Finally, certain types of bacteria in the soil can convert nitrogen into a gas, which is returned to the atmosphere.

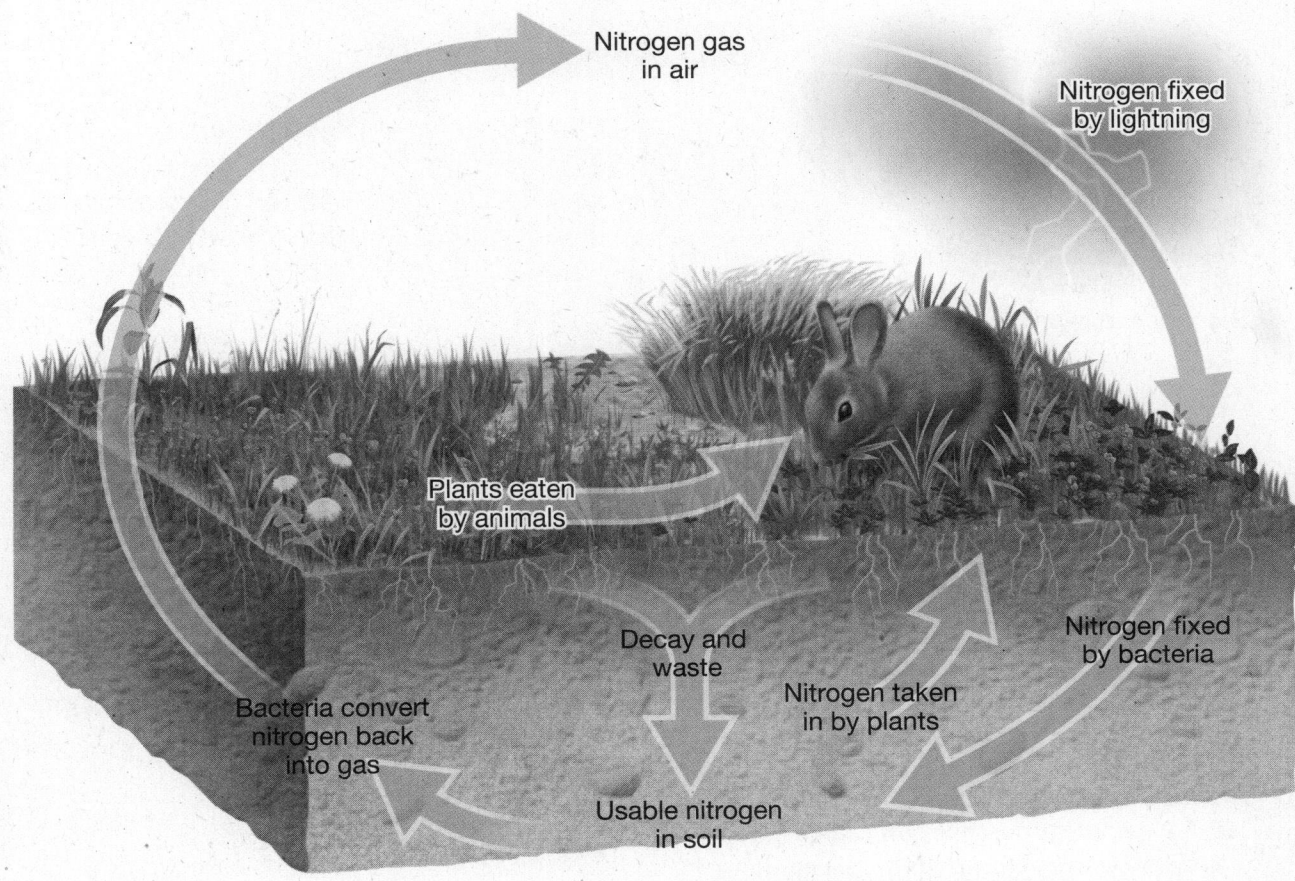

Nitrogen gas in air

Nitrogen fixed by lightning

Plants eaten by animals

Decay and waste

Nitrogen taken in by plants

Nitrogen fixed by bacteria

Bacteria convert nitrogen back into gas

Usable nitrogen in soil

In the nitrogen cycle, nitrogen gas is converted into usable nitrogen by bacteria and lightning. Plants take in the usable nitrogen. Consumers get the nitrogen they need from the organisms they eat.

Visualize It! Inquiry

14 Hypothesize What would happen to the ecosystem if there were no nitrogen-fixing bacteria?

_____

_____

_____

_____

What is the carbon cycle?

Carbon is an important building block of organisms. It is found in sugars, which store the chemical energy that organisms need to live. It also is found in the atmosphere (as carbon dioxide gas), in bodies of water, in rocks and soils, in organisms, and in fossil fuels. Carbon moves through organisms and between organisms and the physical environment in the **carbon cycle**.

Active Reading **15 List** Identify five places where carbon may be found.

_____

_____

_____

Respiration

Photosynthesis

Photosynthesis

During photosynthesis, producers in the water and on land take in light energy from the sun and use carbon dioxide and water to make sugars. These sugars contain carbon and store chemical energy. Oxygen gas is also a product of photosynthesis.

Respiration

Cellular respiration occurs in producers and consumers on land and in water. During respiration, sugars are broken down to release energy. The process uses oxygen gas. Energy, carbon dioxide, and water are released.

carbon in organisms

carbon dioxide dissolved in water

Visualize It!

16 Relate Briefly describe how carbon enters and exits a consumer, such as the sheep shown in this diagram.

_____

_____

_____

_____

_____

Combustion

Combustion is the burning of materials, including wood and fossil fuels. Burning once-living things releases carbon dioxide, water, heat, and other materials into the environment. It may also produce pollution.

carbon dioxide in air

Combustion

Photosynthesis

Respiration

Decomposition

carbon in organisms

Decomposition

Decomposition is the breakdown of dead organisms and wastes. Decomposers get energy from this material by respiration. Decomposition returns carbon dioxide, water, and other nutrients to the environment.

carbon in fossil fuels

Fossil Fuels

Fossil fuels formed from decomposing organisms that were buried deeply millions of years ago. Fossil fuels are burned during combustion, releasing carbon dioxide into the air.

Think Outside the Book Inquiry

17 **Apply** With a partner, choose an ecosystem with which you are familiar. Make a diagram of how carbon cycles in the ecosystem and how energy flows through it. Be sure to label your diagram.

Visual Summary

To complete this summary, fill in the blanks with the correct word or phrase. Then use the key below to check your answers. You can use this page to review the main concepts of the lesson.

Energy and Matter in Ecosystems

Organisms get energy and matter from different sources.

18 Many _____ get energy from sunlight.

19 _____ get energy by eating other organisms.

Water moves between Earth's surface and the atmosphere in the water cycle.

20 Water that flows over the surface of the ground is called _____

Nitrogen moves from the atmosphere, to organisms, and back to the atmosphere in the nitrogen cycle.

21 _____ is the process by which bacteria turn nitrogen gas into compounds plants can use.

Carbon cycles through organisms, into the physical environment, and back again.

22 Dead organisms that were buried may turn into _____ after millions of years.

23 Carbon from this material reenters the atmosphere by _____

Answers: 18 producers; 19 Consumers; 20 runoff; 21 Nitrogen fixation; 22 fossil fuels; 23 combustion

24 **Explain** If energy and matter cannot be destroyed, what happens to energy and matter when an organism is eaten?

Lesson Review

Vocabulary

Fill in the blanks with the term that best completes the following sentences.

1 The ability to do work is called _____

2 _____ is anything that has mass and takes up space.

3 A(n) _____ can be used to trace the flow of energy through an ecosystem.

Key Concepts

4 Describe Explain the difference between a producer, a consumer, and a decomposer.

_____
_____
_____

5 Compare How are the law of conservation of energy and the law of conservation of mass similar?

_____
_____
_____
_____
_____

6 Explain Why do organisms need nitrogen?

_____
_____
_____
_____
_____

Critical Thinking

7 Analyze In an ecosystem, which would have a larger population: producers or primary consumers? Explain.

_____
_____
_____

Use the graph to answer the following questions.

Average Carbon Dioxide Levels at Mauna Loa, Hawaii

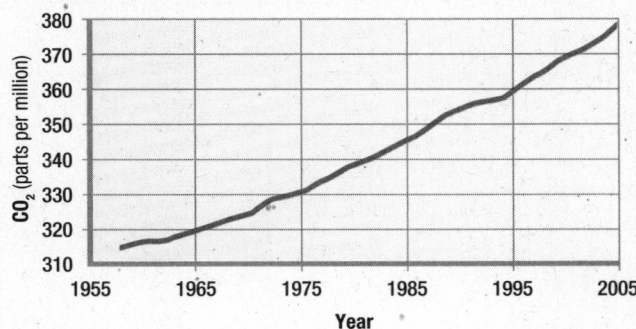

Source: *NOAA 2004*

8 Analyze What process of the carbon cycle is likely causing the increase in carbon dioxide levels shown in the graph above?

_____
_____

9 Identify What is the most likely source of the increase in carbon dioxide in the atmosphere shown in the graph above?

_____
_____

10 Evaluate If people planted huge numbers of trees and other plants, how might the carbon dioxide levels in the graph above change? Explain your answer.

_____
_____
_____
_____
_____

11 Apply Water is traveling up a tree carrying nutrients. Use the water cycle to explain how that water later becomes groundwater.

_____
_____
_____
_____
_____

My Notes

Engineering Design Process

Skills
Identify a need
✔ Conduct research
Brainstorm solutions
✔ Select a solution
✔ Build a prototype
✔ Test and evaluate
✔ Redesign to improve
✔ Communicate results

Objectives

• Explain the flow of energy in an ecosystem.

• Build and analyze a closed ecosystem.

Design an Ecosystem

An ecosystem is a community of organisms that interact with each other and with the nonliving environment in a specific area. Factors, such as temperature, the amount of sunlight, water, and minerals, determine which species can live in an ecosystem. Populations of organisms in an ecosystem can be classified by their function. Some producers, such as algae and green plants, make their own food by using sunlight through a process called photosynthesis. Consumers can be carnivores, herbivores, or omnivores. Decomposers, such as fungi and some bacteria, are consumers that break down dead plants and animals and recycle them as nutrients that other organisms can use.

1 Identify On the illustration of the ecosystem, label A through D as a producer, a consumer, or a decomposer.

A

B

Energy in Ecosystems

A food web is the feeding relationship among organisms within an ecosystem. Energy and nutrients are transferred within a food web as organisms feed. Producers form the base of the food web. When producers, such as plants, are consumed, only one tenth of the energy they get from the sun is passed up the food web to primary consumers. The primary consumers, for example herbivores, use the energy they get from plants to grow, reproduce, and live. In turn, when herbivores are eaten, only about one tenth of the energy is passed to secondary consumers, which are carnivores. The decreasing amounts of energy transferred to higher levels is shown by the energy pyramid here.

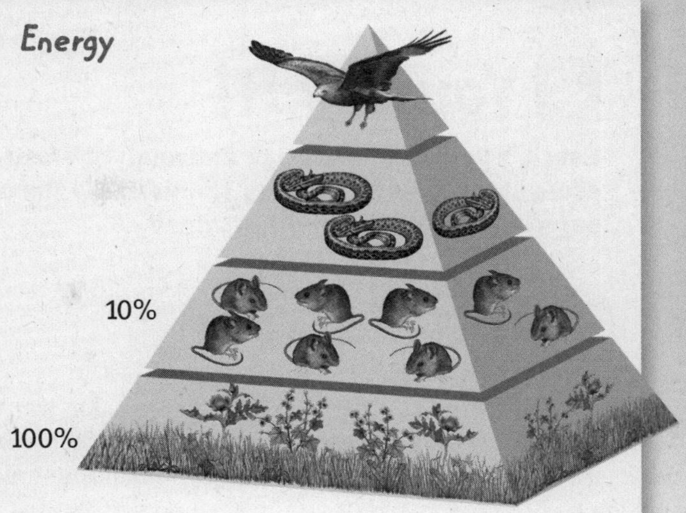

Energy

10%

100%

2 Infer In this example, what percentage of the energy that was available in the grass would reach the snakes? What percentage would reach the eagle? Explain your reasoning.

_____

_____

_____

C

D

✋ **You Try It!** ⟶

Now it's your turn to design a self-contained aquatic ecosystem.

 # You Try It!

Now it's your turn to design and analyze a self-contained aquatic ecosystem. Your ecosystem should allow the occupants to survive just from the light provided.

You Will Need

✓ one-gallon glass jar with tight-fitting lid or sealable clear plastic container

✓ fresh water; can use tap water, but water from natural source is preferable

✓ gravel

✓ aquatic plants and animals to be selected by students

✓ light source if needed

✓ decorative aquarium items (optional)

(1) Conduct Research

Write down the plants and animals that you want to put into your ecosystem. Use fast-growing plants to provide oxygen and food for the animals. Also, write down how decomposers get into the system.

_____

_____

_____

_____

(2) Select a Solution

Based on the flow of energy and biomass in an ecosystem, determine the rough proportion of producers and consumers needed in the ecosystem you are designing. Write down how many plants to animals you think that you will need. Explain your reasoning.

_____

_____

_____

_____

(3) Build a Prototype

Follow these steps to build a prototype of your system.

- Clean your container, and record its mass.
- Put enough gravel in to cover the bottom.
- Fill the container with water, and add decorative items.
- Let the water and decorative items settle for at least 24 hours to allow the chemicals in the water to evaporate and the water to come to room temperature.
- Add your plants, and wait 24 hours.

- Before releasing the animals into the tank, float the containers holding the animals in the water in the tank for a few hours. This allows the animals to adjust to the temperature of the water in the tank.
- Close the lid tightly to prevent evaporation, and then record the mass of your ecosystem.
- Store your ecosystem where it will receive indirect sunlight.

(4) Test and Evaluate

List five things that you think would be important to record before you close your system completely. Keep a journal in which you record daily observations of your ecosystem for several weeks.

_____

_____

_____

_____

_____

(5) Redesign to Improve

After observing your system and keeping a journal for several weeks, what would you change about your system?

_____

_____

_____

_____

_____

_____

_____

(6) Communicate Results

Summarize the observations you made in your journal. Consider these questions: What things do you think made your ecosystem successful or unsuccessful? What things, if any, would you change to improve your ecosystem even more? Finally, make a report of your ecosystem to present to the class.

_____

_____

_____

_____

_____

_____

_____

Lesson 4

Land Biomes

ESSENTIAL QUESTION

What are land biomes?

By the end of this lesson, you should be able to describe the characteristics of different biomes that exist on land.

The North American prairie is an example of a grassland biome. It is home to grazing animals such as the bison.

Herds of thousands of bison used to roam the prairies. Bison became rare as people hunted them and developed the prairie into farmland.

OHIO **7.LS.2** In any particular biome, the number, growth and survival of organisms and populations depend on biotic and abiotic factors.

OHIO **7.SIA.5** Develop descriptions, models, explanations and predictions.

👋 Lesson Labs

Quick Labs
• Climate Determines Plant Life
• Identify Your Land Biome

Field Lab
• Survey of a Biome's Biotic and Abiotic Factors

🧠 Engage Your Brain

1 Compare How are the two biomes in the pictures at right different from each other?

_____
_____
_____
_____
_____
_____

2 Infer Which of these biomes gets more rain? Explain your answer.

_____
_____
_____
_____
_____

A

B

✏️ Active Reading

3 Word Parts Parts of words that you know can help you find the meanings of words you don't know. The suffix *-ous* means "possessing" or "full of." Use the meanings of the root word and suffix to write the meaning of the term *coniferous tree*.

Root Word	Meaning
conifer	tree or shrub that produces cones

coniferous tree:

_____
_____
_____

Vocabulary Terms

• biome
• tundra
• taiga
• coniferous tree
• desert
• grassland
• deciduous tree

4 Apply As you learn the definition of each vocabulary term in this lesson, create your own definition or sketch to help you remember the meaning of the term.

Home Sweet Biome

The taiga is a northern latitude biome that has low average temperatures, nutrient-poor soil, and coniferous trees.

What is a biome?

If you could travel Earth from pole to pole, you would pass through many different biomes. A **biome** is a region of Earth where the climate determines the types of plants that live there. The types of plants in a biome determine the types of animals that live there. Deserts, grasslands, tundra, taiga, temperate forests, and tropical forests are all types of biomes.

What makes one biome different from another?

Each biome has a unique community of plants and animals. The types of organisms that can live in a biome depend on the biome's climate and other abiotic, or nonliving, factors.

Climate

Climate is the main abiotic factor that characterizes a biome. Climate describes the long-term patterns of temperature and precipitation in a region. The position of a biome on Earth affects its climate. Biomes that are closer to the poles receive less annual solar energy and have colder climates. Biomes that are near the equator receive more annual solar energy and have warmer climates. Biomes that are close to oceans often have wet climates.

Earth's Major Land Biomes

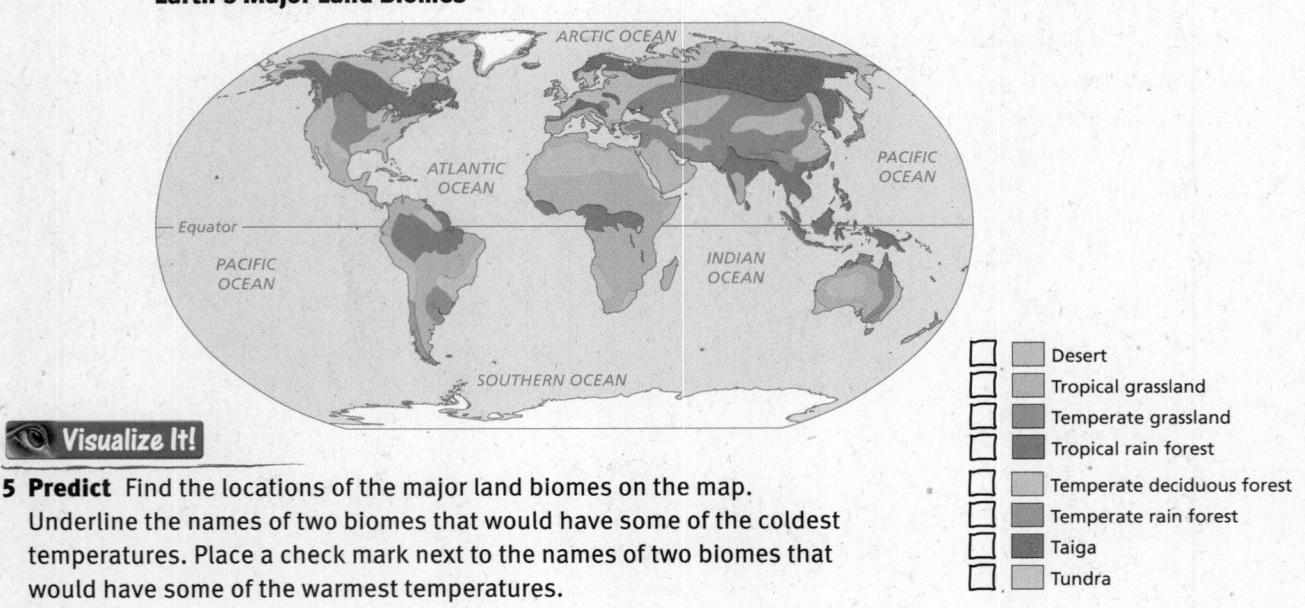

- ☐ Desert
- ☐ Tropical grassland
- ☐ Temperate grassland
- ☐ Tropical rain forest
- ☐ Temperate deciduous forest
- ☐ Temperate rain forest
- ☐ Taiga
- ☐ Tundra

🔍 **Visualize It!**

5 Predict Find the locations of the major land biomes on the map. Underline the names of two biomes that would have some of the coldest temperatures. Place a check mark next to the names of two biomes that would have some of the warmest temperatures.

Other Abiotic Factors

Other abiotic factors that characterize a biome include soil type, amount of sunlight, and amount of water that is available. Abiotic factors affect which organisms can live in a biome.

Plant and Animal Communities

Adaptations are features that allow organisms to survive and reproduce. Plants and animals that live in a biome have adaptations to its unique conditions. For example, animals that live in biomes that are cold all year often grow thick fur coats. Plants that live in biomes with seasonal temperature changes lose their leaves and become inactive in winter. Plants that live in warm, rainy biomes stay green and grow all year long.

Active Reading

6 Identify As you read, underline the abiotic factors besides climate that characterize a biome.

Visualize It!

7 Infer Place a check mark in each box to predict the average temperature range for each of the biomes shown.

☐ Warm All Year

☐ Cool All Year

☐ Seasonal Temperatures

☐ Warm All Year

☐ Cool All Year

☐ Seasonal Temperatures

☐ Warm All Year

☐ Cool All Year

☐ Seasonal Temperatures

Life in a Biome

How are ecosystems related to biomes?

Most biomes stretch across huge areas of land. Within each biome are smaller areas called ecosystems. Each *ecosystem* includes a specific community of organisms and their physical environment. A temperate forest biome can contain pond or river ecosystems. Each of these ecosystems has floating plants, fish, and other organisms that are adapted to living in or near water. A grassland biome can contain areas of small shrubs and trees. These ecosystems have woody plants, insects, and nesting birds.

Visualize It!

Three different ecosystems are shown in this temperate rain forest biome. Different organisms live in each of these ecosystems.

8 Identify List three organisms that you see in the picture that are part of each ecosystem within the biome.

Tree Canopy Ecosystem

_____

_____

Stream Ecosystem

_____

_____

Forest Floor Ecosystem

_____

_____

What are the major land biomes?

There are six major land biomes. These include tundra, taiga, desert, grassland, temperate forest, and tropical forest.

 **9 Identify** Underline the abiotic features that characterize tundra and taiga biomes.

Tundra

Tundra has low average temperatures and very little precipitation. The ground contains permafrost, a thick layer of permanently frozen soil beneath the surface. Tundra is found in the Arctic and in high mountain regions. Tundra plants include mosses and woody shrubs. These plants have shallow roots, since they cannot grow into the permafrost. Tundra winters are dark, cold, and windy. Animals such as musk oxen have thick fur and fat deposits that protect them from the cold. Some animals, such as caribou, migrate to warmer areas before winter. Ground squirrels hibernate, or become dormant, underground.

Taiga

Taiga is also called the boreal forest. **Taiga** has low average temperatures like those in the tundra biome, but more precipitation. The soil layer in taiga is thin, acidic, and nutrient-poor. Taiga biomes are found in Canada and northern Europe and Asia. Taiga plants include **coniferous trees**, which are trees that have evergreen, needlelike leaves. These thin leaves let trees conserve water and produce food all year long. Migratory birds live in taiga in summer. Wolves, owls, and elk live in taiga year-round. Some animals, such as snowshoe hares, experience a change in fur color as the seasons change. Hares that match their surroundings are not seen by predators as easily.

Visualize It!

10 Describe Below each picture, describe how organisms that you see are adapted to the biome in which they live.

Tundra

_____
_____
_____
_____

Taiga

_____
_____
_____
_____

Desert

Desert biomes are very dry. Some deserts receive less than 8 centimeters (3 inches) of precipitation each year. Desert soil is rocky or sandy. Many deserts are hot during the day and cold at night, although some have milder temperatures. Plants and animals in this biome have adaptations that let them conserve water and survive extreme temperatures. Members of the cactus family have needlelike leaves that conserve water. They also contain structures that store water. Many desert animals are active only at night. Some animals burrow underground or move into shade to stay cool during the day.

Active Reading

11 Identify As you read, underline the characteristics of deserts.

Visualize It!

12 Describe List the ways that each plant or animal in the picture is adapted to the desert biome.

Saguaro Cactus

_____
_____
_____
_____
_____

Desert Tortoise

A tortoise can crawl into shade or retreat into its shell to avoid the heat. A tortoise has thick skin that prevents water loss.

Kangaroo Rat

_____
_____
_____
_____
_____

Tropical Grassland

A **grassland** is a biome that has grasses and few trees. Tropical grasslands, such as the African savanna, have high average temperatures throughout the year. They also have wet and dry seasons. Thin soils support grasses and some trees in this biome. Grazing animals, such as antelope and zebras, feed on grasses. Predators such as lions hunt grazing animals. Animals in tropical grasslands migrate to find water during dry seasons. Plants in tropical grasslands are adapted to survive periodic fires.

Temperate Grassland

Temperate grasslands, such as the North American prairie, have moderate precipitation, hot summers, and cold winters. These grasslands have deep soils that are rich in nutrients. Grasses are the dominant plants in this biome. Bison, antelope, prairie dogs, and coyotes are common animals. Periodic fires sweep through temperate grasslands. These fires burn dead plant material and kill trees and shrubs. Grasses and other nonwoody plants are adapted to fire. Some of these plants regrow from their roots after a fire. Others grow from seeds that survived the fire.

Visualize It!

13 Describe Write captions to explain how fire shapes a temperate grassland biome.

Between fires, small trees begin to grow in a temperate grassland.

_____
_____
_____
_____
_____
_____
_____

Temperate Deciduous Forest

Temperate deciduous forests have moderate precipitation, hot summers, and cold winters. These forests are located in the northeastern United States, East Asia, and much of Europe. This biome has **deciduous trees**, which are broadleaf trees that drop their leaves as winter approaches. Fallen leaves decay and add organic matter to the soil, making it nutrient-rich. Songbirds nest in these forests during summer, but many migrate to warmer areas before winter. Animals such as chipmunks and black bears hibernate during winter. Deer and bobcats are active year-round.

Temperate Rain Forest

Temperate rain forests have a long, cool wet season and a relatively dry summer. Temperate rain forests exist in the Pacific Northwest and on the western coast of South America. This biome is home to many coniferous trees, including Douglas fir and cedar. The forest floor is covered with mosses and ferns and contains nutrient-rich soil. Plants grow throughout the year in the temperate rain forest. Animals in this biome include spotted owls, shrews, elk, and cougars.

👁 Visualize It!

14 Summarize Fill in the missing information on the cards to describe each of these temperate forest biomes.

Temperate Rain Forest

A. Climate: _____

B. Soil: _____

C. Plants: _____

D. Animals: _____

Temperate Deciduous Forest

A. Climate: _____

B. Soil: _____

C. Plants: _____

D. Animals: _____

Think Outside the Book Inquiry

15 Apply With a classmate, compare the adaptations of animals that migrate, hibernate, or stay active year-round in a temperate deciduous forest.

Tropical Rain Forest

Tropical rain forests are located near Earth's equator. This biome is warm throughout the year. It also receives more rain than any other biome on Earth. The soil in tropical rain forests is acidic and low in nutrients. Even with poor soil, tropical rain forests have some of the highest biological diversity on Earth. Dense layers of plants develop in a tropical rain forest. These layers block sunlight from reaching the forest floor. Some plants such as orchids grow on tree branches instead of on the dark forest floor. Birds, monkeys, and sloths live in the upper layers of the rain forest. Leaf-cutter ants, jaguars, snakes, and anteaters live in the lower layers.

Visualize It!

16 **Display** Color in the band labeled *Light Level* next to the picture of the tropical rain forest. Make the band darkest at the level where the forest would receive the least light. Make the band lightest at the level where the forest would receive the most light.

Light Level

Emergent Layer

Canopy

Understory

Forest Floor

Visual Summary

To complete this summary, fill in the answers to the questions. Then, use the key below to check your answers. You can use this page to review the main concepts of the lesson.

Land Biomes

A biome is a region of Earth characterized by a specific climate and specific plants and animals.

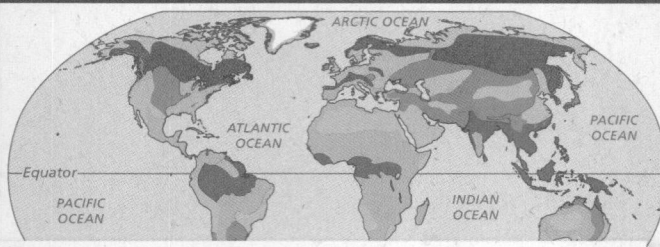

17 What are the major land biomes?

_____

_____

_____

Each biome can contain many ecosystems.

18 How are ecosystems different from biomes?

_____

_____

_____

Plants and animals are adapted to the conditions in their biome.

19 The plant below is adapted to what conditions?

_____

_____

_____

Sample answers: 17 tundra, taiga, desert, grassland, temperate forest, tropical forest; 18 Ecosystems are smaller areas within biomes that include communities of organisms and their nonliving environment.; 19 dry conditions

20 Predict Describe what might happen to the organisms in a desert if the climate changed and rainfall increased.

Lesson Review

Vocabulary

Define Draw a line to connect the following terms to their definitions.

1 a region that has a specific climate and a specific community of plants and animals

A taiga

2 a region with low average temperatures and little precipitation

B climate

3 long-term temperature and precipitation patterns in a region

C biome

Key Concepts

4 Identify What are the abiotic factors that help to characterize a biome?

_____

_____

_____

5 Describe Describe a tropical grassland biome.

_____

_____

_____

_____

6 Explain How does climate determine the organisms that live in a biome?

_____

_____

_____

7 Summarize Why can many ecosystems exist in one biome?

_____

_____

_____

Critical Thinking

Use the Venn diagram to answer the following questions.

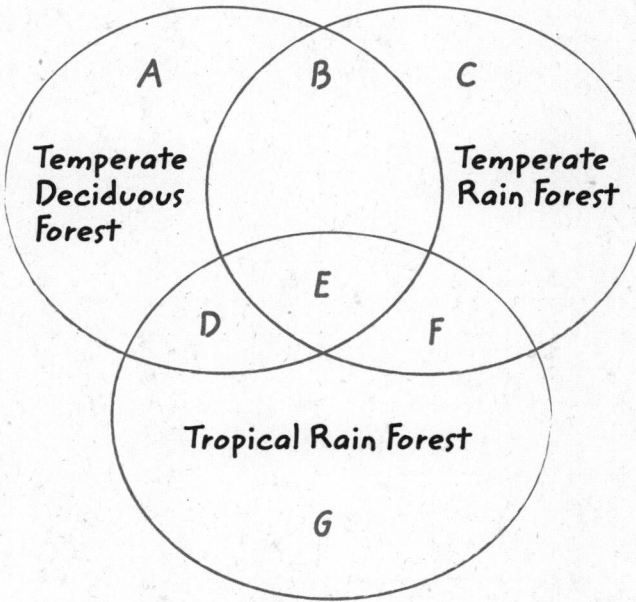

8 Infer In which space on the Venn diagram would you write *coniferous trees*?

_____

9 Analyze What is common among all three types of forests in the diagram?

_____

_____

10 Relate What biome do you think you live in? Explain your answer.

_____

_____

_____

_____

_____

My Notes

Lesson 5

Aquatic Ecosystems

ESSENTIAL QUESTION

What are aquatic ecosystems?

By the end of this lesson, you should be able to describe the characteristics of marine, freshwater, and other aquatic ecosystems.

Coral reefs are coastal ocean ecosystems that are located in many tropical areas. Coral reefs have some of the highest biological diversity on Earth.

OHIO **7.LS.2** In any particular biome, the number, growth and survival of organisms and populations depend on biotic and abiotic factors.

OHIO **7.SIA.5** Develop descriptions, models, explanations and predictions.

390

© Houghton Mifflin Harcourt Publishing Company • Image Credits: (bg) ©Jeffrey Rotman/Corbis

Engage Your Brain

1 Predict Check T or F to show whether you think each statement is true or false.

T   F

☐ ☐ Wetlands can protect areas close to shorelines from flooding.

☐ ☐ Most ponds contain both salt water and fresh water.

☐ ☐ Plants and animals cannot live in fast-moving waters.

☐ ☐ The deep ocean is colder and darker than other marine ecosystems.

2 Predict How do you think organisms like this squid are adapted to life in the deep ocean?

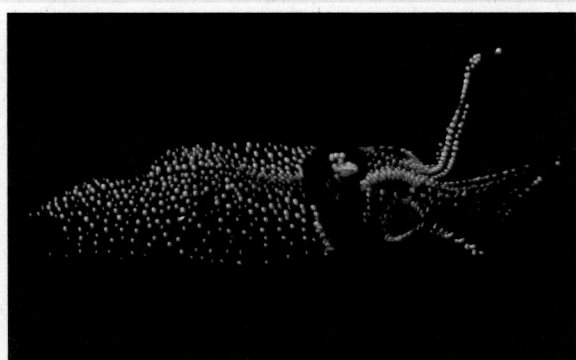

_____

_____

_____

3 Synthesize You can often define an unknown word if you know the meaning of its word parts. Use the word parts and sentence below to make an educated guess about the meaning of the word *wetland*.

Word part	Meaning
wet-	having water or liquid on the surface
-land	solid part of Earth's surface

Example sentence:
Many species of birds and mammals rely on <u>wetlands</u> for food, water, and shelter.

wetland:

_____

_____

Vocabulary Terms
- wetland
- estuary

4 Identify As you read, place a question mark next to any words that you don't understand. When you finish reading the lesson, go back and review the text you marked. Work with a classmate to define the words that are still unclear.

Splish Splash

What are the major types of aquatic ecosystems?

Have you ever gone swimming in the ocean, or fishing on a lake? Oceans and lakes support many of the aquatic ecosystems on Earth. An *aquatic ecosystem* includes any water environment and the community of organisms that live there.

The three main types of aquatic ecosystems are freshwater ecosystems, estuaries, and marine ecosystems. Freshwater ecosystems can be found in rivers, lakes, and wetlands. Marine ecosystems are found in oceans. Rivers and oceans form estuaries where they meet at a coastline.

What abiotic factors affect aquatic ecosystems?

Abiotic factors are the nonliving things in an environment. The major abiotic factors that affect aquatic ecosystems include water temperature, water depth, amount of light, oxygen level, water pH, salinity (salt level), and the rate of water flow. An aquatic ecosystem may be influenced by some of these factors but not others. For example, a river would be influenced by rate of water flow but not typically by salinity.

Visualize It!

5 Identify Fill in the major types of aquatic ecosystems in the picture.

Freshwater and marine ecosystems meet at a coastline. These ecosystems form estuaries, which have a mixture of fresh water and salt water.

A _____

estuary

B _____

6 Compare What is the main difference in the water that is in freshwater ecosystems, estuaries, and marine ecosystems?

_____
_____
_____

Where are examples of freshwater ecosystems found?

Freshwater ecosystems contain water that has very little salt in it. Freshwater ecosystems are found in lakes, ponds, wetlands, rivers, and streams. Although freshwater ecosystems seem common, they actually contain less than one percent of all the water on Earth.

In Lakes and Ponds

Lakes and ponds are bodies of water surrounded by land. Lakes are larger than ponds. Some plants grow at the edges of these water bodies. Others live underwater or grow leaves that float on the surface. Protists such as algae and amoebas float in the water. Frogs and some insects lay eggs in the water, and their young develop there. Clams, bacteria, and worms live on the bottom of lakes and ponds and break down dead materials for food. Frogs, turtles, fish, and ducks have adaptations that let them swim in water.

7 Identify As you read, underline the names of organisms that live in or near lakes and ponds.

8 Describe Pick a plant and animal in the picture. Describe how each is adapted to a pond.

Plant

_____

_____

_____

Animal

_____

_____

_____

In Wetlands

A **wetland** is an area of land that is saturated, or soaked, with water for at least part of the year. Bogs, marshes, and swamps are types of wetlands. Bogs contain living and decomposing mosses. Many grasslike plants grow in marshes. Swamps have trees and vines. Plants that live in wetlands are adapted to living in wet soil.

Wetlands have high species diversity. Common wetland plants include cattails, duckweed, sphagnum moss, sedges, orchids, willows, tamarack, and black ash trees. Animals found in wetlands include ducks, frogs, shrews, herons, and alligators. Water collects and slowly filters through a wetland. In this way, some pollutants are removed from the water. Since wetlands can hold water, they also protect nearby land and shore from floods and erosion.

Think Outside the Book Inquiry

9 Apply Use library and Internet resources to put together an identification guide to common wetland plants.

Visualize It!

Wetland

Development That Replaced Wetland

10 Describe What can happen when a wetland is replaced by a development in an area?

_____

_____

_____

_____

_____

In Rivers and Streams

Water moves in one direction in a stream. As water moves, it interacts with air and oxygen is added to the water. A large stream is called a river. Rivers and streams are home to many organisms, including fish, aquatic insects, and mosses. Freshwater ecosystems in streams can have areas of fast-moving and slow-moving water. Some organisms that live in fast-moving water have adaptations that let them resist being washed away. Immature black flies can attach themselves to rocks in a fast-moving stream. Rootlike rhizoids let mosses stick to rocks. In slow-moving waters of a stream, water striders are adapted to live on the water's surface.

The slope of a river's channel and the river's depth determine how quickly water moves.

Visualize It!

11 Match Match the correct captions to the pictures showing areas of fast-moving and slow-moving water.

A Water striders move across the surface of a pool of water in a river.

B Rocks form small waterfalls in areas of some streams.

C Aquatic plants can live below the surface of a river.

D Mosses can grow on the surface of rocks even in fast-moving water.

Inquiry

12 Infer Why might stream water have more oxygen in it than pond water does?

_____

Where River Meets Sea

What is an estuary?

An **estuary** is a partially enclosed body of water formed where a river flows into an ocean. Because estuaries have a mixture of fresh water and salt water, they support ecosystems that have a unique and diverse community of organisms. Seagrasses, mangrove trees, fish, oysters, mussels, and water birds all live in estuaries. Fish and shrimp lay eggs in the calm waters of an estuary. Their young mature here before moving out into the ocean. Many birds feed on the young shrimp and fish in an estuary.

Organisms in estuaries must be able to survive in constantly changing salt levels due to the rise and fall of tides. Some estuary grasses, such as smooth cordgrass, have special structures in their roots and leaves that let them get rid of excess salt.

Visualize It!

13 Describe Fill in the rest of the name tags for each estuary organism. List at least one way the organism uses an estuary to survive.

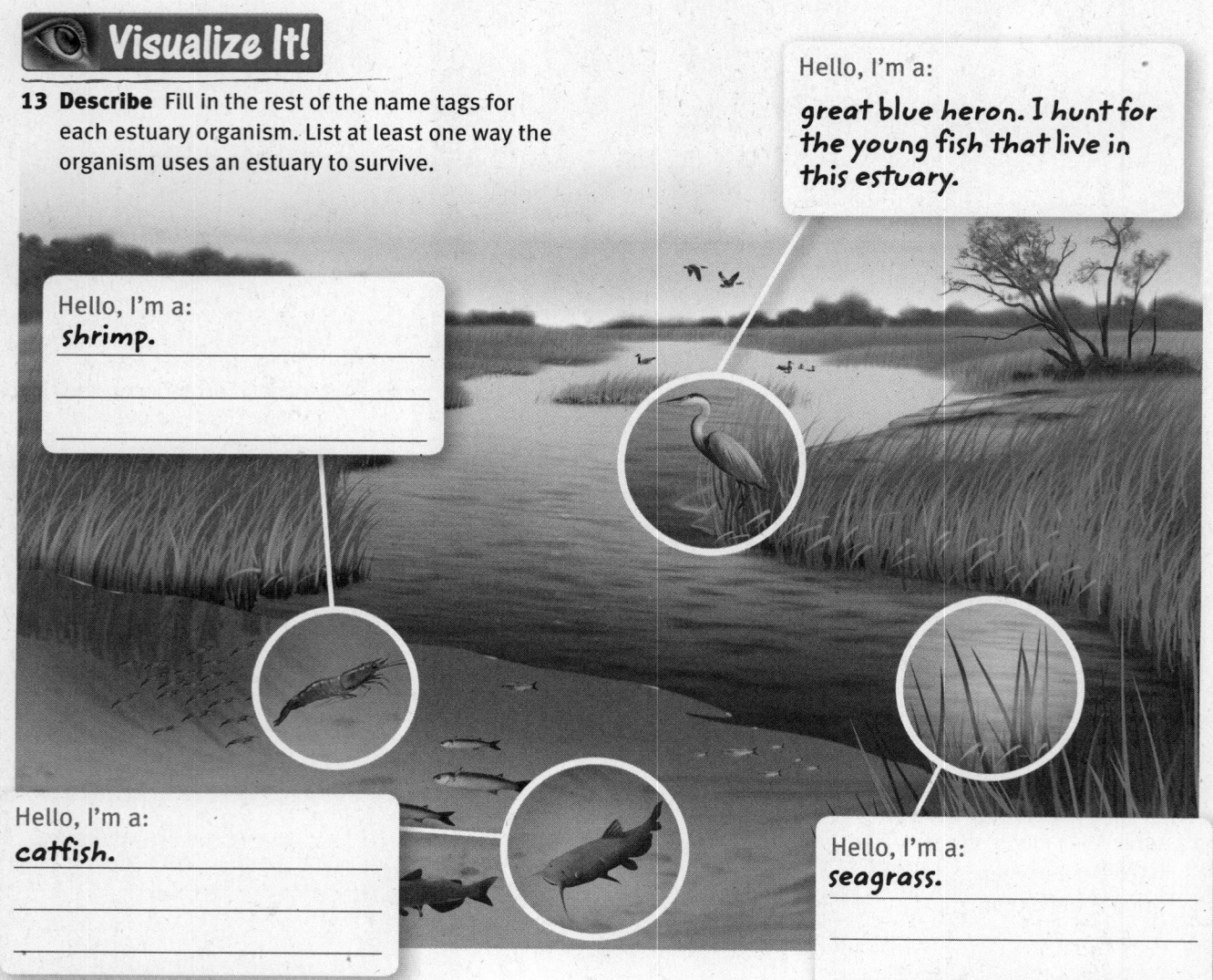

Hello, I'm a:
great blue heron. I hunt for the young fish that live in this estuary.

Hello, I'm a:
shrimp.

Hello, I'm a:
catfish.

Hello, I'm a:
seagrass.

Protecting Estuaries

Why are estuaries important? The mixture of salt water and nutrient-rich fresh water in an estuary supports breeding grounds for birds, commercial fish, and shellfish such as crabs and shrimp. The grasses in estuaries also protect coastal areas from erosion and flooding.

Oil Spill!

In 2010, a major oil spill occurred in the Gulf of Mexico. Oil flowed into the ocean for almost three months.

Coastal Damage

Estuaries along the northern Gulf Coast were affected. Oil killed birds and other animals. It soaked seagrasses and damaged fish and shellfish nurseries.

Cleaning Up

A large cleanup effort began after the spill. Continuing work will be important to restore ecosystems and protect fishing and tourism jobs in the area.

Extend

Inquiry

14 Explain What are the economic benefits from estuaries?

15 Research Find out about another damaged estuary ecosystem. How has the estuary been restored?

16 Hypothesize Form a hypothesis about how the loss of estuaries can increase erosion along shorelines.

© Houghton Mifflin Harcourt Publishing Company • Image Credits: (b) ©NASA Image by Jeff Schmaltz, MODIS Rapid Response Team; (t) ©Chfile Delmar/Alamy; (c) ©Sean Gardner/Reuters/Corbis

By the Beautiful Sea

The open ocean is vast and contains a variety of life forms. The ocean's largest, fastest, and deepest-diving organisms are found here.

Where are examples of marine ecosystems found?

Marine ecosystems are saltwater ecosystems. They cover more than 70 percent of Earth's surface. Marine ecosystems are found in the coastal ocean, the open ocean, and the deep ocean. Different abiotic, or nonliving, factors affect each marine ecosystem.

In and Along Coastal Oceans

Marine ecosystems in and along coastal oceans include the intertidal zone and the neritic zone. The intertidal zone is the land between high and low tides that includes beaches and rocky shores. Organisms that live in this zone are often adapted to changing water depth, wave action, exposure to air, and changing salinity. Crabs and seagrasses live on beaches. Barnacles and anemones live in tidal pools on rocky shores.

The neritic zone is the underwater zone from the shore to the edge of the continental shelf. Light reaches the bottom of the neritic zone, allowing algae and many plants to live there. Coral reefs and kelp forests are found in the neritic zone. Coral reefs are located mainly in warm tropical areas. They support many species of colorful fish, anemones, and coral. Kelp forests are found in cold, nutrient-rich waters. Kelp forests support brown and red algae, shrimp, fish, brittle stars, and sea otters.

Visualize It!

17 List Below each photo, list abiotic factors that affect the coastal ocean ecosystem that is shown.

Sandy Beach

Ⓐ

Rocky Shore

Ⓑ

Coral Reef

Ⓒ

Kelp Forest

Ⓓ

_____   _____   _____   _____
_____   _____   _____   _____
_____   _____   _____   _____

In Open Oceans

The open ocean includes all surface waters down to a depth of about 2,000 meters (6,562 feet). Ecosystems at the surface are often dominated by tiny floating organisms called plankton. Organisms that are adapted to dark and cold conditions live at greater depths. Because the open ocean is so large, the majority of sea life is found there. Animals found in open ocean ecosystems include sharks, whales, dolphins, fish, and sea turtles. Ecosystems in the bathyal zone, which extends from the edge of the continental shelf to its base, are also considered open ocean ecosystems.

In Deep Oceans

The deep ocean has the coldest and darkest conditions. Deep ocean ecosystems include those in the abyssal zone, which is the part of the ocean below 2,000 meters (6,562 feet). Some species that live in the deep ocean have bioluminescence, which lets them produce a glowing light to attract mates or prey. Female anglerfish attract prey using bioluminescent structures that act as bait.

No light can reach the deep ocean, so no photosynthesis can happen there. Organisms in the deep ocean must get energy in other ways. Some feed on the organic material that is constantly falling from shallower ocean depths. Microorganisms living near hydrothermal vents use chemicals in the water as an energy source.

Active Reading

18 Infer How do organisms in the deep ocean get energy to live?

_____

_____

Hydrothermal vents release super-hot, acidic water in the deep ocean. Microorganisms called archaea convert chemicals from the vents into food using chemosynthesis. Archaea, tube worms, crabs, clams, and shrimp are part of hydrothermal vent communities.

Visual Summary

To complete this summary, fill in the answer to each question. Then, use the key below to check your answers. You can use this page to review the main concepts of the lesson.

Aquatic Ecosystems

Freshwater ecosystems contain still or moving fresh water.

19 Where are freshwater ecosystems found?

_____

_____

An estuary is an ecosystem that forms where a river empties into an ocean.

Marine ecosystems are located in or near oceans.

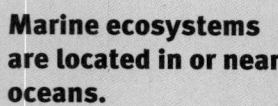

20 Where are ecosystems found in the ocean?

_____

_____

21 Which abiotic factor would likely have the greatest effect on an estuary?

_____

_____

Sample answers: 19 In lakes, ponds, wetlands, rivers, and streams; 20 In the coastal ocean, open ocean, and deep ocean; 21 changing salinity

22 Compare How are estuaries and coral reefs similar?

_____

Lesson Review

Vocabulary

Fill in the blank with the term that best completes the following sentences.

1 A(n) _____ is a partially enclosed body of water formed where a river flows into an ocean.

2 A(n) _____ is an area of land that is covered or saturated with water for at least part of the year.

Key Concepts

3 Identify What kinds of organisms live in estuaries?

_____

_____

_____

_____

4 Describe What types of adaptations would be needed by organisms that live in a river?

_____

_____

_____

_____

5 Describe Describe the characteristics of the four zones found in the ocean.

_____

_____

_____

_____

_____

_____

_____

_____

Critical Thinking

Use the photo to answer the following question.

6 Predict Organisms in the aquatic ecosystem in the picture must be adapted to which abiotic factors?

_____

_____

_____

7 Draw Draw an organism that is adapted to the abyssal zone of the ocean, and label its adaptations.

8 Analyze Salt water is denser than fresh water. What ecosystem would be most affected by this fact? Explain your answer.

_____

_____

_____

_____

My Notes

Interpreting Circle Graphs

Scientists display data in tables and graphs in order to organize it and show relationships. A *circle graph*, also called a *pie graph*, is used to show and compare the pieces of a whole.

OHIO **7.SIA.3** Use appropriate mathematics, tools and techniques to gather data and information.
OHIO **7.SIA.4** Analyze and interpret data.
OHIO **7.SIA.5** Develop descriptions, models, explanations and predictions.

Tutorial

In a circle graph, the entire circle represents the whole, and each piece is called a *sector*. Follow the instructions below to learn how to interpret a circle graph.

1 Evaluating Data Data on circle graphs may be given in one of two ways: as values (such as dollars, days, or numbers of items) or as percentages of the whole.

2 Changing Percentage to Value The word *percent* means "per hundred," so 25% means 25 per 100, or 25/100. To find the total volume represented by a sector, such as the volume of fresh water in surface water, multiply the whole value by the percent of the sector, and then divide by 100.

$$35{,}030{,}000 \text{ km}^3 \times \frac{0.3}{100} = 105{,}090 \text{ km}^3 \text{ of Earth's fresh water is in surface water.}$$

3 Changing Value to Ratio The sum of the sectors, 35,030,000 km³, is the whole, or total value. Divide the value of a sector, such as the icecaps and glaciers sector, by the value of the whole. Simplify this fraction to express it as a ratio.

$$\frac{24{,}065{,}610 \text{ km}^3}{35{,}030{,}000 \text{ km}^3} \approx \frac{25}{35} = \frac{5}{7}$$

About $\frac{5}{7}$ of Earth's fresh water is in icecaps and glaciers.

This ratio can be expressed as $\frac{5}{7}$, 5:7, or 5 to 7.

4 Changing Value to Percentage The whole circle graph is 100%. To find the percentage of a sector, such as the world's fresh water that is found as groundwater, divide the value of the sector by the value of the whole and then multiply by 100%.

$$\frac{10{,}544{,}030 \text{ km}^3}{35{,}030{,}000 \text{ km}^3} \times 100\% = 30.1\% \text{ of Earth's fresh water is groundwater.}$$

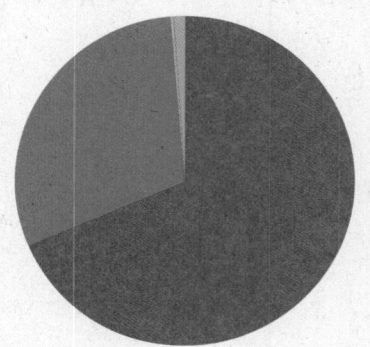

Distribution of Fresh Water (in values)

- Icecaps and Glaciers 24,065,610 km³
- Ground Water 10,544,030 km³
- Surface Water 105,090 km³
- Other 315,270 km³

Source: Gleick, P. H., 1996: Water resources. In Encyclopedia of Climate and Weather, ed. by S. H. Schneider, Oxford University Press, New York, vol. 2, pp.817-823

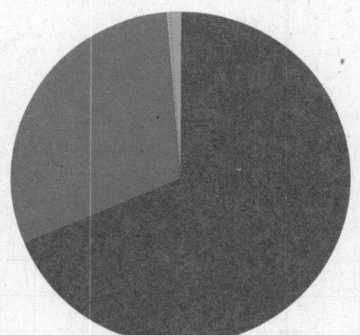

Distribution of Fresh Water (in percentages)

- Icecaps and Glaciers 68.7%
- Ground Water 30.1%
- Surface Water 0.3%
- Other 0.9%

Source: Gleick, P. H., 1996: Water resources. In Encyclopedia of Climate and Weather, ed. by S. H. Schneider, Oxford University Press, New York, vol. 2, pp.817-823

You Try It!

Use the circle graphs below to answer the following questions.

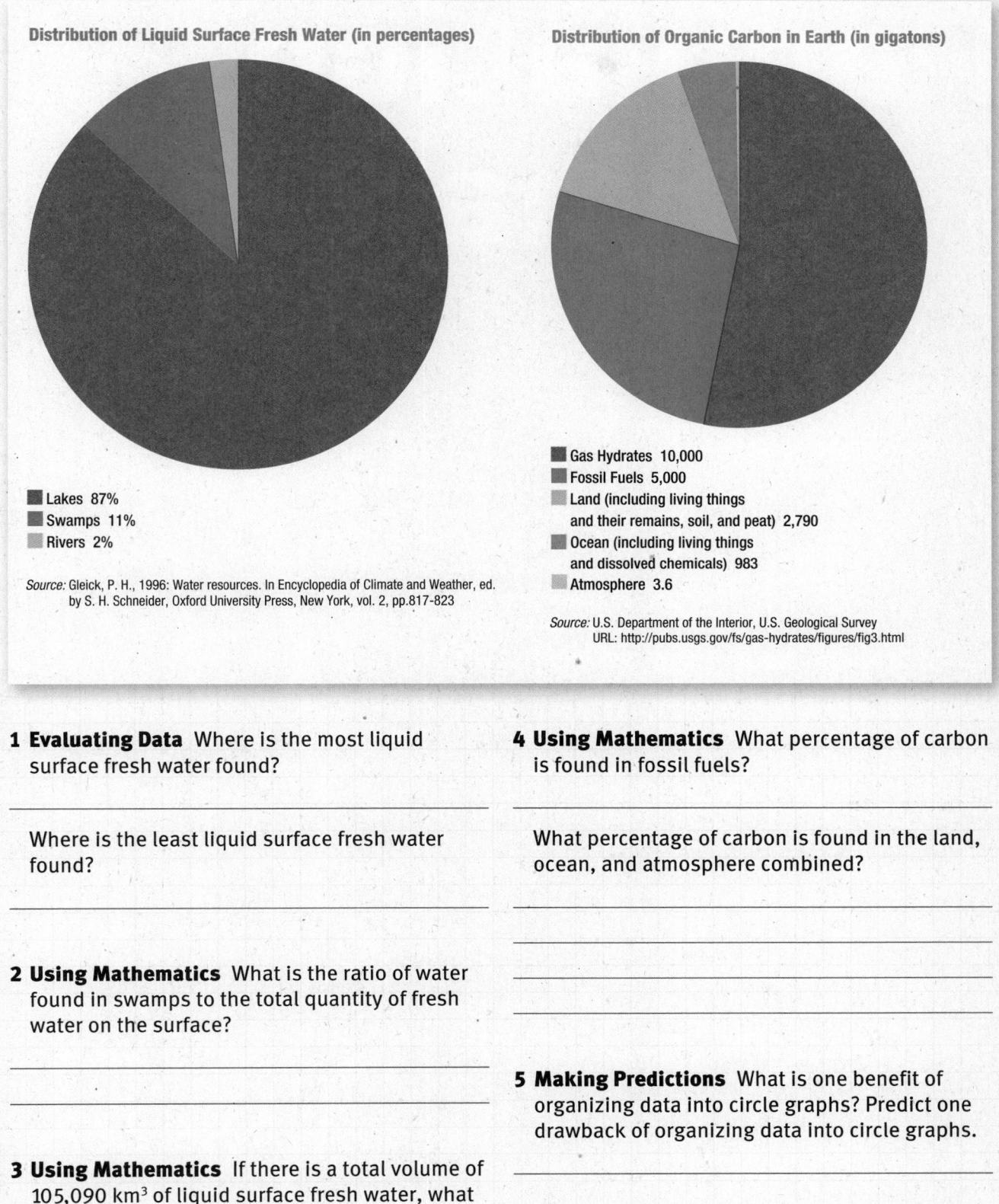

Distribution of Liquid Surface Fresh Water (in percentages)

Distribution of Organic Carbon in Earth (in gigatons)

- Lakes 87%
- Swamps 11%
- Rivers 2%

Source: Gleick, P. H., 1996: Water resources. In Encyclopedia of Climate and Weather, ed. by S. H. Schneider, Oxford University Press, New York, vol. 2, pp.817-823

- Gas Hydrates 10,000
- Fossil Fuels 5,000
- Land (including living things and their remains, soil, and peat) 2,790
- Ocean (including living things and dissolved chemicals) 983
- Atmosphere 3.6

Source: U.S. Department of the Interior, U.S. Geological Survey URL: http://pubs.usgs.gov/fs/gas-hydrates/figures/fig3.html

1 Evaluating Data Where is the most liquid surface fresh water found?

_____

Where is the least liquid surface fresh water found?

_____

2 Using Mathematics What is the ratio of water found in swamps to the total quantity of fresh water on the surface?

_____

_____

3 Using Mathematics If there is a total volume of 105,090 km³ of liquid surface fresh water, what volume is found in swamps?

_____

_____

4 Using Mathematics What percentage of carbon is found in fossil fuels?

_____

What percentage of carbon is found in the land, ocean, and atmosphere combined?

_____

_____

_____

_____

5 Making Predictions What is one benefit of organizing data into circle graphs? Predict one drawback of organizing data into circle graphs.

_____

_____

_____

_____

Population Dynamics

ESSENTIAL QUESTION

What determines a population's size?

By the end of this lesson, you should be able to explain how population size changes in response to environmental factors and interactions between organisms.

By looking like a snake, this caterpillar may scare off predators. However, the effectiveness of this defense depends on population size. If there are few real snakes, predators won't be fooled for long.

OHIO **7.LS.2** In any particular biome, the number, growth and survival of organisms and populations depend on biotic and abiotic factors.

OHIO **7.SIA.5** Develop descriptions, models, explanations and predictions.

Lesson Labs

Quick Labs
- What Factors Influence a Population Change?
- Investigate an Abiotic Limiting Factor

Exploration Lab
- How Do Populations Interact?

Engage Your Brain

1 Predict Check T or F to show whether you think each statement is true or false.

T   F

☐   ☐   Plants compete for resources.

☐   ☐   Populations of organisms never stop growing.

☐   ☐   Animals never help other animals survive.

☐   ☐   Living things need the nonliving parts of an environment to survive.

2 Explain When a chameleon eats a butterfly, what happens to the number of butterflies in the population? How could a sudden decrease in butterflies affect chameleons?

_____

_____

_____

Active Reading

3 Synthesize You can often define an unknown word if you know the meaning of its word parts. Use the word parts and sentences below to make an educated guess about the meaning of the words *immigrate* and *emigrate*.

Word part	Meaning
im-	into
e-	out
-migrate	move

Example sentence
Many deer will <u>immigrate</u> to the new park.

immigrate:

_____

Example sentence
Birds will <u>emigrate</u> from the crowded island.

emigrate:

_____

Vocabulary Terms

- carrying capacity
- limiting factor
- competition
- cooperation

4 Identify This list contains the vocabulary terms you'll learn in this lesson. As you read, circle the definition of each term.

Movin' Out

How can a population grow or get smaller?

Active Reading **5 Identify** As you read, underline the processes that can cause a population to grow or to get smaller.

A population is a group of organisms of one species that lives in the same area at the same time. If new individuals are added to the population, it grows. The population gets smaller if individuals are removed from it. The population stays at about the same size if the number of individuals that are added is close to the number of individuals that are removed.

By Immigration and Emigration

Populations change in size when individuals move to new locations. *Immigration* occurs when individuals join a population. For example, fruit flies may travel on fruit to a new island. The population of fruit flies on the new island grows as fruit flies immigrate. *Emigration* occurs when individuals leave a population. The population of fruit flies on the original island decreases when fruit flies emigrate.

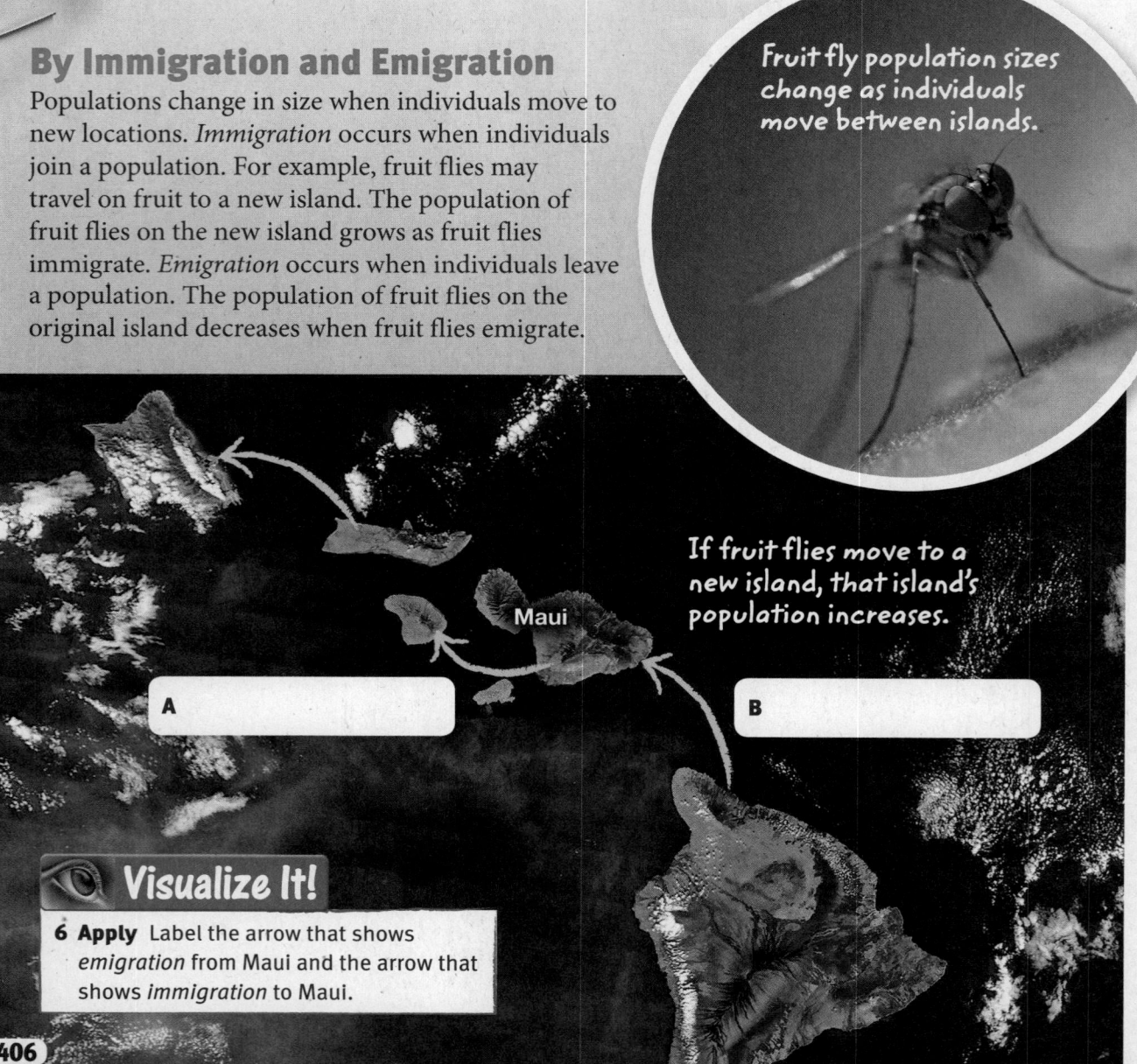

Fruit fly population sizes change as individuals move between islands.

Maui

If fruit flies move to a new island, that island's population increases.

A

B

Visualize It!

6 Apply Label the arrow that shows *emigration* from Maui and the arrow that shows *immigration* to Maui.

By Birth and Death

Populations increase as individuals are born. For example, consider a population of 100 deer in a forest. The population will increase if 20 fawns are born that year. But what if 12 deer are killed by predators or disease that year? Populations decrease as individuals die. If 20 deer are added and 12 are lost, the population will have an overall increase. At the end of the year, there will be 108 deer. The number of births compared to the number of deaths helps to determine if a population is increasing or decreasing.

Visualize It!

7 Apply Use the terms *birth*, *death*, and *immigration* to label each way that this population is changing.

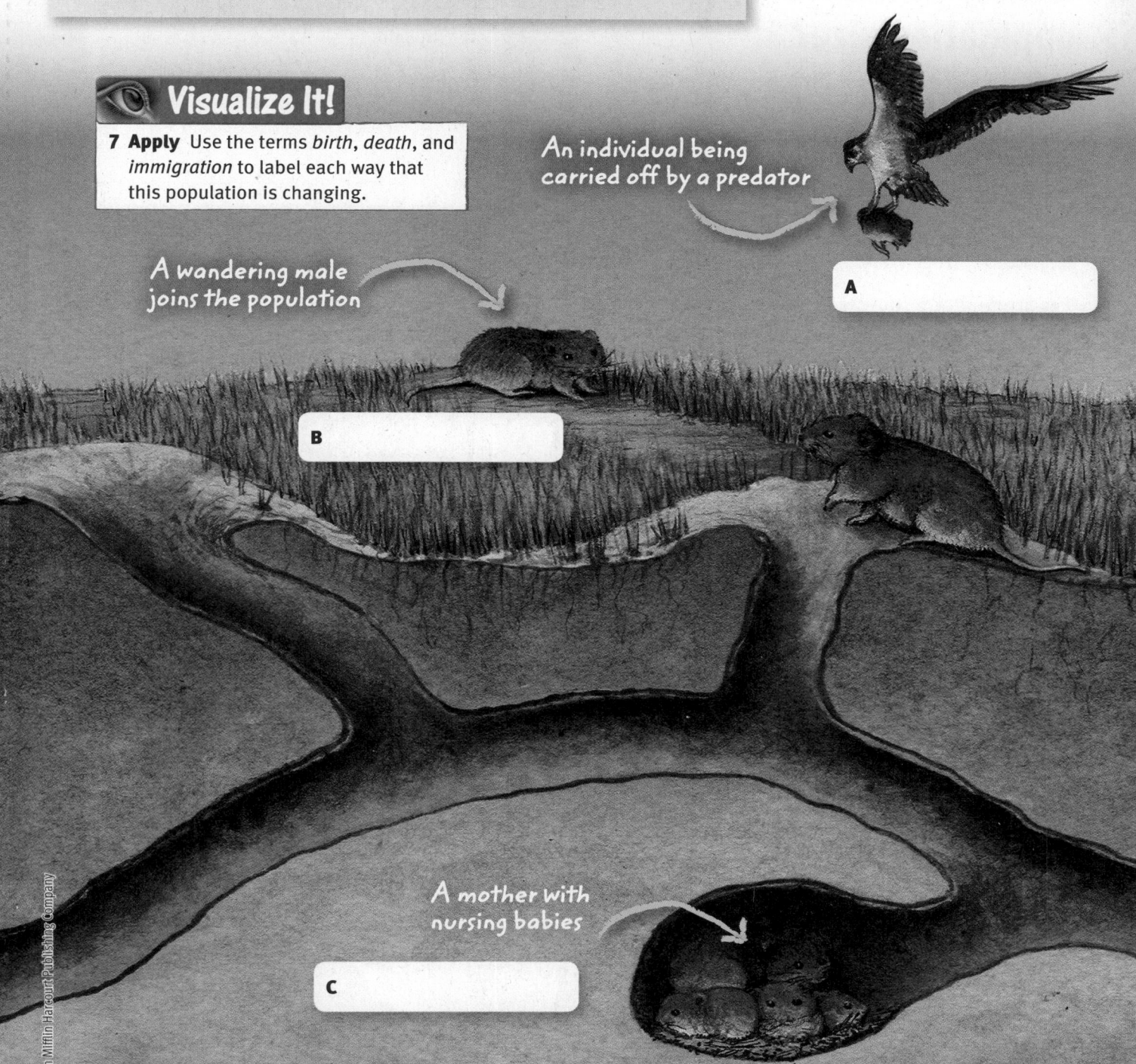

An individual being carried off by a predator

A

A wandering male joins the population

B

A mother with nursing babies

C

Know Your Limits

What environmental factors influence population size?

A tropical rain forest can support large populations of trees. A desert, however, will probably support few or no trees. Each environment has different amounts of the resources that living things need, such as food, water, and space.

Resource Availability

The amount of resources in an area influences the size of a population. If important resources are lost from the environment, a population may shrink. The population may grow if the amount of resources in the environment is increased. But if the population continues to grow, the individuals would eventually run out of resources. The **carrying capacity** is the maximum number of individuals of one species that the environment can support. For example, the carrying capacity, or the number of owls that a forest can support, depends on how many mice are available to eat and how many trees are available for the owls to live in.

Deforestation causes a sudden change in resource availability.

Visualize It!

8 Identify Make a list of each population in the image that would be affected by drought.

_____

_____

_____

_____

Animals use plants as food and shelter. Plants depend on sunlight and water as resources.

Changes in the Environment

The carrying capacity can change when the environment changes. For example, after a rainy season, plants may produce a large crop of leaves and seeds. This large amount of food may allow an herbivore population to grow. But what if important resources are destroyed? A population crash occurs when the carrying capacity of the environment suddenly drops. Natural disasters, such as forest fires, and harsh weather, such as droughts, can cause population crashes. The carrying capacity can also be reduced when new competitors enter an area and outcompete existing populations for resources. This would cause existing populations to become smaller or crash.

Active Reading **9 Describe** What are two ways in which the environment can influence population size?

_____

_____

_____

_____

Drought slowly reduces the amount of water available as a resource to different populations.

Think Outside the Book

10 Apply With a classmate, discuss how the immigration of new herbivores might affect the carrying capacity of the local zebra population.

Maximum Capacity

What factors can limit population size?

A part of the environment that keeps a population's size at a level below its full potential is called a **limiting factor**. Limiting factors can be living or nonliving things in an environment.

Abiotic Factors

The nonliving parts of an environment are called *abiotic factors*. Abiotic factors include water, nutrients, soil, sunlight, temperature, and living space. Organisms need these resources to survive. For example, plants use sunlight, water, and carbon dioxide to make food. If there are few rocks in a desert, lizard populations that use rocks for shelter will not become very large.

Biotic Factors

Relationships among organisms affect each one's growth and survival. A *biotic factor* is an interaction between living things. For example, zebras interact with many organisms. Zebras eat grass, and they compete with antelope for this food. Lions prey on zebras. Each of these interactions is a biotic factor that affects the population of zebras.

Inquiry

11 **Apply** Think about how people limit the populations of pests such as insects and mice. List one abiotic factor and one biotic factor that humans use to limit these pest populations.

Abiotic _____

Biotic _____

12 **Identify** Label each of the following factors that limits plant population growth as abiotic or biotic.

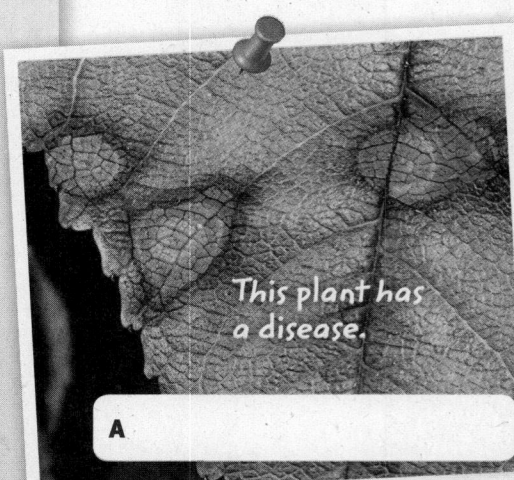

This plant has a disease.

A _____

This plant grows between the rocks.

B _____

Herbivores are eating this leaf.

C _____

A Fungus Among Us!

In many parts of the world, frog populations are shrinking. We now know that many of these frogs have died because of a fungal infection.

Meet the fungus
Chytrid fungi [KY•trid FUHN•jy] live in water. They are important decomposers. One of them, called Bd, infects frogs.

Stop the Spread
Bd is found in wet mud. If you go hiking in muddy places, washing and drying your boots can help stop Bd from spreading.

Deadly Disease
Frogs take in oxygen and water through their skin. Bd interferes with this process. The fungus also affects an infected frog's nervous system.

Extend

Inquiry

13 Describe How does Bd fungus harm frogs?

14 Recommend Imagine that an endangered frog lives near an area where Bd was just found. How could you help protect that frog species?

15 Apply Design an experiment to test whether using soap or using bleach is the better way to clean boots to prevent Bd contamination. What are the independent and dependent variables? Remember to include a control in designing your experiment.

Teamwork

Animals compete for access to water.

What interactions between organisms can influence population size?

As living things try to gather the resources they need, they often interact with each other. Sometimes interactions help one individual and harm another. At other times, all of the organisms benefit by working together.

Competition

When two or more individuals or populations try to use the same limited resource, such as food, water, shelter, space, or sunlight, it is called **competition**. Competition can happen among individuals within a population. The elk in a forest compete with each other for the same food plants. This competition increases in winter when many plants die. Competition also happens among populations. For example, different species of trees in a forest compete with each other for sunlight and space.

Visualize It!

16 Predict The image above shows individuals from two populations competing for access to water.

What would happen to the size of the lion population if elephants usually won this competition?

_____

_____

_____

What would happen to each population if lions usually won this competition?

_____

_____

_____

17 Identify As you read, underline how cooperation can influence population dynamics.

Cooperation

Cooperation occurs when individuals work together. Some animals, such as killer whales, hunt in groups. Emperor penguins in Antarctica stay close together to stay warm. Some populations have a structured social order that determines how the individuals work with each other. For example, ants live in colonies in which the members have different jobs. Some ants find food, others defend the colony, and others take care of the young. Cooperation helps individuals get resources, which can make populations grow.

18 Compare Make an analogy between an ant colony and a sports team. How does each group work together to achieve a goal?

_____

_____

_____

_____

_____

_____

These ants cooperate to protect aphids that produce a substance that ants eat.

Visual Summary

To complete this summary, fill in the blanks with the correct word or phrase. Then use the key below to check your answers. You can use this page to review the main concepts of the lesson.

Population Dynamics

Populations grow due to birth and immigration and get smaller due to death and emigration.

19 If more individuals are born in a population than die or emigrate, the population will _____

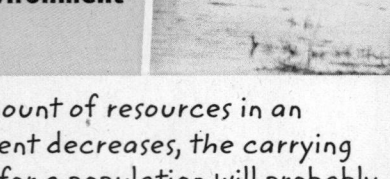

The carrying capacity is the maximum number of individuals of one species an environment can support.

20 If the amount of resources in an environment decreases, the carrying capacity for a population will probably _____

Both populations and individuals can compete or cooperate.

21 Some birds warn other birds when predators are close. This type of interaction is called

_____

Answers: 19 grow; 20 decrease; 21 cooperation

22 Synthesize Describe how a change in the environment could lead to increased immigration or emigration.

Lesson Review

Vocabulary

Circle the term that best completes the following sentences.

1 Individuals joining a population is an example of *emigration / immigration*.

2 A part of the environment that prevents a population from growing too large is a(n) *abiotic / limiting / biotic* factor.

3 Individuals *cooperate / compete* when they work together to obtain resources.

Key Concepts

4 Identify What is a limiting factor?

_____

_____

_____

5 Describe How do limiting factors affect the carrying capacity of an environment?

_____

_____

_____

_____

_____

_____

6 Explain Give one example of how cooperation can help organisms survive.

_____

_____

_____

7 Provide Name two factors that increase population size and two factors that decrease population size.

_____

_____

_____

_____

Critical Thinking

Use the illustration to answer the following questions.

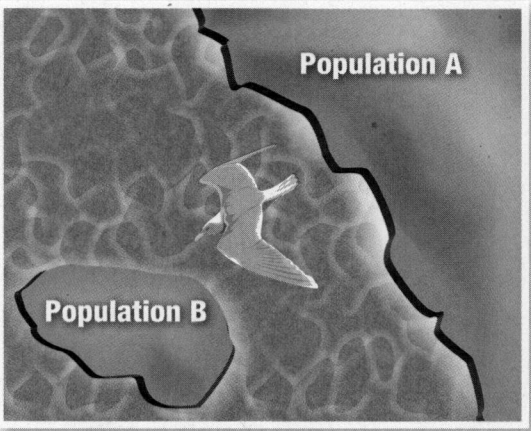

8 Infer What might cause birds in Population A to immigrate to the island?

_____

_____

9 Predict How will the level of competition among birds in Population B change if many birds from Population A join Population B?

_____

_____

_____

10 Conclude Explain how a change in the environment could cause a population crash.

_____

_____

_____

_____

11 Relate How does population size relate to resource availability in an environment?

_____

_____

_____

_____

_____

My Notes

Changes in Ecosystems

ESSENTIAL QUESTION

How do ecosystems change?

By the end of this lesson, you should be able to describe how natural processes change ecosystems and help them develop after a natural disturbance.

Ecosystems are always changing. Many changes in ecosystems are due to natural disturbances. This forest fire in Yellowstone National Park was caused by lightning.

OHIO **7.LS.2** In any particular biome, the number, growth and survival of organisms and populations depend on biotic and abiotic factors.

OHIO **7.SIA.5** Develop descriptions, models, explanations and predictions.

 **Lesson Labs**

Quick Labs
- Measuring Species Diversity
- Investigate Evidence of Succession

Field Lab
- Predicting How Succession Follows a Human Disturbance

Engage Your Brain

1 Predict Check T or F to show whether you think each statement is true or false.

T	F	
☐	☐	Some damaged ecosystems can recover after a disturbance.
☐	☐	Ecosystems only change slowly after natural disturbances.
☐	☐	Changes in ecosystems proceed in a fairly predictable way after a disturbance occurs.
☐	☐	Ecosystems eventually stop changing.

2 Describe Use the picture below to describe how beavers change their environment.

_____

_____

_____

Active Reading

3 Synthesize A compound term is a term made from two or more words. The term *pioneer species* is a compound term. Use the definitions and sentence below to make an educated guess about the meaning of the compound term *pioneer species*.

Word	Meaning
pioneer	the first ones to do something
species	a group of very similar organisms

Example sentence
Lichens and other <u>pioneer species</u> break down rock and leave organic matter that mix together to make soil.

pioneer species:

_____

_____

Vocabulary Terms
- eutrophication
- succession
- pioneer species
- biodiversity

4 Identify As you read, create a reference card for each vocabulary term. On one side of the card, write the term and its meaning. On the other side, draw a picture that illustrates or makes a connection to the term. These cards can be used as bookmarks in the text. You can also refer to the cards while studying.

Nothing Stays the Same

How quickly do ecosystems change?

Ecosystems and organisms are constantly changing and responding to daily, seasonal, and long-term changes in the environment. Most ecosystem changes are gradual. Some are sudden and irregular.

 **Active Reading** **5 Describe** As you read, underline one example of a slow change and one example of a sudden change in an ecosystem.

Ecosystems May Change Slowly

Some changes happen slowly. Over time, a pond can develop into a meadow. **Eutrophication** (yoo•trohf•ih•KAY• shuhn) is the process in which organic matter and nutrients slowly build up in a body of water. The nutrients increase the growth of plants and microorganisms. When these organisms die, decaying matter sinks to the bottom of the pond. This organic matter can eventually fill the pond and become soil that grasses and other meadow plants can grow in.

Ecosystem changes can also be caused by seasonal or long-term changes in climate.

Ecosystems May Change Suddenly

Ecosystems can suddenly change due to catastrophic natural disturbances. A hurricane's strong winds can blow down trees and destroy vegetation in a few hours. Lightning can start a forest fire that rapidly clears away plants and alters animal habitats. A volcano, such as Washington's Mount St. Helens, can erupt and cause massive destruction to an ecosystem. But destruction is not the end of the story. Recovery brings new changes to an ecosystem and the populations that live in it.

Visualize It! Inquiry

6 Hypothesize What natural ecological change might happen to the meadow that forms where the pond was?

_____

_____

The organic matter growing in a pond dies and falls to the bottom. The pond gets shallower as the matter piles up.

Eventually, the pond fills in, and land plants grow there. The pond becomes a level meadow.

Ruin and Recovery

Ecosystems can change very fast. The volcanic eruption of Mount St. Helens in southern Washington devastated the mountain on May 18, 1980, killing 57 people. The hot gas and debris also killed native plant and animal species and damaged 596 square kilometers (230 square miles) of forest.

1979

Today

A Changed Landscape

The eruption changed the ecosystem dramatically. Trees fell and forests burned. Much of the ice and snow melted. The water mixed with ash and dirt that covered the ground. Thick mud formed and slid down the mountain. Flowing mud removed more trees and changed the shape of the landscape.

Road to Recovery

How did the ecosystem recover? Snow patches and ice protected some species. Some small mammals were sheltered in burrows. With the trees gone, more sunlight reached the ground. Seeds sprouted, and the recovery began.

Extend

Inquiry

7 Explain How do sudden catastrophes such as the eruption of Mount St. Helens change the landscape of ecosystems?

8 Research Find out about how natural catastrophic events, such as volcanic eruptions, can affect the climate on Earth.

9 Hypothesize Form a hypothesis based on your research in question 8 about how changes in climate can lead to changes in ecosystems.

What are the two types of ecological succession?

Ecosystems can develop from bare rock or cleared land. This development is the result of slow and constructive gradual changes. The slow development or replacement of an ecological community by another ecological community over time is called **succession**.

Primary Succession

A community may start to grow in an area that has no soil. This process is called primary succession. The first organisms to live in an uninhabited area are called **pioneer species**. Pioneer species, such as lichens, grow on rock and help to form soil in which plants can grow.

👁 Visualize It!

10 Label Write a title for each step of primary succession.

A _____

A slowly retreating glacier exposes bare rock where nothing lives, and primary succession begins.

B _____

Acids from lichens break down the rock into particles. These particles mix with the remains of dead lichens to make soil.

C _____

After many years, there is enough soil for mosses to grow. The mosses replace the lichens. Insects and other small organisms begin to live there, enriching the soil.

D _____

As the soil deepens, mosses are replaced by ferns. The ferns may slowly be replaced by grasses and wildflowers. If there is enough soil, shrubs and small trees may grow.

E _____

After hundreds or even thousands of years, the soil may be deep and fertile enough to support a forest.

Secondary Succession

Succession also happens to areas that have been disturbed but that still have soil. Sometimes an existing ecosystem is damaged by a natural disaster, such as a fire or a flood. Sometimes farmland is cleared but is left unmanaged. In either case, if soil is left intact, the original community may regrow through a series of stages called secondary succession.

Think Outside the Book

12 Describe Find an example of secondary succession in your community, and make a poster that describes each stage.

11 Identify Underline one or two distinctive features of each stage of secondary succession.

A

The first year after a farmer stops growing crops or the first year after some other major disturbance, wild plants start to grow. In farmland, crabgrass often grows first.

B

By the second year, new wild plants appear. Their seeds may have been blown into the field by the wind, or they may have been carried by insects or birds. Horseweed is common during the second year.

C

In 5 to 15 years, small conifer trees may start growing among the weeds. The trees continue to grow, and after about 100 years, a forest may form.

D

As older conifers die, they may be replaced by hardwoods, such as oak or maple trees, if the climate can support them.

It's a Balancing Act

What are two signs of a mature ecosystem?

In the early stages of succession, only a few species live and grow in an area. As the ecosystem matures, more species become established.

Climax Species

Succession can happen over decades or over hundreds of years. A community of producers forms first. These organisms are followed by decomposers and consumers. Over time, a stable, balanced ecosystem develops.

As a community matures, it may become dominated by well-adapted *climax species*. The redwoods in a temperate rain forest are a climax species. An ecosystem dominated by climax species is stable until the ecosystem is disturbed.

Biodiversity

As succession moves along, richer soil, nutrients, and other resources become available. This increase in resource availability lets more species become established. By the time climax species are established, the resources in the area support many different kinds of organisms. The number and variety of species that are present in an area is referred to as **biodiversity**.

A diverse forest is more stable and less likely to be destroyed by sudden changes, such as an insect invasion. Most plant-damaging insects attack only one kind of plant. The presence of a variety of plants can reduce the impact of the insects. Even if an entire plant species dies off, other similar plant species may survive.

Active Reading **13 Summarize** How is biodiversity beneficial to an ecosystem?

_____

_____

_____

Rain forests are not just found at the equator. Temperate rain forests along the Pacific Northwest host a diversity of life. Temperate rain forests are often dominated by conifers. Rain forests can receive 350 cm or more of rain annually.

Ferns and other small plants live on the wet, shady forest floor.

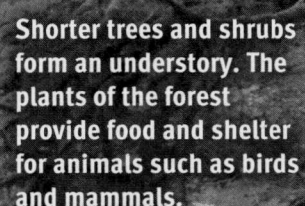

Shorter trees and shrubs form an understory. The plants of the forest provide food and shelter for animals such as birds and mammals.

A desert is very different from a rain forest, but it can also be an example of a mature ecosystem. Deserts receive as little as 8 cm of rain per year. But a desert has climax species well-adapted to its dry climate. These species form a balanced ecosystem.

Large cactuses are climax species in deserts.

Desert plants are adapted to live in hot, dry conditions and provide food and shelter for animals.

14 Compare Use the Venn diagram to compare and contrast deserts and rain forests.

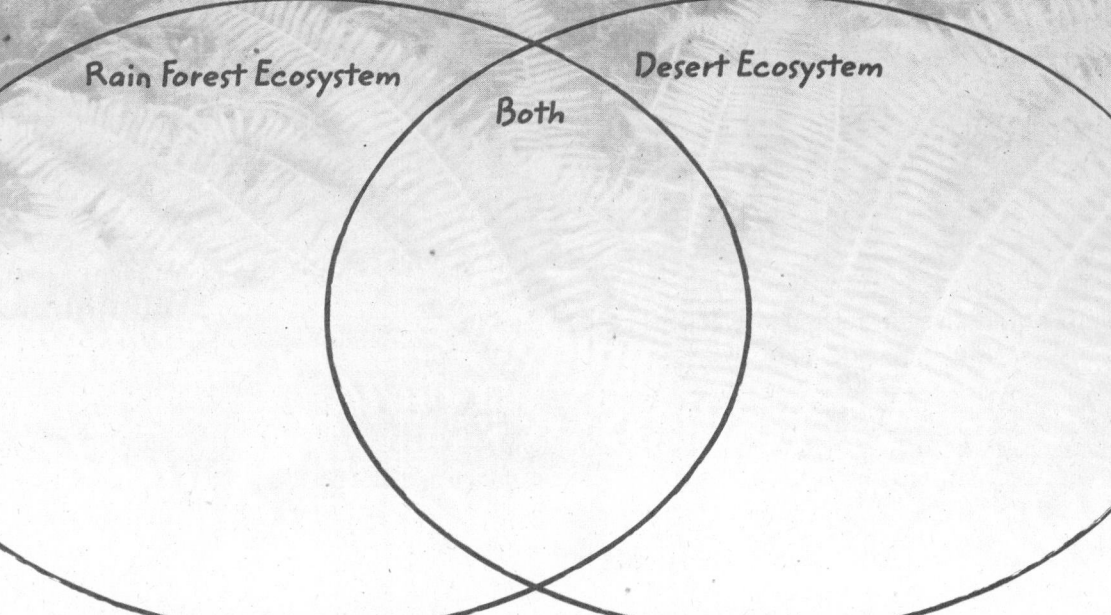

Rain Forest Ecosystem

Both

Desert Ecosystem

Visual Summary

To complete this summary, fill in the blanks with the correct word or phrase. Then use the key below to check your answers. You can use this page to review the main concepts of the lesson.

Changes in Ecosystems

Ecosystems are always changing.

Ecosystems can change rapidly or slowly.

15 A pond fills in with organic matter during _____

Primary succession begins with bare rock.

16 In primary succession, _____ grow on bare rock.

Secondary succession occurs in damaged ecosystems that still have soil.

17 Soil in damaged ecosystems enables _____ to grow right away.

Mature ecosystems include many kinds of diverse organisms living in balance.

18 Many mature ecosystems are dominated by a community of _____

Answers: 15 eutrophication; 16 lichens; 17 plants; 18 climax species

19 Relate How is diversity related to changes in ecosystems?

Lesson Review

Vocabulary

Fill in the blank with the term that best completes the following sentences.

1 _____ are the first organisms to live in an uninhabited area.

2 _____ is the number and variety of species that are present in an area.

3 The gradual development or replacement of one ecological community by another is called

_____

Key Concepts

4 **Describe** Explain how eutrophication can change an aquatic ecosystem into a land ecosystem.

_____

_____

_____

_____

_____

_____

5 **Compare** What is the major difference between primary and secondary succession?

_____

_____

_____

_____

6 **Summarize** Explain the important role a pioneer species plays in succession.

_____

_____

_____

_____

_____

Critical Thinking

Use the diagram to answer the following questions.

Visit 1 | Visit 2 | Visit 3 | Visit 4 | Visit 5 | Visit 6 | Visit 7

7 **Analyze** Between visits 1 and 7, what kind of ecological succession is shown? Explain your answer.

_____

_____

_____

8 **Predict** If a fire occurs at visit 5, what kind of ecological succession is more likely to occur thereafter?

_____

_____

_____

9 **Synthesize** How might biodiversity help an ecosystem recover from a volcanic eruption?

_____

_____

_____

_____

_____

_____

My Notes

Unit 6 ◀ Big Idea ◀ Matter and energy together support life within an environment.

Lesson 1
ESSENTIAL QUESTION
How do cells get and use energy?

Explain how cells capture and release energy.

Lesson 2
ESSENTIAL QUESTION
How does energy flow through an ecosystem?

Describe how energy is transferred between organisms in food chains and food webs within an ecosystem.

Lesson 3
ESSENTIAL QUESTION
How do energy and matter move through ecosystems?

Explain the flow of energy and the cycles of matter in ecosystems.

Lesson 4
ESSENTIAL QUESTION
What are land biomes?

Describe the characteristics of different biomes that exist on land.

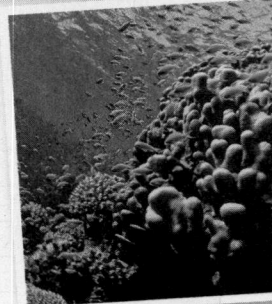

Lesson 5
ESSENTIAL QUESTION
What are aquatic ecosystems?

Describe the characteristics of marine, freshwater, and other aquatic ecosystems.

Lesson 6
ESSENTIAL QUESTION
What determines a population's size?

Explain how population size changes in response to environmental factors and interactions between organisms.

Lesson 7
ESSENTIAL QUESTION
How do ecosystems change?

Describe how natural processes change ecosystems and help them develop after a natural disturbance.

Connect ESSENTIAL QUESTIONS
Lessons 6 and 7

1 Explain How might human activity cause secondary succession? In your answer, discuss population changes.

_____

_____

_____

_____

Think Outside the Book

2 Synthesize Choose one of these activities to help synthesize what you have learned in this unit.

☐ Using what you learned in lessons 4 and 5, create a brochure that describes the characteristics of the biome in which you live. In your brochure, list what aquatic systems, if any, can also be found where you live.

☐ Using what you learned in lessons 2, 3, 4, and 5, choose a biome or aquatic ecosystem and draw or make a collage of an energy pyramid that might be found in it. Label each tier of the energy pyramid, and identify the species shown.

Unit 6 Review

Name _____

Vocabulary

Check the box to show whether each statement is true or false.

T	F	
☐	☐	**1** An <u>ecosystem</u> is a community of organisms at a major regional or global level.
☐	☐	**2** A <u>deciduous</u> tree has leaves that drop in the winter as an adaptation to cold temperatures.
☐	☐	**3** A <u>food chain</u> is the feeding relationships among all of the organisms in an ecosystem.
☐	☐	**4** A <u>pioneer species</u> is one of the first species of organisms to live in an area.
☐	☐	**5** The <u>law of conservation of energy</u> states that energy cannot be created or destroyed.

Key Concepts

Choose the letter of the best answer.

6 Some grass species need fire in order for their seeds to germinate. Why might this adaptation be useful for grasses?

  A Fire allows trees to grow and provide shade for the grasses.

  B The hot temperature of the fire helps the grasses grow faster.

  C Seeds can germinate in an area that has been cleared by a fire.

  D Fire discourages grazing by large animals so grass can grow higher.

7 In a diagram of a food chain, where does a producer, such as a tree, get the energy it needs to survive?

  A from the air

  B from the sun

  C from the organisms it eats

  D from the remains of organisms

Unit 6 Review continued

8 The following table lists the number and variety of organisms in four different ecosystems.

	Plants		Animals	
	# of organisms	# of species	# of organisms	# of species
Ecosystem 1	500	5	300	4
Ecosystem 2	300	10	100	7
Ecosystem 3	100	2	200	5
Ecosystem 4	50	6	30	4

Predict what would happen to Ecosystem 3 immediately after a volcanic eruption.

A The number and variety of organisms in the ecosystem would be greater than those in Ecosystem 1.

B The number and variety of organisms in the ecosystem would be greater than those in Ecosystem 2.

C Its biodiversity would not change.

D Its biodiversity would decrease.

9 Jose observed a puddle in a schoolyard. He gathered a sample of the water in the puddle and used a microscope to study the organisms that live in this microhabitat. The table below shows his results.

Name	Sketch	# Legs	Size
Ostracods		>8	2 mm
Copepods		>8	0.5 - 3 mm
Water fleas		>8	0.3 - 3 mm
Water bears		8	<1 mm
Water mites		8	0.5 - 5 mm
Mosquito larvae		0	1 - 20 mm

What is true of the organisms in this puddle?

A They are all small.

B They are all mammals.

C They are all the same shape.

D They are all the same species.

10 A student is studying interactions between organisms in a food web. She wonders what could happen in a prairie ecosystem if foxes suddenly disappeared. Which of the following is the best answer to her question?

A If foxes disappear, all other populations will grow.

B If foxes disappear, all other populations will shrink.

C If foxes disappear, the population of an organism that fed on foxes will likely grow.

D If foxes disappear, the population of an organism on which foxes fed will likely grow.

11 Below is a diagram of the carbon cycle.

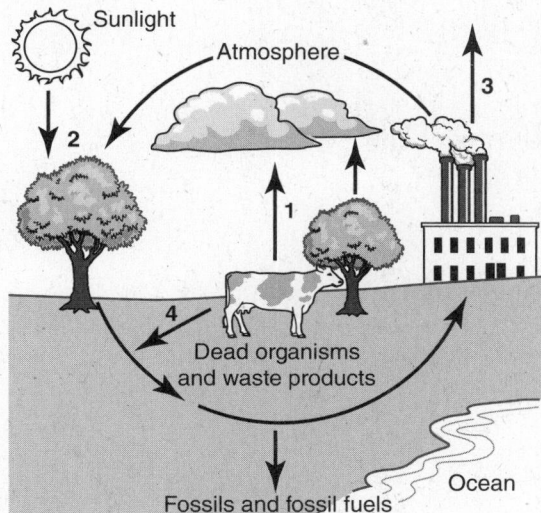

Which number corresponds to combustion that results in the release of CO_2 and water and the loss of energy as heat into the environment?

A 1

B 2

C 3

D 4

12 Bees have a society in which different members have different responsibilities. The interaction among bees is an example of what type of behavior?

A cooperation

B competition

C consumerism

D commensalism

13 The following diagram shows a common cell organelle.

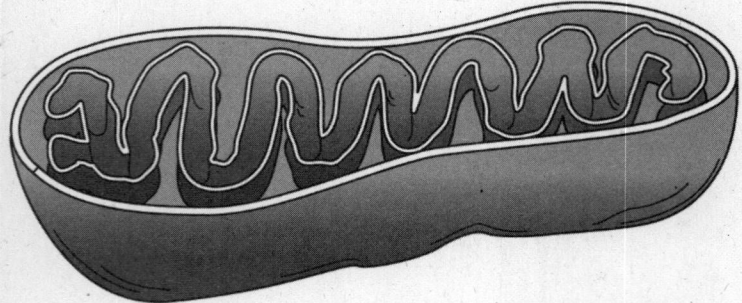

What process takes place in the organelle shown?

A photosynthesis

B protein synthesis

C cellular respiration

D packaging of proteins

14 Which of the following is the most likely reason that a population might crash?

A The competition for the same resource suddenly drops.

B The number of prey suddenly increases.

C The number of predators suddenly decreases.

D The carrying capacity of the environment suddenly drops.

Name _____

Critical Thinking

Answer the following questions in the spaces provided.

15 The diagram below shows an example of a food web.

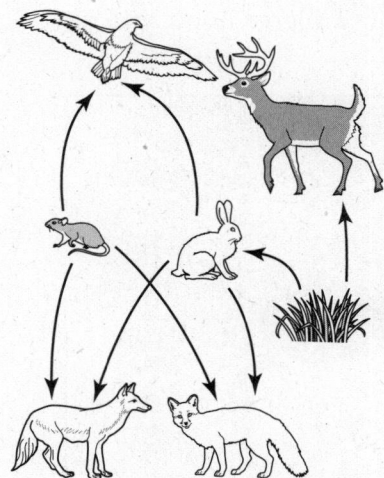

What are common traits of the prey shown that help them survive?

_____
_____
_____

What important ecological group is missing from this food web?

_____
_____

What might happen if the rabbit population suddenly shrank due to disease?

_____
_____
_____

16 How is a wetland ecosystem different from other types of aquatic ecosystems?

_____
_____
_____

Describe three functions of wetlands.

_____
_____
_____

Connect ESSENTIAL QUESTIONS
Lessons 6 and 7

Answer the following questions in the spaces provided.

17 The picture below shows a land ecosystem that experienced a large flood several months before.

Is the ecosystem shown more likely a result of primary succession or secondary succession? Explain why.

_____

_____

_____

_____

How could you tell if this is a mature ecosystem? Describe two signs of a mature ecosystem.

_____

_____

_____

_____

Properties of Matter

Big Idea

The properties of matter are determined by the arrangement of atoms.

At room temperature, gold is a solid. But at very high temperatures, solid gold becomes a liquid that flows.

What do you think?

Gold is a shiny metal that can be used to make jewelry. Water is a clear liquid that makes up over half of the human body. Though gold and water have different properties, they are both made of matter. What is matter?

Unit 7
Properties of Matter

Matter Up Close

Matter is anything that has mass and takes up space. All things, large and small, on Earth are made up of matter! Atoms are the smallest parts of the matter you see. You can't see atoms with your eyes alone.

Fly, about 7×10^{-3} m
The eye of a fly has been magnified so that you can see more detail. Magnification allows us to see things we cannot see with the human eye alone.

Grain of salt, about 5×10^{-4} m

This seasoning and preservative can be harvested from seawater.

Table salt

Rhinovirus, about 3×10^{-8} m

Watch out for this virus—it causes the common cold.

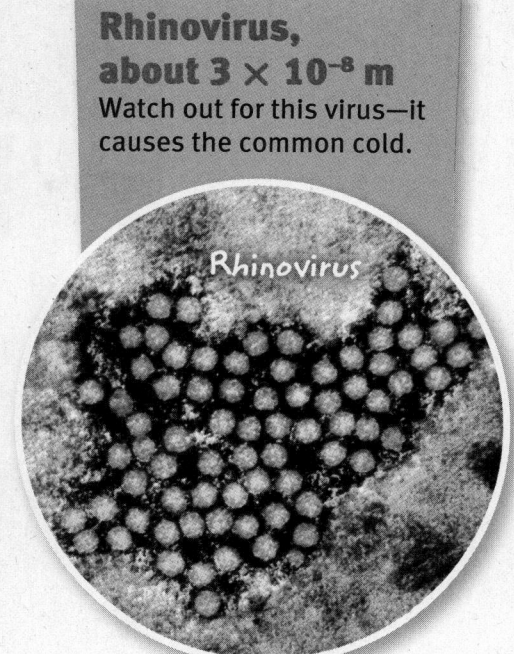

Rhinovirus

Helium atom, about 3×10^{-11} m

Atoms are so small that they cannot be viewed with traditional microscopes. Often, they are represented by models such as this one.

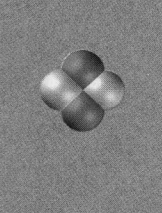

Object	Width
Grain of salt	5×10^{-4} m (or 0.0005 m)
Rhinovirus	3×10^{-8} m (or 0.00000003 m)
Helium atom	3×10^{-11} m (or 0.00000000003 m)

Take It Home — Size Is Relative

By looking at ratios of sizes, you can compare the relative sizes of objects. How many times greater is the size of a grain of salt than a rhinovirus particle? You can write a ratio to find the answer:

$$\frac{\text{grain of salt}}{\text{rhinovirus}} = \frac{0.0005 \text{ m}}{0.00000003 \text{ m}} \approx 17{,}000$$

A grain of salt is about 17,000 times the size of a rhinovirus.

A Determine how many times greater a rhinovirus is than a helium atom.

B Measure the width of one of your textbooks to the nearest millimeter. How many helium atoms could you line up across the book?

Physical and Chemical Changes

ESSENTIAL QUESTION

What are physical and chemical changes of matter?

By the end of this lesson, you should be able to distinguish between physical and chemical changes of matter.

Rusty beams are all that remain of these large boats. The rust is the result of an interaction of the iron beams with water and air.

OHIO **7.PS.1** The properties of matter are determined by the arrangement of atoms.

OHIO **7.SIA.5** Develop descriptions, models, explanations and predictions.

Engage Your Brain

1 Predict Check T or F to show whether you think each statement is true or false.

T   F

☐ ☐ When an ice cube melts, it is still water.

☐ ☐ Matter is lost when a candle is burned.

☐ ☐ When your body digests food, the food is changed into new substances.

2 Describe Write a word or phrase beginning with each letter of the word CHANGE that describes changes you have observed in everyday objects.

C _____

H _____

A _____

N _____

G _____

E _____

Active Reading

3 Apply Use context clues to write your own definitions for the words *interact* and *indicate*.

Example sentence
As the two substances <u>interact</u>, gas bubbles are given off.

interact:

_____

_____

_____

Example sentence
A color change may <u>indicate</u> that a chemical change has taken place.

indicate:

_____

_____

_____

Vocabulary Terms

• physical change
• chemical change
• law of conservation of mass

4 Apply As you learn the definition of each vocabulary term in this lesson, create your own definition or sketch to help you remember the meaning of the term.

Change of Appearance

What are physical changes of matter?

A physical property of matter is any property that can be observed or measured without changing the chemical identity of the substance. A **physical change** is a change that affects one or more physical properties of a substance. Physical changes occur when a substance changes from one form to another. When a substance undergoes a purely physical change, the chemical identity of the substance remains the same.

Changes in Observable Properties

The appearance, shape, or size of a substance may be altered during a physical change. For example, the process of turning wool into a sweater requires that the wool undergo physical changes. Wool is sheared from the sheep. The wool is then cleaned, and the wool fibers are separated from one another. Shearing and separating the fibers are physical changes that change the shape, volume, and texture of the wool.

Active Reading

5 Explain What happens to a substance during a physical change?

_____

_____

_____

Physical Changes Turn Wool into a Sweater

A Wool is sheared from the sheep. The raw wool is then cleaned and placed into a machine that separates the wool fibers from one another.

B The wool fibers are spun into yarn. Again, the shape and volume of the wool change. The fibers are twisted so that they are packed more closely together and are intertwined with one another.

C The yarn is dyed. The dye changes the color of the wool, but it does not change the wool into another substance. This type of color change is a physical change.

Changes That Do Not Alter the Chemical Identity of the Substance

Physical changes do not change the chemical identity of a substance. For example, during the process of turning wool into a sweater, many physical changes occur in the wool. However, the wool does not change into a different substance.

Another example of a physical change happens when you fill an ice cube tray with water and place it inside a freezer. Freezing water does not change its chemical makeup. In fact, you could melt the ice cube and have liquid water again! Changes of state are physical changes that affect matter.

Some physical changes, such as freezing and melting, are reversible. However, some are not. For example, if you wash a wool sweater in hot water, and then dry it at a high temperature, the fibers contract and the sweater shrinks. This is a physical change, but the sweater can't be returned to its original size.

6 Identify The list below gives several examples of physical changes. Write your own examples of physical changes on the blank lines.

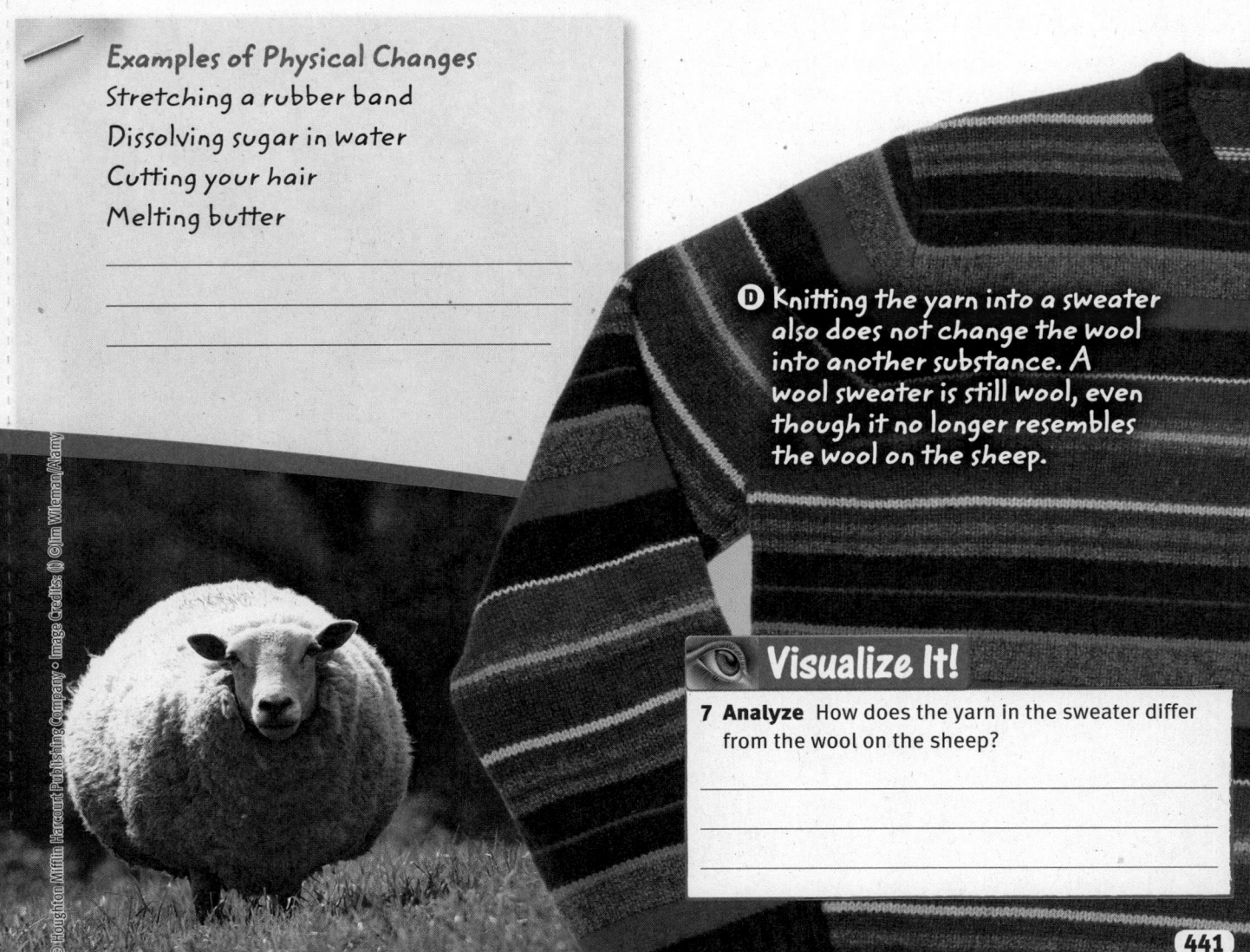

Examples of Physical Changes
Stretching a rubber band
Dissolving sugar in water
Cutting your hair
Melting butter

_____

_____

_____

D Knitting the yarn into a sweater also does not change the wool into another substance. A wool sweater is still wool, even though it no longer resembles the wool on the sheep.

Visualize It!

7 Analyze How does the yarn in the sweater differ from the wool on the sheep?

_____

_____

_____

© Houghton Mifflin Harcourt Publishing Company • Image Credits: © ©Jim Wileman/Alamy

Change from

What are chemical changes of matter?

Think about what happens to the burning logs in a campfire. They start out dry, rough, and dense. After flames surround them, the logs emerge as black and powdery ashes. The campfire releases a lot of heat and smoke in the process. Something has obviously happened, something more than simply a change of appearance. The wood has stopped being wood. It has undergone a chemical change.

Changes in Substance Identity

A **chemical change** occurs when one or more substances change into entirely new substances with different properties. For example, in the campfire, the dry, dense wood became the powdery ashes—new substances with different properties. When a cake is baked, the liquid cake batter becomes the solid, spongy treat. Whenever a new substance is formed, a chemical change has occurred.

Be aware that chemical *changes* are not exactly the same as chemical *properties*. Burning is a chemical change; flammability is a chemical property. The chemical properties of a substance describe which chemical changes can or cannot happen to that substance. Chemical changes are the *processes* by which substances actually change into new substances. You can learn about a substance's chemical properties by watching the chemical changes that substance undergoes.

© Houghton Mifflin Harcourt Publishing Company • Image Credits: ©Nina Strataki/Flcs/Corbis

Visualize It!

8 Identify Use the boxes provided to identify the wood, ashes, and flames involved in the chemical change. Then write a caption describing the chemical changes you see in the photo.

_____

_____

_____

_____

the inside

A _____

B _____

C _____

Changes to the Chemical Makeup of a Substance

In a chemical change, a substance's identity changes because its chemical makeup changes. This happens as the particles and chemical bonds that make up the substance get rearranged. For example, when iron rusts, molecules of oxygen from the air combine with iron atoms to form a new compound. Rust is not iron or oxygen. It is a new substance made up of oxygen and iron joined together.

Because chemical changes involve changes in the arrangements of particles, they are often influenced by temperature. At higher temperatures, the particles in a substance have more average kinetic energy. They move around a lot more freely and so rearrange more easily. Therefore, at higher temperatures, chemical reactions often happen more quickly. Some chemical changes can not happen at all without the addition of energy in the form of heat. Think of baking a cake. Without heat, the batter will not slowly change to become cake.

Active Reading **9 Explain** How do higher temperatures influence a chemical change?

_____

_____

_____

Think Outside the Book Inquiry

10 Infer Think of ways you control temperature to influence chemical changes during a typical day. (Hint: Cooking, Art class)

Look for the signs

How can you tell a chemical change has happened?

A physical change can happen without a chemical change. But all chemical changes are accompanied by some kind of change in the physical properties of the substances. This is because chemical changes result in new substances with new physical properties. The following are examples of observable changes that often accompany chemical changes. If you observe two or more of these changes, it is likely that you are observing a chemical change.

Active Reading **11 Compare** How are physical and chemical changes different?

_____

_____

_____

Production of an Odor

Some chemical changes produce odors. The chemical change that occurs when an egg is rotting, for example, produces the smell of sulfur. Milk that has soured also has an unpleasant smell—because bacteria have formed new substances in the milk. And if you've gone outdoors after a thunderstorm, you've probably noticed a distinct smell. This odor is an indication that lightning has caused a chemical change in the air.

Production of a Gas

Chemical changes often cause fizzing or foaming. For example, a chemical change is involved when an antacid tablet is dropped into a glass of water. As the tablet makes contact with the water and begins to react with it, bubbles of gas appear. One of the new substances that is formed is carbon dioxide gas, which forms the bubbles that you see.

It is important to note that some physical changes, such as boiling, can also produce gas bubbles. Therefore, the only way to know for sure whether a chemical change has taken place is to identify new substances.

Bubbles form when an antacid tablet reacts with water. The bubbles contain a new, gaseous substance, which signals that a chemical change has happened.

Formation of a Precipitate

Chemical changes may result in products in different physical states. Liquids sometimes combine to form a solid called a *precipitate*. For example, colorless potassium iodide and lead nitrate combine to form the bright yellow precipitate lead iodide, as shown below.

Bright yellow lead iodide precipitate forms when these liquids mix.

Change in Color

A change in color is often an indication of a chemical change. For example, when gray iron rusts, the product that forms is brown.

Change in Energy

Chemical changes can cause energy to change from one form into another. For example, in a burning candle, the chemical energy stored in the candle converts to heat and light energy.

A change in temperature is often a sign of a chemical change. The change need not always be as dramatic as the one in the photo, however.

The reaction of powdered aluminum with a metal oxide releases so much heat that it is often used to weld metals together. Here it is being used to test the heat-resistant properties of steel.

12 Infer List the observations you might make as you witness each of the changes below. Then identify whether the physical changes you observed also included a chemical change.

Change	Physical changes observed	Chemical change: Yes/No
Boiling water		
Baking a cake		
Burning wood		
Painting a door		

Conservation is the Law

What is the law of conservation of mass?

If you freeze 5 mL of water and then let the ice melt, you have 5 mL of water again. You can freeze and melt the water as much as you like. The mass of water will not change.

This does not always seem true for chemical changes. The ashes remaining after a fire contain much less mass than the logs that produced them. Mass seems to vanish. In other chemical changes, such as those that cause the growth of plants, mass seems to appear out of nowhere. This puzzled scientists for years. Where did the mass go? Where did it come from?

In the 1770s, the French chemist Antoine Lavoisier (an•TWAHN luh•VWAH•zee•ay) studied chemical changes in which substances seemed to lose or gain mass. He showed that the mass was most often lost to or gained from gases in the air. Lavoisier demonstrated this transformation of mass by observing chemical changes in sealed glass bulbs. This was the first demonstration of the *law of conservation of mass*. The **law of conservation of mass** states that in ordinary chemical and physical changes, mass is not created or destroyed but is only transformed into different substances.

The examples at the right will help you understand how the law works in both physical and chemical changes. In the top example, the second robot may have a different shape than the first, but it clearly has the same parts. In the second example, vinegar and baking soda undergo a chemical change. Mix the baking soda with the vinegar in the flask, and mass seems to vanish. Yet the balloon shows that what really happens is the production of a gas—carbon dioxide gas.

Active Reading 13 **Identify** What is the law of conservation of mass?

_____

_____

_____

The water may freeze or the ice may melt, but the amount of matter in this glass will stay the same.

Conservation of Mass in Physical Changes

When the long gray piece is moved from its arms to its waist, the toy robot gets a new look. It's still a toy robot—its parts are just rearranged. Many physical changes are reversible. All physical changes follow the law of conservation of mass.

Before 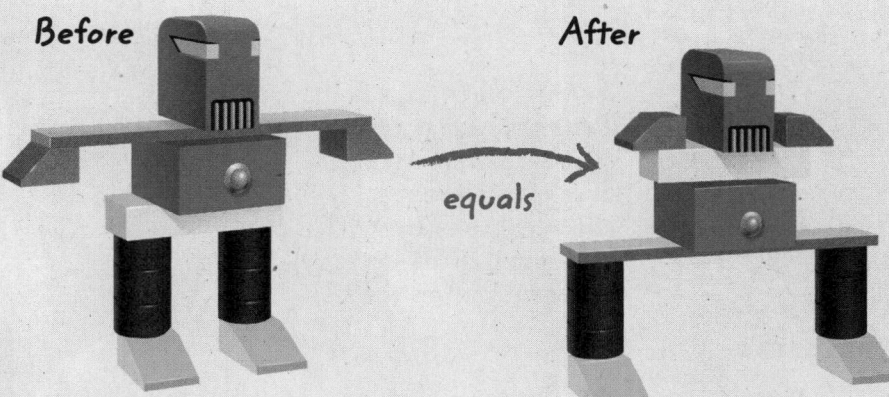 **After**

equals

👁 **Visualize It!**

14 **Describe** How is the physical change in the robot reversible, and how can you tell that the change follows the law of conservation of mass?

_____

_____

_____

_____

Conservation of Mass in Chemical Changes

When vinegar and baking soda are combined, they undergo a chemical change. The balloon at the right is inflated with carbon dioxide gas that was produced as a result of the change. The mass of the starting materials is the same as the mass of the products. Without the balloon to catch it, however, the gas would seem to disappear.

Before  **After**

vinegar

baking soda

equals

When vinegar and baking soda combine, carbon dioxide gas is produced.

👁 **Visualize It!**

15 **Infer** What would you observe about the mass in the flask if you did not put the balloon on top? Why?

_____

_____

Visual Summary

To complete this summary, circle the correct word or phrase. Then use the key below to check your answers. You can use this page to review the main concepts of the lesson.

How Matter Changes

A physical change is a change in the physical properties of matter, which can occur with or without a chemical change.

16 Burning / Dying wool is an example of a physical change.

A chemical change is a change of matter that occurs when one or more substances change into entirely new substances with different properties.

17 The formation of a precipitate signals a physical / chemical change.

Chemical changes often cause the production of an odor, fizzing or foaming, the formation of a precipitate, or changes in color or temperature.

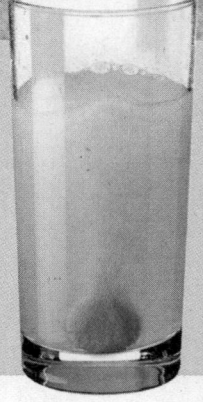

18 This physical / chemical change results in the formation of new substances.

The law of conservation of mass states that mass cannot be created or destroyed in ordinary chemical and physical changes.

19 The mass of the toy on the right is the same as / different from the mass of the toy on the left.

Answers: 16 Dying; 17 chemical; 18 chemical; 19 the same as

20 Explain Do changes that cannot be easily reversed, such as burning, observe the law of conservation of mass? Explain.

Lesson Review

Vocabulary

In your own words, define the following terms.

1 physical change

_____

_____

_____

2 chemical change

_____

_____

_____

3 law of conservation of mass

_____

_____

_____

_____

Key Concepts

4 Identify Give an example of a purely physical change and an example of a chemical change.

_____

_____

_____

_____

_____

5 Compare How is a chemical change different from a physical change?

_____

_____

_____

_____

6 Apply Suppose a log's mass is 5 kg. After burning, the mass of the ash is 1 kg. Explain what may have happened to the other 4 kg.

_____

_____

_____

_____

_____

Critical Thinking

Use this photo to answer the following question.

7 Analyze As the bright sun shines upon the water, the water slowly disappears. The same sunlight gives energy to the surrounding plants to convert water and carbon dioxide into sugar and oxygen gas. Which change is purely physical and which is both physical and chemical?

_____

_____

_____

8 Compare Relate the statement "You can't get something for nothing" to the law of the conservation of mass.

_____

_____

_____

_____

9 Infer Sharpening a pencil leaves behind pencil shavings. What type of change has occurred? Explain.

_____

_____

_____

_____

My Notes

The Atom

ESSENTIAL QUESTION

How do we know what parts make up the atom?

By the end of this lesson, you should be able to describe how the development of the atomic theory has led to the modern understanding of the atom and its parts.

This sandcastle is made up of tiny grains of sand. Each grain of sand is made up of particles called atoms, which are too small to see.

OHIO 7.PS.1 The properties of matter are determined by the arrangement of atoms.

OHIO 7.SIA.5 Develop descriptions, models, explanations and predictions.

Engage Your Brain

1 Identify Read over the following vocabulary terms. In the spaces provided, place a + if you know the term well, a ~ if you have heard the term but are not sure what it means, and a ? if you are unfamiliar with the term. Then, write a sentence that includes the word you are most familiar with.

_____ atom

_____ electron

_____ neutron

_____ proton

_____ nucleus

Sentence using known word:

_____

_____

2 Compare Use the figure below to answer the questions. Check T or F to show whether you think each statement is true or false.

T   F

☐ ☐ Electrons move in orbits in the same way planets orbit the sun.

☐ ☐ If this were a model of the atom, the nucleus would be in the same place as the sun.

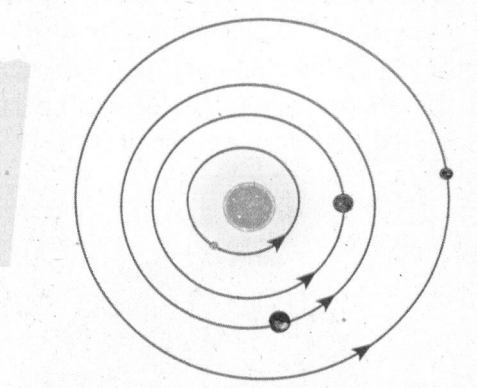

Active Reading

3 Apply Use context clues to write your own definition for the words *theory* and *revise*.

Example sentence
The scientist developed a <u>theory</u> to explain the structure of the atom.

theory:

_____

_____

Example sentence
As scientists learned new information about atoms, they had to <u>revise</u> the model of the atom.

revise:

_____

_____

Vocabulary Terms

• atom
• electron
• nucleus
• proton
• neutron
• electron cloud
• atomic number
• mass number

4 Apply As you learn the definition of each vocabulary term in this lesson, create your own definition or sketch to help you remember the meaning of the term.

As a Matter of Fact

What makes up matter?

Imagine that you are cutting fabric to make a quilt. You cut a piece of fabric in half. Then, you cut each half in half again. Could you keep cutting the pieces in half forever? Around 400 BCE, a Greek philosopher named Democritus (dih·MAHK·rih·tuhs) thought that you would eventually end up with a particle that could not be cut. He called this particle *atomos,* a Greek word meaning "not able to be divided." Aristotle (AIR·ih·staht'l), another Greek philosopher, disagreed. He did not believe that such a particle could make up all substances found in nature.

Neither Democritus nor Aristotle did experiments to test their ideas. It would be centuries before scientists tested these hypotheses. Within the past 200 years, scientists have come to agree that matter is made up of small particles. Democritus's term *atom* is used to describe these particles.

Active Reading

5 Describe Who was Democritus?

_____

_____

_____

_____

There is a limit to how small you can cut a piece of fabric. Even the smallest piece of fabric you can cut is made up of a huge number of particles of many different elements.

© Houghton Mifflin Harcourt Publishing Company • Image Credits: ©HMH

Atoms

An **atom** is the smallest particle into which an element can be divided and still be the same element. People used to think that atoms could not be divided into anything simpler. Scientists now know that atoms are made of even smaller particles. But the atom is still considered to be the basic unit of matter because it is the smallest unit that has the chemical properties of an element.

You cannot see individual atoms. But they make up everything you do see. The food you eat and the water you drink are made of atoms. Plants, such as moss, are made of atoms. Even things you cannot see are made of atoms. The air you breathe is made of atoms. There are many types of atoms that combine in different ways to make all substances.

You can use a light microscope to see the cells that make up a tiny moss leaf. But you cannot see the atoms that make up the substances in the cells. Atoms are so small that you cannot see them with an ordinary microscope. Only powerful instruments can make images of atoms. How small are atoms? Think about a penny. A penny contains about 2×10^{22}, or 20,000,000,000,000,000,000,000 atoms of copper and zinc. That's almost 3,000 billion times more atoms than there are people living on Earth!

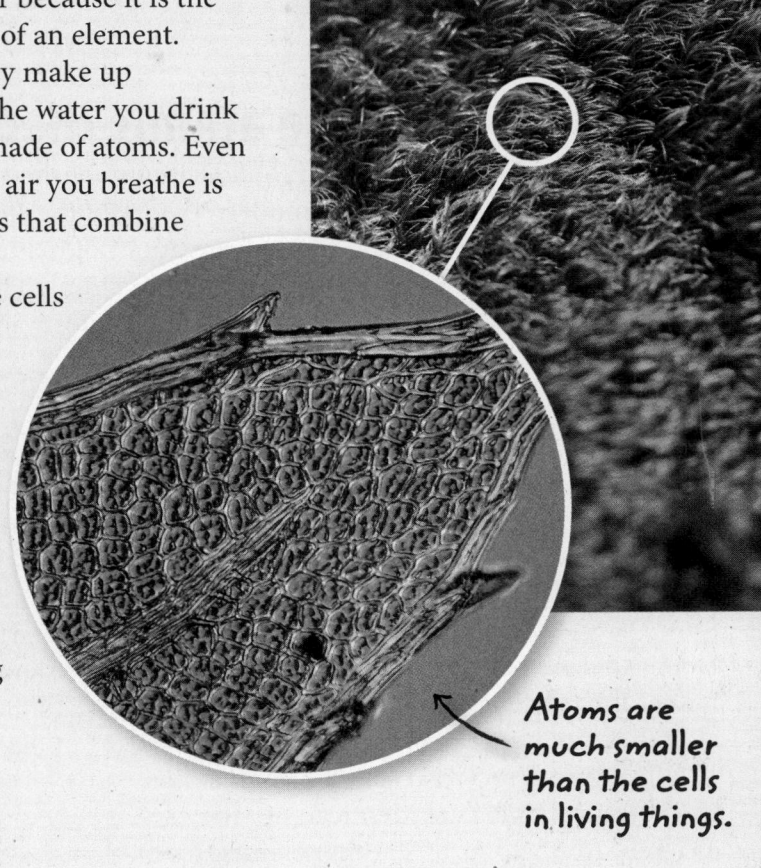

Moss

Atoms are much smaller than the cells in living things.

Visualize It! Inquiry

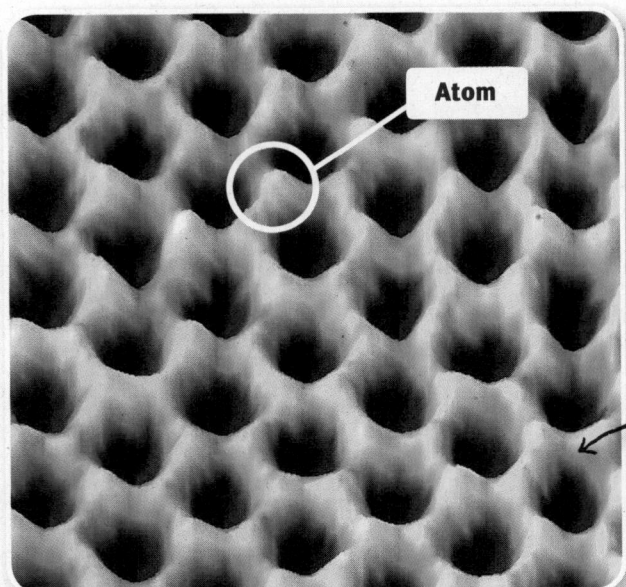

Atom

This image shows how carbon atoms are connected in a substance. It was taken with a special type of electron microscope.

6 Analyze What can you infer about atoms from this image? What can't you infer from the image?

_____

_____

_____

_____

_____

_____

Something Old, Something New

Who developed the atomic theory?

In 1808, a British chemist named John Dalton published an atomic theory. This was the start of the modern theory of the atom. Dalton's theory could explain most observations of matter at that time. Over time, scientists learned more about atoms. The atomic theory was revised as scientists discovered new information.

John Dalton

Active Reading **7 Identify** As you read, underline the four main ideas of Dalton's theory of the atom.

Unlike the ideas of Democritus and Aristotle, John Dalton's theory was based on evidence from experiments. Dalton's theory stated that all matter is made up of atoms. He also thought that atoms cannot be created, divided, or destroyed.

Dalton's theory also stated that all atoms of a certain element are identical. But they are different from atoms of all other elements. For example, every atom of carbon is the same as every other atom of carbon. However, every atom of carbon is different from any atom of oxygen. Dalton also thought that atoms join with other atoms to make new substances. For example, an oxygen atom combines with two hydrogen atoms to form water. Every substance is made up of atoms combined in certain ways.

1808

J. J. Thomson

J. J. Thomson's experiments provided evidence that atoms are made up of even smaller particles. He found particles within the atom that have a negative charge. These negatively charged particles later became known as **electrons**. Thomson thought that an atom was a positive sphere with the electrons mixed through it, as shown below.

1897

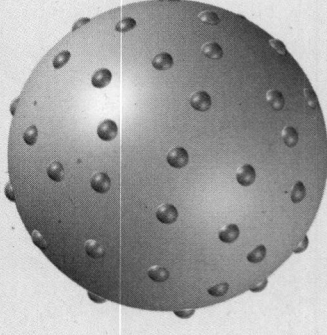

8 Model Describe how you would show J. J. Thomson's model of the atom using small beads and clay.

_____

_____

_____

_____

_____

Ernest Rutherford

In 1909, Ernest Rutherford conducted an experiment to study the parts of the atom. His experiment suggested that atoms have a **nucleus**—a small, dense center that has a positive charge and is surrounded by moving electrons. Rutherford later found that the nucleus is made up of smaller particles. He called the positively charged particles in the nucleus **protons**.

Niels Bohr

Niels Bohr made observations that led to a new theory of how the electrons in the atom behaved. Bohr agreed that an atom has a positive nucleus surrounded by electrons. In his model, electrons move around the nucleus in circular paths. Each path is a certain distance from the nucleus. Bohr's model helped scientists predict the chemical properties of elements. However, scientists have since made observations that could not be explained by Bohr's model. The model of the atom has been revised to explain these observations.

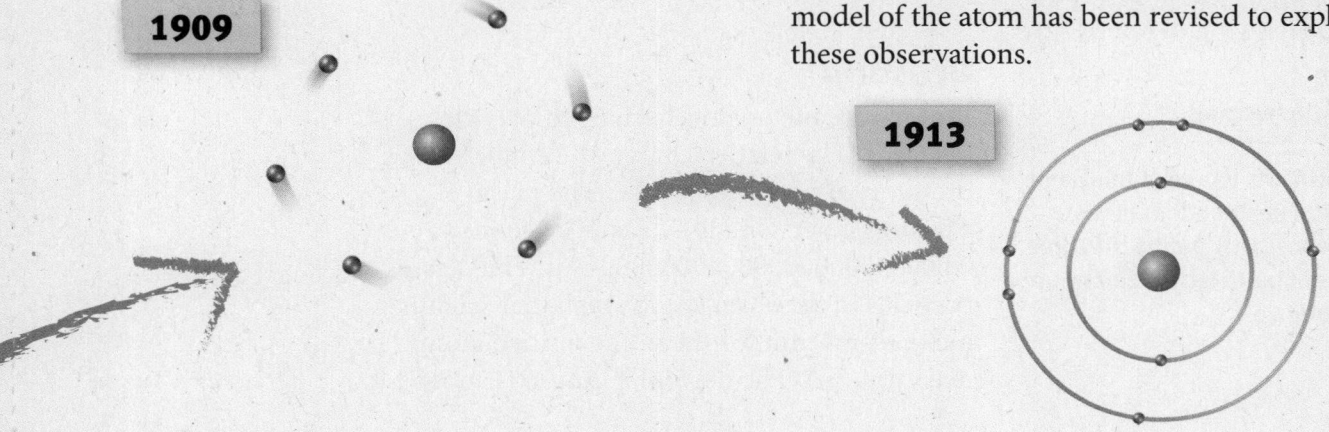

1909

1913

What is the current atomic theory?

Modern atomic theory is based on the work of many scientists. It keeps Dalton's ideas that atoms are the basic unit of matter and that the atoms of each element are unique. The experiments of Thomson and Rutherford showed that atoms are made up of electrons and protons. James Chadwick was Rutherford's student. In 1932, Chadwick discovered that the nucleus contains uncharged particles called **neutrons**. In the current atomic theory, electrons do not move in circular paths around the nucleus as Bohr thought. Instead, the current theory suggests that electrons move within an area around the nucleus called the **electron cloud**.

9 **Analyze** Today's model of the atom looks different from the models that came before it. Why has the model of the atom changed?

_____

_____

_____

_____

Up and Atom!

What are the parts of an atom?

This model of an atom shows where protons, neutrons, and electrons are found within the atom. Protons and neutrons are found in the center of the electron cloud. The particles in this model are not shown in their correct proportions. If they were, the protons and neutrons would be too small to see.

Protons

Protons are the positively charged particles of atoms. The relative charge of a single proton is often written as 1+. The mass of a proton is very small—1.7×10^{-24} g, or 0.0000000000000000000000017 g. The masses of particles in the atom are so small that scientists made a new unit for them: the unified atomic mass unit (u). The mass of a proton is about 1 u.

Neutrons

Neutrons are particles that have no electric charge. They are a little more massive than protons are. But the mass of a neutron is still very close to 1 u. Atoms usually have at least as many neutrons as they have protons.

Together, protons and neutrons form the nucleus of the atom. The nucleus is located at the center of an atom. This model of a beryllium atom shows that the nucleus of this atom is made up of four protons and five neutrons. Because each proton has a 1+ charge, the overall charge of this nucleus is 4+. (Remember: neutrons have no electric charge.) The volume of the nucleus is very small compared to the rest of the atom. But protons and neutrons are the most massive particles in an atom. So the nucleus is very dense. If it were possible to have a nucleus the volume of a grape, that nucleus would have a mass greater than 9 million metric tons!

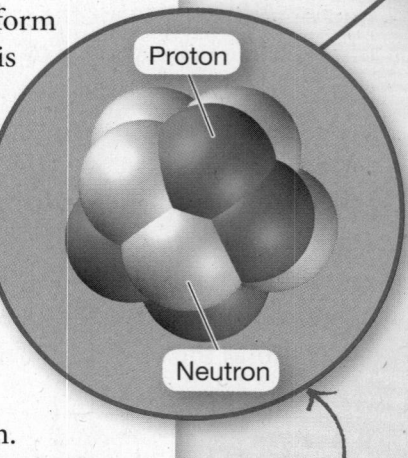

Proton

Neutron

Nucleus

The Electron Cloud

The negatively charged particles of the atom are called electrons. Electrons move around the nucleus very quickly. Scientists have found that it is not possible to determine both their exact positions and speed at the same time. This is why we picture the electrons as being in an electron cloud around the nucleus.

Compared with protons and neutrons, electrons have very little mass. It takes more than 1,800 electrons to equal the mass of 1 proton. The mass of an electron is so small that it is usually thought of as almost 0 u.

The charge of a single electron is represented as 1−. The charges of protons and electrons are opposite but equal. The number of protons in an atom equals the number of electrons. So the atom has a net, or overall, charge of 0. For example, this beryllium atom contains four electrons. The combined charge of the electrons is 4−. But remember that the charge of the nucleus is 4+.

$$(4+) + (4-) = 0$$

The net charge of the atom is 0.

An atom can lose or gain electrons. When this happens, we refer to the atom as an *ion*. Ions have a net charge that is not 0.

11 Summarize Complete the following table with information about the parts of the atom.

Part of the atom	Location in the atom	Electric charge	Relative mass
Proton			Slightly less massive than a neutron
	Nucleus		
		1−	

Take a Number!

How can we describe atoms?

Think of all the substances you see and touch every day. Are all of these substances the same? No. The substances that make up this book are quite different from the substances in the air you are breathing. If all atoms are composed of the same particles, how can there be so many different types of substances? Different combinations of protons, neutrons, and electrons produce atoms with different properties. The number of each kind of particle within an atom determines its unique properties. In turn, these different atoms combine to form the different substances all around us.

By Atomic Number

The number of protons distinguishes the atoms of one element from the atoms of another. For example, every hydrogen atom contains one proton. And every carbon atom has exactly six protons in its nucleus.

The number of protons in the nucleus of an atom is the **atomic number** of that atom. Hydrogen has an atomic number of 1 because each of its atoms contains just one proton. Carbon has an atomic number of 6 because each of its atoms contains six protons.

Active Reading 12 **Compare** How are two atoms of the same element alike?

_____

_____

_____

_____

_____

_____

Think Outside the Book · Inquiry

13 **Apply** Research how scientists make new types of atoms using particle accelerators. Choose one element that has been made by scientists. Create a brochure that describes its properties and how it was made.

By Mass Number

The atoms of a certain element always have the same number of protons. But they may not always have the same number of neutrons. For example, all chlorine atoms have 17 protons. But some chlorine atoms have 18 neutrons. Other chlorine atoms have 20 neutrons. These two types of chlorine atoms are called isotopes. *Isotopes* are atoms of the same element that have different numbers of neutrons. Some elements have many isotopes, and other elements have just a few.

The total number of protons and neutrons in an atom's nucleus is its **mass number**. Different isotopes of chlorine have different mass numbers. What is the mass number of a chlorine atom that contains 18 neutrons?

$$17 + 18 = 35$$

The mass number of this atom is 35.

The helium in these balloons is less massive than an equal volume of the nitrogen in the air, so the balloons float.

---

14 Calculate Use this model of a helium atom to find its atomic number and mass number.

Proton

Neutron

Atomic number: [ ]

Mass number: [ ]

Visual Summary

To complete this summary, check the box that indicates true or false. Then, use the key below to check your answers. You can use this page to review the main concepts of the lesson.

The Atom

An atom is the smallest particle of an element. All substances are made up of atoms.

T   F
15 ☐   ☐   You can use a light microscope to see the atoms in fabric.

Atomic theory has changed over time as scientists learned more about the particles that make up matter.

T   F
16 ☐   ☐   According to current atomic theory, electrons are in fixed locations.

Atoms contain a positively charged nucleus surrounded by a negatively charged electron cloud.

T   F
17 ☐   ☐   The nucleus contains neutrons and electrons.

Atomic number and mass number are used to describe atoms.

T   F
18 ☐   ☐   Every atom of the same element has the same atomic number.

19 **Predict** Explain why you think the current model of the atom will or will not change over time.

Lesson Review

Vocabulary

Draw a line to connect the following terms to their definitions.

1 atom

2 proton

3 neutron

A a positively charged atomic particle

B an uncharged atomic particle

C the smallest particle of an element that has the chemical properties of that element

Key Concepts

4 Compare Compare the charges and masses of protons, neutrons, and electrons.

_____

_____

_____

_____

_____

_____

5 Explain How can atoms make up all of the substances around you?

_____

_____

_____

_____

6 Compare How does the current model of the atom differ from J. J. Thomson's model?

_____

_____

_____

_____

_____

_____

7 Calculate What is the atomic number of a sodium atom that has 11 protons and 12 neutrons?

_____

_____

Critical Thinking

Use this diagram to answer the following questions.

8 Analyze The red sphere represents a proton. What is the atomic number of this atom? Explain how you found the atomic number.

_____

_____

_____

9 Apply What is the mass number of an isotope of this atom that has 2 neutrons?

_____

_____

10 Analyze Where are the nucleus and the electrons located in this atom?

_____

_____

_____

_____

_____

_____

11 Infer If atoms are made of smaller parts such as electrons, why are atoms considered the basic unit of matter?

_____

_____

_____

_____

My Notes

The Periodic Table

ESSENTIAL QUESTION

How are elements arranged on the periodic table?

By the end of this lesson, you should be able to describe the relationship between the arrangement of elements on the periodic table and the properties of those elements.

In this market, similar foods are arranged in groups. Can you identify some of the properties each group shares?

OHIO **7.PS.1** The properties of matter are determined by the arrangement of atoms.

OHIO **7.SIA.3** Use appropriate mathematics, tools and techniques to gather data and information.

OHIO **7.SIA.4** Analyze and interpret data.

🧠 Engage Your Brain

1 Describe Write a word or phrase beginning with each letter of the word GOLD that describes the properties of these gold coins.

G _____

O _____

L _____

D _____

2 Describe As you will learn in this lesson, elements are arranged by their properties on the periodic table. What other objects are often arranged by their properties?

_____

_____

_____

_____

_____

_____

✏️ Active Reading

3 Preview Before you begin reading this lesson, look through the pages and read the headings and subheadings. The headings show how information is organized in the lesson. After you read the headings and subheadings, write a short description of what the lesson will cover.

_____

_____

_____

_____

Vocabulary Terms

• periodic table
• chemical symbol
• average atomic mass
• metal
• nonmetal
• metalloid
• group
• period

4 Apply As you learn the definition of each vocabulary term in this lesson, create your own definition or sketch to help you remember the meaning of the term.

Get Organized!

What are elements?

People have long sought to find the basic substances of matter. It was once believed that fire, wind, earth, and water, in various combinations, made up all objects. By the 1860s, however, scientists considered there to be at least 60 different basic substances, or elements. They saw that many of these elements shared certain physical and chemical properties and began classifying them. Knowing what you know about the properties of matter, try classifying the elements below.

Bismuth

Sulfur

Chlorine

Mercury

Visualize It!

5 Identify Observe the appearance of these six elements. Create two or three categories that group the elements by similar properties. Below each element, write the name of the category in which the element belongs.

Copper

Bromine

© Houghton Mifflin Harcourt Publishing Company • Image Credits: (tl) ©Russell Lappa/Photo Researchers, Inc.; (tr) ©Charles D. Winters/Photo Researchers, Inc.; (bl) ©Harry Taylor/Dorling Kindersley/Getty Images; (bc) ©Charles D. Winters/Photo Researchers, Inc.

How are the elements organized?

Around this time, a Russian chemist named Dmitri Mendeleev (dih•MEE•tree men•duh•LAY•uhf) began thinking about how he could organize the elements based on their properties. To help him decide how to arrange the elements, Mendeleev made a set of element cards. Each card listed the mass of an atom of each element as well as some of the element's properties. Mendeleev arranged the cards in various ways, looking for a pattern to emerge. When he arranged the element cards in order of increasing atomic mass, the properties of those elements occurred in a *periodic,* or regularly repeating, pattern. For this reason, Mendeleev's arrangement of the elements became known as the **periodic table**. Mendeleev used the periodic pattern in his table to predict elements that had not yet been discovered.

In the early 1900s, British scientist Henry Moseley showed how Mendeleev's periodic table could be rearranged. After determining the numbers of protons in the atoms of the elements, he arranged the elements on the table in order of increasing number of protons, or *atomic number.* Moseley's new arrangement of the elements corrected some of the flaws in Mendeleev's table.

The periodic table is a useful tool to scientists because it makes clear many patterns among the elements' properties. The periodic table is like a map or a calendar of the elements.

6 Explain How did Henry Moseley revise Mendeleev's periodic table?

_____

_____

_____

_____

7 Apply What are you doing this week? Fill in the calendar with activities or plans you have for this week and next. Do any events occur periodically? Explain.

_____

_____

_____

What does the periodic table have in common with a calendar? They both show a periodic pattern. On a calendar, the days of the week repeat in the same order every 7 days.

Sunday	Monday	Tuesday	Wednesday	Thursday	Friday	Saturday

The Periodic Table of Elements

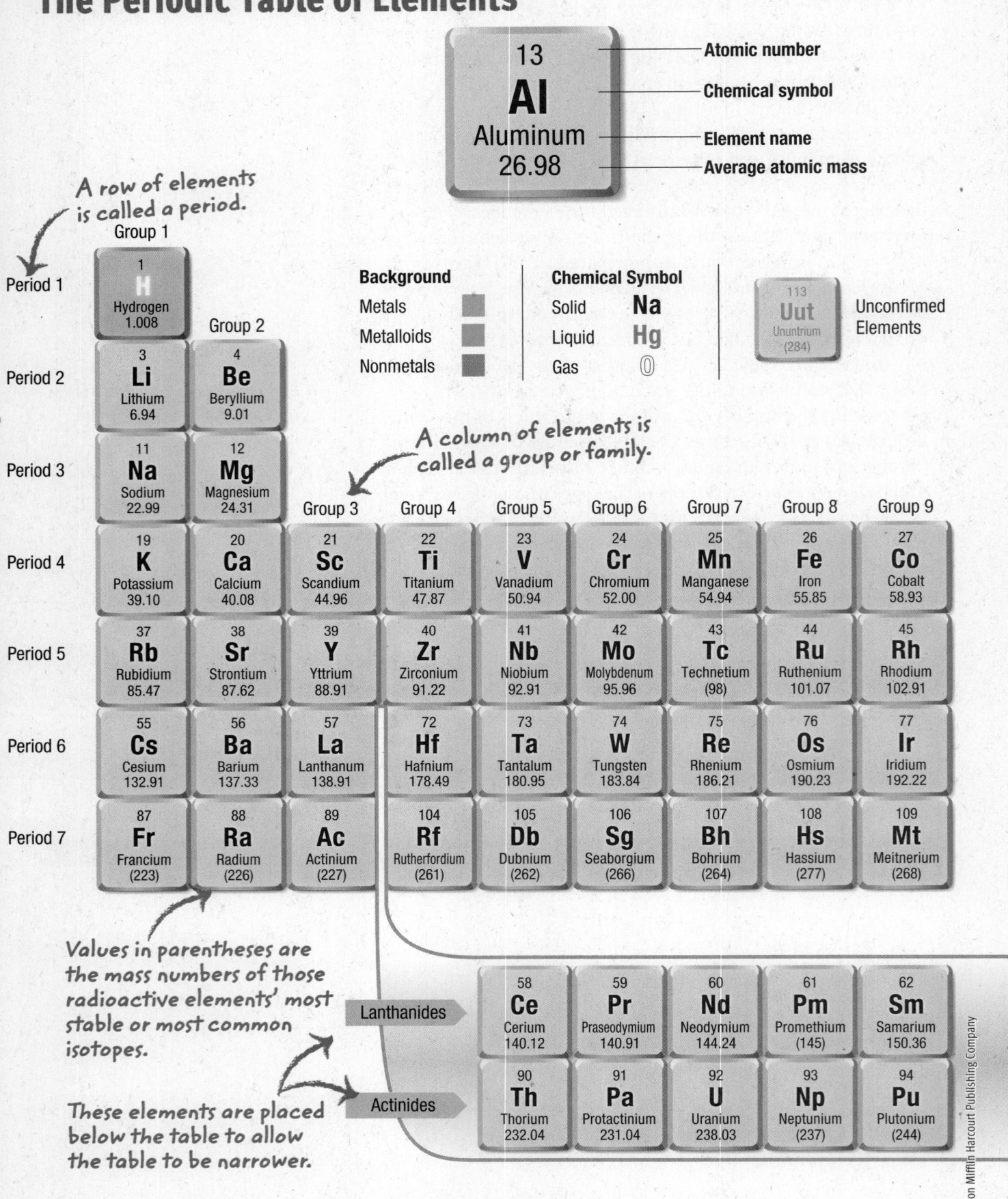

13
Al
Aluminum
26.98

— Atomic number
— Chemical symbol
— Element name
— Average atomic mass

A row of elements is called a period.

Group 1

Period 1 —
| 1 |
| **H** |
| Hydrogen |
| 1.008 |

Group 2

Period 2
3	4
Li	**Be**
Lithium	Beryllium
6.94	9.01

Background
- Metals
- Metalloids
- Nonmetals

Chemical Symbol
- Solid **Na**
- Liquid **Hg**
- Gas ⓪

| 113 |
| **Uut** |
| Ununtrium |
| (284) |

Unconfirmed Elements

Period 3
11	12
Na	**Mg**
Sodium	Magnesium
22.99	24.31

A column of elements is called a group or family.

Group 3	Group 4	Group 5	Group 6	Group 7	Group 8	Group 9

Period 4
19	20	21	22	23	24	25	26	27
K	**Ca**	**Sc**	**Ti**	**V**	**Cr**	**Mn**	**Fe**	**Co**
Potassium	Calcium	Scandium	Titanium	Vanadium	Chromium	Manganese	Iron	Cobalt
39.10	40.08	44.96	47.87	50.94	52.00	54.94	55.85	58.93

Period 5
37	38	39	40	41	42	43	44	45
Rb	**Sr**	**Y**	**Zr**	**Nb**	**Mo**	**Tc**	**Ru**	**Rh**
Rubidium	Strontium	Yttrium	Zirconium	Niobium	Molybdenum	Technetium	Ruthenium	Rhodium
85.47	87.62	88.91	91.22	92.91	95.96	(98)	101.07	102.91

Period 6
55	56	57	72	73	74	75	76	77
Cs	**Ba**	**La**	**Hf**	**Ta**	**W**	**Re**	**Os**	**Ir**
Cesium	Barium	Lanthanum	Hafnium	Tantalum	Tungsten	Rhenium	Osmium	Iridium
132.91	137.33	138.91	178.49	180.95	183.84	186.21	190.23	192.22

Period 7
87	88	89	104	105	106	107	108	109
Fr	**Ra**	**Ac**	**Rf**	**Db**	**Sg**	**Bh**	**Hs**	**Mt**
Francium	Radium	Actinium	Rutherfordium	Dubnium	Seaborgium	Bohrium	Hassium	Meitnerium
(223)	(226)	(227)	(261)	(262)	(266)	(264)	(277)	(268)

Values in parentheses are the mass numbers of those radioactive elements' most stable or most common isotopes.

Lanthanides
58	59	60	61	62
Ce	**Pr**	**Nd**	**Pm**	**Sm**
Cerium	Praseodymium	Neodymium	Promethium	Samarium
140.12	140.91	144.24	(145)	150.36

Actinides
90	91	92	93	94
Th	**Pa**	**U**	**Np**	**Pu**
Thorium	Protactinium	Uranium	Neptunium	Plutonium
232.04	231.04	238.03	(237)	(244)

These elements are placed below the table to allow the table to be narrower.

8 Analyze According to the periodic table, how many elements are a liquid at room temperature?

_____

9 Analyze According to the periodic table, how many elements are metalloids?

_____

The zigzag line separates metals from nonmetals.

				Group 13	Group 14	Group 15	Group 16	Group 17	Group 18
									2 **He** Helium 4.003
				5 **B** Boron 10.81	6 **C** Carbon 12.01	7 **N** Nitrogen 14.01	8 **O** Oxygen 16.00	9 **F** Fluorine 19.00	10 **Ne** Neon 20.18
Group 10	Group 11	Group 12		13 **Al** Aluminum 26.98	14 **Si** Silicon 28.09	15 **P** Phosphorus 30.97	16 **S** Sulfur 32.06	17 **Cl** Chlorine 35.45	18 **Ar** Argon 39.95
28 **Ni** Nickel 58.69	29 **Cu** Copper 63.55	30 **Zn** Zinc 65.38	31 **Ga** Gallium 69.72	32 **Ge** Germanium 72.63	33 **As** Arsenic 74.92	34 **Se** Selenium 78.96	35 **Br** Bromine 79.90	36 **Kr** Krypton 83.80
46 **Pd** Palladium 106.42	47 **Ag** Silver 107.87	48 **Cd** Cadmium 112.41	49 **In** Indium 114.82	50 **Sn** Tin 118.71	51 **Sb** Antimony 121.76	52 **Te** Tellurium 127.60	53 **I** Iodine 126.90	54 **Xe** Xenon 131.29
78 **Pt** Platinum 195.08	79 **Au** Gold 196.97	80 **Hg** Mercury 200.59	81 **Tl** Thallium 204.38	82 **Pb** Lead 207.2	83 **Bi** Bismuth 208.98	84 **Po** Polonium (209)	85 **At** Astatine (210)	86 **Rn** Radon (222)
110 **Ds** Darmstadtium (271)	111 **Rg** Roentgenium (272)	112 **Cn** Copernicium (285)	113 **Uut** Ununtrium (284)	114 **Fl** Flerovium (289)	115 **Uup** Ununpentium (288)	116 **Lv** Livermorium (293)	117 **Uus** Ununseptium (294)	118 **Uuo** Ununoctium (294)

63 **Eu** Europium 151.96	64 **Gd** Gadolinium 157.25	65 **Tb** Terbium 158.93	66 **Dy** Dysprosium 162.50	67 **Ho** Holmium 164.93	68 **Er** Erbium 167.26	69 **Tm** Thulium 168.93	70 **Yb** Ytterbium 173.05	71 **Lu** Lutetium 174.97
95 **Am** Americium (243)	96 **Cm** Curium (247)	97 **Bk** Berkelium (247)	98 **Cf** Californium (251)	99 **Es** Einsteinium (252)	100 **Fm** Fermium (257)	101 **Md** Mendelevium (258)	102 **No** Nobelium (259)	103 **Lr** Lawrencium (262)

Ma**K**ing Arrangements

What information is contained in each square on the periodic table?

The periodic table is not simply a list of element names. The table contains useful information about each of the elements. The periodic table is usually shown as a grid of squares. Each square contains an element's chemical name, atomic number, chemical symbol, and average atomic mass.

Atomic Number

The atomic number is the number of protons in the nucleus of an atom of that element. All atoms of an element have the same atomic number. In this way, the number of protons determines the identity of the element. For example, every aluminum atom has 13 protons, so its atomic number is 13.

Chemical Symbol

The **chemical symbol** is an abbreviation for the element's name. The first letter is always capitalized. Any other letter is always lowercase. For most elements, the chemical symbol is a one- or two-letter symbol. However, some elements have temporary three-letter symbols. These elements will receive permanent one- or two-letter symbols once they have been reviewed by an international committee of scientists.

13

Al

Aluminum

26.98

Chemical Name

The names of the elements come from many sources. Some elements, such as mendelevium, are named after scientists. Others, such as californium, are named after places.

Average Atomic Mass

All atoms of a given element contain the same number of protons. But the number of neutrons in those atoms can vary. So different atoms of an element can have different masses. The **average atomic mass** of an atom is the weighted average of the masses of all the naturally occurring isotopes of that element. A weighted average accounts for the percentages of each isotope. Atomic mass is measured using the unified atomic mass unit (u).

🖋 **Active Reading**

10 Apply What is the average atomic mass of aluminum?

_____

How are the elements arranged on the periodic table?

Have you ever noticed how items in a grocery store are arranged? Each aisle contains a different kind of product. Within an aisle, similar products are grouped together on shelves. Because the items are arranged in categories, it is easy to find your favorite brand of cereal. Similarly, the elements are arranged in a certain order on the periodic table. If you understand how the periodic table is organized, you can easily find and compare elements.

Metals, Nonmetals, and Metalloids Are Found in Three Distinct Regions

Elements on the periodic table can be classified into three major categories: metals, nonmetals, and metalloids. The zigzag line on the periodic table can help you identify where these three classes of elements are located. Except for hydrogen, the elements to the left of the zigzag line are metals. **Metals** are elements that are shiny and conduct heat and electricity well. Most metals are solid at room temperature. Many metals are *malleable,* or able to be formed into different shapes. Some metals are *ductile,* meaning that they can be made into wires. The elements to the right of the zigzag line are nonmetals. **Nonmetals** are poor conductors of heat and electricity. Nonmetals are often dull and brittle. Metalloids border the zigzag line on the periodic table. **Metalloids** are elements that have some properties of metals and some properties of nonmetals. Some metalloids are used to make semiconductor chips in computers.

11 Identify Fill in the blanks below with the word *metal, nonmetal,* or *metalloid.*

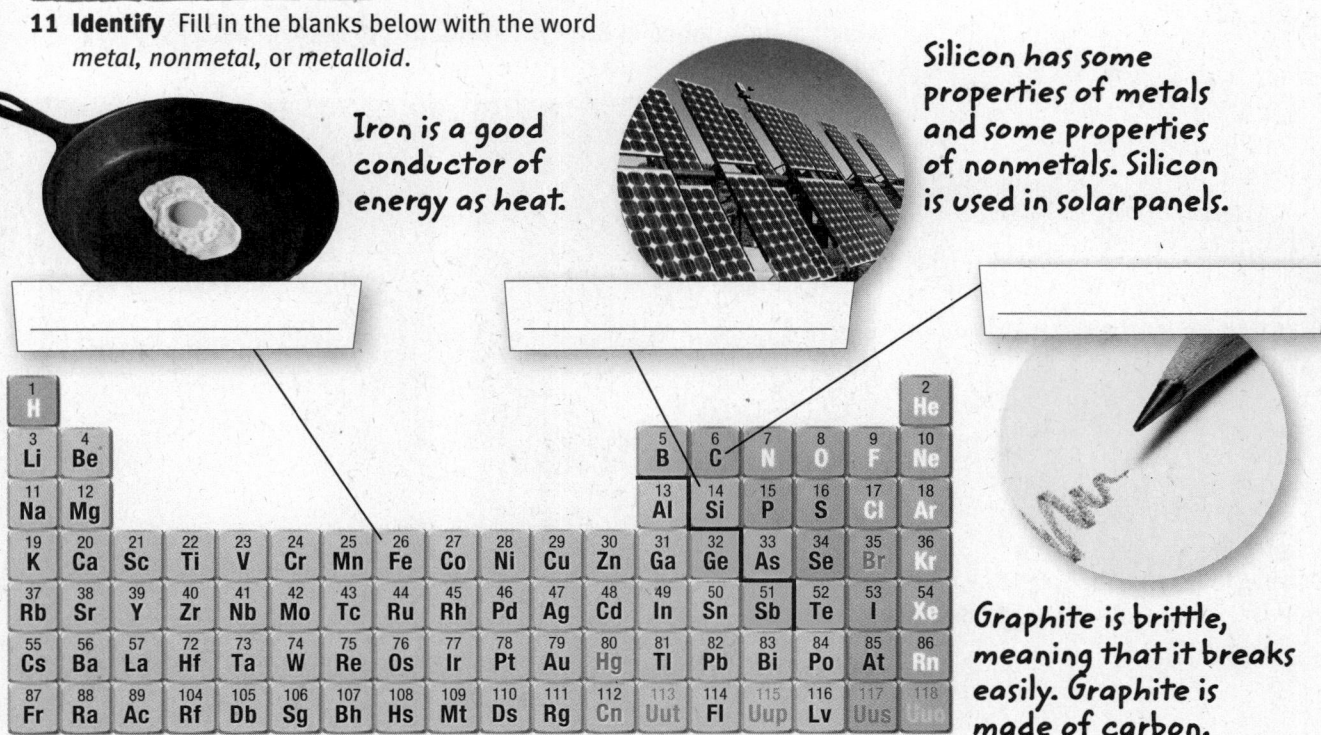

Iron is a good conductor of energy as heat.

Silicon has some properties of metals and some properties of nonmetals. Silicon is used in solar panels.

Graphite is brittle, meaning that it breaks easily. Graphite is made of carbon.

Elements in Each Column Have Similar Properties

The periodic table groups elements with similar properties together. Each vertical column of elements (from top to bottom) on the periodic table is called a **group**. Elements in the same group often have similar physical and chemical properties. For this reason, a group is sometimes called a *family*.

The properties of elements in a group are similar because the atoms of these elements have the same number of *valence electrons*. Valence electrons are found in the outermost portion of the electron cloud of an atom. Because they are far from the the attractive force of the nucleus, valence electrons are able to participate in chemical bonding. The number of valence electrons helps determine what kind of chemical reactions the atom can undergo. For example, all of the atoms of elements in Group 1 have a single valence electron. These elements are very reactive. The atoms of elements in Group 18 have a full set of valence electrons. The elements in Group 18 are all unreactive gases.

Active Reading **12 Explain** Why do elements within a group have similar chemical properties?

_____

_____

_____

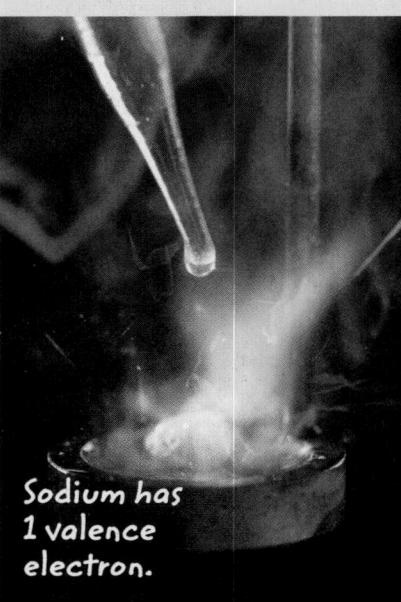

Just as this family is made up of members that have similar characteristics, families in the periodic table are made up of elements that have similar properties.

Groups of Elements Have Similar Properties

Observe the similarities of elements found in Group 1 and in Group 18.

Alkali metals, found in Group 1, share the property of reactivity with water.

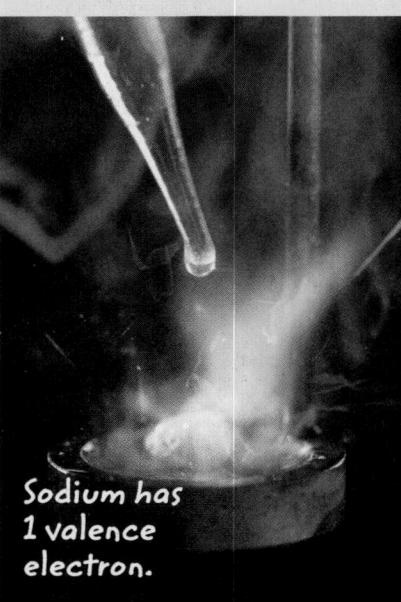

Sodium has 1 valence electron.

Potassium has 1 valence electron.

© Houghton Mifflin Harcourt Publishing Company • Image Credits: (t) ©Hill Street Studios/Getty Images; (bl) ©Charles D. Winters/Photo Researchers, Inc.; (br) ©Charles D. Winters/Photo Researchers, Inc.

Elements in Each Row Follow Periodic Trends

Each horizontal row of elements (from left to right) on the periodic table is called a **period**. The physical and chemical properties of elements change in predictable ways from one end of the period to the other. For example, within any given period on the periodic table, atomic size decreases as you move from left to right. The densities of elements also follow a pattern. Within a period, elements at the left and right sides of the table are the least dense, and the elements in the middle are the most dense. The element osmium has the highest known density, and it is located at the center of the table. Chemists cannot predict the exact size or density of an atom of elements based on that of another. However, these trends are a valuable tool in predicting the properties of different substances.

Elements Are Arranged in Order of Increasing Atomic Number

As you move from left to right within a period, the atomic number of each element increases by one. Once you've reached the end of the period, the pattern resumes on the next period. You might have noticed that two rows of elements are set apart from the rest of the periodic table. These rows, the lanthanides and actinides, are placed below the table to allow it to be narrower. These elements are also arranged in order of increasing atomic number.

Think Outside the Book Inquiry

13 **Apply** Imagine that you have just discovered a new element. Explain where this element would appear on the periodic table and why. Describe the element's properties and propose a chemical symbol and name for the element.

Noble gases, found in Group 18, glow brightly when an electric current is passed through them.

Neon has 8 valence electrons.

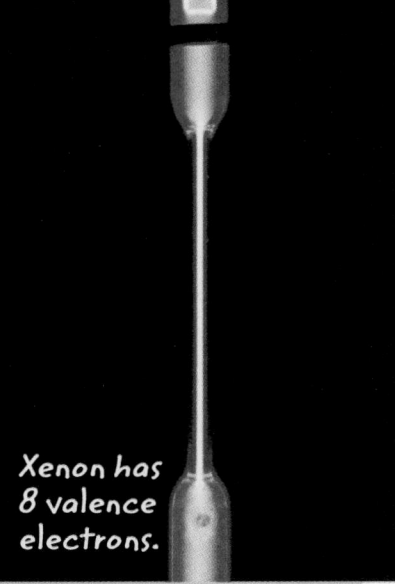

Xenon has 8 valence electrons.

14 **Analyze** List three other elements that have 1 valence electron. (Hint: Refer to the periodic table.)

_____

_____

15 **Analyze** List three other elements that have 8 valence electrons. (Hint: Refer to the periodic table.)

_____

_____

_____

Visual Summary

To complete this summary, fill in the blanks with the correct word or phrase. Then use the key below to check your answers. You can use this page to review the main concepts of the lesson.

The periodic table arranges elements in columns and rows.

16 Elements in the same _____ have similar properties.

17 Rows on the periodic table are known as _____

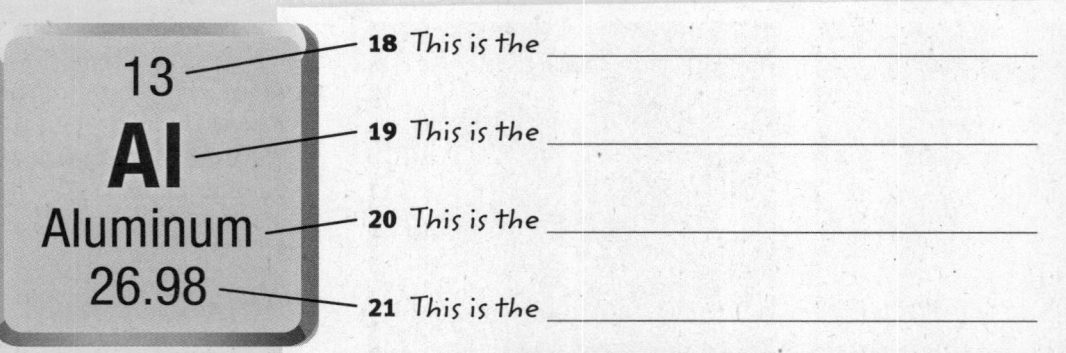

The Periodic Table

The periodic table contains information about each element.

13
Al
Aluminum
26.98

18 This is the _____

19 This is the _____

20 This is the _____

21 This is the _____

22 **Describe** Some elements are highly unstable and break apart within seconds, making them difficult to study. How can the periodic table help scientists infer the properties of these elements?

Lesson Review

Vocabulary

Draw a line to connect the following terms to their definitions.

1 metal

2 nonmetal

3 metalloid

A an element that has properties of both metals and nonmetals

B an element that is shiny and that conducts heat and electricity well

C an element that conducts heat and electricity poorly

Key Concepts

4 Identify Elements in the same _____ on the periodic table have the same number of valence electrons.

5 Identify Properties of elements within a _____ on the periodic table change in a predictable way from one side of the table to the other.

6 Identify The number of _____ in an atom determines the identity of the element.

7 Describe What is the purpose of the zigzag line on the periodic table?

_____

_____

_____

8 Apply Thorium (Th) has an average atomic mass of 232.04 u and an atomic number of 90. In the space below, draw a square from the periodic table to represent thorium.

Critical Thinking

Use this graphic to answer the following questions.

9 Infer What can you infer about copper and silver based on their position relative to each other?

_____

_____

_____

10 Apply How does the nucleus of a copper atom compare to the nucleus of a nickel atom?

_____

_____

11 Explain Explain how chemists can state with certainty that no one will discover an element that would appear on the periodic table between sulfur (S) and chlorine (Cl).

_____

_____

_____

_____

_____

_____

_____

_____

My Notes

Chemical Reactions

ESSENTIAL QUESTION

How are chemical reactions modeled?

By the end of this lesson, you should be able to use balanced chemical equations to model chemical reactions.

A chemical reaction that releases light energy occurs inside lightning bugs.

OHIO **7.PS.1** The properties of matter are determined by the arrangement of atoms.

OHIO **7.PS.2** Energy can be transformed or transferred but is never lost.

OHIO **7.SIA.3** Use appropriate mathematics, tools and techniques to gather data and information.

Engage Your Brain

1 Identify Unscramble the letters below to find two types of energy that can be released when chemical reactions occur. Write your words on the blank lines.

GLITH _____

DSNUO _____

2 Describe Write your own caption to the photo below. Describe what kind of changes have happened to the ship and anchor.

_____
_____
_____
_____

Active Reading

3 Synthesize You can often define an unknown word if you know the meaning of its word parts. Use the word parts and sentence below to make an educated guess about the meaning of the word *exothermic*.

Word part	Meaning
exo-	go out, exit
therm-	heat

Example sentence
Exothermic reactions can sometimes quickly release so much heat that they can melt iron.

exothermic:

_____
_____
_____

Vocabulary Terms

• chemical reaction
• chemical formula
• chemical equation
• reactant
• product
• law of conservation of mass
• endothermic reaction
• exothermic reaction
• law of conservation of energy

4 Identify This list contains the vocabulary terms you'll learn in this lesson. As you read, circle the definition of each term.

Change It Up!

What are the signs of a chemical reaction?

Have you seen leaves change color in the fall or smelled sour milk? The changes in leaves and milk are caused by chemical reactions. A **chemical reaction** is the process in which atoms are rearranged to produce new substances. During a chemical reaction, the bonds that hold atoms together may be formed or broken. The properties of the substances produced in a chemical reaction are different than the properties of the original substances. So, a change in properties is a sign that a chemical reaction may have happened. For example, a solid substance called a *precipitate* may form in a solution. A color change, a change in odor, precipitate formation, and the appearance of gas bubbles are all evidence of a chemical reaction.

 **Visualize It!**

5 Identify In each blank box, identify the evidence that a chemical reaction has taken place.

B
_____
_____

A black column forms when sugar reacts with sulfuric acid.

A yellow liquid and a colorless liquid react to form a red precipitate.

C
_____
_____

New substances that smell bad are produced when milk turns sour.

Gas bubbles form when baking soda and vinegar react.

A
_____
_____

D
_____
_____

© Houghton Mifflin Harcourt Publishing Company • Image Credits: (t) ©Charles D. Winters/Photo Researchers, Inc.; (c) ©Charles D. Winters/Photo Researchers, Inc.; (bl) ©HMH; (br) ©Charles D. Winters/Photo Researchers, Inc.

How are chemical reactions modeled?

You can describe the substances before and after a reaction by their properties. You can also use symbols to identify the substances. Each element has its own chemical symbol. For example, H is the symbol for hydrogen, and O is the symbol for oxygen. You can use the periodic table to find the chemical symbol for any element. A **chemical formula** uses chemical symbols and numbers to represent a given substance. The chemical symbols in a chemical formula tell you what elements make up a substance. The numbers written below and to the right of chemical symbols are called *subscripts*. Subscripts tell you how many of each type of atom are in a molecule. For example, the chemical formula for water is H_2O. The subscript 2 tells you that there are two atoms of hydrogen in each water molecule. There is no subscript on O, so each molecule of water contains only one oxygen atom.

6 Identify Circle the subscript in the chemical formula below.

H_2O

A water molecule has two hydrogen (H) atoms and one oxygen (O) atom.

With Chemical Equations

To model reactions, chemical formulas can be joined together in an equation. A **chemical equation** is an expression that uses symbols to show the relationship between the starting substances and the substances that are produced by a chemical reaction. The chemical equation below shows that carbon and oxygen react to form carbon dioxide. The chemical formulas of carbon and oxygen are written to the left of the arrow. The chemical formula of carbon dioxide is written to the right of the arrow. Plus signs separate the chemical formulas of multiple products or reactants.

👁 **Visualize It!**

Reactants are the substances that participate in a chemical reaction. Their chemical formulas are written on the left.

Products are the substances formed in a reaction. Their chemical formulas are written on the right.

$$C + O_2 \longrightarrow CO_2$$

An arrow known as a *yields sign* points from reactants to products.

7 Analyze Atoms of which elements are involved in this reaction?

8 Apply How many atoms of each element are in one molecule of the product?

A Balancing Act

How do chemical equations show the law of conservation of mass?

The **law of conservation of mass** states that matter is neither created nor destroyed in ordinary physical and chemical changes. This law means that a chemical equation must show the same numbers and kinds of atoms on both sides of the arrow. When writing a chemical equation, you must be sure that the reactants and products contain the same number of atoms of each element. This is called *balancing the equation*.

You use coefficients to balance an equation. A *coefficient* is a number that is placed in front of a chemical formula. For example, $3H_2O$ represents three water molecules. The number 3 is the coefficient. For an equation to be balanced, all atoms must be counted. So, you must multiply the subscript of each element in a formula by the formula's coefficient. There are a total of six hydrogen atoms and three oxygen atoms in $3H_2O$. Only coefficients—not subscripts—can be changed when balancing equations. Changing the subscripts in the chemical formula of a compound would change the identity of that compound. For example, H_2O_2 represents the compound hydrogen peroxide, not water.

Active Reading **9 Compare** What is the difference between a coefficient and a subscript?

_____

_____

_____

_____

_____

Do the Math — Sample Problem

Follow these steps to write a balanced chemical equation.

Identify

A Count the atoms of each element in the reactants and in the product. You can see that there are more oxygen atoms in the reactants than in the product.

$$C \quad + \quad O_2 \quad \longrightarrow \quad CO$$

$$C = 1 \qquad O = 2 \qquad\qquad C = 1 \quad O = 1$$

Solve

B To balance the number of oxygen atoms, place the coefficient 2 in front of CO. Now the number of oxygen atoms in the reactants is the same as in the product. Next, the number of carbon atoms needs to be balanced. Place the coefficient 2 in front of C. Finally, be sure to double-check your work!

$$2C \quad + \quad O_2 \quad \longrightarrow \quad 2CO$$

$$C = 2 \qquad O = 2 \qquad\qquad C = 2 \quad O = 2$$

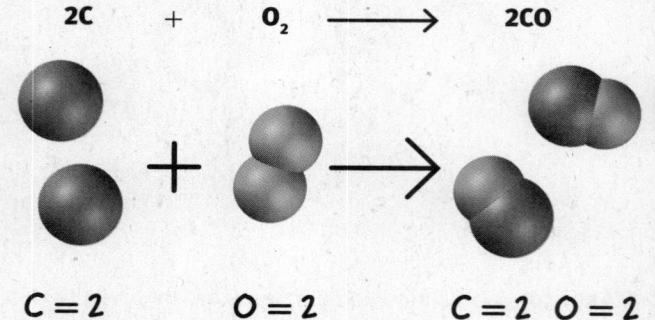

Do the Math You Try It

10 Calculate Fill in the blanks below to balance this chemical equation. Sketch the products and reactants to show that the number of each type of atom is the same.

Identify

A Count the atoms of each element in the reactants and product in the unbalanced equation.

H_2 + O_2 ⟶ H_2O

H = _____ O = _____   H = _____ O = _____

Solve

B To balance the number of each type of atom, place coefficients in front of the appropriate chemical formulas. Sketch the products and reactants, showing the correct number of molecules of each.

_____ H_2 + _____ O_2 ⟶ _____ H_2O

+   ⟶

H = _____ O = _____   H = _____ O = _____

Hydrogen and oxygen release energy when they react to form water, which forms the cloud shown. The released energy helped to propel this space shuttle.

Think Outside the Book (Inquiry)

11 Apply Research hydrogen-powered vehicles. Create a poster that describes the advantages and disadvantages of vehicles that use hydrogen as a fuel. Be sure to include a balanced chemical equation to represent the use of hydrogen fuel.

Energy, Energy

Plants absorb energy when they carry out photosynthesis.

What happens to energy during chemical reactions?

Changes in energy are a part of all chemical reactions. Chemical reactions can either release energy or absorb energy. Energy is needed to break chemical bonds in the reactants. As new bonds form in the products, the reactants release energy. Reactions are described by the overall change in energy between the products and reactants.

Energy Can Be Absorbed

A chemical reaction that requires an input of energy is called an **endothermic reaction**. The energy taken in during an endothermic reaction is absorbed from the surroundings, usually as heat. This is why endothermic reaction mixtures often feel cold.

Photosynthesis is an example of an endothermic process that absorbs light energy. In photosynthesis, plants use energy from the sun to change carbon dioxide and water to oxygen and the sugar glucose. Overall, more energy is absorbed during photosynthesis than is released to the surroundings. Some of the absorbed energy is stored in the products: oxygen and glucose.

Energy Can Be Released

A chemical reaction in which energy is released to the surroundings is called an **exothermic reaction**. Exothermic reactions can give off energy in several forms. For example, you feel warmth and see a glow when a candle burns. Burning is an exothermic reaction. The products of the reaction are lower in energy than the reactants. Some of the energy in the bonds of the reactants changes to energy as heat and light. Exothermic reaction mixtures often feel warm when heat is released to the surroundings.

12 List Name three everyday exothermic chemical reactions.

_____

_____

_____

_____

Burning a candle releases energy as heat and light.

Energy Is Always Conserved

The **law of conservation of energy** states that energy cannot be created or destroyed. However, energy can change form. The total amount of energy does not change in endothermic or exothermic reactions. For example, light energy from the sun changes into energy stored in chemical bonds during photosynthesis.

Methane (CH_4) burns when it reacts with oxygen (O_2). This reaction produces carbon dioxide (CO_2) and water (H_2O), as shown below. The reaction of methane and oxygen is exothermic. Burning methane releases energy as heat and light into the surroundings. This energy was first stored in the chemical bonds of the reactants. The energy that was stored in the bonds of the reactants is equal to the energy released plus the energy stored in the bonds of the products. The total amount of all of the types of energy is the same before and after every chemical reaction.

13 Describe What happens to the energy absorbed during an endothermic reaction?

_____

_____

_____

_____

Exothermic Reaction of Methane and Oxygen

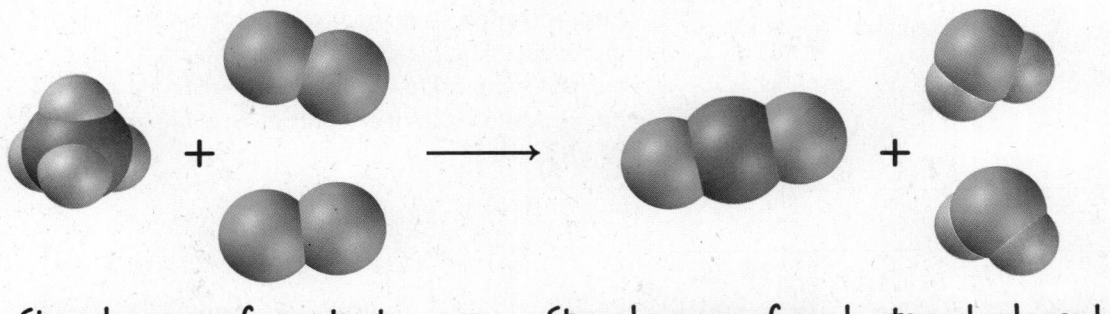

Stored energy of reactants = Stored energy of products and released energy

---

14 Compare Complete the Venn diagram to compare endothermic and exothermic reactions.

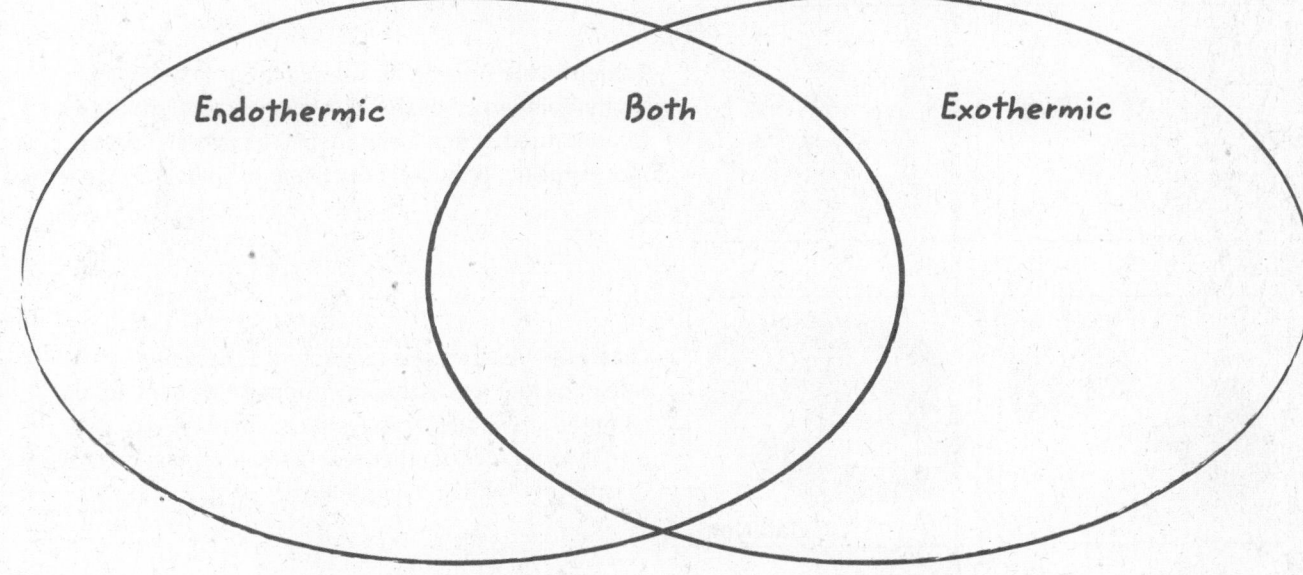

Endothermic   Both   Exothermic

The Need for Speed

What affects the rates of reactions?

Some chemical reactions occur in less than a second. Others may take days. The rate of a reaction describes how fast the reaction occurs. For a reaction to occur, particles of the reactants must collide. Reaction rates are affected by how often the particles collide. Factors that affect reaction rates include concentration, surface area, temperature, and the presence of a catalyst.

Changing the Rate of Reaction

Decreased Rate	Increased Rate	Factors That Affect Reaction Rates
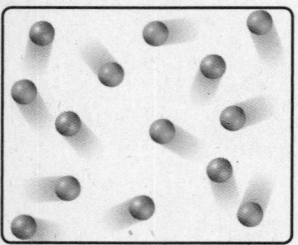	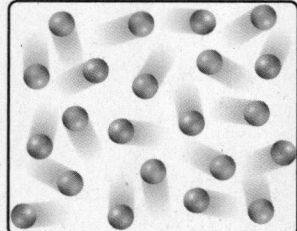	**Concentration** At higher concentrations, there are more reactants in a given volume. The reactants are more likely to collide and react. The reaction rate is higher when reactant concentration is higher.
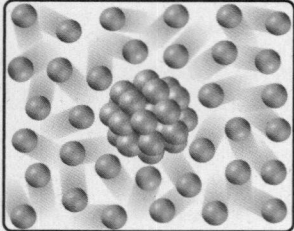	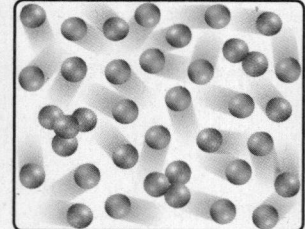	**Surface Area** The reaction rate increases when more reactant particles are exposed to one another. Crushing or grinding solids increases their surface area and the reaction rate.
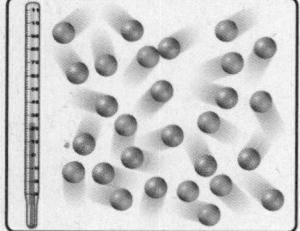	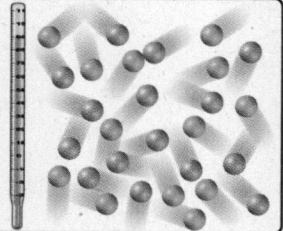	**Temperature** Reactions usually occur faster at higher temperatures. Particles move faster at higher temperatures. Because the reactant particles move more quickly, they are more likely to collide and react.
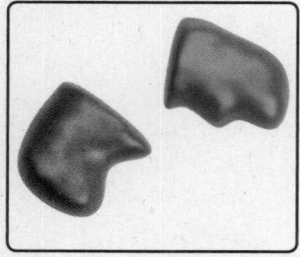	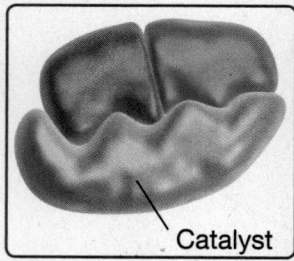 Catalyst	**Catalysts** A catalyst is a substance that changes the rate of a chemical reaction without being used up or changed very much. Catalysts can increase reaction rate by bringing together reactants. Enzymes are a type of catalyst found in living things.

Enzymes

Enzymes that increase the rates of reactions keep your body going. They help digest food so your body has the energy it needs. They also help build the molecules your body needs to grow.

Energy

All living things need energy to function. This energy is released when food molecules break down. Enzymes speed up reactions so energy is readily available.

Medical Conditions

Problems with enzymes can cause medical conditions or changes in the body. Albinism, a lack of pigment, occurs when a certain enzyme in animals does not work the way it should work.

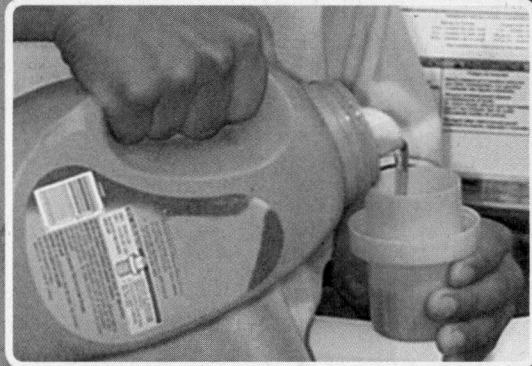

Cleaners

Enzymes are not only found in living things. They can be used outside of the body, too. The enzymes in some cleaners help break down substances such as grease.

Extend

Inquiry

16 Describe Explain how enzymes affect reactions.

17 Research Lactose intolerance is a condition that occurs when people are unable to digest milk products. Investigate the cause of lactose intolerance. Write a summary of your findings.

18 Design Create a project that explains how lactose intolerance affects people and why it occurs. Present your project as a written report, a poster, or an oral report.

Visual Summary

To complete this summary, fill in the blanks with the correct word or phrase. Then, use the key below to check your answers. You can use this page to review the main concepts of the lesson.

Bonds are broken and formed during chemical reactions to produce new substances.

19 One sign of a chemical reaction is the formation of a solid _____

A chemical equation uses symbols to show the relationship between the products and the reactants.

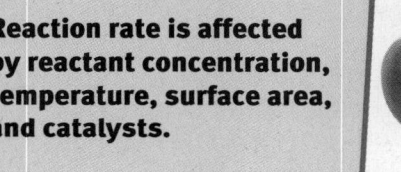

$$C + O_2 \longrightarrow CO_2$$

20 A balanced chemical equation shows that chemical reactions follow the law of conservation of _____

Chemical Reactions

Exothermic reactions release energy to the surroundings, and endothermic reactions absorb energy from the surroundings.

21 The total amount of energy before and after a chemical reaction is _____

Reaction rate is affected by reactant concentration, temperature, surface area, and catalysts.

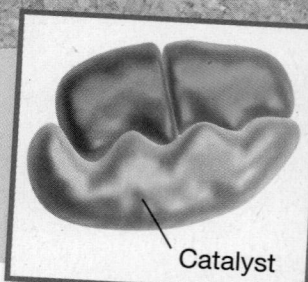

Catalyst

22 A _____ is not changed much by a chemical reaction.

23 The rate of reaction is _____ at higher temperatures because particles collide more often.

Answers: 19 precipitate; 20 mass; 21 the same; 22 catalyst; 23 faster

24 Design Write a procedure for how you would measure the effect of reactant concentration on the reaction rate.

Lesson Review

Vocabulary

Draw a line to connect the following terms to their definitions.

1 reactant

2 product

A a substance that is produced by a chemical reaction

B a substance that participates in a chemical reaction

Key Concepts

3 Describe What happens to the atoms in the reactants during a chemical reaction?

_____

_____

_____

4 Explain How does a balanced chemical equation show that mass is never lost or gained in a chemical reaction?

_____

_____

_____

_____

_____

5 Relate Describe four ways you could increase the rate of a chemical reaction.

_____

_____

_____

_____

_____

6 Compare How do exothermic and endothermic reactions differ?

_____

_____

_____

Critical Thinking

Use this diagram to answer the following questions.

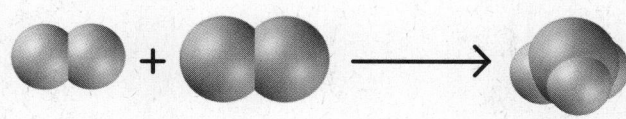

7 Model The reactants in the above reaction are hydrogen (H_2) and nitrogen (N_2). The product is ammonia (NH_3). In the space below, write a balanced chemical equation that represents the reaction.

8 Analyze This reaction releases energy as heat. Explain whether the reaction is exothermic or endothermic and whether it obeys the law of conservation of energy.

_____

_____

_____

_____

_____

9 Evaluate Two colorless solutions are mixed together. Bubbles form as the solution is stirred. Give two possible explanations for this result.

_____

_____

_____

_____

_____

10 Apply The chemical formula of glucose is $C_6H_{12}O_6$. What are the names of the elements in glucose, and how many atoms of each element are present in a glucose molecule?

_____

_____

_____

My Notes

Shirley Ann Jackson

PHYSICIST AND EDUCATOR

How can you make contributions to many areas of science all at once? One way is to promote the study of science by others. This is precisely what physicist Dr. Shirley Ann Jackson does as the president of Rensselaer Polytechnic Institute in Troy, New York.

Earlier in her career, she was a research scientist, investigating the electrical and optical properties of matter. Engineers used her research to help develop products for the telecommunications industry. She later became a professor of physics at Rutgers University in New Jersey.

In 1995, President Bill Clinton appointed Dr. Jackson to chair the U.S. Nuclear Regulatory Commission (NRC). The NRC is responsible for promoting the safe use of nuclear energy. At the NRC, Dr. Jackson used her knowledge of how the particles that make up matter interact and can generate energy. She also used her leadership skills. She helped to start the International Nuclear Regulators Association. This group made it easier for officials from many nations to discuss issues of nuclear safety.

Dr. Jackson's interest in science started when she observed bees in her backyard. She is still studying the world around her, making careful observations, and taking actions based on what she learns. These steps for learning were the foundation for all her later contributions to science. As a student, Dr. Jackson learned the same things about matter and energy that you are learning.

Nuclear power plant

Language Arts Connection

Research how nuclear energy is generated, what it can be used for, and what concerns surround it. Write a summary report to the government outlining the risks and benefits of using nuclear energy.

JOB BOARD

Chemical Technician

What You'll Do: Help chemists and chemical engineers in laboratory tests, observe solids, liquids, and gases for research or development of new products. You might handle hazardous chemicals or toxic materials.

Where You Might Work: Mostly indoors in laboratories or manufacturing plants, but may do some research outdoors.

Education: An associate's degree in applied science or science-related technology, specialized technical training, or a bachelor's degree in chemistry, biology, or forensic science is needed.

Other Job Requirements: You need to follow written steps of procedures and to accurately record measurements and observations. You need to understand the proper handling of hazardous materials.

Chef

What You'll Do: Prepare, season, and cook food, keep a clean kitchen, supervise kitchen staff, and buy supplies and equipment.

Where You Might Work: Restaurants, hotels, the military, schools, and in your own kitchen as a private caterer.

Education: Many chefs gain on-the-job training without formal culinary school training. However, you can also learn cooking skills at culinary institutes and earn a two-year or four-year degree.

Other Job Requirements: Your job will require you to be on your feet for many hours and lift heavy equipment and boxes of food.

PEOPLE IN SCIENCE NEWS

Andy Goldsworthy

Changing Matter Is Art

Andy Goldsworthy is interested in how matter changes over time. He is inspired by the changes that occur in nature. As a sculptor, he uses materials found in nature, like snow, ice, twigs, and leaves. Many of his sculptures do not last for very long, but these materials show the changing state of matter. For example, for one of his art projects, he made 13 large snowballs in the winter and placed them in cold storage. In the middle of summer, he placed the snowballs around London. It took five days for the snowballs to melt. During that time they were reminders of a wider world of nature. Movement, change, light, growth, and decay are factors that affect his pieces. Because his work is constantly changing, Goldsworthy takes photographs of his sculptures.

Solutions

ESSENTIAL QUESTION

What is a solution?

By the end of this lesson, you should be able to summarize the characteristics of a solution.

Glass forms when sand, soda ash, and limestone are heated to become liquids and are mixed to form a solution. The solution is cooled to form solid glass. The resulting glass is an example of a solid solution.

OHIO **7.PS.1** The properties of matter are determined by the arrangement of atoms.

OHIO **7.SIA.3** Use appropriate mathematics, tools and techniques to gather data and information.

Lesson Labs

Quick Labs
- Investigate Solutions
- Solution Concentration

Exploration Lab
- Investigate Solubility

Engage Your Brain

1 Explain What happens when you combine a powdered drink mix with water?

_____

_____

_____

_____

_____

_____

_____

_____

2 Describe Write a caption describing the mixture being made in the jar.

_____

_____

_____

_____

Active Reading

3 Apply Many scientific words, such as *solution*, also have everyday meanings. Use context clues to write your own definition for each meaning of solution.

Example sentence
Emily worked hard on the <u>solution</u> to a math problem.

solution:

_____

_____

Example sentence
Connor made a <u>solution</u> by mixing salt and water.

solution:

_____

_____

Vocabulary Terms

- mixture
- solution
- solute
- solvent
- concentration
- solubility

4 Apply As you learn the definition of each vocabulary term in this lesson, create your own definition or sketch to help you remember the meaning of the term.

Mix It Up

The bronze statue is an example of a solid solution. The air that surrounds it is a gas solution, and salt water in the ocean it overlooks is a liquid solution.

What is a Mixture?

Active Reading

5 Identify As you read, underline characteristics that would help you identify different types of mixtures.

A **mixture** is a combination of two or more substances that are not chemically combined. The substances in a mixture retain their separate atomic compositions and can be separated from each other based on their properties. There are several types of mixtures. A **solution** is a mixture in which two or more substances are so completely blended that it looks like it is made of only one substance. A solution is a *homogeneous* mixture. Light passes through gas and liquid solutions, so you can see through them. Particles in a solution are so small that they cannot be separated by a filter.

A *colloid* is another type of mixture. It contains medium-sized particles mixed into a gas, liquid, or solid. The particles are large enough to scatter light passing through the mixture but small enough not to settle or be separated by a filter. In a *suspension*, large particles are mixed into a gas or liquid. The particles block light and the mixture appears cloudy. Particles eventually settle out of a suspension, or they can be separated out by a filter.

Visualize It!

6 Compare On the note cards below, write down three characteristics of each example of a mixture.

Lemonade

Heavy cream

Flour and water

Solution

_____
_____
_____

Colloid

_____
_____
_____

Suspension

_____
_____
_____

What are the two parts of a solution?

Solutions have two parts: the solute and the solvent. As a solution forms, solute particles become evenly distributed in the solvent. A homogeneous mixture is formed. After a solution forms, it is not possible to visibly distinguish between the solute and the solvent.

Solute

A solute can be a liquid, gas, or solid. The **solute** is the substance that is being dissolved in a solution. Vinegar is a solution of a liquid solute, acetic acid, dissolved in liquid water. Carbonated soda water is a solution of a gas solute, carbon dioxide, dissolved in liquid water. Salt water is a solution of a solid solute, sodium chloride, dissolved in liquid water.

Solvent

A solvent can also be a liquid, gas, or solid. The **solvent** is the substance in the solution that does the dissolving. Water is the most common liquid solvent, but there are many others. Air is a solution in which a gas solvent, nitrogen, dissolves gaseous solutes such as oxygen and carbon dioxide. Solid solvents, such as copper, can be melted in order to dissolve a melted metal solute, such as tin. When the solution cools back to a solid, the result is a solid metal solution called bronze.

Solid tin

Solid copper

Solid bronze is a solution of tin dissolved in copper.

7 Categorize Fill in spaces A, B, C, and D in the table with the appropriate state—*solid*, *liquid*, or *gas*.

Solution	Solute	State of solute	Solvent	State of solvent
air	oxygen	**A**	nitrogen	gas
carbonated water	carbon dioxide	gas	water	**B**
salt water	salt	**C**	water	liquid
bronze	tin	**D**	copper	solid

Concentrate!

How can the concentration of a solution vary?

As a solute dissolves, its small particles are distributed evenly between particles of the solvent. The measure of the amount of solute dissolved in a solvent is called **concentration**. One way the concentration of a solution can be calculated is with the equation:

$$\text{Concentration} = \frac{\text{mass of solute}}{\text{volume of solvent}}$$

When using this equation, the units of concentration are often expressed as grams per milliliter (g/ml).

A Solution Can Be Dilute

A dilute solution contains a small amount of solute in a given volume of solvent. For example, compare ocean water to water from a well. Ocean water tastes salty, but well water does not. The well water also contains salt, but in such a small amount that you cannot taste it. A dilute solution, like well water, has a low concentration of the solute salt.

A Solution Can Be Concentrated

A concentrated solution contains a large amount of solute in a given volume of solvent. If you make a glass of lemonade by adding three scoops of drink mix to one glass of water, the lemonade will have a very strong flavor. You have added a lot of solute, the powdered drink mix, to a solvent, water. The lemonade is a concentrated solution. It has a high concentration of solute.

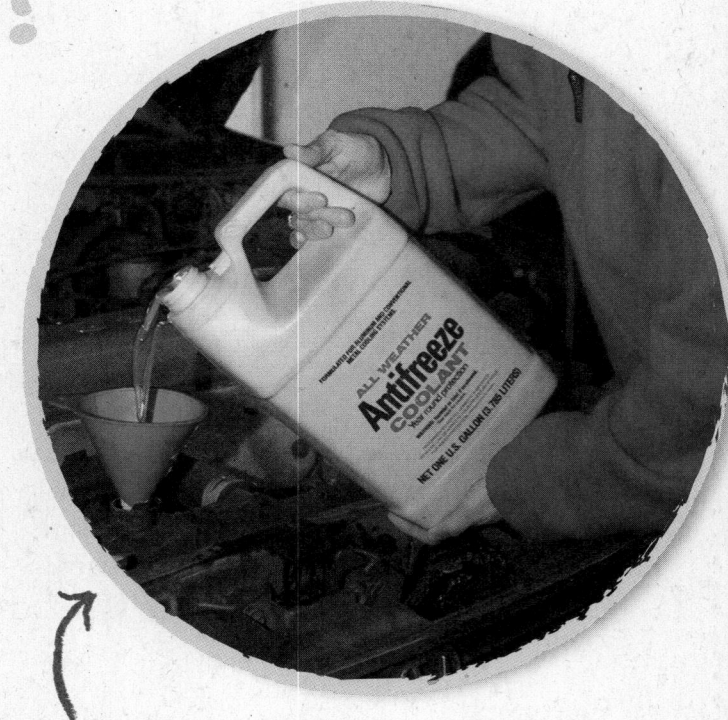

Adding just the right concentration of antifreeze to the water in a car radiator is important for keeping the engine from freezing in the winter and overheating in the summer.

8 Compare What is the difference between a dilute solution and a concentrated solution?

_____

_____

_____

_____

_____

_____

Think Outside the Book Inquiry

9 Research Identify some common household items that are solutions. Try to categorize each as a dilute or concentrated solution. Create a poster illustrating the items you find.

A Solution Can Be Saturated

A saturated solution contains the most solute that can be completely dissolved in a given amount of a solvent at a given temperature and pressure. If more solute is added to a container of a saturated solution, it will settle to the bottom without dissolving. Have you ever wondered how much sugar you can add to a glass of tea at room temperature? When you first add spoonfuls of sugar, they will dissolve in the tea. However, as you keep adding sugar, eventually the sugar does not dissolve. Instead, solid sugar falls to the bottom of the glass. The tea contains as much sugar as it can hold at room temperature. You have made a saturated sugar solution. Adding more sugar to the tea will not increase the concentration of sugar in the solution.

A Solution Can Be Supersaturated

Sometimes a solution contains more solute than is normally possible. This type of solution is said to be supersaturated. Raising the temperature of a saturated solution often allows more solute to dissolve. If the solution is cooled very slowly, the extra solute might stay dissolved. This supersaturated solution is very unstable. If even a single crystal of solute is added, all the extra solute will quickly solidify, so that it is no longer dissolved in the solution. The result is often the formation of beautiful crystals of the solute.

Sodium acetate crystals form as a supersaturated solution of sodium acetate and water is cooled.

Visualize It!

Dilute solution

More concentrated solution

Even more concentrated solution

10 Predict Draw a picture to illustrate what might happen when more solute is added to a saturated solution.

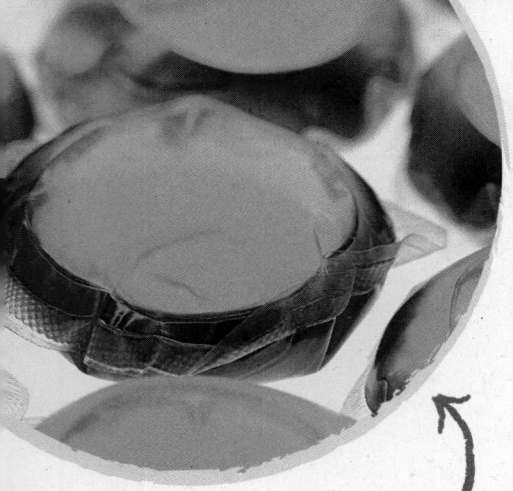

Both the liquid laundry detergent and the gel capsule it is packaged in are soluble in water.

What factors affect solubility?

The amount of solute needed to make a saturated solution depends on the solubility of a solute in a particular solvent. The **solubility** of a solute is its ability to dissolve in a given amount of solvent at a certain temperature and pressure. For example, a large amount of ammonia gas can dissolve in liquid water. Ammonia has a high solubility in water. In comparison, only a small amount of carbon dioxide gas can dissolve in liquid water. Carbon dioxide has a low solubility in water. Some substances, such as oil, hardly dissolve in water at all, and are considered to be insoluble in water.

Temperature

An increase in temperature has two effects on most solid solutes—they dissolve more quickly, and a greater amount can be dissolved in a given amount of liquid solvent. Sugar dissolves faster in water that is hot than in water that is cold. The opposite is true for gases—an increase in temperature makes a gas less soluble in water. Soda water loses its fizz faster as it warms up. The carbon dioxide gas cannot stay dissolved in water as the temperature increases. So the gas escapes, and the drink becomes "flat."

Pressure

Pressure changes do not usually change the solubility of solids or liquids. But the solubility of a gas increases at higher pressures and decreases at lower pressures. Carbon dioxide is added to cans and bottles of soda water under high pressure. The pressure decreases when you open the bottle, letting carbon dioxide bubbles escape.

Do the Math   You Try It!

11 Graph Plot a line graph using the data at the right to show the relationship between the solubility of O_2 in water and pressure at 10°C.

12 Describe Explain the relationship between pressure and solubility.

_____

_____

_____

_____

_____

_____

_____

Solubility of Oxygen in 100 g of Water (H_2O)	
Amount of O_2 dissolved (mg)	Pressure (kPa)
10.0	100
16.0	200
22.0	300
30.0	400
35.0	500

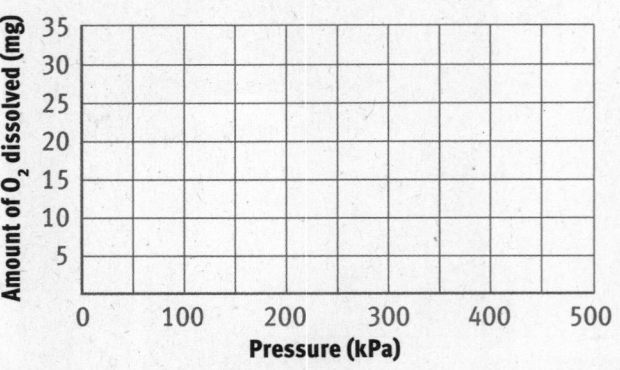

© Houghton Mifflin Harcourt Publishing Company • Image Credits: ©Ocean/Corbis

What helps solids dissolve faster in liquids?

13 Identify As you read, underline factors that affect how fast a solid solute dissolves in a liquid solvent.

When a solid dissolves in a liquid, the particles of the solid separate and spread out among the particles of the liquid until the solid is evenly distributed throughout the liquid. You cannot see any solid particles in the final solution.

Several things can help a solid dissolve more quickly in a liquid. An increase in temperature, an increase in surface area, and an increase in motion can all help a dissolving solid to dissolve more quickly. Each method helps the solid particles separate and spread out among the liquid particles. Dissolving sugar in hot water before adding it to a pitcher of lemonade and ice lets you enjoy your drink sooner. Heating a mixture can help a solid dissolve very quickly in a liquid. If only large sugar cubes are available, they can be crushed into smaller pieces before they are added to lemonade. Crushing increases the surface area of solute that is exposed to the liquid solvent. Crushing helps solids dissolve faster. Solids also dissolve faster when you stir or shake a mixture. Stirring or shaking lemonade after you add sugar will help the sugar dissolve faster.

Visualize It!

14 Describe Write a caption to describe each method of dissolving sugar in water.

A

_____

_____

_____

_____

B

_____

_____

_____

_____

Crushing the sugar cubes increases their surface area, and helps the sugar to dissolve more quickly in water.

Visual Summary

To complete this summary, fill in the blanks with the correct word or phrase. Then, use the key below to check your answers. You can use this page to review the main concepts of the lesson.

Solutions

A solution is a homogeneous mixture of two or more substances.

15 A solute dissolves in a(n) _____

Concentration is a measure of the amount of solute dissolved in a solvent.

16 A solution in which no more solute can dissolve is _____

Temperature and pressure affect solubility.

17 At higher temperatures, the solubility of a solid _____

---

18 Synthesize Suppose you want to serve fruit juice mixed with carbonated water at a picnic. Describe what you could do to be sure the drinks keep their fizz for as long as possible. Explain why your method would work.

Lesson Review

Lesson **5**

Vocabulary

Draw a line to connect the word to its definition.

1 mixture

2 solvent

3 solute

4 concentration

5 solubility

A a substance that can be dissolved in another substance

B the ability of a substance to dissolve in another at a given temperature and pressure

C the substance in a solution that dissolves the solute

D a combination of two or more substances that are not chemically combined

E a measure of the amount of a substance dissolved in another substance

Key Concepts

6 Identify In a solution of water and salt, which substance is the solute?

7 Describe How does pressure affect the solubility of gases?

8 Explain How could you dissolve more solid solute in a saturated solution in a liquid solvent? Explain.

Critical Thinking

9 Predict Which would dissolve sugar faster: hot tea or iced tea? Explain your answer.

Use this table to answer the following questions.

Solid solute	Solubility in 100 g H_2O at 25 °C (g)	Solubility in 100 g H_2O at 100 °C (g)
Sodium chloride	36	40
Potassium nitrate	39	246
Cerium sulfate	20	0

10 Analyze How does an increase in temperature affect the solubility of each compound in 100 g H_2O?

11 Infer How can you influence the rate at which the solutes dissolve in 100 g H_2O at either temperature?

12 Predict Suppose the temperature was lowered to 18 °C. How do you think this would affect the solubility of each solute?

© Houghton Mifflin Harcourt Publishing Company

Lesson 5 Solutions **497**

My Notes

Acids, Bases, and Salts

ESSENTIAL QUESTION

What are the properties of acids, bases, and salts?

By the end of this lesson, you should have an understanding of the physical and chemical properties of acids, bases, and salts and how these chemicals are commonly used.

Lemons, oranges, limes, and grapefruits contain citric acid, which explains their "pucker power." A sour taste is a characteristic of an acid.

OHIO 7.PS.1 The properties of matter are determined by the arrangement of atoms.

OHIO 7.SIA.5 Develop descriptions, models, explanations and predictions.

✋ Lesson Labs

Quick Labs
- Household Acids and Bases
- Making Salt

Exploration Lab
- Acids, Bases, and Fruit Oxidation

🧠 Engage Your Brain

1 Identify Unscramble the letters below to find five common items containing acids, bases, or salts. Write your words on the blank lines.

GIRNEAV _____

NLOME _____

APOS _____

ANAMOIM _____

KAHCL _____

2 Describe Describe the taste of vinegar. Do you think vinegar is acidic or a basic?

_____

_____

_____

_____

_____

_____

✏️ Active Reading

3 Apply Many scientific words, such as *neutral*, also have everyday meanings. Use context clues to write your own definition for each meaning of the word *neutral*.

Example sentence
Scott was <u>neutral</u> on the subject of which class play to produce.

neutral:

_____

_____

Example sentence
The solution formed when table salt is dissolved in water is <u>neutral</u>.

neutral:

_____

_____

Vocabulary Terms
- acid
- base
- neutralization reaction
- salt

4 Identify As you read, place a question mark next to any words that you don't understand. When you finish reading the lesson, go back and review the text that you marked. If the information is still confusing, consult a classmate or your teacher.

Donations ACCEPTED

What are acids and bases?

Though you may not realize it, you are probably familiar with many common acids and bases already. Lemon juice and vinegar both contain acid. Shampoo and window cleaner both contain bases. Acids and bases are chemicals that increase the number of ions present when they dissolve in water.

Active Reading **5 Identify** What are two common substances that contain an acid?

How do acids and bases interact with water?

Water is made up of molecules of H_2O. In any given sample of water, a small number of these molecules break apart and recombine to form hydronium ions, H_3O^+, and hydroxide ions, OH^-. An **acid** increases the number of positively charged H_3O^+ ions when it dissolves in water. A **base** increases the number of negatively charged OH^- ions when it dissolves in water.

Soap bubbles form when a thin skin of soap molecules surrounds a bit of air. Soap is an example of a base.

Acids Increase Hydronium Ions Present in Water

Recall that a water sample contains mostly whole H_2O molecules. There are only a few H_3O^+ ions and OH^- ions, as shown in the first beaker at the right. Many acids contain at least one atom of hydrogen that can be pulled off by a water molecule to form H_3O^+ ions. For example, when an acid such as hydrochloric acid, or HCl, is added to water, the water molecules pull apart the HCl molecules and recombine to form H_3O^+ ions and Cl^- ions. The result is an acidic solution that contains positively charged hydronium ions and negatively charged chloride ions.

Adding an acid to water increases the number of hydronium ions in the solution.

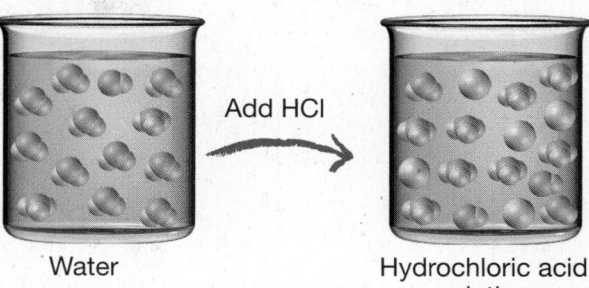

Water → Add HCl → Hydrochloric acid solution

Cl^-	
OH^-	
H_2O	
H_3O^+	

Visualize It!

6 Identify What ions form when HCl dissolves in water?

_____

_____

Bases Increase Hydroxide Ions Present in Water

The particles of many bases contain at least one hydroxide group. When these bases dissolve in water, they break apart to release OH^- ions. Other bases such as ammonia, which is found in many household cleaners, do not contain hydroxide groups. But when these bases dissolve in water, they can remove hydrogen atoms from water molecules to form OH^- ions.

Look at the beakers to the right. Compare the solution containing the base sodium hydroxide, NaOH, with the sample of pure water. You will notice that the sodium hydroxide solution contains many more hydroxide ions than pure water does.

Adding a base to water increases the number of hydroxide ions in the solution.

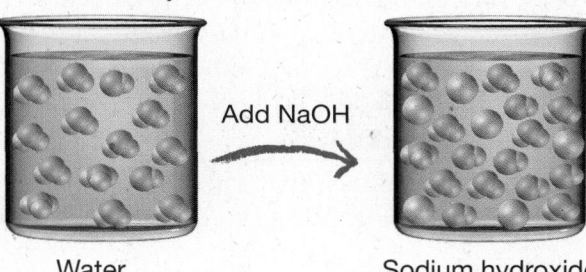

Water → Add NaOH → Sodium hydroxide solution

Na^+	
OH^-	
H_2O	
H_3O^+	

Visualize It!

7 Identify What ions form when sodium hydroxide dissolves in water?

_____

_____

8 Label On each of the labeled cards, write the chemical formula of each ion.

Hydronium ion

Hydroxide ion

What is the difference between strong and weak acids and bases?

Active Reading

9 Classify As you read, underline the factor that determines the strength of an acid or base.

Some acids and bases are dangerous and can burn your skin or eyes, but others are found in many of the foods you eat and cleansers you use. What makes some acids and bases more dangerous than others?

The strength of an acid or base depends on the percentage of its particles that break apart to form ions in a solution. The strength of an acid or base is not the same as its concentration. Diluted hydrochloric acid is still strong and can damage your skin, but concentrated citric acid does not harm your skin.

Strong Acids and Bases Break Apart Completely

In water, all of the particles of a strong acid break apart, forming many H_3O^+ ions. All of the particles of a strong base also break apart in water to form OH^- ions. The diagrams below of HCl and NaOH show how strong acids and bases behave in water. Notice that all of the particles have broken apart to form ions in water.

Weak Acids and Bases Remain Mostly Intact

In weak acids and bases, only some of the particles break apart to form ions in water. Therefore, few hydronium ions or hydroxide ions are produced. The diagrams of acetic acid (vinegar) and ammonia show how weak acids and bases behave in water. Notice that there are still whole molecules in each beaker.

Visualize It!

All of the particles of strong acids and bases break apart in water. Only some of the particles of weak acids and bases break apart in water.

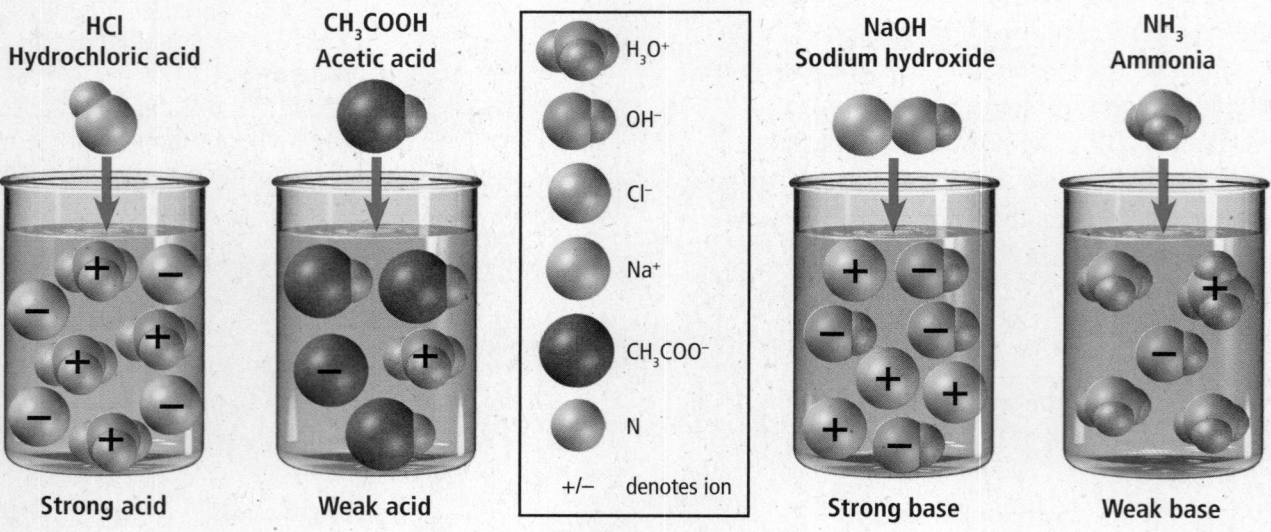

10 Explain Describe what happens when a weak acid dissolves in water.

_____

11 Contrast How does a strong base behave differently from a weak base?

_____

No-Nonsense Self Defense

Many insects and sea animals use acids or bases to protect themselves from predators. Some animals spray the acids or bases at their enemies. Other animals have acids in their skin. One small taste, and a predator looks for a different meal!

Fire Ants

When fire ants sting, it hurts! Fire ants use a structure on their abdomen to inject a toxic base into their victim. They hold on to its skin with their pincers and sting again and again.

Whip Scorpions

To protect themselves, these scorpions spray acetic acid at small predators that want to eat them.

Nudibranchs

Nudibranchs, or shell-less sea slugs, recycle toxic substances from species they eat as a form of protection. They can also secrete acid from their skin in self defense.

Extend

Inquiry

12 Infer Do you think the acid secreted from the nudibranch is as strong a protection as the hard outer shell that some other slugs have? Explain.

13 Research Investigate another animal that produces acid to protect itself.

14 Compose Choose one of the species shown on this page. Write a short description of a possible encounter with a predator. Explain how this creature uses acids or bases to defend itself.

What are the physical properties of acids?

Like all substances, acids have certain properties that help identify them. Physical properties can help us to identify chemicals as acids.

Acids Taste Sour

Vinegar, lemon juice, and tomatoes all have a sour taste. They taste sour because they are acidic. The term *acid* comes from the Latin word for sour. However, you should NEVER use taste, touch, or smell to identify an unknown chemical. Some acids can damage body tissue. Most strong acids are poisonous.

Acids Conduct an Electric Current

When a strong acid is dissolved in water, it breaks apart and forms ions in solution. The ions make it possible for the solution to conduct an electric current. A car battery is one example of how an acid can be used to produce an electric current. The sulfuric acid in the battery conducts an electric current to help start the car's engine and run all the electrical systems in the car.

What are some chemical properties of acids?

Acids are *corrosive*, which means that they can react with and destroy body tissue, clothing, and other things. They react violently with many metals. Hydrogen gas bubbles are released as the metal is "eaten away" by the acid.

Acids react with certain compounds called acid-base indicators. They cause the indicators to change color. Using an indicator is a good way to determine whether a solution is acidic. For example, litmus paper is a type of indicator. Blue litmus paper turns red in the presence of an acid.

Visualize It!

15 Classify Label each image as either a physical property or a chemical property of an acid.

A

When a metal such as zinc is added to a strong acid such as HCl, a violent reaction occurs. As the metal corrodes, hydrogen gas bubbles are released.

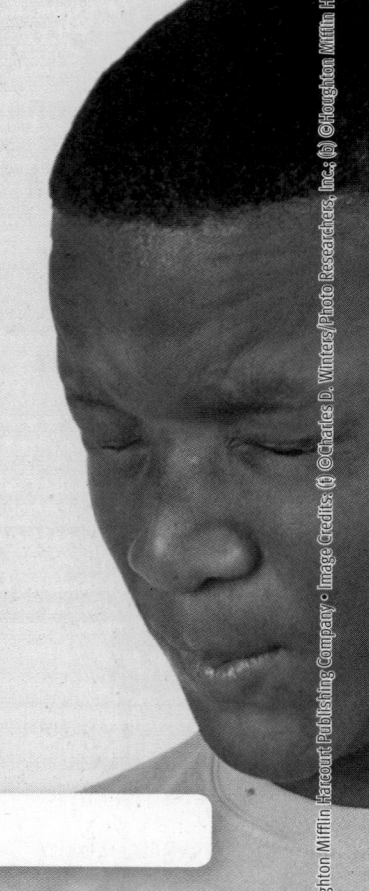

Lemons contain citric acid. Sour taste is a property of acids.

B

What are the physical properties of bases?

Bases also have certain identifiable properties. It is these physical properties that help us determine if a chemical is a base.

Bases Taste Bitter

Have you ever accidentally tasted soap? The bitter taste left in your mouth is a property of a base. NEVER use taste, touch, or smell to identify a base because many bases are caustic and cause burns.

Bases Feel Slippery

When you wash your hands with soap, they feel slippery. This characteristic is another physical property of a base. If your hands feel slippery while working with a base during a lab activity, immediately rinse your hands with water and tell an adult.

Bases Conduct an Electric Current

Like acids, solutions of bases conduct an electric current. A solution must contain ions for it to conduct a current. Remember that strong bases completely break up into ions in water. Alkaline batteries contain solutions of bases.

17 Identify List the physical and chemical properties of acids and bases on the index cards below.

Acids

_____
_____
_____
_____
_____
_____

What are some chemical properties of bases?

Bases are *caustic*. This property means that they can burn or corrode other substances. Bases also change the color of acid-base indicators. Most indicators turn a different color in the presence of a base than they do in the presence of an acid. For example, a base causes red litmus paper to turn blue.

Active Reading **16 Explain** What type of indicators can you use to determine the presence of an acid or base in solution?

_____
_____
_____

Soap is a base. Bases are slippery, making it easy for this dog to plan an escape!

Bases

_____
_____
_____
_____
_____
_____

What is a neutralization reaction?

Once in a while, your stomach may produce too much acid, which causes discomfort. An antacid can help you feel better. When the weak base in the antacid solution meets the excess acid in your stomach, the acid is neutralized. A **neutralization reaction** is the reaction between an acid and a base in a water solution.

A Reaction Between an Acid and a Base

Active Reading **18 Identify** As you read, underline the products that form in a neutralization reaction.

Two products of a neutralization reaction are water and a salt. Water molecules form when the hydrogen ions from the acid combine with the hydroxide ions from the base to make H_2O.

What happens to the remaining ions from the acid and base? They combine to form a salt. A **salt** is an ionic compound that forms from the negative ion of the acid and the positive ion of the base.

Neutralization reaction between an antacid and stomach acid, HCl:

$$NaHCO_3 + HCl \rightarrow NaCl + CO_2 + H_2O$$

| weak base | strong acid | salt | carbon dioxide | water |

Some antacid tablets must be dissolved in water to act as a base. The dissolved base reacts with HCl in the stomach.

 Visualize It!

19 Describe The photo at the right shows an antacid tablet dissolving in water. Describe what is taking place. What ions do you think are forming?

_____

_____

_____

_____

What are some examples of salts?

Thousands of salts are formed in chemistry. The salt you sprinkle on your food, sodium chloride, is only one kind of salt. The identity of the salt that forms in a neutralization reaction depends on the identities of the acid and base. For example, sodium chloride forms from the neutralization of HCl and NaOH, while calcium chloride forms from the neutralization of HCl with calcium hydroxide, $Ca(OH)_2$. Salts have many uses in industry and in homes. Sodium chloride is used to make baking soda as well as to season your food. Sodium nitrate is a salt that preserves food. Calcium sulfate is used to make plasterboard, which is an important component in the construction of homes and buildings. Calcium chloride is used to help keep ice from forming on roads and sidewalks in winter. And the chalk used to decorate the sidewalk in the photo below is calcium sulfate.

Think Outside the Book

21 **Research** Natural chalk is no longer used to make blackboard and sidewalk chalk. Find out what natural chalk is, where it is found, and how it forms. Explain why natural chalk is no longer used for drawing on sidewalks.

Active Reading 20 **Explain** What determines the identity of the salt that forms in a neutralization reaction?

_____

_____

_____

The artist creates a colorful portrait with sidewalk chalk. The chalk she is using is made by compressing the salt calcium sulfate into colored sticks.

Visualize It!

Common Acids, Bases, and Salts

22 Classify On these two pages, you can read about some common acids, bases, and salts and their uses. Identify each as an acid, a base, or a salt.

A

Spoiled milk has a sour taste.

Many fruits and vegetables such as these tomatoes contain chemicals that contribute to their sour taste.

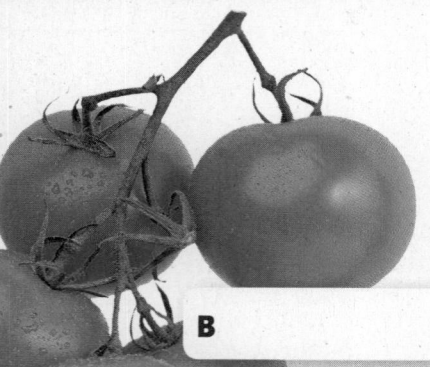

B

Laundry detergent is a type of soap. It feels slippery on your hands.

C

UNSCENTED

LAUNDRY DETERGENT

One Gallon

23 Infer Hydrochloric acid is found in swimming pools and in your stomach. How does it function in each situation?

_____

_____

_____

D

HCl is added to swimming pools to keep the water clean and clear.

Farmers use liquid ammonia to fertilize their crops.

E

F

The potassium hydroxide, KOH, in this battery conducts an electric current.

24 Identify What properties of a substance can you examine to determine whether it is an acid or a base?

_____

_____

_____

G

Calcium chloride is used to help keep ice from forming on roads and sidewalks.

Inquiry

25 Predict What do you think would happen if you spread regular table salt (sodium chloride) on an icy sidewalk?

_____

_____

_____

Sodium chloride is used to flavor food.

H

Visual Summary

To complete this summary, fill in the blank with the correct word or phrase. Then use the key below to check your answers. You can use this page to review the main concepts of the lesson.

Acids, Bases, and Salts

In strong acids and bases, all particles break apart to form ions in water. In weak acids and bases, only some particles break apart to form ions in water.

26 When an acid breaks apart in water, a(n) _____ ion is formed.

27 Bases form _____ ions in water.

Acids and bases have unique chemical properties.

29 Acids turn blue litmus paper _____

30 In a neutralization reaction, _____ and a salt are formed.

Acidic solutions have a sour taste. Basic solutions have a bitter taste and feel slippery.

28 Strong acids and bases conduct an electric current because _____

_____

Many foods and other everyday items contain acids, bases, or salts.

31 _____ is used to prevent ice from forming on roads.

32 **Evaluate** Explain the following statement: A concentrated acid is not necessarily a strong acid.

Lesson Review

Vocabulary

Draw a line to connect the following terms to their definitions.

1 acid

2 base

3 salt

4 neutralization reaction

A formed from joining positive and negative ions

B increases OH⁻ ions

C forms a salt and water

D increases H₃O⁺ ions

Key Concepts

5 Identify Which of the following is a chemical property of a base?

A slippery feel

B conducts an electric current

C turns red litmus paper blue

D forms hydronium ions in water

6 Identify What particle increases in number when a base is dissolved in water?

A OH⁻

B H₃O⁺

C H₂O

D H⁺

7 Classify Which of the following is classified as a salt: ammonia or sodium chloride?

_____

8 Classify Are many common foods we eat more likely to be acidic or basic?

_____

9 Contrast Describe the difference between a strong acid and a weak acid.

_____

_____

_____

Critical Thinking

10 Analyze A salt is formed when nitric acid (HNO_3) combines with sodium hydroxide (NaOH). What ions are present in the salt that forms?

_____

_____

_____

Use this photo to answer the following questions.

11 Infer Pickles are preserved by soaking cucumbers in a vinegar solution. What are some properties of these pickles?

_____

_____

_____

12 Infer How might the vinegar solution help keep pickles fresh for a long period of time?

_____

_____

_____

_____

_____

_____

_____

My Notes

Measuring pH

ESSENTIAL QUESTION

What is pH a measure of?

By the end of this lesson, you should be able to describe the pH scale and how it is used to classify a solution as either acidic, basic, or neutral.

River otters survive on fish from rivers. Changes in the pH of river water might kill fish that live there. Without enough fish in the river, otters will struggle to find food.

OHIO **7.PS.1** The properties of matter are determined by the arrangement of atoms.

OHIO **7.SIA.3** Use appropriate mathematics, tools and techniques to gather data and information.

OHIO **7.SIA.4** Analyze and interpret data.

Lesson Labs

Quick Labs
- Determining pH Levels
- Investigating Respiration with Chemical Indicators
- Investigating the Effects of Acid Precipitation

Engage Your Brain

1 Identify Unscramble the letters below to find household substances that are acidic. Write your words on the blank lines.

GRAVEIN _____

NOMEDEAL _____

TUPCHEK _____

OLAC _____

2 Describe Explain why you think a scientist might test the water quality in a river or stream.

_____
_____
_____
_____
_____

Active Reading

3 Apply Use context clues to write your own definition for the words *precise* and *estimate*.

Example sentence
Chan measured the length of the leaf carefully because he wanted a <u>precise</u> measurement.

precise:

_____
_____

Example sentence
Jarred did not need an exact answer, so he made an <u>estimate</u> of the height of the tree.

estimate:

_____
_____

Vocabulary Term

- pH

4 Apply As you learn the definition of the vocabulary term in this lesson, create your own definition or sketch to help you remember the meaning of the term.

What's Your Number?

What is the pH scale?

5 Identify As you read, underline the pH values that indicate an acidic solution, a neutral solution, and a basic solution.

To properly take care of fish in a fish tank, you need to provide food, air, and clean water. But clean water is not enough—the water must also have the correct pH. The **pH** of a solution is a measure of how acidic or basic a solution is. The numbers on the pH scale relate to the concentration of hydronium, H_3O^+, ions present in a solution.

The pH scale has values ranging from 0 to 14. A solution that has a pH value of exactly 7 is neutral—neither acidic nor basic. A solution with a pH value of less than 7 is acidic. An acidic solution has more H_3O^+ ions than OH^- ions in the solution. The lower the pH value, the more H_3O^+ ions are present, and the more acidic the solution. A solution with a pH value greater than 7 is basic. There are more OH^- ions than H_3O^+ ions in the solution. The higher the pH value, the more OH^- ions are present, and the more basic the solution.

A change of one number on the pH scale represents a tenfold change in H_3O^+ concentration. For example, a solution with a pH of 3 has ten times more H_3O^+ ions than a solution with a pH of 4. So a change of one number on the pH scale is significant.

Do the Math

For each decrease of one pH unit, the H_3O^+ concentration increases ten times.

Sample Problem

What is the change in H_3O^+ concentration from pH 7 to pH 5?

A. What do you know?
The pH is decreasing by 2 units.

B. What do you want to find out?
The change in H_3O^+ concentration.

C. Calculate: The H_3O^+ concentration would increase by a factor of 10 for each decrease in pH unit.
$10 \times 10 = 100$

D. Solve: The concentration of H_3O^+ is 100 times greater at pH 5 than at pH 7.

You Try It

6 Calculate If the pH of a solution changes from pH 8 to pH 3, what is the change in H_3O^+ concentration?

A. What do you know?

B. What do you want to find out?

C. Calculate

D. Solve

What is the pH of some common solutions?

Every water-based solution has a pH. Lemon juice is a common acidic solution. It has a pH of about 2. It is slightly more acidic than another common food item, vinegar. Milk is also acidic. It has a pH of about 6.5. But milk that has gone sour has a pH of about 4. Pure water is neither acidic nor basic; it is neutral. It has a pH of 7. Ammonia, a household cleaning solution, is an example of a basic solution. A solution of ammonia has a pH of around 12. Antacid tablets dissolve in water to form a basic solution of about pH 8.

The pH of the water in the fish tank must be kept within a set range so the fish stay healthy.

7 Identify Write the name of each item in the appropriate column in the table to identify the solution as acidic, neutral, or basic.

The pH of Some Common Materials

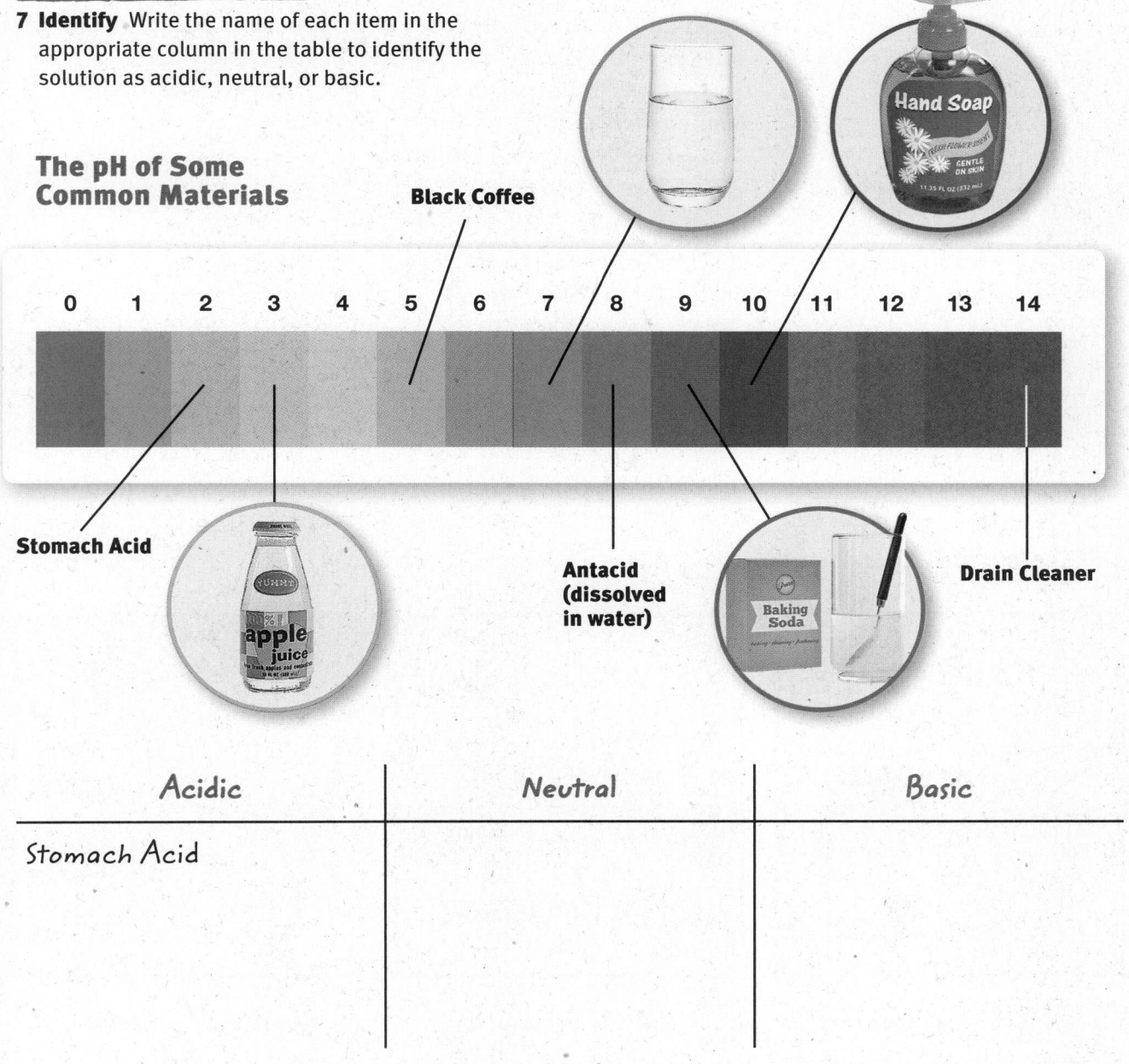

Black Coffee

Hand Soap

0 1 2 3 4 5 6 7 8 9 10 11 12 13 14

Stomach Acid

apple juice

Antacid (dissolved in water)

Baking Soda

Drain Cleaner

Acidic	Neutral	Basic
Stomach Acid		

How is pH measured?

The pH of a solution can be measured using different techniques. One method is to use an acid-base indicator. These indicators are chemical dyes that change color at certain pH ranges, but they do not give you a specific pH value. The pH can be estimated by placing a few drops of indicator in a solution. The color of the solution changes according to its pH. The indicator bromthymol (brohm•THY•mawl) blue is blue above pH 7.6, green between pH 7.6 and 6.0, and yellow below pH 6.0. Another indicator, phenol (FEE•nawl) red, changes from bright pink to orange to yellow as the pH changes from basic to acidic.

Universal pH paper is a strip of dry paper that has been infused with several acid-base indicators. A drop of solution is placed on the paper strip, and the paper turns a specific color depending on the pH of the solution. The color is compared to a reference card that shows the pH indicated by each color.

An electronic pH meter has a probe that is placed into the solution being measured. A precise pH value is measured, and the number is displayed on the meter.

Visualize It!

8 Describe Write a caption to explain each method of measuring pH. Then place a check next to the method you think is the most accurate.

_____   _____   _____

_____   _____   _____

_____   _____   _____

_____   _____   _____

_____   _____   _____

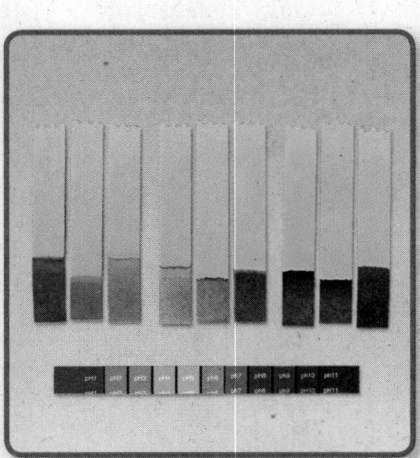

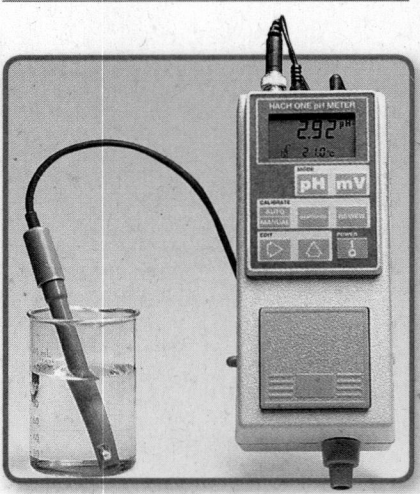

☐ Acid-base indicators   ☐ Universal pH paper   ☐ Electronic pH meter

A Natural pH Meter

The pH of soil could be measured using pH paper or an electronic pH meter. But if you have certain flowering plants in your garden, there is an easier way. You can just look at the color of the flowers!

For some hydrangea plants, the color of the flowers depends on the pH of the soil. Aluminum, the mineral needed to produce the blue color, can not be absorbed by the plant in basic soil. As a result, hydrangeas act as acid-base indicators in nature.

This hydrangea plant has blue flowers. The blue color indicates that the soil pH is less than 5.5. It is acidic.

This hydrangea plant has pink flowers. The pink color indicates that the soil pH is greater than 6.5. It is basic.

Extend

Inquiry

9 Describe Explain how hydrangeas may help gardeners decide what else to plant in their garden.

10 Research How does the pH of soil affect plant growth?

11 Discuss Gardeners often measure the pH of soil. Discuss why gardeners want to know the pH of soil. How might gardeners use this information?

In Our World

What role does pH play in the environment?

Plants and animals are healthiest when their environment is within a certain pH range. The pH of soil in any environment is important. If soil pH is too acidic or too basic, the nutrients that plants need do not dissolve into the water in the soil. When plants do not get the nutrients they need, they do not grow well. When plants cannot thrive, the population of animals that depends on the plants as a food source also suffers, and an entire food web may collapse.

In most ocean environments, the water has a pH of about 8. If too much carbon dioxide is absorbed by the water, the ocean pH may be slightly lowered. This lower pH could harm sea animals such as mollusks by causing their hard outer shells to dissolve. Other sea creatures that depend on mollusks as a food source would also suffer.

Visualize It!

12 Predict A decrease in the pH of the soil might affect the ecosystem shown. Choose two species other than the blue heron that could be affected and explain why.

The blue heron eats fish from this pond to survive. The fish may struggle to survive if the worms that they eat no longer get proper nutrients from the soil.

What causes acid rain?

Rain is not pure water because it has carbon dioxide from the atmosphere dissolved in it. Normal rain has a pH between 5 and 6. Acid rain is any form of precipitation, such as rain, sleet, or snow, that has a lower pH than normal. When fossil fuels such as coal and petroleum are burned, they release certain chemicals into the air. These chemicals, which include sulfur oxides and nitrogen oxides, combine with water in the atmosphere to produce sulfuric acid and nitric acid. These acids in the atmosphere form acid rain when they dissolve in precipitation such as raindrops.

Active Reading **13 Describe** How does acid rain form?

Chemicals released into the air when fossil fuels are burned combine with water in the atmosphere to form acid rain.

What are the effects of acid rain?

Acid rain can cause harm directly. For example, it can cause buildings to erode faster, and it can damage trees. Acid rain also affects living things by causing changes in the environment.

Acid Rain Can Harm Ecosystems

Acid rain can lower the pH of lakes, ponds, and streams. This decrease in pH can harm aquatic species, as well as other organisms that rely on the water for survival. Acid rain can harm plants by damaging their leaves. It can also harm plants and other living things by lowering soil pH.

Acid Rain Can Harm Human-Made Structures

Acid rain can damage buildings and sculptures made of limestone and marble. Acid rain reacts with the stone that makes up these structures. This reaction causes the structures to erode. Acid rain can also damage paint and cause metals to corrode faster.

If acid rain has a low enough pH, it can severely damage trees and other plants.

Acid rain can destroy the details of limestone sculptures.

Think Outside the Book Inquiry

14 Research With a partner, research a specific area or environment that has been affected by acid rain. Present your research to the class.

Body in Balance

Where does pH play an important role in the human body?

For the human body to work properly, its pH must be in balance. If the pH is too high or too low, your body has problems functioning, and you can feel ill. Not all parts of the body need the same pH.

In Your Stomach

Food is digested and broken down by many substances in your digestive tract, including hydrochloric acid in the stomach. The stomach is a very acidic environment. It usually has a pH of about 2.5. But if food that is difficult to digest is eaten, more stomach acid is made. The acidity can drop as low as 1.2. Difficulty digesting food and a low stomach pH can cause an uncomfortable feeling in your stomach, called indigestion. The pH can be increased to healthier levels by consuming antacid tablets. Antacid tablets are basic. They restore the pH in the stomach back to a normal level.

Active Reading

15 Identify As you read, underline ways in which pH affects our health.

Visualize It!

16 Infer Use information from this lesson to fill in the missing pH level of the antacid in the diagram below.

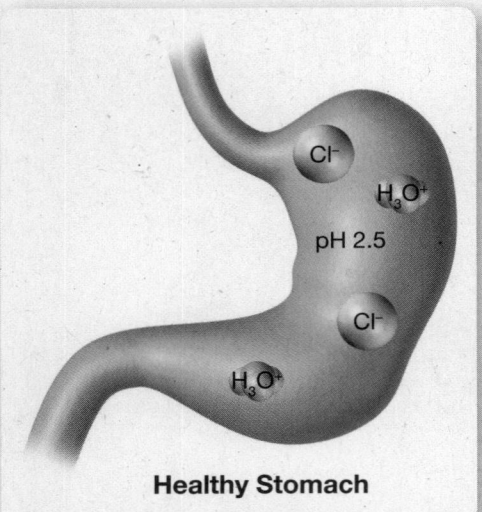

Healthy Stomach

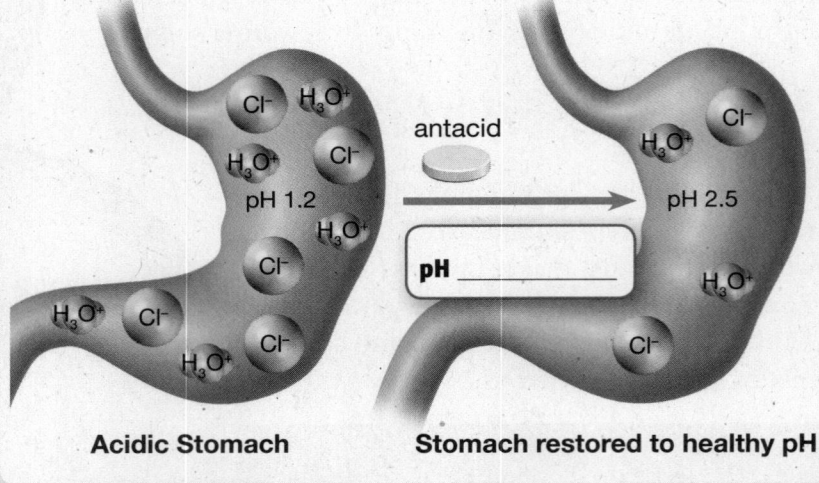

pH 1.2

antacid

pH _____

pH 2.5

Acidic Stomach   **Stomach restored to healthy pH**

17 Explain Antacid tablets help restore the stomach to normal pH levels. What property of the antacid allows for this?

_____

_____

_____

In Your Blood

Normal blood pH ranges from 7.35 to 7.45. The pH must be within this small range to maintain good health. If blood pH falls below 7.35, it is too acidic. This condition is called *acidosis* (as•ih•DOH•sis). If blood pH rises above 7.45, it is too basic, or alkaline. This condition is called *alkalosis* (al•kuh•LOH•sis). Both conditions make a person feel ill. The lungs and kidneys keep the blood's pH within the correct range. The kidneys remove acids made during normal cell functions. The lungs remove carbon dioxide. If a person's kidneys or lungs do not work properly, blood CO_2 levels can increase, lowering blood pH. The person develops acidosis. Alkalosis is usually caused by an increased breathing rate. The person's blood CO_2 levels decrease, raising their blood pH.

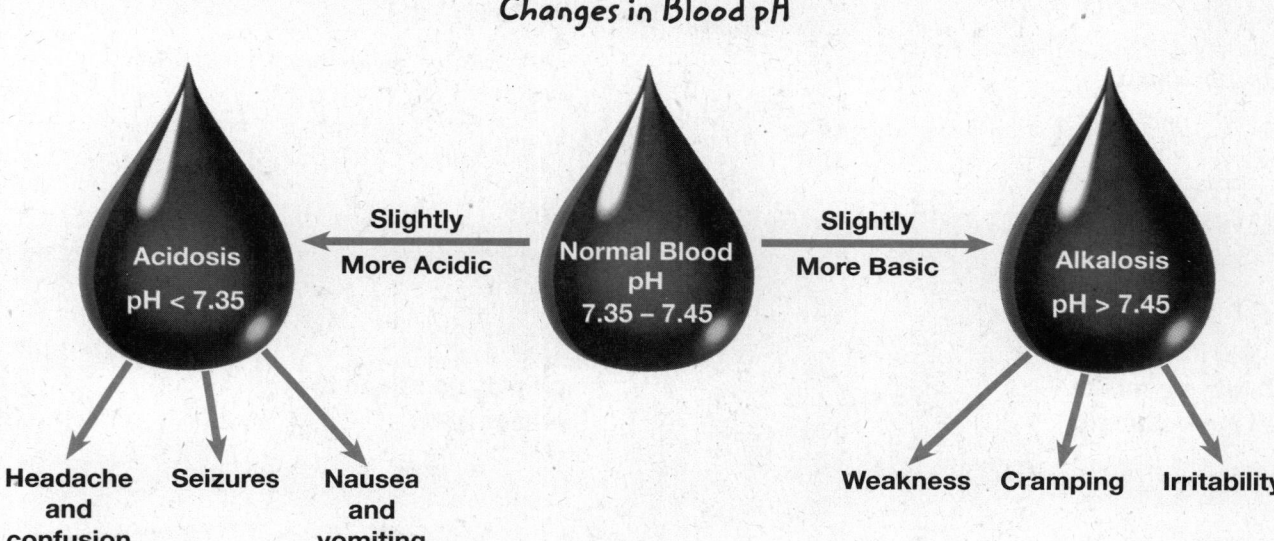

Changes in Blood pH

Acidosis pH < 7.35 — Slightly More Acidic ← **Normal Blood pH** 7.35 – 7.45 → Slightly More Basic — **Alkalosis** pH > 7.45

Headache and confusion Seizures Nausea and vomiting

Weakness Cramping Irritability

18 Analyze Decide whether each condition would result in acidosis or alkalosis. Place a check in the box to show your diagnosis.

A **Condition:** Poor breathing (slow breathing)
Effect: Increase in blood CO_2

☐ acidosis ☐ alkalosis

C **Condition:** Prolonged vomiting
Effect: Decrease in stomach acid

☐ acidosis ☐ alkalosis

B **Condition:** Hyperventilation (fast breathing)
Effect: Decrease in blood CO_2

☐ acidosis ☐ alkalosis

D **Condition:** Untreated diabetes
Effect: Build up of acid in the blood

☐ acidosis ☐ alkalosis

Visual Summary

To complete this summary, fill in the blanks with the correct word. Then use the key below to check your answers. You can use this page to review the main concepts of the lesson.

Measuring pH

The pH of a solution is a measure of its acidity or basicity.

19 The pH of a solution depends on the concentration of _____ ions.

The pH scale ranges from 0 to 14.

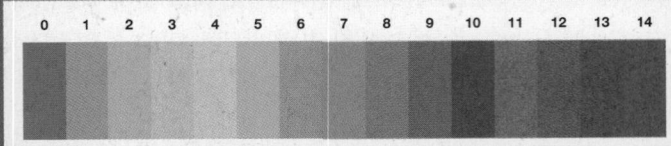

21 A solution with a pH less than 7 is _____

22 A solution with a pH greater than 7 is _____

pH plays a role in the environment.

20 The pH of soil and streams can decrease because of _____ rain.

pH plays a role in the human body.

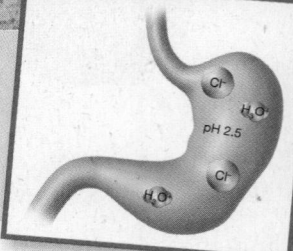

23 A blood pH of greater than 7.45 leads to the condition called _____

24 **Support** Use an example to support the following statement: Living things may be unable to survive if their environment is not kept within a suitable pH range.

© Houghton Mifflin Harcourt Publishing Company • Image Credits: (t) ©petographer/Alamy Images; (b) ©Will & Deni McIntyre/Corbis

Lesson Review

Vocabulary

In your own words, define the following term.

1 pH

_____

_____

Key Concepts

2 Describe What might cause stomach pH to become more acidic than normal?

_____

_____

_____

_____

3 Compare How is the concentration of H_3O^+ ions and OH^- ions different in an acid solution and a basic solution?

_____

_____

_____

_____

_____

4 Decide Myra wants to measure the pH of a sample of drinking water as accurately as possible. What method should she use?

_____

_____

_____

_____

5 Conclude A student uses universal pH paper to find the pH of three solutions. Solution A has a pH of 5, solution B has a pH of 11, and solution C has a pH of 7. Identify which solution is acidic, which solution is neutral, and which solution is basic.

_____

_____

_____

Critical Thinking

6 Evaluate Devon says that acid in your stomach will make you unhealthy. Do you agree or disagree? Explain.

_____

_____

_____

_____

Use this photograph to answer the following questions.

7 Analyze When a volcano erupts, sulfur oxides are released into the atmosphere. How does this volcanic eruption affect precipitation?

_____

_____

_____

8 Apply If the volcanic eruption lowers the pH of the water in a nearby lake, how might this lowered pH harm living things in the lake?

_____

_____

_____

_____

_____

My Notes

Unit 7　Big Idea

The properties of matter are determined by the arrangement of atoms.

Lesson 1

ESSENTIAL QUESTION
What are physical and chemical changes of matter?

Distinguish between physical and chemical changes of matter.

Lesson 2

ESSENTIAL QUESTION
How do we know what parts make up the atom?

Describe how the development of the atomic theory has led to the modern understanding of the atom and its parts.

Lesson 3

ESSENTIAL QUESTION
How are elements arranged on the periodic table?

Describe the relationship between the arrangement of elements on the periodic table and the properties of those elements.

Lesson 4

ESSENTIAL QUESTION
How are chemical reactions modeled?

Use balanced chemical equations to model chemical reactions.

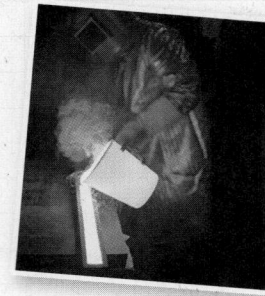

Lesson 5

ESSENTIAL QUESTION
What is a solution?

Summarize the characteristics of a solution.

Lesson 6

ESSENTIAL QUESTION
What are the properties of acids, bases, and salts?

Understand the physical and chemical properties of acids, bases, and salts and how these chemicals are commonly used.

Lesson 7

ESSENTIAL QUESTION
What is pH a measure of?

Describe the pH scale and how it is used to classify a solution as either acidic, basic, or neutral.

Connect　ESSENTIAL QUESTIONS
Lessons 2 and 3

1 Synthesize How is chemical bonding related to the organization of the periodic table?

_____
_____
_____
_____
_____

Think Outside the Book

2 Synthesize Choose one of these activities to help synthesize what you have learned in this unit.

☐ Using what you learned in lessons 2 and 3, explain how the structure of the atom is related to the periodic table by putting together a poster presentation. Include captions and labels on your poster.

☐ Using what you learned in lessons 3 and 4, make a model of a water molecule. Label each part of the model. Provide a caption that gives the chemical formula of water.

Name _____

Vocabulary

Fill in the blank with the term that best completes the sentence.

1 Elements in the periodic table are arranged in columns,

or _____.

2 A(n) _____ is the smallest particle of an element that has the chemical properties of that element.

3 A(n) _____ is a negatively charged subatomic particle.

4 A chemical _____ occurs when one or more substances change into entirely new substances with different properties.

5 A combination of chemical symbols and numbers to represent a substance is a chemical _____.

Key Concepts

Choose the letter of the best answer.

6 The chart below gives the atomic number and mass number of two elements.

	Element A	Element B
Atomic number	10	9
Mass number	20	19

How many protons does Element B have?

A 9

B 10

C 19

D 20

7 Which of the following is an example of an endothermic reaction?

A a cake baking

B a candle burning

C a firework exploding

D a piece of wood smoldering

8 Which model of an atom is correctly labeled?

A

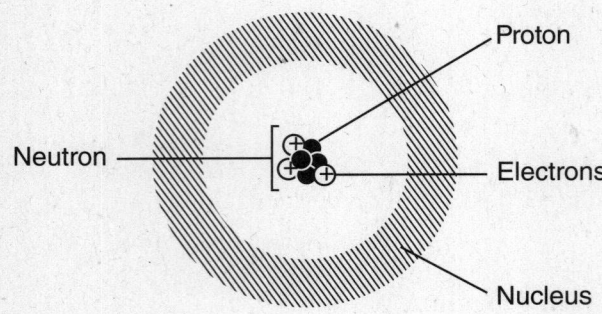

B

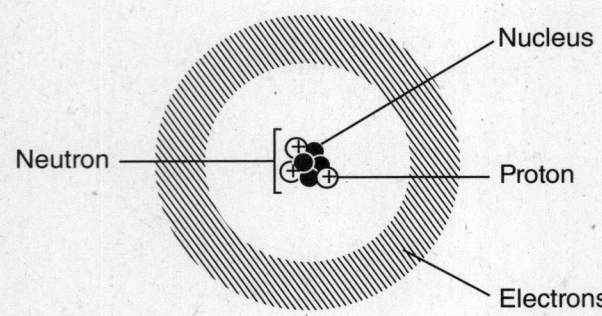

C

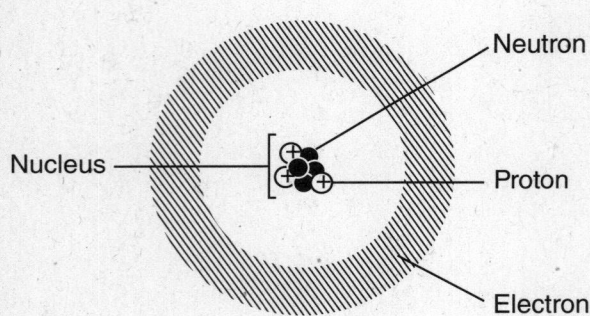

D

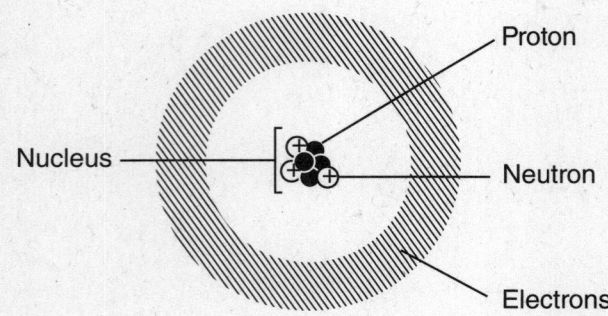

9 Phenolphthalein is pink in the presence of a base and colorless when a base is not present. A student injected a solution of a base containing phenolphthalein into a lemon. When she cut the lemon open, there was no pink color inside. What must have happened?

   A The acid in the lemon neutralized the base.

   B The base changed into an acid in the lemon.

   C The phenolphthalein stopped working inside the lemon.

   D The lemon absorbed the base but not the phenolphthalein.

10 In our bodies, stomach acids help break down food and release nutrients. Sometimes, people take antacids to do what?

   A make their stomach more acidic

   B make their stomach less basic

   C neutralize their stomach acids

   D release more nutrients from their food

11 Below is a scale used in characterizing a solution.

pH Scale

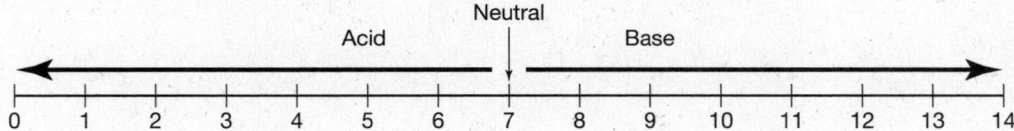

An acidic solution undergoes a 100-fold decrease in hydronium ion concentration. Which of the following intervals could represent this change?

   A 0–1

   B 2–4

   C 8–10

   D 9–12

12 Which observation is a sign of a chemical change?

   A A rotting potato gives off a bad smell.

   B A melting block of ice leaves a large puddle.

   C A cloud changes shape when blown by wind.

   D A plaster statue breaks when it falls onto the floor.

13 What is a solution that has a relatively low amount of solute called?

   A saturated

   B concentrated

   C dilute

   D suspension

14 The diagram below shows how atomic theory has changed over time.

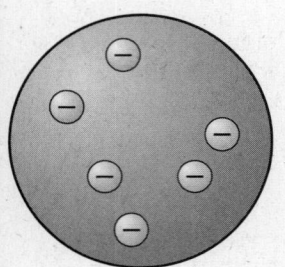 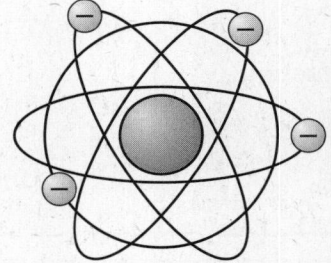 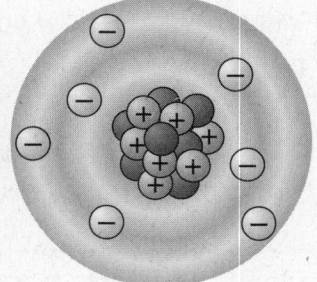

Thomson's model of atom   Rutherford's model of atom   Current model of atom

How is the current understanding of atomic structure different from both Thomson's model and Rutherford's model?

   A Electrons move only in the current model of the atom.

   B Electrons are fixed only in the current model of the atom.

   C Electrons travel in orbits only in the current model of the atom.

   D Electrons travel in an electron cloud only in the current model of the atom.

15 Which of the following forms during a neutralization reaction?

A a salt

B a base

C an acid

D a metal

16 Trini adds 10 g of baking soda to 100 g of vinegar. The mixture begins to bubble. When the bubbling stops, Trini finds the mass of the resulting mixture. She determines its mass is 105 g.

Before mixing		After mixing
Mass, baking soda	Mass, vinegar	Mass, mixture
10 g	100 g	105 g

Why has the mass changed?

A A gas has formed and left the mixture.

B Vinegar evaporated during the experiment.

C Mixtures always are less massive than their parts.

D Mass was destroyed when vinegar reacted with baking soda.

Critical Thinking

Answer the following questions in the spaces provided.

17 List three properties of metals that nonmetals typically do not have.

_____

_____

Describe where metals and nonmetals are found on the periodic table.

_____

_____

What are elements that have some properties of metals and some properties of nonmetals called?

_____

18 How is acid rain formed?

_____

_____

What happens to the pH of soil, lakes, ponds, and streams when acid rain falls?

_____

_____

Give an example of how acid rain may affect a living organism.

_____

_____

What could be done to reduce the amount of acid rain that falls on Earth?

_____

_____

_____

Connect **ESSENTIAL QUESTIONS**
Lessons 6 and 7

Answer the following questions in the spaces provided.

19 Name two ways in which acids are different from bases.

_____

_____

Give an example of a base and a common use of that base.

_____

_____

Give an example of an acid and a common use of that acid.

_____

_____

Energy

Lightning is the discharge of static electricity that builds up in clouds during a storm.

Big Idea

Energy is always conserved but can change forms and can be transferred.

What do you think?

Static electricity can make your hair stand on end. What other effects of static electricity can you think of?

This Van de Graaff generator makes a safe but hair-raising demonstration.

CITIZEN SCIENCE

Be Lightning Safe

Lightning can be an impressive display, but it is also very dangerous. Lightning strikes carry a great deal of energy that can split apart trees, damage property, and start fires. People can be injured or killed if they are struck by lightning.

1 Define the Problem

Research how people can protect themselves from lightning while participating in outdoor activities.

A What are some signs that lightning may occur?

_____

_____

_____

B Where and for how long should people take shelter from lightning?

_____

_____

_____

To be safe from lightning, people should wait out a storm by going inside a school building that is completely enclosed.

Game Canceled due to severe weather

② Ask Some Questions

A Where is your school's lightning-safety plan posted?

_____
_____

B Are students and teachers aware of your school's plan for lightning safety?

_____
_____

C What is your school's current policy for canceling outdoor events when there is a risk of lightning?

_____
_____
_____

D Is your school's current plan for lightning safety adequate?

_____
_____
_____

③ Make a Plan

A What are two ways in which your school's lightning-safety plan could be improved?

_____
_____
_____
_____

B Describe two steps that you could take to promote your improved lightning-safety plan at your school.

_____
_____
_____
_____

Take It Home

With an adult, make a lightning-safety plan for your family. And, discuss the weather conditions that would cause you to put your plan into action.

Energy Transformation and Transfer

ESSENTIAL QUESTION

How can energy be transformed and transferred?

By the end of this lesson, you should be able to analyze how energy is conserved through transformations and transfer.

An electric bass guitar converts sound energy into electrical energy. The guitar's amplifier converts the electrical energy back into sound energy.

OHIO 7.PS.2 Energy can be transformed or transferred but is never lost.

OHIO 7.SIA.5 Develop descriptions, models, explanations and predictions.

Engage Your Brain

1 Construct Draw a diagram that shows what might happen when a light bulb is turned on. When making your diagram, think about what happens to the energy.

2 Describe What do you know about energy? Using the first letters of the word *energy*, make an acrostic poem that describes energy.

E _____

N _____

E _____

R _____

G _____

Y _____

Active Reading

3 Apply Many scientific terms, such as *transformation* and *transfer*, also have everyday meanings. Use context clues to write your own definition for the underlined word.

Example Sentence
After she learned how to play soccer, she went through a complete <u>transformation</u>. Now she practices every day.

transformation:

_____

_____

_____

Example Sentence
On the way to visit her friend, she had to <u>transfer</u> from one bus line to another.

transfer:

_____

_____

_____

Vocabulary Terms

- energy
- energy transformation
- law of conservation of energy

4 Apply As you learn the definition of each vocabulary term in this lesson, create your own definition or sketch to help you remember the meaning of the term.

What are some forms of energy?

Remember that **energy** is the ability to do work. Energy is measured in joules (J). Energy can come in many different forms. Some common forms of energy are discussed below.

Active Reading **5 Identify** As you read this page and the next, underline examples of energy provided in the text.

Mechanical Energy

Mechanical energy is the sum of an object's kinetic and potential energy. The energy that a moving car has is kinetic energy. The energy a book has sitting on a desktop is potential energy.

Sound Energy

Sound energy is a type of kinetic energy. It results from the vibration of particles. People are able to detect these tiny vibrations with structures in their ears that vibrate due to the sound. When you hear a car, you are detecting vibrations in the air that transfer sound energy. Sound cannot travel through empty space. If there were no air or other substance between you and the car, then you would not hear sounds from the car.

Electromagnetic Energy

Electromagnetic (ee•LEK•troh•mag•NEH•tik) energy is transmitted through space in the form of electromagnetic waves. Electromagnetic waves can be produced by the vibration of electrically charged particles. Unlike sound, electromagnetic waves can travel through empty space. Light energy is a form of electromagnetic energy. Some examples of electromagnetic energy are visible light, x-rays, and microwaves. X-rays are high-energy waves used by doctors to look at your bones. Microwaves can be used to cook food. The sun releases a large amount of electromagnetic energy, some of which is absorbed by Earth.

The piccolo player is producing sound energy.

Microwaves use electromagnetic energy to warm food.

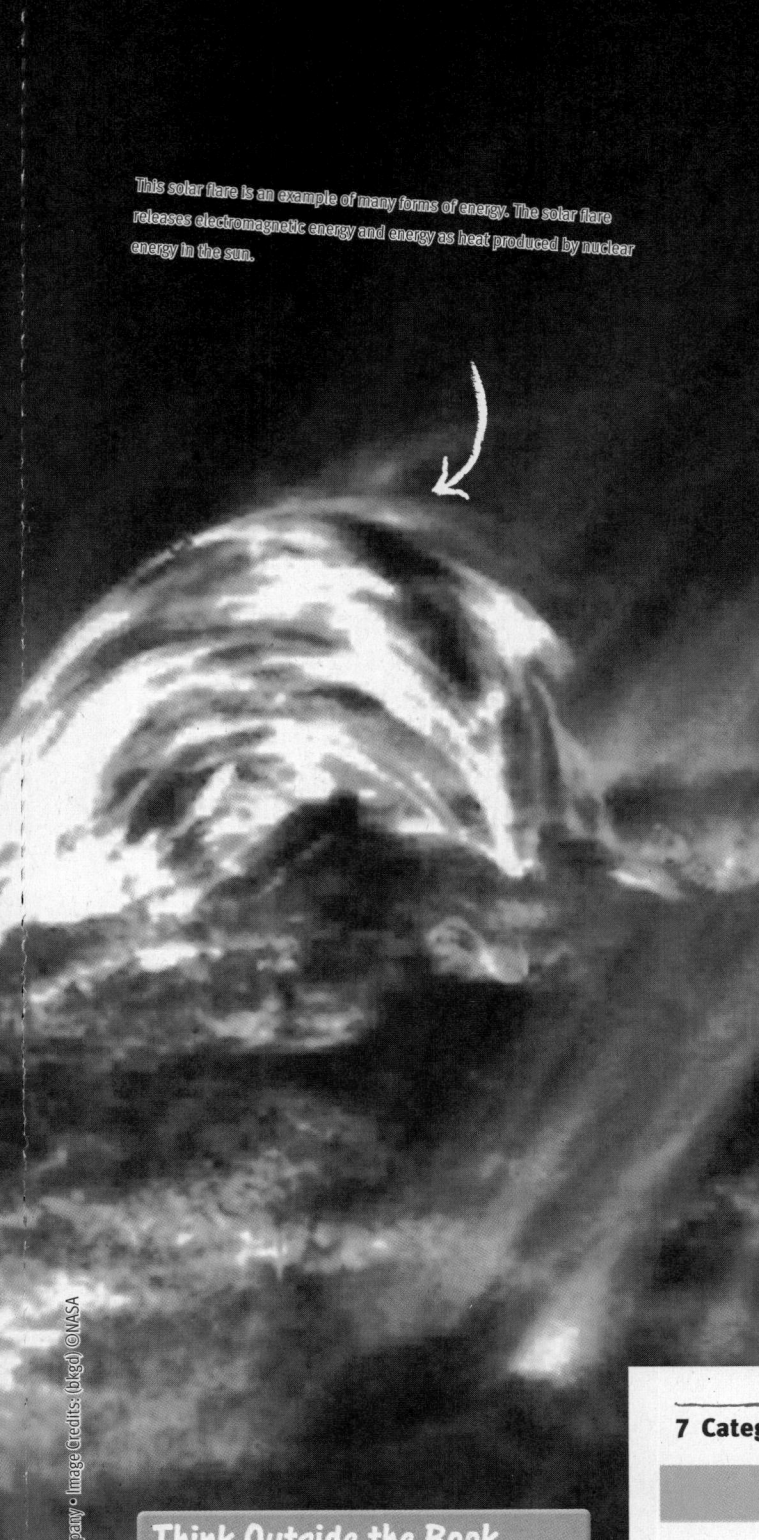

This solar flare is an example of many forms of energy. The solar flare releases electromagnetic energy and energy as heat produced by nuclear energy in the sun.

Chemical Energy

Chemical potential energy is the energy stored in chemical bonds that hold chemical compounds together. As chemical bonds form and are broken, energy can be absorbed or released. Chemical potential energy can be stored in food.

Thermal Energy and Heat

Thermal energy is the energy an object has due to the motion of its molecules. The faster the molecules in an object move, the more thermal energy the object has. Heat is the energy transferred from an object at a higher temperature to an object at a lower temperature.

Electrical Energy

Electrical energy is the energy of moving electrons. When you plug an electrical device, such as a computer, into an outlet and turn it on, electrons moving in the wire provide electrical energy to the device that it needs to operate.

Nuclear Energy

The nucleus of an atom is the source of nuclear (NOO•klee•uhr) energy. When an atom's nucleus breaks apart, or when the nuclei of two small atoms join together, energy is released. The energy given off by the sun comes from nuclear energy. In the sun, hydrogen nuclei join to make a helium nucleus. This reaction gives off a huge amount of energy. The sun's light and heat come from these reactions. Without nuclear energy from the sun, life would not exist on Earth.

Think Outside the Book

6 Apply Keep a journal of ten examples of energy you see during the day. Classify each example as either mechanical, sound, electromagnetic, chemical, thermal, electrical, or nuclear.

7 Categorize Fill in the blank parts of the chart below.

Example	Type of energy
Bicycle going up a hill	
	Electromagnetic
Orchestral music	

Transformers

What is an energy transformation?

An **energy transformation** takes place when energy changes from one form into another. Any form of energy can change into any other form of energy. Often, one form of energy changes into more than one form. For example, when you rub your hands together, you hear a sound, and your hands get warm. The kinetic energy of your moving hands was transformed into both sound energy and thermal energy.

Another example of an energy transformation is when chemical energy is converted in the body. Why is eating breakfast so important? Eating breakfast gives your body the energy needed to help you start your day. Your chemical potential energy comes from the food you eat. Your body breaks down the components of the food to access the energy contained in them. This energy is then changed to the kinetic energy in your muscles. Some of the chemical energy is converted into thermal energy that allows your body to stay warm.

Visualize It!

8 Describe At point A, chemical potential energy from the battery is transformed into electrical energy. Describe the energy transformation that occurs at point B.

_____

_____

_____

_____

_____

Batteries

What transformations occur in renewable energy systems?

Chemical energy in a battery is transformed to the electrical energy needed in a flashlight or cell phone. But what about the electrical energy that you use at home? Renewable energy systems, such as those powered by sunlight, wind, or water, convert electromagnetic energy or mechanical energy to electrical energy.

In a wind power system, moving air pushes against the blades of a turbine, and the turbine rotates. The mechanical energy of the spinning turbine is converted to electrical energy.

In hydroelectric power systems, the mechanical energy of falling water is changed to electrical energy. The water level is higher behind a dam than in front of the dam. The mechanical energy of the water changes from potential energy to kinetic energy as the water moves through the dam. The moving water pushes the blades of a turbine. The mechanical energy of the spinning turbine is converted to electrical energy.

Active Reading **10 Compare** How does the energy transformation in a wind-powered system compare with the energy transformation in a water-powered system?

_____

_____

_____

_____

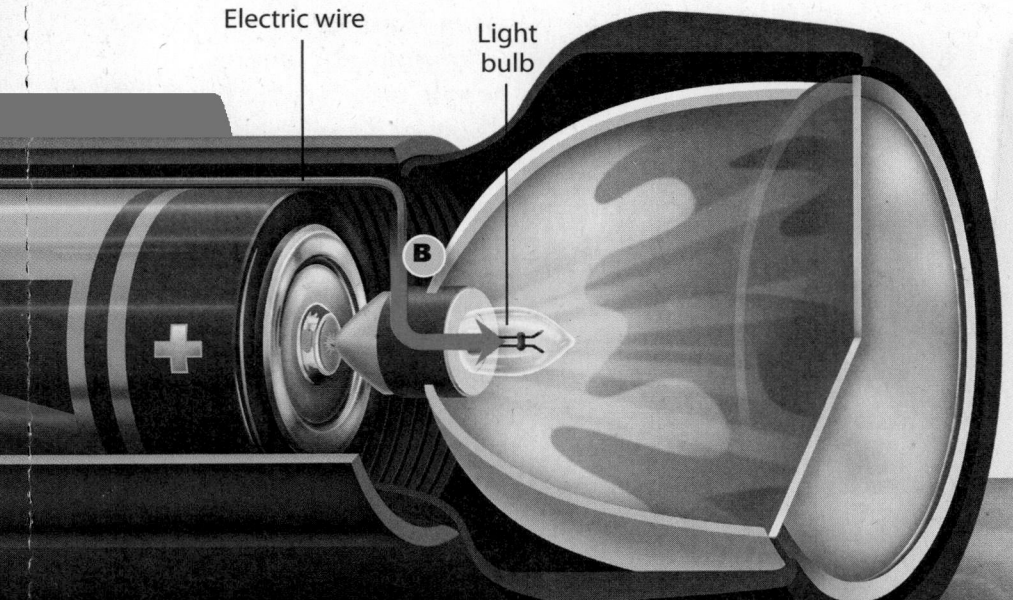

Electric wire

Light bulb

B

+

Think Outside the Book (Inquiry)

9 Apply Have you ever thought about how a television works? What form of energy is used to power a television? What forms of energy are produced by a television? What energy transformations do you think take place inside a television? Construct a diagram showing these transformations.

11 Describe Give another example of electrical energy being transformed into light energy.

_____

_____

_____

_____

_____

From One to Another

What is an energy transfer?

Have you ever accidentally knocked a book off your desk? Then you have seen an energy transfer. An *energy transfer* is the movement of energy from one object or system to another. An example of an energy transfer is when a raindrop hits a leaf and the leaf begins to move. The kinetic energy of the raindrop transfers to the leaf. When you warm your hands by a fire, thermal energy transfers from the burning wood to your skin.

What are some types of energy that can be transferred?

There are many ways in which energy can transfer between objects. A few examples of energy that can be transferred are mechanical energy, electrical energy, electromagnetic energy, and thermal energy.

Active Reading **12 Describe** As you read these pages, underline how each of these types of energy listed can be transferred.

The sun transfers electromagnetic energy, so people wear protective clothing and sunblock.

Mechanical Energy

Mechanical energy can be transferred when objects push or pull on each other over a distance. Mechanical energy includes kinetic energy, gravitational potential energy, and elastic potential energy. For example, sound energy is a type of kinetic energy. Moving air molecules transfer energy to other objects. The mechanical energy of these molecules undergoes an energy transfer when the molecules push against your eardrum. The kinetic energy of the molecules transfers to the eardrum to make it move.

Electrical Energy

Electrical energy can be transferred when an electrical source is connected in a complete electrical circuit to an electronic device. A battery is one type of electrical source. A remote control for a television needs a battery to work. An electrical outlet is another electrical source. Electrical energy transfers to a light bulb when a lamp is plugged into a working outlet and turned on. However, a break in the wire or a missing bulb opens the circuit. No electrical energy can be transferred until the gap in the circuit is closed.

Visualize It!

13 **Label** Fill in the missing forms of energy to complete each image caption.

A The sun transfers _____ energy as heat that warms the water surface.

B The innertube transfers _____ energy to the water it enters.

C The camera battery transfers _____ energy to the other parts of the camera when a photo is taken.

Electromagnetic Energy

Electromagnetic waves transfer energy when they interact with matter. Microwaves are a form of electromagnetic wave. The microwaves transfer energy to a cup of cocoa when they interact with and are absorbed by the cocoa. Visible light waves are also electromagnetic waves. A hawk can see a mouse when visible light waves from the sun bounce off of the mouse and enter the hawk's eyes. The visible light waves interact with the cells in the back of the hawk's eyes, in the retina, and transfer energy to the cells. The hawk can see the mouse, which is the hawk's prey.

Thermal Energy

Thermal energy can be transferred as heat from a hot object to a cooler object. This transfer can occur through radiation, conduction, and convection. You feel warmer when you stand in direct sunlight through the radiation of infrared and visible light waves from the sun. Directly touching a hot bowl of soup allows thermal energy to transfer through conduction from the bowl to your fingers. Thermal energy can be transferred as heat through convection as hot air above a burning candle rises. The hot air rises, and cooler air moves down toward the candle in a convection current.

What is conservation of energy?

The **law of conservation of energy** states that energy cannot be created or destroyed; it can only change forms. When energy is transferred from one system to another, the total amount of energy in all systems before transfer equals the total amount in all systems after transfer. When energy is transformed, the total amount of energy remains the same. Energy may appear to be lost, but it is not. Instead, the energy may change into unwanted or unintended forms, such as heat or sound.

For example, you transfer energy to a ball when you roll it across a rug. If energy is conserved, why doesn't the ball keep rolling? As it rolls, the ball transfers energy to the air and rug. The ball stops when all of its kinetic energy has changed to thermal energy in the ball, air, and rug. But the energy is still present, and the total amount of energy is still the same.

Active Reading **14 Apply** If energy is conserved, why do you have to keep pedaling your bicycle once it starts moving?

_____

_____

_____

Visualize It!

15 Identify Name two energy transformations that take place in the bamboo forest shown here.

_____

_____

_____

_____

Bamboo plants use light energy from the sun to produce sugars, which contain chemical potential energy.

The panda gets chemical potential energy by eating bamboo plants. In order to keep its body functioning, the panda converts this energy into other forms, such as kinetic energy for moving around.

© Houghton Mifflin Harcourt Publishing Company • Image Credits: (bg) ©Keren Su/Stone/Getty Images

How is energy conserved?

Energy is always conserved. Energy can undergo an energy transformation and change to a different form. An energy transfer might happen that could move energy to a different object in the same system or to an object in another system. How energy is conserved can depend on the kind of system you are studying.

Energy Can Be Transformed

Defining a system that is closed to its surroundings is helpful when studying energy. Matter and energy cannot get into or out of a closed system. In a closed system, if energy appears to be gained or lost, the energy has just transformed. Think again about rolling a ball across a rug. Imagine that you, the ball, the air, and the rug form a closed system. Then, the energy that appears to be lost by the ball is still present within the system. In the end, the energy has been transformed into thermal energy in the ball, the air, and the rug, which are all part of the system.

Energy Can Be Transferred

Most natural systems on Earth are open systems. Matter and energy can be transferred into or out of an open system. If energy appears to be gained by or lost from an open system, it has either transformed into a different form or transferred into a different system. To show that energy is conserved, you must add up the energy in all systems that interact. If you look at the rolling ball itself as a system, then the ball is an open system. The energy of the ball decreases. But this example still follows the law of conservation of energy. As the ball rolls, it interacts with the rug and the air. Because you are now considering the ball an open system, you must find the total energy in all of the interacting systems. Then, you see that the ball transfers the missing energy to the air and the rug.

17 Explain Is a sealed jar of water on a sunny windowsill a closed system? Why or why not?

_____

_____

_____

_____

Visualize It!

16 Identify For each illustration, identify whether it is an example of an open system or a closed system.

A _____

B _____

Visual Summary

To complete this summary, fill in the blanks with the correct word or phrase. Then, use the key below to check your answers. You can use this page to review the main concepts of the lesson.

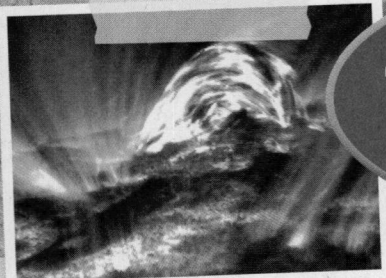

Energy Transformation and Transfer

Energy can come in many different forms, such as mechanical energy, sound energy, electromagnetic energy, thermal energy, chemical energy, electrical energy, and nuclear energy.

18 The light given off by the solar flare is an example of _____ energy.

One form of energy can transform into another form of energy. Energy can be transferred from one object to another.

19 Energy in a flashlight's battery changes from _____ energy to electrical energy.

Energy is always conserved. Matter and energy can go in and out of open systems but not closed systems.

20 Energy cannot be _____ or _____.

Answers: 18. electromagnetic; 19. chemical; 20 created, destroyed;

21 Apply Describe a process in which energy changes form at least two times. Explain how the law of conservation of energy applies to the process you describe.

Lesson Review

Vocabulary

In your own words, define the following terms.

1 energy transformation:

_____

_____

_____

2 law of conservation of energy:

_____

_____

_____

3 energy transfer:

_____

_____

_____

Key Concepts

4 Identify Give one example of energy transformation. Make sure to say which forms of energy are involved.

_____

_____

_____

_____

5 Explain How is energy conserved when a pan of water on an electric stove comes to a boil?

_____

_____

_____

_____

6 Distinguish How does an open system differ from a closed system?

_____

_____

_____

Critical Thinking

Use this photo to answer the following question.

7 Apply List one example of each of the following forms of energy found in this photo.

sound energy:

_____

_____

chemical energy:

_____

_____

mechanical energy:

_____

_____

8 Synthesize In order to keep an automobile operating, it is necessary to keep adding fuel as it is used up. What kind of system is the car? Explain why this doesn't go against the law of conservation of energy.

_____

_____

_____

_____

_____

_____

My Notes

Mechanical Energy

ESSENTIAL QUESTION

How can mechanical energy be transferred?

By the end of this lesson, you will be able to describe how mechanical energy can be transferred when objects push or pull on each other over a distance.

The back-and-forth movement of a swing is caused by the transfer of mechanical energy.

OHIO **7.PS.2** Energy can be transformed or transferred but is never lost.

OHIO **7.PS.3** Energy can be transferred through a variety of ways.

OHIO **7.SIA.3** Use appropriate mathematics, tools and techniques to gather data and information.

✋ **Lesson Labs**

Quick Labs
• Transferring Potential Energy
• The Energy of a Pendulum

S.T.E.M. Lab
• Energy in a Roller Coaster

Engage Your Brain

1. **Describe** Fill in the blank with the word or phrase that you think correctly completes the following sentences.

A squirrel in a tree has gravitational

_____ energy because of its position.

An acorn falling to the ground has

_____ energy because it is moving.

As an acorn falls, its potential energy

_____, and its kinetic

energy _____.

2. **Describe** How do you know that the penguin in the photo has potential energy?

_____

_____

_____

_____

Active Reading

3. **Synthesize** Many English words have their origins in other languages. Use the meaning of the Greek word below to make an educated guess about the meaning of the term *kinetic energy*.

Greek word	Meaning
kinein	to move

Example sentence
The speeding car had a large amount of <u>kinetic energy</u>.

kinetic energy:

_____

_____

Vocabulary Terms

• **kinetic energy**
• **potential energy**
• **mechanical energy**
• **force**
• **work**

4. **Apply** As you learn the definition of each vocabulary term in this lesson, create your own definition or sketch to help you remember the meaning of the term.

Potential to Move!

What is mechanical energy?

Active Reading

5 Identify As you read, underline the two kinds of energy that can make up the mechanical energy of an object.

Although you may not think about it, you encounter mechanical energy every day! To explore mechanical energy, we first have to understand its two components: potential and kinetic energy.

An object has mechanical energy if it is moving, if it is positioned above Earth's surface, or both. **Kinetic energy** is the energy of an object due to the object's motion. **Potential energy** is the energy that an object has because of its position, shape, or chemical composition.

Objects interact with one another and can influence the types of energy other objects have. Consider an archer, his bow, and his arrows. The archer places an arrow in the bow, increasing the arrow's gravitational potential energy as it moves farther from Earth's surface. Drawing the bowstring causes the limbs of the bow to bend, or deform, which increases the elastic potential energy of the bowstring and the bow. The bowstring snaps back to its original position when the archer releases it. The potential energy of the drawn bow becomes the kinetic energy of the moving string and then the moving arrow.

The total energy an object has because of its motion, change of position, or its shape is its mechanical energy. **Mechanical energy** is the sum of an object's kinetic energy and potential energy. Like all forms of energy, mechanical energy is measured in joules (J).

The bow and bowstring have elastic potential energy because their shape changes.

The potential energy of the string transforms to the kinetic energy of the moving arrow.

The bowstring transfers mechanical energy to the arrow when it is released.

How is energy conserved when mechanical energy transforms?

An *energy transformation* occurs when energy changes from one form to another. As a pendulum swings, its mechanical energy changes form, from almost entirely potential energy to almost entirely kinetic energy at specific points in its swing. Energy can change form, but the total amount of energy in the entire system is conserved, or remains constant.

So why doesn't a pendulum keep swinging forever? If all the mechanical energy of the pendulum were conserved, the pendulum would continue swinging. But transformations are not always 100 percent efficient. Some of the mechanical energy is transformed to forms that are not kinetic or potential energy. This energy is transferred to the environment instead of staying within the pendulum system. Eventually the pendulum slows down and stops. This occurs because as the pendulum swings, it pushes through the air particles that surround it. Some of the pendulum's mechanical energy gets transferred to these air particles, increasing their kinetic energy. Over time, the mechanical energy within the pendulum system moves to the environment around it, but the total amount of energy remains constant. Energy is never lost.

6 Describe How is mechanical energy not conserved in a system?

_____

_____

_____

_____

_____

As the arrow flies higher above the ground, its gravitational potential energy increases and its kinetic energy decreases.

Once the arrow hits the target, its kinetic energy transforms to gravitational potential energy, thermal energy, and sound energy.

Visualize It!

7 Distinguish Circle the arrows that have potential energy only.

8 Compare How does the mechanical energy of the arrows in the target compare with the mechanical energy of the arrows on the ground?

_____

_____

_____

_____

When is mechanical energy transferred?

Recall that mechanical energy can be transferred. As well as seeing examples of mechanical energy in everyday life, you experience mechanical energy transfers too! If you fire an arrow from a bow, lift a seashell up from the beach, or pick up an apple from a table, mechanical energy is transferred from you to the object.

When a Force Is Applied

Mechanical energy is transferred when a force acts between objects and one of the objects moves some distance either with or against the force. A **force** is a push or a pull exerted on an object in order to change the motion of the object. A force has both a size and a direction. Forces transfer energy. Energy transfers from the bowstring to the arrow, moving the arrow forward. The transfer of energy stops when the objects no longer exert forces on each other. The amount of energy transferred depends on the strength of the force and the distance through which the force moves the object. Pulling the string farther back allows it to transfer more energy to the arrow.

How are force and energy related to work?

When you lift an apple, you exert a force on the apple and move it a distance in the direction of the force you apply. You do work on the apple. **Work** is the use of force to move an object some distance. Work is described by the equation:

$$\text{work} = \text{force} \times \text{distance}$$

Force is measured in newtons (N), and distance is measured in meters (m). When you multiply newtons by meters, the product is the joule. Therefore, work is measured in joules. By transferring energy to the apple, you've changed the apple's position and increased its gravitational potential energy. You did work on the apple.

Mechanical energy is transferred when work is carried out. You transferred mechanical energy to the apple by moving it upward. But, work is done only by the portion of the force that's in the same direction as the force.

Active Reading **9 Describe** What mechanical energy do you transfer to an object when you lift it?

_____

_____

The boxes are moving in the direction of the pulling and pushing forces the men are applying. Therefore, work is done on the boxes.

How is energy different from work?

Energy is the ability to do work. Work is a measure of how much energy a force transfers when it acts on a moving object. However, if the object does not move in the direction of the force, the force does not do work because mechanical energy is not transferred to the object. For example, if the men in the picture carried the boxes instead of pulling and pushing them, work would not be done on the boxes because the upward lifting force on the boxes is not in the direction of the forward movement. The amount of energy transferred to an object increases as the strength of the force and the distance the object is moved increases. This energy transfer stops when the objects no longer exert forces on each other.

Think Outside the Book Inquiry

10 Apply Sketch five situations in which forces are applied during a day, and identify whether work is done in each instance.

 Do the Math Sample Problem

Trudy picks up a puppy from the floor and lifts it 1.2 m into a basket. She lifts the puppy using a force of 22 N. How much energy does Trudy transfer to the puppy?

Identify

What do you know?

distance = 1.2 m; force = 22 N

What do you want to find out?

The amount of energy transferred (the work done)

Plan

Write the formula:

work = force × distance

Substitute into the formula:

work = 22 N × 1.2 m

Solve

Calculate and simplify:

work = 26.4 J

Check that your units agree:

N × m = J

(Joules is the unit for energy and also for work.)

Answer: Trudy transfers 26.4 J of energy to the puppy.

You Try It

11 Calculate Trudy uses a force of 44 N to pick up a heavier puppy. She lifts the puppy 1.2 m into the same basket. How much energy does Trudy transfer to the heavier puppy?

Identify

What do you know?

What do you want to find out?

Plan

Write the formula:

Substitute into the formula:

Solve

Calculate and simplify:

Check that your units agree:

Answer:

Visual Summary

To complete this summary, fill in the blank with the correct word or phrase. Then use the key below to check your answers. You can use this page to review the main concepts of the lesson.

Mechanical Energy

An object's mechanical energy is the sum of its kinetic energy and potential energy.

13 The mechanical energy of a speeding arrow is mostly _____ energy.

Work is the product of a force applied to an object and the distance the object moves with or against the force: work = force × distance.

15 To find the work done by a force, you must multiply the force by the _____ the object moves as the force is acting on it.

Mechanical energy is transferred when a force acts between objects and one of the objects moves some distance either with or against the force.

14 You can transfer mechanical energy when you push a cart forward because you exert a forward _____ that moves the cart in the same direction.

Mechanical energy is transferred when one object does work on another object.

16 The crane transferred mechanical energy to the bricks as it did _____ on the bricks to raise them 15 meters.

Answers: 13 kinetic; 14 force; 15 distance; 16 work

17 Diagram Sketch two images of a person jumping on a trampoline. The person should be at different heights above the trampoline in each image. Describe the transfer of mechanical energy taking place.

Lesson Review

Vocabulary

Draw a line to connect the following terms to their definitions.

1 work

2 potential energy

3 mechanical energy

A the energy that an object has because of its position, shape, or chemical composition

B the sum of an object's kinetic and potential energies

C the transfer of energy to an object by using a force that causes the object to move in the direction of the force

Key Concepts

4 Identify Describe the transformation of mechanical energy in a ball when it is thrown straight up and then comes back down.

_____

_____

_____

_____

5 Explain Is mechanical energy conserved as a playground swing moves? Why or why not?

_____

_____

_____

_____

6 List Describe the two forms of energy that make up the mechanical energy of an object.

_____

_____

_____

_____

_____

Critical Thinking

Use the graph below to answer the following questions.

Energy Graph for Ideal Pendulum

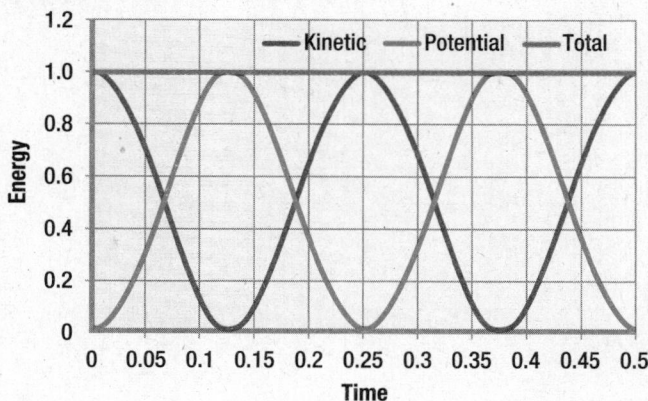

7 Analyze What can you determine about mechanical energy from this graph?

_____

_____

8 Infer This graph shows the energy transformations of an *ideal* pendulum system. How does this differ from a real-word example?

_____

_____

_____

9 Relate Brianna pushes against a door that is stuck and does not move. Describe the mechanical energy of the door in terms of force, energy, and work.

_____

_____

_____

10 Calculate Pablo lifts a bag of flour 0.8 m from the floor to a table. He lifted the bag using a force of 20 N. How much work did Pablo do on the bag of flour?

My Notes

Thermal Energy and Heat

ESSENTIAL QUESTION

What is the relationship between heat and temperature?

By the end of this lesson, you should be able to analyze the relationship between heat, temperature, and thermal energy.

The Afar Depression, in Eastern Africa, is one of the hottest places on Earth. In the summer, temperatures average over 100 °F!

OHIO **7.PS.3** Energy can be transferred through a variety of ways.

✋ **Lesson Labs**

Quick Labs
• Simple Heat Engine
• Observing the Transfer of Energy
• Exploring Thermal Conductivity
Field Lab
• Building a Solar Cooker

 Engage Your Brain

1 Describe Fill in the blanks with the words that you think correctly complete the following sentences.

When you put your hands on a cold object, like a glass of ice water, your hands become

_____ The glass of water

becomes _____ if you

leave your hands on it for a long time. If you

leave the glass of ice water out in the sun, the

ice will start to _____

2 Describe Write your own caption for this photo.

_____

_____

_____

_____

✏️ Active Reading

3 Apply Many scientific words, such as *conductor*, also have everyday meanings. Use context clues to write your own definition for each meaning of the word *conductor*.

Example sentence
That school's band is very good because its conductor is a great teacher.

conductor:

_____

_____

Example sentence
That metal spoon is a good conductor, so it will get hot if you put it into boiling soup.

conductor:

_____

_____

Vocabulary Terms

• thermal energy   • conductor
• heat   • insulator
• calorie   • convection
• conduction   • radiation

4 Apply As you learn the definition of each vocabulary term in this lesson, create your own definition or sketch to help you remember the meaning of the term.

There are more water molecules in this lake than in the glass of water on the right.

What is thermal energy?

Thermal energy is the total kinetic energy of all particles in a substance. In the SI system, thermal energy is measured in joules (J). Remember that temperature is not energy, but it does give a measure of the average kinetic energy of all the particles in a substance. If you have two identical glasses of water and one is at a higher temperature than the other, the particles in the hotter water have a higher average kinetic energy. The water at a higher temperature will have a higher amount of thermal energy.

What is the difference between thermal energy and temperature?

Temperature and thermal energy are different from each other. Temperature is related to the average kinetic energy of particles, while thermal energy is the total kinetic energy of all the particles. A glass of water can have the same temperature as Lake Superior, but the lake has much more thermal energy because the lake contains many more water molecules.

After you put ice cubes into a pitcher of lemonade, energy is transferred from the warmer lemonade to the colder ice. The lemonade's thermal energy decreases and the ice's thermal energy increases. Because the particles in the lemonade have transferred some of their energy to the particles in the ice, the average kinetic energy of the particles in the lemonade decreases. Thus, the temperature of the lemonade decreases.

Active Reading **5 Explain** What are two factors that determine the thermal energy of a substance?

_____

_____

Houghton Mifflin Harcourt Publishing Company • Image Credits: ©John Warden/SuperStock

Under Where?

There are fewer water molecules in this glass than in the lake.

6 Apply For each object pair in the table below, circle the object that has more thermal energy. Assume that both objects are at the same temperature.

| bowl of soup | small balloon | tiger |
| pot of soup | large balloon | house cat |

Heat It Up!

Energy in the form of heat flows from the warm drinks to the cold ice. The ice melts.

What is heat?

You might think of the word *heat* as having to do with things that feel hot. But heat also has to do with things that feel cold. Heat causes objects to feel hot or cold or to get hot or cold under the right conditions. You probably use the word *heat* every day to mean different things. However, in science, **heat** is the energy transferred from an object at a higher temperature to an object at a lower temperature.

When two objects at different temperatures come into contact, energy is always transferred from the object that has the higher temperature to the object that has the lower temperature. Energy in the form of heat always flows from hot to cold. For example, if you put an ice cube into a glass of water, energy is transferred from the warmer water to the colder ice cube.

7 **Apply** For each object pair in the table below, draw an arrow in the direction in which energy in the form of heat would flow.

Object 1	Direction of heat flow	Object 2
metal rod		fire
hat		snowman
ice cube		glass of warm water

Energy in the form of heat flows from the hot fire to the marshmallow. The marshmallow gets so hot that it catches on fire!

Energy in the form of heat flows from the warm mugs to the girls' cold hands. Their hands get warmer.

Visualize It!

8 Apply What is another heat exchange happening in this picture?

_____

_____

_____

_____

How is heat measured?

Heat is measured in two ways. One way is the calorie (cal). One **calorie** is equal to the amount of energy needed to raise the temperature of 1 g of water by 1 °C. Heat can also be measured in joules (J) because heat is a form of energy. One calorie is equal to 4.18 J.

You probably think of calories in terms of food. However, in nutrition, one Calorie—written with a capital C—is actually one kilocalorie, or 1,000 calories. This means that one Calorie (Cal) contains enough energy to raise the temperature of 1 kg of water by 1 °C. Each Calorie in food contains 1,000 cal of energy.

To find out how many Calories are in an apple, the apple is burned inside an instrument called a calorimeter. A thermometer measures the increase in temperature, which is used to calculate how much energy is released. This amount is the number of Calories.

How is heat related to thermal energy?

Adding or removing heat from a substance will affect its temperature and thermal energy. Heat, however, is not the same as thermal energy and temperature. These are properties of a substance. Heat is the energy involved when these properties change.

Think of what happens when two objects at different temperatures come into contact. Energy as heat flows from the object at the higher temperature to the object at the lower temperature. When both objects come to the same temperature, no more energy as heat flows. Just because the temperature of the two objects is the same does not mean they have the same thermal energy. One object may be larger than the other and thus have more particles in motion.

Active Reading **9 Relate** What will happen if two objects at different temperatures come into contact?

_____

_____

_____

© Houghton Mifflin Harcourt Publishing Company • Image Credits: (t) ©Darren Kemper/Corbis; (tc) ©Getty Images/Jupiterimages; (b) ©Jose Luis Pelaez Inc/Blend Images/Age Fotostock

How can heat affect the state of an object?

The matter that makes up a frozen juice bar is the same whether the juice bar is frozen or has melted. The matter is just in a different form, or state. Remember that the kinetic theory of matter states that the particles that make up matter move around at different speeds. The state of a substance depends on the speed of its particles. Adding energy in the form of heat to a substance may result in a change of state. The added energy may cause the bonds between particles to break. This is what allows the state to change. Adding energy in the form of heat to a chunk of glacier may cause the ice to melt into water. Removing energy in the form of heat from a substance may also result in a change of state.

Active Reading 11 **Predict** What are two ways to change the state of a substance?

_____

_____

Think Outside the Book Inquiry

10 **Compare** Have you ever needed to touch a very hot object? What did you use to touch it without burning yourself? Make a list. Have you ever needed to protect yourself from being cold? What sorts of things did you use? Make a list. Now, looking at the two lists, what do the things have in common?

Some of this ice is changing state. It is melting into water.

How do polar bears stay warm?

Keep Your Cool

What is conduction?

There are three main ways to transfer energy as heat: conduction, convection, and radiation. **Conduction** is the transfer of energy as heat from one substance to another through direct contact. It occurs any time that objects at different temperatures come into contact with each other. The average kinetic energy of particles in the warmer object is greater than the average kinetic energy of the particles in the cooler object. As the particles collide, some of the kinetic energy of the particles in the warmer object is transferred to the cooler object. As long as the objects are in contact, conduction continues until the temperatures of the objects are equal.

Conduction can also occur within a single object. In this case, energy in the form of heat is transferred from the warmer part of the object to the cooler part of the object. Imagine you put a metal spoon into a cup of hot cocoa. Energy will be conducted from the warm end of the spoon to the cool end until the temperature of the entire spoon is the same.

This is a photo of polar bear hair magnified about 350 times! Notice that it is hollow inside. The air inside is a good insulator.

Conductors

Some materials transfer the kinetic energy of particles better than others. A **conductor** is a material that transfers heat very well. Metals are typically good conductors. You know that when one end of a metal object gets hot, the other end quickly becomes hot as well. Consider pots or pans that have metal handles. A metal handle becomes too hot to touch soon after the pan is placed on a hot stove.

Insulators

An **insulator** (IN•suh•lay•ter) is a material that is a poor conductor of heat. Some examples of insulators are wood, paper, and plastic foam. Plastic foam is a good insulator because it contains many small spaces that are filled with air. A plastic foam cup will not easily transfer energy in the form of heat by conduction. That is why plastic foam is often used to keep hot drinks hot. Think about the metal pan handle mentioned above. It can be dangerous to have handles get hot so quickly. Instead, pot handles are often made of an insulator, such as wood or plastic. Although a plastic handle will also get hot when the pot is on the stove, it takes a much longer time for it to get hot than it would for a metal handle.

12 Classify Decide whether each object below is a conductor or an insulator. Then check the correct box.

Flannel shirt	☐ Conductor ☐ Insulator
Iron skillet	☐ Conductor ☐ Insulator
Copper pipe	☐ Conductor ☐ Insulator
Oven mitt	☐ Conductor ☐ Insulator

© Houghton Mifflin Harcourt Publishing Company • Image Credits: ©Andrew Syred/Photo Researchers, Inc.

13 Identify As you read, underline examples of heat transfer.

This pot of boiling water shows how convection currents move.

What is convection?

Energy in the form of heat can also be transferred through the movement of gases or liquids. **Convection** (kuhn•VEK•shuhn) is the transfer of energy as heat by the movement of a liquid or gas. In most substances, as temperature increases, the density of the liquid or gas decreases. Convection occurs when a cooler, denser mass of a gas or liquid replaces a warmer, less dense mass of a gas or liquid by pushing it upward.

When you boil water in a pot, the water moves in roughly circular patterns because of convection. The water at the bottom of the pot gets hot because there is a source of heat at the bottom. As the water heats, it becomes less dense. The warmer water rises through the denser, cooler water above it. At the surface, the warm water begins to cool. The particles move closer together, making the water denser. The cooler water then sinks back to the bottom, is heated again, and the cycle repeats. This cycle causes a circular motion of liquids or gases. The motion is due to density differences that result from temperature differences. The motion is called a *convection current*.

What is radiation?

Radiation is another way in which heat can be transferred. **Radiation** is the transfer of energy by electromagnetic waves. Some examples of electromagnetic waves include visible light, microwaves, and infrared light. The sun is the most significant source of radiation that you experience on a daily basis. However, all objects—even you—emit radiation and release energy.

When radiation is emitted from one object and then absorbed by another, the result is often a transfer of heat. Like conduction and convection, radiation can transfer heat from warmer to cooler objects. However, radiation differs from conduction and convection in a very significant way. Radiation can travel through empty space, as it does when it moves from the sun to Earth.

14 Classify Fill in the blanks in the chart below.

Example	Conduction, Convection, or Radiation
When you put some food in the microwave, it gets hot.	
	Conduction
A heater on the first floor of the school makes the air on the second floor warm.	

Practical Uses of Radiation

Do you think that you could cook your food using the energy from the sun? Using a device called a solar cooker, you could! A solar cooker works by concentrating the radiation from the sun into a small area using mirrors. Solar cookers aren't just fun to use—they also help some people eat clean food!

In a refugee camp
This woman, who lives in a refugee camp in Sudan, is making tea with water that she boiled in a solar cooker. For many people living far from electricity or a source of clean water, a solar cooker provides a cheap and portable way to sterilize their water. This helps to prevent disease.

As a hobby
This woman demonstrates how her solar cooker works. Many people like to use solar cookers because they do not require any fuel. They also do not release any emissions that are harmful to the planet.

Extend

Inquiry

15 Identify Two examples of radiation are shown in the photos above. What is the source of the radiation in the examples?

16 Relate Research other places throughout the world where solar cookers are being used.

17 Produce Explain how solar cookers are useful to society by doing one of the following:
• Make a solar cooker and demonstrate how it works.
• Write a story about a family who uses a solar cooker to stay healthy and safe.

Visual Summary

To complete this summary, circle the correct word or phrase. Then use the key below to check your answers. You can use this page to review the main concepts of the lesson.

Thermal energy is the total kinetic energy of all particles in a substance.

18 If two objects are at the same temperature, the one with more / fewer / the same amount of particles will have a higher thermal energy.

Heat is the energy transferred from an object at a higher temperature to an object at a lower temperature.

19 Heat always flows from cold to hot / hot to cold / left to right.

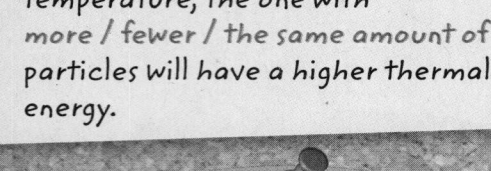

Heat

Heat can change the state of a substance.

20 Adding heat to an object causes bonds between particles to form / break / combine. This is what allows the state change.

There are three main ways to transfer energy as heat: conduction, convection, and radiation.

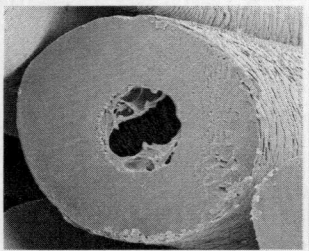

conduction

convection

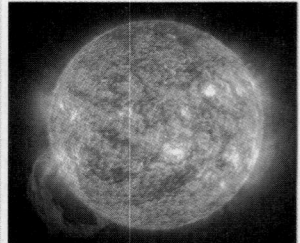

radiation

21 Conduction is the transfer of energy from a warmer object to a cooler object through a gas / empty space / direct contact.

22 Energy from the sun travels to Earth through conduction / convection / radiation.

23 **Conclude** Suppose you are outside on a hot day and you move into the shade of a tree. Which form of energy transfer are you avoiding? Explain.

Lesson Review

Vocabulary

In your own words, define the following terms.

1 heat

_____

_____

_____

2 thermal energy

_____

_____

_____

3 conduction

_____

_____

_____

4 convection

_____

_____

_____

5 radiation

_____

_____

_____

Key Concepts

6 **Compare** What is the difference between heat and temperature?

_____

_____

_____

_____

7 **Predict** If two objects at different temperatures are in contact with each other, what happens to their temperatures?

_____

_____

_____

_____

Use this photo to answer the following questions.

8 **Classify** Which type of energy transfer is occurring at each lettered area?

A _____

B _____

C _____

Critical Thinking

9 **Synthesize** Describe the relationships among temperature, heat, and thermal energy.

_____

_____

_____

_____

10 **Synthesize** Do you think that solids can undergo convection? Explain.

_____

_____

_____

_____

_____

_____

My Notes

Engineering Design Process

Skills
Identify a need
Conduct research
✓ Brainstorm solutions
✓ Select a solution
✓ Design a prototype
✓ Build a prototype
✓ Test and evaluate
Redesign to improve
✓ Communicate results

Objectives
• List and rank insulation materials according to effectiveness.
• Design a technological solution to keep an ice cube frozen.
• Test a prototype insulated ice cooler and communicate whether it achieved the desired results.

Building an Insulated Cooler

What do freezers, ovens, and polar bears have in common? They are all insulated! *Insulation* is a type of material that slows the transfer of energy such as heat. Refrigerators and freezers use insulation to keep the food inside cold. Insulation around ovens keeps energy inside the oven. And some animals have hair, fur, and fat layers that provide them with insulation, too.

1 Apply Which items in this picture provide insulation?

_____

_____

_____

_____

_____

2 List Name other everyday objects not shown here where insulation is used to keep objects warm or cool.

_____

_____

_____

_____

_____

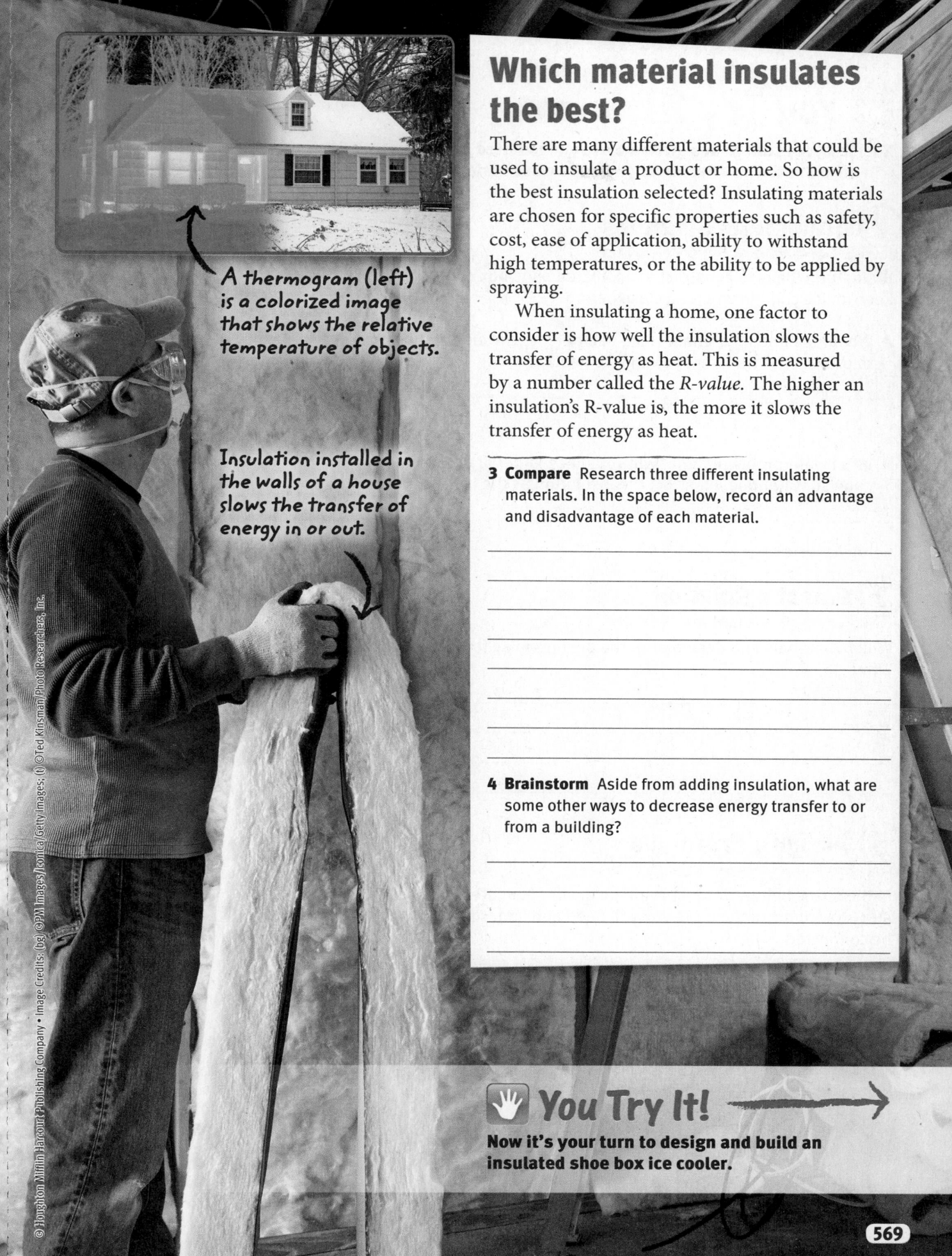

A thermogram (left) is a colorized image that shows the relative temperature of objects.

Insulation installed in the walls of a house slows the transfer of energy in or out.

Which material insulates the best?

There are many different materials that could be used to insulate a product or home. So how is the best insulation selected? Insulating materials are chosen for specific properties such as safety, cost, ease of application, ability to withstand high temperatures, or the ability to be applied by spraying.

When insulating a home, one factor to consider is how well the insulation slows the transfer of energy as heat. This is measured by a number called the *R-value*. The higher an insulation's R-value is, the more it slows the transfer of energy as heat.

3 Compare Research three different insulating materials. In the space below, record an advantage and disadvantage of each material.

_____

_____

_____

_____

_____

_____

_____

_____

4 Brainstorm Aside from adding insulation, what are some other ways to decrease energy transfer to or from a building?

_____

_____

_____

_____

✋ **You Try It!** ⟶

Now it's your turn to design and build an insulated shoe box ice cooler.

 You Try It!

Now it's your turn to design and build an insulated cooler that will keep an ice cube frozen for an entire class period.

You Will Need

✔ balance

✔ duct tape or packing tape

✔ ice cube

✔ insulation material

✔ plastic bag or waterproof container

✔ shoe box, empty

(1) Brainstorm Solutions

Brainstorm ideas to construct an insulated shoe box cooler that will keep an ice cube frozen for a class period.

A What insulation materials could you put into the empty shoe box to prevent the transfer of energy as heat?

_____

_____

B What waterproof container will you place under or around the ice cube so water doesn't affect the insulation as the ice cube melts?

_____

_____

(2) Select a Solution

Which materials and design offer the best promise for success? Why?

_____

_____

_____

(3) Design a Prototype

In the space below, draw a prototype of your insulated cooler. Be sure to include all the parts you will need and show how they will be connected.

(4) Build a Prototype

Now build your insulated cooler. What parts, if any, did you have to revise as you were building the prototype?

_____

_____

_____

_____

(5) Test and Evaluate

A At the beginning of a class period, find the mass of an ice cube. Record your result below.

_____

B Place the ice cube in your cooler and close it. At the end of the class period, open the cooler and observe the ice cube. Find the ice cube's mass and record your result below.

_____

C Was part of the ice still frozen? Calculate the fraction of the ice cube that remained frozen.

_____

_____

(6) Communicate Results

A Did your cooler provide effective insulation? Explain.

_____

_____

_____

_____

B Is there anything you could have done to increase the amount of ice remaining?

_____

_____

_____

_____

_____

_____

_____

Lesson 4

Waves and Energy

ESSENTIAL QUESTION

How do waves transfer energy?

By the end of this lesson, you should be able to distinguish between different types of waves and describe the amplitude, wavelength, frequency, and speed of a wave.

The energy in ocean waves can cause great destruction. This painting illustrates a great wave off the coast of Japan.

OHIO **7.PS.3** Energy can be transferred through a variety of ways.

OHIO **7.SIA.3** Use appropriate mathematics, tools and techniques to gather data and information.

Engage Your Brain

1 Predict Check T or F to show whether you think each statement is true or false.

T	F	
☐	☐	The air around you is full of waves.
☐	☐	Ocean waves carry water from hundreds of miles away.
☐	☐	Sound waves can travel across empty space.
☐	☐	Visible light is a wave.
☐	☐	Waves that carry more energy are closer together.

2 Illustrate Draw a diagram of a wave in the space below. How would you describe your wave so that a friend on the phone could duplicate your drawing?

Active Reading

3 Distinguish Many scientific words, such as *medium*, also have everyday meanings. Use context clues to write your own definition for each meaning of the word *medium*.

This is a <u>medium</u> pizza.

medium:

_____

_____

_____

He prefers DVDs as a storage <u>medium</u>.

medium:

_____

_____

_____

Vocabulary Terms

- medium
- longitudinal wave
- transverse wave
- mechanical wave
- electromagnetic wave
- amplitude
- wavelength
- wave period
- frequency
- wave speed

4 Identify This list contains the vocabulary terms you'll learn in this lesson. As you read, circle the definition of each term.

What are waves?

The world is full of waves. Water waves are just one of many kinds of waves. Sound and light are also waves. What do water waves, sound waves, and light waves have in common?

Waves Are Vibrations in a Medium

Waves are caused by vibrations of a medium. A **medium** is the material—solid, liquid, or gas—through which a wave can travel.

You can create waves on a rope by shaking the end up and down. When the particles at one end of the rope move, they cause the particles next to them to move up and down, too. These moving particles then cause their neighbors to move. In this way, the wave passes as a vibration down the whole length of the rope.

Think about one small piece in the middle of the rope. The piece moves up and down as a wave goes by. After each wave passes, the piece has returned back to where it was before. A wave transfers energy from one place to another. It does not transfer matter.

The points where the wave is highest are called *crests*. The points where the wave is lowest are called *troughs*.

Active Reading

5 Identify Underline the names for the highest and lowest points of a wave.

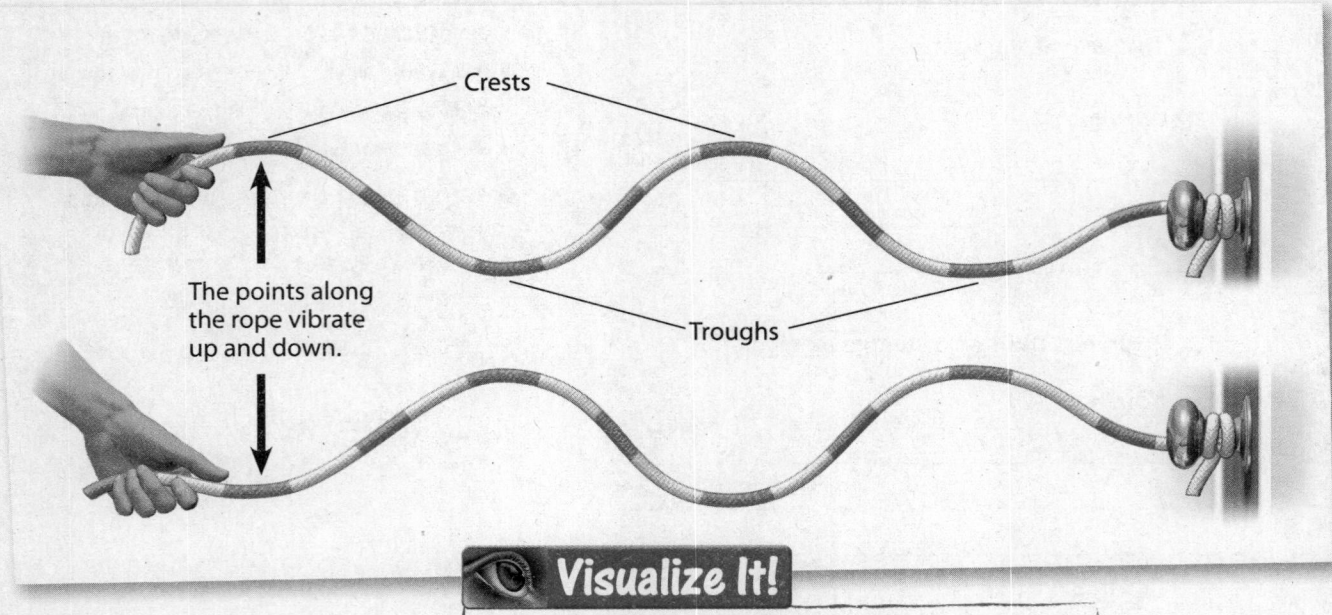

Crests

The points along the rope vibrate up and down.

Troughs

Visualize It!

6 Label Draw an arrow to show the direction the wave energy travels.

Waves Are Also a Transfer of Energy

A wave is a disturbance that transfers energy. Waves that need a medium to transfer energy include ocean waves, which move through water, and sound waves, which are carried on guitar or cello strings when they vibrate. Some waves can transfer energy without a medium. One example is visible light. Light waves from the sun transfer energy to Earth across empty space.

 Visualize It!

Each snapshot below shows the passage of a wave. The leaf rises and falls as crests and troughs carry it.

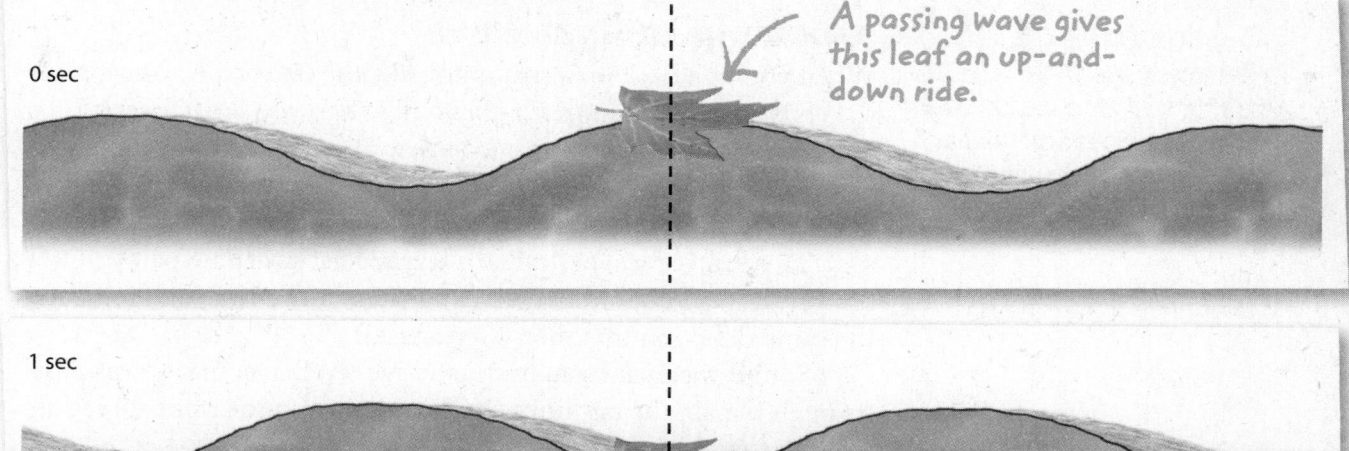

0 sec

A passing wave gives this leaf an up-and-down ride.

1 sec

7 Illustrate In the picture below, draw the leaf in the location it will be after 2 seconds.

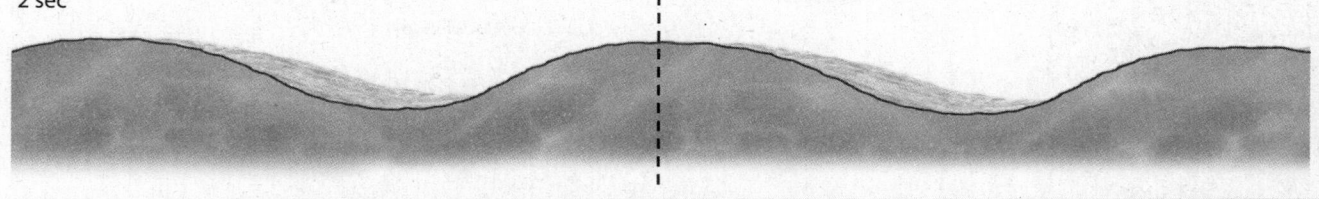

2 sec

8 Model In the space below, draw the leaf and wave as they will appear after 3 seconds.

3 sec

Different Ways

How do waves transfer energy?

All waves transfer energy from one place to another by repeated vibrations. However, not all vibrations are the same. Waves can be classified by comparing the direction that they cause particles in the medium to move with the direction in which the wave moves.

As a Longitudinal Wave

When you pull back on a spring toy like the one below, you spread the coils apart (creating a *rarefaction*). When you push forward, you compress the coils closer together. The compression you make when you push travels along the spring toy. As a result, energy is transferred from one end of the spring toy to the other.

This kind of wave is called a **longitudinal wave** (lawn•ji•TOOD•ehn•uhl). In a longitudinal wave, particles move back and forth in the same direction that the wave travels.

Sound waves are longitudinal waves. When sound waves pass through the air, the air moves back and forth in the same direction that the sound waves travel.

 **Visualize It!**

10 Apply In the longitudinal wave below, circle the arrow that shows the direction in which the wave travels, and draw a box around the arrow that shows the direction in which the spring is disturbed.

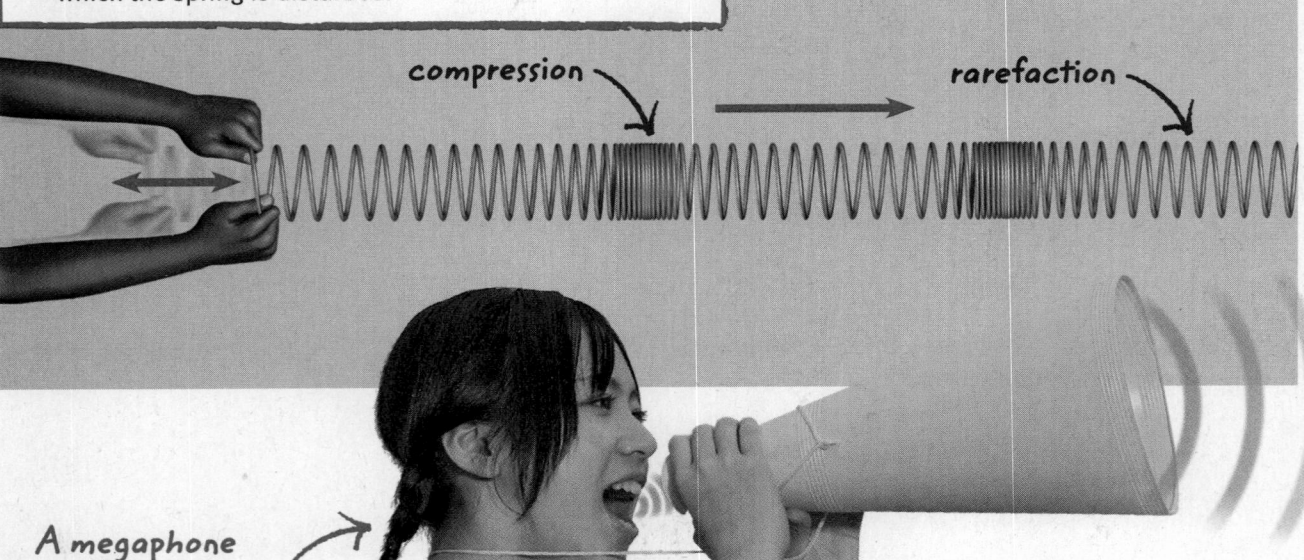

compression

rarefaction

A megaphone amplifies sound waves.

As a Transverse Wave

The same spring toy can be used to make other kinds of waves. If you move the end of the spring toy up and down, a wave also travels along the spring. In this wave, the spring's coils move up and down as the wave passes. This kind of wave is called a **transverse wave**. In a transverse wave, particles move perpendicularly to the direction the wave travels.

Transverse waves and longitudinal waves often travel at different speeds in a medium. In a spring toy, longitudinal waves are usually faster. An earthquake sends both longitudinal waves (called P-waves) and transverse waves (called S-waves) through Earth's crust. In this case, the longitudinal waves are also faster. During an earthquake, the faster P-waves arrive first. A little while later the S-waves arrive. The S-waves are slower but usually more destructive.

A transverse wave and a longitudinal wave can combine to form another kind of wave called a *surface wave*. Ripples on a pond are an example of a surface wave.

When these fans do "The Wave" in a stadium, they are modeling the way a disturbance travels through a medium.

11 Categorize Is the stadium wave at right a transverse or longitudinal wave?

_____

Visualize It!

12 Apply In the transverse wave below, circle the arrow that shows the direction in which the wave travels, and draw a box around the arrow that shows the direction in which the spring is disturbed.

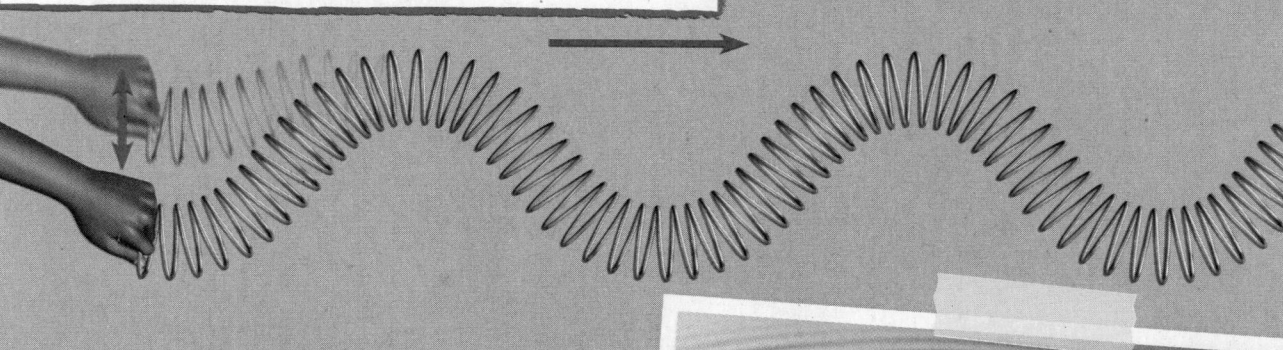

Water waves are surface waves, a combination of transverse and longitudinal waves.

Making Waves

What are some types of waves?

As you have learned, waves are disturbances that transfer energy. These disturbances can be classified by the type of motion they create. But they can also be classified by what they are disturbing.

Mechanical Waves

Most of the waves we have talked about so far are waves in a medium. For water waves, water is the medium. For earthquake waves, Earth's crust is the medium. Waves that require a medium are called **mechanical waves**.

Some mechanical waves can travel through more than one medium. For example, sound waves can move through air, through water, or even through a solid wall. The waves travel at different speeds in the different media. Sound waves travel much faster in a liquid or a solid than in air.

Mechanical waves can't travel without a medium. If all the air is removed from a jar, no sound waves will escape it. Because the inside of the jar is a vacuum, there is no air to transmit sound waves. The sound made inside the bell jar in the photograph below can't be heard.

Electromagnetic Waves

Are there any waves that can travel without a medium? Yes. Sunlight travels from the sun to Earth through empty space. Sunlight is an example of an **electromagnetic wave**. Unlike other waves, electromagnetic (EM) waves are not disturbances in a physical medium. Instead, they are vibrations of electric and magnetic fields. Also, EM waves do not lose energy as they move through a vacuum.

Examples of EM waves include

- visible light
- radio waves
- microwaves
- ultraviolet (UV) light
- x-rays

In empty space, all these waves travel at the same speed. This speed is referred to as the speed of light, about 300 million meters per second!

The sound from the toy cannot be heard, because there is no air to transmit the sound.

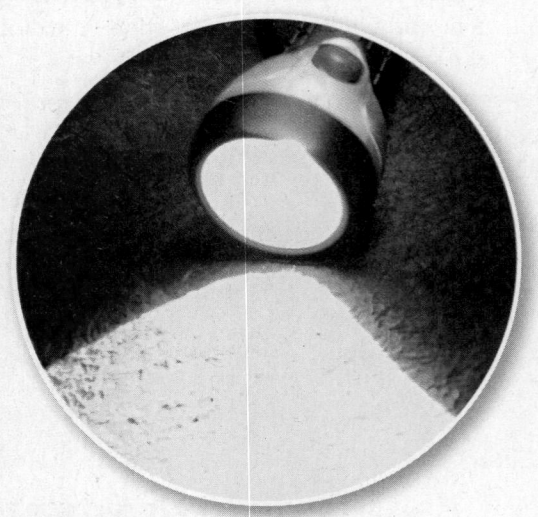

Visible light is a type of wave called an electromagnetic wave.

13 Classify Identify each example of waves in these three photographs as mechanical or electromagnetic.

Sunlight is a(n)

_____

Water waves are

_____

A towel waving displays a(n)

_____

Vocal sounds are

_____

Music is a(n)

_____

Firelight is a(n)

_____

Amp It UP!

How can we describe a wave?

Suppose you are talking to a friend who was at the beach. You want to know what the waves were like. Were they big or small? How often did they come? How far apart were they? Each of these is a basic property used to describe waves.

Wave direction

Amplitude

Wavelength

Amplitude

As a wave passes, particles in the medium vibrate up and down or back and forth. A wave's **amplitude** is a measure of how far particles in the medium move from their rest position. The highest points of a transverse wave are called crests and the lowest are troughs. For a transverse wave, amplitude is the height of a crest or a trough. In a longitudinal wave, amplitude is how far a particle travels in one direction. In mechanical waves, amplitude is related to the amount of energy in the wave. The greater the amplitude, the more energy the wave carries.

Wavelength

The amplitude of a wave describes the amount of up-and-down or side-to-side displacement. **Wavelength** is defined as the distance from any point on a wave to the next identical point on the same wave. It is the distance over which the wave's shape repeats. For example, in a transverse wave, wavelength can be measured as the distance from one crest to another, or one trough to another. In a longitudinal wave, a wavelength can be measured from any point on a wave, such as the point of greatest compression, to the same point on the next wave.

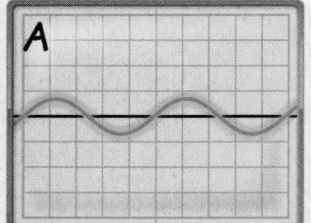
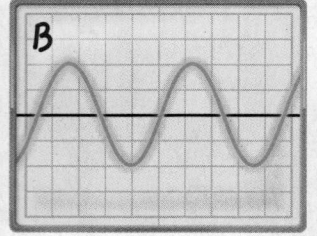
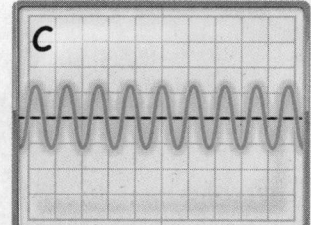
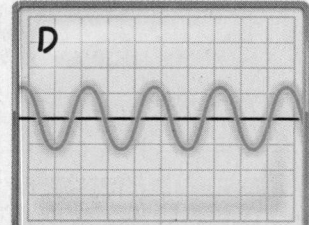

Visualize It!

14 Identify Label the amplitude in diagrams A and B, and circle the wave that has the greater amplitude.

15 Identify Label the wavelength in diagrams C and D and draw a box around the wave that has the longer wavelength.

Frequency

The time required for identical parts of consecutive waves to pass a given point is called the **wave period** (usually just "period"). For example, if you were floating in a boat, you could start a stopwatch when one crest passed and stop it when the next crest passed. The time between two crests is the period.

Frequency is the number of waves that pass a point in a given amount of time, usually one second. Frequency is measured in hertz (Hz). One hertz is equal to one wavelength per second.

> Frequency and period are closely related. Frequency is the inverse of period:
>
> $$\text{frequency} = \frac{1}{\text{period}}$$

In the example shown at the right, suppose the time from one crest to another—the period—is five seconds. The frequency is then 0.2 Hz. Only two-tenths of a wave pass per second.

The amount of energy in an electromagnetic wave is related to frequency. The higher the frequency, the more energy is carried by the wave.

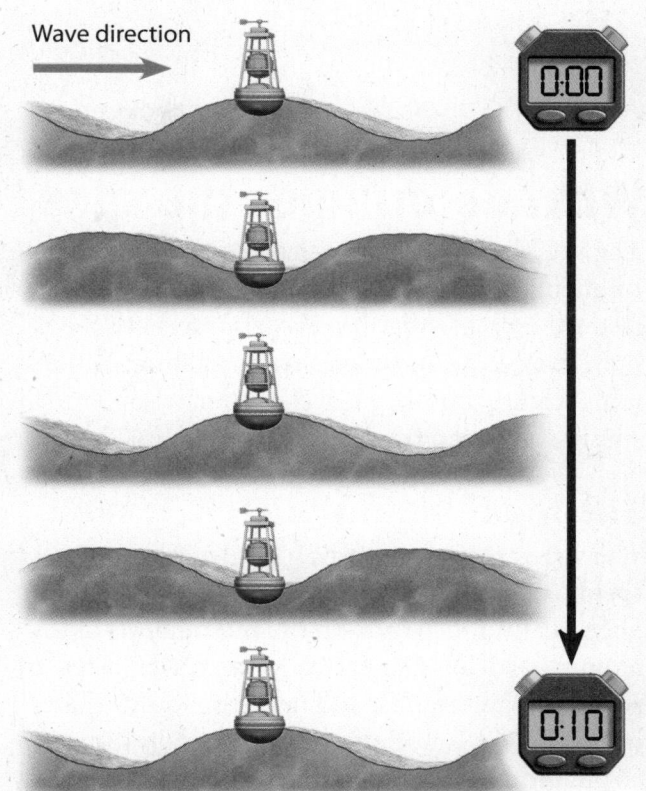

The buoy moves down and back up as waves pass every five seconds.

Visualize It!

16 Apply On the grid below, draw a wave that has twice the frequency as the wave shown.

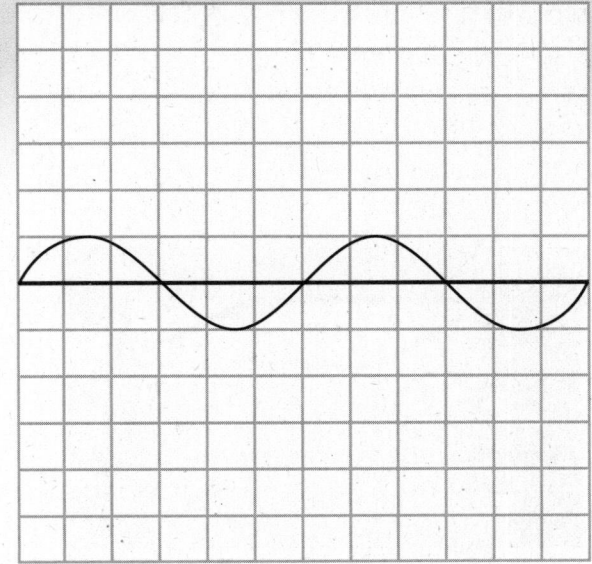

17 Apply On the grid below, draw a wave that has twice the amplitude as the wave shown.

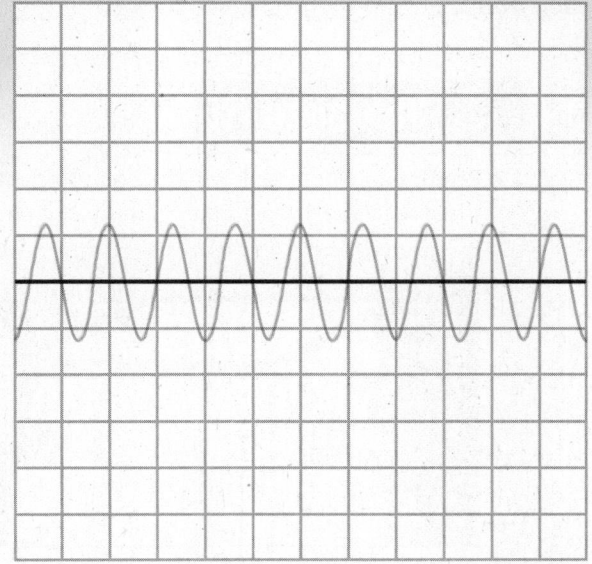

A Happy Medium

What determines the speed of a wave?

The speed of a wave is determined by its wavelength and frequency. For a given frequency, the longer the wavelength, the faster the speed. Waves travel at different speeds in different media. For example, sound waves travel at about 340 m/s in air at room temperature, but they travel at nearly 1,500 m/s in water. In a solid, sound waves can travel even faster.

The more flexible a medium is, the slower it transmits waves.

The Medium in Which It Travels

The speed that waves travel—called **wave speed**—depends on the properties of the medium. Specifically, it depends on the interactions of the atomic particles. Generally, waves travel faster in solids than in liquids, and faster in liquids than in gases. This is because solids generally have the strongest interactions between particles.

When you compare two materials in the same state, wave speed is also dependent on the density of the medium. Waves usually travel slower in the denser medium because the particles are more resistant to the motion that transfers waves. Water is more dense than oil. Sound travels slower through water than through oil. The state of matter has more effect on speed than does density. Sound travels faster through steel than through water even though steel is much denser.

As with solids and liquids, wave speed in a gas depends on density but also on temperature. Particles in hot air move faster than particles in cold air, so they collide more often with other particles. Therefore, waves pass through hot air more quickly than through cold air.

Electromagnetic waves don't require a medium, so they can travel in empty space. All electromagnetic waves travel at the same speed in empty space. This speed, called *the speed of light*, is about 300,000,000 m/s. While passing through a medium such as air or glass, EM waves move slightly slower than that.

Active Reading **18 Identify** Does sound travel faster or slower when the air gets warmer?

_____

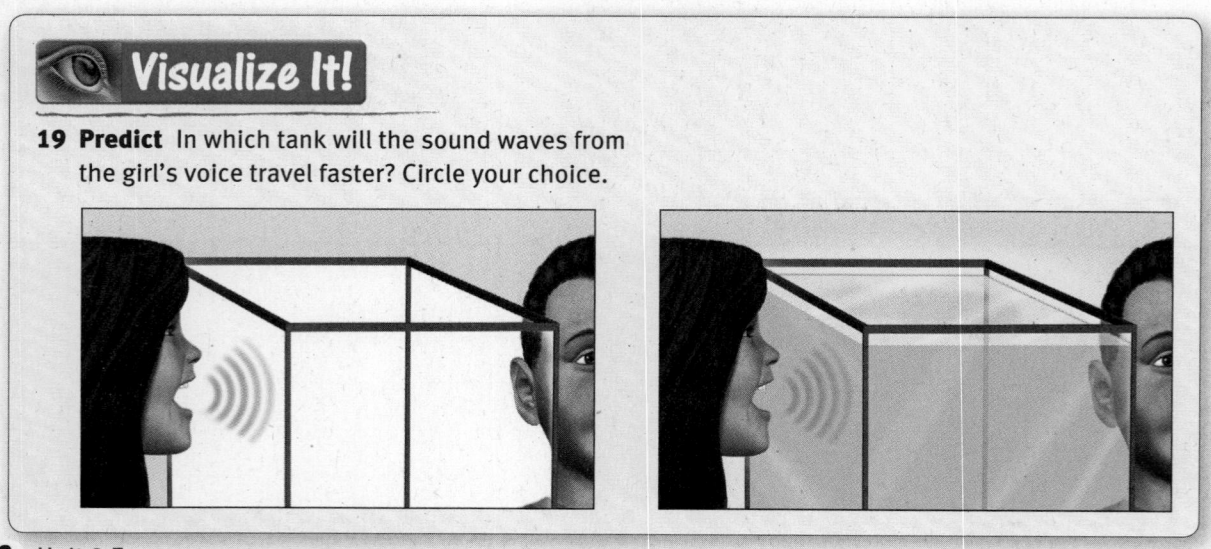

Visualize It!

19 Predict In which tank will the sound waves from the girl's voice travel faster? Circle your choice.

As a person bounces on a trampoline, he or she models a particle being moved by a wave.

Imagine if the tension on the trampoline were much lower: each bounce would take longer, because the person would sink much lower.

Its Frequency and Wavelength

Wave speed can be calculated from frequency and wavelength. To understand how, it helps to remember that speed is defined as distance divided by time.

$$speed = \frac{distance}{time}$$

So, if a runner runs 8 m in 2 s, then the runner's speed is 8 m ÷ 2 s = 4 m/s. In the case of waves, a wavelength is the distance the disturbance travels in one period, and the period is the time it takes for one wavelength to pass.

$$wave\ speed = \frac{wavelength}{wave\ period}$$

So, if a wave with a wavelength of 8 m takes 2 s to pass by, the wave speed is calculated just like the runner's speed: 8 m ÷ 2 s = 4 m/s. Finally, remember that frequency is the inverse of the wave period. So this relationship can be rewritten like this:

$$wave\ speed = frequency \times wavelength$$
$$or$$
$$wavelength = \frac{wave\ speed}{frequency}$$

If you already know the wave speed, you can use this equation to solve for frequency or wavelength.

 **Do the Math** You Try It

20 Calculate Elephants can communicate over great distances. They use sound with very low frequency (5 cycles per second). If the speed of sound at 20 °C is 340 m/s, how long is the wavelength of an elephant call at a frequency of 5 cycles per second?

Visual Summary

To complete this summary, fill in the blanks with the correct word or phrase. Then, use the key below to check your answers. You can use this page to review the main concepts of the lesson.

Waves and Energy

Waves are vibrations that carry energy through a medium.

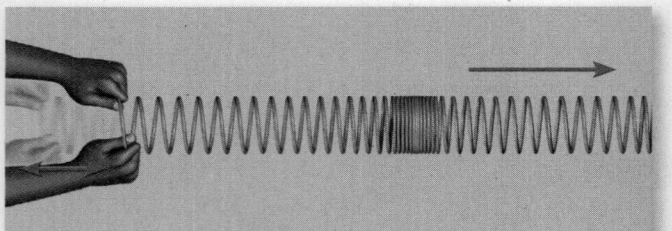

21 The diagram shows a _____ wave in which the energy moves parallel to direction in which the wave travels.

Wave speed depends on the properties of the medium.

22 wave speed = frequency × _____

A wave can be described by its amplitude, period, and frequency.

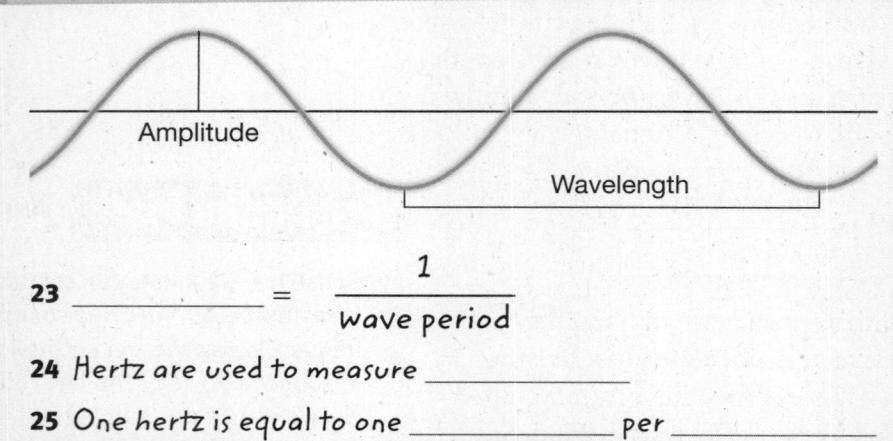

Amplitude

Wavelength

23 _____ = $\dfrac{1}{\text{wave period}}$

24 Hertz are used to measure _____

25 One hertz is equal to one _____ per _____

26 Support Use an example to support the following statement:
Waves transfer energy. Waves do not transfer matter.

Lesson Review

Vocabulary

Circle the term that best completes the following sentences.

1 A *medium/period* is the material through which a wave travels.

2 In a *longitudinal/transverse* wave, particles move at right angles to the direction the wave travels.

3 *Mechanical / Electromagnetic* waves require a medium in which to travel.

4 The amount of energy in a mechanical wave is related to its *frequency/amplitude*.

Key Concepts

Identify the medium for each type of wave for Questions 5–7.

Type of wave	Medium
ocean waves	**5 Identify**
earthquake waves	**6 Identify**
sound waves from a speaker	**7 Identify**

8 Describe How can you use a rope to produce transverse waves? Then describe how pieces of the rope move as waves pass.

_____

_____

_____

9 Contrast Mechanical waves travel as disturbances in a physical medium. How do electromagnetic waves travel?

_____

_____

_____

Critical Thinking

10 Relate Describe the relationship between wavelength, frequency, and the speed of a wave.

_____

_____

Use the diagram of ocean waves to answer Questions 11 and 12.

Frequency = 0.5 Hz

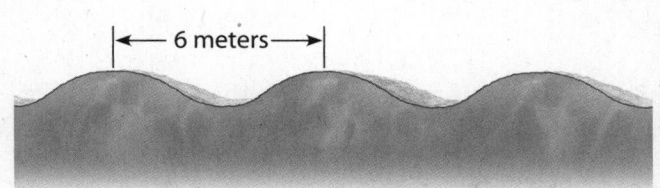

11 Analyze What is the wavelength of these waves? _____

12 Calculate If you were sitting in a boat as these waves passed by, how many seconds would pass between wave crests?

13 Infer Why does the speed of sound depend on air temperature?

_____

_____

My Notes

James West

RESEARCH SCIENTIST

James West's parents wanted him to be a medical doctor, but he wanted to study physics. His father was sure he'd never find a job that way. But Dr. West wanted to study what he loved. He did study physics, and he did find a job. He worked for Bell Laboratories and developed a microphone called the electret microphone. Today, Dr. West's microphone is in almost all telephones, cell phones, and other equipment that records sound.

Dr. West's interest in the microphone started with a question about hearing. A group of scientists wanted to know how close together two sounds could be before the ear would not be able to tell them apart. At the time, there was no earphone sensitive enough for their tests. Dr. West and fellow scientist Dr. Gerhard Sessler found that they could make a more sensitive microphone by using materials called *electrets*. Electrets are the electrical counterparts of permanent magnets. Some metals can become magnetic. Electrets can store electric charge. This eliminates the need for a battery. The new microphones were cheaper, more reliable, smaller, and lighter than any microphone before them.

Dr. West enjoys the thrill of discovery. He should know. To date, he holds more than 200 U.S. and foreign patents. In 1999 he was inducted into the National Inventors Hall of Fame. Dr. West retired from Bell Laboratories in 2001 and is now on the faculty at Johns Hopkins University. He has won many awards for his work, including both the Silver and Gold Medals from the Acoustical Society of America, the National Medal of Technology, and the Benjamin Franklin Medal in Electrical Engineering.

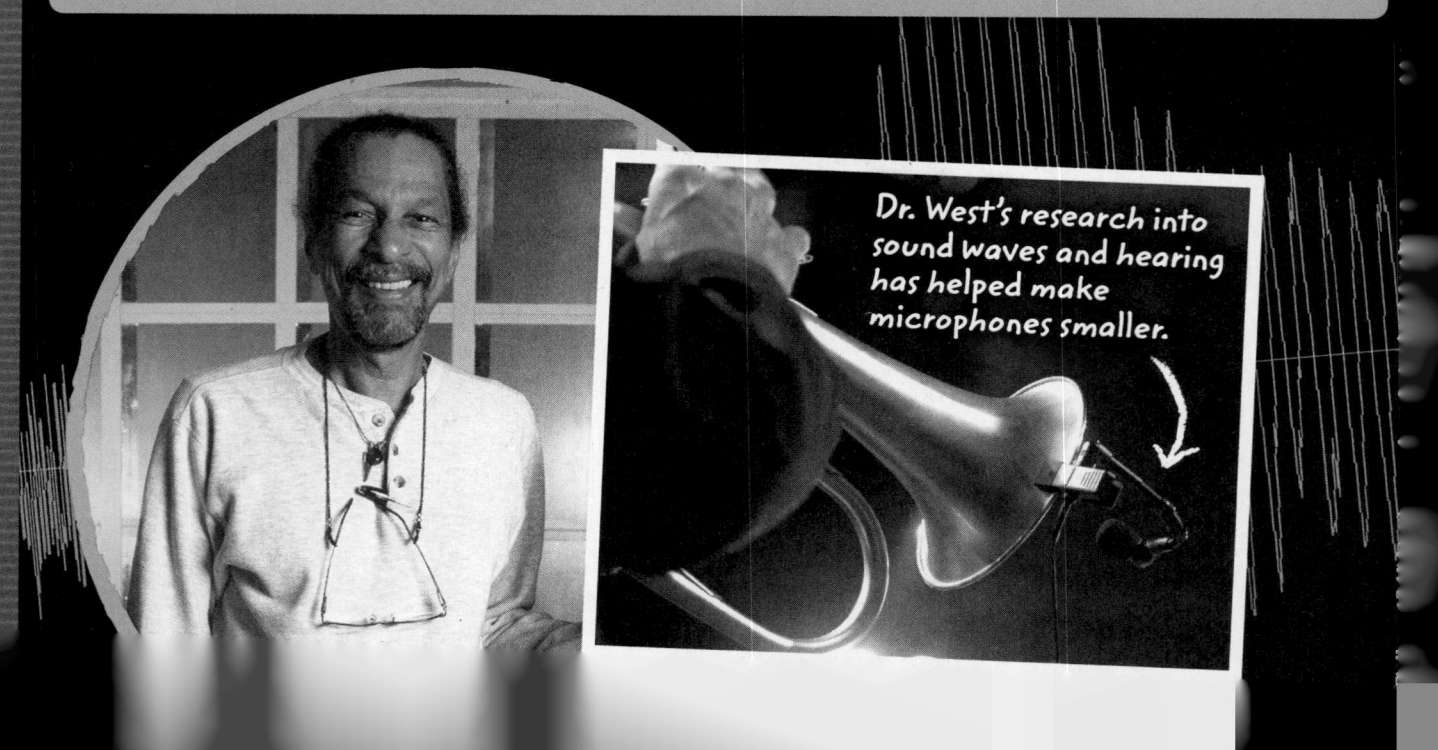

Dr. West's research into sound waves and hearing has helped make microphones smaller.

JOB BOARD

Dispensing Optician

What You'll Do: Help select and then fit eyeglasses and contact lenses.

Where You Might Work: Medical offices, or optical, department, or club stores

Education: Most training is on the job or through apprenticeships that last two years or longer. Some employers prefer graduates of postsecondary training programs in opticianry.

Other Job Requirements: A good eye for fashion, face shape, and color is a plus, as opticians help people find glasses they like.

Lighting Designer

What You'll Do: Work in theater, television, or film to make what happens on stage or on set visible to audiences. Lighting designers also use lighting and shadow to create the right tone or mood.

Where You Might Work: Theaters, television and film studios and sets, concerts and other special events

Education: A diploma or certificate in lighting design or technical stage management from a college or performing arts institute

Other Job Requirements: Experience lighting stage productions, the ability to work in a team

---

PEOPLE IN SCIENCE NEWS

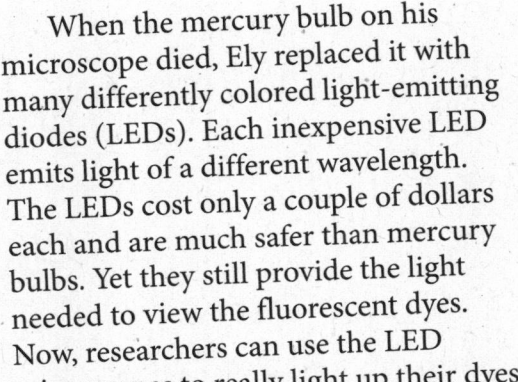

ELY Stone

A New Light on Microscopy

Doctors and medical researchers use fluorescent microscopes to see colored or fluorescent dyes in medical research. These microscopes use expensive and dangerous mercury light bulbs to illuminate the dyes. But Ely Stone, a retired computer programmer and inventor in Florida, found a less expensive source of light.

When the mercury bulb on his microscope died, Ely replaced it with many differently colored light-emitting diodes (LEDs). Each inexpensive LED emits light of a different wavelength. The LEDs cost only a couple of dollars each and are much safer than mercury bulbs. Yet they still provide the light needed to view the fluorescent dyes. Now, researchers can use the LED microscopes to really light up their dyes!

Electric Current

ESSENTIAL QUESTION

What flows through an electric wire?

By the end of this lesson, you should be able to describe how electric charges flow as electric current.

Electric current sent over wires from power plants supplies this city with energy for lights and other uses.

OHIO **7.PS.3** Energy can be transferred through a variety of ways.

Lesson Labs

Quick Labs
• Investigate Electric Current
• Lemon Battery

S.T.E.M. Lab
• Voltage, Current, and Resistance

Engage Your Brain

1 Identify Unscramble the letters below to find terms related to electric current. Write your words on the blank lines.

SGARCHE _____

EGATOVL _____

EERPAM _____

EIRW _____

2 Describe Describe what makes this electric sign light up when it is in use.

_____
_____
_____
_____

Active Reading

3 Apply Many scientific words such as *resistance* also have everyday meanings. Use context clues to write your own definition for the word *resistance*.

Example sentence
John's request to go to the movies met with <u>resistance</u> from his friends.

resistance:

_____

_____

Example sentence
The composition of a wire determines its electrical <u>resistance</u>.

resistance:

_____
_____
_____

Vocabulary Terms

• electric current • resistance
• voltage

4 Identify As you read, place a question mark next to any words that you do not understand. When you finish reading the lesson, go back and review the text that you marked. If the information is still confusing, consult a classmate or a teacher.

Current Events

What is an electric current?

When you watch TV, use a computer, or even turn on a light bulb, you depend on moving charges to provide the electrical energy that powers them. *Electrical energy* is the energy of electric charges. In most devices that use electrical energy, the electric charges flow through wires. The rate of flow of electric charges is called **electric current**.

How is electric current measured?

To understand an electric current, think of people entering the seating area for a sporting event through turnstiles. A counter in each turnstile records the number of people who enter. The number of people who pass through a turnstile each minute describes the rate of flow of people into the stadium. Similarly, an electric current describes the rate of flow of charges, such as the slow flow of many electrons through a wire. Electric current is the amount of charge that passes a location in the wire every second. Electric current is expressed in units called *amperes* (AM•pirz), which is often shortened to "amps." The symbol for ampere is A. A wire with a current of 2 A has twice as much charge passing by each second as a wire with a current of 1 A.

© Houghton Mifflin Harcourt Publishing Company • Image Credits: ©Elsa/Staff/Getty Images Sport/Getty Images

What are two kinds of current?

Two kinds of electric current are *direct current* (DC) and *alternating current* (AC). Both kinds of current carry electrical energy. They differ in the way that the charges move.

Direct Current (DC)

In direct current, charges always flow in the same direction. The electric current generated by batteries is DC. Some everyday devices that use DC from batteries are flashlights, cars, and cameras.

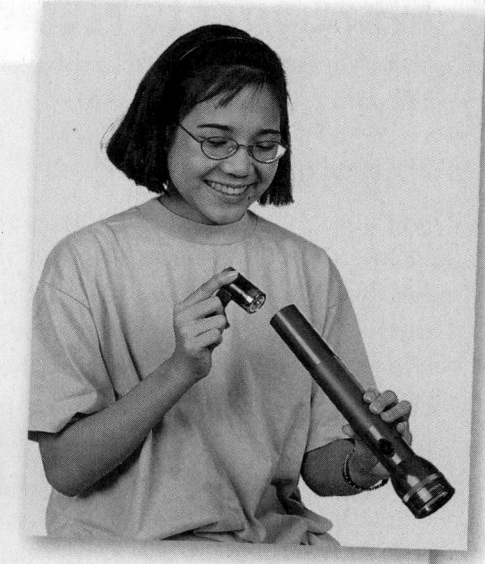

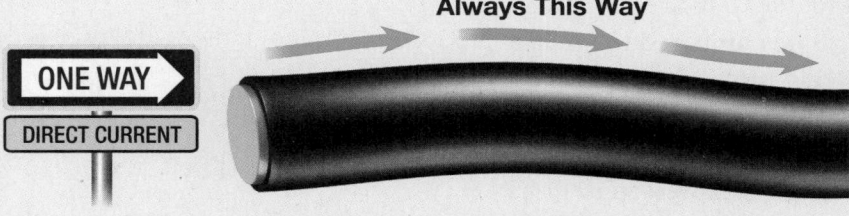

Always This Way

ONE WAY ▶
DIRECT CURRENT

Charges move in one direction in DC.

Alternating Current (AC)

In alternating current, charges repeatedly shift from flowing in one direction to flowing in the reverse direction. The current *alternates* direction. The electric current from outlets in your home is AC. So, most household appliances run on alternating current. In the United States, the alternating current reverses direction and then returns back to the original direction 60 times each second.

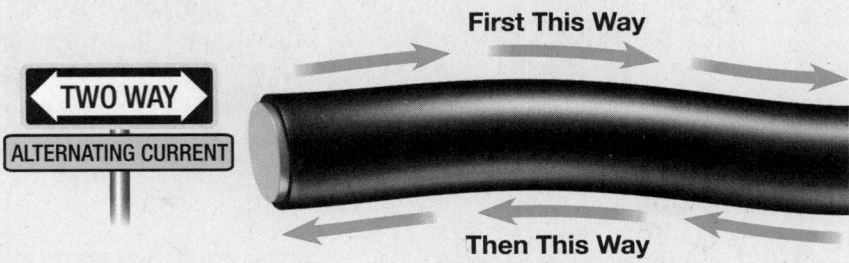

First This Way

◀ TWO WAY ▶
ALTERNATING CURRENT

Then This Way

Charges repeatedly change direction in AC.

 **Active Reading**

7 Explain What alternates in alternating current?

_____

_____

You've Got *Potential*

What affects electric current?

Two factors that can affect the current in a wire are *voltage* and *resistance*.

Voltage

Compare the two drink containers below. If you pour lemonade from a full container, your glass fills quickly. If the container is nearly empty, the flow of lemonade is weaker. The lemonade in the full container exerts more pressure due to its weight, causing a higher rate of flow. This pressure can be compared to voltage. **Voltage** is the amount of work required to move each unit of charge between two points. Just as higher pressure produces a higher rate of flow of lemonade, higher voltage produces a higher rate of flow of electric charges in a given wire. Voltage is expressed in units of volts (V). Voltage is sometimes called *electric potential* because it is a measure of the electric potential energy per unit charge.

Visualize It!

8 Analyze How does the flow of the lemonade coming out of these containers relate to current and voltage?

_____

_____

_____

_____

_____

_____

Resistance

Think about the difference between walking around your room and walking around in waist-deep water. The water resists your movement more than the air, so you have to work harder to walk through water. If you walked in waist-deep mud, you would have to work even harder. Similarly, some materials do not allow electric charges to move freely. The opposition to the flow of electric charge is called **resistance**. Resistance is expressed in ohms (Ω, the Greek letter *omega*). Higher resistance at the same voltage results in lower current.

Think Outside the Book Inquiry

9 Apply In a small group, create a skit that illustrates the idea of electrical resistance. Be sure to compare high resistance and low resistance.

What affects electrical resistance?

A material's composition affects its resistance. Some metals, such as silver and copper, have low resistance and are very good electrical conductors. Other metals, such as iron and nickel, have a higher resistance. Electrical insulators such as plastic have such a high resistance that electric charges cannot flow in them at all. Other factors that affect the resistance of a wire are thickness, length, and temperature.

- A thin wire has higher resistance than a thicker wire.
- A long wire has higher resistance than a shorter wire.
- A hot wire has higher resistance than a cooler wire.

Conductors with low resistance, such as copper, are used to make wires. But conductors with high resistance are also useful. For example, an alloy of nickel and chromium is used in heating coils. Its high resistance causes the wire to heat up when it carries electric current.

Like lemonade in a drinking straw, electric charges move more easily through a short, wide pathway than through a long, narrow one.

Visualize It!

10 Predict For each pair of images, place a check mark in the box that shows the material that has higher electrical resistance.

Composition Wires made from different materials have different uses in electronic devices.	Pure copper	Nickel and chromium alloy
Thickness A three-way light bulb contains a thin filament and a thick filament. Charges move through one filament or the other or both to produce different brightness levels.	Thin filament	Thick filament
Temperature The electrical resistance of this heating element changes as its temperature increases.		

Visual Summary

To complete this summary, fill in the blanks with the correct word or phrase. Then use the key below to check your answers. You can use this page to review the main concepts of the lesson.

Electric current is the rate of flow of electric charges.

First This Way

Then This Way

11 In _____ current, the flow of charge changes direction and then reverses back to the original direction.

The opposition to the flow of electric charges is called resistance.

13 Four factors that determine the resistance of a wire are

_____

_____

_____

Voltage is the amount of work to move an electric charge between two points.

12 If the voltage applied to a given wire increases, its current will

_____

Electric Current

14 Apply What might happen if a wire in an electronic device is replaced with a thinner, longer wire? Explain.

Lesson Review

Vocabulary

Draw a line to connect the following terms to their definitions.

1 electric current

2 voltage

3 resistance

A the opposition to the flow of electric charges

B the rate of flow of electric charges

C the amount of work required to move each unit of electric charge between two points

Key Concepts

4 Compare How does direct current differ from alternating current?

_____

_____

_____

_____

_____

5 Summarize Describe how resistance affects electric current.

_____

_____

_____

_____

_____

6 Apply What happens to the electric current in a wire as voltage is increased?

_____

_____

_____

7 Apply List two everyday devices that use DC and two everyday devices that use AC.

_____

_____

_____

Critical Thinking

Use the diagram to answer the following questions.

Electrical Resistance of Various Materials

Copper   Germanium   PVC Plastic

Low resistance → High resistance

8 Analyze Which material is likely to slow the flow of electric charges the most? Explain.

_____

_____

_____

9 Infer A certain voltage is applied to a copper wire and to a germanium wire of the same thickness and length. How will the current in the two wires compare?

_____

_____

_____

_____

_____

_____

10 Compare How do the currents produced by a 1.5 V flashlight battery and a 12 V car battery compare if the resistance is the same?

_____

_____

_____

_____

11 Infer What does it mean to say that the electric current from a wall socket is "120 V AC?"

_____

_____

_____

_____

My Notes

OHIO **7.SIA.3** Use appropriate mathematics, tools and techniques to gather data and information.

OHIO **7.SIA.4** Analyze and interpret data.

Mean, Median, Mode, and Range

You can analyze both the measures of central tendency and the variability of data using mean, median, mode, and range.

Tutorial

Imagine that a group of students records the light levels at various places within a classroom.

Classroom Light Levels	
Area	**Illuminance (lux)**
1	800
2	300
3	150
4	300
5	200

Mean The mean is the sum of all of the values in a data set divided by the total number of values in the data set. The mean is also called the *average*.	$$\frac{800 + 300 + 150 + 300 + 200}{5}$$ **mean** = 350 lux
Median The median is the value of the middle item when data are arranged in order by size. In a range that has an odd number of values, the median is the middle value. In a range that has an even number of values, the median is the average of the two middle values.	If necessary, reorder the values from least to greatest: 150, 200, **300**, 300, 800 ⟶ ⟵ **median** = 300 lux
Mode The mode is the value or values that occur most frequently in a data set. If all values occur with the same frequency, the data set is said to have no mode. Values should be put in order to find the mode.	If necessary, reorder the values from least to greatest: 150, 200, 300, 300, 800 The value 300 occurs most frequently. **mode** = 300 lux
Range The range is the difference between the greatest value and the least value of a data set.	800 − 150 **range** = 650 lux

You Try It!

The data table below shows the data collected for rooms in three halls in the school.

Illuminance (lux)				
	Room 1	**Room 2**	**Room 3**	**Room 4**
Science Hall	150	250	500	400
Art Hall	300	275	550	350
Math Hall	200	225	600	600

Using Formulas Find the mean, median, mode, and range of the data for the school.

Analyzing Methods The school board is looking into complaints that some areas of the school are too poorly lit. They are considering replacing the lights. If you were in favor of replacing the lights, which representative value for the school's data would you use to support your position? If you were opposed to replacing the lights, which representative value for the school's data would you choose to support your position? Explain your answer.

_____

_____

_____

_____

_____

_____

_____

_____

_____

_____

_____

Language Arts Connection

On flashcards, write sentences that use the keywords *mean, median, mode,* and *range.* Cover the keywords with small sticky notes. Review each sentence, and determine if it provides enough context clues to determine the covered word. If necessary, work with a partner to improve your sentences.

Lesson 6

Electric Circuits

ESSENTIAL QUESTION

How do electric circuits work?

By the end of this lesson, you should be able to describe basic electric circuits and how to use electricity safely.

Microscopic electric circuits inside these computer chips carry electric charges that can power computers, video games, and home appliances.

OHIO 7.PS.3 Energy can be transferred through a variety of ways.

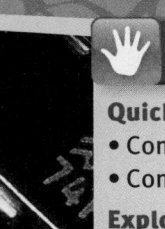 **Lesson Labs**

Engage Your Brain

1 Predict Check T or F to show whether you think each statement is true or false.

T	F	
☐	☐	A circuit must form a closed loop to have an electric current.
☐	☐	Electricity is dangerous only when it is labeled as high voltage.
☐	☐	Every electric circuit must have an energy source.

2 Describe Write a caption explaining how these light bulbs are connected.

_____

_____

_____

_____

Active Reading

3 Apply Many scientific words, such as *current*, also have everyday meanings. Use context clues to write your own definition for each meaning of the word *current*.

Example sentence
The magazine covered <u>current</u> events.

current:

_____

_____

Example sentence
The circuit had an electric <u>current</u> in it.

current:

_____

_____

Vocabulary Terms
- electric circuit
- series circuit
- parallel circuit

4 Apply As you learn the definition of each vocabulary term in this lesson, create your own definition or sketch to help you remember the meaning of the term.

A Complete Circuit

What are the parts of an electric circuit?

Think about a running track. It forms a loop. The spot where you start running around the track is the same as the spot where you end. This kind of closed loop is called a circuit. Like a track, an electric circuit also forms a loop. An **electric circuit** is a complete, closed path through which electric charges can flow. All electric circuits contain three basic parts: an energy source, an electrical conductor, and a load.

Energy Source

The energy source converts some type of energy, such as chemical energy, into electrical energy. One common household energy source is a battery. A battery changes chemical energy stored inside the battery into electrical energy. A solar cell is an energy source that changes light energy into electrical energy.

Inside a power plant, a form of energy such as chemical or nuclear energy is changed into mechanical energy. Electric generators in the power plant change the mechanical energy into electrical energy. Power transmission lines deliver this energy to wall outlets in homes, schools, and other buildings.

Active Reading

5 Identify As you read this page and the next, underline examples of energy sources, electrical conductors, and electrical loads used in an electric circuit.

Solar cell

Battery

Think Outside the Book Inquiry

6 Research Learn how your local power plant uses turbines and generators to produce electrical energy. Then write a short article about how the power plant generates the mechanical energy for the turbines.

Power plant

Electrical Conductor

Materials in which electric charges can move easily are called *electrical conductors*. Most metals are good conductors of electric current. Electric wires are often made of copper. Copper is a metal that is a good conductor and is inexpensive compared to many other metals. Conducting wires connect all the parts of an electric circuit.

To protect people from harmful electrical shocks, copper wire is often covered with an insulator. An *electrical insulator* is a material, such as glass, plastic, or rubber, through which electric charges cannot move easily.

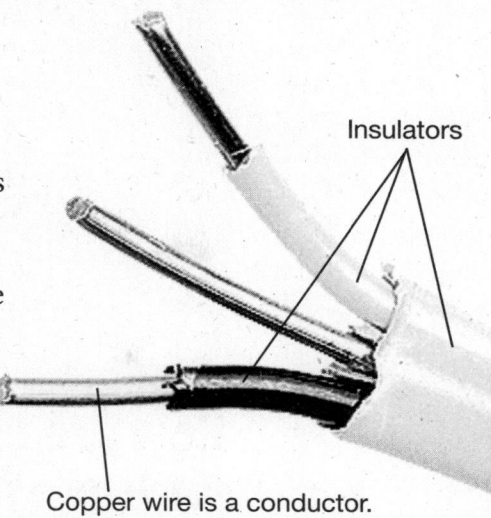

Insulators

Copper wire is a conductor.

Load

A complete circuit also includes a *load*, a device that uses electrical energy to operate. The conductor connects the energy source to the load. Examples of loads include light bulbs, radios, computers, and electric motors. The load converts electrical energy into other forms of energy. A light bulb, for example, converts electrical energy into light and energy as heat. A doorbell produces sound waves, energy that is transmitted through the air to your ear. A cell phone converts electrical energy into electromagnetic waves that carry information.

Visualize It!

7 Identify List the devices in the photograph that could be a load in an electric circuit.

_____

_____

_____

_____

_____

_____

_____

Around and Around

How are electric circuits modeled?

Active Reading

8 Identify As you read, underline the descriptions of symbols used in circuit diagrams.

To make an electric circuit, you need only three basic parts: an energy source, an electrical conductor, and a load. Most electric circuits, however, have more than one load. A circuit in your home might connect a desk lamp, clock radio, computer, and TV set. The circuit may even include devices in more than one room. Circuits can be complex. A single computer chip can have many millions of parts. One tool that can be used to model electric circuits is a circuit diagram.

Circuit Diagram Symbols

Wire

Load

Energy Source

Open switch

Closed switch

With Circuit Diagrams

A circuit diagram helps engineers and electricians design and install electric circuits so that they function correctly and safely. Sometimes, special software is used to create complex circuit designs on computers. A diagram for an electric circuit shows all the parts in the complete circuit and the relationships among the different parts. The chart at the left shows how each part of a circuit can be represented in a circuit diagram. The energy source can be represented by two parallel lines of different length. A wire or other conductor is shown as a line. A load is represented by a zigzag line segment. A small circle shows where two wires are connected. A straight line between two circles shows an on-off switch. When the line of the switch symbol is slanted up, the switch is open. When the line for the switch symbol connects two dots, the switch is closed.

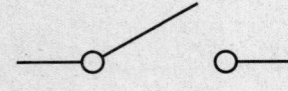

Symbols are put together to show the arrangement of parts in a circuit. A circuit diagram is like a road map for the moving charges.

How does current stop and start?

Electric charges move continuously in the closed loop of an electric circuit. What do you do if you want the charges to stop flowing? You open the switch! A switch is a device that turns electrical devices on and off. A switch is usually made of a piece of conducting material that can move. When the switch is open, the circuit is open. That means it does not form a closed loop, so charges cannot flow. When you turn a light switch on, the switch closes the circuit. Charges flow through the light bulb. If you turn a light switch off, the switch opens the circuit, and the charges stop flowing.

9 Explain Why does an open light switch turn off the light?

_____
_____
_____
_____

Visualize It!

10 Identify Label the parts in this circuit diagram. Then draw a switch to match the circuit shown in the photograph.

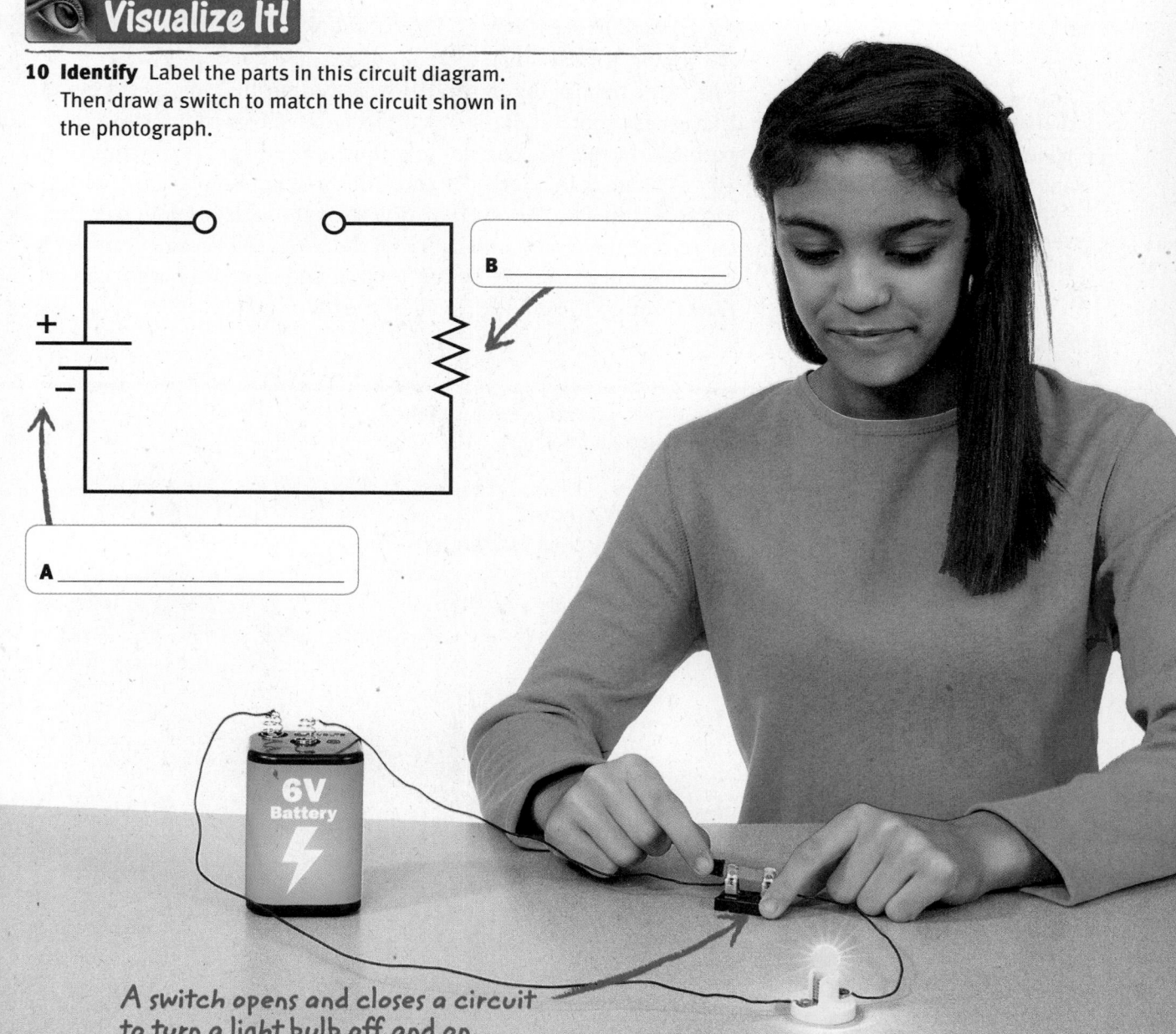

B _____

A _____

A switch opens and closes a circuit to turn a light bulb off and on.

All Together?

How do series circuits and parallel circuits differ?

Most electric circuits have more than one load. Simple electric circuits that contain one energy source and more than one load are classified as either a series circuit or a parallel circuit.

In Series Circuits, Charges Follow a Single Path

The three light bulbs shown below are connected in a series circuit. In a **series circuit**, all parts are connected in a row that forms one path for the electric charges to follow. The current is the same for all of the loads in a series circuit. All three light bulbs glow with the same brightness. However, adding a fourth bulb would lower the current in the circuit and cause all the bulbs to become dimmer. If one bulb burns out, the circuit is open and electric charges cannot flow through the circuit. So all of the bulbs go out.

Visualize It!

12 Apply In these two circuit illustrations, draw an *X* over the bulbs that would not glow if the bulb closest to the battery burned out.

Series circuit with battery and switch

The bulbs are connected to one another in a single loop.

In Parallel Circuits, Charges Follow Multiple Paths

Think about what would happen if all of the lights in your home were connected in series. If you needed to turn on a light in your room, all other lights in the house would have to be turned on, too! Instead of being wired in series, circuits in buildings are wired in parallel. In a **parallel circuit**, electric charges have more than one path that they can follow. Loads in a parallel circuit are connected side by side. In the parallel circuit shown below, any bulb can burn out without opening the circuit.

Unlike the loads in a series circuit, the loads in a parallel circuit can have different currents. However, each load in a parallel circuit experiences the same voltage. For example, if three bulbs were hooked up to a 12-volt battery, each would have the full voltage of the battery. Each light bulb would glow at the same brightness no matter how many more bulbs were added to the circuit.

13 Compare In the table below, list the features of series and parallel circuits.

Series circuits	Parallel circuits

Parallel circuit
with battery and switch

The bulbs are connected side by side.

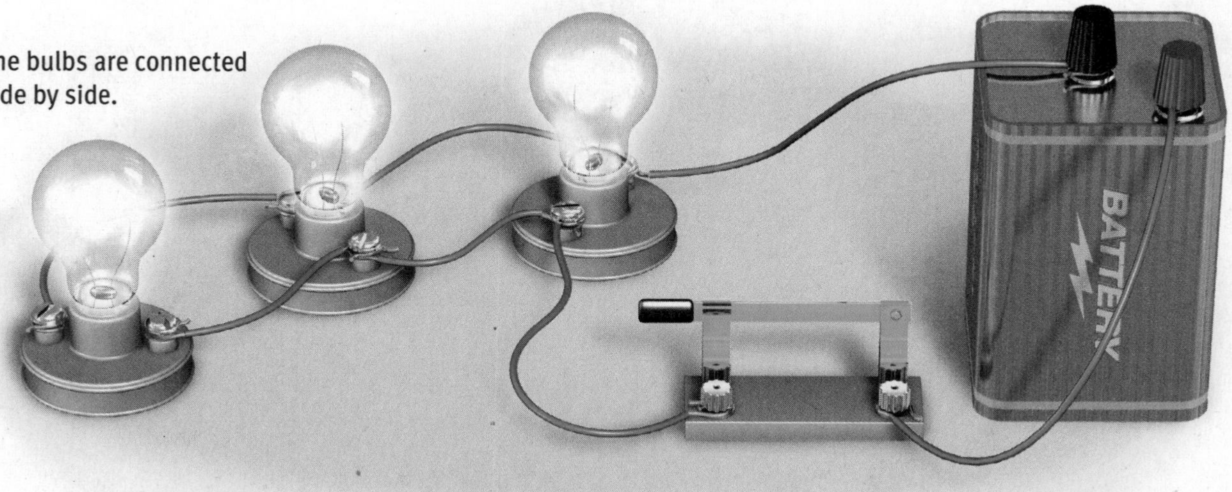

Safety First!

How can I use electricity safely?

You use many electrical devices every day. It is important to remember that electrical energy can be hazardous if it is not used correctly. Electric circuits in buildings have built-in safeguards to keep people safe. You can stay safe if you are careful to avoid electrical dangers and pay attention to warning signs and labels.

By Avoiding Exposure to Current

Pure water is a poor conductor of electric current. But water usually has substances such as salt dissolved in it. These substances make water a better conductor. This is especially true of fluids inside your body. The water in your body is a good conductor of electric current. This is why you should avoid exposure to current. Even small currents can cause severe burns, shock, and even death. A current can prevent you from breathing and stop your heart.

Following basic safety precautions will protect you from exposure to electric current. Never use electrical devices around water. Do not use any appliance if its power cord is worn or damaged. Always pay attention to warning signs near places with high-voltage transmission lines. You do not actually have to touch some high-voltage wires to receive a deadly shock. Even coming near high-voltage wires can do serious harm to your body.

A damaged cord exposes the metal wires that conduct electric charges.

Stay away from places where there is high-voltage electrical equipment.

DANGER
High Voltage
Trespassers may be electrocuted

By Using Electrical Safety Devices

Damage to wires can cause a "short circuit," in which charges do not pass through all the loads. When this happens, current increases and wires can get hot enough to start a fire.

Fuses, circuit breakers, and ground fault circuit interrupters (GFCIs) are safety devices that act like switches. When the current is too high in a fuse, a metal strip that is part of the circuit heats up and melts. Circuit breakers are switches that open when the current reaches a certain level. A GFCI is a type of circuit breaker. GFCIs are often built into outlets that are used near water, such as in a kitchen or bathroom.

Active Reading **15 Identify** Name three safety devices that you might find in electric circuits at home.

_____

_____

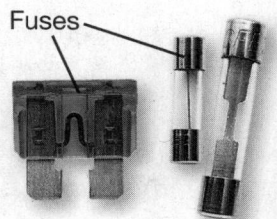

Fuses

When the current is too high in the fuse, the metal strip melts and opens the circuit.

Ground fault circuit interrupter (GFCI)

The lightning rod attached to the top of this building helps to protect it from a lightning strike.

By Taking Precautions during a Lightning Storm

When lightning strikes, electric charges can travel between a cloud and the ground. Lightning often strikes objects that are taller than their surroundings, such as skyscrapers, trees, barns, or even a person in an open field. During a thunderstorm, be sure to stay away from trees and other tall objects. The best place to seek shelter during a thunderstorm is indoors.

Many buildings have lightning rods. These are metal rods at the highest part of the building. The rod is connected to the ground by a thick conducting wire. The rod and wire protect the building by _grounding_ it, or providing a path that allows charges to flow into the ground.

16 Infer What would happen if there were no electrical path from the top of the building to the ground?

_____

_____

_____

Visual Summary

To complete this summary, fill in the blanks with the correct word or phrase. Then, use the key below to check your answers. You can use this page to review the main concepts of the lesson.

Electric Circuits

Circuits can be connected in series or in parallel.

19 When one of several bulbs in a series circuit burns out, the other bulbs _____

20 When one of several bulbs in a parallel circuit burns out, the other bulbs _____

An electric circuit has three basic parts: an energy source, an electric conductor, and a load.

17 Batteries are an example of an _____ in an electric circuit.

18 To open and close a circuit, a _____ can be used.

Taking precautions when using electricity and during a lightning storm can keep you safe from electrical dangers.

21 This outlet contains a GFCI, which acts as a _____ to protect people from short circuits.

22 Synthesize Compare the function of a switch in an electric circuit to the function of a water faucet. How are they alike and how are they different?

Lesson Review

Vocabulary

Draw a line to connect the following terms to their definitions.

1 series circuit

2 parallel circuit

A a circuit with two or more paths for charges

B a circuit with a single path for charges

Key Concepts

3 Explain Why is an energy source needed in order to have a working electric circuit?

_____

_____

_____

_____

4 Compare Describe the difference between a closed circuit and an open circuit.

_____

_____

_____

_____

5 Apply Why does removing one bulb from a string of lights in a series circuit cause all the lights to go out?

_____

_____

_____

_____

6 Describe How does a lightning rod protect a building from lightning damage?

_____

_____

_____

_____

Critical Thinking

Use this drawing to answer the following questions.

Energy source

7 Identify Circuits can be either series or parallel. What type of circuit is shown above?

_____

_____

8 Infer Imagine that a circuit breaker opened the circuit every time that you operated the light, coffee maker, and microwave at the same time. What could be causing this?

_____

_____

_____

_____

9 Predict What electrical safety device could be used in this kitchen to decrease risk of electric shock? Explain.

_____

_____

_____

_____

_____

_____

My Notes

Unit 8 — Big Idea — Energy is always conserved but can change forms and can be transferred.

Lesson 1
ESSENTIAL QUESTION
How can energy be transformed and transferred?

Analyze how energy is conserved through transformations and transfer.

Lesson 2
ESSENTIAL QUESTION
How can mechanical energy be transferred?

Describe how mechanical energy can be transferred when objects push or pull on each other over a distance.

Lesson 3
ESSENTIAL QUESTION
What is the relationship between heat and temperature?

Analyze the relationship between heat, temperature, and thermal energy.

Lesson 4
ESSENTIAL QUESTION
How do waves transfer energy?

Distinguish between different types of waves, and describe the amplitude, wavelength, frequency, and speed of a wave.

Lesson 5
ESSENTIAL QUESTION
What flows through an electric wire?

Describe how electric charges flow as electric current.

Lesson 6
ESSENTIAL QUESTION
How do electric circuits work?

Describe basic electric circuits and how to use electricity safely.

Connect ESSENTIAL QUESTIONS
Lessons 1 and 3

1 Synthesize Give an example of energy conservation involving thermal energy.

_____

_____

_____

_____

Think Outside the Book

2 Synthesize Choose one of these activities to help synthesize what you have learned in this unit.

☐ Using what you learned in lessons 1, 5, and 6, make a poster presentation showing how electrical energy is safely transferred from a power station to a lamp. Include captions and labels.

☐ Using what you learned in lessons 2 and 4, write a story about a mechanical wave traveling through different media. Include energy transfers that may occur along the way.

Unit 8 Review

Name _____

Vocabulary

Fill in each blank with the term that best completes the following sentences.

1 _____ is the energy transferred from an object at a higher temperature to an object at a lower temperature.

2 The amount of work required to move a unit electric charge between two points is called _____.

3 A(n) _____ is an electric circuit in which all the parts are connected in a single loop.

4 The transfer of energy to an object by using a force that causes the object to move in the direction of the force is _____.

5 The total amount of energy an object has because of its motion, its position, and its shape is _____.

Key Concepts

Choose the letter of the best answer.

6 The graph below shows the speeds of three waves in air and water.

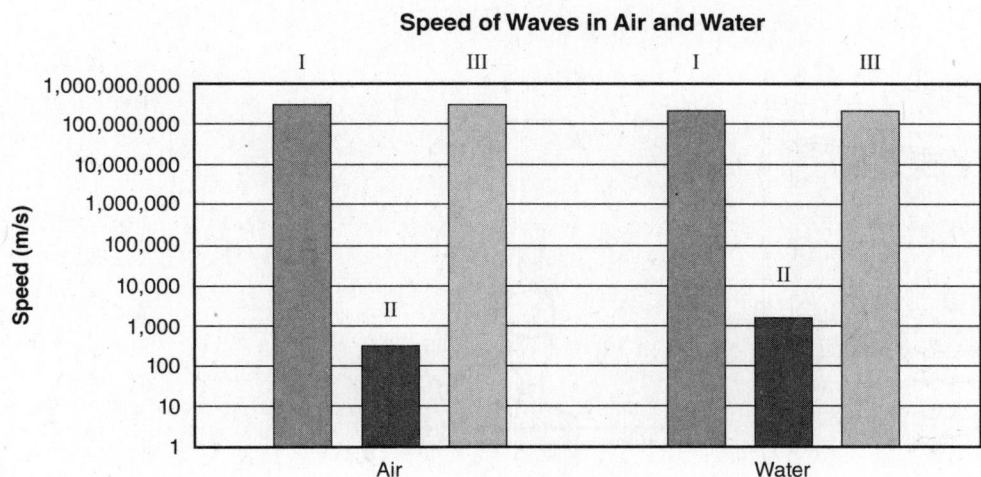

Speed of Waves in Air and Water

Which wave or waves are electromagnetic waves?

A II only

B I, II, and III

C I and II only

D I and III only

7 Which of the following is the transfer of energy as heat by the movement of a liquid or gas?

A radiation

C convection

B emission

D conduction

8 Which of the following wires has the lowest resistance?

A a short, thick copper wire at 25 °C

B a long, thick copper wire at 35 °C

C a long, thin copper wire at 35 °C

D a short, thin iron wire at 25 °C

9 There are many devices in the home that use electricity. Below is a diagram of four common electrical devices.

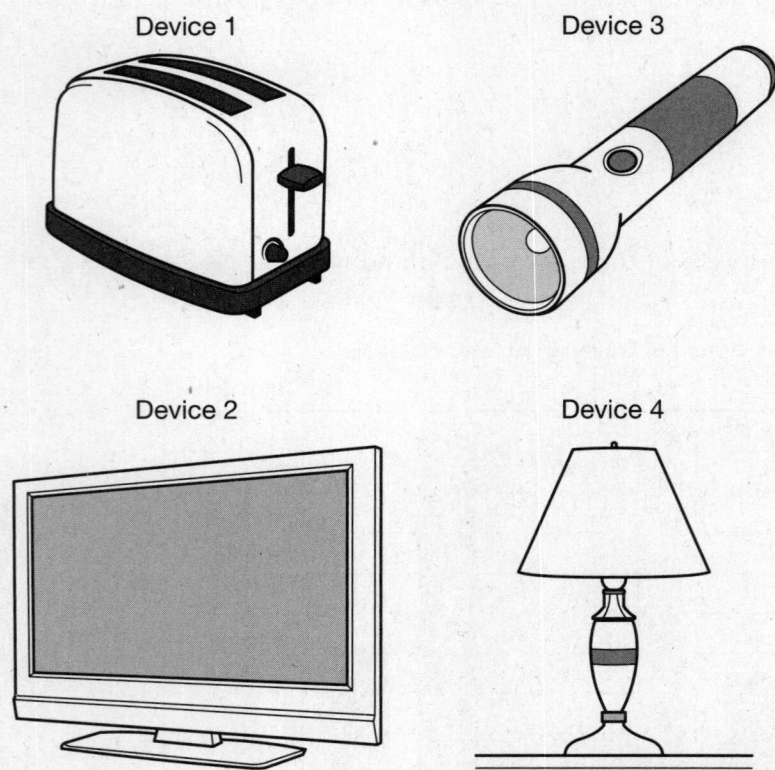

Device 1

Device 3

Device 2

Device 4

Which electrical device runs on direct current?

A Device 1

C Device 3

B Device 2

D Device 4

10 The diagram below shows two examples of electrical circuits.

Circuit 1

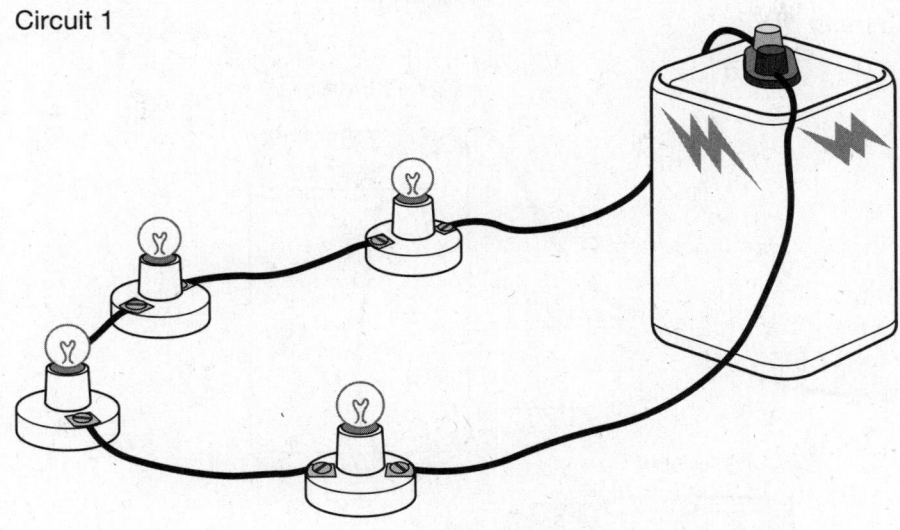

Circuit 2

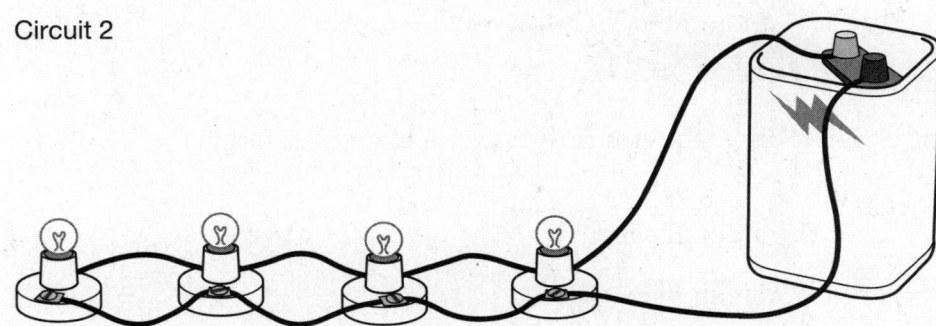

Which of the following statements about the circuits is correct?

A Circuit 1 is a parallel circuit, and Circuit 2 is a parallel circuit.

B Circuit 1 is a series circuit, and Circuit 2 is a parallel circuit.

C Circuit 1 is a parallel circuit, and Circuit 2 is a series circuit.

D Circuit 1 is a series circuit, and Circuit 2 is a series circuit.

11 It is important to practice electrical safety. Which of the following choices is unsafe?

A only using electrical cords that have proper insulation

B seeking shelter on a beach or under a tree during a lightning storm

C keeping electrical appliances away from sinks and bathtubs

D using ground fault circuit interrupters (GFCIs) in the home

12 Here is a diagram of a simple electric circuit. There are four elements to the
circuit. They are labeled Circuit Element 1, Circuit Element 2, Circuit
Element 3, and Circuit Element 4.

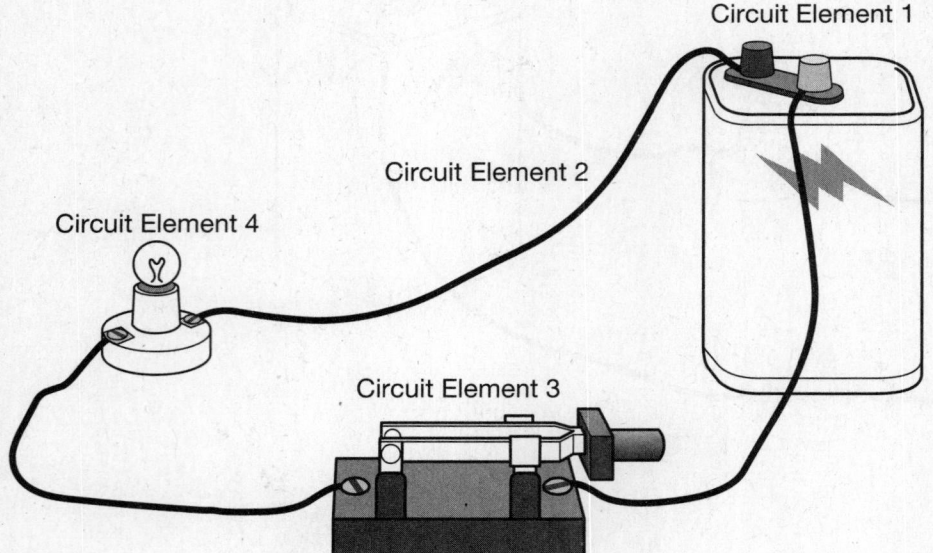

Circuit Element 1

Circuit Element 2

Circuit Element 4

Circuit Element 3

What part of an electric circuit changes the electrical energy into another form
of energy?

A Circuit Element 1   **C** Circuit Element 3

B Circuit Element 2   **D** Circuit Element 4

13 A scientist places a block of hot metal in a jar of cool water, and the jar is then
sealed shut. Because energy is conserved, what must happen?

A The sum of the thermal energy of the water and the thermal energy of the
metal will increase.

B The thermal energy of the water and the thermal energy of the metal will
remain the same.

C Some of the metal's thermal energy is transferred to the water as heat, but a
small amount changes to mass.

D The thermal energy of the water will increase by the same amount that the
thermal energy of the metal decreases.

14 When mechanical energy is not conserved, which form of energy might be
responsible for the apparent loss of energy?

A kinetic energy   **C** elastic potential energy

B sound energy   **D** gravitational potential energy

15 Which statement best shows that waves carry energy?

A Sounds can be recorded.

B A rainbow shows a spectrum of colors.

C You feel vibrations if loud sounds are played.

D Light shining through some trees makes shadows.

16 In which situation would you be doing work on the box?

A You hold a box and carry it across the room.

B You push a box, but it does not move.

C You pull a box that slides toward you.

D You hold a box while you stand still.

Critical Thinking

Answer the following questions in the spaces provided.

17 An athlete does work to lift a heavy ball to the top of a hill. He says, "I did work against a gravitational field to move a heavy ball from one location to another." He claims that this situation is an analogy for a concept related to electricity. For which electrical concept is this an analogy?

_____

_____

How could you rewrite his statement so that it accurately defines this electrical concept?

_____

_____

_____

18 An ice cube sits in an open container of water placed outside on a sunny day.

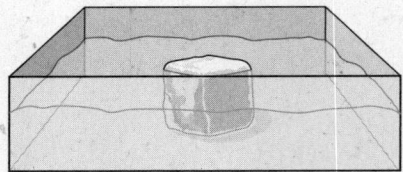

The warmer water contacting the ice cube transfers energy to the ice cube through what process? Use the setup shown in the diagram to give two examples of how adding energy as heat to a system may result in a change of state.

_____

_____

Connect ESSENTIAL QUESTIONS
Lessons 1 and 3

Answer the following question in the space provided.

19 A student wants to test heat transfer in different materials. She places four spoons in a bowl of hot water, as shown below.

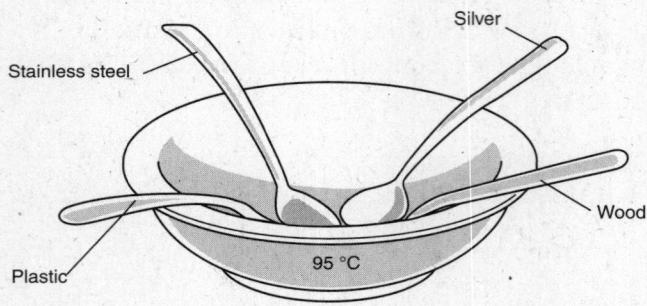

Identify and describe the type of heat transfer that occurs between the hot water and the spoons.

_____

After the spoons have been in the water for a couple of minutes, what will the student most likely observe about the temperature of each spoon?

_____

_____

Classify each of the materials that the student is testing as a conductor or an insulator.

_____

_____

Look It Up!

References

Mineral Properties

Here are five steps to take in mineral identification:

1 Determine the color of the mineral. Is it light-colored, dark-colored, or a specific color?

2 Determine the luster of the mineral. Is it metallic or nonmetallic?

3 Determine the color of any powder left by its streak.

4 Determine the hardness of your mineral. Is it soft, hard, or very hard? Using a glass plate, see if the mineral scratches it.

5 Determine whether your sample has cleavage or any special properties.

TERMS TO KNOW	DEFINITION
adamantine	a nonmetallic luster like that of a diamond
cleavage	how a mineral breaks when subject to stress on a particular plane
luster	the state or quality of shining by reflecting light
streak	the color of a mineral when it is powdered
submetallic	between metallic and nonmetallic in luster
vitreous	glass-like type of luster

Silicate Minerals

Mineral	Color	Luster	Streak	Hardness	Cleavage and Special Properties
Beryl	deep green, pink, white, bluish green, or yellow	vitreous	white	7.5–8	1 cleavage direction; some varieties fluoresce in ultraviolet light
Chlorite	green	vitreous to pearly	pale green	2–2.5	1 cleavage direction
Garnet	green, red, brown, black	vitreous	white	6.5–7.5	no cleavage
Hornblende	dark green, brown, or black	vitreous	none	5–6	2 cleavage directions
Muscovite	colorless, silvery white, or brown	vitreous or pearly	white	2–2.5	1 cleavage direction
Olivine	olive green, yellow	vitreous	white or none	6.5–7	no cleavage
Orthoclase	colorless, white, pink, or other colors	vitreous	white or none	6	2 cleavage directions
Plagioclase	colorless, white, yellow, pink, green	vitreous	white	6	2 cleavage directions
Quartz	colorless or white; any color when not pure	vitreous or waxy	white or none	7	no cleavage

Nonsilicate Minerals					
Mineral	**Color**	**Luster**	**Streak**	**Hardness**	**Cleavage and Special Properties**
Native Elements					
Copper	copper-red	metallic	copper-red	2.5–3	no cleavage
Diamond	pale yellow or colorless	adamantine	none	10	4 cleavage directions
Graphite	black to gray	submetallic	black	1–2	1 cleavage direction
Carbonates					
Aragonite	colorless, white, or pale yellow	vitreous	white	3.5–4	2 cleavage directions; reacts with hydrochloric acid
Calcite	colorless or white to tan	vitreous	white	3	3 cleavage directions; reacts with weak acid; double refraction
Halides					
Fluorite	light green, yellow, purple, bluish green, or other colors	vitreous	none	4	4 cleavage directions; some varieties fluoresce
Halite	white	vitreous	white	2.0–2.5	3 cleavage directions
Oxides					
Hematite	reddish brown to black	metallic to earthy	dark red to red-brown	5.6–6.5	no cleavage; magnetic when heated
Magnetite	iron-black	metallic	black	5.5–6.5	no cleavage; magnetic
Sulfates					
Anhydrite	colorless, bluish, or violet	vitreous to pearly	white	3–3.5	3 cleavage directions
Gypsum	white, pink, gray, or colorless	vitreous, pearly, or silky	white	2.0	3 cleavage directions
Sulfides					
Galena	lead-gray	metallic	lead-gray to black	2.5–2.8	3 cleavage directions
Pyrite	brassy yellow	metallic	greenish, brownish, or black	6–6.5	no cleavage

References

Geologic Time Scale

Geologists developed the geologic time scale to represent the 4.6 billion years of Earth's history that have passed since Earth formed. This scale divides Earth's history into blocks of time. The boundaries between these time intervals (shown in millions of years ago, or mya, in the table below), represent major changes in Earth's history. Some boundaries are defined by mass extinctions, major changes in Earth's surface, and/or major changes in Earth's climate.

The four major divisions that encompass the history of life on Earth are Precambrian time, the Paleozoic era, the Mesozoic era, and the Cenozoic era. The largest divisions are eons. **Precambrian time** is made up of the first three eons, over 4 billion years of Earth's history.

The **Paleozoic era** lasted from 542 mya to 251 mya. All major plant groups, except flowering plants, appeared during this era. By the end of the era, reptiles, winged insects, and fishes had also appeared. The largest known mass extinction occurred at the end of this era.

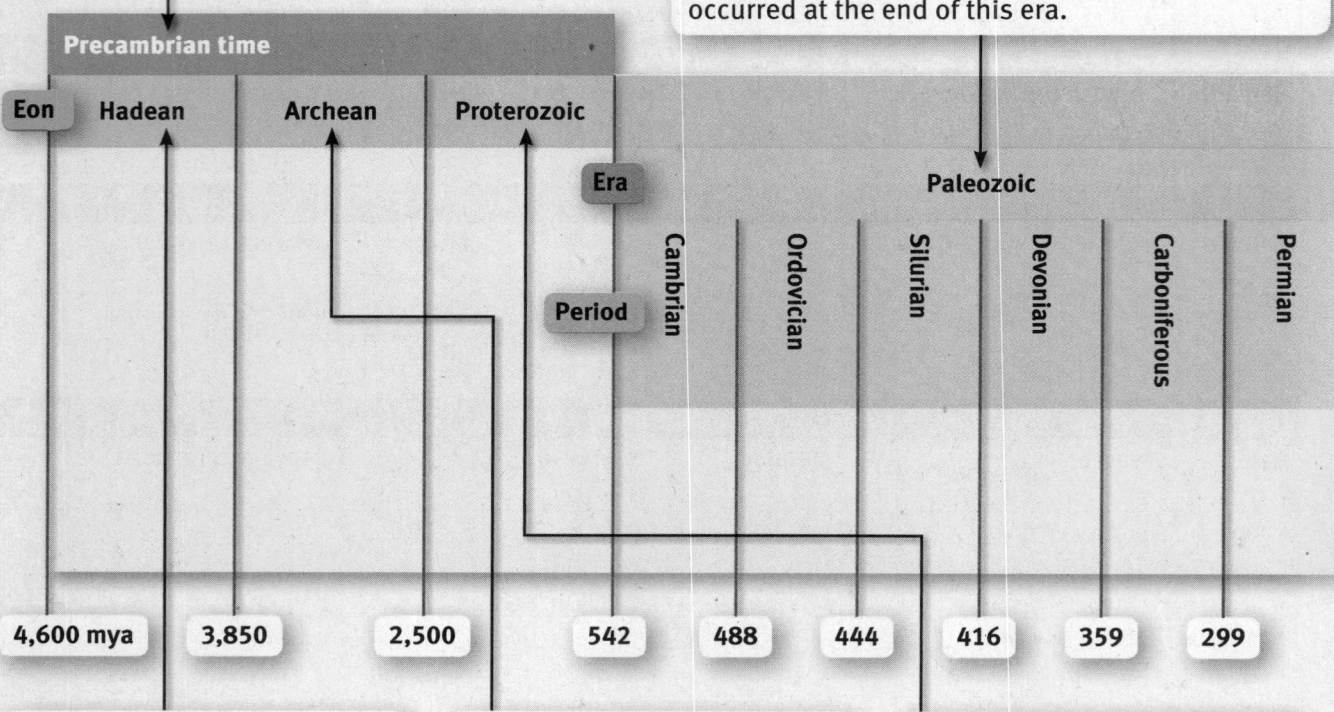

The **Hadean eon** lasted from about 4.6 billion years ago (bya) to 3.85 bya. It is described based on evidence from meteorites and rocks from the moon.

The **Archean eon** lasted from 3.85 bya to 2.5 bya. The earliest rocks from Earth that have been found and dated formed at the start of this eon.

The **Proterozoic eon** lasted from 2.5 bya to 542 mya. The first organisms, which were single-celled organisms, appeared during this eon. These organisms produced so much oxygen that they changed Earth's oceans and Earth's atmosphere.

Divisions of Time

The divisions of time shown here represent major changes in Earth's surface and when life developed and changed significantly on Earth. As new evidence is found, the boundaries of these divisions may shift. The Phanerozoic eon is divided into three eras. The beginning of each of these eras represents a change in the types of organisms that dominated Earth. And each era is commonly characterized by the types of organisms that dominated the era. These eras are divided into periods, and periods are divided into epochs.

The **Mesozoic era** lasted from 251 mya to 65.5 mya. During this era, many kinds of dinosaurs dominated land, and giant lizards swam in the ocean. The first birds, mammals, and flowering plants also appeared during this time. About two-thirds of all land species went extinct at the end of this era.

The **Phanerozoic eon** began 542 mya. We live in this eon.

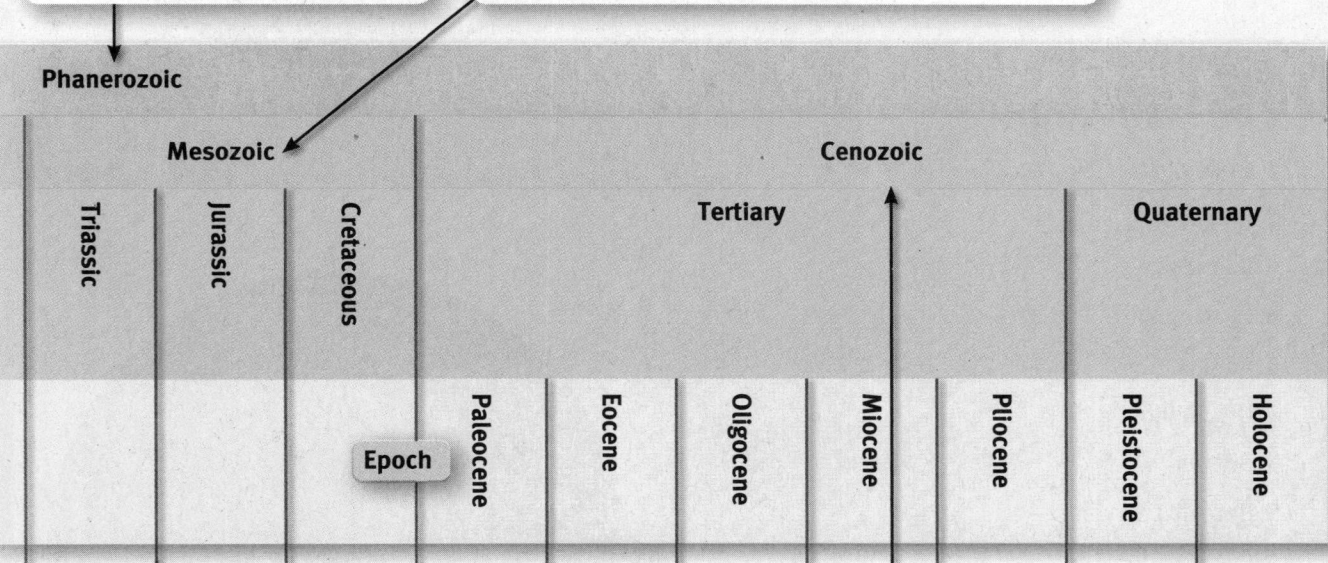

The **Cenozoic era** began 65.5 mya and continues today. Mammals dominate this era. During the Mesozoic era, mammals were small in size but grew much larger during the Cenozoic era. Primates, including humans, appeared during this era.

Star Charts for the Northern Hemisphere

A star chart is a map of the stars in the night sky. It shows the names and positions of constellations and major stars. Star charts can be used to identify constellations and even to orient yourself using Polaris, the North Star.

Because Earth moves through space, different constellations are visible at different times of the year. The star charts on these pages show the constellations visible during each season in the Northern Hemisphere.

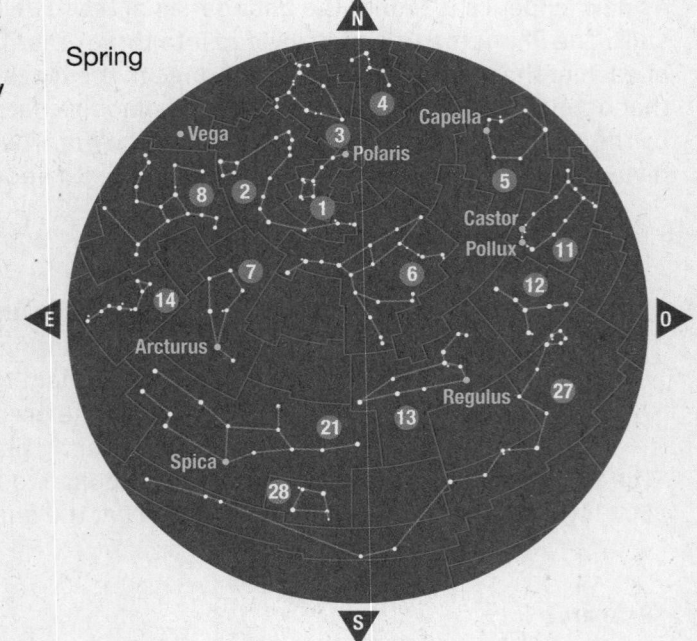

Spring

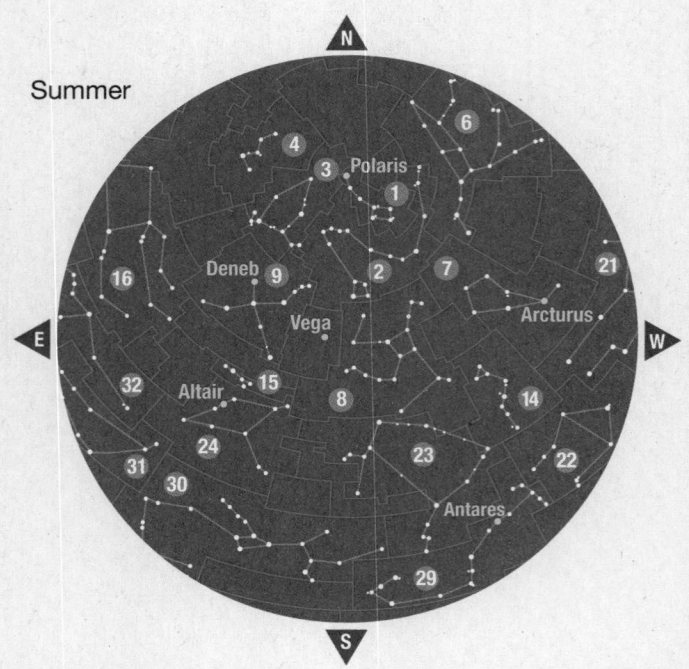

Summer

Constellations

1 Ursa Minor

2 Draco

3 Cepheus

4 Cassiopeia

5 Auriga

6 Ursa Major

7 Boötes

8 Hercules

9 Cygnus

10 Perseus

11 Gemini

12 Cancer

13 Leo

14 Serpens

15 Sagitta

16 Pegasus

17 Pisces

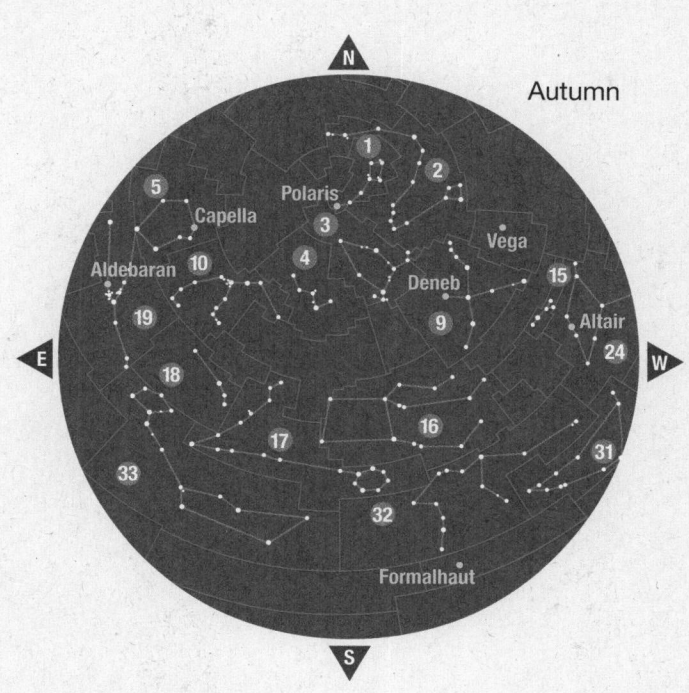

Autumn

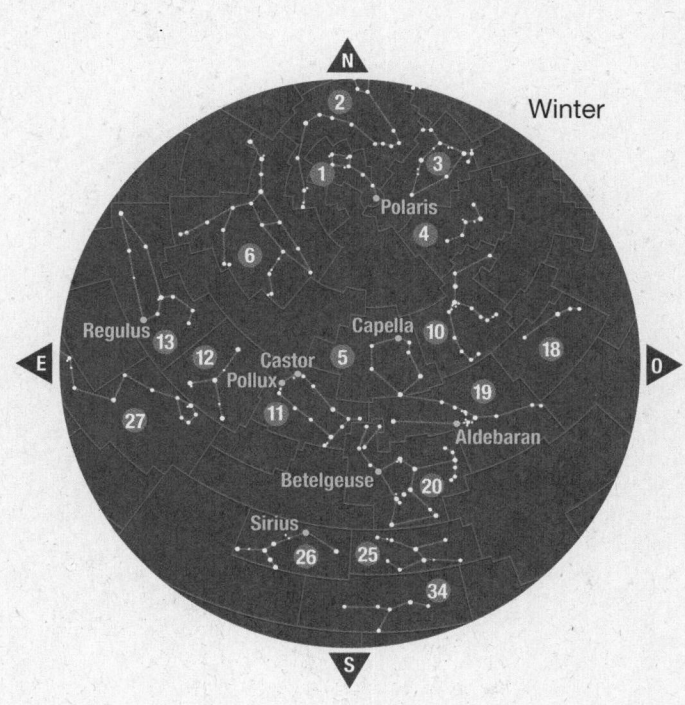

Winter

Constellations

18 Aries

19 Taurus

20 Orion

21 Virgo

22 Libra

23 Ophiuchus

24 Aquila

25 Lepus

26 Canis Major

27 Hydra

28 Corvus

29 Scorpius

30 Sagittarius

31 Capricornus

32 Aquarius

33 Cetus

34 Columba

World Map

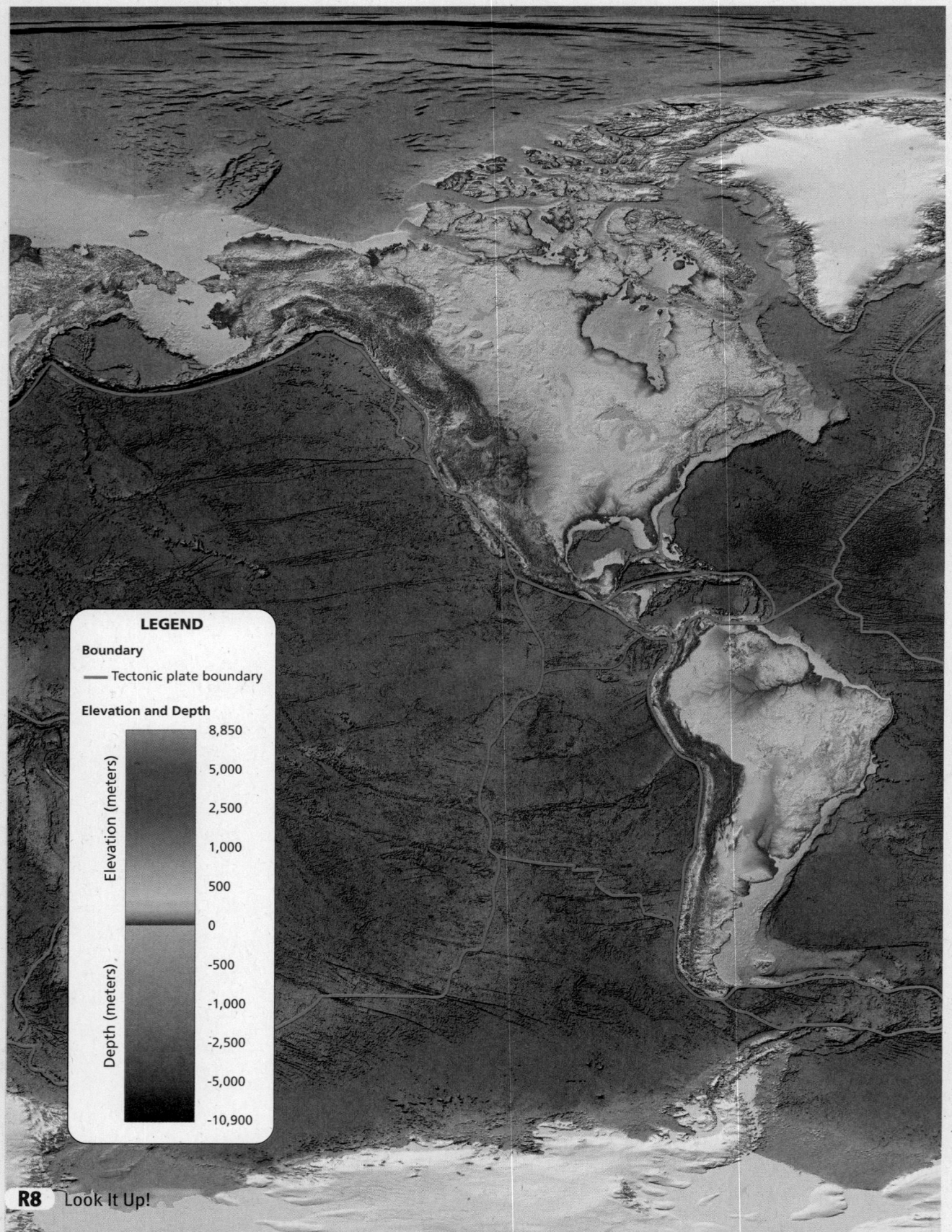

LEGEND

Boundary

—— Tectonic plate boundary

Elevation and Depth

Elevation (meters)
- 8,850
- 5,000
- 2,500
- 1,000
- 500
- 0

Depth (meters)
- -500
- -1,000
- -2,500
- -5,000
- -10,900

Classification of Living Things

Domains and Kingdoms

All organisms belong to one of three domains: Domain Archaea, Domain Bacteria, or Domain Eukarya. Some of the groups within these domains are shown below. (Remember that genus names are italicized.)

Domain Archaea

The organisms in this domain are single-celled prokaryotes, many of which live in extreme environments.

Archaea		
Group	**Example**	**Characteristics**
Methanogens	*Methanococcus*	produce methane gas; can't live in oxygen
Thermophiles	*Sulfolobus*	require sulfur; can't live in oxygen
Halophiles	*Halococcus*	live in very salty environments; most can live in oxygen

Domain Bacteria

Organisms in this domain are single-celled prokaryotes and are found in almost every environment on Earth.

Bacteria		
Group	**Example**	**Characteristics**
Bacilli	*Escherichia*	rod shaped; some bacilli fix nitrogen; some cause disease
Cocci	*Streptococcus*	spherical shaped; some cause disease; can form spores
Spirilla	*Treponema*	spiral shaped; cause diseases such as syphilis and Lyme disease

Domain Eukarya

Organisms in this domain are single-celled or multicellular eukaryotes.

Kingdom Protista Many protists resemble fungi, plants, or animals but are smaller and simpler in structure. Most are single celled.

Protists		
Group	**Example**	**Characteristics**
Sarcodines	*Amoeba*	radiolarians; single-celled consumers
Ciliates	*Paramecium*	single-celled consumers
Flagellates	*Trypanosoma*	single-celled parasites
Sporozoans	*Plasmodium*	single-celled parasites
Euglenas	*Euglena*	single celled; photosynthesize
Diatoms	*Pinnularia*	most are single celled; photosynthesize
Dinoflagellates	*Gymnodinium*	single celled; some photosynthesize
Algae	*Volvox*	single celled or multicellular; photosynthesize
Slime molds	*Physarum*	single celled or multicellular; consumers or decomposers
Water molds	powdery mildew	single celled or multicellular; parasites or decomposers

Kingdom Fungi Most fungi are multicellular. Their cells have thick cell walls. Fungi absorb food from their environment.

Fungi		
Group	**Examples**	**Characteristics**
Zygote fungi	bread mold	spherical zygote produces spores; decomposers
Sac fungi	yeast; morels	saclike spore structure; parasites and decomposers
Club fungi	mushrooms; rusts; smuts	club-shaped spore structure; parasites and decomposers
Lichens	British soldier	a partnership between a fungus and an alga

Kingdom Plantae Plants are multicellular and have cell walls made of cellulose. Plants make their own food through photosynthesis. Plants are classified into divisions instead of phyla.

Plants		
Group	**Examples**	**Characteristics**
Bryophytes	mosses; liverworts	no vascular tissue; reproduce by spores
Club mosses	*Lycopodium;* ground pine	grow in wooded areas; reproduce by spores
Horsetails	rushes	grow in wetland areas; reproduce by spores
Ferns	spleenworts; sensitive fern	large leaves called fronds; reproduce by spores
Conifers	pines; spruces; firs	needlelike leaves; reproduce by seeds made in cones
Cycads	*Zamia*	slow growing; reproduce by seeds made in large cones
Gnetophytes	*Welwitschia*	only three living families; reproduce by seeds
Ginkgoes	*Ginkgo*	only one living species; reproduce by seeds
Angiosperms	all flowering plants	reproduce by seeds made in flowers; fruit

Kingdom Animalia Animals are multicellular. Their cells do not have cell walls. Most animals have specialized tissues and complex organ systems. Animals get food by eating other organisms.

Animals		
Group	**Examples**	**Characteristics**
Sponges	glass sponges	no symmetry or specialized tissues; aquatic
Cnidarians	jellyfish; coral	radial symmetry; aquatic
Flatworms	planaria; tapeworms; flukes	bilateral symmetry; organ systems
Roundworms	*Trichina;* hookworms	bilateral symmetry; organ systems
Annelids	earthworms; leeches	bilateral symmetry; organ systems
Mollusks	snails; octopuses	bilateral symmetry; organ systems
Echinoderms	sea stars; sand dollars	radial symmetry; organ systems
Arthropods	insects; spiders; lobsters	bilateral symmetry; organ systems
Chordates	fish; amphibians; reptiles; birds; mammals	bilateral symmetry; complex organ systems

References

Periodic Table of the Elements

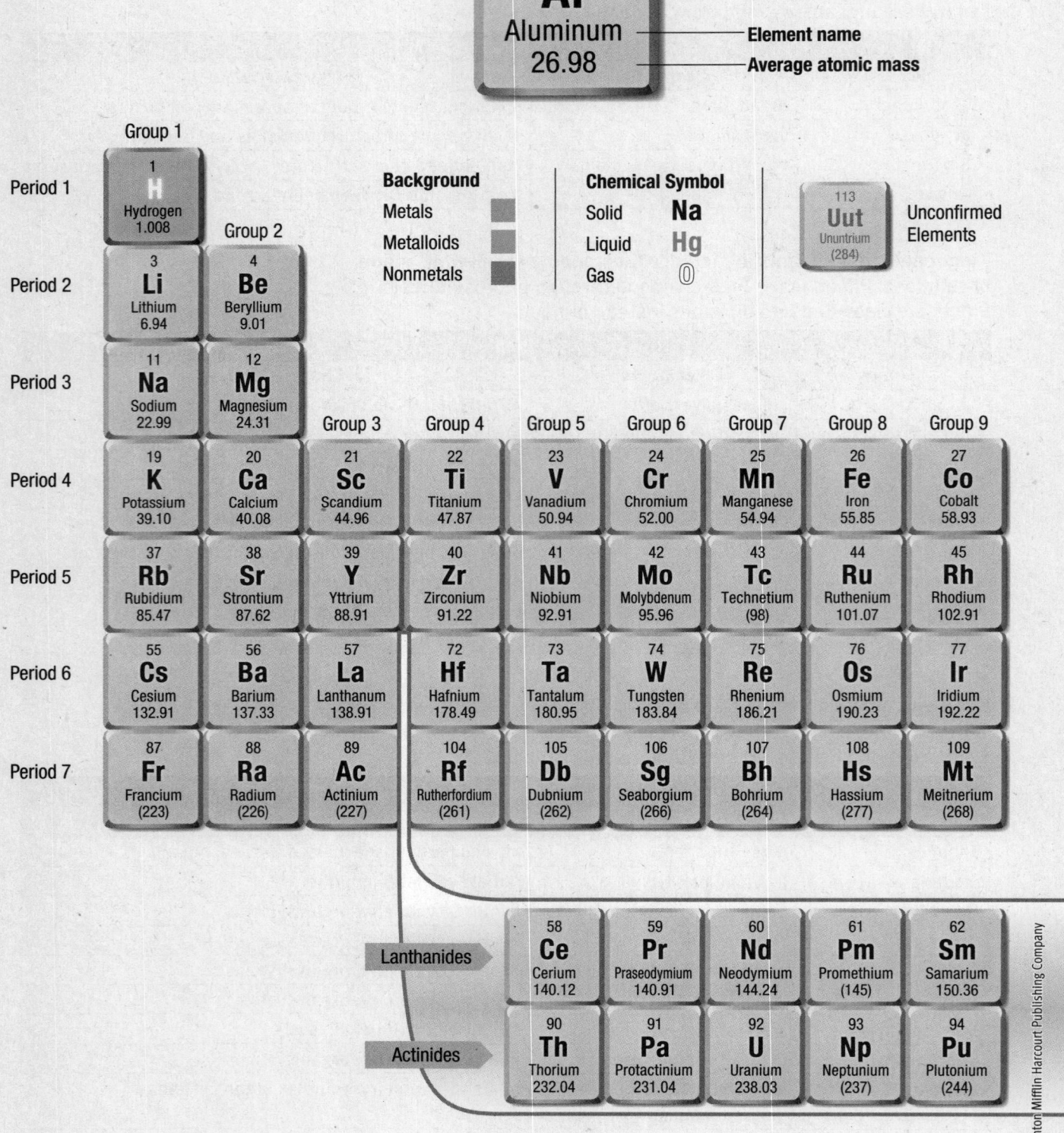

Sample element box:

13
Al
Aluminum
26.98

- Atomic number
- Chemical symbol
- Element name
- Average atomic mass

Background
- Metals
- Metalloids
- Nonmetals

Chemical Symbol
- Solid   **Na**
- Liquid   **Hg**
- Gas   Ⓞ

113
Uut
Ununtrium
(284)
Unconfirmed Elements

Group 1

| Period 1 | 1 **H** Hydrogen 1.008 |

Group 2

| Period 2 | 3 **Li** Lithium 6.94 | 4 **Be** Beryllium 9.01 |
| Period 3 | 11 **Na** Sodium 22.99 | 12 **Mg** Magnesium 24.31 |

			Group 3	Group 4	Group 5	Group 6	Group 7	Group 8	Group 9
Period 4	19 **K** Potassium 39.10	20 **Ca** Calcium 40.08	21 **Sc** Scandium 44.96	22 **Ti** Titanium 47.87	23 **V** Vanadium 50.94	24 **Cr** Chromium 52.00	25 **Mn** Manganese 54.94	26 **Fe** Iron 55.85	27 **Co** Cobalt 58.93
Period 5	37 **Rb** Rubidium 85.47	38 **Sr** Strontium 87.62	39 **Y** Yttrium 88.91	40 **Zr** Zirconium 91.22	41 **Nb** Niobium 92.91	42 **Mo** Molybdenum 95.96	43 **Tc** Technetium (98)	44 **Ru** Ruthenium 101.07	45 **Rh** Rhodium 102.91
Period 6	55 **Cs** Cesium 132.91	56 **Ba** Barium 137.33	57 **La** Lanthanum 138.91	72 **Hf** Hafnium 178.49	73 **Ta** Tantalum 180.95	74 **W** Tungsten 183.84	75 **Re** Rhenium 186.21	76 **Os** Osmium 190.23	77 **Ir** Iridium 192.22
Period 7	87 **Fr** Francium (223)	88 **Ra** Radium (226)	89 **Ac** Actinium (227)	104 **Rf** Rutherfordium (261)	105 **Db** Dubnium (262)	106 **Sg** Seaborgium (266)	107 **Bh** Bohrium (264)	108 **Hs** Hassium (277)	109 **Mt** Meitnerium (268)

Lanthanides

| 58 **Ce** Cerium 140.12 | 59 **Pr** Praseodymium 140.91 | 60 **Nd** Neodymium 144.24 | 61 **Pm** Promethium (145) | 62 **Sm** Samarium 150.36 |

Actinides

| 90 **Th** Thorium 232.04 | 91 **Pa** Protactinium 231.04 | 92 **U** Uranium 238.03 | 93 **Np** Neptunium (237) | 94 **Pu** Plutonium (244) |

The International Union of Pure and Applied Chemistry (IUPAC) has determined that, because of isotopic variance, the average atomic mass is best represented by a range of values for each of the following elements: hydrogen, lithium, boron, carbon, nitrogen, oxygen, silicon, sulfur, chlorine, and thallium. However, the values in this table are appropriate for everyday calculations.

			Group 13	Group 14	Group 15	Group 16	Group 17	Group 18
								2 **He** Helium 4.003
			5 **B** Boron 10.81	6 **C** Carbon 12.01	7 **N** Nitrogen 14.01	8 **O** Oxygen 16.00	9 **F** Fluorine 19.00	10 **Ne** Neon 20.18
Group 10	Group 11	Group 12	13 **Al** Aluminum 26.98	14 **Si** Silicon 28.09	15 **P** Phosphorus 30.97	16 **S** Sulfur 32.06	17 **Cl** Chlorine 35.45	18 **Ar** Argon 39.95
28 **Ni** Nickel 58.69	29 **Cu** Copper 63.55	30 **Zn** Zinc 65.38	31 **Ga** Gallium 69.72	32 **Ge** Germanium 72.63	33 **As** Arsenic 74.92	34 **Se** Selenium 78.96	35 **Br** Bromine 79.90	36 **Kr** Krypton 83.80
46 **Pd** Palladium 106.42	47 **Ag** Silver 107.87	48 **Cd** Cadmium 112.41	49 **In** Indium 114.82	50 **Sn** Tin 118.71	51 **Sb** Antimony 121.76	52 **Te** Tellurium 127.60	53 **I** Iodine 126.90	54 **Xe** Xenon 131.29
78 **Pt** Platinum 195.08	79 **Au** Gold 196.97	80 **Hg** Mercury 200.59	81 **Tl** Thallium 204.38	82 **Pb** Lead 207.2	83 **Bi** Bismuth 208.98	84 **Po** Polonium (209)	85 **At** Astatine (210)	86 **Rn** Radon (222)
110 **Ds** Darmstadtium (271)	111 **Rg** Roentgenium (272)	112 **Cn** Copernicium (285)	113 **Uut** Ununtrium (284)	114 **Fl** Flerovium (289)	115 **Uup** Ununpentium (288)	116 **Lv** Livermorium (293)	117 **Uus** Ununseptium (294)	118 **Uuo** Ununoctium (294)

63 **Eu** Europium 151.96	64 **Gd** Gadolinium 157.25	65 **Tb** Terbium 158.93	66 **Dy** Dysprosium 162.50	67 **Ho** Holmium 164.93	68 **Er** Erbium 167.26	69 **Tm** Thulium 168.93	70 **Yb** Ytterbium 173.05	71 **Lu** Lutetium 174.97
95 **Am** Americium (243)	96 **Cm** Curium (247)	97 **Bk** Berkelium (247)	98 **Cf** Californium (251)	99 **Es** Einsteinium (252)	100 **Fm** Fermium (257)	101 **Md** Mendelevium (258)	102 **No** Nobelium (259)	103 **Lr** Lawrencium (262)

References

Physical Science Refresher

Atoms and Elements

Every object in the universe is made of matter. **Matter** is anything that takes up space and has mass. All matter is made of atoms. An **atom** is the smallest particle into which an element can be divided and still be the same element. An **element**, in turn, is a substance that cannot be broken down into simpler substances by chemical means. Each element consists of only one kind of atom. An element may be made of many atoms, but they are all the same kind of atom.

Atomic Structure

Atoms are made of smaller particles called **electrons**, **protons**, and **neutrons**. Electrons have a negative electric charge, protons have a positive charge, and neutrons have no electric charge. Together, protons and neutrons form the **nucleus**, or small dense center, of an atom. Because protons are positively charged and neutrons are neutral, the nucleus has a positive charge. Electrons move within an area around the nucleus called the **electron cloud**. Electrons move so quickly that scientists cannot determine their exact speeds and positions at the same time.

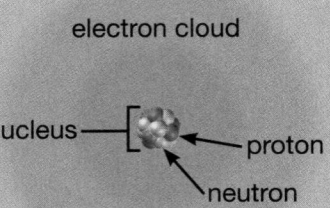

electron cloud

nucleus — proton
neutron

Atomic Number

To help distinguish one element from another, scientists use the atomic numbers of atoms. The **atomic number** is the number of protons in the nucleus of an atom. The atoms of a certain element always have the same number of protons.

When atoms have an equal number of protons and electrons, they are uncharged, or electrically neutral. The atomic number equals the number of electrons in an uncharged atom. The number of neutrons, however, can vary for a given element. Atoms of the same element that have different numbers of neutrons are called **isotopes**.

Periodic Table of the Elements

In the periodic table, each element in the table is in a separate box. And the elements are arranged from left to right in order of increasing atomic number. That is, an uncharged atom of each element has one more electron and one more proton than an uncharged atom of the element to its left. Each horizontal row of the table is called a **period**. Changes in chemical properties of elements across a period correspond to changes in the electron arrangements of their atoms.

Each vertical column of the table is known as a **group.** A group lists elements with similar physical and chemical properties. For this reason, a group is also sometimes called a family. The elements in a group have similar properties because their atoms have the same number of electrons in their outer energy level. For example, the elements helium, neon, argon, krypton, xenon, and radon all have similar properties and are known as the noble gases.

© Houghton Mifflin Harcourt Publishing Company

Molecules and Compounds

When two or more elements join chemically, they form a **compound**. A compound is a new substance with properties different from those of the elements that compose it. For example, water, H_2O, is a compound formed when hydrogen (H) and oxygen (O) combine. The smallest complete unit of a compound that has the properties of that compound is called a **molecule**. A chemical formula indicates the elements in a compound. It also indicates the relative number of atoms of each element in the compound. The chemical formula for water is H_2O. So each water molecule consists of two atoms of hydrogen and one atom of oxygen. The subscript number after the symbol for an element shows how many atoms of that element are in a single molecule of the compound.

Chemical Equations

A chemical reaction occurs when a chemical change takes place. A chemical equation describes a chemical reaction using chemical formulas. The equation indicates the substances that react and the substances that are produced. For example, when carbon and oxygen combine, they can form carbon dioxide, shown in the following equation: $C + O_2 \longrightarrow CO_2$

Acids, Bases, and pH

An **ion** is an atom or group of chemically bonded atoms that has an electric charge because it has lost or gained one or more electrons. When an acid, such as hydrochloric acid, HCl, is mixed with water, it separates into ions. An **acid** is a compound that produces hydrogen ions, H^+, in water. The hydrogen ions then combine with a water molecule to form a hydronium ion, H_3O^+. A **base**, on the other hand, is a substance that produces hydroxide ions, OH^-, in water.

To determine whether a solution is acidic or basic, scientists use pH. The **pH** of a solution is a measure of the hydronium ion concentration in a solution. The pH scale ranges from 0 to 14. Acids have a pH that is less than 7. The lower the number, the more acidic the solution. The middle point, pH $= 7$, is neutral, neither acidic nor basic. Bases have a pH that is greater than 7. The higher the number is, the more basic the solution.

The pH of Some Common Materials

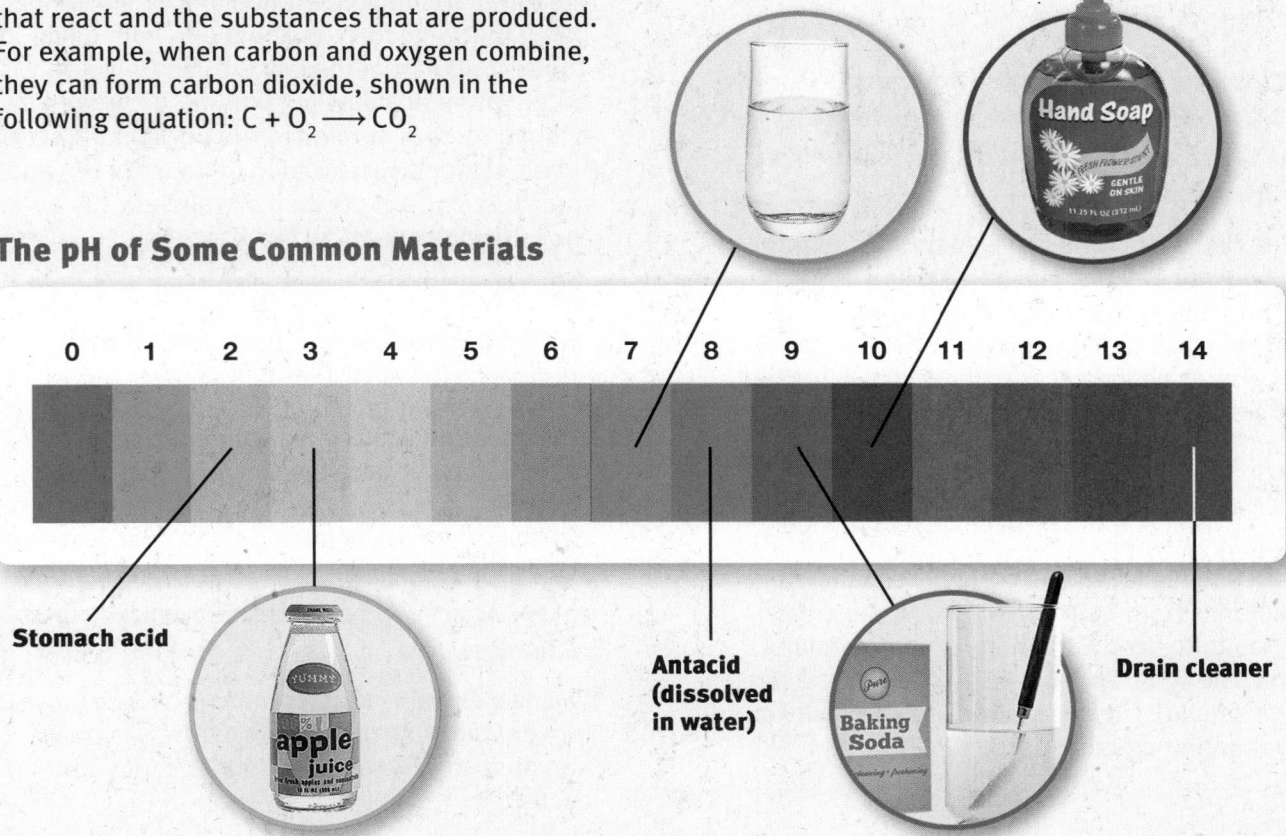

0 1 2 3 4 5 6 7 8 9 10 11 12 13 14

Stomach acid

apple juice

Antacid (dissolved in water)

Baking Soda

Drain cleaner

References

Physical Laws and Useful Equations

Law of Conservation of Mass

Mass cannot be created or destroyed during ordinary chemical or physical changes.

The total mass in a closed system is always the same no matter how many physical changes or chemical reactions occur.

Law of Conservation of Energy

Energy can be neither created nor destroyed.

The total amount of energy in a closed system is always the same. Energy can be changed from one form to another, but all of the different forms of energy in a system always add up to the same total amount of energy, no matter how many energy conversions occur.

Law of Universal Gravitation

All objects in the universe attract each other by a force called gravity. The size of the force depends on the masses of the objects and the distance between the objects.

The first part of the law explains why lifting a bowling ball is much harder than lifting a marble. Because the bowling ball has a much larger mass than the marble does, the amount of gravity between Earth and the bowling ball is greater than the amount of gravity between Earth and the marble.

The second part of the law explains why a satellite can remain in orbit around Earth. The satellite is placed at a carefully calculated distance from Earth. This distance is great enough to keep Earth's gravity from pulling the satellite down, yet small enough to keep the satellite from escaping Earth's gravity and wandering off into space.

Newton's Laws of Motion

Newton's first law of motion states that an object at rest remains at rest and that an object in motion remains in motion at constant speed and in a straight line unless acted on by an unbalanced force.

The first part of the law explains why a football will remain on a tee until it is kicked off or until a gust of wind blows it off. The second part of the law explains why a bike rider will continue moving forward after the bike comes to an abrupt stop. Gravity and the friction of the sidewalk will eventually stop the rider.

Newton's second law of motion states that the acceleration of an object depends on the mass of the object and the amount of force applied.

The first part of the law explains why the acceleration of a 4 kg bowling ball will be greater than the acceleration of a 6 kg bowling ball if the same force is applied to both balls. The second part of the law explains why the acceleration of a bowling ball will be greater if a larger force is applied to the bowling ball. The relationship of acceleration (a) to mass (m) and force (F) can be expressed mathematically by the following equation:

$$\text{acceleration} = \frac{force}{mass}, \text{ or } a = \frac{F}{m}$$

This equation is often rearranged to read $force = mass \times$ acceleration, or $F = m \times a$

Newton's third law of motion states that whenever one object exerts a force on a second object, the second object exerts an equal and opposite force on the first.

This law explains that a runner is able to move forward because the ground exerts an equal and opposite force on the runner's foot after each step.

Average Speed

$$\text{average speed} = \frac{\text{total distance}}{\text{total time}}$$

Example:
A bicycle messenger traveled a distance of 136 km in 8 h. What was the messenger's average speed?

$$\frac{136 \text{ km}}{8 \text{ h}} = 17 \text{ km/h}$$

The messenger's average speed was **17 km/h.**

Average Acceleration

$$\text{average acceleration} = \frac{\text{final velocity} - \text{starting velocity}}{\text{time it takes to change velocity}}$$

Example:
Calculate the average acceleration of an Olympic 100 m dash sprinter who reached a velocity of 20 m/s south at the finish line. The race was in a straight line and lasted 10 s.

$$\frac{20 \text{ m/s} - 0 \text{ m/s}}{10 \text{ s}} = 2 \text{ m/s/s}$$

The sprinter's average acceleration was **2 m/s/s south.**

Pressure

Pressure is the force exerted over a given area. The SI unit for pressure is the pascal. Its symbol is Pa.

$$\text{pressure} = \frac{\text{force}}{\text{area}}$$

Net Force
Forces in the Same Direction

When forces are in the same direction, add the forces together to determine the net force.

Example:
Calculate the net force on a stalled car that is being pushed by two people. One person is pushing with a force of 13 N northwest, and the other person is pushing with a force of 8 N in the same direction.

$$13 \text{ N} + 8 \text{ N} = 21 \text{ N}$$

The net force is **21 N northwest.**

Forces in Opposite Directions

When forces are in opposite directions, subtract the smaller force from the larger force to determine the net force. The net force will be in the direction of the larger force.

Example:
Calculate the net force on a rope that is being pulled on each end. One person is pulling on one end of the rope with a force of 12 N south. Another person is pulling on the opposite end of the rope with a force of 7 N north.

$$12 \text{ N} - 7 \text{ N} = 5 \text{ N}$$

The net force is **5 N south.**

Example:
Calculate the pressure of the air in a soccer ball if the air exerts a force of 10 N over an area of 0.5 m².

$$\text{pressure} = \frac{10 \text{ N}}{0.5 \text{ m}^2} = \frac{20 \text{ N}}{\text{m}^2} = 20 \text{ Pa}$$

The pressure of the air inside the soccer ball is **20 Pa.**

Reading and Study Skills

A How-To Manual for Active Reading

This book belongs to you, and you are invited to write in it. In fact, the book won't be complete until you do. Sometimes you'll answer a question or follow directions to mark up the text. Other times you'll write down your own thoughts. And when you're done reading and writing in the book, the book will be ready to help you review what you learned and prepare for tests.

Active Reading Annotations

Before you read, you'll often come upon an Active Reading prompt that asks you to underline certain words or number the steps in a process. Here's an example.

Active Reading

12 Identify In this paragraph, number the sequence of sentences that describe replication.

Marking the text this way is called **annotating,** and your marks are called **annotations.** Annotating the text can help you identify important concepts while you read.

There are other ways that you can annotate the text. You can draw an asterisk (*) by vocabulary terms, mark unfamiliar or confusing terms and information with a question mark (?), and mark main ideas with a <u>double underline</u>. And you can even invent your own marks to annotate the text!

Other Annotating Opportunities

Keep your pencil, pen, or highlighter nearby as you read so you can make a note or highlight an important point at any time. Here are a few ideas to get you started.

- Notice the headings in red and blue. The blue headings are questions that point to the main idea of what you're reading. The red headings are answers to the questions in the blue ones. Together these headings outline the content of the lesson. After reading a lesson, you could write your own answers to the questions.

- Notice the bold-faced words that are highlighted in yellow. They are highlighted so that you can easily find them again on the page where they are defined. As you read or as you review, challenge yourself to write your own sentence using the bold-faced term.

- Make a note in the margin at any time. You might
  - Ask a "What if" question
  - Comment on what you read
  - Make a connection to something you read elsewhere
  - Make a logical conclusion from the text

Use your own language and abbreviations. Invent a code, such as using circles and boxes around words to remind you of their importance or relation to each other. Your annotations will help you remember your questions for class discussions, and when you go back to the lesson later, you may be able to fill in what you didn't understand the first time you read it. Like a scientist in the field or in a lab, you will be recording your questions and observations for analysis later.

Active Reading Questions

After you read, you'll often come upon Active Reading questions that ask you to think about what you've just read. You'll write your answer underneath the question. Here's an example.

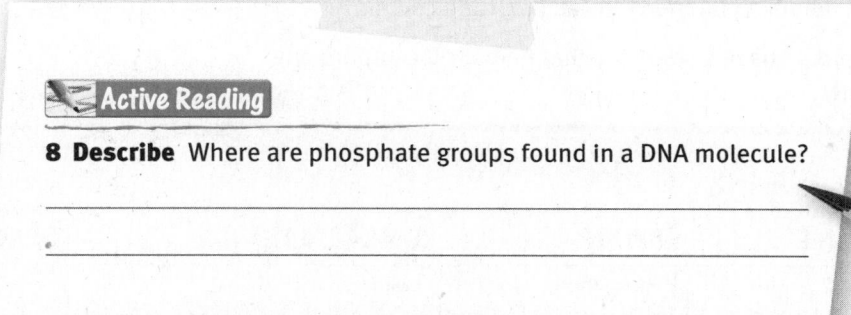

Active Reading

8 Describe Where are phosphate groups found in a DNA molecule?

_____

_____

This type of question helps you sum up what you've just read and pull out the most important ideas from the passage. In this case, the question asks you to **describe** the structure of a DNA molecule that you have just read about. Other times you may be asked to do such things as **apply** a concept, **compare** two concepts, **summarize** a process, or **identify a cause-and-effect** relationship. You'll be strengthening those critical thinking skills that you'll use often in learning about science.

Reading and Study Skills

Using Graphic Organizers to Take Notes

Graphic organizers help you remember information as you read it for the first time and as you study it later. There are dozens of graphic organizers to choose from, so the first trick is to choose the one that's best suited to your purpose. Following are some graphic organizers to use for different purposes.

To remember lots of information	To relate a central idea to subordinate details	To describe a process	To make a comparison
• Arrange data in a Content Frame • Use Combination Notes to describe a concept in words and pictures	• Show relationships with a Mind Map or a Main Idea Web • Sum up relationships among many things with a Concept Map	• Use a Process Diagram to explain a procedure • Show a chain of events and results in a Cause-and-Effect Chart	• Compare two or more closely related things in a Venn Diagram

Content Frame

1 Make a four-column chart.

2 Fill the first column with categories (e.g., snail, ant, earthworm) and the first row with descriptive information (e.g., group, characteristic, appearance).

3 Fill the chart with details that belong in each row and column.

4 When you finish, you'll have a study aid that helps you compare one category to another.

Invertebrates

NAME	GROUP	CHARACTERISTICS	DRAWING
snail	mollusks	mantle	
ant	arthropods	six legs, exoskeleton	
earthworm	segmented worms	segmented body, circulatory and digestive systems	
heartworm	roundworms	digestive system	
sea star	echinoderms	spiny skin, tube feet	
jellyfish	cnidarians	stinging cells	

Combination Notes

1 Make a two-column chart.

2 Write descriptive words and definitions in the first column.

3 Draw a simple sketch that helps you remember the meaning of the term in the second column.

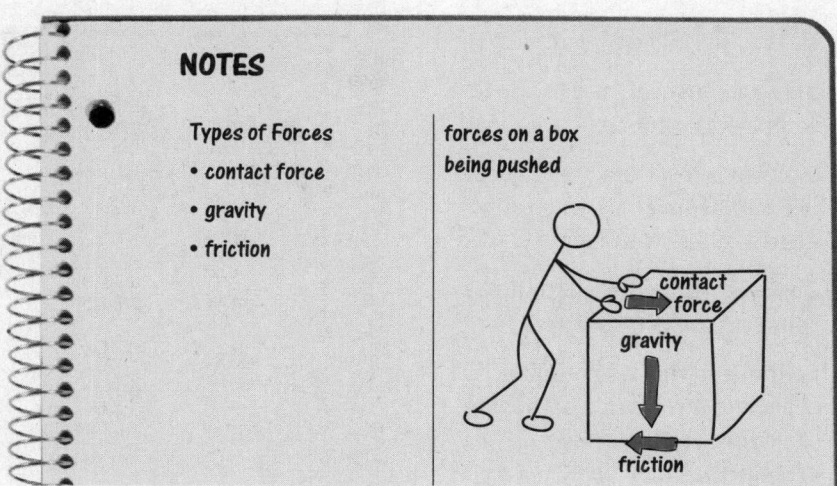

Mind Map

1 Draw an oval, and inside it write a topic to analyze.

2 Draw two or more arms extending from the oval. Each arm represents a main idea about the topic.

3 Draw lines from the arms on which to write details about each of the main ideas.

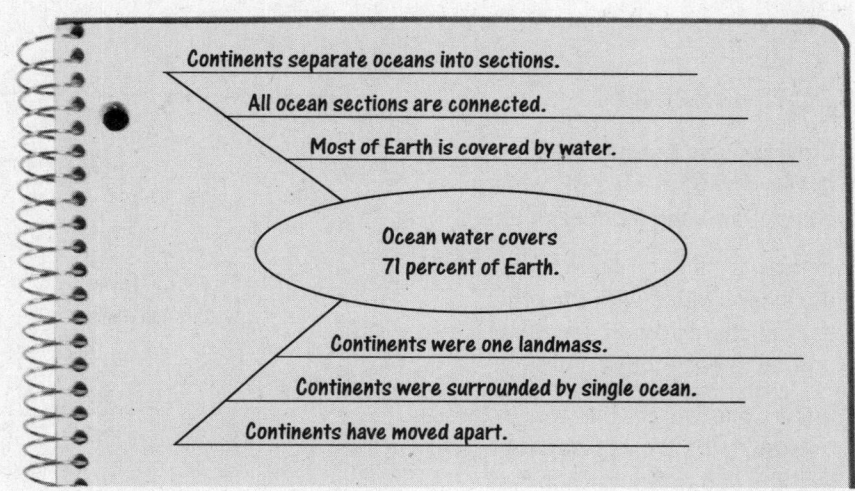

Main Idea Web

1 Make a box, and write a concept you want to remember inside it.

2 Draw boxes around the central box, and label each one with a category of information about the concept (e.g., definition, formula, descriptive details).

3 Fill in the boxes with relevant details as you read.

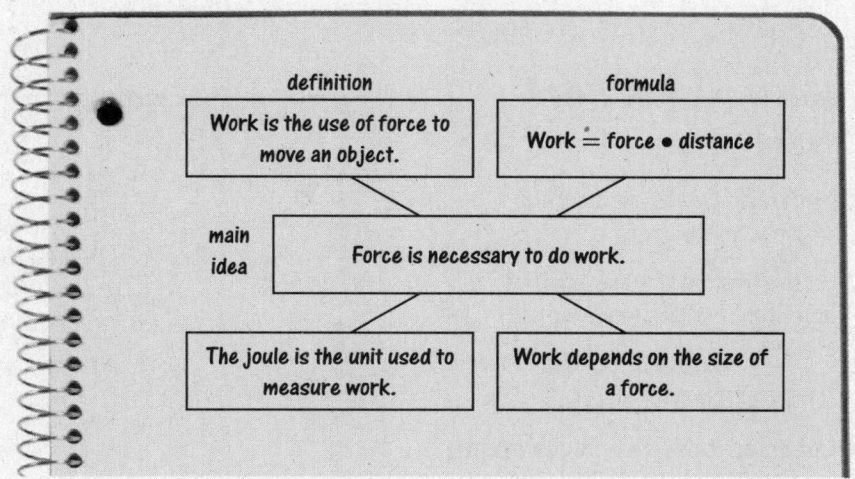

Reading and Study Skills

Concept Map

1 Draw a large oval, and inside it write a major concept.

2 Draw an arrow from the concept to a smaller oval, in which you write a related concept.

3 On the arrow, write a verb that connects the two concepts.

4 Continue in this way, adding ovals and arrows in a branching structure, until you have explained as much as you can about the main concept.

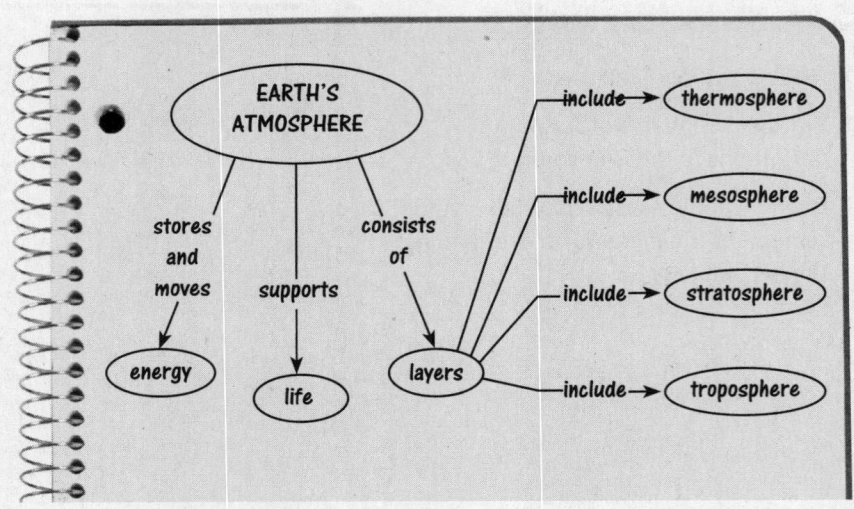

Venn Diagram

1 Draw two overlapping circles or ovals—one for each topic you are comparing—and label each one.

2 In the part of each circle that does not overlap with the other, list the characteristics that are unique to each topic.

3 In the space where the two circles overlap, list the characteristics that the two topics have in common.

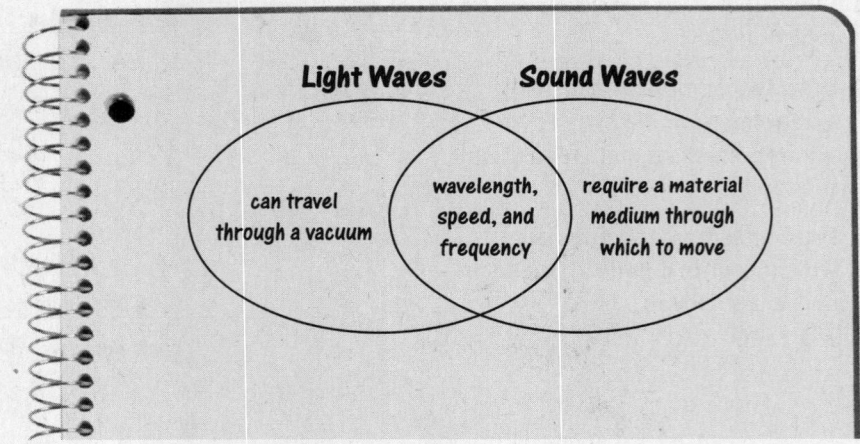

Cause-and-Effect Chart

1 Draw two boxes, and connect them with an arrow.

2 In the first box, write the first event in a series (a cause).

3 In the second box, write a result of the cause (the effect).

4 Add more boxes when one event has many effects or vice versa.

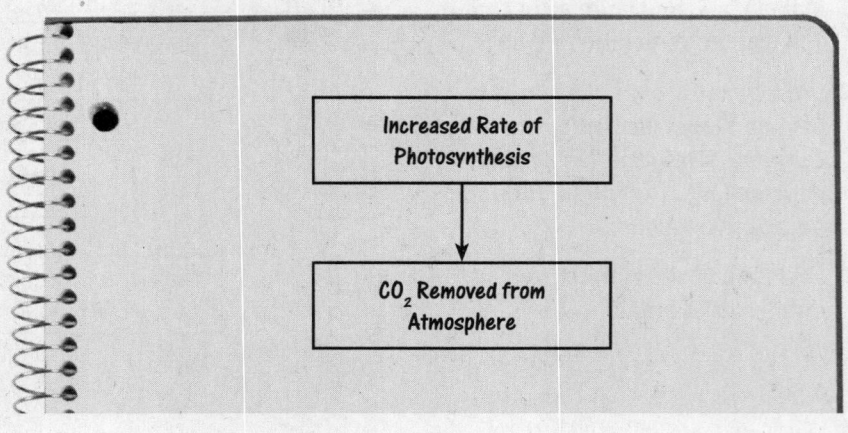

Process Diagram

A process can be a never-ending cycle. As you can see in this technology design process, engineers may backtrack and repeat steps, they may skip steps entirely, or they may repeat the entire process before a usable design is achieved.

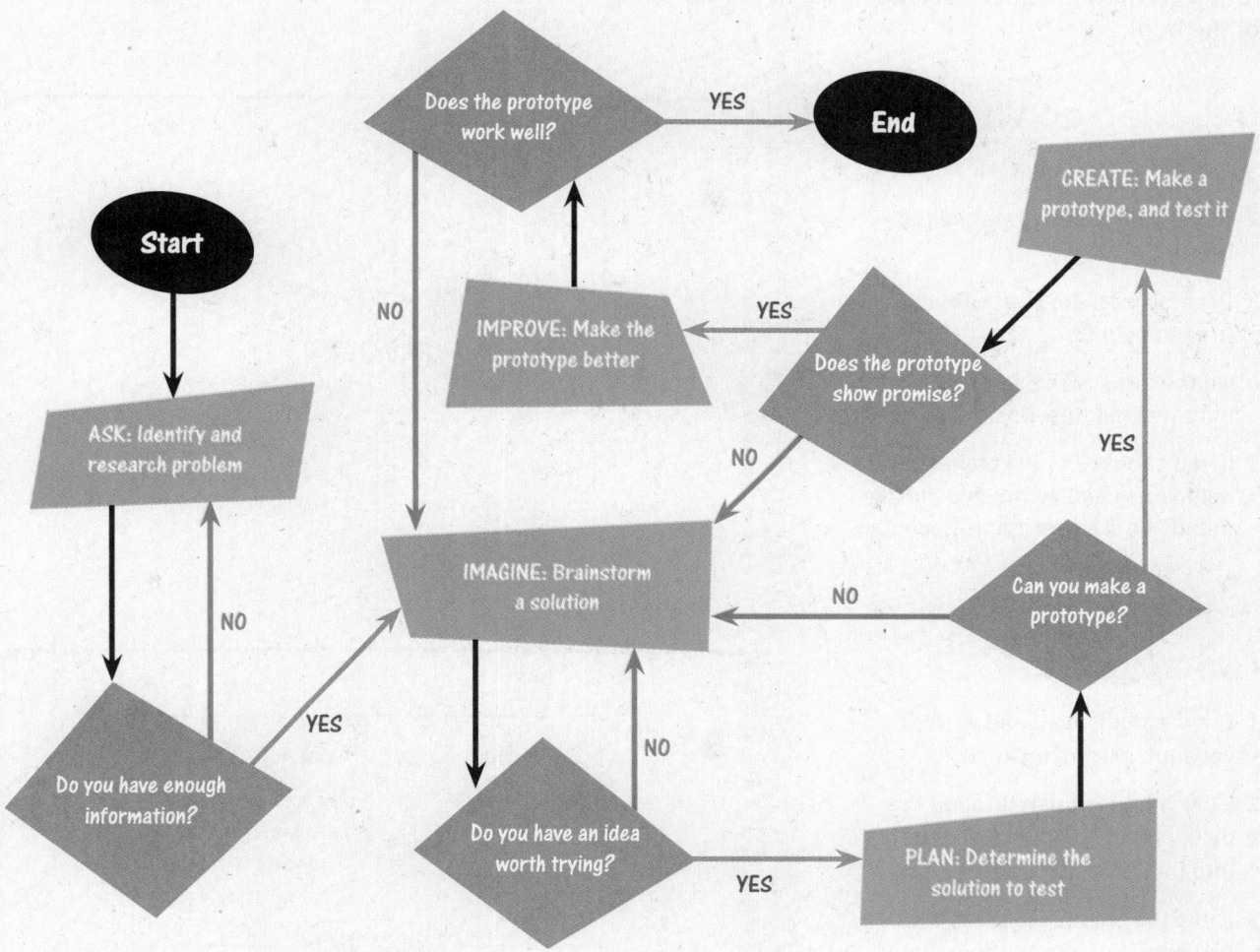

Reading and Study Skills

Using Vocabulary Strategies

Important science terms are highlighted where they are first defined in this book. One way to remember these terms is to take notes and make sketches when you come to them. Use the strategies on this page and the next for this purpose. You will also find a formal definition of each science term in the Glossary at the end of the book.

Description Wheel

1 Draw a small circle.

2 Write a vocabulary term inside the circle.

3 Draw several arms extending from the circle.

4 On the arms, write words and phrases that describe the term.

5 If you choose, add sketches that help you visualize the descriptive details or the concept as a whole.

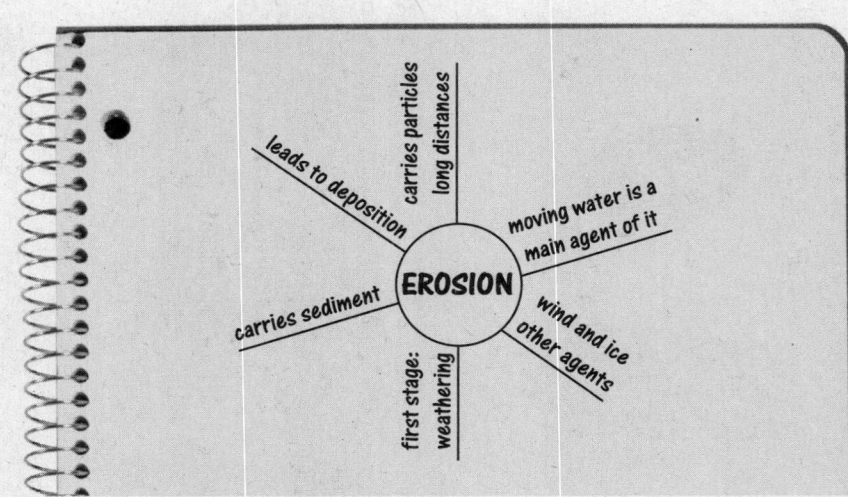

Four Square

1 Draw a small oval, and write a vocabulary term inside it.

2 Draw a large square around the oval, and divide the large square into four smaller squares.

3 Label the smaller squares with categories of information about the term, such as definition, characteristics, examples, non-examples, appearance, and root words.

4 Fill the squares with descriptive words and drawings that will help you remember the overall meaning of the term and its essential details.

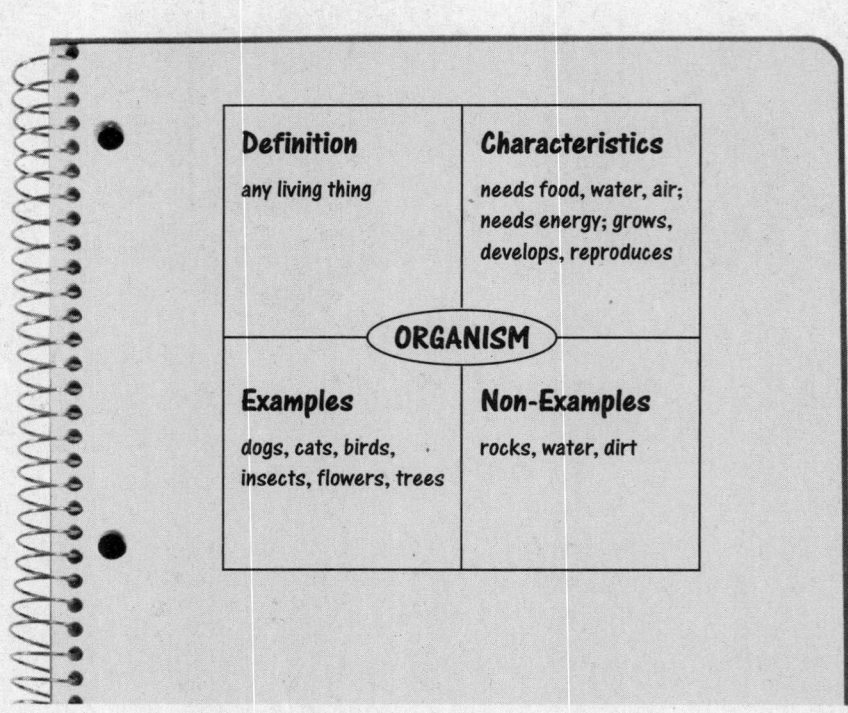

Frame Game

1 Draw a small rectangle, and write a vocabulary term inside it.

2 Draw a larger rectangle around the smaller one. Connect the corners of the larger rectangle to the corners of the smaller one, creating four spaces that frame the word.

3 In each of the four parts of the frame, draw or write details that help define the term. Consider including a definition, essential characteristics, an equation, examples, and a sentence using the term.

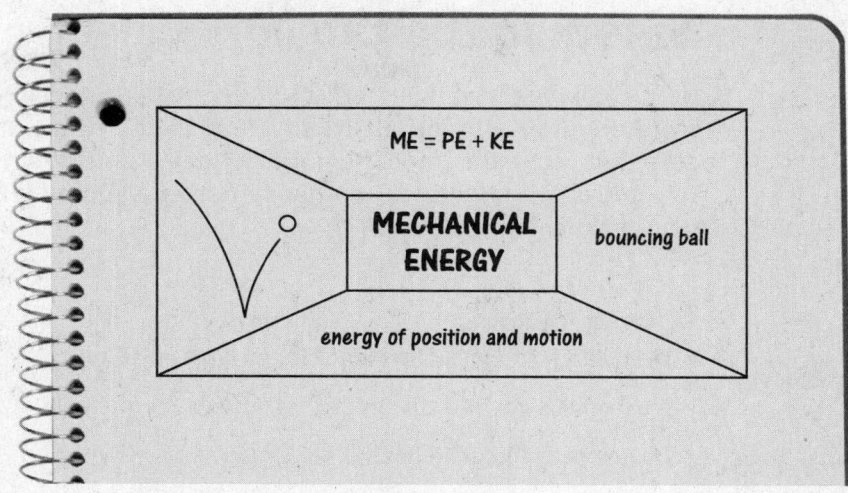

Magnet Word

1 Draw horseshoe magnet, and write a vocabulary term inside it.

2 Add lines that extend from the sides of the magnet.

3 Brainstorm words and phrases that come to mind when you think about the term.

4 On the lines, write the words and phrases that describe something essential about the term.

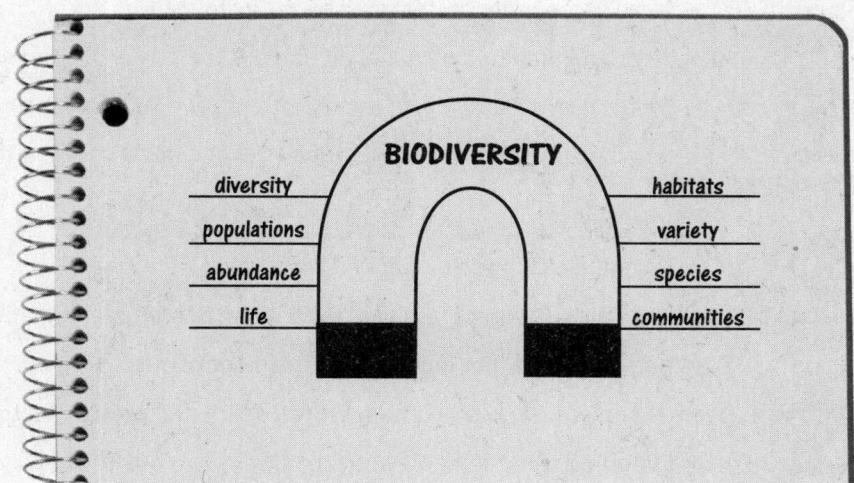

Word Triangle

1 Draw a triangle, and add lines to divide it into three parts.

2 Write a term and its definition in the bottom section of the triangle.

3 In the middle section, write a sentence in which the term is used correctly.

4 In the top section, draw a small picture to illustrate the term.

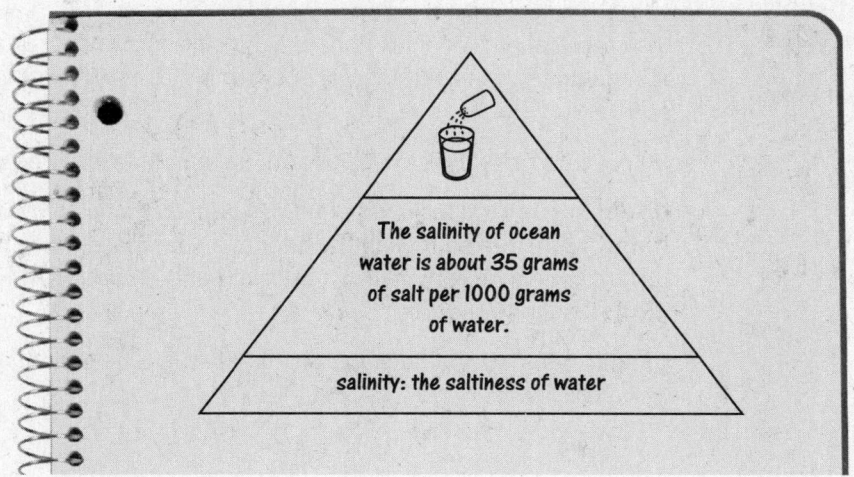

Science Skills

Safety in the Lab

Before you begin work in the laboratory, read these safety rules twice. Before starting a lab activity, read all directions, and make sure that you understand them. Do not begin until your teacher has told you to start. If you or another student are injured in any way, tell your teacher immediately.

Dress Code

Eye Protection

Hand Protection

Clothing Protection

- Wear safety goggles at all times in the lab as directed.
- If chemicals get into your eyes, flush your eyes immediately.
- Do not wear contact lenses in the lab.
- Do not look directly at the sun or any intense light source or laser.
- Do not cut an object while holding the object in your hand.
- Wear appropriate protective gloves as directed.
- Wear an apron or lab coat at all times in the lab as directed.
- Tie back long hair, secure loose clothing, and remove loose jewelry.
- Do not wear open-toed shoes, sandals, or canvas shoes in the lab.

Glassware and Sharp Object Safety

Glassware Safety

Sharp Objects Safety

- Do not use chipped or cracked glassware.
- Use heat-resistant glassware for heating or storing hot materials.
- Notify your teacher immediately if a piece of glass breaks.
- Use extreme care when handling all sharp and pointed instruments.
- Cut objects on a suitable surface, always in a direction away from your body.

Chemical Safety

Chemical Safety

- If a chemical gets on your skin, on your clothing, or in your eyes, rinse it immediately (shower, faucet, or eyewash fountain), and alert your teacher.
- Do not clean up spilled chemicals unless your teacher directs you to do so.
- Do not inhale any gas or vapor unless directed to do so by your teacher. If you are instructed to note the odor of a substance, wave the fumes toward your nose with your hand. This is called wafting. Never put your nose close to the source.
- Handle materials that emit vapors or gases in a well-ventilated area.

Electrical Safety

Electrical Safety

- Do not use equipment with frayed electrical cords or loose plugs.
- Do not use electrical equipment near water or when clothing or hands are wet.
- Hold the plug housing when you plug in or unplug equipment.

Heating and Fire Safety

Heating Safety

- Be aware of any source of flames, sparks, or heat (such as flames, heating coils, or hot plates) before working with any flammable substances.
- Know the location of lab fire extinguishers and fire-safety blankets.
- Know your school's fire-evacuation routes.
- If your clothing catches on fire, walk to the lab shower to put out the fire.
- Never leave a hot plate unattended while it is turned on or while it is cooling.
- Use tongs or appropriate insulated holders when handling heated objects.
- Allow all equipment to cool before storing it.

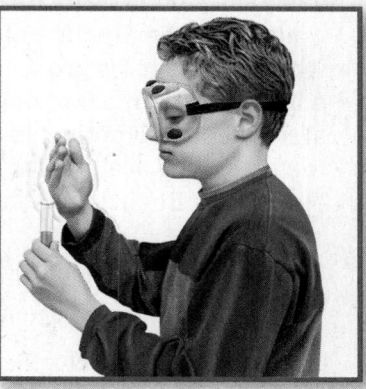

Wafting

Plant and Animal Safety

Plant Safety

Animal Safety

- Do not eat any part of a plant.
- Do not pick any wild plants unless your teacher instructs you to do so.
- Handle animals only as your teacher directs.
- Treat animals carefully and respectfully.
- Wash your hands thoroughly after handling any plant or animal.

Cleanup

Proper Waste Disposal

Hygienic Care

- Clean all work surfaces and protective equipment as directed by your teacher.
- Dispose of hazardous materials or sharp objects only as directed by your teacher.
- Keep your hands away from your face while you are working on any activity.
- Wash your hands thoroughly before you leave the lab or after any activity.

Science Skills

Designing, Conducting, and Reporting an Experiment

An experiment is an organized procedure to study something under specific conditions. Use the following steps of the scientific method when designing or conducting a controlled experiment.

1 Identify a Research Problem

Every day, you make observations by using your senses to gather information. Careful observations lead to good questions, and good questions can lead you to an experiment. Imagine, for example, that you pass a pond every day on your way to school, and you notice green scum beginning to form on top of it. You wonder what it is and why it seems to be growing. You list your questions, and then you do a little research to find out what is already known. A good place to start a research project is at the library. A library catalog lists all of the resources available to you at that library and often those found elsewhere. Begin your search by using:

- keywords or main topics.

- words similar to, or synonyms of, your keyword.

The types of resources that will be helpful to you will depend on the kind of information you are interested in. And some resources are more reliable for a given topic than others. Some different kinds of useful resources are:

- magazines and journals (or periodicals)—articles on a topic.

- encyclopedias—a good overview of a topic.

- books on specific subjects—details about a topic.

- newspapers—useful for current events.

The Internet can also be a great place to find information. Some of your library's reference materials may even be online. When using the Internet, however, it is especially important to make sure you are using appropriate and reliable sources. Websites of universities and government agencies are usually more accurate and reliable than websites created by individuals or businesses. Decide which sources are relevant and reliable for your topic. If in doubt, check with your teacher.

Take notes as you read through the information in these resources. You will probably come up with many questions and ideas for which you can do more research as needed. Once you feel you have enough information, think about the questions you have on the topic. Then write down the problem that you want to investigate. Your notes might look like those at the top of the next page.

Research Questions	Research Problem	Library and Internet Resources
• How do algae grow? • How do people measure algae? • What kind of fertilizer would affect the growth of algae? • Can fertilizer and algae be used safely in a lab? How?	How does fertilizer affect the algae in a pond?	Pond fertilization: initiating an algal bloom—from University of California Davis website. Blue-green algae in Wisconsin waters—from the Department of Natural Resources of Wisconsin website.

As you gather information from reliable sources, record details about each source, including author name(s), title, date of publication, and/or web address. Make sure to also note the specific information that you use from each source. Staying organized in this way will be important when you write your report and create a bibliography or works cited list. Recording this information and staying organized will help you credit the appropriate author(s) for the information that you have gathered.

Representing someone else's ideas or work as your own (without giving the original author credit) is known as plagiarism. Plagiarism can be intentional or unintentional. The best way to make sure that you do not commit plagiarism is to always do your own work and to always give credit to others when you use their words or ideas.

Current scientific research is built on scientific research and discoveries that have happened in the past. This means that scientists are constantly learning from each other and combining ideas to learn more about the natural world through investigation. But a good scientist always credits the ideas and research gathered from other people to those people. There are more details about crediting sources and creating a bibliography under step 9.

2 Make a Prediction

A prediction is a statement of what you expect will happen in your experiment. Before making a prediction, you need to decide in a general way what you will do in your procedure. You may state your prediction in an if-then format.

Prediction

If the amount of fertilizer in the pond water is increased, then the amount of algae will also increase.

Science Skills

3 Form a Hypothesis

Many experiments are designed to test a hypothesis. A hypothesis is a tentative explanation for an expected result. You have predicted that additional fertilizer will cause additional algae growth in pond water; your hypothesis should state the connection between fertilizer and algal growth.

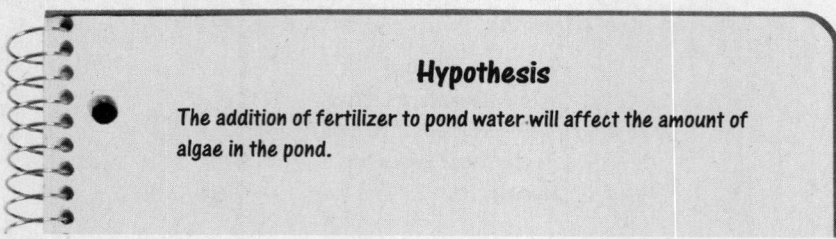

Hypothesis

The addition of fertilizer to pond water will affect the amount of algae in the pond.

4 Identify Variables to Test the Hypothesis

The next step is to design an experiment to test the hypothesis. The experimental results may or may not support the hypothesis. Either way, the information that results from the experiment may be useful for future investigations.

Experimental Group and Control Group

An experiment to determine how two factors are related has a control group and an experimental group. The two groups are the same, except that the investigator changes a single factor in the experimental group and does not change it in the control group.

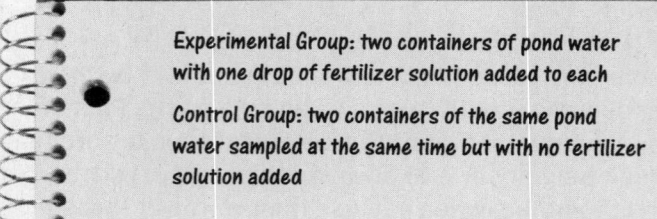

Experimental Group: two containers of pond water with one drop of fertilizer solution added to each

Control Group: two containers of the same pond water sampled at the same time but with no fertilizer solution added

Variables and Constants

In a controlled experiment, a variable is any factor that can change. Constants are all of the variables that are kept the same in both the experimental group and the control group.

The independent variable is the factor that is manipulated or changed in order to test the effect of the change on another variable. The dependent variable is the factor the investigator measures to gather data about the effect.

Independent Variable	Dependent Variable	Constants
Amount of fertilizer in pond water	Growth of algae in the pond water	• Where and when the pond water is obtained • The type of container used • Light and temperature conditions where the water is stored

5 Write a Procedure

Write each step of your procedure. Start each step with a verb, or action word, and keep the steps short. Your procedure should be clear enough for someone else to use as instructions for repeating your experiment.

Procedure

1. Use the masking tape and the marker to label the containers with your initials, the date, and the identifiers "Jar 1 with Fertilizer," "Jar 2 with Fertilizer," "Jar 1 without Fertilizer," and "Jar 2 without Fertilizer."

2. Put on your gloves. Use the large container to obtain a sample of pond water.

3. Divide the water sample equally among the four smaller containers.

4. Use the eyedropper to add one drop of fertilizer solution to the two containers labeled "Jar 1 with Fertilizer" and "Jar 2 with Fertilizer."

5. Cover the containers with clear plastic wrap. Use the scissors to punch ten holes in each of the covers.

6. Place all four containers on a window ledge. Make sure that they all receive the same amount of light.

7. Observe the containers every day for one week.

8. Place a ruler over the opening of the jar and measure the diameter of the largest clump of algae in each container. Record your measurements daily.

Science Skills

6 Experiment and Collect Data

Once you have all of your materials and your procedure has been approved, you can begin to experiment and collect data. Record both quantitative data (measurements) and qualitative data (observations), as shown below.

Algal Growth and Fertilizer

Date and Time	Experimental Group		Control Group		Observations
	Jar 1 with Fertilizer (diameter of algal clump in mm)	Jar 2 with Fertilizer (diameter of algal clump in mm)	Jar 1 without Fertilizer (diameter of algal clump in mm)	Jar 2 without Fertilizer (diameter of algal clump in mm)	
5/3 4:00 p.m.	0	0	0	0	condensation in all containers
5/4 4:00 p.m.	0	3	0	0	tiny green blobs in Jar 2 with fertilizer
5/5 4:15 p.m.	4	5	0	3	green blobs in Jars 1 and 2 with fertilizer and Jar 2 without fertilizer
5/6 4:00 p.m.	5	6	0	4	water light green in Jar 2 with fertilizer
5/7 4:00 p.m.	8	10	0	6	water light green in Jars 1 and 2 with fertilizer and Jar 2 without fertilizer
5/8 3:30 p.m.	10	18	0	6	cover off of Jar 2 with fertilizer
5/9 3:30 p.m.	14	23	0	8	drew sketches of each container

Drawings of Samples Viewed Under Microscope on 5/9 at 100x

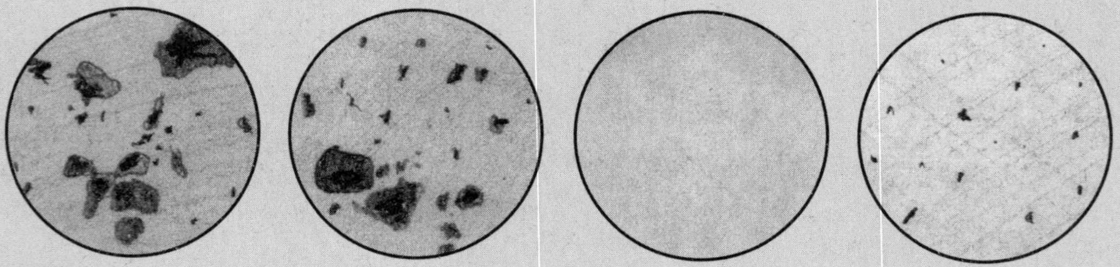

Jar 1 with Fertilizer

Jar 2 with Fertilizer

Jar 1 without Fertilizer

Jar 2 without Fertilizer

7 Analyze Data

After you complete your experiment, you must analyze all of the data you have gathered. Tables, statistics, and graphs are often used in this step to organize and analyze both the qualitative and quantitative data. Sometimes, your qualitative data are best used to help explain the relationships you see in your quantitative data.

Computer graphing software is useful for creating a graph from data you have collected. Most graphing software can make line graphs, pie charts, or bar graphs from data that have been organized in a spreadsheet. Graphs are useful for understanding relationships in the data and for communicating the results of your experiment.

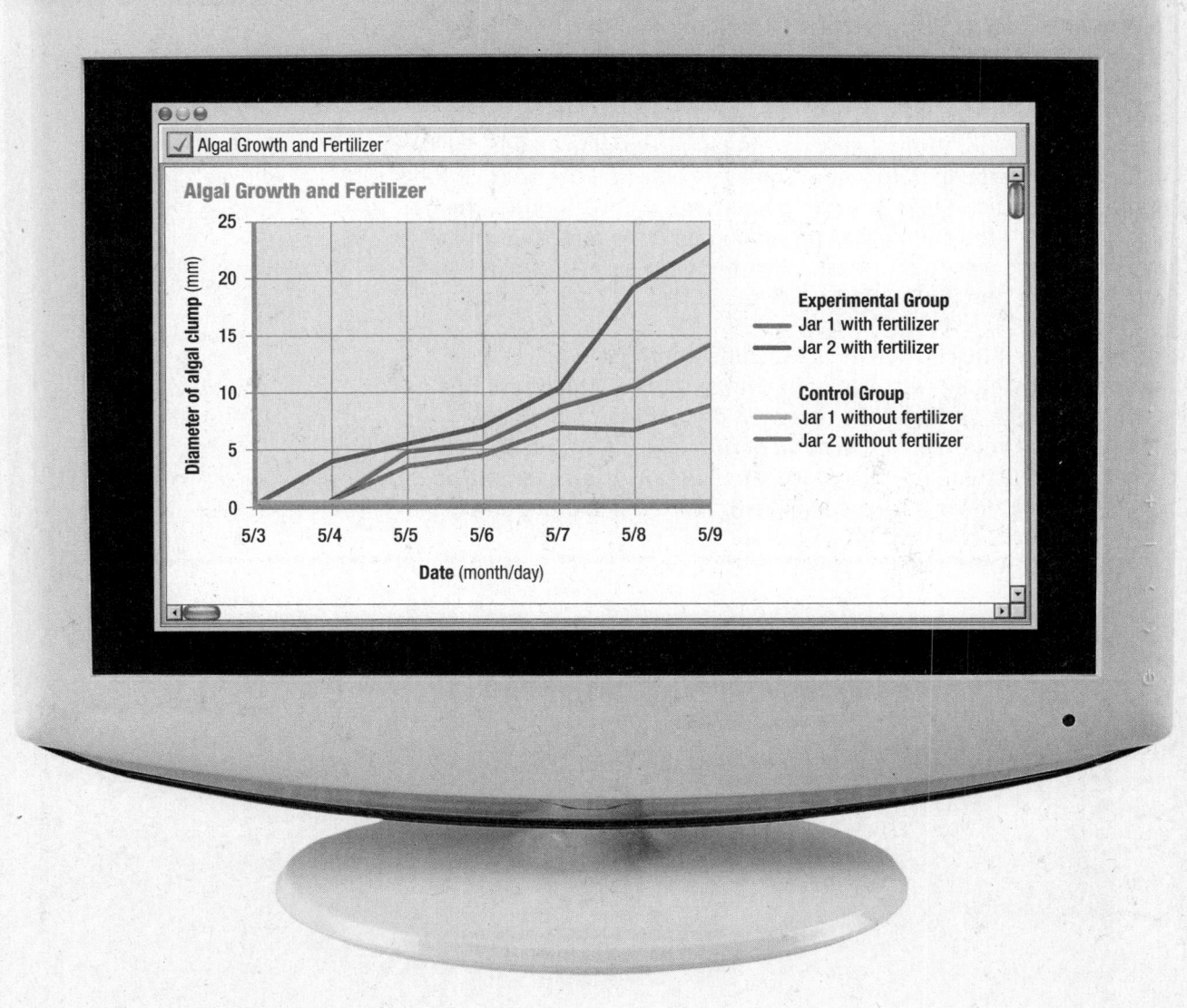

Science Skills

8 Make Conclusions

To draw conclusions from your experiment, first, write your results. Then, compare your results with your hypothesis. Do your results support your hypothesis? What have you learned?

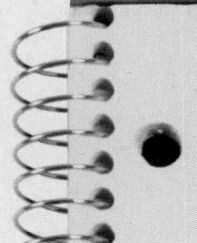

Conclusion

More algae grew in the pond water to which fertilizer had been added than in the pond water to which fertilizer had not been added. My hypothesis was supported. I conclude that it is possible that the growth of algae in ponds can be influenced by the input of fertilizer.

9 Create a Bibliography or Works Cited List

To complete your report, you must also show all of the newspapers, magazines, journals, books, and online sources that you used at every stage of your investigation. Whenever you find useful information about your topic, you should write down the source of that information. Writing down as much information as you can about the subject can help you or someone else find the source again. You should at least record the author's name, the title, the date and where the source was published, and the pages in which the information was found. Then, organize your sources into a list, which you can title Bibliography or Works Cited.

Usually, at least three sources are included in these lists. Sources are listed alphabetically, by the authors' last names. The exact format of a bibliography can vary, depending on the style preferences of your teacher, school, or publisher. Also, books are cited differently than journals or websites. Below is an example of how different kinds of sources may be formatted in a bibliography.

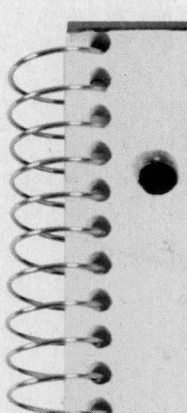

BOOK: Hauschultz, Sara. Freshwater Algae. Brainard, Minnesota: Northwoods Publishing, 2011.

ENCYCLOPEDIA: Lasure, Sedona. "Algae is not all just pond scum." Encyclopedia of Algae. 2009.

JOURNAL: Johnson, Keagan. "Algae as we know it." Sci Journal, vol 64. (September 2010): 201-211.

WEBSITE: Dout, Bill. "Keeping algae scum out of birdbaths." Help Keep Earth Clean. News. January 26, 2011. <www.SaveEarth.org>.

Using a Microscope

Scientists use microscopes to see very small objects that cannot easily be seen with the eye alone. A microscope magnifies the image of an object so that small details may be observed. A microscope that you may use can magnify an object 400 times—the object will appear 400 times larger than its actual size.

Eyepiece Objects are viewed through the eyepiece. The eyepiece contains a lens that commonly magnifies an image 10 times.

Body The body separates the lens in the eyepiece from the objective lenses below.

Nosepiece The nosepiece holds the objective lenses above the stage and rotates so that all lenses may be used.

High-Power Objective Lens This is the largest lens on the nosepiece. It magnifies an image approximately 40 times.

Coarse Adjustment This knob is used to focus the image of an object when it is viewed through the low-power lens.

Fine Adjustment This knob is used to focus the image of an object when it is viewed through the high-power lens.

Low-Power Objective Lens This is the smallest lens on the nosepiece. It magnifies images about 10 times.

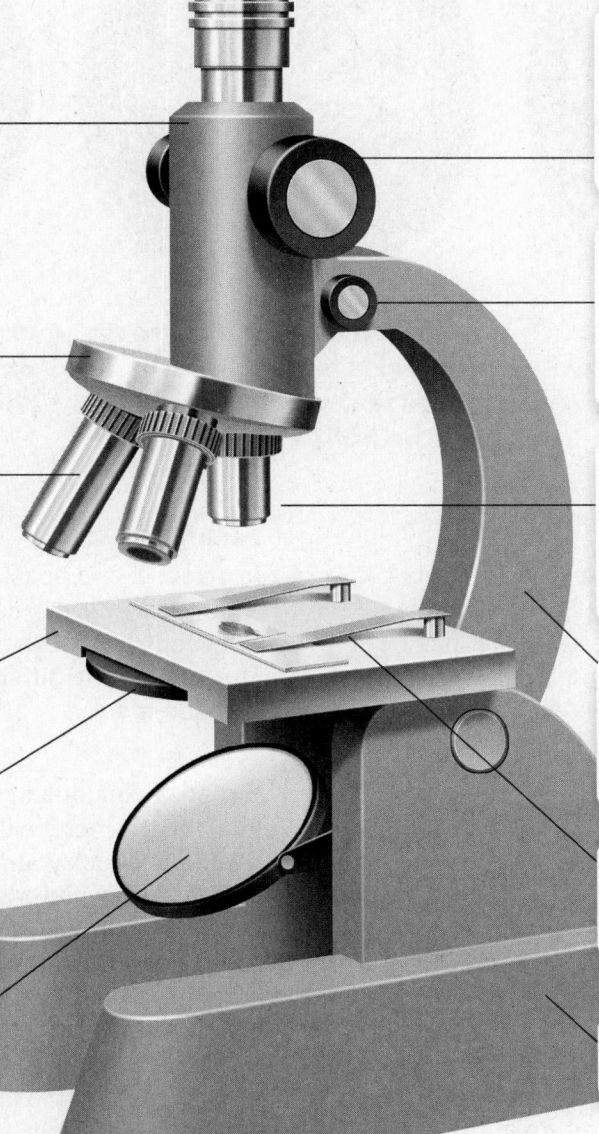

Stage The stage supports the object being viewed.

Diaphragm The diaphragm is used to adjust the amount of light passing through the slide and into an objective lens.

Mirror or Light Source Some microscopes use light that is reflected through the stage by a mirror. Other microscopes have their own light sources.

Arm The arm supports the body above the stage. Always carry a microscope by the arm and base.

Stage Clip The stage clip holds a slide in place on the stage.

Base The base supports the microscope.

Science Skills

Measuring Accurately

Precision and Accuracy

When you do a scientific investigation, it is important that your methods, observations, and data be both precise and accurate.

Low precision: The darts did not land in a consistent place on the dartboard.

Precision but not accuracy: The darts landed in a consistent place but did not hit the bull's eye.

Precision and accuracy: The darts landed consistently on the bull's eye.

Precision

In science, *precision* is the exactness and consistency of measurements. For example, measurements made with a ruler that has both centimeter and millimeter markings would be more precise than measurements made with a ruler that has only centimeter markings. Another indicator of precision is the care taken to make sure that methods and observations are as exact and consistent as possible. Every time a particular experiment is done, the same procedure should be used. Precision is necessary because experiments are repeated several times and if the procedure changes, the results might change.

Example

Suppose you are measuring temperatures over a two-week period. Your precision will be greater if you measure each temperature at the same place, at the same time of day, and with the same thermometer than if you change any of these factors from one day to the next.

Accuracy

In science, it is possible to be precise but not accurate. *Accuracy* depends on the difference between a measurement and an actual value. The smaller the difference, the more accurate the measurement.

Example

Suppose you look at a stream and estimate that it is about 1 meter wide at a particular place. You decide to check your estimate by measuring the stream with a meter stick, and you determine that the stream is 1.32 meters wide. However, because it is difficult to measure the width of a stream with a meter stick, it turns out that your measurement was not very accurate. The stream is actually 1.14 meters wide. Therefore, even though your estimate of about 1 meter was less precise than your measurement, your estimate was actually more accurate.

Graduated Cylinders

How to Measure the Volume of a Liquid with a Graduated Cylinder

- Be sure that the graduated cylinder is on a flat surface so that your measurement will be accurate.

- When reading the scale on a graduated cylinder, be sure to have your eyes at the level of the surface of the liquid.

- The surface of the liquid will be curved in the graduated cylinder. Read the volume of the liquid at the bottom of the curve, or meniscus (muh•NIHS•kuhs).

- You can use a graduated cylinder to find the volume of a solid object by measuring the increase in a liquid's level after you add the object to the cylinder.

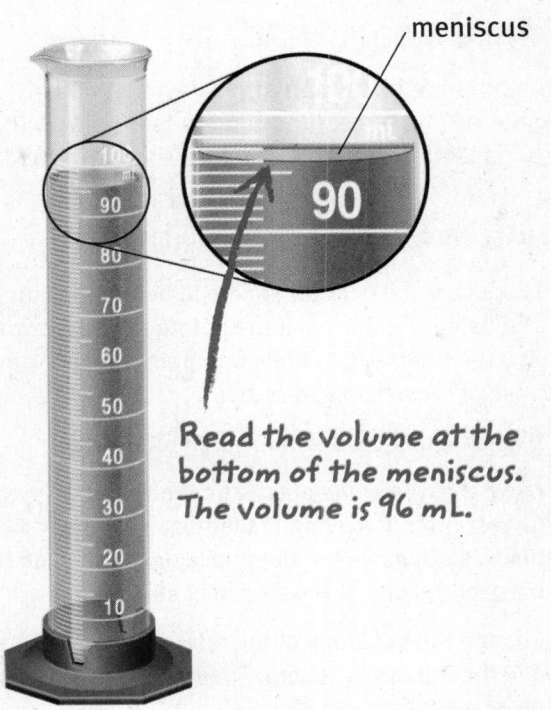

meniscus

Read the volume at the bottom of the meniscus. The volume is 96 mL.

Metric Rulers

How to Measure the Length of a Leaf with a Metric Ruler

1 Lay a ruler flat on top of the leaf so that the 1-centimeter mark lines up with one end. Make sure the ruler and the leaf do not move between the time you line them up and the time you take the measurement.

2 Look straight down on the ruler so that you can see exactly how the marks line up with the other end of the leaf.

3 Estimate the length by which the leaf extends beyond a marking. For example, the leaf below extends about halfway between the 4.2-centimeter and 4.3-centimeter marks, so the apparent measurement is about 4.25 centimeters.

4 Remember to subtract 1 centimeter from your apparent measurement, since you started at the 1-centimeter mark on the ruler and not at the end. The leaf is about 3.25 centimeters long (4.25 cm − 1 cm = 3.25 cm).

Not to scale

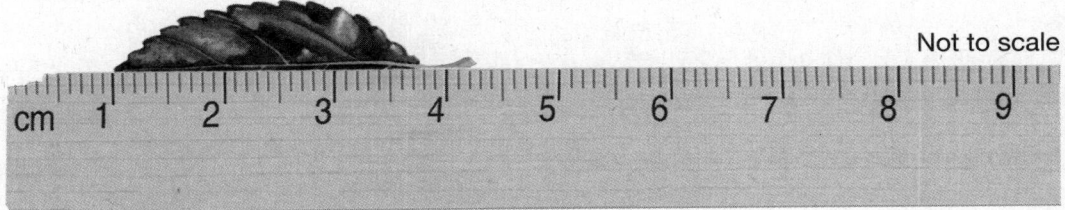

Science Skills

Triple Beam Balance

This balance has a pan and three beams with sliding masses, called riders. At one end of the beams is a pointer that indicates whether the mass on the pan is equal to the masses shown on the beams.

How to Measure the Mass of an Object

1 Make sure the balance is zeroed before measuring the mass of an object. The balance is zeroed if the pointer is at zero when nothing is on the pan and the riders are at their zero points. Use the adjustment knob at the base of the balance to zero it.

2 Place the object to be measured on the pan.

3 Move the riders one notch at a time away from the pan. Begin with the largest rider. If moving the largest rider one notch brings the pointer below zero, move the rider back one notch and begin measuring the mass of the object with the next smaller rider.

4 Change the positions of the riders until they balance the mass on the pan and the pointer is at zero. Then add the readings from the three beams to determine the mass of the object.

300 g	position of largest rider
90 g	position of middle rider
+ 3 g	position of smallest rider
393 g	mass of beaker and water

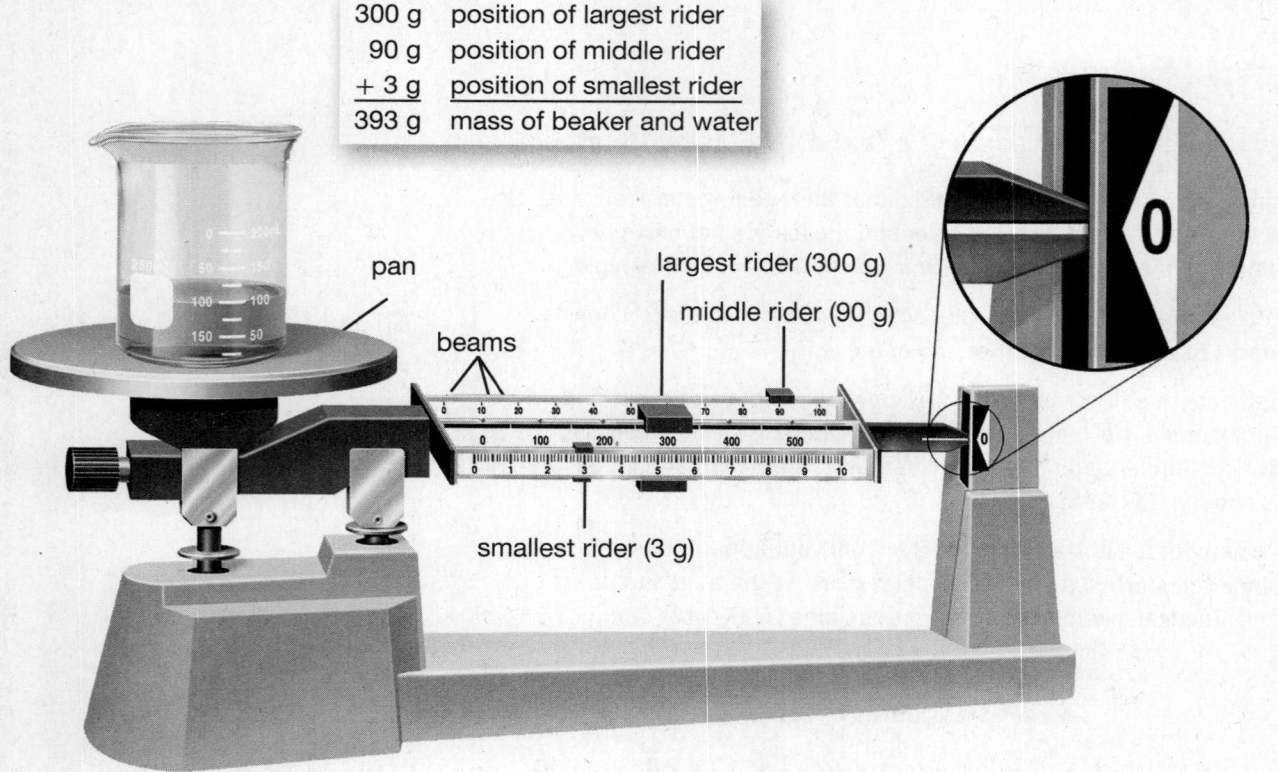

pan

beams

largest rider (300 g)

middle rider (90 g)

smallest rider (3 g)

Electronic Balance

How to Measure the Mass of an Object

1 Be sure the balance is on a flat, stable surface.

2 Zero, or *tare*, the balance using the appropriate key. If you are measuring a specific quantity of a substance using a weigh boat or other container, place the weigh boat or container on the balance pan before zeroing the balance.

3 When the readout on the balance is steady and within a few thousandths of zero grams, place the object to be measured on the balance. If you are measuring out chemicals or other substances, wear gloves and use a clean spatula or similar tool to transfer the substance. Do not reach into containers or touch chemicals with your hands.

4 Record the mass of the object to the nearest milligram (1/1000 of one gram).

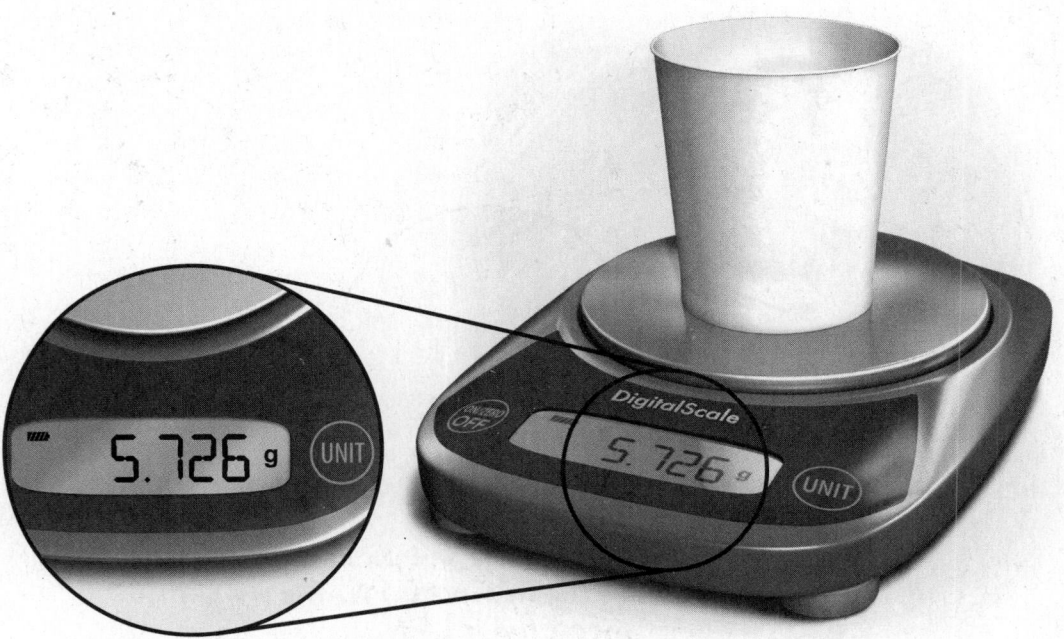

Record the mass of an object to the nearest milligram (mg). The mass measured is 5.726 grams.

Science Skills

Spring Scale

Spring scales are tools that measure forces, such as weight, or the gravitational force exerted on an object. A spring scale indicates an object's weight by measuring how far the spring stretches when an object is suspended from it. This type of scale is often used in grocery stores or to measure the weights of large loads of crops or industrial products. Spring scales are useful for measuring the weight of larger objects as well.

How to Measure the Weight of an Object

- Be sure the spring scale is securely suspended and is not touching the ground, wall, or desk. The pointer should be at zero.

- Hang the object to be weighed from the hook at the free end of the spring scale.

- When the object is still—not bouncing, swinging, or otherwise moving—read the object's weight to the nearest 0.5 N.

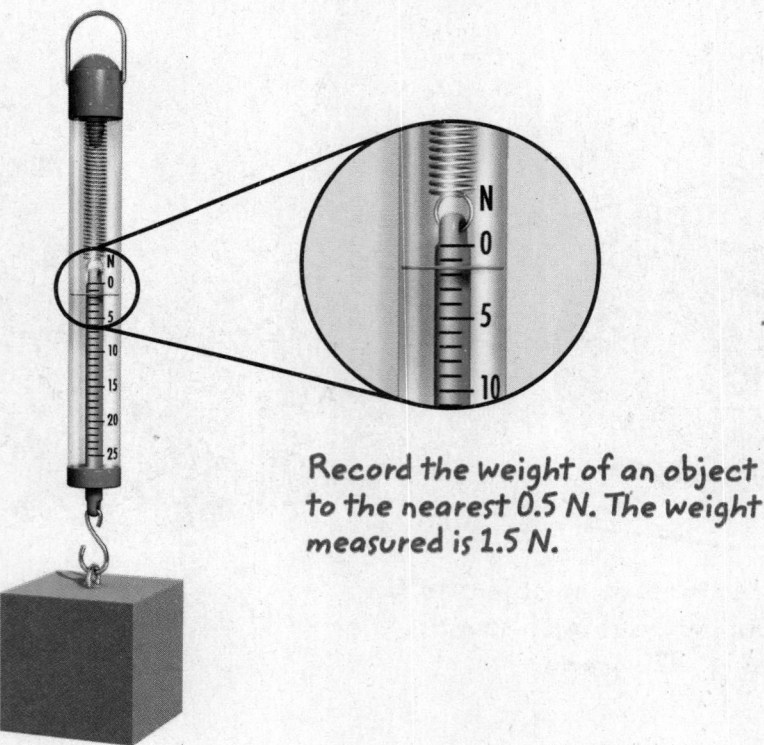

Record the weight of an object to the nearest 0.5 N. The weight measured is 1.5 N.

Thermometer

Many laboratory thermometers are the bulb type shown below. The sensing bulb of the thermometer is filled with a colored liquid (alcohol) that expands as it is heated. When the liquid expands, it moves up the stem of the thermometer through the capillary tube. Thermometers usually measure temperature in degrees Celsius (°C).

How to Measure the Temperature of a Substance

Caution: Do not hold the thermometer in your hand while measuring the temperature of a heated substance. Never use a thermometer to stir a solution. Always consult your teacher regarding proper laboratory techniques and safety rules when using a thermometer.

- Carefully lower the bulb of the thermometer into the substance. The stem of the thermometer may rest against the side of the container, but the bulb should never rest on the bottom. If the thermometer has an adjustable clip for the side of the container, use the clip to suspend the thermometer in the liquid.

- Watch the colored liquid as it rises in the thermometer's capillary tube. When the liquid stops rising, note the whole-degree increment nearest the top of the liquid column.

- If your thermometer is marked in whole degrees, report temperature to the nearest half degree.

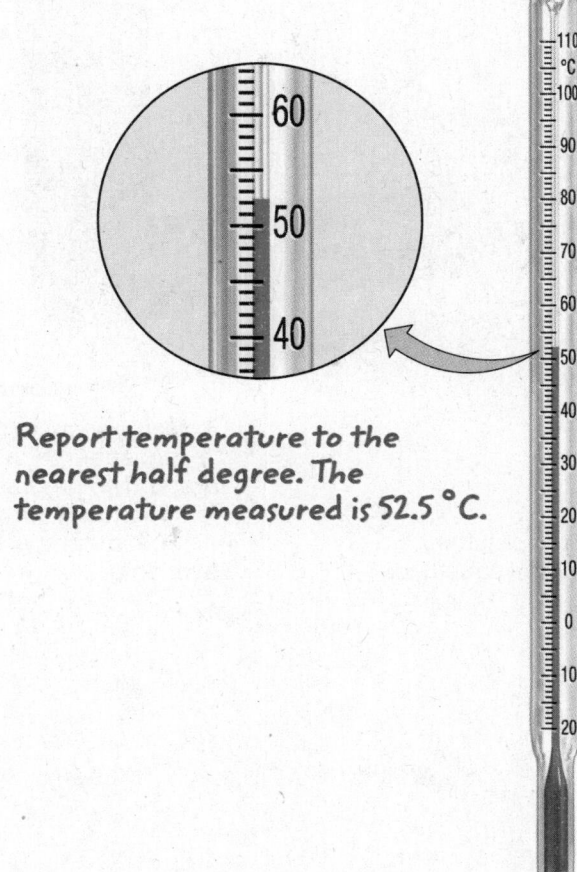

Report temperature to the nearest half degree. The temperature measured is 52.5 °C.

Introduction to Probeware

Probeware is a system of tools that offers a way to measure and analyze various physical properties, such as pressure, pH, temperature, or acceleration. Most probeware systems consist of a sensor, or probe, that is connected to a device such as a computer. As the sensor takes measurements, a computer program records the data. Users can then analyze data using tables, charts, or graphs. Some systems allow you to analyze more than one variable at a time.

Temperature Probe

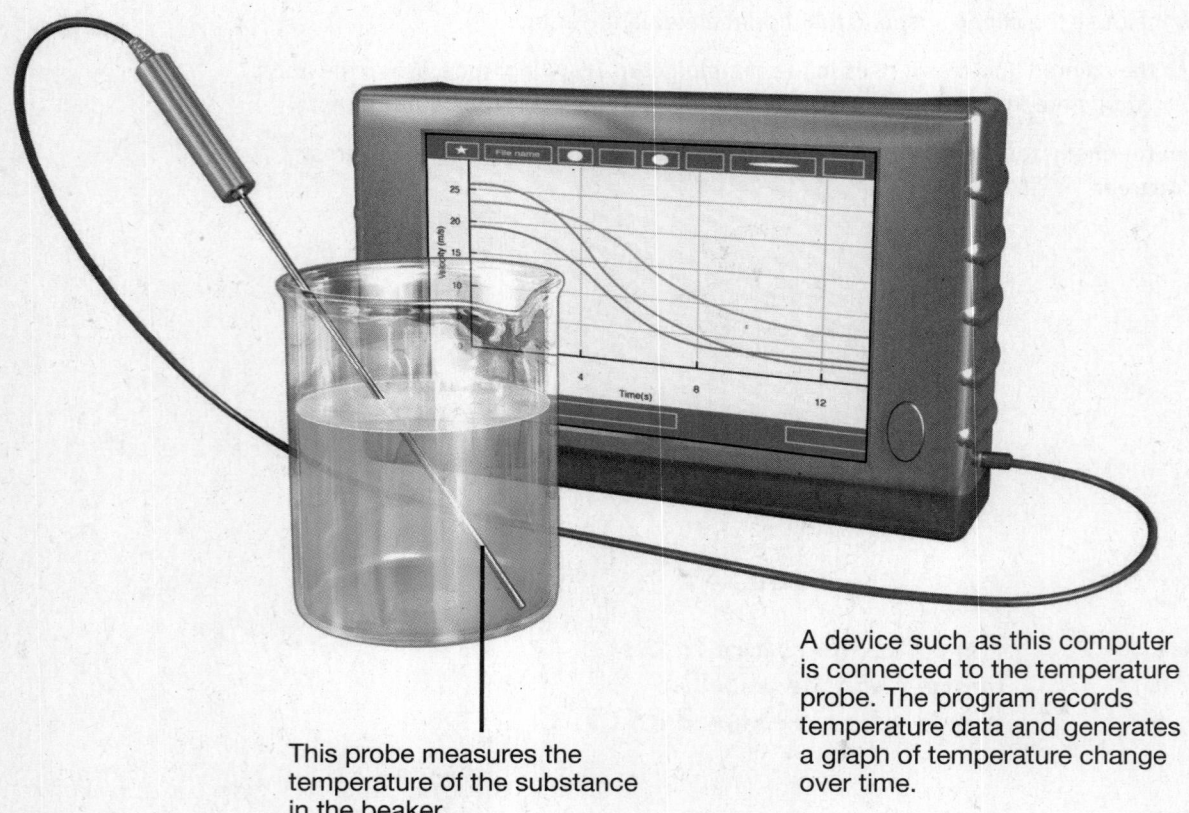

This probe measures the temperature of the substance in the beaker.

A device such as this computer is connected to the temperature probe. The program records temperature data and generates a graph of temperature change over time.

Motion Detector

Use a motion detector to gather information about an object's velocity, position, or acceleration.

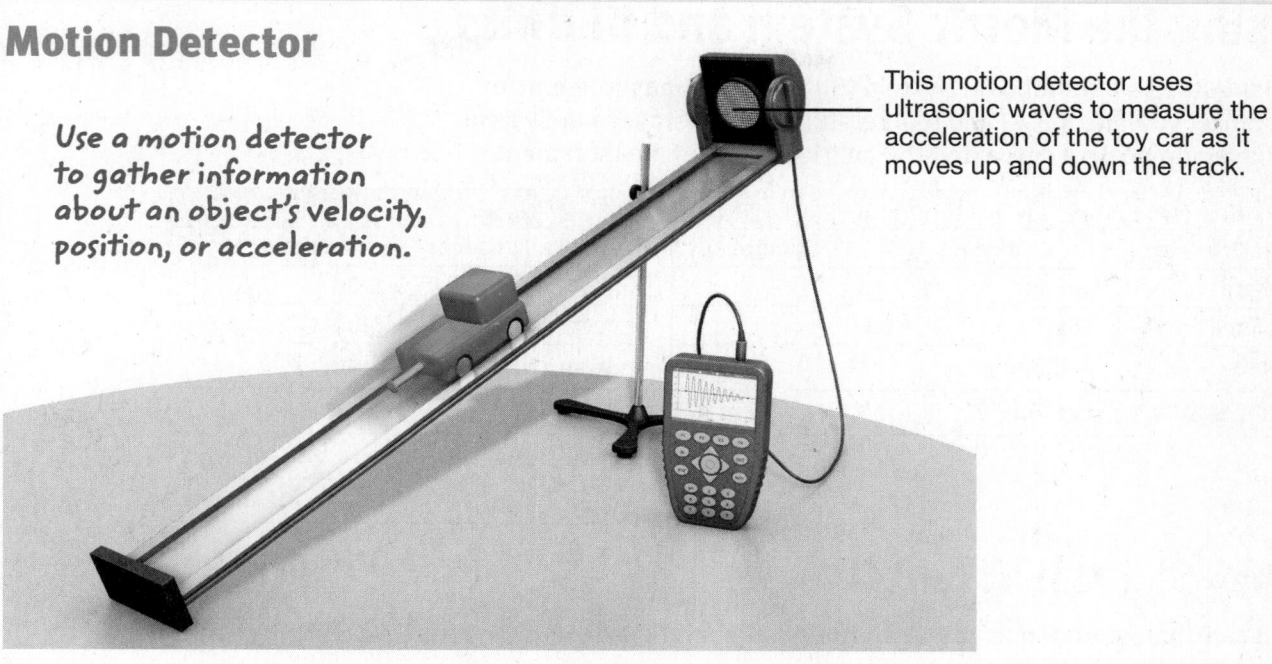

This motion detector uses ultrasonic waves to measure the acceleration of the toy car as it moves up and down the track.

pH Probe

Use a pH probe to determine whether a substance is acidic, neutral, or basic.

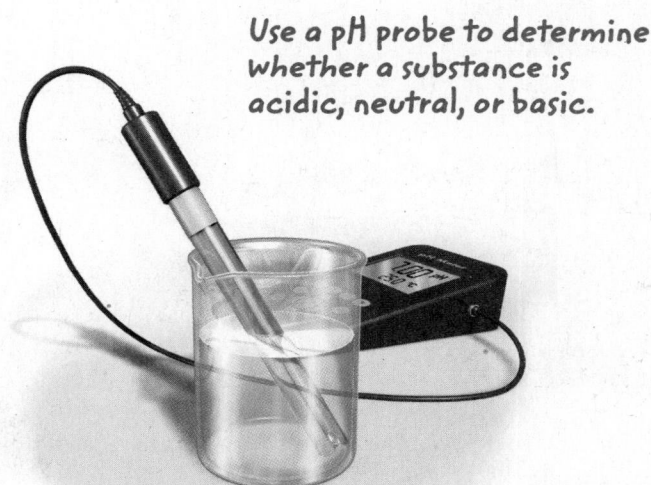

pH probes measure the concentration of hydrogen ions in a liquid, such as the substance in the beaker shown here.

The tip of a pH probe is a thin glass membrane that should not be allowed to dry out. Store pH probes in the appropriate container and solution when you are finished with your investigation.

Caution: Probeware equipment should always be handled carefully. Be sure to follow your teacher's instructions regarding the use and storage of all probeware equipment.

Science Skills

Using the Metric System and SI Units

Scientists use International System (SI) units for measurements of distance, volume, mass, and temperature. The International System is based on powers of ten and the metric system of measurement.

Basic SI Units		
Quantity	Name	Symbol
length	meter	m
volume	liter	L
mass	kilogram	kg
temperature	kelvin	K

SI Prefixes		
Prefix	Symbol	Power of 10
kilo-	k	1000
hecto-	h	100
deca-	da	10
deci-	d	0.1 or $\frac{1}{10}$
centi-	c	0.01 or $\frac{1}{100}$
milli-	m	0.001 or $\frac{1}{1000}$

Changing Metric Units

You can change from one unit to another in the metric system by multiplying or dividing by a power of 10

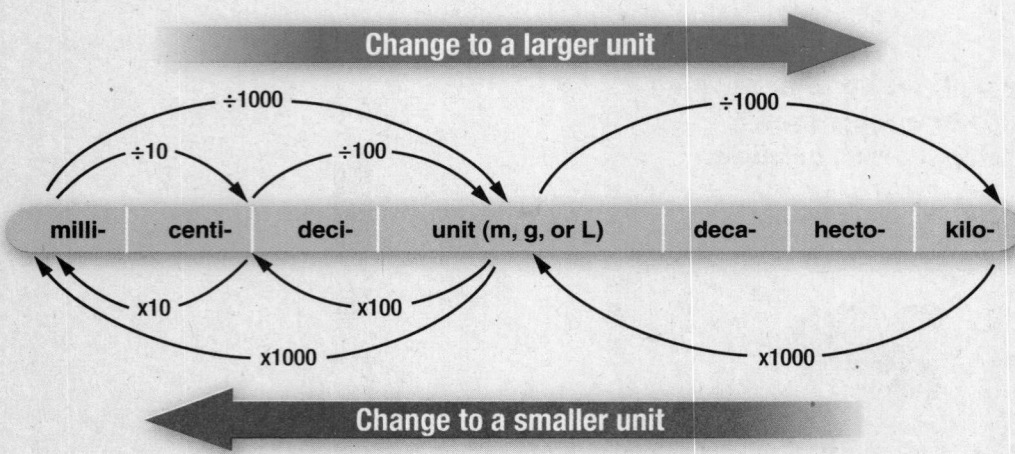

Example

Change 0.64 liters to milliliters.
1 Decide whether to multiply or divide.
2 Select the power of 10.

Change to a smaller unit by multiplying

mL ◄── x 1000 ── L

0.64 x 1000 = 640.

ANSWER 0.64 L = 640 mL

Example

Change 23.6 grams to kilograms.
1 Decide whether to multiply or divide.
2 Select the power of 10.

Change to a larger unit by dividing

g ── ÷ 1000 ──► kg

26.3 ÷ 1000 = 0.0263

ANSWER 23.6 g = 0.0236 kg

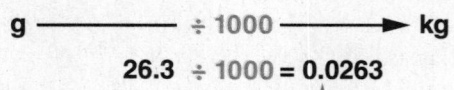

Converting Between SI and U.S. Customary Units

Use the chart below when you need to convert between SI units and U.S. customary units

SI Unit	From SI to U.S. Customary			From U.S. Customary to SI		
Length	**When you know**	**multiply by**	**to find**	**When you know**	**multiply by**	**to find**
kilometer (km) = 1000 m	kilometers	0.62	miles	miles	1.61	kilometers
meter (m) = 100 cm	meters	3.28	feet	feet	0.3048	meters
centimeter (cm) = 10 mm	centimeters	0.39	inches	inches	2.54	centimeters
millimeter (mm) = 0.1 cm	millimeters	0.04	inches	inches	25.4	millimeters
Area	**When you know**	**multiply by**	**to find**	**When you know**	**multiply by**	**to find**
square kilometer (km²)	square kilometers	0.39	square miles	square miles	2.59	square kilometers
square meter (m²)	square meters	1.2	square yards	square yards	0.84	square meters
square centimeter (cm²)	square centimeters	0.155	square inches	square inches	6.45	square centimeters
Volume	**When you know**	**multiply by**	**to find**	**When you know**	**multiply by**	**to find**
liter (L) = 1000 mL	liters	1.06	quarts	quarts	0.95	liters
	liters	0.26	gallons	gallons	3.79	liters
	liters	4.23	cups	cups	0.24	liters
	liters	2.12	pints	pints	0.47	liters
milliliter (mL) = 0.001 L	milliliters	0.20	teaspoons	teaspoons	4.93	milliliters
	milliliters	0.07	tablespoons	tablespoons	14.79	milliliters
	milliliters	0.03	fluid ounces	fluid ounces	29.57	milliliters
Mass and Weight	**When you know**	**multiply by**	**to find**	**When you know**	**multiply by**	**to find**
kilogram (kg) = 1000 g	kilograms	2.2	pounds	pounds	0.45	kilograms
gram (g) = 1000 mg	grams	0.035	ounces	ounces	28.35	grams

Temperature Conversions

Even though the kelvin is the SI base unit of temperature, the degree Celsius will be the unit you use most often in your science studies. The formulas below show the relationships between temperatures in degrees Fahrenheit (°F), degrees Celsius (°C), and kelvins (K).

$$°C = \frac{5}{9} \ (°F - 32) \qquad °F = \frac{9}{5} \ °C + 32 \qquad K = °C + 273$$

Examples of Temperature Conversions		
Condition	**Degrees Celsius**	**Degrees Fahrenheit**
Freezing point of water	0	32
Cool day	10	50
Mild day	20	68
Warm day	30	86
Normal body temperature	37	98.6
Very hot day	40	104
Boiling point of water	100	212

Math Refresher

Performing Calculations

Science requires an understanding of many math concepts. The following pages will help you review some important math skills.

Mean

The mean is the sum of all values in a data set divided by the total number of values in the data set. The mean is also called the *average*.

Example

Find the mean of the following set of numbers: 5, 4, 7, and 8.

Step 1   Find the sum.

$$5 + 4 + 7 + 8 = 24$$

Step 2   Divide the sum by the number of numbers in your set. Because there are four numbers in this example, divide the sum by 4.

$$24 \div 4 = 6$$

Answer The average, or mean, is 6.

Median

The median of a data set is the middle value when the values are written in numerical order. If a data set has an even number of values, the median is the mean of the two middle values.

Example

To find the median of a set of measurements, arrange the values in order from least to greatest. The median is the middle value.

13 mm   14 mm   16 mm   21 mm   23 mm

Answer The median is 16 mm.

Mode

The mode of a data set is the value that occurs most often.

Example

To find the mode of a set of measurements, arrange the values in order from least to greatest, and determine the value that occurs most often.

13 mm, 14 mm, 14 mm, 16 mm,
21 mm, 23 mm, 25 mm

Answer The mode is 14 mm.

A data set can have more than one mode or no mode. For example, the following data set has modes of 2 mm and 4 mm:

2 mm   2 mm   3 mm   4 mm   4 mm

The data set below has no mode because no value occurs more often than any other.

2 mm   3 mm   4 mm   5 mm

Ratios

A **ratio** is a comparison between numbers, and it is usually written as a fraction.

Example

Find the ratio of thermometers to students if you have 36 thermometers and 48 students in your class.

Step 1   Write the ratio.

$$\frac{36 \text{ thermometers}}{48 \text{ students}}$$

Step 2   Simplify the fraction to its simplest form.

$$\frac{36}{48} = \frac{36 \div 12}{48 \div 12} = \frac{3}{4}$$

The ratio of thermometers to students is 3 to 4 or 3:4. So there are 3 thermometers for every 4 students.

Proportions

A **proportion** is an equation that states that two ratios are equal.

$$\frac{3}{1} = \frac{12}{4}$$

To solve a proportion, you can use cross-multiplication. If you know three of the quantities in a proportion, you can use cross-multiplication to find the fourth.

Example

Imagine that you are making a scale model of the solar system for your science project. The diameter of Jupiter is 11.2 times the diameter of the Earth. If you are using a plastic-foam ball that has a diameter of 2 cm to represent the Earth, what must the diameter of the ball representing Jupiter be?

$$\frac{11.2}{1} = \frac{x}{2 \text{ cm}}$$

Step 1   Cross-multiply.

$$\frac{11.2}{1} = \frac{x}{2}$$

$$11.2 \times 2 = x \times 1$$

Step 2   Multiply.

$$22.4 = x \times 1$$

$$x = 22.4 \text{ cm}$$

You will need to use a ball that has a diameter of 22.4 cm to represent Jupiter.

Rates

A **rate** is a ratio of two values expressed in different units. A unit rate is a rate with a denominator of 1 unit.

Example

A plant grew 6 centimeters in 2 days. The plant's rate of growth was $\frac{6 \text{ cm}}{2 \text{ days}}$.

To describe the plant's growth in centimeters per day, write a unit rate.

Divide numerator and denominator by 2:

$$\frac{6 \text{ cm}}{2 \text{ days}} = \frac{6 \text{ cm} \div 2}{2 \text{ days} \div 2}$$

Simplify:

$$= \frac{3 \text{ cm}}{1 \text{ day}}$$

Answer   The plant's rate of growth is 3 centimeters per day.

Math Refresher

Percent

A **percent** is a ratio of a given number to 100. For example, 85% = 85/100. You can use percent to find part of a whole.

Example
What is 85% of 40?

Step 1 Rewrite the percent as a decimal by moving the decimal point two places to the left.

$$0.85$$

Step 2 Multiply the decimal by the number that you are calculating the percentage of.

$$0.85 \times 40 = 34$$

85% of 40 is 34.

Decimals

To **add** or **subtract decimals**, line up the digits vertically so that the decimal points line up. Then add or subtract the columns from right to left. Carry or borrow numbers as necessary.

Example
Add the following numbers: 3.1415 and 2.96.

Step 1 Line up the digits vertically so that the decimal points line up.

$$\begin{array}{r} 3.1415 \\ + 2.96 \\ \hline \end{array}$$

Step 2 Add the columns from right to left, and carry when necessary.

$$\begin{array}{r} 3.1415 \\ + 2.96 \\ \hline 6.1015 \end{array}$$

The sum is 6.1015.

Fractions

A **fraction** is a ratio of two whole numbers. The top number is the numerator. The bottom number is the denominator. The denominator must not be zero.

Example
Your class has 24 plants. Your teacher instructs you to put 5 plants in a shady spot. What fraction of the plants in your class will you put in a shady spot?

Step 1 In the denominator, write the total number of parts in the whole.

$$\frac{?}{24}$$

Step 2 In the numerator, write the number of parts of the whole that are being considered.

$$\frac{5}{24}$$

So $\frac{5}{24}$ of the plants will be in the shade.

Simplifying Fractions

It is usually best to express a fraction in its simplest form. Expressing a fraction in its simplest form is called **simplifying a fraction**.

Example
Express the fraction $\frac{30}{45}$ in its simplest form.

Step 1   Find the largest whole number that will divide evenly into both the numerator and denominator. This number is called the greatest common factor (GCF).

Factors of the numerator 30:
1, 2, 3, 5, 6, 10, 15, 30

Factors of the denominator 45:
1, 3, 5, 9, 15, 45

Step 2   Divide both the numerator and the denominator by the GCF, which in this case is 15.

$$\frac{30}{45} = \frac{30 \div 15}{45 \div 15} = \frac{2}{3}$$

Thus, $\frac{30}{45}$ written in its simplest form is $\frac{2}{3}$.

Adding and Subtracting Fractions

To **add** or **subtract fractions** that have the same denominator, simply add or subtract the numerators.

Examples
$\frac{3}{5} + \frac{1}{5} = ?$ and $\frac{3}{4} - \frac{1}{4} = ?$

Step 1   Add or subtract the numerators.
$$\frac{3}{5} + \frac{1}{5} = \frac{4}{} \text{ and } \frac{3}{4} - \frac{1}{4} = \frac{2}{}$$

Step 2   Write in the common denominator, which remains the same.
$$\frac{3}{5} + \frac{1}{5} = \frac{4}{5} \text{ and } \frac{3}{4} - \frac{1}{4} = \frac{2}{4}$$

Step 3   If necessary, write the fraction in its simplest form.
$\frac{4}{5}$ cannot be simplified, and $\frac{2}{4} = \frac{1}{2}$.

To **add** or **subtract** fractions that have **different denominators,** first find the least common denominator (LCD).

Examples
$\frac{1}{2} + \frac{1}{6} = ?$ and $\frac{3}{4} - \frac{2}{3} = ?$

Step 1   Write the equivalent fractions that have a common denominator.
$$\frac{3}{6} + \frac{1}{6} = ? \text{ and } \frac{9}{12} - \frac{8}{12} = ?$$

Step 2   Add or subtract the fractions.
$$\frac{3}{6} + \frac{1}{6} = \frac{4}{6} \text{ and } \frac{9}{12} - \frac{8}{12} = \frac{1}{12}$$

Step 3   If necessary, write the fraction in its simplest form.
$\frac{4}{6} = \frac{2}{3}$, and $\frac{1}{12}$ cannot be simplified.

Multiplying Fractions

To **multiply fractions**, multiply the numerators and the denominators together, and then simplify the fraction if necessary.

Example
$\frac{5}{9} \times \frac{7}{10} = ?$

Step 1   Multiply the numerators and denominators.
$$\frac{5}{9} \times \frac{7}{10} = \frac{5 \times 7}{9 \times 10} = \frac{35}{90}$$

Step 2   Simplify the fraction.
$$\frac{35}{90} = \frac{35 \div 5}{90 \div 5} = \frac{7}{18}$$

Math Refresher

Dividing Fractions

To **divide fractions,** first rewrite the divisor (the number you divide by) upside down. This number is called the reciprocal of the divisor. Then multiply and simplify if necessary.

Example

$$\frac{5}{8} \div \frac{3}{2} = ?$$

Step 1   Rewrite the divisor as its reciprocal.

$$\frac{3}{2} \rightarrow \frac{2}{3}$$

Step 2   Multiply the fractions.

$$\frac{5}{8} \times \frac{2}{3} = \frac{5 \times 2}{8 \times 3} = \frac{10}{24}$$

Step 3   Simplify the fraction.

$$\frac{10}{24} = \frac{10 \div 2}{24 \div 2} = \frac{5}{12}$$

Using Significant Figures

The **significant figures** in a decimal are the digits that are warranted by the accuracy of a measuring device.

When you perform a calculation with measurements, the number of significant figures to include in the result depends in part on the number of significant figures in the measurements. When you multiply or divide measurements, your answer should have only as many significant figures as the measurement with the fewest significant figures.

Examples

Using a balance and a graduated cylinder filled with water, you determined that a marble has a mass of 8.0 grams and a volume of 3.5 cubic centimeters. To calculate the density of the marble, divide the mass by the volume.

Write the formula for density: $\text{Density} = \dfrac{mass}{volume}$

Substitute measurements: $= \dfrac{8.0 \text{ g}}{3.5 \text{ cm}^3}$

Use a calculator to divide: $\approx 2.285714286 \text{ g/cm}^3$

Answer Because the mass and the volume have two significant figures each, give the density to two significant figures. The marble has a density of 2.3 grams per cubic centimeter.

Using Scientific Notation

Scientific notation is a shorthand way to write very large or very small numbers. For example, 73,500,000,000,000,000,000,000 kg is the mass of the moon. In scientific notation, it is 7.35×10^{22} kg. A value written as a number between 1 and 10, times a power of 10, is in scientific notation.

Examples

You can convert from standard form to scientific notation.

Standard Form	Scientific Notation
720,000	7.2×10^5
5 decimal places left	Exponent is 5.
0.000291	2.91×10^{-4}
4 decimal places right	Exponent is −4.

You can convert from scientific notation to standard form.

Scientific Notation	Standard Form
4.63×10^7	46,300,000
Exponent is 7.	7 decimal places right
1.08×10^{-6}	0.00000108
Exponent is −6.	6 decimal places left

Making and Interpreting Graphs

Circle Graph

A circle graph, or pie chart, shows how each group of data relates to all of the data. Each part of the circle represents a category of the data. The entire circle represents all of the data. For example, a biologist studying a hardwood forest in Wisconsin found that there were five different types of trees. The data table at right summarizes the biologist's findings.

Wisconsin Hardwood Trees	
Type of tree	**Number found**
Oak	600
Maple	750
Beech	300
Birch	1,200
Hickory	150
Total	3,000

How to Make a Circle Graph

1 To make a circle graph of these data, first find the percentage of each type of tree. Divide the number of trees of each type by the total number of trees, and multiply by 100%.

$$\frac{600 \text{ oak}}{3,000 \text{ trees}} \times 100\% = 20\%$$

$$\frac{750 \text{ maple}}{3,000 \text{ trees}} \times 100\% = 25\%$$

$$\frac{300 \text{ beech}}{3,000 \text{ trees}} \times 100\% = 10\%$$

$$\frac{1,200 \text{ birch}}{3,000 \text{ trees}} \times 100\% = 40\%$$

$$\frac{150 \text{ hickory}}{3,000 \text{ trees}} \times 100\% = 5\%$$

2 Now, determine the size of the wedges that make up the graph. Multiply each percentage by 360°. Remember that a circle contains 360°.

$$20\% \times 360° = 72° \qquad 25\% \times 360° = 90°$$

$$10\% \times 360° = 36° \qquad 40\% \times 360° = 144°$$

$$5\% \times 360° = 18°$$

3 Check that the sum of the percentages is 100 and the sum of the degrees is 360.

$$20\% + 25\% + 10\% + 40\% + 5\% = 100\%$$

$$72° + 90° + 36° + 144° + 18° = 360°$$

4 Use a compass to draw a circle, and mark the center of the circle.

5 Then, use a protractor to draw angles of 72°, 90°, 36°, 144°, and 18° in the circle.

6 Finally, label each part of the graph, and choose an appropriate title.

A Community of Wisconsin Hardwood Trees

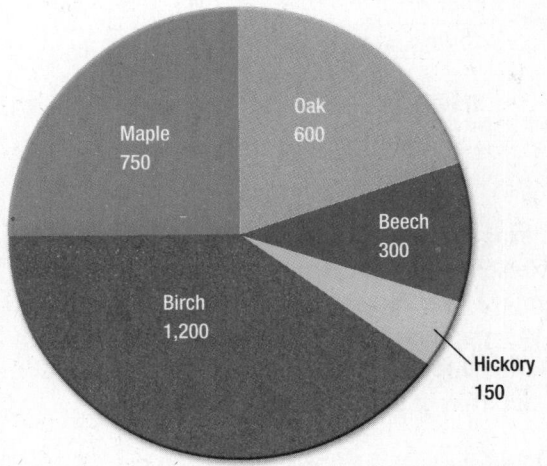

Math Refresher

Line Graphs

Line graphs are most often used to demonstrate continuous change. For example, Mr. Smith's students analyzed the population records for their hometown, Appleton, between 1910 and 2010. Examine the data at right.

     Because the year and the population change, they are the variables. The population is determined by, or dependent on, the year. Therefore, the population is called the **dependent variable,** and the year is called the **independent variable**. Each year and its population make a **data pair**. To prepare a line graph, you must first organize data pairs into a table like the one at right.

Population of Appleton, 1910–2010	
Year	**Population**
1910	1,800
1930	2,500
1950	3,200
1970	3,900
1990	4,600
2010	5,300

How to Make a Line Graph

1 Place the independent variable along the horizontal (x) axis. Place the dependent variable along the vertical (y) axis.

2 Label the x-axis "Year" and the y-axis "Population." Look at your greatest and least values for the population. For the y-axis, determine a scale that will provide enough space to show these values. You must use the same scale for the entire length of the axis. Next, find an appropriate scale for the x-axis.

3 Choose reasonable starting points for each axis.

4 Plot the data pairs as accurately as possible.

5 Choose a title that accurately represents the data.

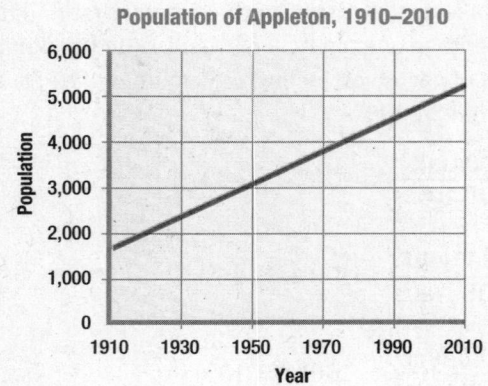

How to Determine Slope

Slope is the ratio of the change in the y-value to the change in the x-value, or "rise over run."

1 Choose two points on the line graph. For example, the population of Appleton in 2010 was 5,300 people. Therefore, you can define point A as (2010, 5,300). In 1910, the population was 1,800 people. You can define point B as (1910, 1,800).

2 Find the change in the y-value.
(y at point A) − (y at point B) =
5,300 people − 1,800 people =
3,500 people

3 Find the change in the x-value.
(x at point A) − (x at point B) =
2010 − 1910 = 100 years

4 Calculate the slope of the graph by dividing the change in y by the change in x.

$$slope = \frac{change\ in\ y}{change\ in\ x}$$

$$slope = \frac{3,500\ people}{100\ years}$$

$$slope = 35\ people\ per\ year$$

In this example, the population in Appleton increased by a fixed amount each year. The graph of these data is a straight line. Therefore, the relationship is **linear**. When the graph of a set of data is not a straight line, the relationship is **nonlinear**. As a result, the slope varies at different points on the graph.

Bar Graphs

Bar graphs can be used to demonstrate change that is not continuous. These graphs can be used to indicate trends when the data cover a long period of time. A meteorologist gathered the precipitation data shown here for Summerville for April 1–15 and used a bar graph to represent the data.

Precipitation in Summerville, April 1–15			
Date	**Precipitation (cm)**	**Date**	**Precipitation (cm)**
April 1	0.5	April 9	0.25
April 2	1.25	April 10	0.0
April 3	0.0	April 11	1.0
April 4	0.0	April 12	0.0
April 5	0.0	April 13	0.25
April 6	0.0	April 14	0.0
April 7	0.0	April 15	6.50
April 8	1.75		

How to Make a Bar Graph

1 Use an appropriate scale and a reasonable starting point for each axis.

2 Label the axes, and plot the data.

3 Choose a title that accurately represents the data.

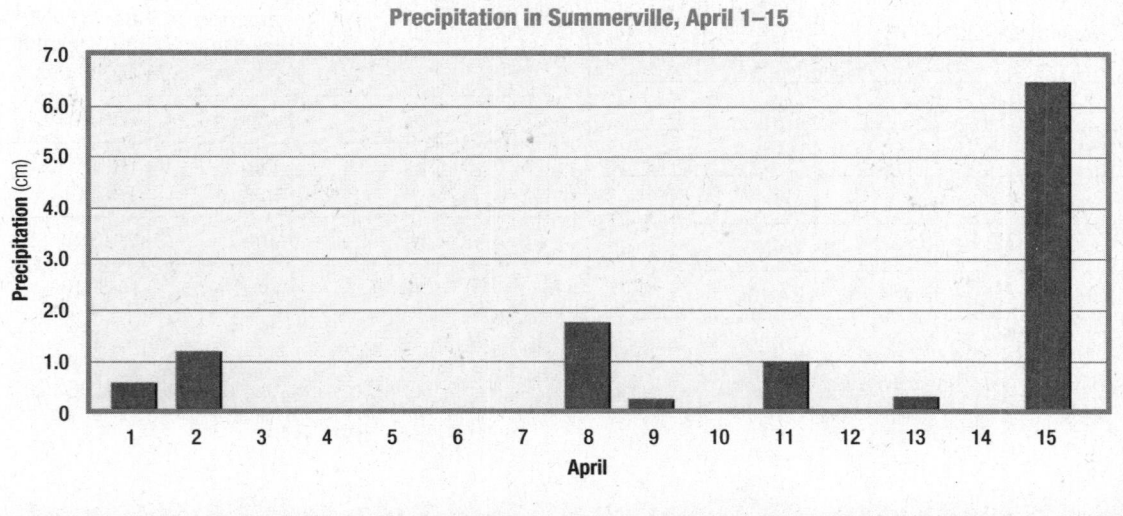

Precipitation in Summerville, April 1–15

Glossary

		Pronunciation Key					
Sound	**Symbol**	**Example**	**Respelling**	**Sound**	**Symbol**	**Example**	**Respelling**
ă	a	pat	PAT	ŏ	ah	bottle	BAHT•l
ā	ay	pay	PAY	ō	oh	toe	TOH
âr	air	care	KAIR	ô	aw	caught	KAWT
ä	ah	father	FAH•ther	ôr	ohr	roar	ROHR
är	ar	argue	AR•gyoo	oi	oy	noisy	NOYZ•ee
ch	ch	chase	CHAYS	ŏŏ	u	book	BUK
ĕ	e	pet	PET	ōō	oo	boot	BOOT
ĕ (at end of a syllable)	eh	settee lessee	seh•TEE leh•SEE	ou	ow	pound	POWND
ĕr	ehr	merry	MEHR•ee	s	s	center	SEN•ter
ē	ee	beach	BEECH	sh	sh	cache	CASH
g	g	gas	GAS	ŭ	uh	flood	FLUHD
ĭ	i	pit	PIT	ûr	er	bird	BERD
ĭ (at end of a syllable)	ih	guitar	gih•TAR	z	z	xylophone	ZY•luh•fohn
ī	y eye (only for a complete syllable)	pie island	PY EYE•luhnd	z	z	bags	BAGZ
				zh	zh	decision	dih•SIZH•uhn
îr	ir	hear	HIR	ə	uh	around broken focus	uh•ROWND BROH•kuhn FOH•kuhs
j	j	germ	JERM	ər	er	winner	WIN•er
k	k	kick	KIK	th	th	thin they	THIN THAY
ng	ng	thing	THING	w	w	one	WUHN
ngk	ngk	bank	BANGK	wh	hw	whether	HWETH•er

A

accuracy (AK•yer•uh•see) a description of how close a measurement is to the true value of the quantity measured (41)
exactitud término que describe qué tanto se aproxima una medida al valor verdadero de la cantidad medida

acid (AS•id) any compound that increases the number of hydronium ions when dissolved in water (500)
ácido cualquier compuesto que aumenta el número de iones de hidrógeno cuando se disuelve en agua

acid precipitation (AS•id prih•sip•ih•TAY•shuhn) rain, sleet, or snow that contains a high concentration of acids (205)
precipitación ácida lluvia, aguanieve o nieve que contiene una alta concentración de ácidos

adhesion (ad•HEE•zhuhn) the attractive force between two bodies of different substances that are in contact with each other (88)
adhesión la fuerza de atracción entre dos cuerpos de diferentes sustancias que están en contacto

air mass (AIR MAS) a large body of air throughout which temperature and moisture content are similar (236)
masa de aire un gran volumen de aire, cuya temperatura y cuyo contenido de humedad son similares en toda su extensión

air pollution (AIR puh•LOO•shuhn) the contamination of the atmosphere by the introduction of pollutants from human and natural sources (203)
contaminación del aire la contaminación de la atmósfera debido a la introducción de contaminantes provenientes de fuentes humanas y naturales

air pressure (AIR PRESH•er) the measure of the force with which air molecules push on a surface (161, 228)
presión del aire la medida de la fuerza con la que las moléculas del aire empujan contra una superficie

air quality (AIR KWAHL•ih•tee) a measure of the pollutants in the air that is used to express how clean or polluted the air is (206)
calidad de aire una medida de los contaminantes presentes en el aire que se usa para expresar el nivel de pureza o contaminación del aire

amplitude (AM•plih•tood) the maximum distance that the particles of a wave's medium vibrate from their rest position (580)
amplitud la distancia máxima a la que vibran las partículas del medio de una onda a partir de su posición de reposo

aquifer (AH•kwuh•fer) a body of rock or sediment that stores groundwater and allows the flow of groundwater (110)
acuífero un cuerpo rocoso o sedimento que almacena agua subterránea y permite que fluya

atmosphere (AT•muh•sfir) a mixture of gases that surrounds a planet, moon, or other celestial body (160)
atmósfera una mezcla de gases que rodea un planeta, una luna, u otras cuerpos celestes

atom (AT•uhm) the smallest unit of an element that maintains the properties of that element (453)
átomo la unidad más pequeña de un elemento que conserva las propiedades de ese elemento

atomic number (uh•TAHM•ik NUM•ber) the number of protons in the nucleus of an atom; the atomic number is the same for all atoms of an element (455)
número atómico el número de protones en el núcleo de un átomo; el número atómico es el mismo para todos los átomos de un elemento

average atomic mass (AV•er•ij uh•TAHM•ik MAS) the weighted average of the masses of all naturally occurring isotopes of an element (468)
masa atómica promedio el promedio ponderado de las masas de todos los isótopos de un elemento que se encuentran en la naturaleza

B

base (BAYS) any compound that increases the number of hydroxide ions when dissolved in water (500)
base cualquier compuesto que aumenta el número de iones de hidróxido cuando se disuelve en agua

biodiversity (by•oh•dih•VER•sih•tee) the number and variety of organisms in a given area during a specific period of time (420)
biodiversidad el número y la variedad de organismos que se encuentran en un área determinada durante un período específico de tiempo

biome (BY•ohm) a large region characterized by a specific type of climate and certain types of plant and animal communities (380)
bioma una región extensa caracterizada por un tipo de clima específico y ciertos tipos de comunidades de plantas y animales

C

calorie (KAL•uh•ree) the amount of energy needed to raise the temperature of 1 g of water 1 °C; the Calorie used to indicate the energy content of food is a kilocalorie (561)
caloría la cantidad de energía que se requiere para aumentar la temperatura de 1 g de agua en 1 °C; la Caloría que se usa para indicar el contenido energético de los alimentos es la kilocaloría

carbon cycle (KAR•buhn SY•kuhl) the movement of carbon from the nonliving environment into living things and back (370)

ciclo del carbono el movimiento del carbono del ambiente sin vida a los seres vivos y de los seres vivos al ambiente

carnivore (KAR•nuh•vohr) an organism that eats animals (351)

carnívoro un organismo que se alimenta de animales

carrying capacity (KAIR•ee•ing kuh•PAS•ih•tee) the largest population that an environment can support at any given time (408)

capacidad de carga la población más grande que un ambiente puede sostener en cualquier momento dado

cellular respiration (SEL•yuh•luhr res•puh•RAY•shuhn) the process by which cells use oxygen to produce energy from food (340)

respiración celular el proceso por medio del cual las células utilizan oxígeno para producir energía a partir de los alimentos

channel (CHAN•uhl) the path that a stream follows (108)

canal el camino que sigue un arroyo

chemical change (KEM•ih•kuhl CHAYNJ) a change that occurs when one or more substances change into entirely new substances with different properties (442)

cambio químico un cambio que ocurre cuando una o más sustancias se transforman en sustancias totalmente nuevas con propiedades diferentes

chemical equation (KEM•ih•kuhl ih•KWAY•zhuhn) a representation of a chemical reaction that uses symbols to show the relationship between the reactants and the products (477)

ecuación química una representación de una reacción química que usa símbolos para mostrar la relación entre los reactivos y los productos

chemical formula (KEM•ih•kuhl FOHR•myuh•luh) a combination of chemical symbols and numbers to represent a substance (477)

fórmula química una combinación de símbolos químicos y números que se usan para representar una sustancia

chemical reaction (KEM•ih•kuhl re•AK•shuhn) the process in which atoms are rearranged and chemical bonds are broken and formed to produce a chemical change of a substance (476)

reacción química el proceso por el cual los átomos cambian su disposición y se rompen y forman enlaces químicos de manera que se produce un cambio químico en una sustancia

chemical symbol (KEM•ih•kuhl SIM•buhl) a one-, two-, or three-letter abbreviation of the name of an element (468)

símbolo químico una abreviatura de una, dos o tres letras del nombre de un elemento

chlorophyll (KLOHR•uh•fil) a green pigment that captures light energy for photosynthesis (339)

clorofila un pigmento verde que capta la energía luminosa para la fotosíntesis

climate (KLY•mit) the weather conditions in an area over a long period of time (250)

clima las condiciones del tiempo en un área durante un largo período de tiempo

cohesion (koh•HEE•zhuhn) the force that holds molecules of a single material together (88)

cohesión la fuerza que mantiene unidas a las moléculas de un solo material

competition (kahm•pih•TISH•uhn) ecological relationship in which two or more organisms depend on the same limited resource (412)

competencia la relación ecológica en la que dos o más organismos dependen del mismo recurso limitado

concentration (kahn•suhn•TRAY•shuhn) the amount of a particular substance in a given quantity of a solution (492)

concentración la cantidad de una determinada sustancia en una cantidad dada de una solución

condensation (kahn•den•SAY•shuhn) the change of state from a gas to a liquid (97)

condensación el cambio de estado de gas a líquido

conduction (kuhn•DUHK•shuhn) the transfer of energy as heat through a material (180, 563)

conducción la transferencia de energía en forma de calor a través de un material

conductor (kuhn•DUK•ter) a material that transfers energy easily (563)

conductor un material a través del cual se transfiere energía

coniferous tree (kuh•NIF•er•uhs TREE) a cone-bearing tree that usually keeps its leaves or needles during all seasons of the year (383)

árbol conífero un árbol que produce conos o piñas y que generalmente conserva sus hojas o agujas durante todas las estaciones del año

constant (KAHN•stuhnt) a condition or factor that is assumed to have one value, or remain unchanged, throughout a particular investigation (23)

constante condición o factor que tiene un valor fijo o que permanece invariable en una investigación determinada

consumer (kuhn•SOO•mer) an organism that eats other organisms or organic matter (351)

consumidor un organismo que se alimenta de otros organismos o de materia orgánica

convection (kuhn•VEK•shuhn) the movement of matter due to differences in density; the transfer of energy due to the movement of matter (178, 564)

convección el movimiento de la materia debido a diferencias en la densidad; la transferencia de energía debido al movimiento de la materia

convection current (kuhn•VEK•shuhn KER•uhnt)
any movement of matter that results from differences
in density; may be vertical, circular, or cyclical (123)
corriente de convección cualquier movimiento de la
materia que se produce como resultado de diferencias
en la densidad; puede ser vertical, circular o cíclico

cooperation (koh•ahp•uh•RAY•shuhn) an interaction
between two or more living things in which they are
said to work together (413)
cooperación la interacción entre dos o más
organismos vivos en la cualse dice que trabajan juntos

Coriolis effect (kohr•ee•OH•lis ih•FEKT) the curving of
the path of a moving object from an otherwise straight
path due to Earth's rotation (119, 187)
efecto de Coriolis la desviación de la trayectoria recta
que experimentan los objetos en movimiento debido a
la rotación de la Tierra

data (DAY•tuh) information gathered by observation or
experimentation that can be used in calculating or
reasoning (23)
datos la información recopilada por medio de la
observación o experimentación que puede usarse para
hacer cálculos o razonar

day (DAY) the time required for Earth to rotate once
on its axis (290)
día el tiempo que se requiere para que la Tierra rote
una vez sobre su eje

deciduous tree (dih·SIJ·oo·uhs TREE) a tree that sheds
and regrows its leaves in response to seasonal
changes (386)
árbol caducifolio un árbol que pierde sus hojas
cuando llega el otoño; las hojas vuelven a salir cuando
llega la primavera

decomposer (dee•kuhm•POH•zer) an organism that
gets energy by breaking down the remains of dead
organisms or animal wastes and consuming or
absorbing the nutrients (350)
descomponedor un organismo que, para obtener
energía, desintegra los restos de organismos muertos
o los desechos de animales y consume o absorbe los
nutrientes

deep current (DEEP KER•uhnt) a streamlike movement of
ocean water far below the surface (122)
corriente profunda un movimiento del agua del
océano que es similar a una corriente y ocurre debajo
de la superficie

dependent variable (dih•PEN•duhnt VAIR•ee•uh•buhl)
in a scientific investigation, the factor that changes as
a result of manipulation of one or more independent
variables (23)
variable dependiente en una investigación
científica, el factor que cambia como resultado de la
manipulación de una o más variables independientes

desert (DEZ•ert) a region characterized by a very dry
climate and extreme temperatures (384)
desierto una región que se caracteriza por tener un
clima muy seco y temperaturas extremas

dew point (DOO POYNT) at constant pressure and water
vapor content, the temperature at which the rate of
condensation equals the rate of evaporation (225)
punto de rocío a presión y contenido de vapor de
agua constantes, la temperatura a la que la tasa de
condensación es igual a la tasa de evaporación

divide (dih•VYD) the boundary between drainage areas
that have streams that flow in opposite directions (109)
división el límite entre áreas de drenaje que tienen
corrientes que fluyen en direcciones opuestas

eclipse (ih•KLIPS) an event in which the shadow of one
celestial body falls on another (306)
eclipse un suceso en el que la sombra de un cuerpo
celeste cubre otro cuerpo celeste

ecosystem (EE•koh•sis•tuhm) a community of organisms
and their abiotic, or nonliving, environment (348)
ecosistema una comunidad de organismos y su
ambiente abiótico o no vivo

electric circuit (ee•LEK•trik SER•kit) a set of electrical
components connected such that they provide one
or more complete paths for the movement of charges
(600)
circuito eléctrico un conjunto de componentes
eléctricos conectados de modo que proporcionen
una o más rutas completas para el movimiento de las
cargas

electric current (ee•LEK•trik KER•uhnt) the rate at which
electric charges pass a given point (590)
corriente eléctrica la tasa a la que las cargas eléctricas
pasan por un punto dado

electromagnetic wave (ee•lek•troh•mag•NET•ik WAYV)
a wave, consisting of changing electric and magnetic
fields, that is emitted by vibrating electric charges and
can travel through a vacuum (578)
onda electromagnética una onda formada por campos
eléctricos y magnéticos cambiantes, que es emitida
por cargas eléctricas que vibran, y que puede viajar por
un vacío

electron (ee•LEK•trahn) a subatomic particle that has a
negative charge (454)
electrón una partícula subatómica que tiene carga
negativa

electron cloud (ee•LEK•trahn KLOWD) a region around
the nucleus of an atom where electrons are likely to be
found (455)
nube de electrones una región que rodea al núcleo
de un átomo en la cual es probable encontrar a los
electrones

elevation (el•uh•VAY•shuhn) the height of an object above sea level (254)
elevación la altura de un objeto sobre el nivel del mar

empirical evidence (em•PIR•ih•kuhl EV•ih•duhns) the observations, measurements, and other types of data that people gather and test to support and evaluate scientific explanations (8)
evidencia empírica las observaciones, mediciones y demás tipos de datos que se recopilan y examinan para apoyar y evaluar explicaciones científicas

endothermic reaction (en•doh•THER•mik ree•AK•shuhn) a chemical reaction that requires energy input, usually as heat (480)
reacción endotérmica una reacción química que requiere la entrada de energía, generalmente en forma de calor

energy (EN•er•jee) the ability to cause change (364, 538)
energía la capacidad de producir un cambio

energy pyramid (EN•er•jee PIR•uh•mid) a triangular diagram that shows an ecosystem's loss of energy, which results as energy passes through the ecosystem's food chain; each row in the pyramid represents a trophic (feeding) level in an ecosystem, and the area of a row represents the energy stored in that trophic level (366)
pirámide de energía un diagrama con forma de triángulo que muestra la pérdida de energía que ocurre en un ecosistema a medida que la energía pasa a través de la cadena alimenticia del ecosistema; cada hilera de la pirámide representa un nivel trófico (de alimentación) en el ecosistema, y el área de la hilera representa la energía almacenada en ese nivel trófico

energy transformation (EN•er•jee trans•fohr•MAY•shuhn) the process of energy changing from one form into another (540)
transformación de energía el proceso de cambio de un tipo de energía a otro

engineering (en•juh•NIR•ing) the application of science and mathematics to solve real-life problems (62)
ingeniería la aplicación de las ciencias y las matemáticas para resolver problemas de la vida diaria

equinox (EE•kwuh•nahks) the moment when the sun appears to cross the celestial equator (294)
equinoccio el momento en que el Sol parece cruzar el ecuador celeste

estuary (ES•choo•ehr•ee) an area where fresh water mixes with salt water from the ocean (396)
estuario un área donde el agua dulce de los ríos se mezcla con el agua salada del océano

eutrophication (yoo•trohf•ih•KAY•shuhn) an increase in the amount of nutrients, such as nitrates, in a marine or aquatic ecosystem (138, 418)
eutrofización un aumento en la cantidad de nutrientes, tales como nitratos, en un ecosistema marino o acuático

evaporation (ee•vap•uh•RAY•shuhn) the change of state from a liquid to a gas that usually occurs at the surface of a liquid over a wide range of temperatures (96)
evaporación el cambio de estado de líquido a gaseoso que ocurre generalmente en la superficie de un líquido en un amplio rango de temperaturas

exothermic reaction (ek•soh•THER•mik ree•AK•shuhn) a chemical reaction in which energy is released to the surroundings, usually as heat (480)
reacción exotérmica una reacción química en la que se libera energía en el ambiente, generalmente en forma de calor

experiment (ek•SPEHR•uh•muhnt) an organized procedure to study something under controlled conditions (20)
experimento un procedimiento organizado que se lleva a cabo bajo condiciones controladas para estudiar algo

food chain (FOOD CHAYN) the pathway of energy transfer through various stages as a result of the feeding patterns of a series of organisms (353)
cadena alimenticia la vía de transferencia de energía a través de varias etapas, que ocurre como resultado de los patrones de alimentación de una serie de organismos

food web (FOOD WEB) a diagram that shows the feeding relationships between organisms in an ecosystem (354)
red alimenticia un diagrama que muestra las relaciones de alimentación entre los organismos de un ecosistema

force (FOHRS) a push or a pull exerted on an object in order to change the motion of the object; force has size and direction (552)
fuerza una acción de empuje o atracción que se ejerce sobre un objeto con el fin de cambiar su movimiento; la fuerza tiene magnitud y dirección

frequency (FREE•kwuhn•see) the number of cycles, such as waves, in a given amount of time (581)
frecuencia el número de ciclos, tales como ondas, producidas en una determinada cantidad de tiempo

front (FRUHNT) the boundary between air masses of different densities and usually different temperatures (236)
frente el límite entre masas de aire de diferentes densidades y, normalmente, diferentes temperaturas

G

global warming (GLOH•buhl WOHR•ming) a gradual increase in average global temperature (270)
calentamiento global un aumento gradual de la temperatura global promedio

global wind (GLOH•buhl WIND) the movement of air over Earth's surface in patterns that are worldwide (188)
viento global el movimiento del aire sobre la superficie terrestre según patrones globales

grassland (GRAS•land) a region that is dominated by grasses, that has few woody shrubs and trees, that has fertile soils, and that receives moderate amounts of seasonal rainfall (385)
pradera una región en la que predomina la hierba, tiene algunos arbustos leñosos y árboles y suelos fértiles, y recibe cantidades moderadas de precipitaciones estacionales

gravity (GRAV•ih•tee) a force of attraction between objects that is due to their masses (302)
gravedad una fuerza de atracción entre dos objetos debido a sus masas

greenhouse effect (GREEN•hows ih•FEKT) the warming of the surface and lower atmosphere of Earth that occurs when water vapor, carbon dioxide, and other gases absorb and reradiate thermal energy (166, 202, 268)
efecto invernadero el calentamiento de la superficie y de la parte más baja de la atmósfera, el cual se produce cuando el vapor de agua, el dióxido de carbono y otros gases absorben y vuelven a irradiar la energía térmica

groundwater (GROWND•waw•ter) the water that is beneath Earth's surface (106)
agua subterránea el agua que está debajo de la superficie de la Tierra

group (GROOP) a vertical column of elements in the periodic table; elements in a group share chemical properties (470)
grupo una columna vertical de elementos de la tabla periódica; los elementos de un grupo comparten propiedades químicas

H

habitat (HAB•ih•tat) the place where an organism usually lives (349)
hábitat el lugar donde generalmente vive un organismo

heat (HEET) the energy transferred between objects that are at different temperatures (174, 560)
calor la transferencia de energía entre objetos que están a temperaturas diferentes

herbivore (HER•buh•vohr) an organism that eats only plants (351)
herbívoro un organismo que sólo come plantas

humidity (hyoo•MID•ih•tee) the amount of water vapor in the air (225)
humedad la cantidad de vapor de agua que hay en el aire

hypothesis (hy•PAHTH•ih•sis) a testable idea or explanation that leads to scientific investigation (22)
hipótesis una idea o explicación que conlleva a la investigación científica y que se puede probar

I

ice age (EYES AYJ) a long period of climatic cooling during which the continents are glaciated repeatedly (267)
edad de hielo un largo período de enfriamiento del clima, durante el cual los continentes se ven repetidamente sometidos a la glaciación

independent variable (in•dih•PEN•duhnt VAIR•ee•uh•buhl) in a scientific investigation, the factor that is deliberately manipulated (23)
variable independiente en una investigación científica, el factor que se manipula deliberadamente

insulator (IN•suh•lay•ter) a material that reduces or prevents the transfer of energy (563)
aislante un material que reduce o evita la transferencia de energía

J

jet stream (JET STREEM) a narrow band of strong winds that blow in the upper troposphere (190, 241)
corriente en chorro un cinturón delgado de vientos fuertes que soplan en la parte superior de la troposfera

K

kinetic energy (kih•NET•ik EN•er•jee) the energy of an object that is due to the object's motion (550)
energía cinética la energía de un objeto debido al movimiento del objeto

L

latitude (LAT•ih•tood) the distance north or south from the equator; expressed in degrees (252)
latitud la distancia hacia el norte o hacia el sur del ecuador; se expresa en grados

law of conservation of energy (LAW UHV kahn•suhr•VAY•shuhn UHV EN•er•jee) the law that states that energy cannot be created or destroyed but can be changed from one form to another (365, 481, 544)
ley de la conservación de la energía la ley que establece que la energía ni se crea ni se destruye, sólo se transforma de una forma a otra

law of conservation of mass (LAW UHV kahn•suhr•VAY•shuhn UHV MAS) the law that states that mass cannot be created or destroyed in ordinary chemical and physical changes (365, 446, 478)
ley de la conservación de la masa la ley que establece que la masa no se crea ni se destruye por cambios químicos o físicos comunes

limiting factor (LIM•ih•ting FAK•ter) an environmental factor that prevents an organism or population from reaching its full potential of size or activity (410)
factor limitante un factor ambiental que impide que un organismo o población alcance su máximo potencial de distribución o de actividad

local wind (LOH•kuhl WIND) the movement of air over short distances; occurs in specific areas as a result of certain geographical features (192)
viento local el movimiento del aire a través de distancias cortas; se produce en áreas específicas como resultado de ciertas características geográficas

longitudinal wave (lahn•jih•TOOD•n•uhl WAYV) a wave in which the particles of the medium vibrate parallel to the direction of wave motion (576)
onda longitudinal una onda en la que las partículas del medio vibran paralelamente a la dirección del movimiento de la onda

lunar phases (LOO•ner FAYZ•iz) the different appearances of the moon from Earth throughout the month (304)
fases lunares la diferente apariencia que tiene la Luna cuando se ve desde la Tierra a lo largo del mes

mass number (MAS NUM•ber) the sum of the numbers of protons and neutrons in the nucleus of an atom (458)
número de masa la suma de los números de protones y neutrones que hay en el núcleo de un átomo

matter (MAT•er) anything that has mass and takes up space (364)
materia cualquier cosa que tiene masa y ocupa un lugar en el espacio

mean (MEEN) the number obtained by adding up the data for a given characteristic and dividing this sum by the number of individuals (50)
media el número que se obtiene sumando los datos de una característica dada y dividiendo esa suma entre el número de individuos

measurement (MEZH•uhr•muhnt) a quantitative description of something that includes a number and a unit, such as 42 meters (36)
medida una descripción cuantitativa de algo, que incluye un número y una unidad, por ejemplo, 42 metros

mechanical energy (mih•KAN•ih•kuhl EN•er•jee) the sum of an object's kinetic energy and potential energy due to gravity or elastic deformation; does not include chemical energy or nuclear energy (550)
energía mecánica la suma de las energías cinética y potencial de un objeto debido a la gravedad o a la deformación elástica; no incluye la energía química ni nuclear

mechanical wave (mih•KAN•ih•kuhl WAYV) a wave that requires a medium through which to travel (578)
onda mecánica una onda que requiere un medio para desplazarse

medium (MEE•dee•uhm) a physical environment in which phenomena occur; for waves, the material through which a wave can travel (574)
medio un ambiente físico en el que ocurren fenómenos; para las ondas, el medio a través del cual se desplaza una onda

mesosphere (MEZ•uh•sfir) the layer of the atmosphere between the stratosphere and the thermosphere and in which temperature decreases as altitude increases (164)
mesosfera la capa de la atmósfera que se encuentra entre la estratosfera y la termosfera, en la cual la temperatura disminuye al aumentar la altitud

metal (MET•l) an element that is shiny and that conducts heat and electricity well (469)
metal un elemento que es brillante y conduce bien el calor y la electricidad

metalloid (MET•l•oyd) an element that has properties of both metals and nonmetals (469)
metaloide un elemento que tiene propiedades tanto de metal como de no metal

mixture (MIKS•cher) a combination of two or more substances that are not chemically combined (490)
mezcla una combinación de dos o más sustancias que no están combinadas químicamente

model (MAHD•l) a pattern, plan, representation, or description designed to show the structure or workings of an object, system, or concept (54)
modelo un diseño, plan, representación o descripción cuyo objetivo es mostrar la estructura o funcionamiento de un objeto, sistema o concepto

neap tide (NEEP TYD) a tide of minimum range that occurs during the first and third quarters of the moon (319)
marea muerta una marea que tiene un rango mínimo, la cual ocurre durante el primer y el tercer cuartos de la Luna

neutralization reaction (noo•truh•lih•ZAY•shuhn ree•AK•shuhn) the reaction of an acid and a base to form a neutral solution of water and a salt (506)
reacción de neutralización la reacción de un ácido y una base que forma una solución neutra de agua y una sal

neutron (NOO•trahn) a subatomic particle that has no charge and that is located in the nucleus of an atom (455)
neutrón una partícula subatómica que no tiene carga y que está ubicada en el núcleo de un átomo

nitrogen cycle (NY•truh•juhn SY•kuhl) the cycling of nitrogen between organisms, soil, water, and the atmosphere (369)
ciclo del nitrógeno el ciclado del nitrógeno entre los organismos, el suelo, el agua y la atmósfera

nonmetal (nahn•MET•l) an element that conducts heat and electricity poorly (469)
no metal un elemento que es mal conductor del calor y la electricidad

nonpoint-source pollution (nahn•POYNT SOHRS puh•LOO•shuhn) pollution that comes from many sources rather than from a single specific site; an example is pollution that reaches a body of water from streets and storm sewers (138)
contaminación no puntual contaminación que proviene de muchas fuentes, en lugar de provenir de un solo sitio específico; un ejemplo es la contaminación que llega a una masa de agua a partir de las calles y los drenajes

nucleus (NOO•klee•uhs) in physical science, an atom's central region, which is made up of protons and neutrons (455)
núcleo en ciencias físicas, la región central de un átomo, la cual está constituida por protones y neutrones

observation (ahb•zer•VAY•shuhn) the process of obtaining information by using the senses (21)
observación el proceso de obtener información por medio de los sentidos

ocean current (OH•shuhn KER•uhnt) a movement of ocean water that follows a regular pattern (118)
corriente oceánica un movimiento del agua del océano que sigue un patrón regular

omnivore (AHM•nuh•vohr) an organism that eats both plants and animals (351)
omnívoro un organismo que come tanto plantas como animales

ozone layer (OH•zohn LAY•er) the layer of the atmosphere at an altitude of 15 to 40 km in which ozone absorbs ultraviolet solar radiation (163)
capa de ozono la capa de la atmósfera ubicada a una altitud de 15 a 40 km, en la cual el ozono absorbe la radiación solar

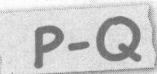

parallel circuit (PAIR•uh•lel SER•kit) a circuit in which the parts are joined in branches such that the voltage across each part is the same (605)
circuito paralelo un circuito en el que las partes están unidas en ramas de manera tal que el voltaje entre cada parte es la misma

particulate (par•TIK•yuh•lit) a tiny particle of solid that is suspended in air or water (203)
material particulado una pequeña partícula de material sólido que se encuentra suspendida en el aire o el agua

penumbra (pih•NUHM•bruh) the outer part of a shadow such as the shadow cast by Earth or the moon in which sunlight is only partially blocked (306)
penumbra la parte exterior de la sombra (como la sombra producida por la Tierra o la Luna) en la que la luz solar solamente se encuentra bloqueada parcialmente

period (PIR•ee•uhd) in chemistry, a horizontal row of elements in the periodic table (471)
período en química, una hilera horizontal de elementos en la tabla periódica

periodic table (pir•ee•AHD•ik TAY•buhl) an arrangement of the elements in order of their atomic numbers such that elements with similar properties fall in the same column, or group (459)
tabla periódica un arreglo de los elementos ordenados en función de su número atómico, de modo que los elementos que tienen propiedades similares se encuentran en la misma columna, o grupo

pH (PEE AYCH) a value that is used to express the acidity or basicity (alkalinity) of a system (514)
pH un valor que expresa la acidez o la basicidad (alcalinidad) de un sistema

photosynthesis (foh•toh•SIN•thih•sis) the process by which plants, algae, and some bacteria use sunlight, carbon dioxide, and water to make food (338)
fotosíntesis el proceso por medio del cual las plantas, las algas y algunas bacterias utilizan la luz solar, el dióxido de carbono y el agua para producir alimento

physical change (FIZ•ih•kuhl CHAYNJ) a change of matter from one form to another without a change in chemical properties (440)
cambio físico un cambio de materia de una forma a otra sin que ocurra un cambio en sus propiedades químicas

pioneer species (py•uh•NIR SPEE•sheez) a species that colonizes an uninhabited area and that starts a process of succession (420)
especie pionera una especie que coloniza un área deshabitada y empieza un proceso de sucesión

point-source pollution (POYNT SOHRS puh•LOO•shuhn) pollution that comes from a specific site (138)
contaminación puntual contaminación que proviene de un lugar específico

polarity (poh•LAIR•ih•tee) a property of a system in which two points have opposite characteristics, such as charges or magnetic poles (86)
polaridad la propiedad de un sistema en la que dos puntos tienen características opuestas, tales como las cargas o polos magnéticos

potential energy (puh•TEN•shuhl EN•er•jee) the energy that an object has because of the position, condition, or chemical composition of the object (550)
energía potencial la energía que tiene un objeto debido a su posición, condición o composición química

precipitation (prih•sip•ih•TAY•shuhn) any form of water that falls to Earth's surface from the clouds (97, 226)
precipitación cualquier forma de agua que cae de las nubes a la superficie de la Tierra

precision (prih•SIZH•uhn) the exactness of a measurement (41)
precisión la exactitud de una medición

producer (pruh•DOO•ser) an organism that can make its own food by using energy from its surroundings (350)
productor un organismo que puede elaborar sus propios alimentos utilizando la energía de su entorno

product (PRAHD•uhkt) a substance that forms in a chemical reaction (477)
producto una sustancia que se forma en una reacción química

proton (PROH•tahn) a subatomic particle that has a positive charge and that is located in the nucleus of an atom; the number of protons in the nucleus is the atomic number, which determines the identity of an element (455)
protón una partícula subatómica que tiene una carga positiva y que está ubicada en el núcleo de un átomo; el número de protones que hay en el núcleo es el número atómico, y éste determina la identidad del elemento

prototype (PROH•tuh•typ) a test model of a product (65)
prototipo prueba modelo de un producto

radiation (ray•dee•AY•shuhn) the transfer of energy as electromagnetic waves (176, 564)
radiación la transferencia de energía en forma de ondas electromagnéticas

reactant (ree•AK•tuhnt) a substance that participates in a chemical reaction (477)
reactivo una sustancia que participa en una reacción química

relative humidity (REL•uh•tiv hyoo•MID•ih•tee) the ratio of the amount of water vapor in the air to the amount of water vapor needed to reach saturation at a given temperature (225)
humedad relativa la proporción de la cantidad de vapor de agua que hay en el aire respecto a la cantidad de vapor de agua que se necesita para alcanzar la saturación a una temperatura dada

resistance (rih•ZIS•tuhns) in physical science, the opposition presented to the current by a material or device (592)
resistencia en ciencias físicas, la oposición que un material o aparato presenta a la corriente

revolution (rev•uh•LOO•shuhn) the motion of a body that travels around another body in space; one complete trip along an orbit (291)
revolución el movimiento de un cuerpo que viaja alrededor de otro cuerpo en el espacio; un viaje completo a lo largo de una órbita

rotation (roh•TAY•shuhn) the spin of a body on its axis (290)
rotación el giro de un cuerpo alrededor de su eje

salt (SAWLT) an ionic compound that forms when a metal atom replaces the hydrogen of an acid (506)
sal un compuesto iónico que se forma cuando un átomo de un metal reemplaza el hidrógeno de un ácido

satellite (SAT•l•yt) a natural or artificial body that revolves around a celestial body that is greater in mass (302)
satélite un cuerpo natural o artificial que gira alrededor de un cuerpo celeste que tiene mayor masa

science (SY•uhns) the knowledge obtained by observing natural events and conditions in order to discover facts and formulate laws or principles that can be verified or tested (6)
ciencia el conocimiento que se obtiene por medio de la observación natural de acontecimientos y condiciones con el fin de descubrir hechos y formular leyes o principios que puedan ser verificados o probados

scientific notation (sy•uhn•TIF•ik noh•TAY•shuhn) a method of expressing a quantity as a number multiplied by 10 to the appropriate power (40)
  notación científica un método para expresar una cantidad en forma de un número multiplicado por 10 a la potencia adecuada

season (SEE•zuhn) a division of the year that is characterized by recurring weather conditions and determined by both Earth's tilt relative to the sun and Earth's position in its orbit around the sun (294)
  estación una de las partes en que se divide el año que se caracteriza por condiciones climáticas recurrentes y que está determinada tanto por la inclinación de la Tierra con relación al Sol como por la posición que ocupa en su órbita alrededor del Sol

series circuit (SIR•eez SER•kit) a circuit in which the parts are joined one after another such that the current in each part is the same (604)
  circuito en serie un circuito en el que las partes están unidas una después de la otra de manera tal que la corriente en cada parte es la misma

simulation (sim•yuh•LAY•shuhn) a method that is used to study and analyze the characteristics of an actual or theoretical system (55)
  simulación un método que se usa para estudiar y analizar las características de un sistema teórico o real

smog (SMAHG) air pollution that forms when ozone and vehicle exhaust react with sunlight (204)
  esmog contaminación del aire que se produce cuando el ozono y sustancias químicas como los gases de los escapes de los vehículos reaccionan con la luz solar

solstice (SOHL•stis) the point at which the sun is as far north or as far south of the equator as possible (294)
  solsticio el punto en el que el Sol está tan lejos del ecuador como es posible, ya sea hacia el norte o hacia el sur

solubility (sahl•yuh•BIL•ih•tee) the ability of one substance to dissolve in another at a given temperature and pressure (494)
  solubilidad la capacidad de una sustancia de disolverse en otra a una temperatura y una presión dadas

solute (SAHL•yoot) in a solution, the substance that dissolves in the solvent (491)
  soluto en una solución, la sustancia que se disuelve en el solvente

solution (suh•LOO•shuhn) a homogeneous mixture throughout which two or more substances are uniformly dispersed (490)
  solución una mezcla homogénea en la cual dos o más sustancias se dispersan de manera uniforme

solvent (SAHL•vuhnt) in a solution, the substance in which the solute dissolves (89, 491)
  solvente en una solución, la sustancia en la que se disuelve el soluto

specific heat (spih•SIF•ik HEET) the quantity of heat required to raise a unit mass of homogeneous material 1 K or 1 °C in a specified way, given constant pressure and volume (89)
  calor específico la cantidad de calor que se requiere para aumentar una unidad de masa de un material homogéneo 1 K ó 1° C de una manera especificada, dados un volumen y una presión constantes

spring tide (SPRING TYD) a tide of increased range that occurs two times a month, at the new and full moons (318)
  marea viva una marea de mayor rango que ocurre dos veces al mes, durante la luna nueva y la luna llena

stratosphere (STRAT•uh•sfir) the layer of the atmosphere that is above the troposphere and in which temperature increases as altitude increases (163)
  estratosfera la capa de la atmósfera que se encuentra encima de la troposfera y en la que la temperatura aumenta al aumentar la altitud

sublimation (suhb•luh•MAY•shuhn) the change of state from a solid directly to a gas (96)
  sublimación cambio de estado por el cual un sólido se convierte directamente en un gas

succession (suhk•SESH•uhn) the replacement of one type of community by another at a single location over a period of time (420)
  sucesión el reemplazo de un tipo de comunidad por otro en un mismo lugar a lo largo de un período de tiempo

surface current (SER•fuhs KER•uhnt) a horizontal movement of ocean water that is caused by wind and that occurs at or near the ocean's surface (118, 257)
  corriente superficial un movimiento horizontal del agua del océano que es producido por el viento y que ocurre en la superficie del océano o cerca de ella

surface water (SER•fuhs WAW•ter) all the bodies of fresh water, salt water, ice, and snow that are found above the ground (106)
  agua superficial todas las masas de agua dulce, agua salada, hielo y nieve que se encuentran arriba del suelo

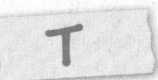

taiga (TY•guh) a region of evergreen, coniferous forest below the arctic and subarctic tundra regions (383)
  taiga una región de bosques siempreverdes de coníferas, ubicado debajo de las regiones árticas y subárticas de tundra

technology (tek•NAHL•uh•jee) the application of science for practical purposes; the use of tools, machines, materials, and processes to meet human needs (63)
  tecnología la aplicación de la ciencia con fines prácticos; el uso de herramientas, máquinas, materiales y procesos para satisfacer las necesidades de los seres humanos

temperature (TEM•per•uh•chur) a measure of how hot (or cold) something is; specifically, a measure of the average kinetic energy of the particles in an object (172)
temperatura una medida de qué tan caliente (o frío) está algo; específicamente, una medida de la energía cinética promedio de las partículas de un objeto

thermal energy (THER•muhl EN•er•jee) the kinetic energy of a substance's atoms (172, 558)
energía térmica la energía cinética de los átomos de una sustancia

thermal expansion (THER•muhl ek•SPAN•shuhn) an increase in the size of a substance in response to an increase in the temperature of the substance (173)
expansión térmica un aumento en el tamaño de una sustancia en respuesta a un aumento en la temperatura de la sustancia

thermal pollution (THER•muhl puh•LOO•shuhn) a temperature increase in a body of water that is caused by human activity and that has a harmful effect on water quality and on the ability of that body of water to support life (138)
contaminación térmica un aumento en la temperatura de una masa de agua, producido por las actividades humanas y que tiene un efecto dañino en la calidad del agua y en la capacidad de esa masa de agua para permitir que se desarrolle la vida

thermosphere (THER•muh•sfir) the uppermost layer of the atmosphere, in which temperature increases as altitude increases (164)
termosfera la capa más alta de la atmósfera, en la cual la temperatura aumenta a medida que la altitud aumenta

tidal range (TYD•l RAYNJ) the difference in levels of ocean water at high tide and low tide (318)
rango de marea la diferencia en los niveles del agua del océano entre la marea alta y la marea baja

tide (TYD) the periodic rise and fall of the water level in the oceans and other large bodies of water (316)
marea el ascenso y descenso periódico del nivel del agua en los océanos y otras masas grandes de agua

topography (tuh•PAHG•ruh•fee) the size and shape of the land surface features of a region, including its relief (254)
topografía el tamaño y la forma de las características de una superficie de terreno, incluyendo su relieve

transpiration (tran•spuh•RAY•shuhn) the process by which plants release water vapor into the air through stomata; *also* the release of water vapor into the air by other organisms (96)
transpiración el proceso por medio del cual las plantas liberan vapor de agua al aire por medio de los estomas; también, la liberación de vapor de agua al aire por otros organismos

transverse wave (TRANS•vers WAYV) a wave in which the particles of the medium move perpendicularly to the direction the wave is traveling (577)
onda transversal una onda en la que las partículas del medio se mueven perpendicularmente respecto a la dirección en la que se desplaza la onda

tributary (TRIB•yuh•tehr•ee) a stream that flows into a lake or into a larger stream (108)
afluente un arroyo que fluye a un lago o a otro arroyo más grande

troposphere (TROH•puh•sfir) the lowest layer of the atmosphere, in which temperature decreases at a constant rate as altitude increases (162)
troposfera la capa inferior de la atmósfera, en la que la temperatura disminuye a una tasa constante a medida que la altitud aumenta

tundra (TUHN•druh) a region found at far northern and far southern latitudes characterized by low-lying plants, a lack of trees, and long winters with very low temperatures (383)
tundra una región que se encuentra en latitudes muy al norte o muy al sur y que se caracteriza por las plantas bajas, la ausencia de árboles y los inviernos prolongados con temperaturas muy bajas

U

umbra (UHM•bruh) a shadow that blocks sunlight, such as the conical section in the shadow of the Earth or the moon (306)
umbra una sombra que bloquea la luz solar, como por ejemplo, la sección cónica en la sombra de la Tierra o la Luna

upwelling (UHP•well•ing) the movement of deep, cold, and nutrient-rich water to the surface (124)
surgencia el movimiento de las aguas profundas, frías y ricas en nutrientes hacia la superficie

visibility (viz•uh•BIL•ih•tee) the distance at which a given standard object can be seen and identified with the unaided eye (229)

visibilidad la distancia a la que un objeto dado es perceptible e identificable para el ojo humano

voltage (VOHL•tij) the amount of work to move a unit electric charge between two points; expressed in volts (592)

voltaje la cantidad de trabajo necesario para transportar una unidad de carga eléctrica entre dos puntos; se expresa en voltios

water cycle (WAW•ter SY•kuhl) the continuous movement of water between the atmosphere, the land, the oceans, and living things (94, 368)

ciclo del agua el movimiento continuo del agua entre la atmósfera, la tierra, los océanos y los seres vivos

water pollution (WAW•ter puh•LOO•shuhn) waste matter or other material that is introduced into water and that is harmful to organisms that live in, drink, or are exposed to the water (138)

contaminación del agua material de desecho u otro material que se introduce en el agua y que daña a los organismos que viven en el agua, la beben o están expuestos a ella

watershed (WAW•ter•shed) the area of land that is drained by a river system (109)

cuenca hidrográfica el área del terreno que es drenada por un sistema de ríos

water table (WAW•ter TAY•buhl) the upper surface of underground water; the upper boundary of the zone of saturation (106)

capa freática el nivel más alto del agua subterránea; el límite superior de la zona de saturación

wavelength (WAYV•lengkth) the distance from any point on a wave to the corresponding point on the next wave (580)

longitud de onda la distancia entre cualquier punto de una onda y el punto correspondiente de la siguiente onda

wave period (WAYV PIR•ee•uhd) the time required for corresponding points on consecutive waves to pass a given point (581)

período de onda el tiempo que se requiere para que los puntos correspondientes de ondas consecutivas pasen por un punto dado

wave speed (WAYV SPEED) the speed at which a wave travels; speed depends on the medium (582)

rapidez de onda la rapidez a la cual viaja una onda; la rapidez depende del medio

weather (WETH•er) the short-term state of the atmosphere, including temperature, humidity, precipitation, wind, and visibility (224, 250)

tiempo el estado de la atmósfera a corto plazo que incluye la temperatura, la humedad, la precipitación, el viento y la visibilidad

wetland (WET•land) an area of land that is periodically underwater or whose soil contains a great deal of moisture (394)

pantano un área de tierra que está periódicamente bajo el agua o cuyo suelo contiene una gran cantidad de humedad

wind (WIND) the movement of air caused by differences in air pressure (186, 228)

viento el movimiento de aire producido por diferencias en la presión barométrica

work (WERK) the transfer of energy to an object by using a force that causes the object to move in the direction of the force (552)

trabajo la transferencia de energía a un objeto mediante una fuerza que hace que el objeto se mueva en la dirección de la fuerza

Y-Z

year (YIR) the time required for Earth to orbit once around the sun (291)

año el tiempo que se requiere para que la Tierra le dé la vuelta al Sol una vez

Index

Note: Italic page numbers represent illustrative material, such as figures, tables, margin elements, photographs, and illustrations. Boldface page numbers represent page numbers for definitions.

ductility, 469
dust storm, 191, *191*

Earth. *See also* climate change.
　appearance of moon from, 303
　average surface temperature, 166,
　　167, 236–237, *237,* 268
　axis tilt, *292,* 292–294, *293*
　computer models of, 21
　conduction on, 181
　convection currents in, *122–123,*
　　123, 179, *179,* 543
　days, 290, *290*
　earthquake waves in, 577
　lunar eclipse, 306, *306*
　lunar phases from, 304, *304–305*
　orbit of, 291, *291,* 302, *302*
　radiation on, 177, *177*
　revolution of, 291, *291*
　rotation of, 119, *119,* 187–188,
　　290, *290*
　seasons, 294, *294–295*
　solar eclipse, 307, *307*
　tides, *316,* 316–320, *317, 318,*
　　319, 320
　years, 291, *291*
Earth–moon–sun system, *302,* 302–
　307, *303, 304, 305, 306, 307*
earthquake wave, 577–578
Earth science, 6
easterlies, *240*
eclipse, 306, *306,* 306–307, *307*
　lunar, 306, *306*
　solar, 307, *307*
ecologist, 360
economy, climate change and, 275
ecosystem, 348. *See also* aquatic
　ecosystems.
　acid precipitation and, 205, *518,*
　　519, 519
　biomes and, 382
　biotic and abiotic factors in, 348,
　　380–381, 392, 410, *410*
　climate change and, 271, *271*
　designing, 374–377
　energy conservation in, 365
　energy pyramid, 366, *366*
　energy transfer in, *346,* 352–353,
　　352–353, 364–366, 375
　food chain in, *352–353,* 353, 366,
　　366
　food web in, *354–355,* 354–356,
　　375
　habitat and niche in, 349, *349*
　invasive species in, 357, *357,* 360,
　　360
　matter cycles in, 364, 367–371,
　　368, 369, 370–371
　mature, 422, *422–423*
　producers, decomposers, and
　　consumers in, 350–353, *352–353,*
　　364

slow and fast changes in, *418,*
　418–419, *419*
succession in, *420,* 420–421, *421*
educator, 486
elastic potential energy, 542
electret, 586
electret microphone, 586
electrical conductor, 601, *601,* 602,
　602
electrical energy, 539, 541, 542, 590
electrical insulator, 593, 601, *601*
electrical thermometer, 224
electric charge
　in atomic particles, 86, *86,*
　　454–457
　in ions, 457
　polarity of molecules and, 86, *86,*
　　88
electric circuit, 600, 600–607
　circuit diagram, 602, *602*
　electrical conductor in, 601, *601,*
　　602, *602*
　energy source in, 600, *600,* 602,
　　602
　gap in, 542
　load in, *601,* 601–602, *602*
　microscopic, *598*
　safe use of, *606,* 606–607, *607*
　series and parallel circuits, *604,*
　　604–605, *605*
　short circuit, 607
　switch in, *602,* 602–603, *603*
electric current, 590, 590–593
　acid and, 504
　base and, 505, *509*
　direct and alternating, 591, *591*
　from hydroelectric dams, 130–131,
　　131
　measurement of, 590
　resistance and, 592–593
　safety precautions, 606, *606*
　switches in, 603, *603*
　voltage and, 592, *592*
　in a wind turbine, 196
electric generator, 600
electricity. *See also* fossil fuels; power
　plants.
　environmental effects of, 15, *15,*
　　196
　static, *533*
　from tides, 310–311
　from wind turbines, 196–197, 541
electric potential, 592
electric scooter, as form of electric
　transportation, 15, *15*
electromagnetic energy, 538, *538,* 543
electromagnetic radiation, 176, *176*
electromagnetic wave, 578
　energy transfer by, 176, *176,* 564
　examples of, 538, 578, *578*
　speed of, 582–583
　travel of, 538
electron, 454
　charge on, 454
　location of, 454–455, *454–455,*
　　457, *457*
　valence, 470, *470–471*

electron cloud, 455, *455,* 456–457,
　457
electronic balance, R39
electron microscope, 42, 43, *453*
element. *See also* periodic table.
　in chemical reactions, 477
　examples of, 464, *464*
　groups of, 466–467, 470, *470–471*
　in periodic table, 465–471,
　　466–467
elevation, 254
　climate and, 254, 255, *255*
　pressure and temperature and, 161,
　　161, 228, *228*
El Niño, 266, *266*
emergencies, weather, 220–221
emergent layer, in rain forests, *387*
emigration, in populations, 406
empirical evidence, 8
endothermic reaction, 480
energy, 364, 538. *See also* energy
　transfer; kinetic energy; thermal
　energy.
　in cells, 336–342, *337, 338–339,*
　　340–341, 342
　chemical, 337, 338–339, 341,
　　539–540
　chemical potential, 540
　in chemical reactions, 445, *445,*
　　480–481
　chemosynthesis, 399
　conservation of, 365, 481, *481,*
　　544–545, *545*
　elastic potential, 542
　electrical, 539, 541, 542, 590
　in electric circuits, 600, *600,* 602,
　　602
　electromagnetic, 538, *538,* 543
　energy pyramid, 366, *366*
　enzymes and, 483
　in food, 337, *340–341,* 340–342,
　　342, 350–351
　force and, 552
　gravitational potential, 542
　heat as transfer of, 174
　from hydroelectric dam, 130–131,
　　131, 541
　law of conservation of, 365, 481,
　　481, 544
　light, 338–339, *338–339,* 364, 538
　mechanical, 538, 541–542,
　　550–551, 550–552
　nuclear, 486, 539
　ocean currents and, *122–123,* 123,
　　127, *127*
　from photosynthesis, 338–339,
　　338–339, 342, *342*
　in plants, 333
　potential, 540–542, 550–551,
　　550–551
　quantifiable change in virtual
　　environment, 55, 272
　renewable, 196–197, 274,
　　310–311, *311,* 541

friction, 130
front (weather), **236**, 236–237, *237*
full moon, 304, *304*, 318
fungi (singular, *fungus*)
  acid precipitation and, 205
  chytrid, 411, *411*
  as decomposers, 337, 350, *350*, 367, 411
  in frog infections, 411, *411*
  in indoor air, *207*
  mushrooms, 350, *350*
fuse, 607, *607*

© Houghton Mifflin Harcourt Publishing Company

light bulb
  electrical resistance in, 593, *593*
  in energy transfer, 542
  load in, 601
  in parallel circuit, 605, *605*
  in series circuit, 604, *604*
light-emitting diode (LED), *62*, 587
light energy, 338–339, *338–339*, 364, 538, 600
lighting designer, 587
light microscope, 42, 43
lightning
  forest fires from, 418
  nitrogen fixation by, 369, *369*
  safety precautions in, 534–535, 607, *607*
  static electricity in, *533*
lightning rod, 607, *607*
limestone, acid rain and, *519*
limiting factor, **410**, *410*
line graph, 50, *50*, 52
liquid, water as, 87, *87*
lithosphere, 94, 99, *100–101*
litmus paper, 504, 505
load, 601, 602, *602*
local wind, **192**, *192*, 192–193, *193*
longitudinal wave, **576**, *576*, 580, *580*
Look It Up! Reference Section, R1–R53
  Classification of Living Things, R10–R11
  Designing, Conducting, and Reporting an Experiment, R28–R34
  Electronic Balance, R39
  Geologic Time Scale, R4–R5
  A How-To Manual for Active Reading, R18–R19
  Introduction to Probeware, R42
  Making and Interpreting Graphs, R51–R53
  Measuring Accurately, R36–R38
  Mineral Properties, R2–R3
  Motion Detector, R43
  Performing Calculations, R47–R50
  Periodic Table of the Elements, R12–R13
  Physical Laws and Useful Equations, R16–R17
  Physical Science Refresher, R14–R15
  Safety in the Lab, R26–R27
  Science Skills, R39–R43
  Sky Charts for the Northern Hemisphere, R6–R7
  Spring Scale, R40
  Thermometer, R41
  Using a Microscope, R35
  Using Graphic Organizers to Take Notes, R20–R23
  Using the Metric System and SI Units, R44–R45
  Using Vocabulary Strategies, R24–R25
  World Map, R8–R9

low-pressure system, *238*, 238–239, *239*
low tide, *316*, 317, *317*
lunar eclipse, 306, *306*
lunar phases, **304**, *304–305*
lungs, blood pH and, 521

M

magnetic resonance imaging (MRI), 43, *43*
magnification, 436–437, *436–437*
Making and Interpreting Graphs, R51–R53
malaria, 271
malleability, 469
mammal. *See also* animal.
  anteater, 387
  antelope, 385, *385*, 410
  badger, 351
  bison, 351, *378*, 385
  black bear, 386
  bobcat, 386
  caribou, 383
  chipmunk, 386
  cougar, 386
  coyote, 349, 385
  deer, 386
  elephant, *412*
  elk, 383, 386, 412
  fox, 271
  gray squirrel, 349
  grizzly bear, *317*
  ground squirrel, 38
  hedgehog, *351*
  jaguar, 387
  kangaroo rat, 384
  killer whale, *354*, 355
  lion, 385, 410, *412*
  monkey, 387
  moose, 351
  musk ox, 383
  otter, 361, *361*, 398, *512*
  panda, *544*
  polar bear, *122*, 262, *262*, 562, *563*
  prairie dog, 385, *385*
  seal, *355*
  sea otter, 398
  showshoe hare, 383
  shrew, 386
  sloth, 387
  wolf, 351, *351*, 383
  zebra, 385, *385*, 409, 410
March equinox, 294–295, *294–295*
marine ecosystem, 392, *392*, 398, 398–399, *399*
marine west coast climate, 258, *258–259*
marsh, 394, *394*
Mars rover, *64*

mass
  of atomic particles, 456–457
  law of conservation of, 365, *446*, 446–447, *447*, 478
  measurement of, *37*, 38, *38*
mass number, **459**, 466–467
mathematical model, 54
mathematics review, R47–R50
Math Refresher, R46–R53
  Making and Interpreting Graphs, R51–R53
  Performing Calculations, R46–R50
matter, **364**
  atoms in, 452–455, *453*, *454–455*
  chemical changes in, 442–445, *444*, *445*, 447
  in ecosystems, 364, 367–371, *368*, *369*, *370–371*
  elements in, 464, *464*
  heat and, 562
  law of conservation of mass, 365, *446*, 446–447, *447*, 478
  physical changes in, *440*, 440–441, *441*, 447, 487
  in plants, 333
  properties of, 364
  states of, 87
matter and energy flow, 367–371
  carbon cycle, 367, 370, *370–371*
  in ecosystems, 367
  nitrogen cycle, 367, 369, *369*
  in the water cycle, 99, *99*, *100–101*, 368, *368*
McCrory, Phil, 361
mean (average), **50**, 51, 596
measurement, **36**. *See also* scientific tools.
  accuracy and precision in, 41, *41*, R36–R38
  as empirical evidence, *8*
  errors in, 29, *29*
  estimation in, 41
  importance of standard units, 36
  Measuring Accurately, R36–R38
  scientific notation, 40
  SI units, *37*, 37–39, *38*, *39*
  of temperature, 7, *29*, 38, *38*, 224
  tools for, *7*, *37*, *38*
measures of central tendency, 596
Measuring Accurately, R36–R38
mechanical energy, **550**
  definition of, 538
  energy transfer of, 542, *552*
  energy transformation in, 550–551, *550–551*
  mechanical work and, 552, *552*
  in renewable energy systems, 541
mechanical wave, **578**, *578*
media, reliability of, 31
median, 596
Mediterranean climate, 258, *258–259*
medium, **574**, 578, 582
megaphone, *576*

melting
  as change of state, 95, *95, 435*
  of glaciers and sea ice, 208, *208,*
    209, 270, *270,* 562
  of ice, *170,* 270, *270*
Mendeleev, Dmitri, 465
mendelevium, 468
mercury, *464*
mesosphere, **164,** *165*
metal, **469,** *469*
  acid precipitation and, 205
  acid reactions with, 205, 504
  alkali, *470*
  as electrical conductor, 601, *601*
  heavy, 141
  in the periodic table, 469, *469*
  properties of, 469
  resistance of, 593
  as thermal conductor, 563
metalloid, **469,** *469*
meteorologist, 55, 246
meterstick, *37, 38*
methane, 268, 481, *481*
metric system, R44–R45. **See also**
  SI units.
microbial load, 138, *140*
microhabitat, 349, *349*
microphone, 586, *586*
microscope
  electron, 42, 43
  fluorescent, 587
  light, 42, 43
  using, R35
microwave (in electromagnetic
  spectrum), 538, *538, 543*
milliliter (mL), 38
mimicry, *404*
mimivirus, *40*
Mineral Properties, R2–R3
Mississippi River watershed, 109
mitochondria (singular, *mitochondrion*),
  340–341, 340–342, *342*
mixture, 490
mode, 596
model, scientific, **54**
  of atoms, *437*
  of chemical reactions, 477, *477*
  of climate change, 272, *272*
  computer, 21
  conceptual, 54
  of DNA, 54, *54*
  physical, 54
  simulation as, 55
  uses of, 26, 54–55, *55*
molecule, water, 86, *86*
monsoon, 242
month, 291
moon (of Earth)
  appearance of surface, 303
  distance to Earth, 302
  gravity and, 11, *11,* 302, *302*
  lunar eclipses, 306, *306*
  orbit of, *302,* 302–303, *303,*
    304–305, 306
  phases of, 304, *304–305*

rotation of, 302, *303*
  as satellite, 302
  shadows on, *300*
  solar eclipses and, 307, *307*
  tides and, *316,* 316–320, *317, 318,*
    319, 320
Moseley, Henry, 465
motion detector, R43
mountain breeze, 193, *193*
mountains, climate and, 193, *193,*
  254, *254*
Mount St. Helens eruption, 418–419,
  419
MRI (magnetic resonance imaging),
  43, *43*
mud flow, 419, *419*

natural disaster, 409, 418
natural resource
  fresh water as, 113, *113*
  population size and, 408, *408*
neap tide, **319,** *319*
near side, of the moon, 303
need, identifying, 66, *68*
neon, *471*
neritic zone, 398
neutralization reaction, **506,** *506*
neutron, **455,** 456, *456,* 468
new moon, 304, *305,* 318
Newton, Isaac, 11, *11*
newton (N), 38, *38,* 552
niche, 349
nickel, 593
nighttime, 290
nitric acid, 519
nitrogen
  in the atmosphere, 160, *160,* 164
  fixation, 369, *369*
  in ocean currents, 127
nitrogen cycle, 367, **369,** *369*
nitrogen dioxide, 203
nitrogen fixation, 369, *369*
nitrogen oxides, 205, *205, 207,* 519
nitrous oxide, as greenhouse gas, 268
noble gas, *471*
nonmetal, **469,** *469*
nonpoint-source pollution, **138,** *139*
North American prairie, *378,* 385, *385*
North Atlantic Current, 243, *243,* 257
North Equatorial Current, *256–257*
Northern Hemisphere
  axis tilt and, *292,* 292–293, *293*
  daylight hours and, 293, *293*
  ocean surface currents and, 119
  pressure systems in, 238, *238*
  sky charts for, R6–R7
  winds in, *187,* 187–190, *189, 190*
North Pole
  axis tilt and, 292, *292*
  solstice and, 294, *294–295*
Norway Current, *257*

NRC (U.S. Nuclear Regulatory
  Commission), 486
nuclear energy, 539
nuclear power plant, 486, *486*
nucleus (atomic), **455,** 539
nutrients
  eutrophication from, 138
  in ocean currents, 127
  in ocean upwelling, 124, *124*

observation, **21**
  creativity in explaining, 11, *11*
  as empirical evidence, 8, 23
  of the natural world, 21, *21*
ocean. *See also* animal; ocean current.
  climate and, 256, *256*
  coastline animals, 321, *321*
  El Niño and La Niña, 266, *266*
  evaporation from, 96, *96*
  marine ecosystems, 392, *392, 398,*
    398–399, 399
  pH of, 518
  sea-level rise, 208, 270, *272*
  surface winds, 118–120, *121*
ocean current, **118,** 118–127
  climate and, 127, *256–257,* 257
  convection, *122–123,* 123, *178,*
    178–179, 543
  deep currents, 94, 122–123,
    122–123
  energy transport by, 99, *122–123,*
    123, 127, *127*
  maps of, *121,* 126–127
  matter transport by, 99, 127
  organism transport by, *125*
  surface currents, *118,* 118–121,
    119, 121, 242–243, 257
  transport time of, 126, *126*
  upwelling, 124, *124*
  in the water cycle, 94, 98
  weather and, *242,* 242–243, *243*
  wind and, *242,* 242–243, *243*
ocean wave, *572, 575, 575*
odor, as sign of chemical change, 444
ohm, 592
oil, solubility of, 494
oil lamp, *62*
oil spills, 361, *361, 397, 397*
omnivore, 351
open ocean (ecosystem), *398,*
  398–399
open system, 367, 545, *545*
organism. *See also* algae; animal;
  archaea; bacteria; fungi; life on
  Earth; plant; protist.
  atmosphere and, 161–162, 202
  in biomes, *380,* 380–381, *381*
  cells in, 336–337
  classification of, R10–R11
  climate and, 250
  in ecosystems, 348–349

in extreme environments, 321, *321*
in food chains, *352–353*, 353, 366, *366*
in food webs, *354–355*, 354–356, 375
pollution impacts on, 205, 209
population interactions, *412*, 412–413, *413*
as producers, decomposers, and consumers, 350–353, *352–353*, 364
water needs of, *134*, 136–138, 144
as water pollutant, 140–141
osmium, 471
outlet, electrical, 542
output, 130
oxygen
in the atmosphere, 160, *160*, 164, 202
in cellular respiration, *340–341*, 340–342, *342*
dissolved, 127, *140*
in fresh water, 20
in ocean water, 127
from photosynthesis, 338–339, *338–339*, 342, *342*
smog formation and, 204
solubility of, *494*, *494*
ozone
as air pollutant, 156, 203–204
in the atmosphere, 163, *163*, 165, 166, 202
ozone layer, **163**
human impact on, 209, *209*
ozone hole, 166, *166*, 209

percent, 402
Performing Calculations, R46–R50
period (in periodic table), *466–467*, **471**
period (of a wave), **581**, *581*, 583
periodic table, 464–471, **465**
atomic number in, 465, 471
element organization in, *464*, 464–465
format of, *466–467*, R12–R13
group of elements in, 470, *470–471*
metals, nonmetals, and metalloids in, 469, *469*
periods in, 471, *471*
permafrost, 137, 383
permeability, 109, 110, *110*
pH, **514**. *See also* acid; base.
acid rain, 138, *139*, 205, 519, *519*
of common solutions, 515, *515*
of the environment, *512*, 518, *518*
in the human body, *520*, 520–521, *521*
hydrangea plants and, 517, *517*
measurement of, 516, *516*
scale, 514, *515*
water quality and, *140*
phases of the moon, 304, *304–305*
phenol, 516
pH meter, 516, *516*
phosphorus, 127
photosynthesis, **338**
asteroid impacts and, 265
in the carbon cycle, 370, *370–371*
carbon dioxide for, 202
conservation of energy in, 481, 544
as endothermic process, 480
energy production from, 338–339, *338–339*, 342, *342*
by producers, 337, 350, *350*, 364, 374
pH paper, 516, *516*
physical change, **440**, *440*, 440–441, *441*, 447
physical characteristic, 504, 505
physical (abiotic) components
in aquatic ecosystems, 392
in biomes, 380–381
in population size, 410, *410*
Physical Laws and Useful Equations, R16–R17
physical model, 54
physical science, 6
Physical Science Refresher, R14–R15
physicist, 486
physics, 6
phytoplankton, 124, 354, *355*
pie chart, 52–53, *53*, 402–403
Pinatubo, Mount, eruption of, 265, *265*
pioneer species, **420**, *420*
pipette, 42
planet, 299
plankton, 124
planning, in investigation, 24

plant
in aquatic ecosystems, *393*, 393–394, *395*
bamboo, *544*
biomes and, 381
cactus, 384, *384*, *423*
cedar, 386
coconut, *125*
crabgrass, *421*
Douglas fir, 386
ferns, 386, *420*, *422*
in gardens, 332–333
horseweed, 421
hydrangea, 517, *517*
kudzu, 357, *357*
mangrove, *331*, 396
maple, 271, *271*, 349
matter for, *364*
mosses, 386, 394, 395, *395*, *420*, *453*
nitrogen in, 369
orchid, 387
pH and, 517, *517*, 518, *518*
photosynthesis by, 202, 338–339, *338–339*, 342, *342*
as producers, 350, 364, 374
redwood, 422
seagrass, *396*, 396–397, *397*, 398
smooth cordgrass, *396*
sugar maple, 271, *271*
sunflower, *334*
transpiration from, 96, 368
in the water cycle, 94
plant cell
energy in, 337, *337*, 338–339, *338–339*, 342, *342*
model of, *55*
plate tectonics, 179, 264, *264*
plus sign, in chemical equation, 477, *477*
point-source pollution, **138**, *139*
polar climate zone, 258, *258–259*
polar easterlies, 188, *189*
polar ice cap climates, 258, *258–259*
polarity, **86**, *86*, 88
polar jet stream, 190, *190*, 241, *241*
polar regions, solar energy in, 252, *252*
political action, climate change and, 275
pollution. *See also* air pollution; water pollution.
biological, 138, *139*
chemical, 138, *139*
indoor air, 206, *207*
point-source and nonpoint-source, 138, *139*
thermal, 138, *139*
pond ecosystem, *393*, *393*, 418, *418*
popcorn, 8–9
population (biological)
carrying capacity and, *408*, 408–409, *409*
diseases in, 411, *411*
habitat and niche for, 349, *349*

© Houghton Mifflin Harcourt Publishing Company

T

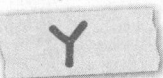